Readings & Cases

IN STATE AND LOCAL POLITICS

Readings & Cases

IN STATE AND LOCAL POLITICS

Richard A. Clucas

Portland State University

Houghton Mifflin Company

Boston New York

To Nathaniel and Alexander.

Publisher: Charles Hartford
Sponsoring Editor: Katherine Meisenheimer
Senior Development Editor: Jeffrey Greene
Editorial Assistant: Kristen Craib
Associate Project Editor: Teresa Huang
Editorial Assistant: Jake Perry
Senior Art and Design Coordinator: Jill Haber
Senior Photo Editor: Jennifer Meyer Dare
Senior Composition Buyer: Sarah Ambrose
Manufacturing Coordinator: Renee Ostrowski
Executive Marketing Manager: Nicola Poser
Marketing Associate: Kathleen Mellon

Cover image: Paul Chesley/Getty Images.

Printed in the U.S.A.

Library of Congress Control Number: 2004114376

ISBN: 0-618-37132-X

123456789-QUF-09 08 07 06 05

BRIEF CONTENTS

CONTENTS

TOPIC CORRELATION CHART

Budgeting and Finance

Bureaucracies

Campaigns and Elections

Civic Engagement and Political Participation

Constitutions and Charters

Courts

Explaining Differences Across the States

Federalism and Intergovernmental Relations

Governors

Initiative, Referendum, and Recall

Interest Groups and Lobbying

Legislative Politics

Local Government and Politics

Political Culture

Political Pathologies, Dysfunctions, and Failures

Political Power

Professional Politics and Politicians

Resurgence of the States

Social Policy

Values in Politics

Women, Minority, and Gay Issues

PREFACE

Textbooks on state and local politics generally fall into two categories. The first category is the introductory textbook that acquaints readers with how state and local governments function and explains the general character of state politics. The second category consists of collections of essays on state and local politics that have been published in magazines and newspapers. These supplementary texts often try to illustrate concepts discussed in the introductory textbooks and to inform students about current events in states and communities.

For instructors who want to provide their students with a deeper understanding of state and local politics, however, the reading options are limited. The introductory textbooks provide a broad overview, but at the expense of depth. The collection of essays can often help bring politics to life, but they rarely provide a deeper examination of the topics covered in the general textbooks. With this book, I try to provide an alternative approach, one that offers an in-depth exploration of selected topics in state and local politics. By focusing on a few topics more thoroughly, the book is designed to provide students with a richer understanding of some critical aspects of state and local politics.

Design and Format

I have tried to design the book in a way that is useful to instructors and appealing to students. The book has been structured so that it can be used to supplement introductory textbooks in state and local politics courses, offering a selection of readings that parallel the framework traditionally used in these texts. The book consists of sixteen chapters, each one focusing on a specific aspect of state and local politics. Paired together in each chapter is a scholarly reading and a related case study. The use of both a reading and a case study is meant to give students firsthand exposure to current concerns of state and local politics scholars, but in a way that makes the material more accessible and meaningful.

The readings explore central concepts in the study of state and local politics, touching on such topics as the resurgence of the states, devolution, political culture, civic engagement, privatization, legislative professionalism, gubernatorial power, and the new judicial federalism. The case studies have been selected to encourage students to think about how the concepts apply to events in the "real world." The case studies have been drawn from book chapters, magazine articles, and newspapers. I have tried to select studies that are longer and more detailed than the essays found in most supplementary texts to provide students with a better understanding of each topic. I have also tried to find studies that should be interesting to students, providing insights into many of the most prominent issues in the states today, from gay marriages to homeland security to the recall of California Governor Gray Davis that led to the election of Arnold Schwarzenegger. Many of the readings and case studies have been drawn from award-winning or influential books.

The book does not have an overt theme that runs through every chapter, but many of the readings and case studies return to a similar point, which is that it is often difficult for state and local governments to fulfill our expectations because there is often conflict in what we expect from government. The reading and case study in the first chapter, for example, emphasize how efforts to democratize state government may make it more difficult for state government to function. The chapter suggests that there can be a tradeoff between our desires to open up state politics to greater public input and the ability of government to function in an efficient and effective manner. In later chapters, however, as I turn to the work on civic engagement, the readings and case studies again look at whether there is a conflict between democracy and effectiveness, or whether these values can go hand in hand. This recurrent emphasis on the conflict in our expectations is included to provide instructors with a focus for an ongoing dialogue about what we want from state and local government and how those goals can be achieved.

I have included introductions to each reading and case study to put the material into a larger context, to explain some of the concepts more fully, and to help students to understand the material. It is in the introductions that I point out the value conflicts that are seen in many of the readings and case studies so that the students can understand the difficulties confronting state and local governments today in meeting our expectations. Each chapter also includes review questions, a list of key terms, suggestions for further reading, and information on relevant web sites. It is my hope that this structure will make the material accessible and of interest both to lower-division students who have little background in politics as well as those who are upper-division political science majors.

Organization and Approach

The chapters in the book could be divided into four separate sections. The first four chapters focus on fundamental topics for understanding state politics generally. The first chapter explores the changes that have been made in state governments over the past few decades leading to what has been called the resurgence of the states. The chapter explores how these changes have affected state politics for both better and worse, and asks students to consider whether states are up to the task of governing. The second chapter examines the concept of political culture to help students understand why there are differences among the states in how politics is practiced. The chapter includes a reading by Daniel Elazar and a case study on Louisiana politics. The third chapter examines trends in federal–state relations and the movement to devolve more power to the states that began in the mid-1990s. The case study looks at homeland security to help explain why power continues to be centralized at the national level. The fourth chapter provides a reading by Alan Tarr on the distinctive character of state constitutions. The case study then examines the problems associated with Alabama's constitution, which is the longest in the nation and the target of frequent criticism by reformers.

The second group of chapters focuses on the various means in which individuals provide input into government. The first of these chapters examines the importance of civic engagement in state and local politics, and includes an excerpt from Robert Putnam's book, *Bowling Alone.* The next chapter relies on an excerpt from Alan Ehrenhalt's *The United States of Ambition* to explore the entrepreneurial character of modern elections. The case study examines the election of former professional wrestler Jesse Ventura as governor of Minnesota. The final chapter in this section examines the power of interest groups across the nation.

The third group of chapters focuses on the structure and character of state and local governments. The chapters in this group examine the professionalization of state legislatures, the power of governors, proposals to privatize bureaucracies, and the spread of the new judicial federalism. I have also included chapters on the ideal structure of city government and the use of regional governments to solve the problems of the central city.

The last section of the book explores three major public policy concerns: budgeting, education, and welfare. The final chapter on welfare raises the question as to whether states are in the best position to address the many problems of welfare. In raising this question, the chapter brings the book back full circle to some of the questions addressed beginning in the first chapter as to whether states are up to the task of governing.

Instructor's Manual

To help instructors in using the book in the classroom, I have prepared an *Instructor's Manual,* which is available from the publisher. The manual provides summaries of each reading and case study, suggestions for classroom use, potential essay questions for exams, and a list of films and videos to use to accompany each topic.

Acknowledgments

I would like to thank the reviewers of this book for their thoughtful suggestions on how to improve the content and structure so that it is more useful in the classroom. I have tried to listen closely to their advice and incorporate their ideas into the final product. These reviewers were:

Steven R. Bayne, *Inver Hills Community College*
Jennifer M. Jensen, *University at Albany, SUNY*
Aubrey Jewett, *University of Central Florida*
Kathryn A. Lee, *Eastern University*
Suzanne Leland, *University of North Carolina at Charlotte*
Ed Miller, *University of Wisconsin–Stevens Point*
Kevan M. Yenerall, *Clarion University*

The folks at Houghton Mifflin have been continuously helpful and supportive. I want to particularly thank Jeff Greene, Teresa Huang, Katherine Meisenheimer, and Terri Wise for their work. I thank Richard Stillman, the editor of *Public Administration: Concept and Cases,* for his insights on working on this project, and Brent Steel, for directing this project my way. I must also thank Alan Ely for putting aside other tasks to help get different drafts into the mail on time. Lastly, I would like to thank my family, especially Nathaniel and Alexander, for their willingness to put up with me when I should be giving them attention. This book is dedicated to the two of them.

R. C.

Readings & Cases

IN STATE AND LOCAL POLITICS

The Changing Position of State Government: The Concept of Resurgence

Civil rights, poverty, education, workplace safety, consumer protection, health care, and environmental protection . . . as the twentieth century comes to a close, it is to state governments that we now look for solutions to many of these same problems. But are the states up to the task?

David M. Hedge

READING 1

Introduction

Perhaps the best place to begin down the road to understanding state and local governments is to examine how state governments have changed over time. Despite the media and public attention that is frequently focused on the federal government, state governments have emerged in recent years to play a large and very important role in American society, providing a broad range of services, regulating the behavior of businesses and private citizens, and addressing a host of social and economic problems. State government leaders have developed a valuable array of resources to help accomplish these tasks, including large staffs, expert policy advisors, and modern technologies. The leaders themselves tend to be well educated and highly experienced in governing, and they frequently communicate with leaders in other states to know how best to address problems. Certainly, there is considerable variation across the nation in the character and capabilities of state governments, but state governments today are generally considered to be well equipped to handle the tasks they are asked to perform. State politics scholars frequently write that the state governments have considerable capacity to do their jobs. By *capacity,* the scholars mean that the states have the ability and resources that are needed. This is quite different, however, from how things were in the past.

The position of state governments in the American political system has changed considerably since the nation was founded. From the late 1700s until the 1930s, the states played a preeminent role in governing the nation, exercising their powers either directly through state institutions or indirectly through control over local governments. Unlike today, the federal government was not involved in many domestic matters; instead, it focused its attention on foreign affairs, war, and a limited number of activities that are clearly enumerated in the U.S. Constitution. The states did not play as large a role in regulating society or providing services as they do today, but in comparison with the federal government, they played the lead role in domestic politics during that period.

The relationship between the states and the federal government changed dramatically during the Great Depression. Whereas the nation had previously been operating under a state-centered form of federalism, the federal government emerged during this period as the dominant power in the nation's political system. During the Great Depression, state governments found they were unable to address the problems confronting the nation by themselves, forcing them to turn to the federal government for help. Under the leadership of President Franklin Roosevelt, the federal government introduced a host of new programs to rebuild the economy and to address the problems confronting the nation. The strong response by the federal government to the Depression led to a change in the position of state governments within the federal system, as they took on a more marginal role. In the years following World War II, the position of state governments declined even further, so much so in fact that the states were seen by many as being incapable of addressing the problems they confronted. Their position had become so inconsequential that by the 1960s some political commentators began to ask whether the states were even needed.

At the same time that these commentators were questioning the value of states, many states began to take steps to improve their governmental institutions to make state government work more effectively and efficiently. As a result of these reforms, the state governments are considered to have gone through a *resurgence* that has made them far more capable and more important in American politics today than they were just a few decades ago. Through the adoption of these reforms, the states have gained the capacity to handle the task they are asked to perform. The effort to bring about change can be seen in all three branches of government.

Within the executive branch, the push for reform has strengthened the role of governors and made bureaucracies more professional than ever before. When the nation was founded, many states were unwilling to grant much power to governors because they feared strong executives. As a result, governors tended to have only limited impact on state politics. By the 1940s, governors had become more powerful than in the past, but they were still constrained by many legal and constitutional factors, including short terms, limited staff support, poor administrative structures, and the existence of other independently elected statewide executives who could challenge their leadership. These other executives include the lieutenant governor, attorney general, state treasurer, and the secretary of state.

Since the 1960s, most states have expanded the lengths of terms that governors can serve from two to four years, giving governors more time to develop policy proposals and to promote their ideas. Governors have been provided larger staffs to help them develop policy and oversee the bureaucracy. Many have received greater power to reorganize the state bureaucracy through executive orders, which allows them to create more rational administrative structures and to demand greater responsiveness from bureaucrats. Most have also been given greater control over the development of the state budget and thus, in turn, the direction of the state. Furthermore, there has been some effort to reduce the number of other separately elected executives, or to introduce what is called the *short ballot*. Along with the changes in the governor's office, state bureaucracies have also experienced change. Historically, state jobs were frequently given out as patronage to reward political supporters, which meant that the bureaucracies often lacked expertise and skilled workers. In recent decades, however, the states have made a more concerted effort to hire better-educated and more skilled employees, and to rely on the merit system for making personnel decisions.

State legislatures have experienced important changes that have improved their ability to function. Four decades ago, most state legislatures met only briefly every other year and were poorly equipped to address state problems. Legislative procedures and internal structures tended to be poorly designed. The legislatures had little space to conduct work and very limited staff support. Legislators were paid token salaries and thus could not devote much time to policymaking. In the 1960s, a legislative reform movement emerged that sought to strengthen the role of the legislature within the state political system. As a result of this movement, the legislatures in many states now meet every year and are provided with better resources. Legislative procedures and structures have been altered to make them more efficient and productive. New facilities have been built, allowing legislators to have private offices and providing sufficient room to work. The legislators in many states are now paid a more livable wage. There has also been considerable growth in professional staff support, which has allowed legislators to play a more effective role in shaping public policy, overseeing the bureaucracy, and responding to the governor's budget. All of these reforms have helped improve the capacity of state legislatures.

As for the judiciary, there has been an effort to unify the court systems in many states so that the number and types of courts are reduced and there is less overlap in court jurisdiction. These *unification* reforms have sought to make the court system more rationally organized and to ensure that the judicial procedures are consistent across the state. Many states have added an appellate court to reduce the caseload on the state supreme court. Finally, there has been some effort to improve the administration of the courts so that they are better managed. The main way this has been accomplished is by giving responsibility for handling the administrative duties of the entire court system to the chief justice of the state supreme court. The states have also been hiring professionals to help manage the court system.

Along with these reforms in government institutions, there have been a variety of other types of changes that have altered the character of state politics over the past few decades. State parties, for example, have become better funded and more active than they were a few decades ago. The political process has been opened up to allow better public participation through the passage of open meeting and open record laws. Participation has also been improved by the passage of the Voting Rights Act of 1965, along with its amendments, which has allowed greater access to politics to African Americans, language minorities, and the disabled. The increased number and diversity of interest groups at the state level has also improved public input into the political process, as has the increased use of the *initiative* to pass legislation. States have also enacted a variety of ethics rules to reduce corruption and limit the impact of interest group money.

Combined, these different reforms and trends have changed the character of state politics and altered the role of state government, making the states more important in American politics than they have been for many decades. One of the most visible signs of these changes has come in the size and complexity of state finances. By some measures, the size of state spending has more than tripled since the end of World War II.[1] In order to fund these expenditures, states have turned to a more diverse array of revenue sources, including a greater reliance on personal income tax and user fees. There has also been an expansion of sales taxes to include previously untaxed goods and services.

In the essay that follows, David Hedge, a professor at the University of Florida, gives an overview of the reforms that states have adopted to improve their position and that have led to the resurgence of the states. Hedge describes the changes in state government institutions, elections, and other aspects of state politics. He points out that these changes were not all caused by the states pulling themselves up by the bootstraps, but that the federal government has also played an important role in the resurgence of the states. He also describes how these changes have led the states to become more active in policymaking, often taking the lead rather than simply following the direction of the federal government.

The reading is the introductory chapter to a book Hedge wrote on the changing position and character of state government. In subsequent chapters, Hedge goes into detail on the reforms that were enacted over the past few decades to strengthen the states' ability to function. Yet Hedge's book, and this introductory chapter, goes beyond simply describing how these reforms have led to a resurgence of the states. Hedge also describes an alternative view of these changes, one that suggests that although these reforms may have given the states greater capacity, they have also had a detrimental effect on state government, leading to greater "political gridlock, parochialism, and PAC-dominated politics." Hedge's work thus provides two distinct perspectives on what these changes have meant for state politics today.

Hedge concludes his introductory chapter by providing an analytical framework to assess the "quality of governing in the states." Hedge argues that these political developments in the states can be judged by using two criteria, or what he calls two benchmarks for governing. These criteria are responsibility and democratic quality. By *responsibility*, he means the extent to which state governments are able to carry out their functions and produce policies that work. By *democratic quality*, he means the extent to which state policies reflect the preferences of state residents. The problem, which Hedge notes, is that these two criteria can often conflict, so that reforms that increase responsibility may limit public participation, and ones that heighten democracy may make government less responsible.

Hedge's work offers a good introduction to the study of state and local politics because by explaining the changes that have transformed state politics over the past four decades, he sheds considerable light on the character of state government today. Perhaps more importantly, Hedge's essay provides a valuable reminder that there are frequently tensions and conflicts in what we, as citizens, expect from state government. The conflict between responsibility and democracy is a common one that can be seen throughout different aspects of state politics. Yet these are not the only goals we seek from government, nor the only ones that can conflict. Among other goals, we want government decision making to be done in the open, not behind closed doors. We want fair representation of different interests and concerns in society. We want state governments to address social and economic problems, yet we also want them to keep taxes low and balance their budgets. There are often no simple answers that allow all of these goals to be obtained at the same time. For citizens, the question they must then consider when evaluating government is which goals are most important and should take precedence. In the chapters that follow, many of the readings have been selected to encourage students to think about the tensions and tradeoffs that exist in state politics.

Questions to Consider

In reading the excerpt from Hedge's work, these are some questions to consider:

- What does Hedge mean when he writes that there has been a resurgence of the states? What are some of the key characteristics of this resurgence?
- What is the "irony" of this resurgence? What is some of the evidence that Hedge offers to suggest that the effects of the resurgence have not all been positive?
- What are the two criteria that Hedge suggests using for assessing state government? Why does he say that these two goals may conflict?
- What types of political reforms may encourage greater responsibility? What types may encourage democracy?
- From what you have seen elsewhere, including in your own state, does there seem to be a relationship between the adoption of the reforms that Hedge describes and the problems seen today in how states are governed? How so?
- What factors do you think are important in creating "good government"? How important is responsibility compared with democracy? What other criteria do you think should be used to judge government?

Governance and the Changing American States

David M. Hedge

American federalism is being turned on its head. After decades of federal dominance, a realignment is occurring in the respective roles of the states and the federal government. Increasingly, the states are becoming the principal focus for policy initiatives in areas as diverse as education, health care, welfare reform, economic development, and insurance reform. Indeed, the major long-term legacy of the tumultuous politics of the 1990s may be the transfer of substantial responsibility for governing to the American states.

The states' increasing prominence is both planned and unplanned. Throughout the 1980s, the Reagan administration's efforts to achieve a less active federal government and a New Federalism shifted considerable responsibility for governing to the states. As the decade wore on, a growing and seemingly uncontrollable federal debt, divided control of Congress and the White House, a lack of presidential leadership, and a Congress that was growing more and more dysfunctional further guaranteed that fewer policy initiatives, particularly spending initiatives, came from the nation's capital. Moreover, what federal policy prescriptions were put forward frequently had a distinctive state "flavor" to them. The centerpiece of Congress's 1988 overhaul of welfare policy, for example, was the workfare program that had been operating in many of the states for well over a decade.

The trend toward a more state-centered federalism continued into the Clinton administration as well. During its first term, many of the administration's proposals, including family leave legislation, managed competition in health care, urban enterprise zones, and national service, were all initiatives that had already been put forward in a number of states. Even when the Clinton White House proposed major new federal initiatives (the president's ill-fated health care proposal, for example), the states were often slated to play a major role in their implementation. Perhaps the clearest signal of the administration's willingness to transfer authority to the states was the president's decision to sign off on the 1996 welfare reform bill, despite misgivings about the harshness of the legislation.

Any doubts that the responsibilities of the states would continue to grow in the next few decades were erased in the wake of the 1994 election and the apparent rejection of a Democratic Congress and an active federal government. Elements of the Republican "Contract with America," as well as the overarching ideological thrust of the new congressional majority, sought to give the states more freedom from federal intrusion and to shift major responsibility back to the states. Once again, the case of welfare reform is instructive. Initially, the welfare reforms contained in the Republican's Contract with America included a series of controversial proposals that amounted to federally prescribed mandates on the states, including provisions that would have removed unwed mothers from the welfare rolls. However, after meeting with more than a dozen GOP governors, Republican leaders in the House agreed to drop many of those requirements and to recast welfare reform in block grant terms that allow the states greater flexibility in implementation.

The political fallout from the 1994 elections has been every bit as dramatic and potentially far reaching at the state level. Following the 1994 elections, Republicans held the governorships in thirty-one states (up from twenty) and controlled half the states' legislatures. In many of those states, governors and legislators have pursued the new conservative agenda with the same vigor as their counterparts in Congress. According to one source (*Washington Post* January 29, 1995, p. A18):

> The same conservative themes of less government, lower taxes, and the devolution of power that now animate the legislative agenda in Washington are resonating with even greater volume in state capitals across the country. Newly fortified by the November election, Republican governors have outlined aggressive agendas for cutting taxes, shrinking government, reforming welfare and education, and rearranging the balance of power among Washington, the states, and local governments.

Several states considered their own "contracts," and a new round of budget and tax cuts were debated and, in many states, adopted. Newly elected governors George Pataki of New York and John Rowland of Connecticut, for instance, pledged to reduce taxes, and incumbent governors, including Howard Dean of Vermont and Christine Todd Whitman of New Jersey, sought additional cuts in their states' taxes. For the first time in more than a decade, state tax cuts in 1995 actually exceeded state tax increases (Van Horn 1996b).

Although the 1996 elections signaled the public's desire for a more moderate approach to solving the nation's problems, the partisan alignment of the 1994 election remained largely intact (Democrats experienced a net gain of five state legislatures, but Congress remained in Republican hands and Republicans controlled the governorship in thirty-two states), and no one expects power to flow back to Washington, D.C. Indeed, the political dynamics of the 1980s and 1990s point to a sea change in the nation's political thinking. Increasingly, the prevailing wisdom is that the states and not the federal government should take the lead in solving the nation's problems. Part of that reflects dissatisfaction with the federal government. But it also reflects a growing respect for the states. Many would agree with Carl Van Horn's (1989:1) assertion that state governments "are arguably the most responsive, innovative, and effective level of government in the American federal system."

The reader will note an irony in all of this. The dramatic growth in the reach of the federal government following World War II came about in large part because state and local governments were either unwilling or unable (or both) to deal with a wide range of social and economic problems—civil rights, poverty, education, workplace safety, consumer protection, health care, and environmental protection. Yet, as the twentieth century comes to a close, it is to state governments that we now look for solutions to many of these same problems. But are the states up to the task? Can the "sometimes governments" provide the political and policy leadership so sorely needed in the United States? Many would say yes.

The Resurgence of the States

There is considerable consensus among scholars and practitioners alike that the states have undergone a dramatic resurgence in recent decades. As a result of forces operating at both the national and subnational levels, state governments have become more representative and better able and more willing to govern. A variety of initiatives and reforms have increased citizen participation and input into state government; blacks, Hispanics, and women enjoy considerably greater representation at the state and local level; and higher levels of interparty competition and a growing diversity of interest groups promise a better linkage between public opinion and public policy. Parallel changes have occurred in the states' political institutions. Governors now have more power than ever before and are more willing to use that power to effect innovative policy solutions. That influence is evidenced by their prominence and visibility; no fewer than a dozen governors and former governors have been serious contenders for the presidency in the past four elections. During the 104th Congress, Republican governors such as Tommy Thompson of Wisconsin and John Engler of Michigan seemed to spend as much time in Washington, D.C., as they did in their state capitals, as they sought to shape and reshape elements of the Republican legislative agenda. For their part, state legislatures are more professional, better staffed, and more assertive. There is a new kind of career legislator who comes to the legislature at an earlier age, stays longer, and is much less willing to defer to governors or party leaders. State courts have also undergone significant structural reform and have demonstrated a willingness to intervene in the decisions and actions of the executive and legislative branches.

Most importantly, the states have taken the lead in addressing a wide range of policy problems, becoming what one author (Osborne 1988) refers to as "laboratories of democracy." When a national education commission declared in the early 1980s that America was a "Nation at Risk," for example, it was the states that adopted innovative educational reforms including curriculum changes, teacher competency requirements, aid equalization, and increased spending. In a parallel fashion, by the time Congress put the final touches on its first major attempt at developing a national AIDS policy in 1988, several of the states had already passed legislation dealing with the more controversial aspects of the AIDS crisis, including confidentiality, discrimination, and AIDS education in the public schools (Bingham and Hedge 1991). More recently, in the wake of the administration's abortive attempt to pass national health care reform, several states, including Florida, Minnesota, Oregon, Washington, and Hawaii, have already considered, and in many cases adopted, dramatic new reforms. Similarly, even before Congress and the president agreed on the 1996 welfare bill, a majority of the states had already sought federal exemptions that allowed them to, among other things, set limits on welfare receipt, extend transitional services and support for families leaving welfare for work, and encourage teen welfare recipients to finish high school (see, e.g., Strawn, Dacey, and McCart 1994).

What prompted the resurgence of the states? Much of the credit lies, ironically, with the federal government. A half century of federal grants-in-aid has increased both the technical capacity and aspirations of state and local officials. Federal grants, together with federal mandates, have also expanded the policy scope of the states. Two other federal actions have been particularly important. Federal civil rights policy and the reapportionment "revolution" triggered by the 1962 *Baker v. Carr* decision have ensured that minorities and urban areas are better represented in state legislatures and have contributed to increased legislative activism, particularly on behalf of the cities. More recently, the Reagan administration's New Federalism, with its emphasis on devolution, deregulation, and "defunding," forced the states to do more with less, a trend that continues today. And if the cohort of new Republican governors and legislators elected in 1994 have their way, the states will enjoy even more flexibility in programming with fewer mandates in the years ahead.

The states have contributed to their own resurgence as well. First, since the 1960s over three-fourths of the states have either enacted new or revised existing constitutions that strengthen their governors, increase legislative sessions and compensation, establish greater fiscal discipline, and provide a basis for protecting individual rights and liberties (Van Horn 1996a). Second, the greater use of the initiative and referendum, efforts to make voting and registration less burdensome, and reforms that increase citizen participation in government between elections, together with state policies that comply with federal reapportionment and civil rights policies, have increased the opportunities for ordinary citizens to access and influence state government. Third, over the last few decades the states have restructured their revenue systems to make them more diverse, less prone to economic cycles, and, in many cases, more equitable. Prodded by the three Rs—tax revolts, recessions, and reductions in federal aid—many states in the 1980s increased existing taxes, most notably income and sales taxes, and found new sources of revenues, including state lotteries and additional user charges.

Perhaps nothing better illustrates the realignment of federal and state policy responsibilities than current models of federalism. Although the particulars may differ, recent visions of federalism afford the states the dominant role in governing America, something unheard of two decades ago. Two models are particularly illustrative of the states' resurgence. Linda Tarr-Whelan has argued that a *progressive federalism* may be emerging in America.[1] According to Tarr-Whelan, states serve as laboratories for policy innovations that are eventually diffused to others through federal incentives and negotiation. Progressive federalism unfolds in several stages. At the outset, a handful of states take the lead in fashioning new and innovative approaches to issues as diverse as welfare, health care reform, and consumer protection. At the federal level, progressives push to extend new state initiatives to the remainder of the states. The result is federal legislation that sets minimum program standards, provides limited federal resources as an incentive to participate, and allows the states maximum flexibility in implementation. The states are then allowed to further innovate beyond the prescribed minimum.

Thomas Dye's (1988) model of *competitive federalism* also views the states as the locus of governing in the United States and provides an even smaller role for the federal government. Extending Charles Tiebout's model of local government to the states, Dye argues that federalism is usefully viewed as a marketplace where states compete with one another for residents and firms by offering the most attractive package of taxes and services. Acting as consumers, voters and firms, armed with the necessary information, can "vote with their feet" and through the ballot box for the state policy package that best satisfies their policy preferences. Competition and the prospect of losing firms and citizens to other states forces the states to be more efficient, responsive, and innovative. Federalism as a marketplace of governments also blunts the federal government's tendency to overproduce goods and services and to respond to narrow interests at the expense of the larger public.

New theories of federalism are increasingly finding their way into more concrete proposals for rearranging functional responsibilities within the United States. Just prior to joining the Clinton administration, Alice Rivlin (1992) proposed a fundamental realignment in the respective policy roles of the federal and state governments. Under Rivlin's proposal, state governments would assume primary responsibility for economic development, including education, job training, infrastructure development, and child care, while the federal government would assume sole responsibility for national health insurance. As part of that, Rivlin proposed eliminating most federal programs in the areas of housing, social services, education, and economic development. On the fiscal side, she proposed that the federal government run a budget surplus and that the states cooperate in developing a common tax pool that would be shared among the states on a formula basis. What is particularly striking about Rivlin's proposal is that it rests less on conventional notions of politics and economics and more on a pragmatic view of American politics. States governments should shoulder greater responsibility for governing because they are better able to do so and federal authorities have demonstrated that they are not.

Passage of the 1996 welfare reform bill reflected that kind of pragmatism as well. The conventional wisdom, supplied by public finance theorists, has long held that programs that redistribute wealth, most notably welfare, are best left at the national level for both equity and efficiency reasons. Yet by replacing the open-end entitlement program that had guaranteed the poor assistance since the 1930s with a closed-end block grant, the president and Congress discarded the conventional wisdom in lieu of a number of more practical considerations—the size of the federal deficit and a corresponding desire to reduce spending, the political clout of Republican governors and the new conservative Republican congressional majority, and Bill Clinton's need to deliver on his 1992 campaign promise to "end welfare as we know it." In addition, as Richard Nathan (1996) points out, the discussion of welfare reform in the 1990s has less to do with the redistribution of wealth than with fashioning effective intervention strategies that will move individuals off welfare rolls and into jobs, a task that many feel the states are better suited to do.

The Irony of Reform: An Alternative View

Despite the apparent resurgence of the states, recent events and developments suggest a less benign view of the states' capacity to govern. Many have argued that political developments and policy activism in the states have produced new problems. As state governments address a wider range of issues, as those issues become more controversial, as each branch of government becomes more assertive, and as the states' political systems become further decentralized and fragmented, a number of political pathologies—political gridlock, parochialism, and political action committee (PAC)–dominated politics—threaten the states' resurgence. As the 1990s unfolded, a number of developments signaled that all was not well with the American states.

- The nation's recession that lingered into the early 1990s caused an overwhelming majority of the American states to face their most severe budget crises in recent history. Politically unable to raise taxes and fees significantly (having done so in the 1980s), faced with rising welfare, education, prison, and Medicaid costs, and limited by constitutional requirements to maintain balanced operating budgets, state lawmakers were forced to make painful cuts in many areas of their budgets. Many states faced crisis levels in several policy areas. In California, for example, the recession, tax limitations, and a population explosion produced serious school overcrowding, teacher layoffs, a real decline in per pupil expenditures, and as one author (Meyer 1992: 70–71) notes, "a lost generation of children." Similarly, in Florida, newly completed (and sorely needed) state prisons remained empty during the early 1990s because there was no money in the budget to staff and operate them.

For many the recession of the late 1980s and early 1990s laid to rest any notion that the states' fiscal houses were in order. Despite the fiscal reforms and tax increases of the 1980s and the recent economic recovery, states in the 1990s still find themselves scrambling to generate new resources to meet escalating costs in a political climate that is even less supportive of new taxes than it was during the Reagan years. And analysts worry that in balancing their operating budgets and providing tax relief to their citizens, too many states have incurred too much short- and long-term debt. New Jersey's popular governor Christine Todd Whitman, for example, was able to deliver on her 1993 promise to cut taxes by 15 percent and balance the budget only by delaying payments to the state employees' retirement fund (payments that will have to be made later) and refinancing 10-year state road bonds to a 20-year maturity. Already analysts and political leaders are warning of potentially bleak days ahead for the states should the nation enter a new recession.

- Some worry that political reforms and other developments have produced new pathologies. Although the increased use of initiatives and referenda, for instance, has ensured that issues such as term limits and tax relief are placed on the public agenda, there is a concern that citizens are being crowded out of issue elections by special interests. Within legislatures, greater careerism and the demands of reelection contribute to legislative fragmentation, open the door to inordinate PAC influence, make leadership more difficult, and undercut the ability of legislatures to reach consensus or fashion coherent public policy. More broadly, developments and reforms on both the supply and demand side of state government magnify the role and importance of money in state politics, producing new ethical challenges and threatening the quality of representation and the ability of state governments to make difficult policy choices. In addition, as each branch of state government grows stronger and more assertive, conflicts between governors, legislatures, and the courts have grown more frequent and intense and too often lead to policy gridlock and inaction. That tendency toward gridlock is further accentuated by increases in the rate of divided government. A more recent development, the adoption of term limits in half of the American states, may also blunt the states' resurgence by reversing the trend toward greater legislative professionalism and making lawmakers more dependent on staff, governors, and interest groups.
- The new Republican majorities in the 104th Congress moved toward a much less restrictive federal presence in state government. One of the earliest elements of the Contract with America to be enacted was legislation limiting the ability of the federal government to impose new mandates on the states. Nonetheless, if elements of the Contract with America are a guide to what will unfold in the next few years, inconsistencies in federal policies toward the states will continue. In the series of crime bills passed in February 1995, for example, House Republicans managed to eliminate one set of mandates (the provision that localities use federal grant monies to hire new police officers) in one piece of legislation while at the same time imposing others (e.g., a requirement that states adopt truth-in-sentencing requirements as a condition for receiving federal prison dollars) in another. In a related fashion, tort reforms adopted in the House in March of 1995 would preempt state liability laws by limiting the amount of punitive damages that can be awarded to successful litigants.
- Perhaps most distressing, there is growing evidence that many of the states' policy initiatives have simply not worked or not worked as well as advocates had hoped. Despite two decades of school reform, for example, many contend that America's schools are still in crisis. The uneven record of state policy initiatives is seen elsewhere as well—studies in the mid-1980s gave a majority of the states low marks in managing the environment (see, e.g., Ridley 1987); critics charge that the states are doing a poor job of enforcing workplace safety standards (Victor 1990); and analyses of economic development policy raise fundamental questions about the ability of state governments to nurture and sustain long-term economic growth (Brace 1993). Moreover, even where state and local policies seem to be working, a lack of resources frequently limits policy effectiveness as services can only be provided to a portion of eligible recipients.

Taken together, the evidence suggests an alternative view of the states' resurgence, one in which the capacity of the states is limited and where state politics and policy frequently mirror the larger political climate of political stalemate and malaise that we have come to associate with politics in Washington, D.C. That should come as a shock to no one. The federal government has long served as the model by which we often reform and judge the states. State legislatures, for example, are given high marks for achieving the kind of "institutionalization" typical of the U.S. Congress. No one should be surprised, therefore, when state legislatures begin to exhibit the same kinds of frailties as the U.S. House and the Senate. Similarly, while state courts are applauded for their activism, that activism contributes to the policy dilemmas and conflict many states now face. In summary, by the mid-1990s state legislative politics looked surprisingly similar to congressional dynamics, governors faced the same kinds of limits with which modern presidents must contend, state courts find themselves at odds with the executive and legislative branches, political gridlock occurs frequently, and a skeptical public still expects governments to solve their problems without raising their taxes.

None of this is meant to suggest that the states have not enjoyed a resurgence (they have) or that they are not more capable of governing than they were three decades ago (they are). Rather, the politics of the 1980s and 1990s illustrate that the resurgent states face a number of limits—a more fragmented and contentious political climate, revenue constraints, citizen dissatisfaction, and a fiscally strapped federal partner—that make governing the states more difficult and complex. Moreover, decades of social programming have demonstrated, if nothing else, that the problems governments must now deal with, including poverty, health care for the poor and the aged, crime, and environmental management, are more intractable than we had first imagined. These are not problems that beg simple solutions. Nor are solutions to these problems likely to come cheap. Cleaning up the environment, rebuilding America's infrastructure, fighting poverty and crime, taking care of the elderly, and meeting the needs of education in an increasingly competitive world economy are costly enterprises and demand a long-term commitment of state resources and attention. They may also require a new way of conducting politics and devising policy.

At a minimum, recent developments, both good and bad, suggest the need for a closer look at state political reforms and developments. The pages that follow look systematically at those changes in an effort to gauge the capacity of the states to govern in the twenty-first century. Over the next several chapters answers are sought to the following questions:

How has the character of state politics changed in recent decades? How much political reform has, in fact, taken place? What other changes have occurred in state politics and government? What are the consequences of those changes for the capacity of state governments to govern in the decades ahead? Are state governments capable of producing policies that effectively address the pressing problems of the day? Are state governments sufficiently representative of and responsive to their citizens? . . .

In discussing the changes that have occurred in state politics in recent decades, the intent is not only to document those changes but to assess their larger consequences for the quality of governing in the states. Toward that end, the remainder of this chapter outlines an analytic framework that will help us to systematically sort those impacts. That framework consists of two related elements: (1) a pair of benchmarks against which reforms and developments can be assessed and (2) a discussion of the conventional wisdom concerning the likely impacts on governing of the many changes that are documented throughout the remaining chapters.

Benchmarks for Governing

Identifying a set of criteria for gauging the governing capacity of the American states is a daunting task. Analytically, there is a need for a set of standards broad enough to encompass the wide range of developments that have occurred on the supply and demand sides of government. Making it easier to register and vote and restructuring the states' court systems are seemingly unrelated developments, yet each conditions the character and quality of state government. The task is made more difficult by a lack of consensus in the 1990s as to what constitutes wise governance. Over the last several years, political conflict has increasingly foundered on fundamental issues concerning the goals governments should pursue and the institutional arrangements appropriate to achieving those goals. Those analytic and normative difficulties aside, most would agree that democratic governments need to do two things—produce effective policies while responding to the needs and preferences of their citizens. Given those twin goals, two sets of criteria—responsibility and democratic quality—are useful benchmarks for assessing the implications for governing of recent political developments in state politics.[2]

Responsibility

Responsibility speaks to the ability of governments to govern wisely. As Leroy Rieselbach (1994: 18) notes: "Responsibility focuses on problem solving. A responsible institution makes policies that are reasonably successful in resolving the major issues confronting the nation." Ultimately, responsible government requires enacting and implementing policies that work, that achieve their goals in an effective and efficient manner. In this sense responsibility focuses on the *products* of government, on the outcomes and consequences of government activities. Against that benchmark, state governments are responsible only when their policies, among other things, improve the education of their children, ensure a clean environment, or maintain acceptable levels of public safety or health. But determining the ultimate impact of public policies can be problematic, particularly in the short run. Policy analysts and public officials have long understood how difficult it is to link policy outcomes to specific policies. Most of the things governments attend to are influenced by a number of variables, of which policies and programs are only a few. We know, for example, that educational outcomes not only reflect what it is that schools do but also what children bring to the classroom and their experiences outside of the school. Moreover, policy analysts have learned that the effects of public policies are often not realized for years. Head Start is a good example of that. Written off as a failure in its formative years, the program is now hailed by liberals and conservatives alike as a program that worked.

For these and other reasons, responsibility is also defined and judged in terms of the *processes* involved in making and carrying out public policies. For some, responsibility entails making policy in a timely fashion. Relatedly, critics of divided government and increasing partisanship often couch calls for greater responsibility in terms of avoiding inaction, gridlock, and stalemate. In recent decades citizens have become increasingly frustrated not so much by what the federal government does, but with the seeming inability of Congress and the president to act at all, to avoid the partisan gridlock that frequently immobilizes the federal government. The most dramatic example of that in recent years, of course, was the budget deadlock that shut down the federal government in the winter of 1995.

Others look for responsibility in innovative programming and policy solutions that represent major departures from the status quo. Inherent in that latter notion of responsibility is a dissatisfaction with incremental policies and an attendant policymaking process that places a premium on compromise. According to this view, although compromise often makes sense from a political perspective, the result is frequently policies that are more symbolic than real, pursue conflicting goals, and are unlikely to produce much change. A desire for what is often radical policy change is not inherently a liberal or conservative trademark. Whereas calls for major changes in policy in the 1960s and 1970s typically referenced liberal policy alternatives, efforts to substantially alter the policy status quo in the 1990s are, often as not, support for conservative policy prescriptions (e.g., calls for a flat tax or the welfare reforms that were enacted in 1996) that are every bit as radical as analogous policies two or three decades earlier.

Kent Weaver and Bert Rockman's (1993) analysis of the governing capacity of the industrial powers in Europe, North America, and Japan suggests additional procedural indicators of responsibility, including the ability of governments to (1) sustain policy innovations over time, (2) target resources, and (3) impose losses on powerful groups. The latter pair of standards usefully acknowledge the limited resources that governments at all levels must contend with in the 1990s. In an era of scarce resources, state governments cannot address every policy problem, and state policymakers must necessarily choose among competing public policy concerns. In the early 1990s, for example, the need to build new prisons to house their states' rapidly growing prison populations meant that states such as Florida and Texas had to place new initiatives in education and health care on hold. In addition, one of the painful realities of governing in the 1990s is the fact that finding responsible policy solutions often means imposing losses on particular, and often powerful, groups. Although policymakers are reluctant to admit as much, shrinking the federal budget deficit, for instance, has meant (or will mean) substantially reducing (in some cases eliminating) benefits to the poor, farmers, the elderly, and others.

Defining responsibility in terms of the processes of governing has considerable virtue; it avoids the difficult and often fruitless task of sorting out the ultimate effects of public policies and it makes it easier to design and judge institutional arrangements that promote program effectiveness. But, as the reader is well aware, there is less agreement on procedural benchmarks. Decisions that are made too quickly, for example, can also be viewed as impulsive, not well thought out, and pandering to the latest public opinion poll. Similarly, proposals that depart substantially from the status quo are often seen as extreme, reckless, and risky. There is also no guarantee that policies that move in big steps will necessarily succeed. Nonetheless, there is good reason to believe that governments that cannot respond in a timely fashion to pressing public problems do not serve their citizenry well. Moreover, there is an emerging consensus that governments at all levels need to find new approaches that depart substantially from the policies of the past. And in the face of scarce resources doing that probably entails saying no to some and yes to others.

Statehouse Democracy

Governing requires more than acting responsibly, however. State governments, as all governments, also need to be judged in terms of the quality of "statehouse democracy." For the most part, democracy in the states is representative democracy; citizen preferences, at least in the ideal, find their way into government policies and decisions through elected and, increasingly, nonelected intermediaries. For that to occur, Kim Quaile Hill (1994: 11–12) contends that four procedural conditions or requirements must be present: (1) equal political rights; (2) free and fair elections; (3) high levels of citizen participation in elections; and (4) the existence of "competing nongovernmental institutions" that will organize and articulate the policy preferences of like-minded citizens. Robert Erikson, Gerald Wright, and John McIver (1993: 1) maintain that democratic practices embody both democratic procedures and their results. As those authors note, "we often gauge the quality of democratic government by the responsiveness of public policy makers to the preferences of the mass public as well as by formal opportunities for, and the practice of, mass participation in political life." For Erikson, Wright, and McIver, a critical test of democratic governments is whether public policies are congruent with public opinion.

Taken together, the analyses of Hill and Erikson, Wright, and McIver, as well as a broader reading of democratic theory and practice, suggest that in gauging the democratic consequences of state political developments, we need to attend to the following:

- the extent to which citizens are able to and actually do participate both directly and indirectly in the decisions of government, through candidate and issue elections and through citizen participation devices that promote citizen input between elections;
- the quality of that participation in terms of the number and kinds of opportunities for participation, the extent to which individuals are presented with meaningful and real choices, and the quality of those choices (i.e., are citizens informed and do they choose in their own best interest?);
- the extent to which political minorities, most notably women and racial and language minorities, are represented in government;
- the extent to which the preferences of ordinary citizens are effectively and accurately transmitted to public officials; and
- the extent to which there is a fit between public opinion and public policy.

Achieving greater democracy and policy responsibility is difficult under the best of circumstances. The problem, however, is compounded by a tension that often emerges between the two benchmarks in the day-to-day workings of government. As we suggest throughout the chapters, providing more opportunities for more citizens and groups to have input into government promotes statehouse democracy but often detracts from the ability of governments to make responsible policy decisions by promoting delay, incrementalism, or stalemate. The tension between responsibility and "democraticness" is particularly troublesome for individual representatives who must somehow balance the needs and preferences of constituents with the broader needs of the state and the need for policy coherence. On the one hand, we expect our representatives to prosecute district and constituent interests. And, to their credit, state legislators in a number of states have become quite adept at doing just that. On the other hand, there is a concern that by focusing on the needs of constituents, lawmakers inevitably produce policies that ignore the broader needs of the state and substitute pork barrel and other particularized benefits for responsible, effective programs.

Political Change and the Art of Governing: The Conventional Wisdom

The critical question is how various reforms and developments on the demand and supply sides of government will affect the ability of the states to be both democratic and responsible. Obviously, there is much disagreement here as well, as recent debates over term limits and balanced budget amendments testify. Nonetheless, there is a growing body of evidence and speculation that the capacity to govern is shaped in large part by the degree to which power is centralized within political systems. The conventional wisdom that has emerged maintains that political and institutional changes that fragment or decentralize political authority contribute to statehouse democracy but also make government less responsible. According to this view, spreading the power and authority to govern across and among multiple political institutions and interests ensures that more citizens and groups, including political and social minorities, will have more opportunities to participate in more decisions. Political fragmentation also protects political minorities from majority rule by making it more difficult for majorities to act. And, therein lies the rub. Decentralizing political authority also makes it more difficult to fashion coherent policies in a timely fashion by (1) promoting compromise and incrementalism, (2) making it more difficult to target resources or impose losses on major interests, (3) encouraging the production of particularized benefits (e.g., pork barrel programs or tax breaks for special interests), and (4) contributing to policy delay and stalemate by making political agreements on major legislation and policy initiatives more difficult to obtain.

The genesis of the conventional wisdom is found, in large part, in the long-standing institutional critique of American government, a critique that is addressed to the national government but which has obvious implications for state governments as well. As all of us learned in our civics and American government classes, the founding fathers purposely set out to create a complex set of checks and balances aimed at ensuring that governing would be difficult. A number of constitutional provisions, most notably a separation of powers, checks and balances, antimajority rules, bicameralism, and federalism, provided the means to check the worst impulses of those who would use government too capriciously and on behalf of narrow interests. Those constitutional features also ensured that diverse interests would have the opportunity to be heard in government. Yet, for decades scholars and practitioners alike have found the decentralization and shared authority inherent in America's constitutional framework cumbersome and unwieldy. In his classic study of Congress, Woodrow Wilson lamented a federal government that "lacks strength because its powers are divided, lacks promptness because its authorities are multiplied, lacks wieldiness because its processes are roundabout, lacks efficiency because its responsibility is indistinct and its actions without competent directions" (Wilson 1981: 206).

A century later, the bipartisan Committee on the Constitutional System (CCS) voiced similar concerns about America's constitutional system. As CCS cochair Lloyd Cutler (1985: 12) complained: "A particular shortcoming in need of a remedy is the structural inability of our government to propose, legislate, and administer a balanced program for governing. In parliamentary terms, one might say that under the U.S. Constitution it is not now feasible to 'form a government.' The separation of powers between the legislative and executive branches, whatever its merits in 1793, has become a structure that almost guarantees stalemate today." The problem of decentralization and fragmentation is made worse by recent political developments, including a more assertive Supreme Court, the increased decentralization of Congress, and most notably perhaps, the propensity toward divided government.

Although institutional critiques have been aimed at the national government, their relevance to state governments seems obvious. In the first place, state governments share a common constitutional framework. Like their national counterpart, the states have devised systems of separation of powers and checks and balances and, with the exception of Nebraska, have bicameral legislatures. In addition, many of the changes that have occurred in state government, including the growing diversity of interest groups, the resurgence of state parties, and institutional reforms and developments in each branch of state government, contribute to the centralization or decentralization of state government.

At the same time, the model of governance outlined here only begins to capture the kinds of changes that have occurred at the state level and their likely effects on governing. Many of the changes that have occurred, for example increased compensation for legislators or merit selection for judges, are as much about increasing institutional capacity as they are about centralization or decentralization. Nor does the brief discussion of the positive impacts of decentralization for democratic development address the complex issues and concerns surrounding representation. Moreover, not everyone agrees with the major premise of the framework, that is, that decentralization detracts from responsibility. There is some evidence, for example, that divided government can promote policy innovation by encouraging competition between branches of government and ensuring effective oversight of the executive branch (Weaver and Rockman 1993; Fiorina 1996). These and other caveats aside, the model of governance implicit in the conventional wisdom represents a useful reference point for making sense in a larger fashion of the changes that are occurring throughout the states. It is to those developments we now turn.

Notes

1. Reported in Peirce 1991.
2. Readers who are familiar with Leroy Rieselbach's (1994) excellent text on congressional reform will instantly recognize my intellectual debt to that author. Rieselbach argues that three sets of criteria can be used to assess congressional behavior—responsibility, responsiveness, and accountability. Those same criteria, however, seem appropriate to the kinds of changes that have occurred in the states' political institutions and processes. However, in utilizing those concepts, I have chosen to subsume responsiveness and accountability under the rubric of democratic quality.

References

Bingham, Richard D., and David Hedge. 1991. *State and Local Government in a Changing Society*, 2nd ed. New York: McGraw-Hill.

Brace, Paul. 1993. *State Government and Economic Performance*. Baltimore: Johns Hopkins University Press.

Cutler, Lloyd N. 1985. "To Form a Government." In Donald L. Robinson, ed., *Reforming American Government: The Bicentennial Papers of the Committee on the Constitutional System*. Boulder: Westview Press.

Dye, Thomas R. 1988. "A Theory of Competitive Federalism." Presented at the annual meeting of the Southern Political Science Association, Atlanta, November 3–5.

Erikson, Robert S., Gerald C. Wright, and John P. McIver. 1993. *Statehouse Democracy: Public Opinion and Policy in the American States*. New York: Cambridge University Press.

Fiorina, Morris. 1996. *Divided Government*, 2nd ed. Needham Heights, MA: Simon & Schuster.

"Governors Add Conservative Themes to Their Agendas for Next Few Years: States Look for Ways to Cut Taxes, Reform Welfare, Shrink Government." *Washington Post*, January 29, 95: A18.

Hill, Kim Quaile. 1994. *Democracy in the Fifty States*. Lincoln: University of Nebraska Press.

Meyer, Michael. 1992. "Another Lost Generation." *Newsweek*, May 4: 70–72.

Nathan, Richard P. 1996. "The Role of the States in American Federalism." In Carl Van Horn, ed., *The State of the States*, 3rd ed. Washington, DC: CQ Press.

Osborne, David. 1988. *Laboratories of Democracy: A New Breed of Governor Creates Models for National Growth*. Boston: Harvard Business School Press.

Peirce, Neal. 1991. "State Leadership for the Nation." *The Journal of State Government* (Jan./March): 27–29.

Ridley, Scott. 1987. *The State of the States*. Washington, DC: Fund for Renewable Energy and the Environment.

Rieselbach, Leroy N. 1994. *Congressional Reform: The Changing Modern Congress*. Washington, DC: CQ Press.

Rivlin, Alice M. 1992. *Reviving the American Dream: The Economy, the States, and the Federal Government*. Washington, DC: Brookings Institution.

Robinson, Donald L., ed. 1985. *Reforming American Government: The Bicentennial Papers of the Committee on the Constitutional System*. Boulder: Westview Press.

Strawn, Julie, Sheila Dacey, and Linda McCart. 1994. *Final Report: The National Governors' Association Survey of State Welfare Reforms*. Washington, DC: National Governors' Association.

Van Horn, Carl E. 1989. "The Quiet Revolution." In Carl E. Van Horn, ed., *The State of the States*. Washington, DC: CQ Press.

———. 1996a. "The Quiet Revolution." In Carl E. Van Horn, ed., *The State of the States*, 3rd ed. Washington, DC: CQ Press.

———. 1996b. "Power to the States." In Carl E. Van Horn, ed., *The State of the States*, 3rd ed. Washington, DC: CQ Press.

Victor, Kirk. 1990. "State-Style Safety." *National Journal*, February 24: 440–443.

Weaver, R. Kent, and Bert A. Rockman, eds. 1993. *Do Institutions Matter? Government Capabilities in the United States and Abroad*. Washington, DC: Brookings Institution.

Wilson, Woodrow. 1981. *Congressional Government: A Study in American Politics*. Baltimore: Johns Hopkins University Press.

CASE STUDY 1

Introduction

In the preceding essay, Professor Hedge provides two different perspectives on the broad changes that have transformed state governments over the past four decades. The first perspective suggests that state governments are in a much better position today to handle the tasks they are asked to perform than they have ever been. There has been a resurgence of the states, which has increased their capacity to govern. The second perspective is less positive. It suggests that the states have become affected by some of the same "pathologies" that seem to be stifling government at the national level, as well as some of their own. State finances are in disarray. Special interests seem to dominate politics. There is gridlock and conflict. Many state policy initiatives have simply not worked.

California's experiences in recent years provide a good example of Hedge's argument. On the one hand, California has developed a very capable and active state government, one that has frequently created innovative policies that have become models for the nation. Yet on the other hand, California's government often seems to be unable to function, stifled by partisan conflict and distracted by the demands to raise ever-growing amounts of campaign contributions. With a professional legislature and a well-staffed executive branch, the state government clearly has the institutional structures and support personnel necessary to govern well, but it often seems incapable of doing so. To those who have followed California politics over the past two decades, the recall of California Governor Gray Davis in 2003 may have seemed less of a surprise than simply a continuation of the chaos that has beset the state's politics for many years.

In the case study that follows, Sacramento-based journalist Peter Schrag describes the transformation of California over the past few decades from being a model for other states to a state in despair. The essay was published in 1999, so it does not describe the most recent problems in the state, which led to Davis's recall. Yet there are two different trains of thought in Schrag's essay that make it a particularly valuable case study. One is that it simply describes the problems that are making it difficult today for California's government to function. Hedge's essay, which you just read, raises the question as to whether states are up to the task of governing. Schrag's study of California provides an answer to that question, one that is not particularly optimistic. Despite its past history of innovative policies and politics, California has developed a governmental structure that has grown increasingly "unmanageable and incomprehensible." Second, Schrag's essay is of interest because it illustrates what Hedge describes as the potential conflict between the goals of responsibility and statehouse democracy. Schrag argues that one of the main factors that has led to the problems in California has been the increased use of the initiative process since the 1978 passage of Proposition 13, which placed strict limits on property taxes in the state. The initiative process is often hailed as a way for average citizens to have a greater voice in politics. Through the initiative, citizens can develop their own proposals for new laws and place them on the ballot through a petition drive. Many see the process as a type of governing structure that increases democracy because it allows for direct public involvement in lawmaking. Yet Schrag writes that the frequent use of initiatives in California has severely restricted the state government's ability to function. Ballot measures, such as Proposition 13, have reduced the discretion of the state government, making it more difficult for it to act. Thus, although the initiative process may be increasing democracy, it has not increased government responsibility.

California is often viewed as an exceptional case, one whose experiences are quite different from those of other states. It certainly has some distinctive characteristics: Its population is far larger and more diverse than other states. It also faces a much broader and more diverse set of social problems. Its government is larger than most state governments and even those of many nations. And its politics often seem much different from that practiced elsewhere. Even though California's experiences may often be the exception, the problems that Schrag describes are not particularly different from problems confronting other states. The concerns he voices about initiatives are certainly heard in other states that have the initiative process. Moreover, even many states that do not have the initiative are confronting some of the same neopopulist trends that he describes, making it difficult for the government to function. Thus, Schrag may be right that California offers a valuable cautionary tale, one that raises questions as to the ability of state governments to handle their tasks despite their increased capacity.

Questions to Consider

When reading Schrag's essay, these are some questions to consider:

- Schrag's essay is taken from his book *Paradise Lost: California's Experience, America's Future.* What does he mean that paradise has been lost? What was California once like? What is it like today?
- What was Proposition 13? Why does Schrag use that as a dividing point between the old and new California?
- What different factors does Schrag blame for the problems in California today?
- How does Schrag's essay illustrate Hedge's argument that there can be a conflict between responsibility and democracy? Explain what has happened in California to create this conflict.

- What does Schrag mean when he writes that one group of citizens depends on public services, while another group dominates voter rolls? Who belongs to these different groups? What does he say are the consequences of this situation?
- What is neopopulism? What are some of its characteristics? Is neopopulism prominent in your state? What effect has it had on your state government?
- Is it possible that the problems encountered by state governments today are not caused by a resurgence of state governments, per se, but by other forces? Think about Schrag's essay; does it provide any alternative explanations? Or is there indeed something about this resurgence that encourages political pathologies?

Paradise Lost: California's Experience, America's Future

Peter Schrag

I

In the generation immediately following World War II, and to some extent even before, California was widely regarded as both model and magnet for the nation—in its economic opportunities, its social outlook, and its high-quality public services and institutions. With a nearly free and universally accessible system of public higher education, a well-supported public school system, an ambitious agenda of public works projects—in irrigation and flood control; in highway construction and park development—and a wide array of social services and human rights guarantees that had no parallel in any other state, California seemed to have an optimism about its population, possibilities, and future whose largest flaw was the very excess of expectations on which it rested.

Now, forty years on, having come through the sharp recession of the early 1990s, the state, with a robust but substantially different economic base, is again at the world's economic and technological frontiers: in electronics and software, in biotechnology and a vast array of other scientifically based industries, in foreign trade, and in the convergence of the old Hollywood and the new computer-based graphics and design ventures that have grown up around it. It is even enjoying a revival of the aerospace industries that were devastated by the recession and defense cutbacks of the late 1980s and early 1990s.

But California, even with a large burst of new postrecession revenue, is no longer the progressive model in its public institutions and services, or in its social ethic, that it once was—had indeed ceased to hold that position long before the last recession began. California's schools, which, thirty years ago, had been among the most generously funded in the nation, are now in the bottom quarter among the states in virtually every major indicator—in their physical condition, in public funding, in test scores—closer in most of them to Mississippi than to New York or Connecticut or New Jersey. The state, which has almost doubled in population since the early 1960s, has built some twenty new prisons in the past two decades. But it has not opened one new campus of the University of California for nearly three decades. Its once-celebrated freeway system is now rated as among the most dilapidated road networks in the country. Many of its public libraries operate on reduced hours, and some have closed altogether. The state and county parks charge hefty admission fees. The state's social benefits, once among the nation's most generous, have been cut, and cut again, and then cut again. And what had once been a tuition-free college and university system, while still among the world's great public educational institutions, struggles for funds and charges as much as every other state university system, and in some cases more.

Peter Schrag, *Paradise Lost: California's Experience, America's Future* (Berkeley: University of California Press, 1998), pp. 7–23.

In 1994, Californians, who, after World War II had reveled in their own growth and appeared to welcome every comer, voted overwhelmingly to exclude all illegal-alien children from their public schools. Two years later, they voted to prohibit every form of race- or gender-based affirmative action in public employment, contracting, and education. In 1997, California's Industrial Welfare Commission, a body appointed by the governor, abolished a rule dating back to the Progressive Era that required most non-farm employers to pay overtime to any worker who worked more than an eight-hour day. In the meantime, the gap between the state's upper-income groups and its poorest workers is growing even more rapidly than the national average, not so much because the affluent are making so much more (though they are making more) but because the incomes of the bottom ten percent of the working population have fallen so much further. Thus, as the state begins to celebrate its sesquicentennial—the 150th anniversary of the gold rush of 1848–49; admission to the Union in 1850—California's social policies and governmental structures can be seen more readily as an urgent cautionary tale, and as a high-stakes test for a nation that will increasingly be faced with similar challenges—indeed already is—than as a shining standard.

The most obvious question arising here is as complex in the answering as it is short in the asking: What happened? Why now, why in California, why in this form? What happened in the decades between the ebullient 'fifties and 'sixties and the anxious 'eighties and 'nineties? What occurred particularly in the interplay between the monumental demographic changes of a California where whites will soon be a minority among other minorities and the state's political evolution? What's the relationship between those changes, the enactment of the radical tax limits in Proposition 13 in 1978, the orgy of other voter initiatives that followed in its wake and that have gripped California for the better part of a generation, and the erosion of public services that they brought with them? Can a system that was created, and that flourished, for one kind of population maintain (or regain) its optimism and vitality for another? Put another way, are California's once-splendid public services and its promise of social equity sputtering and coughing because they became overloaded with social burdens? Or is the problem caused by some combination of hostility and indifference on the part of a body of voters that isn't sure it wants to carry this kind of load for *those kinds* of people? Californians seem to have regained a little of their optimism, but many of the effects of the changes of the past generation will last long into the future. Could it all have been negotiated to better ends with better leadership?

Some twenty years have passed since the passage of California's Proposition 13, which set in motion not merely the holy crusade against taxes in which much of the country now seems irretrievably stuck, but a condition of permanent neopopulism in California, and to some extent elsewhere, for which there is no real precedent, even in the Progressive Era of the early years of the twentieth century. During the two decades since the passage of 13, California has been in nearly constant revolt against representative government. During that period, voters have passed one initiative after another—tax limitation initiatives; initiatives capping state and local spending; measures imposing specified minimum spending formulas for schools; term limits for legislative and statewide offices; three-strikes sentencing laws; land conservation measures; the measures abolishing affirmative action in public education, contracting, and employment, and seeking to deny public schooling and other services to illegal immigrants, and dozens of others—each of them mandating or prohibiting major programs and policies, or imposing supermajority requirements. Collectively, those initiatives sharply circumscribed the authority and discretion of the legislature, county boards of supervisors, school boards, city councils, and the courts. In addition, countless reform measures have emanated from the legislature that were themselves spurred by the plebiscitary populism that has marked California politics in the past generation. Because of the constraints those initiatives impose on governmental discretion both at the state and local levels, California, in the words of one policy analyst, can be prosperous "and still be in a budget squeeze." At a time when responsibility for welfare and other major federal programs is being shifted down to the states and local governments, those constraints have left many of California's counties, where the ultimate burden of serving needy people resides, in particularly tough circumstances.

The passage of Proposition 13 serves as a convenient way of dividing the post–World War II era in California between that postwar period of optimism, with its huge investment in public infrastructure and its strong commitment to the development of quality education systems and other public services, and a generation of declining confidence and shrinking public services. Just as significantly, the state's latter-day populism, and the squeeze on taxes and public services it brought, occurred precisely during the period when the state was undergoing those demographic changes: from a society that thought of itself (and in many ways was) overwhelmingly white and middle class to one in which whites will soon be just another minority and where Hispanics, Asians, and blacks already constitute a sizeable majority in school enrollment and in the use of many other public services.

It is hard to prove that those demographic changes produced the political reaction and social neglect. There are other sources of stress in crime, the emergence of crack and other virulent street drugs, and the pressure that increased health costs have put on public budgets. And there are other states—Texas, Florida, New York—that have also been heavily affected by new waves of non-European immigrants. But no state has lived with such extraordinary expectations of social perfection or been subject to such large gaps between what its people once thought they ought, almost as a matter of right, to have, and the burdens they are willing to bear to get it. Those who now disproportionately depend on public services and who suffer the consequences when they're reduced are those new California immigrants and their children. Meanwhile, those who dominate the voter rolls are still white and middle class.

Because of the semipermanent revolt against government that Proposition 13 helped set in motion, and the growing use of the initiative that accompanied it, what had been designed (in 1911) as a Progressive Era instrument whereby "the people" could from time to time check the excesses of a state government that was then dominated by the Southern Pacific Railroad and a handful of other powerful interest groups has increasingly become the prevailing instrumentality of government itself. In the past two decades, the initiative has more often been used by well-organized political and economic entities, on the left and the right, and by incumbent politicians, from the governor down, than by anything that can be called "the people." It is still "the people" that vote on the initiatives that appear on the ballot. But it is those interest groups, backed by media consultants, direct mail specialists, pollsters, and others, that usually finance the costly signature drives, running into the millions, to get measures on the ballot, and the advertising campaigns that put them over—or that block the measures of opponents.

II

Paradoxically, the further the initiative process goes, the more difficult and problematic effective citizenship becomes. California has not just seen a sharp decline in the quality of public services—education, public parks, highways, water projects—that were once regarded as models for the nation. It has also seen the evolution of an increasingly unmanageable and incomprehensible structure of state and local government that exacerbates the same public disaffection and alienation that have brought it on, thus creating a vicious cycle of reform and frustration.

Each measure, because it further reduces governmental discretion, and because it moves control further from the public—from local to state government, from the legislature to the constitution, from simple majorities to supermajorities—makes it even harder to write budgets, respond to changing needs, and set reasonable priorities. And since many of those measures have irrationally—though sometimes necessarily—divided authority between state and local governments and among scores of different agencies, the opportunity for buck passing is nearly unlimited. To cite the most glaring example, because Proposition 13 specifically (and ironically) transferred a great deal of effective spending authority from local governments to the state, the state legislature, itself increasingly constrained by constitutional limits and mandates, allocates funds for local schools. But local school boards have, at least in theory, and, again, within the constraints of their own limits, the authority for spending it.

Thus, when funds run low or programs have to be cut, it is nearly impossible to determine whether accountability rests with the state's elected politicians for not providing enough or with the local board for spending it wastefully. Something similar is true for county governments. And since spending is so hopelessly tangled in formulas that have been written into the constitution—directly by measures like Proposition 98, which established mandatory minimum state funding requirements for the schools; indirectly by a three-strikes initiative that threatens to devour a large part of the state's discretionary funds in escalating prison costs—the system often runs largely on autopilot, beyond the control of any elected official. The whole fiscal system, in the view of Elizabeth Hill, California's nonpartisan Legislative Analyst, has become "dysfunctional." It "does not work together to achieve the public's goals."

Those problems have been compounded by the passage of the nation's most stringent legislative term limits, Proposition 140 in 1990, under which no member of the assembly may serve more than three two-year terms in a lifetime and no state senator more than two four-year terms, and which sharply cut the legislative budget and the professional staff that had once made California a national model as well. California does very little of consequence without excess.

Even before term limits passed, the state legislature had begun to lose a good deal of its luster. Beginning in the early 1980s, it had been afflicted by a series of scandals and embarrassments, including convictions for bribery and extortion that sent a number of its members to jail. More broadly, its effectiveness and stature visibly deteriorated, partly because of the increased complexity and diversity of the state; partly because of the fiscal constraints of Proposition 13 and other constitutional restrictions on legislative discretion and accountability, and the increased partisanship they brought with them; partly because of the increasing cost of campaigns and the political "arms races" they fostered; and partly because of the wider incivility in all public life. But rather than bringing on the "Citizen Legislature" promised by some of its advocates, term limits has generated even more partisanship and incivility among members, a growing inability to compromise, a legislative leadership with greatly reduced powers, and a sharp decline in legislators' comprehension of, and interest in, the complexities of the issues that they are supposed to deal with. When major fiscal committees handling billions of dollars or trying to deal with the intricacies of insurance regulation, school finance, welfare policy, or water law are chaired by people who have been there for no more than six months; when the speaker of the assembly will necessarily be someone with four years' experience or less, and when the professional staff is as thin as it has become, the quality of the work is almost certain to decline.

In 1997, after all assembly members first elected in 1990 or before were already "termed out," a federal trial judge overturned part of the law, ruling that its lifetime ban is unnecessary to achieve its prime objective, which is to enhance rotation in office and reduce the power of incumbency. Yet even if the decision is ultimately sustained by higher courts, it's likely that there will be some form of legislative term limits in California, and almost certain that the sharp cuts in professional staffs, which were not challenged in federal court, will remain unchanged. The net effect in both cases is increased power for interest group lobbyists and agency bureaucrats, who are under no term-limit restraints and who will increasingly become the major source of legislative information. What is likely to increase even more in the face of legislative deprofessionalization—as in some respects it already has—is the power of chance, of error, of gridlock, and of nonfeasance.

But that's only the beginning of this story, which is as much about process as about outcome, as much about unexpected consequences as about those that were intended. Because Proposition 13 froze property values at 1975 levels and only allows them to be reassessed when title changes hands, the owners of identical parcels—say, two neighboring homes of precisely equal value—can pay vastly different amounts in property taxes, and often do. The same is true for business property, something that puts an increasingly large burden on new business and business development, rewards speculative land-holding, and discourages new investment. And because the state has allowed local jurisdictions to keep the sales tax but has shifted a large chunk of property tax revenues (already curtailed by Proposition 13) to pay for its constitutionally mandated school support, many jurisdictions prefer sales-tax paying businesses—shopping malls particularly—to new manufacturing plants and other industry, even though the latter usually generate better jobs. The one pays for itself in new tax revenues, the other does not. Thus, in many communities, the developer of a shopping center has often gotten warmer treatment from zoning boards, planning commissions, and city councils than has the new assembly plant. In California, it's called the fiscalization of land use, and its skewing effect on patterns of development appears to be considerable. Although California's economy has grown vigorously in recent years, a lot of people in the business community believe it might grow more vigorously and rationally if the nexus between economic development and improved local public services were more apparent.

Despite these and other distortions, however, Proposition 13 and its progeny remain sacrosanct, icons of a public policy that no politician dare attack. For a whole generation of middle-aged and elderly home owners, the escalating property taxes of the mid-1970s were a searing experience similar to the impact of the Depression on an older generation, and Proposition 13 akin to the New Deal, a measure credited with preserving the homes and economic security of millions of people. In the 1996 election, the voters, rather than easing property tax restrictions, made them even tighter, requiring votes of property owners (in one case) or of the general electorate (in others) for *any* assessment increasing property-based fees or other exactions. In California, no taxation without representation has been replaced by no taxation without a vote—in many cases without a two-thirds vote—of the people.

This book focuses on this neopopulism, its roots in the state's changing political economy and demographics—white, affluent, elderly taxpayers who vote, as against the younger, preponderantly black and Latino people who use the services but vote in much lower numbers—and its consequences in public services, many of them services used primarily by children. The most obvious of those consequences is the relative slide, already mentioned above, in California school spending from sixth to eighth in the nation per pupil to fortieth; the crowded classrooms, the unmaintained buildings with leaking roofs, falling ceiling tiles, and unusable toilets; the layoffs of school counselors, librarians, and nurses; and the reductions in course offerings in everything from art to zoology. Writer Jonathan Kozol found rotting school facilities in the inner cities; California has them in the suburbs as well.

But the consequences of the state's political shifts also include the ironic decision of the financially strapped University of California to offer across-the-board early retirement to thousands of professors whose salaries it could no longer afford, among them some of the same stars that it had so proudly recruited a generation before. They include the reduced hours and resources of the public libraries; the deteriorating highways; and the increasing reliance on fees to run public parks, pools, and other amenities that had once been virtually free (and the broader anticommunitarian fee ethic that comes with them). And they are reflected in the various efforts of a growing number of people, through gated communities and the creation of new secessionist "cities," to withdraw from the larger commonweal altogether. Some of these things have also occurred, and are still occurring, in other states, but in none has the difference between before and after been anywhere near as great as it has been in the Golden State.

Inevitably, the story also touches on the roles of the principal players in this complex drama, from the California Progressives who led the drive to write the initiative into the state constitution, to Governor Edmund G. "Pat" Brown, the master builder and exemplar of California's public dynamism of the 1950s and 1960s. The cast also includes Howard Jarvis and Paul Gann, the antitax organizers, often called "antitax crusaders" in the media, who invented Proposition 13 and whose professional campaign managers created new political technologies in the effort to get it passed. And it includes people like Gerald Meral of the Planning and Conservation League, who adapted them for environmental, medical, and other causes generally described as liberal.

Together the men and women who refined the uses of the initiative and made it the centerpiece of latter-day California politics have brought into existence a whole new set of political practices and organizations. On the one hand, there is a large network of consulting and initiative marketing firms that not merely work for groups seeking to pass ballot measures (or to block them) but sometimes test market issues for their feasibility to generate funds through direct mailings, and then shop for a group to back them. On the other hand, California has witnessed the creation of semi-private legislative practices whereby an environmental organization will package hundreds of locally backed projects into a statewide bond measure—acquisition of park land, for example, or designation of wildlife refuges—in return for financial and other support from local sponsor-groups in getting the measure on the ballot and getting it passed.

All of this, of course, has had—and continues to have—broader national influence and implications. Just as Howard Jarvis and Paul Gann began the national tax revolt of the late 1970s and helped point the way for the presidential policies of Ronald Reagan, so California's hyperpopulism, its off-again, on-again forays into immigrant exclusion and its growing penchant for autopilot solutions, have resonated at the federal level—in the push for a balanced budget amendment and for a constitutional amendment requiring congressional supermajorities to increase public revenues; in term limits; in the drive for more restrictive immigration policies and against race- and gender-based affirmative action; in flat tax proposals; in mandatory judge-proof criminal sentencing laws, and in the wider neopopulist climate that underlies them. These things did not all originate in California, but they have generally found their most powerful launching platforms there.

From its start in America in the 1890s, that populism has had both its dark and its affirmative, optimistic sides. Both have been opportunities for some of the nation's most influential politicians: from William Jennings Bryan, Robert M. LaFollette, and Hiram Johnson to Huey Long, George Wallace, and Pat Buchanan—as well as those, like Governor Pete Wilson of California, who, though they are not of it and are temperamentally unsuited for it, have nonetheless exploited it. Proposition 187, which passed in 1994, was hardly the first instance when California tried to have the cake of its cheap immigrant labor and shut those workers and their families out at the same time. Californians excluded Asians from a whole range of economic and educational rights—in issuing business licenses, in the right to attend school with whites, and in a variety of other areas—and the Progressives were hardly immune to such temptations. Less than three years after California's Progressive revolt emerged triumphant in the election of 1910, Hiram Johnson, who had pushed scores of reforms, including tougher utility and railroad regulation, direct democracy through the initiative and referendum, and women's suffrage, gave in to the pressure of the Asiatic Exclusion League and signed the Alien Land Law that denied Japanese aliens the right to own land in California. That dark side has always been inseparably interwoven with the more hopeful elements.

But California's latter-day populism nonetheless tends to be a different kind of political impulse, not because it is primarily a populism of the right whose prime objective is the enervation of government itself, but because it is not particularly interested in civic engagement or in increasing the effectiveness of the citizen in government at all. It is not primarily a movement to cleanse and regain control of the affairs of state through governmental institutions more responsive to the popular will. It is often more like a parody of the Newtonian system of checks and balances written by the framers into the U.S. Constitution, a mechanical device that's supposed to run more or less by itself and spares the individual the bother and complexities of any sort of political engagement.

Woven through that California-style populism is the seemingly irresistible myth of excessive taxation. When he came into the governor's office in 1991, Pete Wilson was forced by recession and a looming $14 billion state deficit—and by the need to deal with a Democratic legislature—to balance spending cuts with a set of temporary state tax increases. But he took a terrible pummeling for those tax increases, particularly from members of his own party. He has pushed, with considerable success, for major tax cuts ever since. Those cuts have disproportionately favored corporations and higher-income taxpayers. Along the way, he continues to insist—and most voters continue to believe—that Californians are overtaxed compared to people in neighboring states, despite the fact that as a percentage of personal income, Californians' taxes are now at just about the national average, and that they pay a smaller share of their personal income in state and local taxes than all but one of their Western neighbors. (Something similar is true, of course, for the myth that this country is overtaxed as a nation.) It is hard to imagine that those arguments would be made with as much vehemence if the beneficiaries of the public services that those taxes support were believed to be the same people, or the same sort of people, as those who go to the polls and vote, or if more voters had someone living at home who is under eighteen.

But the new populism also reflects (and reinforces) the declining stature of, and respect for, virtually all major public institutions and establishments, from the judicial system and the media, to the universities, to the ideal of commonweal itself. We appear to be on the verge of a time when unedited information and unmediated media—the talk show, the computer news group and bulletin board—will radically change (and perhaps undermine) traditional politics and social relations. For the first time in history, the unfounded rumor, the fragment of suspicion, the wildly false "fact," is something not just shared over the back fence but spread in megabytes and milliseconds, without editing, review, or check, to an audience of millions—peasants with pitchforks on the Internet.

It's impossible to determine exactly how all those forces contribute to the new populism; they are evolving too fast and reacting on one another in too many ways. But there's not much doubt that all have contributed to the anticommunitarian, market-oriented ethic of our politics. The recent history of the California initiative system has demonstrated the essential irony of that process: that as the public trusts the system less and less, it becomes ever more susceptible to untested quick-fix remedies that, instead of resolving the problems of the moment, limit public choice and make long-term solutions even more difficult. But it has hardly deterred it.

III

This book attempts to look at those forces, and at how they have shaped California in the past forty years, and particularly at the period since the beginning of the tax revolt in the mid-1970s. . . .

This is primarily a journalist's book, not a work of social science. It comes from intense observation and analysis, spanning more than a generation, of developments in what may well be the democratic world's most fascinating political community. The observations have included conversations with most—if not indeed all—of the major public figures in that community: politicians and community leaders at all levels, among them three governors, a former governor, and countless would-be governors; scholars, social activists, and hundreds of representatives of every major interest group: from the bar, from business, from environmental and health organizations, from public employee and other labor groups, from a broad range of minority and ethnic groups, from the universities, the community colleges, and the public schools, and from county welfare offices and public libraries, not to mention the taxpayer organizations, the professional policy analysts, the lobbyists, and the political consultants. And since most of those conversations, backed by thousands of reports and studies and countless follow-up interviews, were conducted from what may well be the best single vantage point in the state—the editorial board of one of the state's major newspapers, as well the major state capital newspaper—they surely qualify, at the very least, as that first rough cut of history that journalism modestly claims for itself.

Given the complexity of the issues in California and the rapid way that event follows event, history's first cut may turn out to be very rough indeed. Yet the changes that have occurred—in government, in public services, in public outlook—are stark and dramatic. And the questions they raise for the nation as a whole are equally stark. Joan Didion was echoing historian Frederick Jackson Turner's classic invocation of the frontier as the crucial influence in American democracy when she declared a generation ago that things had better work in California because it is there that we run out of continent. But that has to be accompanied by another, equally portentous—and much more urban—wish: Things had better work here, where the new American society is first coming into full view, because if it fails here, it may never work anywhere else either. California is America's most important test for that emerging society, and so far the outcome of that test remains very much in doubt.

Chapter 1 Review Questions

1. What is meant by the "resurgence of the states"? What are some of the reforms that are associated with this resurgence? What factors caused it to occur?

2. What impact has this resurgence had on the ability of states to govern? What are the two different perspectives on this resurgence as described by Hedge?
3. What are the two different criteria that Hedge suggests using to assess governing? What is the "conventional wisdom" he describes, and how is it related to these two criteria?
4. How has California changed over time? According to Schrag, why is California's government having such trouble functioning today?
5. From reading these works, do you think that the state governments are up to the task of governing today? Why or why not? Thinking about your state government, does it seem capable of governing? Explain.
6. What types of reforms do you think are needed to make state governments work better? What criteria do you use in preferring these reforms? For instance, do they encourage greater responsibility or more democracy? Are these reforms likely to have some harmful consequences along with their benefits?

Key Terms

capacity
state-centered federalism
resurgence
independently elected executives
short ballot
patronage
merit system
legislative reform movement
court unification
open meeting laws
open record laws
Voting Rights Act of 1965
initiative
responsibility
democratic quality
New Federalism
mandates
Contract with America
laboratories of democracy
Baker v. *Carr*
devolution
defunding
referendum
progressive federalism
competitive federalism
term limits
divided government
institutionalization
benchmarks for governing
statehouse democracy
centralized power
fragmentation
separation of powers
Proposition 13
neopopulism
plebiscite

Suggestions for Further Reading

Baldassare, Mark. *A California State of Mind: The Conflicted Voter in a Changing World.* Berkeley: University of California Press, 2002. Illuminating book on citizen attitudes and the political climate in the Golden State today.

Beyle, Thad L. "Enhancing Executive Leadership in the States." *State and Local Government Review 27* (Winter 1995): 18–35. Provides an overview of the changes that have transformed state politics in recent years, with particular attention devoted to gubernatorial reforms.

Bowman, Ann O'M., and Richard C. Kearney. *The Resurgence of the States.* Englewood Cliffs, N.J.: Prentice-Hall, 1986. This is one of the best studies of the transformation of state government and politics. It was also one of the major influences in shaping Hedge's work.

Broder, David S. *Democracy Derailed: Initiative Campaigns and the Power of Money*. Harvest Books, 2001. *Washington Post* columnist David Broder examines the undemocratic character of the initiative process.

Ellis, Richard J. *Democratic Delusion: The Initiative Process in America*. Lawrence: University Press of Kansas, 2002. This recent study provides a critical examination of ballot initiatives.

Glick, Henry R. "The Politics of Court Reform: In a Nutshell." *Policy Studies Journal* 10 (1982): 680–689. Concise essay on the concerns of state court reformers.

Jewell, Malcolm E., and Sarah M. Morehouse. *Political Parties and Elections in American States*. 4th ed. Washington, D.C.: CQ Press, 2001. This is the most comprehensive book on state parties and elections in print. It includes detailed information on the strengthening of state parties over the past few decades.

Moncrief, Gary F., and Joel A. Thompson, eds. *Changing Patterns in State Legislative Careers*. Ann Arbor: University of Michigan Press, 1992. This is the most comprehensive book on the changes that have transformed state legislatures over the past several decades.

Rosenthal, Alan. *The Decline of Representative Democracy: Process, Participation and Power in State Legislatures*. Washington, D.C.: CQ Press, 1999. Provides an excellent introduction to the changes that have transformed state legislatures over the past few decades. Its theme is similar to Hedge's as it links the move toward greater democracy with a decline in legislative capacity.

Sabato, Larry. *Goodbye to Good-time Charlie: The American Governor Transformed.* 2d ed. Washington, D.C.: Congressional Quarterly Books, 1983. Superb study on the changes that have transformed the governor's office over time.

Sanford, Terry. *Storm Over the Nation*. New York: McGraw-Hill, 1967. Frequently cited book on the dismal state of state governments in the 1960s.

Van Horn, Carl E. "The Quiet Revolution," in Carl Van Horn, ed. *The State of the States*. 3d ed. Washington, D.C.: CQ Press, 1996. Provides a thoughtful overview of the reforms that have strengthened state governments, but have also led to greater conflict.

Related Web Sites

http://www.firstgov.gov/Agencies/State_and_Territories.shtml
U.S. Government's official web portal with links to the home page for every state government.

http://www.stateline.org
Stateline.org is an on-line news publication with articles on politics in all 50 states. The site includes statistics, gubernatorial speeches, and a wide cross section of valuable links. Stateline.org also produces an annual report on the "State of the States," which is available on-line by searching through the web site of the Pew Charitable Trusts (www.pewtrusts.com).

LexisNexis Academic
A searchable database with access to articles from newspapers and other sources from every state. Available in many university and college libraries.

http://www.igs.berkeley.edu/
The Institute of Governmental Studies provides a good source for more information on California politics, including a superb list of links.

http://www.iandrinstitute.org/
The Initiative & Referendum Institute at the University of Southern California provides research findings and other information on initiatives, referenda, and recalls nationwide.

2

Understanding Differences Across the States: The Concept of Political Culture

The national political culture of the United States is itself a synthesis of three major political subcultures. These subcultures jointly inhabit the country, existing side by side or sometimes overlapping one another.

Daniel J. Elazar

READING 2

Introduction

Why do states differ in their politics and the public policies they enact? For example, how is it that the state of Wisconsin can develop a reputation for clean politics, when its next-door neighbor, Illinois, has developed an image of being tolerant of corruption and unethical behavior? Or why have some states, such as New York and Michigan, created professional legislatures, ones that meet year-round and in which the legislators are well paid, whereas other states, including New Hampshire and Wyoming, have legislatures that meet infrequently and pay token salaries. Or looking at public policy, why have some states, such as Missouri, placed considerable restrictions on access to abortion, whereas others, such as Oregon, have worked to protect access?

The question as to why states differ is of central concern to scholars who study state politics. For political scientists, it is not enough to know that states differ in their politics and policies. It is also important to be able to explain why differences exist. Only by continually questioning why there are differences across the states is it possible to develop a more realistic understanding of the forces that shape state politics.

Over the years, scholars have identified a myriad of factors to explain political differences across the states. A large body of research has focused on the importance of socioeconomic factors on shaping differences in public policy, encouraging some states to adopt more liberal policies and others more conservative ones. The extent of urbanization in a state, the diversity of the population, the strength of a state's economy, the types of industry and business in a state, and the wealth of state residents are among the key factors that generate differences in policy and politics across the states.

The importance of urbanization should be clear to anyone who watched the map repeatedly broadcast on television after the 2004 presidential election showing the distribution of votes for Democrat John Kerry and Republican George W. Bush. The blue areas of the map showed support for Kerry and were concentrated in urban areas and along the coasts. The red areas indicated support for Bush and were concentrated in more rural areas of the nation. What is true in the presidential election is also true in the states. States with a larger urban population tend to support more liberal policies.

Urbanization is only one aspect of state population that is important in shaping politics. Also important is the size and diversity of the population. States that have fewer residents or a more homogenous population are not going to face the same type of political and social conflict as larger states that have more ethnic, racial, and religious diversity. The larger, more diverse states confront a wider range of attitudes about government's role in society and particular policy proposals than states with smaller and less diverse populations. The governments in larger states may also find themselves having to address more diverse, and often more difficult, social and economic problems than exist elsewhere. These differences in population can spur differences in policies.

A state's economy is one of the most important forces in shaping differences in policy. States that have weak economies may not be able to afford the same level of services that wealthier states provide. For example, spending on public education tends to be lower in states where personal income levels are lower. Although some of the difference in education spending reflects other factors, including differences in values, it is difficult for states to fund education if the tax base is limited. In addition to the strength of the economy, the character of the business community and the level of industrialization can also affect state politics. Political leaders in states that are dependent on only a few types of businesses and industries experience different pressures and concerns from those in which the economies are more diverse and complex. Moreover, the specific types of businesses that exist in a state influence politics. For example, states that are more dependent on international trade may have considerably different attitudes about trade-related issues from those that are not. The importance of agriculture to a state's economy can have a similar effect on farm policies.

Along with these socioeconomic factors, many political scientists argue that state politics is also affected by differences in the historical development and political culture of the states. Daniel Elazar, who was a distinguished political scientist at Temple University, has been one of the leaders in this school of thought. Elazar argues that the nation has one general political culture, but that within it are three important subcultures, which he labels *individualistic, moralistic,* and *traditionalistic.* These three subcultures spread across the United States, following historical patterns of migration and settlement, with each one developing stronger ties in particular regions of the country. The character of each subculture reflects the historical experiences of the people living within them. These subcultures are a kind of "second nature," he writes, shaping people's attitudes about government and politics and influencing the way that politics is ultimately practiced in each state. The differences in culture matter because they shape such things as the extent to which the average citizen can participate in politics, the reach of government into society, and the direction of public policy.

Elazar first laid out his arguments on the impact of political culture on state politics in the mid-1960s with the publication of *American Federalism: A View from the States.* Elazar focused on political culture in that book in order to explain how and why states differ in their relationships with the federal government. Since Elazar's work appeared, many scholars have used his categories of political culture to explain differences across the states, from variations in public opinion, to competition between political parties, to the direction of public policy. By the early 1990s, more than 100 articles had been published examining Elazar's thesis, with more appearing since.[1] For example, a recent study found that Elazar's categorization of state culture provided a good prediction for differences in state welfare reform efforts in the 1980s and 1990s.[2]

Not everyone, however, believes that political culture is as significant as Elazar maintains, especially when compared with some of the socioeconomic variables. Even some who agree that culture matters have criticized aspects of Elazar's argument, including his historical analysis and the lack of rigor in categorizing the states' political cultures. Although other factors may provide a good or better explanation for many of the political differences across the states, Elazar's work provides a valuable place to begin talking about the different forces that shape state politics. What makes his work especially helpful is that his argument does a good job in stimulating readers to think about the character of their own state and why its politics may differ from others'.

Questions to Consider

The selection presented below is taken from Elazar's *The American Mosaic,* a 1994 book that traces the impact of political culture, geography, and history in shaping American life over time. As you read the essay, here are some questions to consider:

- What are the three political subcultures that Elazar says exist in the United States? How do they differ in their views toward government, political participation, and politics?
- Elazar differentiates these political subcultures by their concern for the "marketplace" versus the "commonwealth." What do these two terms mean? How do the subcultures differ in their attitudes toward these concerns?
- Why have the states developed these different subcultures? Where did they come from? How did they spread?
- How have recent trends in immigration, migration, and political attitudes affected these subcultures?
- Which one of Elazar's subcultures best describes the state and community in which you live? If Elazar specifically discusses the political culture in your state, how well do you think he captures your state? Would you prefer a different political culture? Why or why not?

- Do you think that political culture provides a good explanation for how politics is practiced in your state, or are there other factors that seem to be more important, including socioeconomic ones? What are these factors and where do you see them affecting politics or policy?

The Political Subcultures of the United States

Daniel J. Elazar

The national political culture of the United States is itself a synthesis of three major political subcultures. These subcultures jointly inhabit the country, existing side by side or sometimes overlapping one another. All three are of nationwide proportions, having spread, in the course of time, from coast to coast. Yet each subculture is strongly tied to specific sections of the country, reflecting the streams and currents of migration that have carried people of different origins and backgrounds across the continent in more or less orderly patterns.

Given the central characteristics that define each of the subcultures and their centers of emphasis, the three political subcultures may be called individualistic, moralistic, and traditionalistic. Each reflects its own particular synthesis of the marketplace and the commonwealth.

It is important, however, not only to examine this description and the following ones very carefully but also to abandon the preconceptions associated with such idea-words as individualistic, moralistic, marketplace, and so on. Thus, for example, nineteenth-century individualistic conceptions of minimum intervention were oriented toward *laissez-faire,* with the role of government conceived to be that of a policeman with powers to act in certain limited fields. And in the twentieth century, the notion of what constitutes minimum intervention has been drastically expanded to include such things as government regulation of utilities, unemployment compensation, and massive subventions to maintain a stable and growing economy—all within the framework of the same political culture. The demands of manufacturers for high tariffs in 1865 and the demands of labor unions for worker's compensation in 1965 may well be based on the same theoretical justification that they are aids to the maintenance of a working marketplace. Culture is not static. It must be viewed dynamically and defined so as to include cultural change in its very nature.

The Individualistic Political Culture

The *individualistic political culture* emphasizes the conception of the democratic order as a marketplace. It is rooted in the view that government is instituted for strictly utilitarian reasons, to handle those functions demanded by the people it serves. According to this view, government need not have any direct concern with questions of the "good society" (except insofar as the government may be used to advance some common conception of the good society formulated outside the political arena, just as it serves other functions). Emphasizing the centrality of private concerns, the individualistic political culture places a premium on limiting community intervention—whether governmental or nongovernmental—into private activities, to the minimum degree necessary to keep the marketplace in proper working order. In general, government action is to be restricted to those areas, primarily in the economic realm, that encourage private initiative and widespread access to the marketplace.

The character of political participation in systems dominated by the individualistic political culture reflects the view that politics is just another means by which individuals may improve themselves socially and economically. In this sense politics is a "business," like any other that competes for talent and offers rewards to those who take it up as a career. Those individuals who choose political careers may rise by providing the governmental services demanded of them and, in return, may expect to be adequately compensated for their efforts.

Interpretation of officeholders' obligations under the individualistic political culture vary among political systems and even among individuals within a single political system. Where the standards are high, such people are expected to provide high-quality government services for the general public in the best possible manner in return for the status and economic rewards considered their due. Some who choose political careers clearly commit themselves to such norms; others believe that an officeholder's primary responsibility is to serve him- or herself and those who have supported him or her directly, favoring them at the expense of others. In some political systems, this view is accepted by the public as well as by politicians.

Political life within an individualistic political culture is based on a system of mutual obligations rooted in personal relationships. Whereas in a simple civil society those relationships can be direct ones, those with individualistic political cultures in the United States are usually too complex to maintain face-to-face ties. So the system of mutual obligation is harnessed through political parties, which serve as "business corporations" dedicated to providing the organization necessary to maintain that system. Party regularity is indispensable in the individualistic political culture because it is the means for coordinating individual enterprise in the political arena; it is also the one way of preventing individualism in politics from running wild.

In such a system, an individual can succeed politically, not by dealing with issues in some exceptional way or by accepting some concept of good government and then by striving to implement it, but by maintaining his or her place in the system of mutual obligations. A person can do this by operating according to the norms of his or her particular party, to the exclusion of other political considerations. Such a political culture encourages the maintenance of a party system that is competitive, but not overtly so, in the pursuit of office. Its politicians are interested in office as a means of controlling the distribution of the favors or rewards of government rather than as a means of exercising governmental power for programmatic ends; hence competition may prove less rewarding than accommodation in certain situations.

Since the individualistic political culture eschews ideological concerns in its "business-like" conception of politics, both politicians and citizens tend to look upon political activity as a specialized one—as essentially the province of professionals, of minimum and passing concern to laypersons, and with no place for amateurs to play an active role. Furthermore, there is a strong tendency among the public to believe that politics is a dirty—albeit necessary—business, better left to those who are willing to soil themselves by engaging in it. In practice, then, where the individualistic political culture is dominant, there is likely to be an easy attitude toward the limits of the professional's perquisites. Since a fair amount of corruption is expected in the normal course of things, there is relatively little popular excitement when any is found, unless it is of an extraordinary character. It is as if the public were willing to pay a surcharge for services rendered, rebelling only when the surcharge becomes too heavy. Of course, the judgments as to what is "normal" and what is "extraordinary" are themselves subjective and culturally conditioned.

Public officials, committed to "giving the public what it wants," are normally not willing to initiate new programs or open up new areas of government activity on their own initiative. They will do so when they perceive an overwhelming public demand for them to act, but only then. In a sense, their willingness to expand the functions of government is based on an extension of the *quid pro quo* "favors" system, which serves as the central core of their political relationships. New and better services are the reward they give the public for placing them in office. The value mix and legitimacy of change in the individualistic political culture are directly related to commercial concerns.

The individualistic political culture is ambivalent about the place of bureaucracy in the political order.[1] In one sense, the bureaucratic method of operation flies in the face of the favor system that is central to the individualistic political process. At the same time, the virtues of organizational efficiency appear substantial to those seeking to master the market. In the end, bureaucratic organization is introduced within the framework of the favor system; large segments of the bureaucracy may be insulated from it through the merit system, but the entire organization is pulled into the political environment at crucial points through political appointment at the upper echelons and, very frequently, also through the bending of the merit system to meet political demands.[2]

The individualistic political culture is a product of the Middle States stream, with its overriding commitment to commercialism and acceptance of ethnic, social, and religious pluralism. It has been reinforced by the English, Continental, East European, Mediterranean, and Irish streams, whose products either brought that political culture with them or adapted to it as their traditional cultures broke down. Most recently, substantial segments of the Southern and African-American streams are adapting to it for similar reasons, as they are transplanted from their original areas of settlement. The individualistic political culture is strong or dominant in those areas where the products of the streams manifesting its characteristics are strong or dominant.

The Moralistic Political Culture

. . . The *moralistic political culture* emphasizes the commonwealth conception as the basis for democratic government. Politics, to this political culture, is considered one of the great human activities: the search for the good society. True, it is a struggle for power, but it is also an effort to exercise power for the betterment of the commonwealth. Accordingly, in the moralistic political culture, both the general public and the politicians conceive of politics as a public activity centered on some notion of the public good and properly devoted to the advancement of the public interest. Good government, then, is measured by the degree to which it promotes the public good and in terms of the honesty, selflessness, and commitment to the public welfare of those who govern.

In the moralistic political culture, individualism is tempered by a general commitment to utilizing communal (preferably nongovernmental, but governmental if necessary) power to intervene in the sphere of "private" activities when it is considered necessary to do so for the public good or the well-being of the community. Accordingly, issues have an important place in the moralistic style of politics, functioning to set the tone for political concern. Government is considered a positive instrument with a responsibility to promote the general welfare, although definitions of what its positive role should be may vary considerably from era to era.

As in the case of the individualistic political culture, the change from nineteenth- to twentieth-century conceptions of what government's positive role should be has been great; for example, support for Prohibition has given way to support for wage and hour regulation. At the same time, care must be taken to distinguish between a predisposition toward communal activism and a desire for federal government activity. For example, many representatives of the moralistic political culture oppose federal aid for urban renewal without in any way opposing community responsibility for urban redevelopment. The distinction they make (implicitly, at least) is between what they consider legitimate community responsibility and what they believe to be central government encroachment; or between communitarianism, which they value, and "collectivism," which they abhor. Thus, on some public issues we find certain such representatives taking highly conservative positions despite their positive attitudes toward public activity generally. Such representatives may also prefer government intervention in the social realm—that is, censorship or screening of books and movies—over government intervention in the economy, holding that the former is necessary for the public good and the latter, harmful.

Since the moralistic political culture rests on the fundamental conception that politics exists primarily as a means for coming to grips with the issues and public concerns of civil society, it embraces the notion that politics is ideally a matter of concern for all citizens, not just those who are professionally committed to political careers. Indeed, this political culture considers it the duty of every citizen to participate in the political affairs of his or her commonwealth.

Accordingly, there is a general insistence within this political culture that government service is public service, which places moral obligations upon those who participate in government that are more demanding than the moral obligations of the marketplace. There is an equally general rejection of the notion that the field of politics is a legitimate realm for private economic enrichment. Of course, politicians may benefit economically because of their political careers, but they are not expected to *profit* from political activity; indeed, they are held suspect if they do.

Since the concept of serving the community is the core of the political relationship, politicians are expected to adhere to it even at the expense of individual loyalties and political friendships. Consequently, party regularity is not of prime importance. The political party is considered a useful political device, but it is not valued for its own sake. Regular party ties can be abandoned with relative impunity for third parties, special local parties, or nonpartisan systems if such changes are believed to be helpful in gaining larger political goals. People can even shift from party to party without sanctions if such change is justified by political belief.

In the moralistic political culture, rejection of firm party ties is not to be viewed as a rejection of politics as such. On the contrary, because politics is considered potentially good and healthy within the context of that culture, it is possible to have highly political nonpartisan systems. Certainly nonpartisanship is instituted not to eliminate politics but to improve it, by widening access to public office for those unwilling or unable to gain office through the regular party structure.[3]

In practice, where the moralistic political culture is dominant today, there is considerably more amateur participation in politics. There is also much less of what Americans consider to be corruption in government and less tolerance of those actions considered to be corrupt. Hence politics does not have the taint it so often bears in the individualistic environment.

By virtue of its fundamental outlook, the moralistic political culture creates a greater commitment to active government intervention in the economic and social life of the community. At the same time, the strong commitment to *communitarianism*[4] characteristic of that political culture tends to channel the interest in government intervention into highly localistic paths, such that a willingness to encourage local government intervention to set public standards does not necessarily reflect a concomitant willingness to allow outside governments equal opportunity to intervene. Not infrequently, public officials themselves will seek to initiate new government activities in an effort to come to grips with problems as yet unperceived by a majority of the citizenry. The moralistic political culture is not committed to either change or the status quo *per se* but, rather, will accept either depending upon the morally defined ends to be gained.

The major difficulty of this political culture in adjusting bureaucracy to the political order is tied to the potential conflict between communitarian principles and the necessity for large-scale organization to increase bureaucratic efficiency, a problem that could affect the attitudes of moralistic culture states toward federal activity of certain kinds. Otherwise, the notion of a politically neutral administrative system creates no problem within the moralistic value system and even offers many advantages. Where merit systems are instituted, they are rigidly maintained.

The moralistic political culture is a product of Puritan New England and the Yankee stream derived from it. It has been strongly reinforced by the North Sea and Jewish streams, who shared the same political culture when they came to the United States. Finally, it is strong or dominant in those areas where Yankees, Scots, Dutch, Scandinavians, Swiss, and Jews are strong or dominant.

The Traditionalistic Political Culture

The *traditionalistic political culture* is rooted in an ambivalent attitude toward the marketplace coupled with a paternalistic and elitist conception of the commonwealth. It reflects an older, precommercial attitude that accepts a substantially hierarchical society as part of the ordered nature of things, authorizing and expecting those at the top of the social structure to take a special and dominant role in government. Like its moralistic counterpart, the traditionalistic political culture accepts government as an actor with a positive role in the community, but in a very limited sphere—mainly that of securing the continued maintenance of the existing social order. To do so, it functions to confine real political power to a relatively small and self-perpetuating group drawn from an established elite who often inherit their "right" to govern through family ties or social position. Accordingly, social and family ties are paramount in a traditionalistic political culture; in fact, their importance is greater than that of personal ties in the individualistic political culture, where, after all is said and done, a person's first responsibility is to him- or herself. At the same time, those who do not have a definite role to play in politics are not expected to be even minimally active as citizens. In many cases, they are not even expected to vote. In return, they are guaranteed that, outside of the limited sphere of politics, family rights (usually labeled "individual rights") are paramount, not to be taken lightly or ignored. As in the individualistic political culture, those active in politics are expected to benefit personally from their activity, though not necessarily through direct pecuniary gain.

Political parties are of minimal importance in a traditionalistic political culture, inasmuch as they encourage a degree of openness and competition that goes against the fundamental grain of an elite-oriented political order. Their major utility is to recruit people to fill the formal offices of government not desired by the established power-holders. Political competition in a traditionalistic political culture is usually conducted through factional alignments, as an extension of the personalistic politics that is characteristic of the system; hence political systems within the culture tend to have a loose one-party orientation if they have political parties at all.

Practically speaking, a traditionalistic political culture is found only in a society that retains some of the organic characteristics of the pre-industrial social order. "Good government" in the political culture involves the maintenance and encouragement of traditional patterns and, if necessary, their adjustment to changing conditions with the least possible upset. Where the traditionalistic political culture is dominant in the United States today, political leaders play conservative and custodial rather than initiatory roles unless pressed strongly from the outside.

Whereas the individualistic and moralistic political cultures may encourage the development of bureaucratic systems of organization on the grounds of "rationality" and "efficiency" in government (depending on their particular situations), traditionalistic political cultures tend to be instinctively anti-bureaucratic. The reason is that bureaucracy by its very nature interferes with the fine web of informal interpersonal relationships that lie at the root of the political system and have been developed by following traditional patterns over the years. Where bureaucracy is introduced, it is generally confined to ministerial functions under the aegis of the established power-holders.

The traditionalistic political culture is a product of the plantation agrarianism of the Southern stream. It was supplemented by the African-American stream, whose "products" were originally absorbed into the Southern way of life as slaves. Secondary reinforcement has come from the Hispanic stream. The traditionalistic political culture is strong only where it has become the dominant political culture in those areas settled almost exclusively by the streams that manifest its characteristics. When those streams have moved into environments where other political cultures have been dominant, the traditionalistic political culture has tended to break down. In fact, as the possibilities for maintaining more than semblances of traditionalistic life have continued to decline in the United States, traditionalistic political culture has also diminished, undergoing subtle but serious changes—generally in the direction of the individualistic political culture, except where strong secondary tendencies toward the moralistic political culture have been present. . . .

The "Geology" of Political Culture

The individualistic, moralistic, and traditionalist political subcultures arose out of very real sociocultural differences found among the peoples who came to America over the years—differences that date back to the very beginnings of settlement in this country and even back to the Old World. Because the various ethnic and religious groups that came to these shores tended to congregate in their own settlements, and because they continued to settle together as they or their descendants moved westward, the political patterns they bore with them are today distributed geographically. Indeed, it is the geographic distribution of political cultures as modified by local conditions that has laid the foundations for American sectionalism. Sectional concentrations of distinctive cultural groups have helped create the social interests that tie contiguous states to one another even in the face of rather marked differences in the standard measures of similarity.

In order to portray the overall pattern of political culture, we must draw upon the full understanding of location presented in this book: Not only spacial but also temporal and cultural location have to be considered. Geography, too, must be taken into account. There is also a kind of human or cultural "geology" that adds another dimension to the problem. In the course of time, the different streams of migration have passed over the American landscape in response to the various frontiers of national development. Those streams, which in themselves are relatively clear-cut, have left residues of population in various places—residues that, in a sense, have become the equivalent of geological strata. As these populations settled in the same location, sometimes side by side, sometimes overlapping, and frequently on top of one another, they created hardened cultural mixtures that must be sorted out for analytical purposes, city by city and county by county, from the Atlantic to the Pacific.

Quite clearly, the various sequences of migration in each locale have determined the particular layering of its cultural geology. Yet even as the strata were being deposited over generations and centuries, externally generated events, such as depressions, wars, and internal cultural conflicts, caused upheavals that altered the relative positions of the various groups in the community. Beyond that, the passage of time and the impact of new events have eroded some cultural patterns, intensified others, and modified still others, to make each local situation even more complex. The simple mapping of such patterns has yet to be done for more than a handful of states and communities; and although the gross data that can be used to outline the grand patterns as a whole are available in various forms, they have been only partially correlated. However, by utilizing the available data, we can sketch with reasonable clarity the nationwide geography of political culture.

The Distribution and Impact of Political Subcultures

. . . The basic patterns of political culture were set during the period of the rural-land frontier by three great streams of American migration that began on the East Coast and moved westward after the colonial period. Each stream moved from east to west along more or less fixed paths, following lines of least resistance that generally led them due west from the immediately previous area of settlement.

Greater New England

Across the northern part of the United States, thrusting westward and slightly southwestward, is an area settled initially by the Puritans of New England and their Yankee descendants. From the first, they established a moralistic political culture.

After five generations of pioneering in New England, where they established several versions of their commonwealth in the New England states, the Puritans had developed a set of deeply rooted cultural patterns. Then, moving westward into New York State, the Yankees began their great cross-country migration. Across New York, northern Pennsylvania, and the upper third of Ohio, the Yankee current moved into the states of the upper Great Lakes and Mississippi Valley. There they established a greater New England in Michigan, Wisconsin, Minnesota, and Iowa, and attempted to do the same by settling in northern Illinois.

Beginning in the mid-nineteenth century, the Yankees were joined by Scandinavians and other Northern Europeans who, stemming from a related tradition (particularly in its religious orientation), reinforced the basic patterns of Yankee political culture, sealing them into the political systems of those states. Pressing westward, the Yankees settled Oregon, then Washington, and were the first "Anglos" to settle California. As Mormons, they settled Utah; then, as abolitionists, they settled Kansas. They became the leaders of the permanent settlements in Colorado and Montana, and even moved into northern Arizona. In each of these states, they were joined or followed by

The Regional Distribution of Political Cultures Within the States
Source: From *The American Mosaic* by Daniel Elazar. Copyright © 1994 by Westview Press, a member of the Perseus Books Group. Reprinted by permission of Westview Press, a member of Perseus Books, L.L.C.

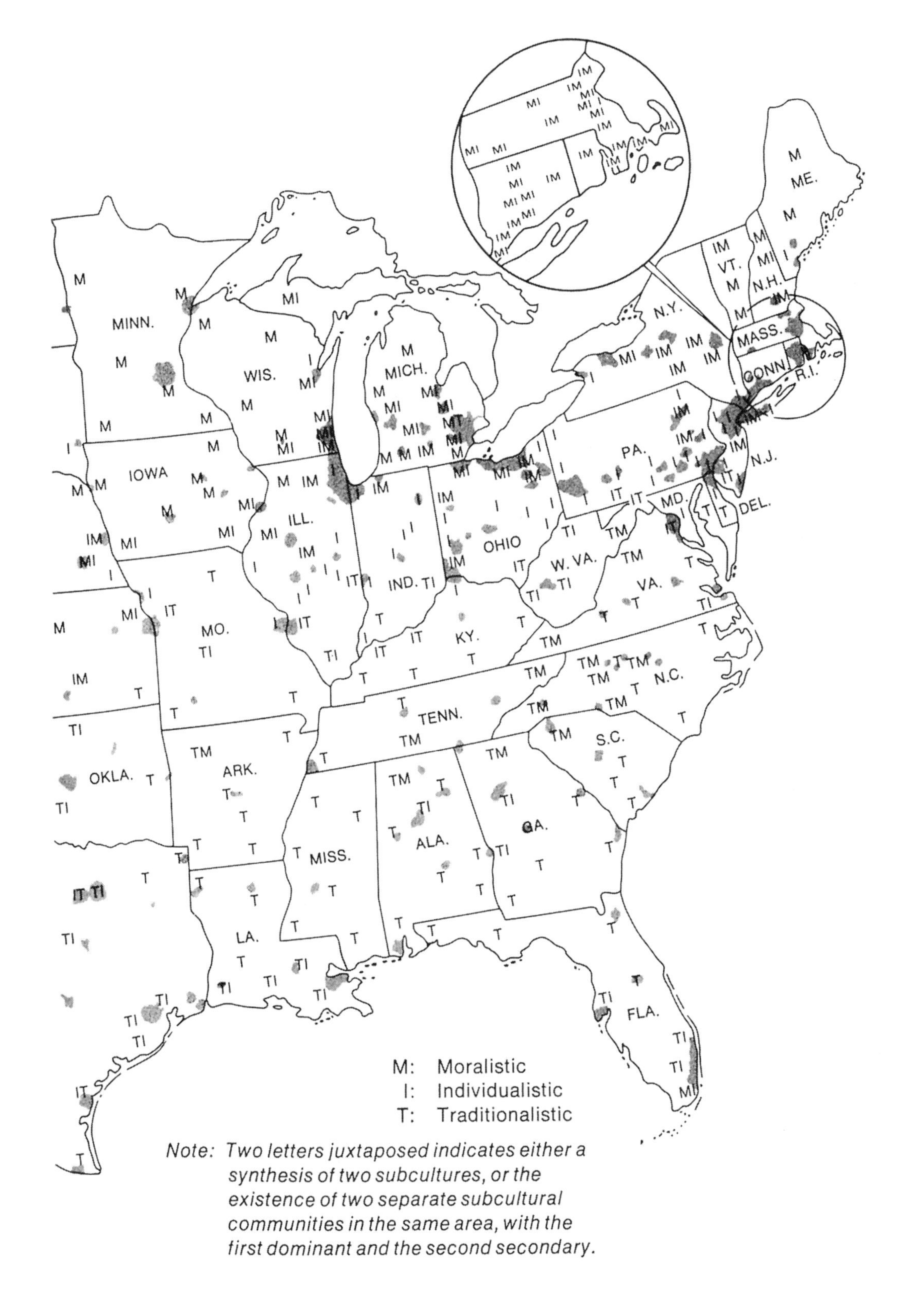

MINN.
WIS.
MICH.
IOWA
ILL.
IND.
OHIO
PA.
N.Y.
VT.
N.H.
ME.
MASS.
CONN.
R.I.
N.J.
DEL.
MD.
W. VA.
VA.
KY.
MO.
OKLA.
ARK.
TENN.
N.C.
S.C.
GA.
ALA.
MISS.
LA.
FLA.
M: Moralistic
I: Individualistic
T: Traditionalistic
Note: Two letters juxtaposed indicates either a synthesis of two subcultures, or the existence of two separate subcultural communities in the same area, with the first dominant and the second secondary.

the same Scandinavian–Northern European group; and in each they established the moralistic political culture to the extent of their influence. Within these states and the smaller ones colonized from them, the moralistic political culture flourishes even today.[5]

The Middle States

Groups of quite different ethnic and religious backgrounds, primarily from England and the interior Germanic states, settled the middle parts of the nation, beginning with the Middle Atlantic states of New York, New Jersey, Pennsylvania, Delaware, and Maryland. Together the majority of these highly diverse groups established the basic patterns of American pluralism. They were united by one common bond in particular—the search for individual opportunity in the New World. Unlike the Puritans who sought communal as well as individualistic goals in their migrations, the pursuit of private ends predominated among the settlers of the Middle States.

Though efforts were made to establish morally purposeful communities, particularly in Pennsylvania, the very purpose of those communities was to develop pluralistic societies dedicated to the individual freedom to pursue private goals, to the point of making religion a private matter (an unheard-of step at the time). The political culture of the Middle States reflected this distinctive emphasis on private pursuits from the first. By the end of the colonial period, a whole system of politics designed to accommodate itself to such a culture had been developed with distinctive state-by-state variations, modified by moralistic traits only in Pennsylvania and by traditionalistic ones in Maryland and Delaware.

These groups also moved westward across Pennsylvania into the central parts of Ohio, Indiana, and Illinois, and then on into Missouri. There, reinforced by immigrants from Western Europe and the lower Germanic states who shared the same attitudes, they developed extensions of their pluralistic patterns. Since these states, too, were settled by representatives of the other two political cultures, giving no single culture clear predominance, pluralism became the only viable alternative. So the individualistic political culture became dominant at the state level in the course of time, whereas the moralistic and traditionalistic political cultures retained pockets of influence in the northern and southern sections of each state.

After crossing the Mississippi, this middle current jumped across the continent to northern California during the 1849 gold rush (an activity highly attractive to individualistic types). Its groups subsequently helped to populate the territory in between. The areas of Nebraska and South Dakota bordering the Missouri River attracted settlers from Illinois and Missouri; the Union Pacific railroad populated central Nebraska and Wyoming; and Nevada was settled by migrants from the California gold fields. Today there is a band of states (or sections of states) across the belt of the country in which the individualistic political culture is dominant.[6]

The South

The people who settled the Southern tier of states were seeking individual opportunity in ways similar to those of their brethren to the immediate north. But whereas the latter sought their opportunities in commercial pursuits, either in business or in a commercially oriented agriculture, those who settled the South sought opportunity in a plantation-centered agricultural system based on slavery and essentially anti-commercial attitudes. This system, as an extension of the landed-gentry agrarianism of the Old World, provided a natural environment for the development of an American-style traditionalistic political culture in which the new landed gentry progressively assumed ever-greater roles in the political process at the expense of the small landholders, while a major segment of the population, the slaves, were totally excluded from any political role. Elitism within this culture reached its apogee in Virginia and South Carolina. In North Carolina and Georgia, meanwhile, a measure of equalitarianism was introduced by the arrival of significant numbers of migrants from the moralistic and individualistic cultures, respectively.

This peculiarly Southern agrarian system and its traditionalistic political culture was carried westward by the southern current. Virginia's people dominated in the settlement of Kentucky; North Carolina's influence was heavy in Tennessee; and settlers from all four states covered the southern parts of Ohio and Illinois as well as most of Indiana and Missouri. Georgians, with a mixture of other settlers, moved westward into Alabama and Mississippi. Louisiana presented a unique situation in that it contained a concentration of non-Anglo-Saxons rare in the South, but its French settlers shared the same political culture as the other Southerners, regardless of their other cultural differences. Ultimately, the Southern political culture spread through Texas, where it was diluted on that state's western fringes by individualistic-type European immigrants, and Oklahoma; into southern Kansas, where it clashed directly with the Yankee political culture; then across New Mexico and into Arizona, eventually over-lapping the Yankee current in southern and central California.[7]

The character and degree of complexity of the geology of specific local settlements in the United States determine whether a particular state or civil community comes closer to resembling one of the three political-culture models or combines elements of more than one within its boundaries. Most states, except those on the peripheries of the country, are situated geo-historically such that representatives of all three political subcultures have contributed to their settlement and development in significant numbers. Settlements and bands of settlements dominated by all three can be found in those states in varying conditions of cultural development and change. Accordingly, their present statewide political cultures were amalgams created out of varying degrees of conflict generated by the initial meeting of the representatives of the three and by the struggle between them for the dominant position of influence within the emerging state political systems.

The general outcome of that original struggle has long since been determined. It created a relationship between political culture and political system in each of the states that continues to set the limits for political behavior within them. At the same time, within the framework of the statewide political subculture, a conflict between products of the original political cultures (substantially modified and disguised though it may be) continues to be waged. Indeed, the very conflict itself has become institutionalized as one of the "moving parts" of the state political system.

The only major departures from the east-west pattern of cultural diffusion during the settlement of the land frontier came when the emigrants encountered the country's great mountain systems. The mountains diffused the cultural patterns because they were barriers to easy east-west movement. Thus, in the East, the Appalachian chain deflected the moralistic Scotch-Irish emigrants southward from Pennsylvania, where they were isolated in the Southern mountains. There they developed traditionalistic patterns of culture over a moralistic base and created special cultural pockets dominated by a synthesis of the traditionalistic and moralistic cultures, especially in the Piedmont areas of Virginia, the Carolinas, Georgia, and even Alabama.

In the West, the Rocky Mountains blocked the neat westward flow of the cultural currents and diverted people from all three political cultures into their valleys, from north to south, in search of fortunes in mining and specialized agricultural pursuits. There the more individualistic types from all three subcultures diffused from Montana to Arizona, creating cultural pockets in all the mountain states of the West that in some cases—Wyoming, for example—altered the normal regional patterns of political culture.

The development of the urban-industrial frontier coincided with the arrival of other immigrant groups that concentrated in the burgeoning cities of the industrializing states. These groups, primarily from Ireland, Italy, Eastern Europe, and the Balkans, also moved from east to west but settled in urban pockets, thereby adding new cultural strata to communities scattered throughout the country. Most of these settlers, though bound at first by traditional ties, soon adopted more individualistic attitudes and goals, which brought them into the individualistic political culture. Since most of them settled in cities, their cultural impact was less universal in scope but more concentrated in force. In some states (such as Massachusetts) they disrupted established cultural patterns to create new ones; in others (such as New York) they simply reinforced the existing individualistic-dominated pluralism; and in still others (such as Illinois) they tipped the balance between competing cultural groups. . . .

Ethnicity, Political Culture, and Contemporary Migration Patterns

Migration as a social phenomenon continues to be of the utmost importance in American life. When the number of immigrants drops internal migration once again comes to the fore as a means of reshaping local social and political patterns. Internal migration today has two aspects. On the one hand, there is the continuing cross-country flow of people seeking better opportunities of one sort or another. On the other hand, the predominant cross-country flow is still westward. From the end of World War II until the late 1960s, the northern flow from the greater South was a close second. Since then, it has been replaced by a northern flow southward. At the same time, intrametropolitan migration has become an even more important phenomenon.[8]

With the advent of the metropolitan frontier after World War II, Americans abandoned sedentary patterns that had become widespread between 1910 and 1945 and began to move again. About one-fifth of the American people change their residence every year. These migrations from farm to city to suburb and from section to section no longer follow a simple east to west pattern.

The first kind of migration—from farm to city, from town to metropolis, or from city to suburb—usually takes place within the same section of the country, if not the same state. It barely alters the local patterns of political culture, even though it may lead to substantial internal changes in the political culture itself. Iowans moving off their farms to Des Moines or Philadelphians moving from the central city to the suburban counties may simply reinforce existing patterns of culture.[9]

The second kind of migration may lead to the alteration of the cultural geology of particular areas. Southerners moving to Detroit have brought a traditionalistic culture into a moralistic environment, whereas Northerners moving southward have altered the states of the Lower and Western South in important ways. In some cases this movement cannot be identified as group migration, but in others the continuity of older modes of cultural diffusion and change is marked.

California is a case in point.[10] Its cultural patterns remain in flux because of the continuous intensity of migration into the state (the highest in the nation since 1910), even though fairly well-defined cultural lines had been established within it by the turn of the century. In a reversal of the national pattern, southern California became the center of the moralistic culture because the Yankees and their midwestern descendants predominated there. Northern California, on the other hand, attracted the Middle State migrants and became the locus of the individualistic culture, whereas central California attracted many Southerners who brought to the region strong traces of the traditionalistic culture. The sharp cultural division between north and south (the central area was still too weak to be of importance) had already helped intensify the well-known conflict between the two sections of the state that came strongly to the fore during the Progressive era.

Until recently, at least, the great migrations of the twentieth century have generally reinforced the original patterns of culture in California. Midwesterners from moralistic culture states continued to seek the Los Angeles area, and individualistic culture types, particularly from the East, flocked to the San Francisco Bay area. Each group has generally blended in well with the original political culture of its area of choice.

During the Great Depression, "Okies" and "Arkies"—migrants from the Western South—settled in great numbers in central California. After World War II, the increased migration of Southerners into all parts of the state, with greatest intensity in the southern part and progressively less intensity moving northward, added a strong strain of the traditionalistic culture (or the particular individualistic manifestation that occurs when its people leave their traditionalistic environment) in areas where that strain was previously weak or nonexistent. What happened in those cases was the development of a conflict between the two cultures as a consequence of the contrast between them. By and large, the radical right of southern California consists of former Southerners in revolt against what were, to them, unacceptable patterns of political and social life created by the dominant non-Southerners.

Two other significant migrational streams became stronger in California after World War II. The Latino migration from Mexico—at first principally illegal, but then publicly recognized—grew to mass proportions to the extent that, by the 1980s, it was projected that Spanish would become the most widely spoken language in the state sometime in the early twenty-first century. Southern California, in particular, acquired a major Hispanic presence.[11]

Beginning in the 1970s, immigration from Asia assumed major proportions. First triggered by the collapse of the American military effort in Southeast Asia, it also featured many Koreans, Filipinos, and others who simply came in search of opportunity, as generations of immigrants from all over the world had done before them. Although the Asians settled throughout the state, they continued to concentrate in northern California.[12] The Hispanics settled in areas already strongly influenced by the traditionalistic political culture as modified, whereas the Asians joined those reflecting the individualistic political culture. Hence these groups, too, tended to reinforce previous patterns rather than bringing major cultural changes with them.

Thus, although the major impact of the three native streams came in the early days of settlement, the streams themselves persist. Since World War I, the Southern stream, transformed into one segment of the overall rural-to-urban migratory movement, has sent fingers northward again, establishing significant colonies of Southerners, particularly unskilled Southern mountain folk in the North, even where none existed before. These groups did not become politically articulate in their new homes until the beginning of the twelfth generation, with the rise of the religious fundamentalists in politics; but their presence and somewhat "alien" ways had presented the civil communities with substantial minority-group problems even earlier.

To a lesser extent, the migration from the farms to the cities has also represented a continuation of the nineteenth-century streams. The original cultural patterns of those streams were best preserved in the rural areas where families, friendship cliques, and religious ties were most stable, having encountered less pressure to change. Thus many of the descendants of the original Yankee, Middle States, and Southern settlers, moving into the cities two, three, or more generations later, have brought with them infusions of a more faithfully preserved form of the original native cultures.

Although continued migration has helped maintain the fluid nature of cultural patterns, the values of the various political cultures have undergone internal change. Moral demands have generally stiffened within the American political culture as a whole. For example, what is today considered to be conflict of interest was considered perfectly proper even by the moralistic political culture in the days of Daniel Webster. Though an authentic Yankee, Webster, without any qualms, could take an annual retainer from a leading Boston bank while serving in the U.S. Senate. At the same time, the moralistic subculture has kept at least a step ahead of the others in its demands for political morality. On another level, when the general culture was so oriented as to demand public standards of social and sexual morality, governments within the orbit of the moralistic political culture tended to enforce the law as fully as possible. Once the general cultural styles changed, the same governments could zealously support the canons of the permissive society on the grounds of individual freedom of choice as a paramount good.

Politicians who developed within the individualistic political culture are suffering most from the new standards of political morality. These new standards have opened up opportunities for everyone—from the FBI to rival politicians in their own bailiwicks—to investigate or entrap them and then drive them out of office for practices that were formerly considered standard behavior in their circles. At the same time, the recent decline in the role of political party organizations has introduced some elements previously associated with the traditionalistic subculture into individualistic culture areas; one such element is the organization of politics around individuals who are able to appeal to the voters and who thereby attract followings among the politicians. In another context, the individualistic political culture, originally the home of the rugged individualist, has taken on something of a collectivist tinge in the twentieth century. Many of those within it have come to believe that big government offers opportunities for individuals that are unobtainable in any other way. Thus its representatives are often found at the forefront of the drive for greater government intervention in the economy.

Meanwhile, the traditionalistic political culture has tended to adopt individualistic elements as its traditional social bases have eroded. With its older elites no longer in positions of power because of economic and social changes, many of its traditionalistic attitudes were transformed into bigotries designed to maintain the old racial caste system, or became unchallenged efforts, by individuals seeking personal profit from the changes, to maintain the political status quo. On the other side of the coin, traditionalistic modes of operation have been adapted by the economic leadership in major Southern cities to create organized business-dominated oligarchies committed to civic progress as a means of economic betterment. The Dallas Citizens' Council is one of the best known of these organizations; others can be found in most major Southern cities.

A certain amount of assimilation from one culture to another is based on changes in individual interests and attitudes. Under certain circumstances, cultural values change because of changing social status. There is some evidence to suggest that, as some people move upward into the middle- to upper-middle-class range, they may adopt, at least for external purposes, some of the values of the moralistic political culture (which has always been a middle-class phenomenon), particularly if those values are the more acceptable ones in their communities. In true frontier fashion, such change often occurs in conjunction with a change of residence, such as migration to the suburbs. This phenomenon was reflected during the 1950s and 1960s in the rise of new-style Republican parties in the suburbs that gained a measure of power by opposing, on moralistic grounds, the old-style machine politics of the Democrats and the GOP old guard, both of which symbolized the individualistic political culture in its least attractive form.

The most visible ethnic manifestations in the United States are found among those people who are products of the later set of European streams. Generally speaking, there are substantial communities of first- and second-generation Americans drawn from those streams that can still be identified without much difficulty. The flow of the European streams radically diminished in intensity with the close of mass immigration after World War I but reintensified briefly after World War II. The trickle that persists today continues to follow the same patterns as the earlier streams: Like attracts like to each locality. Since the revision of immigration laws in the 1960s, there has been an increase in immigration. Approximately 7.5 million immigrants from Europe have entered the United States since 1945, of whom a substantial percentage settled among or near their brethren who had preceded them generations earlier.

In many states and localities where ethnic groups representing different cultural streams have come to rest within the same political system, early conflicts between the groups have given way to cultural synthesis as their descendants have found some common ground of communication. For example, in Massachusetts, where the conflict of political cultures between the moralistic Yankees and the individualistic Irish was extraordinarily intense, the present generation has witnessed a kind of rapprochement in which many of the descendants of the Yankees have adopted the political techniques of the Irish, while many of the descendants of the Irish have adopted the sense of political goals and purposes of the Yankees. The Kennedys illustrate this point. John F. Kennedy was at one and the same time a quintessential Yankee and the leader of an "Irish mafia." Former Senator and Secretary of State Edmund Muskie of Maine, of Polish descent, is another such example. Only by becoming the galvanized Yankee that he is could he have been the first Democrat to break the grip of the Republican party on that state in the 1900s. More recently, Michael Dukakis, of Greek descent, became governor of Massachusetts and the 1988 Democratic candidate for the presidency by doing the same. The Yankees and the Irish, such formidable antagonists in generations past, could begin to meet on common ground because they shared many common values from their respective general cultures, not the least of which was a common "puritanism." . . .

The Implications of American Diversity

As a new society the United States consists of an extraordinary diversity of religious, ethnic, and cultural groups, many of whose original members made more or less conscious decisions to settle in America. However, although a common citizenship, language, and culture unites these groups, considerable differences remain; indeed, they remain because they are tolerated and at various times even encouraged by the society as a whole, and because the groups themselves often insist on retaining subcommunal identities of varying degrees. It is important to note that ethnicity rests not only on country-of-origin but also on racial, sociocultural, socioreligious, and sociolinguistic bases. Ethnic groups have maintained their distinctiveness for various reasons, whether religious, communal, political, associational, and/or fraternal. Ethnicity becomes politically important when (1) a group is large and has potential power; (2) a group is small but highly visible or well organized; or (3) a group is conscious of being a minority and of being surrounded by other well-organized ethnic groups.

The migration of these groups to and within the United States is responsible for settlement of the country. Continuing internal migration has contributed to social mobility and to a national identity by eroding static provincialism. At the same time, the fifteen migrational streams that have flowed across the United States have created a mosaic of cultural patterns consisting of three basic ethnocultural strata: (1) the primary political sub-cultures of the Southern, Middle, and New England states; (2) the discrete European ethnocultural groups such as the Irish; and (3) the non-European ethnocultural groups such as the Chinese. The bases for the coexistence of these groups have shifted over the course of American history from territorial pluralism during the colonial period, to an attempt to impose Protestant republicanism during the nineteenth century, and then to an increasing emphasis on open religious, ethnic, and racial pluralism during the twentieth century.

Political culture has been defined as the summation of persistent patterns of underlying political attitudes and characteristic responses to political concerns within a particular political order. Thus political culture is a kind of "second nature" that is generally unperceived by those who are part of that order. Its origins date back to the beginnings of the people who share it. Political culture influences people's perceptions and expectations about the proper roles of politics and government, the recruitment of specific kinds of people into political life, and the actual practice of government and politics.

Notes

1. The "good" meaning of *bureaucracy:* Administration of a government chiefly through bureaus staffed with nonelective officials, selected on the basis of merit. The "bad" meaning: Any administration in which the need to follow complex procedures impedes effective action.
2. Political leaders in such an environment often argue that merit systems are impersonal, rigid, and ultimately inefficient. As Thomas Whelan, former mayor of Jersey City (1963–1971), once remarked: "You have to have the power to hire and fire. Civil Service examinations may measure intelligence but they don't measure courage, drive or curiosity. You wind up with a guy with nine heads who can't even get the men out of the garage." In 1972, Whelan and several other leaders of this highly individualistic city were convicted of various charges of conspiracy and accepting kickbacks on public contracts.
3. In this context, it should be noted that regular party systems are sometimes abandoned in local communities dominated by the individualistic political culture so that nonpartisan electoral systems can be instituted in an effort to make local governments more "business-like" and to take local administration "out of politics." Such anti-political efforts are generally products of business-dominated reform movements and reflect the view that politics is necessarily "dirty" and illegitimate.
4. On communitarianism, see Robert N. Bellah et al., *Habits of the Heart: Individualism and Commitment in American Life* (New York: Harper and Row, 1985); and Daniel J. Elazar, *The American Constitutional Tradition* (Lincoln: University of Nebraska Press, 1988).
5. See Stewart H. Holbrook, *The Yankee Exodus* (Seattle: University of Washington Press, 1968); James R. Gibson, ed., *European Settlement and Development in North America* (Toronto: University of Toronto Press, 1978); and Louis K. Matthews, *Expansion of New England* (New York: Russell and Pursell, 1936).
6. See Eric F. Goldman, "Middle States Regionalism and American Historiography: A Suggestion," in Eric F. Goldman, ed., *Historiography and Urbanization* (Baltimore: Johns Hopkins University Press, 1941).
7. See W. J. Cash, *The Mind of the South* (New York: Alfred A. Knopf, 1960).
8. See Richard Bensel, *Sectionalism and American Political Development* (Madison: University of Wisconsin Press, 1984); Everett C. Ladd, Jr., with Charles D. Halley, *The Transformation of the American Party System: Political Coalitions from the New Deal to the 1970s* (New York: W. W. Norton, 1975); Everett C. Ladd, Jr.,

American Political Parties: Social Change and Political Response (New York: W. W. Norton, 1970); Jeff Fishel, ed., *Parties and Elections in the Anti-Party Age* (Bloomington: Indiana University Press, 1978); and Seymour Martin Lipset, ed., *Party Coalitions in the 1980s* (San Francisco: Institute of Contemporary Studies, 1981).

9. See, for example, Elazar, *Cities of the Prairie Revisited,* ch. 3.
10. On postwar California, see Gladwin Hall, *Dancing Bear: An Inside Look at California Politics* (Cleveland: World Publishing Company, 1968); and Michael P. Ragin, *Political Change in California: Critical Elections and Social Movements,* 1890–1996 (Westport, Conn.: Greenwood, 1970).
11. On the Hispanic migration, see John J. Burma, *Mexican Americans in the United States* (Cambridge, Mass.: Schenkman Publishing Co., 1970); Lyle Saunders, "The Social History of Spanish-Speaking People in Southwestern United States 1846," First Congress of Historians from Mexico and the United States, *Memoria* (1950); Carey McWilliams, *North from Mexico: The Spanish-Speaking People of the United States* (Philadelphia: J. B. Lippincott, 1949); Kingsley Davis and Clarence Senior, "Immigration from the Western Hemisphere," *American Academy of Political and Social Science: Annals,* no. 262 (March 1949); Norman S. Goldner, *The Mexican in the Northern Urban Area: A Comparison of Two Generations* (San Francisco: R and E Research Associates, 1974); and T. Allen Caine, *Social Life in a Mexican-American Community* (San Francisco: R and E Research Associates, 1974).
12. See June D. Holmquist, ed., *They Chose Minnesota* (St. Paul: Minnesota Historical Society Press, 1981); and Oscar Handlin, *Immigration as a Factor in American History* (Englewood Cliffs, N.J.: Prentice-Hall, 1959).

CASE STUDY 2

Introduction

Louisiana voters faced a choice at the polls in 1991 that would be unthinkable in many states. The Democratic Party candidate for governor was Edwin Edwards, a three-term, fast-talking former governor with a fondness for gambling and women, who had been repeatedly indicted on corruption-related charges. The Republican candidate was David Duke, a former Ku Klux Klan grand wizard.

How could a state find itself in a situation in which the choice for governor was between, as some commentators called it, a crook and a fascist? To those who study Louisiana politics, the answer is simple. The situation was a reflection of the state's political culture or heritage. Since the 1920s, when the populist Huey Long was first elected governor, state voters have repeatedly been willing to elect corrupt or colorful candidates to office. Some commentators say that Louisiana voters simply like to have entertaining politics.

In the article you just read, Elazar argues that political culture plays a significant role in shaping politics in each state. Louisiana is no exception to this rule. In the essay that follows, Victor Gold provides a fascinating glimpse at this political culture as he examines the political career and legal problems of former Louisiana Governor Edwin Edwards. Echoing some of Elazar's themes, Gold traces the state's political climate, and its tolerance for Edwards's behavior, to the state's historical development and the experiences of its people. Elazar categorizes Louisiana as having a mixture of both individualistic and traditionalistic subcultures. Gold's essay reveals aspects of both of these cultures. On the one hand, Edwards's concern for power and the perquisites of office are consistent with an individualistic culture, as is the public's acceptance of his behavior. On the other hand, the paternalistic attitude of Louisiana governors, which dates back at least to Huey Long, is more typical of the traditionalistic culture than of an individualistic one.

The events surrounding Edwards's career, and the state's reaction to those events, make an insightful case study because they provide a vivid example of the importance of the historical development of a state and political culture in shaping a state's politics. Gold's essay also hints at another type of political dynamic that is also important in shaping Louisiana's politics, one that is more consistent with the argument that socioeconomic factors are especially important in shaping state politics. The nomination of David Duke as Edwards's run-off opponent in the 1991 gubernatorial election suggests that race and diversity also play an important role in Louisiana politics.

Questions to Consider

Victor Gold is the national correspondent for *The American Spectator.* In reading this case study, consider the following questions:

- How would you describe Edwards's character? What is he like?
- What different charges were lodged against Edwards? How was he able to retain voter support, given his past actions and legal problems?
- What does Edwards's continued success say about the nature of Louisiana politics?
- Elazar has categorized Louisiana as having a combination of traditionalistic and individualistic culture. Does his categorization seem correct? Why or why not?
- How successful do you think Edwards would be in your state? What is your state's political culture like? Would someone like Edwards be elected? Why or why not?

American Hayride

Victor Gold

Edwards Pleads Innocent in Federal Fraud Case

Edwards Grand Jury Delves into New Terrain

—Headlines, autumn 1999,
New Orleans Times-Picayune

I return home to Louisiana every year or so to rekindle old memories and ponder the future of American politics. My first stop, within hours after arriving, is either Felix's in the Quarter, or The Pearl on St. Charles, where my wife indulges an incredible appetite for raw oysters while I fill up on gumbo and crawfish. Later, though stuffed, we head for the Café du Monde, on the riverfront, for a nightcap round (or two) of café au lait and beignets.

A great deal has changed in New Orleans over the past quarter-century, much to my regret: Canal Street has run down, streetcar fares have gone up; the fabled Roosevelt Hotel is now a mere link in the Fairmont chain; my old neighborhood Tivoli is a funeral parlor, and the K&B drug stores, a local institution, have sold out to Rite-Aid.

Victor Gold, "American Hayride," *The American Spectator* (March 2000): 34–39. Reprinted by permission of the author.

Yet, reassuringly, some things of memory never change: fresh Gulf oysters, savory gumbo, robust coffee, the dinner line outside Galatoire's; and the headlines on any given day, month, or year that Dale and I return, which tell of Governor Edwin Edwards, whether in or out of office, either facing indictment or standing trial at some nearby federal courthouse.

I wasn't very smart, but I knew as a six-year-old I didn't want to farm. You have to work too hard. I wanted to be a politician and a lawyer so I wouldn't have to work.

—Edwin Edwards to Louisiana farm audiences, 1971–1991

As a boy growing up in the small Louisiana town of Marksville (pop. 2,500), Edwin Washington Edwards once had to hide under his house to escape giggling girls intent on kissing him. "He was *so* cute," recalled one in later years. "If we had caught him, we'd have eaten him up."

The record shows that young Edwin, given time, got over his shyness with the opposite sex. But Marksville stayed with him through his law school years at Louisiana State University. "He was as country as you could get," according to a former classmate. "Pure Cajun in the way he dressed and the way he talked. His father, he would say, was a *shar*-cropper. But Edwin's *brain*"—a tap of the head—"that boy was pure hustler, always playing some angle."

Not much different, all in all, from any other LSU law student with an urge to live in the governor's mansion. But Edwards, this classmate adds, entered the Louisiana political arena with assets his future rivals could only envy.

Traditionally, the regional divide in Louisiana's electorate—northern Protestant and redneck, southern Catholic and Cajun—had worked against downstate candidates running for governor. Edwards, however, was an ethnic rarity—a south Louisiana Cajun with a non-Gallic surname that didn't turn off Scots-Irish voters upstate. Through his Cajun mother—a Brouillette—he appealed to Catholic voters in the bayou parishes (*Un de nous Autres*—"He's one of us"), while his father "Boboy," of mixed Welsh heritage, along with a sister married to a Nazarene minister, gave him Protestant credentials.

Add to that the good looks that drove little girls crazy and the roguish charm of a shell-game operator at a parish carnival—a certain gleam that Louisianians, north and south, relish in their politicians; the eye-winking *joie de vivre* that seems to say, *Pay your money, take your choice, catch me if you can.*

Philandering is a habit normally associated with politicians, but so is hypocritical Puritanism. Edwards never fell into that trap. You could say or write what you wanted of his personal life but you didn't call him a hypocrite. . . . Asked by reporters outside a federal courthouse if he thought his phone was tapped, he said no but added, "Except by jealous husbands." His image and his resulting immunity were so firmly established by the end of his first term that he could tell a reporter the only personal scandal that could hurt him would have him "caught in bed with either a dead girl or a live boy."

—John Maginnis, *The Last Hayride*

The parallels are striking: A Southern governor of rural origin whose passion for power is rivaled only by his relentless pursuit of campaign funds and extra-marital sex; whose fundraising involves sizable and frequent contributions from agents of an Asian country intent on influencing the political process in this country; whose obsessive womanizing is so uncontrolled as to alienate his wife and lead personal aides (used as procurers) to worry about its effect on his career; whose public charm and quicksilver tongue allow him, time and again, to survive scandals that would end the careers of most politicians.

"Slick Willie" Clinton and "Fast Eddie" Edwards: So much in common, yet different as piney woods and Spanish moss, hog jowl and crawfish etouffé, Orval Faubus and Huey Long. For Clinton, the hypocritical Puritanism of the political weasel; for Edwards, no hot denials that he ever had "sexual relations with that woman," no solemn meetings with Reverend Fix-it, Jesse Jackson, for drive-by absolution. Not even, for the benefit of prayer-breakfast soulmates, a lip-biting promise to reform his philandering ways.

Instead, for the entertainment, indeed enlightenment, of the churchly bourgeoisie of Louisiana, from Bible Belt north to Mass-going south, there is the spectacle of their once-and-future governor, the Cajun

King, slyly "poking at other politicians' carefully preserved image of righteousness" while flaunting his own venery:

> EDWARDS (of a well-known politician): *I know for a fact he has a mistress.*
> REPORTER: *You're telling us he cheats on his wife?*
> EDWARDS: *He's not as good at it as I am, but he does.*

Edwards Gambling Trips Probed by IRS Agents

It was T. Harry Williams's contention that, bad press notwithstanding, Louisiana politics is no more corrupt than the politics of any other state. That it appears more corrupt, said Williams, is due to Louisiana politicians practicing their art "with style and flair."

Williams, the LSU professor who wrote a prize-winning biography of Huey Long, shared this unorthodox view with two other authorities on Louisiana political culture, A. J. Liebling and John Maginnis. In his memorable profile of Earl Long (*The Earl of Louisiana*), Liebling saw the state as a misplaced Mediterranean province, picaresque and volatile. Maginnis, in *The Last Hayride,* went back to early nineteenth-century history to explain why Louisiana voters, rather than being shocked by the consistent venality of their chosen leaders, "applaud chicanery and corruption as good political theater."

It all started, according to Maginnis, with Jean Lafitte, the swashbuckling bayou buccaneer best known outside Louisiana for having joined forces with General Andrew Jackson to defeat the British at the Battle of New Orleans, January 1815. "Lafitte was no pirate, but a privateer, operating with letters of marque, to prey on the merchant vessels of Spain," Maginnis tells us. "He and his brother Pierre were smugglers on a grand scale . . . an affront to the newly-installed U.S. government in New Orleans."

Now the Faustian twist, the devil's bargain that turned a high-seas bandit from rogue to role model for future Louisiana politicians: "Lafitte was Louisiana's first Robin Hood. He stole treasure from the Spanish, snuck it past the Americans and sold it cheap to the French. So important was Lafitte to the economic lives of the first settlers that if Congress had allowed free elections in the newly acquired territory, the American [Governor William] Claiborne would have had a hard time holding his job against the wealthy privateer."

Fortunately for Claiborne, Congress had no intention of extending the franchise to what Washington then regarded as a territory of odd-speaking foreigners. As it was, the American governor, a stiff-necked autocrat, had a difficult time just holding onto his dignity. When Claiborne placed a $500 bounty on Lafitte's head, the audacious privateer responded by posting a $1,500 reward for the kidnapping and delivery of the governor to Lafitte's hideaway in Bayou Barataria. Though neither bounty was ever collected, Lafitte's Cajun followers loved the show.

Style, flair, above all audacity. Louisianians have ever prized a brazen irreverence in their leaders, a mocking contempt for the power held by the ruling elite. In Lafitte's day the power was that of the ruling Anglos in distant Washington and their local satraps; a century-plus later there would come a new power elite, John D. Rockefeller's Standard Oil, and not long after, a modern-day Robin Hood who, in Maginnis's words, "played to his audience, the teeming masses of poor folk who took special delight not only in his taxing the rich but in his thumbing his nose at the genteel sensibilities of the privileged class."

> *Over the campaign was the incubus of Huey and his methods. Most of the candidates used Huey's oratorical tactics, retained his platform, worked hard to be "second Hueys." Many have pondered the effect on Louisiana youth of the object lessons in demagogy which Huey held forth so vividly.*
>
> —Harnett T. Kane, *Louisiana Hayride* (1928–1940)

The campaign Kane referred to was the raucous extravaganza of 1939, the year of the greatest Louisiana scandal of them all. Huey Long, the "Kingfish," once said that without his restraining hand the rapacious crew around him would end up in prison. Within four years of his death the prediction proved true, beginning at the top, with Governor Richard Leche and James Monroe Smith, president of the state university.

"Fast Eddie" was twelve years old at the time, an impressionable age in a state where politics is a passion absorbed through the pores. In a 1991 interview he would claim that the Longs, Huey and Earl, had only a passing influence on his political evolution, that his true mentor was Franklin Roosevelt. "I remember," he told *New Orleans* magazine,

> when government made it possible for electricity to be brought to my home. . . . I remember when government made it possible for a bus to pick me up and drive me eight miles into town. I remember when government made it possible for me to eat a free, hot lunch at school. I remember when government made books available to me that I otherwise would not have been able to have.

Pointed memories, but in this instance Edwards's sure sense of where he is and how he got there failed him. Other than rural electrification, every governmental blessing named—the school bus, the free hot lunch, the books—came not from the Great White Father in Washington but the Kingfish in Baton Rouge, bought and paid for by soak-the-rich taxation—privateer's loot taken from Rockefeller's galleon.

Share Our Wealth, Huey called it, the American welfare state ahead of its time. And if the brigand crew should skim a few shares off the top? As Dick Leche said of his predecessor O. K. Allen, "They're saying he stole millions. Suppose he did? Look what the people got."

Edwards Denies Taking Tongsun Park Money

At the conclusion of his third successful race for Louisiana's governorship in the winter of 1983, Edwin Edwards asked his brother Marion to come up with some stylish way to pay off a massive campaign debt. The race against Republican David Treen had cost between four and five million dollars—a record-breaker for state politics at the time—and the Cajun King didn't relish the prospect of spending the next four years attending humdrum dinners to satisfy his creditors.

A decade before, when Edwin had won his first term in the mansion (defeating Bennett Johnston), Marion had broken new ground in imaginative fundraising by putting together a fatcat junket to Latin America to pay the bills. Now he would exceed even that triumph: For a $10,000 fee any fun-loving lobbyist, office-seeker, or corporate CEO doing business with the state could join Governor Edwards and his family on a pleasure jaunt to Paris and Monaco. *Laissez les bons temps rouler.*

In the event, no fewer than 600 revelers took the tour. There would be a grand dinner (with dancing) at the Versailles palace, high-rolling at the casino tables in Monte Carlo. Just the sort of in-your-face excess that made Edwards's strait-laced critics at home cringe in embarrassment. Surely, they thought, this would be too much for even Edwards's Coonass[1] *couzains* in the bayou.

In fact, the *couzains* ate it up, just as Huey's followers had vicariously enjoyed the Kingfish's escapades in New York and Chicago four decades before: One of theirs had made it big. The more he embarrassed the swells the better.

Nothing would come of the federal inquiries (FBI, IRS) into the Paris-Monaco junket. But by that time, a dozen years into the Edwards era, few expected anything else. Questions about inquiries into Edwards's financial affairs, either while he was governor or between terms, had by the mid-eighties become so routine as to be, in some cases, back-page stories. Among the major inquiries:

- *The TEL Affair.* The brainchild of Edwards's closest aide, Clyde Vidrine, TEL Enterprises was a quick-dollar development operation to raise funds, through the cachet of the Governor's Office, toward construction of a 62-story skyscraper in downtown New Orleans. Though Edwards had shares in TEL (the building was to be called One Edwards Square), he would back away when Vidrine's fundraising methods came under press scrutiny.

  Cut cold, Vidrine then turned on his former boss, writing a tell-all book (*Just Takin' Orders*) that went into lurid detail about Edwards's shady fundraising tactics and hyperactive sex life. The book proved embarrassing, but a Baton Rouge grand jury, given Vidrine's own shady background, took no action.
- *The Tongsun Park Affair.* Edwards was just a south Louisiana rice-country congressman when he came to know Park, the smooth-talking South Korean businessman-lobbyist who impressed Washington during the early seventies with lavish

parties and large campaign contributions. When Park, working through Congressman Otto Passman, brokered a huge foreign-aid sale that emptied Louisiana rice bins, Edwards shared the credit and gained a statewide reputation as a man who got things done for his constituents. Questioned after he became governor about a $10,000 gift from Park, "Fast Eddie" uncharacteristically offered a Clintonesque denial, but later reverted to form by admitting that yes, Park had given $10,000 to his wife, but it was no big deal. "Ten thousand might seem like a lot of money to a reporter," he told the press, "but there's a big difference between what's illegal and what causes you people to raise your eyebrows."

REPORTER: *Do you know anything about Tongsun Park supplying congressmen with women?*
EDWARDS: *I'm not aware of that, but it's certainly better than cash.*

- Park would end up indicted on thirty-six separate counts of bribery, illegal lobbying, and violation of federal statutes regarding foreign agents. Passman was indicted, tried, and though acquitted, ended up a broken man. Edwards emerged unscathed.
- *The DCCL Inquiry.* Another case of Edwards getting into bed with a *couzain* hustler, Jules LeBlanc, a campaign contributor fallen on hard times. DCCL—the Deferred Compensation Corporation of Louisiana—was given an exclusive franchise to sell tax-shelter retirement plans to state employees. When LeBlanc bankrupted, then took the Fifth Amendment before a legislative subcommittee, a Baton Rouge grand jury weighed in with a report that DCCL had been "manipulated to funnel money to friends of then-Governor Edwards," who, it developed, "held a financial interest in the company." Hardly a clean bill, but no indictments—just a tongue-clucking suggestion that "This is the kind of activity a state code of ethics should protect against."

And so it went until, by the mid-eighties, "Fast Eddie" had earned, among frustrated political critics and grudging federal investigators, a Teflon label. Unreachable, untouchable, a man gifted with *gris-gris.*

This however, was about to change. With the coming of John Volz, a hot-eyed federal district attorney who had tried, and won, criminal cases against the president of the state senate and the godfather of the local Mafia, Edwards's days as a scofflaw were numbered. Any prosecutor who could send Carlos Marcello to prison could nail a Cajun king.

Or so they said.

Edwards Will Enter Plea in Court Today

In the summer of 1934, at a time when young Edwin Edwards was hiding under houses to get away from girls, nationally syndicated columnist Westbrook Pegler came to Baton Rouge to cover a legislative hearing involving Huey Long. Pegler's initial report was so lacerating that Earl Long, in defense of his brother, threw a roundhouse punch at the columnist. Earl missed, but the incident left the usually insouciant Pegler with a lasting impression of Louisiana politics; as did his visits to the legislature where, after watching the people's representatives at work, he wrote: "They do not permit a house of prostitution to operate within a proscribed distance of the state university, but exempt the state Capitol from the meaning of the act."

Those were days when you drove from New Orleans to Baton Rouge via the Airline Highway, noted in history as the road traveled by speeding black limousines, preceded by wailing police sirens, the night Huey Long was shot; or, closer to home for the under-forty generation, the road traveled by Edwin Edwards's soulmate Jimmy Swaggart, the motel-dwelling evangelist, in his fall from grace.

But Interstate 10, a 75-minute scenic stretch from downtown New Orleans to the campus of Louisiana State University, has no such history, though it does pass Donaldsonville, close by the notorious Sunshine Bridge. The Sunshine, which spans the Mississippi from nowhere-to-nowhere, was built in the sixties to enrich the friends of then-Governor Jimmie Davis the singing cowboy. Three decades later it remains a source of wry amusement in Baton Rouge—steel-and-concrete proof that in politics there is no boodler like the boodler who preaches reform.

On an unseasonably warm October day Dale and I travel up I-10 to meet with the Lafitte scholar himself, John Maginnis—the one observer, we're told, who can lift the fog around the Cajun King's latest brush with the law:

Insurance Indictment Snags Brown, Edwards

This indictment comes, understand, while Edwards, now five years out of office, is still awaiting trial on a year-old charge that he rigged the award of riverboat gambling licenses to benefit, among others, his friend and casino-mate Eddie DeBartolo, of the San Francisco Forty-Niner DeBartolos.

There are questions, many questions, we have for Maginnis, but in the time-honored way of Louisiana (as opposed to Anglo) business lunches, they can wait; the eats come first. Maginnis has recommended Juban, a Creole-Cajun restaurant not far from the LSU campus that offers, to my surprise, a gumbo etouffé that excels even that served at Galatoire's. Since the Baton Rouge of my youth was defined, in terms of good eats, as the home of unsurpassed chili-dogs, it occurs to me that all change in the past four decades has not been for the worse.

Maginnis is an independent journalist in his forties who made his reputation as the foremost expert on Edwin Edwards's political career with publication of *The Last Hayride,* a chronicle of the Edwards-Treen governor's race of 1983. Two years later he would be in the crush of reporters and TV cameras at the federal courthouse in New Orleans, on hand to cover the trial of the first Louisiana governor under criminal indictment in nearly half a century.

As John Volz and his team of federal attorneys saw it at the time, they had built an airtight case, one that involved Edwards in a scheme to sell—cash upfront—state approval for the construction of hospital projects. Volz was tenacious, a bulldog prosecutor who reminded old-timers of O. John Rogge, the incorruptible federal prosecutor sent down by Washington in 1939 to nail the remnants of the Long gang.

Rogge, however, had more than law on his side; by the time he arrived in New Orleans the court of public opinion had already convicted Leche and his cronies. Volz, on the other hand, was dealing with a sitting governor only a year after he had won not simply election but an unprecedented third term by a landslide.

The year was 1985. Ronald Reagan sat in the Oval Office. Few Louisiana political observers were surprised when—after Edwards's lawyers portrayed Volz as the tool of a rich-folks' Republican Justice Department out to crucify a populist governor—the case ended in a mistrial. Or when, a year later, Volz's streak of high-profile criminal convictions ended with Edwards's complete acquittal by a second jury.

Not that the Teflon Governor emerged from the trials unscathed. Having spent half his four-year term dividing time between the Capitol and the courthouse, Edwards would run for re-election in 1987 with his poll numbers at an all-time low. Defeated by Charles "Buddy" Roemer, a onetime aide, he entered the private practice of law and seemed, by all Las Vegas odds, to be a man whose time had passed. Not only would he be nearing Social Security retirement age by the next election, but after twenty years and four campaigns, "Fast Eddie's" act, for all its style and flair, had played out.

Or so they said.

I'm a wizard under the sheets myself.

—Edwin Edwards, campaigning
in 1991 against David Duke

Luck, as Branch Rickey famously defined it, is but the residue of preparation; perhaps in sports, but in politics, more often than not, luck is a matter of being blessed with the right enemy at the right time. Case in point: "Fast Eddie's" comeback in the 1991 Louisiana governor's race, in which Edwards, given only a marginal chance to defeat incumbent "Buddy" Roemer, was instead blessed with David Duke as a run-off opponent.

Duke, who by that year had acquired a reputation for—as Earl Long once said of an opponent—"running for any office not nailed down," had edged into the run-off by virtue of Louisiana's bloc-favoring Open Primary system. Running as a Republican, the neo-Nazi/ex-Kluxer was swept away in one of the greatest landslides in state history. Though hardly a mandate for Edwards—Dick Leche resurrected would have done as well—the Cajun King took it as such.

The hayride, more garish than ever, would roll again.

Two Targets May Cut Deal with Prosecution

John Maginnis tells the story of Edwin Edwards campaigning at a Pentecostal revival meeting outside the town of Tioga on a Fourth of July. Dressed in summer white with a white Bible in hand and a stunning blonde nearby, he quoted scripture, then handed the preacher a "love offering"—an envelope with a $5,000 contribution. The crowd was on its feet, clapping, cheering. "It was more than I could take," Maginnis recalls. "I wandered backstage and ran into the Reverend C. D. Bates, a Pentecostal preacher who learned politics from Earl Long and was 100 percent behind Edwin Edwards. Tell me, I asked, how can pious people support a man who is known to gamble, chase women, and constantly face investigation for corruption? The Reverend looked at me as if I'd just checked in from another planet. 'Well,' he said, 'he don't drink or smoke.' "

There is a Republican governor now, Mike Foster, fairly popular, north and south; but five years and two indictments after Edwin Edwards left the mansion for (by all odds) the last time, there are still those who will tell you, at Mother's in New Orleans, or Mulate's in Breaux Bridge, that for all his gambling, cheating and loose way with a solemn oath, "Fast Eddie" was the best damned governor Louisiana ever had. Or, at least, the best since John McKeithen. Or since Uncle Earl, before he went crazy. Or, if they're old enough to remember the Great Flood of '27, since the Kingfish himself.

True believers. Presumably they'll say the same if, as now seems possible, "Fast Eddie's" run of luck plays out at the federal courthouse this round of indictments. John Maginnis, though he's covered Edwards long enough to hedge his guesses, sees signs, portents of an outcome different from the jury verdict of thirteen years ago: for one, the venue is Baton Rouge, not jury-friendly New Orleans; the prosecutor is a Democratic, not a Republican appointee; the judge a no-nonsense fast-tracker who, when asked for a two-month discovery period, simply banged his gavel and snapped, "Are you kidding?"

Add to that the prospect of two trials on separate, unrelated charges, a double gauntlet made more hazardous by the sworn testimony of former cronies gone over to the federal enemy: the Teflon worn down, so thin there is even talk that Edwards, side-by-side with his son and co-defendant Stephen, is resigned to the possibility that he might have to spend his next few birthdays behind prison walls.

Or so they're saying. Me, I wait and see. We have, after all, been here before, and until they show, in open court, the boy live or the girl dead, I'll take my rumors about the Cajun King, like my headlines, with a grain of salt. Or, as it were, a soupçon of Tabasco.

Note

1. "Coonass," for the benefit of the politically correct, is a non-pejorative synonym for "Cajun" widely used by people of French-Acadian stock in Louisiana's bayous—as when Edwards, on the night of his 1971 victory, defined the moment in terms of "The Coonasses have done it!"

Editor's Epilogue

Despite Gold's skepticism that Edwin Edwards would be convicted in the riverboat gambling case, the former Louisiana governor was found guilty of federal racketeering charges in May 2000 and sentenced to ten years in prison. Edwards had been charged with extorting more than $2.5 million from companies seeking gambling licenses, including $400,000 from Eddie DeBarolos. With Edwards's conviction, some political commentators suggested that a new era was dawning in Louisiana's politics, one that was less open to corruption. There has been some evidence of change. Of particular interest, state voters elected Democrat Kathleen Blanco as the first woman governor in November 2003. Blanco, and her opponent, were both well-established politicians without the colorful reputation of previous governors.[3]

Although the outcome of the race may suggest a decline in the state's tolerance for corruption, it provided evidence that race is indeed an important factor in shaping Louisiana's politics. Some initial voting studies on the election outcome indicate that Blanco was supported by many of the same voters who supported the Republican David Duke in 1991. The Republican candidate in 2003 was Bobby Jindal, a son of Indian immigrants.[4]

Chapter 2 Review Questions

1. How does Elazar define political culture? Why does he say that culture is important in shaping state politics?
2. What are the three types of political subcultures Elazar identifies? Describe the characteristics of each one. How well do you think these subcultures capture the political differences across the states?
3. What are the historical roots of these subcultures? Where did they come from? How did they spread across the nation?
4. How well does Elazar's theory of political culture capture Louisiana's politics? Or conversely, how well does this case study support Elazar's ideas about political culture?
5. Write your own definition of political culture. What would you consider to be the key characteristics that define a culture? Now, thinking back to Elazar's reading, how good a job do you think he does in capturing the concept of a political culture?
6. From your experiences and knowledge, how important would you say political culture is in shaping state government and politics? Does some other factor, such as the urban-rural split seen in the 2004 presidential vote, seem more important? How so?

Key Terms

urbanization
political culture
political subculture
individualistic
moralistic
traditionalistic
laissez-faire
marketplace
private activities
quid pro quo
merit system
commercialism
pluralism
commonwealth
public good
communitarianism
collectivism
paternalistic
elitist
agrarianism
human or cultural geology

Suggestions for Further Reading

Almond, Gabriel A. "Comparative Political Systems." *Journal of Politics* 18 (August 1956): 391–409. This seminal piece is credited with introducing the concept of political culture into political science studies. Almond's ideas about political culture are developed more fully in *The Civic Culture: Political Attitudes and Democracy in Five Nations*, by Gabriel A. Almond and Sidney Verba (Thousand Oaks, Calif.: Sage Publications, 1989).

Black, Earl, and Merle Black. *The Rise of Southern Republicans*. Cambridge, Mass.: Belknap Press, 2002. A valuable study on the distinctive regional politics of the South.

Dye, Thomas R. *Politics, Economics, and the Public*. Chicago: Rand McNally, 1966. One of the earliest and most important studies on how economic factors influence state politics and policy. Examines the impact of such factors as urbanization, industrialization, wealth, and levels of educational attainment. More recent information on the impact of economic factors on public policy in the states can be found in Dye's *Understanding Public Policy,* 10th ed. (Englewood Cliffs, N.J.: Prentice-Hall, 2001).

Elazar, Daniel J. *American Federalism: A View from the States.* 3d ed. New York: Harper and Row, 1984. Elazar's typology on the nation's political subcultures was first published in the original edition of this book. The third edition includes a detailed description in the endnotes of previous studies that either used or examined Elazar's typology.

Erickson, Robert S., Gerald C. Wright, and John P. McIver. *Statehouse Democracy: Public Opinion and Policy in the American States.* Cambridge, Mass.: Cambridge University Press, 1993. Oft-cited comparative state study on the impact of public opinion on public policy.

Hero, Rodney. *Faces of Inequality: Social Diversity in American Politics.* Oxford: Oxford University Press, 2000. Important recent study on how the ethnic/racial compositions of states affect state politics and policy.

Lieske, Joel. "Regional Subcultures of the United States." *Journal of Politics* 55 (1993): 888–913. Provides an alternative typology of political subcultures in the United States.

Nardulli, Peter F. "Political Subcultures in the American States." *American Politics Quarterly* 18 (July 1990): 287–315. Critical examination of Elazar's work that uses survey data to test the validity of his typology.

Politics and Governments of the American States series, University of Nebraska Press. This series of textbooks on more than 20 American states relies extensively on Elazar's typology as a common theme.

Sharkansky, Ira. *Regionalism in American Politics.* Madison: University of Wisconsin Press, 1970. Provides an extensive explanation for the importance of studying regions in comparative state research.

Sullivan, John. "Political Correlates of Social, Economic, and Religious Diversity in the American States." *Journal of Politics* 35 (1973): 70–85. One of the earliest studies to focus on the impact of diversity on state politics. The "Sullivan index" is still influential in efforts to rank states by their diversity. An effort to update this index is offered by David R. Morgan and Laura Ann Wilson in "Diversity in the American States: Updating the Sullivan Index," *Publius* 20 (Winter 1990): 71–81.

Thomas, Clive S., ed. *Politics and Public Policy in the Contemporary American West.* Albuquerque: University of New Mexico Press, 1991. Another valuable study on regional politics.

Related Web Sites

http://www.census.gov
The official web site for the U.S. Census Bureau provides statistical data on states, cities, and counties, including on-line versions of the *Statistical Abstracts of the United States* and the *State and Metropolitan Data Book.*

http://www.jcpa.org/djeindex.htm
The Jerusalem Center for Public Affairs provides an on-line library of writings by Daniel Elazar, including work on political culture.

http://www.lib.lsu.edu/govdocs/lougov.html
http://www.library.mcneese.edu/depts/docs/louis.htm
http://library.tulane.edu/about_the_library/departments/government_documents/la_government_sites.php
Louisiana State, McNeese State, and Tulane University Libraries provide good links to information on Louisiana politics.

3

Redistributing Power Among Governments: The Concept of Devolution

The prospects for significant devolution during the foreseeable future are not bright, largely because federal officials are reluctant to relinquish powers they have acquired in the twentieth century to advance national policy objectives.

John Kincaid

READING 3

Introduction

How should power be distributed between the federal government and the states? This question has been the focus of considerable political debate in the nation ever since the federal government began to play an expanded role in society in the 1930s. The debate is important because the outcome may affect the quality of services the public receives from the government, the character of public policy across the nation, and the kind of democracy in which we want to live. In recent years, political reformers have frequently called for *devolution,* or returning greater power and responsibility to the states. For many of these reformers, the national government has grown too large and too distant from average citizens to provide effective services and to hear what the public wants. Returning power to the states will improve the delivery of public services and produce a system of government that is more responsive to citizen demands. Using Hedge's terminology from Chapter 1, devolution is often promoted as a way both to improve responsibility and democracy.

Despite the warm portrait that supporters paint of devolution, not everyone believes that greater power should be given to the states. For opponents, many state governments are still not capable of providing many of the services demanded by the public, despite the increased capacity of these governments. Moreover, many see devolution as promoting an unhealthy competition among the states, one in which the state governments will reduce government services and regulations to attract business or to repel undesirable newcomers, such as welfare recipients. Others also see the federal government as providing a forum where more diverse interests can be heard, whereas some groups of citizens may be too small for their voices to be heard at the state level. These opponents see devolution as actually producing a less democratic system of government.

To understand the debate between these two sides, it is helpful to learn about the relationship between the federal and state governments throughout the nation's history. The term that is often used to describe this relationship prior to the 1930s is *dual federalism.* Many scholars argue that during the first part of the nation's history, the federal and state governments concentrated their efforts on different policy concerns, with the federal government focused solely on the few activities delegated to it in the U.S. Constitution and with the states focused on other domestic matters. The term *dual federalism* is meant to capture this separate focus and to suggest that the two levels did not work together.

There is some disagreement among scholars on how best to describe this relationship since the 1930s. As a result, the literature is scattered with terms that have been used to try to capture the character of our federal system of government today. For example, in the reading in Chapter 1 of this book, Hedge mentions two such terms: *progressive federalism* and *competitive federalism.* Other terms include *cooperative federalism, picket fence federalism, Creative Federalism, coercive federalism, New Federalism, centralized federalism,* and *pragmatic federalism.*

These different terms convey different interpretations of what the relationship has been like between the levels of government since the 1930s. *Cooperative federalism* is the most commonly used term to describe the relationship during this period. It suggests that the federal and state governments work together on public policy matters. Such terms as *coercive federalism* or *centralized federalism* emphasize that the relationship between the levels is not always cooperative. Rather, the federal government at times compels the states to act, thus leading some scholars to say that the relationship is coercive or that it is centralized at the national level. *Creative Federalism, New Federalism,* and *pragmatic federalism* are terms used to describe the specific programs or orientations of recent presidents. *Creative Federalism* was the term used by President Johnson to describe his array of programs that led to a centralization of power at the national level in the 1960s. *New Federalism* is the name used by both presidents Nixon and Reagan to describe their efforts to return greater power to the states. The term *pragmatic federalism* has been used to describe President George W. Bush's attitude toward federalism.

If there is one period in which the term *cooperative* best describes the relationship between federal and state governments, it was from the 1930s into the mid-1960s. During this period, the federal government began to work with the states in providing public services, with much of the help coming in the form of financial assistance. Certainly, there were some policy areas in which there was an element of coercion in the federal government's action toward the states, but in general, the relationship was marked by cooperation and a sharing of responsibilities.

The term *cooperative* has continued to be used by many to describe federalism since the mid-1960s, but it does not do justice to the shifts that have occurred in federal-state relations since that time; thus some scholars prefer these other terms. Beginning with Johnson's administration, there has been less cooperation between the levels of government and a greater centralization of power at the national level. Johnson's Creative Federalism sought to address many of the nation's ills by direct federal action and closer federal ties with local governments. The result was that the states were not included in the action and were left with a less important role in the nation's political system.

Nixon and Reagan made some effort to return greater responsibility to the states. For example, Nixon introduced general revenue sharing as a way for the federal government to help states address policy concerns but without being coercive. Through general revenue sharing, the federal government simply shared federal funds with the states with no strings attached. Even though both presidents talked about returning power to the states, many federal policies enacted under both were coercive in character and continued the trend of centralization. During Nixon's presidency, for example, there was a large increase in federal regulations on the states. During Reagan's tenure, the federal government began to rely extensively on unfunded or underfunded mandates on the states as a way to create new programs but without having to foot the bill. Under a federal mandate, states are required to perform a task delegated to them by the federal government. Since the mandates did not come with adequate funding, the states not only had to create the new programs, but find ways to pay for them.

Proposals to reduce the federal government's role in society and give greater responsibility to the states reemerged on the nation's political agenda during the Clinton administration, especially after the Republican Revolution in 1994, which gave the Republican Party a majority in both houses of Congress. Political leaders began to use the term *devolution* to refer to returning greater responsibility to the states. The passage of the Personal Responsibility and Work Opportunity Reconciliation Act (PRWORA) of 1996, revamping the nation's welfare system, is often cited as the prime example of the devolution movement.

Even though many scholars believe that PRWORA represented an important change in the direction of federal-state relations, not everyone agrees. There have been several recent events and trends that suggest that there has not been a meaningful shift of power back to the states, despite the talk of devolution. For example, under President George W. Bush's leadership, Congress has passed several broad mandates in recent years, which the states are being forced to implement and fund. These include aspects of homeland security and the Help America Vote Act, which was the law passed by Congress to improve election administration after the problems in the 2000 presidential election. The broadest new mandate, however, is the No Child Left Behind Act, which is considered to be the federal government's most direct involvement in local schools in history. Moreover, the federal government has continued to pass legislation over the past several years preempting state laws. Some scholars even question whether PRWORA itself actually gave much power to the states, a question that is looked at in the final chapter of this book.

In the reading that follows, Professor John Kincaid describes some of the national forces that have emerged in recent years that may help produce a devolution of power to the states. Yet Kincaid also provides an explanation for why it may be unlikely that much power will actually return to the states. Kincaid's work provides a valuable introduction to devolution and the political battles that revolve around it. His work is also valuable because it reveals some of the major arguments both for and against devolution. On the one hand, devolution supporters frequently suspect the concentration of power at the national level and believe that modern state governments have the capacity to handle the job. Moreover, devolution is seen as an important aspect of democratization. On the other hand, the federal government frequently focuses on issues that enjoy widespread support nationwide. Kincaid also examines the argument that devolution may lead to destructive interstate competition.

Questions to Consider

Professor Kincaid is the Director of the Meyner Center for the Study of State and Local Government at Lafayette College in Easton, Pennsylvania. These are some questions to think about as you read his work:

- What are some of the arguments in favor of devolution? What are some of the arguments in opposition? From reading Kincaid's work, do you think that devolution would promote more effective government or greater democracy? How so?
- According to Kincaid, what are some of the major forces for restoring state powers? What are some of the leading forces against restoring these powers?
- How have leaders of the Republican Party felt about strengthening the states since the 1950s? How important is devolution to them compared with other political goals? How have Democratic Party leaders felt about devolution?
- What does Kincaid have to say about the likelihood of devolution producing destructive interstate competition? In reflecting on Kincaid's arguments, does he seem to be a supporter or an opponent of devolution?

The Devolution Tortoise and the Centralization Hare

John Kincaid

There has been much talk in recent years of devolving powers and functions from the federal government to the states. Some observers even proclaim a "devolution revolution" (Nathan 1996), the result of which will be a more efficient and effective federal government and more robust and responsive states. The generally recognized objectives of devolution include (1) more efficient provision and production of public services; (2) better alignment of the costs and benefits of government for a diverse citizenry; (3) better fits between public goods and their spatial characteristics; (4) increased competition, experimentation, and innovation

Excerpted from John Kincaid, "The Devolution Tortoise and the Centralization Hare," *New England Economic Review* (May/June 1998): 13–29. Reprinted with permission from the Federal Reserve Bank of Boston.

in the public sector; (5) greater responsiveness to citizen preferences; and (6) more transparent accountability in policymaking.

These are ambitious objectives, although, to date, no consensus on direction is apparent, no plan of execution is in place, and examples of devolution are scarce. Indeed, there are only two commonly cited examples of devolution: congressional repeal of the national 55-mph speed limit and welfare reform. The prospects for significant devolution during the foreseeable future are not bright, largely because federal officials are reluctant to relinquish powers they have acquired in the twentieth century to advance national policy objectives. Consequently, devolution is plodding along at a turtle's pace while centralization is still racing ahead at a rabbit's pace. . . .

Forces for Restoring State Powers

The most immediate force propelling discussions of shifting powers back to the states was the 1994 midterm elections, which brought a Republican majority into both houses of Congress. The 1994 elections ended more than sixty years of nearly continuous Democratic control of the Congress (with Democratic control of the U.S. House of Representatives having been the longest period of one-party rule in U.S. history) and also unseated an incumbent House Speaker for the only time in this century.

The Republicans' "Contract with America" contained several provisions aimed at curbing federal power and restoring state powers, beginning with mandate reform, which was enacted in 1995 with bipartisan support as the Unfunded Mandates Reform Act (UMRA). The state-friendly provisions of the "Contract with America" reflected long-standing Republican concerns dating back to President Dwight D. Eisenhower, who had likened the centralization of power and rise of the "military industrial complex" in the United States during the New Deal and World War II to the "extreme and dictatorial concentration of power" then occurring in communist Eastern Europe (Coleman and Goldberg 1990, p. 20).

President Eisenhower was not, however, able to tilt power back toward the states. On the contrary, Eisenhower's nomination of Earl Warren to be Chief Justice of the U.S. Supreme Court, his support for the National Defense Highway Act of 1956 and for the National Defense Education Act of 1957, his dispatch of federal troops to Little Rock, Arkansas, in 1957 to enforce desegregation pursuant to the U.S. Supreme Court's ruling in *Brown* v. *Board of Education* (1954), and other policy actions, all enhanced federal power. Thus, federal policymaking during the supposedly conservative 1950s reinforced Alpheus T. Mason's observation that: "For two generations American political and economic life has been moving swiftly toward 'bigness,' toward monolithic organization" (Mason 1952, p. 1).

President Richard M. Nixon's New Federalism, which echoed Eisenhower's federalism sentiments, was, despite General Revenue Sharing (1972 to 1986), no more successful in stemming the growth of federal power. President Ronald Reagan began his Administration with strong, emphatic support for a New Federalism aimed at shifting substantial power back to the states. Reagan's success was modest at best, and the federal government continued to expand its power through mandates, preemptions, and conditions attached to federal aid (Conlan 1988, Kincaid 1993b).

This brief history suggests two hypotheses. First, many of the Republicans elected to the Congress in 1994 arrived with strong commitments to long-frustrated desires to limit federal power, which for some, though not all, also means restoring state powers. This was reinforced by the new Republicans elected from the increasingly Republican South and from the Mountain West—both growing regions historically suspicious of, and often hostile to, the federal government. Second, it is the Congress more often than the White House that alters the balance of power in the federal system. If these conclusions are correct, then some significant restorations of state powers are likely to occur if the Republicans maintain control of the Congress, if the Republicans capture the Presidency in 2000, and if the currently federalism-friendly majority on the U.S. Supreme Court is maintained or increased after 2000.

These prospects are further strengthened by support for rebalancing federal-state power among more members of the Democratic party than was true in the past. In a 1997 statement, for example, the Democratic Leadership Council, with which President Clinton was affiliated, said:

> The New Democrat movement has consistently rejected the old-fashioned liberal prejudice against state governments and state elected officials. . . . Now more than ever, state elected officials represent the future of our party and our country. State capitals are the battlegrounds where the big challenges of American domestic policy on the eve of the 21st century are being met (1997, p. 1).

The 1996 Democratic party platform even claimed that "Republicans talked about shifting power back to the states and communities—Democrats are doing it."

This is a far cry from Governor George Wallace standing in the doorway of the University of Alabama in 1963 defying federal authority, but the states have since experienced a remarkable rehabilitation, which has placed them in a much more favorable light. Well into the 1970s, most Americans expressed more trust and confidence in the federal government than in the states. Since then, however, public trust and confidence to the extent the public has any trust and confidence in any governments—has shifted gradually and substantially from the federal government to the states. For example, a 1995 poll conducted by Princeton Survey Research Associates found that 61 percent of Americans trusted their state government to "do a better job of running things" than the federal government. Nearly every subgroup except black Americans and Jews expressed similar support for the states. Adults under age thirty favored the states by 72 to 21 percent, Democrats, by 48 to 35 percent, and self-described liberals, by 49 to 36 percent (Donahue 1997, p. 13). These findings are consistent with trends in most polls asking similar questions for the past decade.

This opinion change is due partly to the "modernization" of state and local governments and political systems that has occurred since the 1950s, with much assistance and pressure from the federal government. The structural changes highlighted by most observers— such as constitutional revision, legislative reapportionment, professionalized legislatures, four-year tenure for 48 governors, and strengthened judiciaries (ACIR 1985; Reeves 1990)—have been important, but the most significant change has been the altered relationship between citizens and their state and local governments. State and local political systems are more electorally inclusive and representative of diversity than in the past, and they are no less inclusive than the federal arena. Previously excluded groups have more opportunities to win office and gain employment in state and local governments than in the federal government. On average, state and local governments are also more accessible to citizen reform, not simply because they are smaller arenas but also because state constitutions and amendments require popular ratification in 49 states; because state constitutions compel recourse to the people and to supermajority consent on many important matters; and because a number of state constitutions give citizens initiative, referendum, and/or recall powers. The federal government is constitutionally impervious to such direct citizen participation. In addition, state and local governments are better equipped today than in the past to provide more and better services for citizens, and with the appearance of less corruption. Furthermore, state and local tax systems are more diversified than in the past and are often less regressive than the federal tax system, where Social Security and Medicare taxes—the largest tax bites for most Americans—are regressive. In addition, most state and local governments have been more fiscally disciplined than the federal government.

The case for devolution has been bolstered as well by a recovering economy. As a result, most states have had year-end budget surpluses during the 1990s; state budget surpluses amounted to $24 billion at the outset of 1998; state and local government spending has increased by 14.3 percent in real terms since 1990; 31 states reduced taxes in 1996; and state and local government employment has increased by about 1.8 million persons since 1990 while federal government employment has declined by more than 345,000.

Adding force to rebalancing efforts has been migration to the suburbs and to the Sunbelt. The United States has been, and continues to be, a nation of small and medium-size communities. Never in the history of the United States have more than 30 percent of Americans lived in urban places having 100,000 or more residents. The high points of big-city life in America occurred between 1920 and 1970. By the late 1980s, the United States had become a suburban nation. In addition, the center of population continues to migrate southwestward as most Sunbelt states experience tremendous growth.

A political sine qua non of suburban life is local self-government, jealously guarded and combined with stout resistance to metropolitan consolidation or other arrangements perceived as threatening to local autonomy, as well as a proclivity for service-efficient council-manager type governance free of "politics" (see, for example, Baker 1975). Hence, the suburban mentality, whatever the shortfalls and shortcomings of its realization, is receptive to "devolution," and the federal government and most state governments have been deferential to this suburban mentality. This deference is reflected, for instance, in the U.S. Supreme Court's unwillingness to extend court-ordered school busing beyond central-city boundaries, in the Congress's and the states' overwhelmingly preferential funding for highways rather than mass transit, in the unwillingness of both the federal government and the states to enforce fair housing laws with any vigor, in the reduced federal funding since the Reagan era for metropolitan regional structures (for example, councils of governments), and in the unwillingness of state legislatures to mandate jurisdictional consolidations.

Migration to the Sunbelt is having at least two devolutionary effects. For one, given that most Sunbelt states have, historically, been states' rights states, migration into those states has strengthened the states' rights voice in Washington, DC. At the same time, migration has helped to "modernize" those states, to make many of them more progressive and innovative and to soften the hard surfaces, such as racism, historically characteristic of politics in many of those states. Migration has helped to pull the Sunbelt states toward the center of the national political spectrum while simultaneously pulling the national political center slightly rightward.

Stemming in part from this suburban and Sunbelt migration has been the emergence of Republican control of a majority of the governorships . . . [28 in 2004]. On average, Republican governors have been more supportive of restoring state powers than Democratic governors, and Republican governors, for example, played a major role in shaping "welfare reform" in 1996. The governors, however, including Republican governors, do not champion state prerogatives across the board. Most governors continue to advocate federal preemptions of state powers in many areas affecting interstate commerce, and most governors supported the preemption-laden North American Free Trade Agreement (NAFTA) in 1993 and the Uruguay Round of the General Agreement on Tariffs and Trade (GATT) in 1994.

Both Democratic and Republican state and local officials have given strong support to deregulatory measures and other efforts to reduce federal "micromanagement" of state and local affairs. Here, elected state and local officials have been nearly unanimous, as reflected in their concerted lobbying for the Unfunded Mandates Reform Act (UMRA). The state-local coalition constructed to support UMRA was unusual because state and local officials rarely speak with one voice in Washington, DC.

Certain historical imperatives, especially the perceived fiscal crisis of the federal government, have added force to rationales for shifting power toward the states. This was the reality facing President Clinton when he declared the end of the era of "big government." Regardless of one's views about federal budget deficits and the size of the federal government, the weight of public opinion perceives these to be serious problems, even though the public does not endorse draconian remedies. The federal government lacks the fiscal resources, and perhaps the political will as well, to sustain, let alone augment, the kinds of expansive and state-intrusive policies associated with the New Deal of the 1930s and the Great Society of the 1960s. By a combination of default, deaccession, and disinvestment, therefore, certain powers and responsibilities must necessarily flow into the states, and the Congress will likely dump certain fiscally onerous and politically volatile functions onto states and localities.

The growth of entitlement spending, which now dominates the federal budget, adds more pressure on Congress to off-load "discretionary" programs that carry real budget costs. Although the 1996 "welfare reform" ended certain long-standing entitlements, their costs pale in comparison to the costs of Social Security, Medicare, and Medicaid. These entitlements are likely to remain entrenched federal responsibilities not only because they are advocated by influential reformers (Rivlin 1992; Peterson 1995) but also, and more important, because they are predominantly middle-class entitlements. Even Medicaid has become a middle-class entitlement because of the high costs of long-term health and nursing home care for the elderly.

Entitlement pressures on the federal budget will, moreover, begin to skyrocket in 2010 when baby boomers commence retirement.

Public disaffection from the federal government has also contributed to support for restoring state powers. The federal government has experienced an astonishing erosion of legitimacy in recent decades, coupled with disillusionment and skepticism about the efficacy of many federal programs—an attitude reinforced by the generally critical media. Although many federal programs are more successful than is generally believed by voters, reality is what citizens perceive it to be, and this perceived reality underwrote President Clinton's pledge to "reinvent" government and, among other things, "to end welfare as we know it." Whatever its past successes, "welfare as we knew it" became widely viewed as a counterproductive failure.

Undoubtedly, some advocates of restored state powers desire little more than to shrink, even cripple, the federal government, while still others wish to abolish or reduce certain federal policies and programs by using the subterfuge of federalism to turn them over to the states where, they hope, the policies and programs will be dismantled or cut back. Such opportunistic forum shopping has long been common in the federal system, and one can expect the debate over restorations of state powers to continue to be clouded by opportunism.

But such motives are overshadowed by another legitimizing force: namely, the power of an idea. Demands for decentralization, devolution, deregulation, federalism, power sharing, and the like have become prominent worldwide. These demands often come from ethnic, tribal, linguistic, religious, and political groups within multinational states, such as the Baltic states, Belgium, Canada, India, Malaysia, Mexico, Nigeria, Pakistan, the Philippines, Rwanda, Spain, Ukraine, the former Soviet Union, the Sudan, Uganda, the United Kingdom, the former Yugoslavia, and others. Elsewhere, though, as in Denmark, France, Japan, Norway, and Sweden, pressure for decentralization or "deconcentration" has stemmed from escalating national welfare costs, rising unemployment, and a growing belief that regional or local governments can provide services more efficiently and effectively (see, for example, Baldersheim and Stava 1993).

An interesting and somewhat surprising twist on the enthusiasm for decentralization has been its support from the left, such as the Socialist party in France, which promoted extensive devolution (Bernier 1992), and the British Labour party's promotion of successful devolution referenda in Scotland and Wales in 1997. . . .

Decentralization and even federalism have gained substantial legitimacy from the perceived failures of the centralized state (Wunsch and Olowu 1995), failures of planned economies, and weakening of the historic nation-state (Elazar 1995). Pressures for decentralization and federalism are usually linked now to political democratization, economic deregulation, denationalization and dereservation of state enterprises and lands, and decriminalization of previously forbidden market and voluntary sector activities. Hence, while federalism in the United States is often viewed as a conservative idea because of the historical backdrop of reactionary states' rights, federalism (or at least decentralization) in many other countries is frequently viewed as a liberal or progressive concept because of the historical backdrop of centralized tyranny (Kincaid 1995). As Carlos Fuentes wrote along these lines in 1990: "The Federalist Papers should be distributed in the millions."

In summary, support for restoring state powers and rebalancing the federal system arises not only from factors particular to the United States but also from a worldwide trend toward decentralization, which some observers link to a broader trend of "flattening hierarchies" across all political, social, economic, and cultural sectors of postmodern life. . . .

Forces Against Restoring State Powers

A significant obstacle to "devolution" is public opinion. Even though there is a generalized public preference for local and state performance of public functions, just as there is a generalized preference for a balanced federal budget, each particular "devolution" proposal, like each particular item slated for a budget cut, encounters opposition from particular beneficiaries anxious to maintain the status quo while being willing to urge devolution of someone else's programs. Even in welfare reform, for example, despite negative public attitudes toward welfare, half of the respondents to a survey by the Kaiser/Harvard Program (1995) supported granting more flexibility to states to experiment with welfare programs, but also agreed that the "federal government has to set guidelines when it gives money to states . . . in order to assure that the states will treat everyone fairly and do the right thing for poor people."

The devolution of any function or shift of any power to the states poses risks and uncertainties for the interests that benefit from the maintenance of federal control. Opposition is likely to stiffen, moreover, when proposals to shift powers to the states are linked to calls for policy reform, budget cuts, deficit reduction, and downsizing (Weaver 1996).

Devolution is also frustrated because, even though the Republican majority in the Congress has tended to express the most support for devolution, Republicans are often more committed to principles of individualism than of federalism. As U.S. House Speaker Newt Gingrich has expressed it:

> The last sixty years has seen so much centralization in Washington that at this point the best we can do is start by shifting power back to the state capitals. Power in fifty different cities is better than power centralized in one city.
>
> Yet our ultimate goal is to move power even beyond the state capitals. Many governors and county commissioners are deeply suspicious of state governments and would prefer bloc [*sic*] grants and programs that come straight to them. . . .
>
> However, much as I sympathize with both state and local governments, what we really want to do is to devolve power all the way out of government and back to working American families. . . . Republicans envision a decentralized America in which responsibility is returned to the individual (Gingrich 1995, pp. 104–105).

Principles of individualism and federalism frequently collide with each other because the promotion of individualism often requires constraints on state and local governments as well as the federal government. As a result, for example, on grounds of individual liberty, many Republicans as well as some Democrats support federal preemption of state authority to reregulate sectors of the economy deregulated by the Congress.

Politically, the devolution agenda that was set forth by the Republicans encountered numerous obstacles that blocked enactment of nearly the entire agenda. Proposals to devolve various health and social welfare programs, for example, jeopardize the entitlement status of programs for both states and individuals. Many state officials have sought to maintain state entitlements to federal support in order to guarantee adequate and predictable federal aid while many congressional Republicans have sought to reduce expenditures. In turn, numerous advocacy and clientele groups have sought to maintain individual entitlements in order to prevent states from denying or reducing benefits to currently eligible citizens. Entitlement advocates have also expressed concern, for example, "that removing individual entitlement in the Medicaid program would lead states to concentrate resources on popular and powerful clienteles, such as the frail elderly in nursing homes" (Weaver 1996, p. 49).

Conflicts over funding formulas have also frustrated devolution. "Formula fights" are among the most vigorous in Congress, and they pit states and regions against each other. In essence, no state or region wants to be a net loser in devolution. States, however, have generally been united in seeking federal guarantees of increased funding during recessions, while many congressional Republicans have opposed such guarantees. Some devolution proposals have also pitted states against their local governments, as local officials seek to defend their prerogatives and shield their jurisdictions from negative fallouts. Devolution proposals have sparked vigorous debates as well, over maintenance-of-effort requirements, maintenance of federal standards, mandates, and accountability. In the end, many Republicans as well as Democrats are unwilling to let go of policy objectives that might be defeated by devolution to states having different policy objectives.

Additionally, many policy functions that enhance federal power and reduce state powers, such as civil rights, environmental protection, middle-class entitlements, and crime control, enjoy broad and deep public support. Furthermore, issues are often framed in ways that make it politically impossible to refuse federal action. How many members of Congress, for instance, could publicly oppose a federal Megan's Law? However strongly President Reagan wished to shrink federal power, he could hardly refuse to sign the bill supported by Mothers Against Drunk Drivers that made it a condition of federal highway aid that states increase the minimum drinking age to 21 in order to reduce teenage highway fatalities and clean up "blood borders." This political dynamic is currently reflected in President Clinton's proposal, thus far approved by the U.S. Senate, to establish—as a condition of federal highway aid—a national blood-alcohol standard of 0.08 percent for drunk driving, in contrast to the 0.10 standard in force in 33 states. Proponents of the proposed standard regard it as good public policy; many opponents argue that it intrudes upon the historic constitutional prerogatives of the states. Hence, the most viable candidates for devolution are powers and functions that do not enjoy strong public support as well as functions of a more administrative nature that are invisible to the general public.

Similarly, a number of federal policy functions are highly beneficial for members of Congress and serve to benefit the constituency interests of the federal government generally. Thus, for example, "in contrast to the bipartisan embrace of welfare-reform block grants, there has been deafening bipartisan disinterest in major devolution of infrastructure activities, such as highways, to the states, despite the existence of a strong performance rationale and incentives for state leadership of these activities" (Posner and Wrightson 1996, p. 107).

In addition, there continue to be strong incentives to use three key tools of coercive federalism: mandates, conditions of aid, and preemption (Kincaid 1993b). Unfunded and underfunded mandates are especially tempting because they allow the Congress and the White House to claim credit for "feel good" policies and to respond to interest groups while "devolving" the costs of those policies to state and local governments. Although the Unfunded Mandates Reform Act appears to be having some limiting effects on the enactment of new unfunded mandates (National Governors' Association 1996), the act has many exemptions, its point of order can be overridden by a simple majority vote in either house of Congress, and it is no barrier to politically popular or compelling mandates such as the bipartisan support for increasing the federal minimum wage in 1996, which will cost state and local taxpayers about $1.3 billion during the next five years, according to the Congressional Budget Office. Furthermore, Republicans have proved to be no less eager than Democrats to mandate their policy preferences nationwide now that they are in power on Capitol Hill.

Conditions of aid remain one of the most open flanks for federal encroachments upon state powers and for federal accessions of powers wholly outside the Congress's constitutionally enumerated powers. The U.S. Supreme Court has upheld such conditions on the ground that federal aid is voluntarily accepted by the states (*South Dakota* v. *Dole* 1987), even though, as a practical political and fiscal matter, states cannot opt out of the large grant-in-aid programs, such as Medicaid and highways. In the case of highways, moreover, if a state were to decline federal highway aid in order to avoid compliance with objectionable conditions, the state's residents would, presumably, still be required to pay the federal motor fuels tax while deriving no benefit from it. Consequently, the large federal-aid programs like highways and Medicaid become vehicles for expanding federal power.

The single greatest devourer of state-local powers, however, is preemption, namely, federal displacement of state law under the supremacy clause of the U.S. Constitution (Article VI). More than 53 percent of all explicit preemption statutes enacted by the Congress since 1789 have been enacted only since 1969 (ACIR 1992). The new Republican majority in Congress, like previous Democratic majorities, has a healthy appetite for preemption (see, for example, Shenk 1997). Indeed, Republican efforts to preempt state product liability, food and drug labeling, Internet taxation, and medical malpractice laws, among others, have made a number of congressional Democrats ardent states' rights advocates.

Pressure in the federal system for preemption is enormous, primarily for economic reasons. For one, many businesses engaged in interstate commerce would rather be regulated by one 500-pound gorilla in Washington than by 50 monkeys on steroids. Second, deregulation of the economy has increased preemption so as to prohibit state regulators from rushing into regulatory vacuums created by federal withdrawal. Third, rising concern about international economic competition has spurred preemptions of state and local barriers to business competitiveness. For example, as Secretary of the Treasury Nicholas Brady said on introducing

President George [H. W.] Bush's proposals to preempt certain state powers over interstate banking, something is seriously amiss when a bank in California can open a branch in Birmingham, England, but not in Birmingham, Alabama (ACIR 1992, p. 38). Fourth, foreign-trade agreements eliminating not only tariffs but also non-tariff barriers to free trade pose substantial, long-term preemption threats to a broad range of state and local tax, regulatory, and policy powers (Weiler 1994).

All of these mechanisms for expanding federal power also reflect a major structural change in the federal system that first occurred during the 1960s, namely, a shift in federal policymaking from places to persons and a reconceptualization of the federal union as one constituted by individuals, not sovereign states. This shift reflects a long-standing debate in American history that reached a flashpoint during the 1980s when President Reagan declared that "the Federal Government did not create the States; the States created the Federal Government." President Reagan's opponents countered along the lines of William H. Seward in 1850: "The States are not parties to the Constitution as States; it is the Constitution of the people of the United States." As Justice Harry A. Blackmun later put it: "Ours . . . is a federal republic, conceived on the principle of a supreme federal power and constituted first and foremost of citizens, not sovereign states" (*Coleman* v. *Thompson* 1991). This individualist view of the union is one reason why Justice O'Connor has sought to transform the Tenth Amendment from a guarantor of states' rights to a guarantor of individual rights.

Politically, the reorientation of federal policymaking from places to persons has been driven primarily by the U.S. Supreme Court's reapportionment decisions requiring "one person, one vote" electoral districts for the U.S. House and for state legislatures (*Reynolds* v. *Sims* 1964; *Wesberry* v. *Sanders* 1964). Reapportionment—coupled with other developments during the 1960s, especially the rise of the national media and of party primaries—was fully implemented by 1972. The principal consequence for state powers was that reapportionment disconnected members of the U.S. House and, as a result, members of the Senate, too, from their historic electoral ties to state and local party organizations and thereby to elected state and local officials. The electoral incentives for members of Congress shifted from dependence on state and local party and government officials to dependence on national interest-group support and direct appeals to voters. Hence, the greatest federal encroachments upon state powers occurred not during the New Deal, when the federal government vastly expanded its power over the economy, but during and after the Great Society, when members of Congress had growing incentives to legislate directly for the interests of persons regardless of the effects of such legislation on places, namely, state and local governments. Virtually every empirical indicator of expanding federal power (for example, numbers of mandates, conditions of aid, preemptions, and federal court orders) shows unprecedented increases since 1969—increases that continued unabated through Democratic and Republican administrations and shifting balances of partisan power in the Congress (Kincaid 1993a & b).

A bellwether has been the Fair Labor Standards Act of 1938 (FLSA). The act was upheld in *United States* v. *Darby* (1941), in which the U.S. Supreme Court dismissed the Tenth Amendment as merely "a truism." However, the Congress specifically exempted state and local government employees from the FLSA, and Darby concerned only the FLSA's applicability to private employers. In 1968, though, the U.S. Supreme Court permitted the U.S. Department of Labor to apply the FLSA to a limited range of state and local institutions held to be enmeshed in interstate commerce (*Maryland* v. *Wirtz* 1968). In an unexpected decision eight years later, however, the Court struck down the application of the FLSA to state and local governments as a violation of the Tenth Amendment's protection of traditional state governmental functions and sovereignty (*National League of Cities* v. *Usery* 1976). A government that cannot determine the wages of its own employees cannot be said to be sovereign.

Nine years later, the Court reversed course again by overturning *National League of Cities in Garcia* v. *San Antonio Metropolitan Transit Authority* (1985). The principal doctrinal argument was that the Court is obligated to protect individual rights, including the employment rights of state and local government employees, but not states' rights under the Tenth Amendment. Although the states obtained some congressional relief, though not exemption, from Garcia, the "political safeguards" of state powers in the federal system that had long protected state sovereignty from the FLSA had clearly deteriorated by the 1970s, such that the Court's National League of Cities ruling was widely viewed as an anomaly that proved, indeed, to be short-lived (Kincaid 1993a). It was not happenstance, therefore, that seven of the twelve UMRA-eligible mandates identified by the Congressional Budget Office in 1996 and early 1997 concerned wage impacts on state and local government employees.

Still another obstacle to devolution is the set of fears often expressed about the possible consequences of devolution, especially destructive interstate competition, limited state capacities to assume responsibility for devolved functions, accountability for policy and expenditure outcomes of devolved programs, and greater disparities of service provision and quality among jurisdictions.

The Question of Interstate Competition

Devolution talk has already generated doomsday fears of destructive interstate competition (for example, Donahue 1997). Such fears are exaggerated, for several reasons.

For one, little "devolution" has occurred thus far, and what devolution can be said to have occurred is too new to permit proper assessment; hence, doomsday predictions are premature. It is difficult to predict what, if any, interjurisdictional competition might be sparked by devolution and whether such competition would be constructive or destructive in different functional areas and under different degrees of devolution. It is also difficult to predict outcomes, because devolution would not entail a return to pre-federalized circumstances. States and localities are quite different polities and communities today than they were in the 1930s and even the 1960s. So is the federal government, and it is difficult to argue today that the federal government is necessarily the superior repository of policy wisdom and political virtue. Furthermore, with modern communications and the existence of numerous public and private institutions dedicated to "watchdog" tasks and to diffusing policy ideas, any interstate competition stimulated by devolution has a greater chance of yielding positive outcomes—such as experimentation in state "laboratories of democracy," diffusion of innovations, and efficiency enhancement—than at any time in our federal history.

Second, even "welfare reform," the most oft-cited example of "devolution," provides no conclusive evidence, despite much research, that the states have been, are currently, or will become engaged in a race to the bottom over welfare benefits (see, for example, Gresenz 1997; Schram, Nitz, and Krueger 1998). Thus far, reports Donna E. Shalala, Secretary of the U.S. Department of Health and Human Services, "There has been no race to the bottom in state welfare spending" (quoted in Vobejda 1998). Too many other factors influence state welfare decision-making, and the relative positions of most high-benefit and most low-benefit states have not changed over the years, even though the real-dollar value of AFDC has declined in all states. The prospects for such competition are also constrained, first, by the authority of high-benefit states to give migrants during their first year in-state the lower benefits they received in their previous state of residence, and second, by the five-year limit on TANF benefits, although because states can lower this limit, there may be some competitive pressure to do so. Furthermore, Social Security for senior citizens, Medicare, Medicaid (for the most part), and a range of other welfare-type programs were not included in the "welfare reform" measures. The lion's share of redistributive spending still lies with the federal government, thus alleviating disparities that might otherwise stem from interstate competition. It is possible that some states might emphasize dead-end jobs so as not to attract out-of-state TANF recipients seeking better employment, but such a strategy would be counterproductive to a state's self-interest. If TANF beneficiaries migrate to states offering better employment opportunities, such migration would be positive.

Similarly, no systematic evidence has been seen of a race to the bottom in environmental standards (Revesz 1997), although certain Rustbelt states appear to skimp on environmental protection standards that increase industrial production costs. A race to the bottom in environmental protection is also unlikely even with further devolution, because environmental interest groups have clout in most states and because environmental protection is increasingly an economic asset for many states. More generally, the shift toward a service economy places a greater value on quality-of-life assets, such as environmental protection, thus dampening competitive pressures that might otherwise push standards downward and fueling competitive pressures that might push standards upward. Consequently, devolution in the context of a service economy rather than an urban-industrial economy is less likely to trigger environmentally destructive interstate competition.

Third, devolution policies can be designed to minimize destructive interstate competition, to the extent it might occur, as reflected in some of TANF's provisions. Mandates, conditions of aid, performance standards, schedules of fines for falling short of performance standards or for creating negative externalities, and other mechanisms could be fashioned for this purpose.

Fourth, zero-sum competition for business facilities through state and local subsidies, tax abatements, and so on is not likely to be accelerated much, if at all, even with substantial devolution. This form of competition is already common and is being driven more by concerns about international economic competition and by state needs to generate more revenue through economic development so as to limit or avoid tax increases.

Fifth, fears of such zero-sum competition usually overlook the negative consequences that could emerge from suppression of such competition, particularly by the federal government. States would find new ways to compete and, under conditions of substantial devolution, such competition could take place primarily in fields of devolved domestic responsibility, such as welfare. If states cannot compete for business through subsidies (however wasteful or ill-advised such subsidies), they may feel compelled to compete through general tax and expenditure reductions and through reductions aimed at unpopular programs and vulnerable populations. Suppression of such competition would also increase state and local pressure on the federal government to redistribute resources to meet the various competitive needs and interests of the states. The unmediated competition of the interstate marketplace would be replaced by mediated competition within the Congress and executive agencies. The proposition that tax resources can be allocated more efficiently through political competition among the states within the Congress and the federal executive branch rather than through fiscal competition within the interstate marketplace is not credible (Kenyon and Kincaid 1991).

Sixth, given the huge number and range of federal mandates, conditions of aid, preemptions, individual rights protections, court orders, and the like, state and local governments have less room within which to compete and fewer tools with which to compete against each other. Economic deregulation coupled with federal preemptions of state-local regulatory authority is rapidly depriving states of viable tools for regulatory competition. As such, regulatory competition might become more localized because citizens are likely to cling tightly to local regulatory powers, such as zoning, that protect property values and lifestyle choices. Thus, even with further devolution of functional responsibilities, massive federal constraints on interstate competition will continue.

Seventh, devolution could also stimulate some healthy intergovernmental competition between the states and the federal government, thus possibly enriching policymaking with the best ideas of two worlds.

The Question of State Capability

The question of state capability can be addressed both empirically and normatively. One can determine empirically the fiscal and administrative capacities of states to assume responsibilities for devolved functions under maintenance-of-effort assumptions. But the short answer to the question will be: Some states can and some cannot, and some will do a better job than others. Substantial devolution may result in greater diversity and heterogeneity across the states.

The normative question of state capability is whether states should be held to maintenance-of-effort requirements and other federal rules governing policy objectives. True devolution in a federal democracy would leave such decisions to the citizens of each state. Whether a state has the capability to assume responsibility for any devolved function, therefore, depends substantially on whether the state's citizens wish to give their state that capability. Here, the normative question intersects with the empirical question, and causes concern among opponents or skeptics of devolution.

The public's general disaffection from government is being vented within states and localities, which are more accessible to direct citizen activism. Much of this activism might be said to reflect the revenge of the "silent majority"—the public voice that President Nixon sought to activate against what he regarded as a strident liberal minority. The silent majority struck with force in 1978 through voter approval of Proposition 13 in California, which set off a wave of citizen efforts to restrain state taxes and expenditures nationwide. Tax and expenditure limits have found their way into more and more state constitutions along with other restraints on state and local governments, including widespread public support for term limits. These limits do not necessarily mean that citizens would be unwilling to allow their states to assume responsibilities for devolved functions, but the limits will constrain state capacities to do so if they prove workable.

Another significant feature of the revenge of the silent majority is its almost single-minded focus on majoritarian rights—sometimes, though not always, at the expense of minority rights. Tax and expenditure limits reflect efforts to protect taxpaying majorities against "big government." The victims' rights movement was one of the first non-fiscal reflections of the desire of the silent majority to protect its rights in the face of then-increasing rights protections for criminals. State and federal Megan's Laws are the latest manifestation of this desire to protect the majoritarian community against what it regards as previously overprotected predators. Similarly, growing opposition to affirmative action, to equal protection for non-heterosexuals, and the like are efforts to protect majority rights. This revenge of the silent majority does not have much of a civic dimension. Instead, the attitude seems to be: What's in it for me?

The silent majority is likely to be receptive to devolution because it would shift powers and functions from a largely out-of-reach government to more within-reach governments where devolved powers and functions could be constrained by majoritarian rule and directed more toward the interests of the majorities within states and localities. In this respect, devolution could "empower" citizens and enhance majoritarian democracy federally rather than monolithically. Whether such an outcome would be positive or negative depends on one's point of view.

Being largely ignored in the devolution debate is what one scholar has called the challenge "to find ways of restoring the sense of accountability and belonging offered by smaller, more human-scale institutions, institutions that can serve as schools of citizenship while retaining the benefits of national government. This is precisely the promise of federalism" (McClay 1996, p. 24).

Of course, more technical questions of state capability arise as well. Devolution will require, for example, continued intergovernmental cooperation, especially as details of separating and sharing responsibilities within specific programs, such as TANF, are worked out under statutory rules. Significant federal regulations are likely to accompany most devolutions, and the states are likely to remain vulnerable to new policies and rules enacted by the Congress or promulgated by federal agencies with little or no advance warning. States, therefore, will need to maintain an anticipatory and defensive stance. State legislatures will also face control and oversight issues, such as assignments of devolution implementation issues to appropriate legislative committees and, more important, decisions about how much authority to embed in state law and how much authority to delegate to the executive branch to implement and alter programs flexibly, pursuant to federal law (Olson 1996). State legislators are especially concerned that the Congress will bypass the state legislatures and state constitutions by devolving control over spending and programmatic implementation to governors. As noted earlier, state legislators succeeded in convincing the Congress to include the Brown Amendment in the 1996 "welfare-reform" law (Section 901), which requires that new block grant funds be appropriated by the state legislature, but it is by no means certain that the Brown Amendment will become a basic principle of devolution.

The logic and fiscal imperatives of devolution, coupled with deregulation and privatization, will require states to work more closely with local governments, nonprofit institutions, civic organizations, businesses, and other states as well (Feustel 1997). Devolution may also have side effects on state and local governments, such as increased lobbying in state capitols, county courthouses, and city halls, as these governments assume more policy and fiscal responsibility for public functions. This could, in turn, increase voter pressure for lobbying and campaign-finance reform as well as stricter ethics laws (Feustel 1997, p. 25).

Conclusion

To date, there is no evidence of wholesale devolution, although there is a discernible and, until recently, unanticipated nudging toward restoring some state powers and rebalancing federal-state relations in the federal system. It is difficult to predict the outcome if this nudge should become a surge, because such rebalancing will occur within historical circumstances quite different from those that prevailed at the outset of the federal government's twentieth-century power expansion. There is no a priori reason, therefore, to expect that substantial devolution, should it ever occur, would be more malignant than benign.

References

Baker, Earl M., ed. 1975. "The Suburban Reshaping of American Politics." *Publius: The Journal of Federalism,* vol. 5 (Winter), entire issue.

Baldersheim, Harold and Peter Slava. 1993. "Reforming Local Government Policymaking and Management through Organizational Learning and Experimentation: The Case of Norway." *Policy Studies Journal,* vol. 21, no. 1, pp. 104–114.

Bernier, Lynne Louise. 1992. "Socialist Intergovernmental Policy During the Mitterand Era." *Publius: The Journal of Federalism,* vol. 22 (Fall), pp. 47–66.

Buchanan, James, M. 1995. "Federalism as an Ideal Political Order and an Objective for Constitutional Reform." *Publius: The Journal of Federalism,* vol. 25, no. 2 (Spring), pp. 19–27.

City of Boerne v. *Flores,* 117 S.Ct. 2157 (1997).

Coleman, William G. and Delphis C. Goldberg. 1990. "The Eisenhower Years and the Creation of ACIR." *Intergovernmental Perspective,* vol. 16, no. 3 (Summer), pp. 19–23.

Coleman v. *Thompson,* 111 S. Ct. 2546 (1991).

Conlan, Timothy. 1988. *New Federalism: Intergovernmental Reform from Nixon to Reagan.* Washington, DC: The Brookings Institution.

Democratic Leadership Council. 1997. "DLC and the States." *State Focus: Supplement to The New Democrat,* vol. 9 (July/August).

Donahue, John D. 1997. *Disunited States.* New York: Basic Books.

Elazar, Daniel J. 1995. "From Statism to Federalism: A Paradigm Shift." *Publius: The Journal of Federalism,* vol. 25, no. 2 (Spring), pp. 5–18.

Feustel, Bruce. 1997. "What Do We Do Now? Devolution and the Legislative Institution." *State Legislatures,* vol. 23, no. 6 (June), pp. 22–25.

Fuentes, Carlos. 1990. "Federalism Is the Great Healer." *Los Angeles Times,* December 16, p. M1.

Garcia v. *San Antonio Metropolitan Transit Authority,* 469 U.S. 528 (1985).

Gingrich, Newt. 1995. *To Renew America.* New York: HarperCollins.

Gresenz, Charles R. 1997. *An Empirical Investigation of the Role of AFDC Benefits in Location Choice.* Santa Monica, CA: The RAND Corporation.

Kaiser/Harvard Program on the Public and Health/Social Policy. 1995. *Survey on Welfare Reform: Basic Values and Beliefs; Support for Policy Approaches; Knowledge About Key Programs.* The Henry J. Kaiser Family Foundation (January), Table 25.

Kenyon, Daphne A. and John Kincaid, eds. 1991. *Competition among States and Local Governments: Efficiency and Equity in American Federalism.* Washington, DC: The Urban Institute Press.

Kincaid, John. 1993a. "Constitutional Federalism: Labor's Role in Displacing Places to Benefit Persons." *PS: Political Science & Politics,* vol. 26 (June), pp. 172–177.

———. 1993b. "From Cooperation to Coercion in American Federalism: Housing, Fragmentation, and Preemption, 1780–1992." *Journal of Law and Politics,* vol. 9 (Winter), pp. 333–433.

———. 1995. "Values and Value Tradeoffs in Federalism." *Publius: The Journal of Federalism,* vol. 26, no. 2 (Spring), pp. 29–44.

———. 1996. "Intergovernmental Costs and Coordination in U.S. Environmental Protection." In Kenneth M. Holland, F. L. Morton, and Brian Galligan, eds., *Federalism and the Environment: Environmental Policymaking in Australia, Canada, and the United States,* pp. 70–101. Westport, CT: Greenwood Press.

Maryland v. *Wirtz,* 392 U.S. 183 (1968).

Mason, Alpheus T. 1952. "American Individualism: Fact and Fiction." *The American Political Science Review,* vol. XLVI, no. 1 (March), pp. 1–18.

McClay, Wilfred M. 1996. "The Soul of Man Under Federalism." *First Things,* no. 64 (June/July), pp. 21–26.

Nathan, Richard P. 1996. "The Devolution Revolution: An Overview." *Rockefeller Institute Bulletin 1996,* pp. 5–13. Albany, NY: Nelson A. Rockefeller Institute of Government, State University of New York.

National Governors' Association. 1996. "States Feel Relief from Unfunded Mandates." *Governors' Bulletin,* vol. 30, June 17, pp. 1–2.

National League of Cities v. *Usery,* 426 U.S. 833 (1976).

Olson, Gary. 1996. "Federal Focus: Devolution—Ready or Not, Here It Comes." *The Fiscal Letter,* vol. 19 (Spring), pp. 5–6.

Peterson, Paul E. 1995. *The Price of Federalism.* Washington, DC: The Brookings Institution.

Posner, Paul L. and Margaret T. Wrightson. 1996. "Block Grants: A Perennial, But Unstable, Tool of Government." *Publius: The Journal of Federalism,* vol. 26, no. 3 (Summer), pp. 87–108.

Reeves, Mavis Mann. 1990. "The States as Polities: Reformed, Reinvigorated, Resourceful." *Annals of the American Academy of Political and Social Science,* vol. 509 (May), pp. 83–93.

Revesz, Richard L. 1997. "Federalism and Environmental Regulation: A Normative Critique." In John Ferejohn and Barry R. Weingast, eds., *The New Federalism: Can the States Be Trusted*? pp. 97–127. Stanford, CA: Hoover Institution Press.

Reynolds v. *Sims,* 377 U.S. 533 (1964).

Rivlin, Alice. 1992. *Reviving the American Dream: The Economy, the States, and the Federal Government.* Washington, DC: The Brookings Institution.

Schram, Sanford, Lawrence Nitze, and Gary Krueger. 1998. "Without Cause or Effect: Reconsidering Welfare Migration as a Policy Problem." *American Journal of Political Science,* vol. 42, no. 1 (January), pp. 210–229.

Shenk, Joshua Wolf. 1997. "Washington's Counter-Devolutionaries." *U.S. News & World Report,* vol. 123, no. 20 (November 24), p. 34.

South Dakota v. *Dole,* 483 U.S. 203 (1987).

United States v. *Darby,* 312 U.S. 100 (1941).

U.S. Advisory Commission on Intergovernmental Relations. 1985. *The Question of State Government Capability.* Washington, DC: ACIR.

———. 1992. *Federal Statutory Preemption of State and Local Authority: History, Inventory, and Issues.* Washington, DC: ACIR.

Vobejda, Barbara. 1998. "Fewer Welfare Recipients, More Spending on Them." *Washington Post National Weekly Edition,* February 16, p. 35.

Weaver, R. Kent. 1996. "Deficits and Devolution in the 104th Congress." *Publius: The Journal of Federalism,* vol. 26, no. 3 (Summer), pp. 45–85.

Weiler, Conrad. 1994. "Foreign-Trade Agreements: A New Federal Partner?" *Publius: The Journal of Federalism,* vol. 24, no. 3 (Summer), pp. 113–133.

Wesberry v. *Sanders,* 376 U.S. 1 (1964).

Wunsch, James S. and Dele Olowu, eds. 1995. *The Failure of the Centralized State: Institutions and Self-Governance in Africa.* San Francisco, CA: ICS Press.

CASE STUDY 3

Introduction

In the preceding essay, Professor Kincaid describes many of the forces working for and against the devolution of power to the states. Kincaid's essay makes it clear that despite recent talk of returning power to the states, many forces at work will make such a return difficult to achieve. Kincaid's essay was published in the late 1990s. After the terrorist attack on the World Trade Center in New York in 2001, the question as to how power should be distributed between the federal government and the states became a prominent part in discussions on how the nation should combat terrorism.

The debate over the distribution of power in regard to fighting terrorism is interesting because it pits two distinct political perspectives against each other. On the one hand, state and local governments have historically handled many of the governmental services that are needed to cope with a terrorist attack, including police, fire, and emergency health services. For many Americans, the idea of passing these responsibilities on to the national government, including the creation of a national police force, runs up against their suspicions of the federal government and the belief that such activities are best handled at the local and state level. On the other hand, the terrorist threat is national in scope and may require greater federal involvement to address the threat successfully. Thus, there is pressure from some political leaders, and even from private citizens, for a more national response.

In the following essay, Paul Posner provides an overview of the issues surrounding how power should be distributed in fighting terrorism. Posner does not use the term *devolution* in the essay, but at the beginning of the essay he lays out the case for a strong state and local role, including the lack of resources, expertise, and political legitimacy for the fight to be handled solely from Washington. Posner makes the important point that state and local governments have the capacity today to handle most of the traditional functions associated with disasters. But he then explains why the problems in fighting terrorism are likely to encourage greater centralization of power at the federal level.

While Kincaid talks in general terms about the reasons why power is being centralized at the federal level, Posner's essay provides a case study of why centralization is likely to occur in one particular policy area, the fight against terrorism. Posner's explanation for why this centralization is likely is different from those laid out in Kincaid's essay. Whereas Kincaid focuses considerable attention on the political factors that encourage centralization, such as the benefits that it can provide for members of Congress and their constituents, Posner offers a more practical reason: the nation's need for safety. Posner's work is also valuable because it doesn't look at the question as to how power should be distributed from an ideological perspective, as many commentators do, but from an analytical one. In so doing, he encourages readers to think rationally about what services we expect government to provide and which level of government is best able to provide those services.

Questions to Consider

A national expert on federalism, Posner is the Managing Director for Federal Budget Issues for the U.S. General Accounting Office. The essay is from a talk Posner gave at the Rockefeller Institute of Government in Albany, New York. As you read his work, these are some questions to consider:

- What are some of the reasons for why state and local governments need to be involved in homeland security efforts? Why is there a need for the federal government's involvement as well?
- What does Posner mean that how the problem is framed determines the process we use to address it? What are the two ways of framing the problem associated

with homeland security? How important a role does Posner say state and local governments need to play, given the framing of the issue in the strategic plan for homeland security? What does the plan say that supports Posner's argument?
- What model of federalism does Posner think will emerge to address homeland security? Why does he think this? How is Posner's argument similar to and different from the argument presented in Kincaid's reading?
- How do you think power should be distributed in addressing homeland security? What role should state and local governments play? What role should the federal government play? What is your rationale for this distribution of power?
- How well are your city, county, and state prepared for terrorist attacks? How can you find out whether they are?

The Role of "Home" in Homeland Security

Paul Posner

While the response to 9/11 was clearly heroic—firefighters deserve their share of fame and of commendation—the real test is not how we do in crises, but how we institutionalize preparedness to prevent or better prepare for the next event. . . .

. . . This is a national, not a federal challenge. The problem spills over the boundaries of a single agency, even the new DHS at the federal level, and spills over the boundaries of states, local governments, and the private sector as well.

This is . . . not an unfamiliar problem. As with most domestic problems the federal government has taken on in the past sixty years, the national government simply does not have the resources, the legal authority, the expertise, or the political legitimacy to deal with these problems from Washington alone. We don't have control over the drivers licensing authority in this country and yet that's a critical function for controlling access to facilities, information, and other kinds of potentially vulnerable targets. We don't own the physical infrastructure at the federal level by and large. Rather, the infrastructure is owned by local government, state governments, and the private sector. The federal government does not commandeer 650,000 policemen like local governments do. We have an FBI of about 20–30,000. We are critically dependent on, as we are in welfare, health care, and education, among many other areas, third parties to help implement and finance federal initiatives. This doesn't necessarily mean devolution to third parties. This doesn't necessarily mean that the state and local governments are in control as we've found in so many other areas. In fact, the federal involvement engagement of third parties often presages a centralization of services and goal-setting in the system.

So, in some sense, homeland security is more of the same. It epitomizes what we've done in some ways with the rest of domestic government. The difference is that third-party governance and interdependent public management and public administration are sweeping over areas that were heretofore largely separate. National defense was largely the province of the central government. Firefighting was largely the province of local governments. There are very few local functions anymore that have been left untouched by the centralization and nationalization of policy in the past sixty years. Firefighting was one of them, arguably. Now that's been changing in recent years anyway, thanks to

Paul Posner, "Speaker's Remarks," from *The Role of "Home" in Homeland Security: The Federalism Challenge* (Albany, N.Y.: The Rockefeller Institute of Government, 2003), pp. 16–30. Reprinted with permission from the Nelson A. Rockefeller Institute of Government, 411 State Street, Albany, N.Y. 12203.

the firefighters themselves who have lobbied successfully for federal aid. So, in some ways the homeland security crisis has prompted the sweeping tide of intergovernmentalization to wash over one of the last bastions of dual federalism.

At the state and local level, this challenge comes against a backdrop of what they typically do. Traditionally for most typical disasters and problems, state and local governments could contain most of the preparedness and response responsibility. And when they couldn't, they called in the feds for disaster relief. Weapons of mass destruction in particular are very different. They create a mismatch between the scope of the problem and the capacity of individual jurisdictions to deal with it because the size, the scale, and the complexity requires at least a regional sub-state capacity as well as other partnerships with the federal agencies and others. The capabilities are spread. Coordination is critical. . . .

For example in public health, let's examine what a local government faces to prepare for bioterrorism. It has to improve the capacity of its local health departments, the human capital that has been woefully neglected in recent years reportedly. It has to update its technology so that it at least can communicate problems to the CDC in Atlanta over the Internet. It has to achieve agreements with hospitals to develop surge capacity and support from doctors and other medical personnel. It has to develop laboratory infrastructure to at least know where the labs are and reach some kind of agreements on how to process samples of suspicious materials. And most importantly, what we're finding increasingly in the local health departments, it has to develop surveillance systems to produce real-time data on day-to-day incidences, to help get early warning of suspicious health trends and incidents to facilitate an expeditious response to health problems where time is such a critical variable influencing potential health outcomes for those exposed.

Baltimore is one of the pioneers. They can show daily the numbers of admittances to emergency rooms, the veterinarians' reports, daily school absences. They are trying to get pharmacies to report daily on medications prescribed. The point is they can monitor these things and look for variations and look for puzzles and, fortunately, they haven't found any. That's the kind of surveillance system that is under development in some communities and illustrates the political challenges in gaining the cooperation of numerous independent actors at the local level.

Framing the Problem

The way the problem is framed determines the framework and the modality or the process that we use to address it. For example, if we define the homeland security problem as a response problem, as a first responder's problem, then the model will have a local orientation. City managers have told me that when you're dealing with the response to an incident, the most effective thing for the effective management of response is for the federal government to stay out of our way. These managers feel they know their communities best. As one said, "Give us money but let us control the action."

As long as we frame homeland security as a response challenge, then the issue for federal policymakers is how can we get the money and information down to the local level as fast as possible?

However, other phases of homeland security suggest a more national and centralized model. For example, if the challenge is how do we interdict terrorists before they get started, how do we protect and mitigate the damage, how do we change standards for infrastructure and things like that, then that suggests a more national centralized model. Again to quote a city manager of a major Western city "what we actually need is federal leadership and standards in preparedness and mitigation because we don't have the incentives to address those problems nor the expertise."

What this official and other people closer to the frontlines are calling for is more centralization of information for use by local responders, the development of authoritative national standards and guidance which provides local official[s] with some protection internally in answering the sensitive question—how much preparedness is enough? This local call for federal guidance and leadership is not at all atypical. Studies of other federal mandates have also chronicled how local or state officials find federal mandates and standards useful in gaining support from recalcitrant legislators and interest groups.[1]

The Six Mission Areas of Homeland Security

The 2002 strategic plan for homeland security issued by the administration illustrates the point that the intergovernmental partnership necessarily extends well beyond the response phase. In fact, state and local governments are critical players in each of the six major mission areas defined by this plan. The mission areas are:

1. Intelligence and warning, obtaining early notice and advance intelligence of the threats that we have. Clearly, part of that is getting information from state and local governments about threats to their community and advising state and local governments of these threats so they can take real-time action.
2. Border and transportation security, protecting the nation's borders, whether it be airport security, train stations, other forms of transportation like mass transit, and the like. State and local governments have a role to play and obviously are doing this.
3. Domestic counterterrorism was a third important area, to generate intelligence information which states and local governments can often provide and use to help interdict threats and gain advance warning.
4. Protecting critical infrastructure. Again, as I said earlier, state and local governments own the infrastructure and their investment and involvement is critical to national efforts to protect these assets against terrorist attacks. In the post 9/11 era, infrastructure has shifted in public debates from an asset needed to promote community economic development to become "critical national infrastructure"—so a bridge is no longer a way to get to the store; it's a critical national infrastructure. This language, in effect, reflects and perpetuates a nationalization in the debate about how infrastructure is to be financed and managed.
5. Defense against catastrophic threats and bioterrorism. We already went over how important local health departments are.
6. Emergency preparedness and response.

Again, the important thing is, as the Office of Homeland Security laid out, five of the six areas really are pre-disaster, pre-response and with each of those state and local governments are critical.

The Risks and Rewards of Intergovernmental Partnerships

For each of these areas, partnership confers both rewards and risks. From the federal standpoint, engaging state and local governments in all phases of preparedness opens access to the legal, personnel, technical, and political resources of state and local governments. The federal government also gains the opportunity to eliminate gaps in coverage among state and local communities that could be exploited by intelligent terrorists who look to exploit weak spots.

State and local governments get federal money, information, and standards. Very often, standards are called for by those very governments to help better promote a national response and indemnify them from opposition and debate. But there are risks to these partnerships for both sides as well.

From the federal standpoint we face the potential diversion and substitution of effort and resources. For instance, some state and local governments have refused to participate in the Justice Department's initiative to interview immigrants of Arab or Muslim descent. Many local governments have not reportedly observed orange alerts, at least not in a uniform way. We know in the past that when we give large amounts of money for functions that parallel what local governments are doing anyway, there is a great vulnerability for fiscal substitution. In other words, the federal funds do not promote increased activity for the program area; rather it permits state or local governments to free up their money for tax cuts or spending increases in other areas. If we want to provide unrestricted aid for local governments to use as they wish, it is far more efficiently and honestly provided through revenue-sharing than through the back door displacement of federal programmatic dollars. There is also tremendous pressure . . . to spread the money around, not to target it on the places that need it the most or where the vulnerability is greatest.

Another risk from the federal perspective involves the sharing of information, which again is vital because the state and local governments are a partner in law enforcement. On the other hand, federal officials feel there are risks in disclosing too much information.

From the state and local standpoint, the risks are there as well. For instance, federal funds and initiatives are often accompanied by unfunded mandates. Even if states want certain mandates, they don't want to pay for them. While they may want a minimum standard for such areas as training or equipment, they often get highly specific and intrusive regulations that constrain flexibility and limit their ability to tailor initiatives to address unique state or local needs.

I think the greatest risk of this new intergovernmentalization is the area of public accountability. With every area, one of the greatest risks from a partnership is the obfuscation of responsibility, for who is to blame, who is to take credit. For example, when that shooter killed the ticket agent at the counter at the Los Angeles airport on July 4, 2002, considerable confusion arose over who was responsible for preventing this incident. The Transportation Security Administration (TSA) indicated that they were not responsible for this area, only the areas where passengers are screened. Debate ensued over who else might be held responsible, ranging from the airport authority, to the airline itself, to the FAA, to the FBI. The presence of high stakes and multiple actors sharing responsibility lends itself to finger-pointing and blame shifting when problems occur.

It's difficult to tell who is accountable in complex systems where authority is so divided and fragmented. For example, let's look at food safety; there's a whole food safety network. If there's a contamination, where did it start? There are very different responsibilities at different levels of the food chain from a farm to the processor to the retail food establishment to the restaurant. All of those have different regulatory regimes and different responsibilities. We have not figured out a road map to know who is to blame.

Federalism Responses to 9/11

The question that I want to focus on for the remainder of my discussion is what kind of partnership is emerging and clearly there is an *ad hoc* adjustment of roles and responsibilities since 9/11. We are seeing different models start to take shape and compete with one another for what this federal role might look like.

- ***Model 1: Cooperative Federalism***—The first model is what many have called "cooperative federalism," the traditional model where the federal government gives aid to the states, where states and local governments are viewed as partners. Each partner in this relationship has leverage, has some kind of bargaining position vis á vis the others. Local governments can walk away from the grants; the federal government can impose standards. There's a tension between those two that often gets negotiated out.

  Right now quite a bit of tension exists over the existing grants. The president promised and proposed a consolidated first-responder grant that never came about. The Congress appropriated money in this past January, to provide first-responder funding through the existing grant channels. There was no new block grant or consolidated grant created. Rather additional funds were allocated to existing grants from the Justice Department, from FEMA, from HHS for different pieces. Two of those major programs are now consolidated into different directorates in the Homeland Security Department; the Justice grant for preparedness is in one directorate; the FEMA grant is in another. So the grant fragmentation problem has not been solved by the consolidation of the Department of Homeland Security; it's been teed up but it hasn't been solved.

  As we go forward and think about designing a grant to promote this kind of cooperative partnership, let's talk about some of the dilemmas that we face—they are traditional dilemmas in federal grant design. One is targeting. How do you concentrate funds in the places with the highest net risks? A proclivity to spread money around, unfortunately, will provide less additional net protection with a lot of additional local burden.

  A second dilemma involves preventing fiscal substitution. That's a fundamentally vexing area. On the one hand it seems like a no-brainer to say you should require local fire departments and police, whoever gets these grants, to maintain the effort they were making before and use the federal money on top of that. That's pretty straightforward except for one thing. We've seen since 9/11 that many local jurisdictions have taken it onto themselves, taken the initiative, to increase funding and effort dramatically. Do we penalize them by preventing them from getting some fiscal relief for the effort and the initiative they've already taken and thereby give an advantage to the governments that have laid back and avoided taking the initiative? That's a classic grant design problem we're going to face.

A third challenge is sustainability. Local governments think of sustainability as keeping the federal spigot turned permanently to "on." They argue that the urgent will trample the important without federal aid. Well, I'll put my black federal hat on here for a second and say that I think there's an expectation that sustainability responsibility would at least be shared because local governments get internal benefits from these grants just as much as the nation gets protection. One model that might be considered here is the seed money concept where federal money would be available for, say, a four or five year period to change preferences at the local level, possibly with the expectation that they take more of the burden at the end of this period. In fact, the literature on intergovernmental management suggests that federal money succeeds in institutionalizing a commitment to aided goals and purposes over time within states and communities, as professional administrators and clients of these programs take root and gain influence within local political circles.[2]

A fourth challenge involves the issue of accountability. Block grants are often bandied about by those frustrated with federal categorical restrictions and mandates. Yet I think it's probably unlikely that we're going to have a pure block grant in the homeland security area where state or local governments gain the discretion to use federal funds for state or local priorities. We have too many national concerns and criteria and goals for a traditional devolution of responsibility here. I think we probably would get a consolidated grant but a "consolidated categorical," if you will. And one only needs to look again at that Office of Homeland Security's strategic plan to see that the White House itself is calling for national training standards, national interoperability standards, nationally required standards for exercises and regional mutual aid, as a condition of aid. That is not a block grant, in most people's view.

One of the models I find most promising is what EPA piloted several years ago, a so-called performance partnership, where funding streams are consolidated. Under this model, states and local governments have discretion but are held accountable for discrete national or negotiated measures and standards.

The final bulwark of cooperative federalism is what I call "networks." They are the backbone of cooperative federalism. They've been called the "picket fence" by many. Experts talking to experts across levels of government grease the wheel of cooperation. Peterson's model of mature federalism suggests that special education and other programs matured when those networks blossomed and became more professionalized.[3] However, those networks have often not yet been well developed in homeland security. The bonds of trust and familiarity have not been established between the FBI and the local governments, between the northern command of the Defense Department and the states. There is still great reluctance and a distrust even to share information across boundaries. This is true among professionals within local communities as well. Fire and public health professionals, for example, are just getting acquainted as they both realize that they share a responsibility for protection against weapons of mass destruction. We might see some shifts over time as professionals learn to work together and develop routines and norms guiding cooperative behaviors, but this will take time in this area.

- ***Model 2: Coercive Federalism***—The other model that, as a student of federalism, I find less preferable but I think is more inevitable, is the coercive federalism model. Over the past thirty years, this model has become more prominent with the evolution of mandates and preemptions at the federal level. In this area at this time, mandates and preemptions are definitely part of the debate and in fact have already happened. Already federal agencies are talking about preempting what used to be local responsibilities for port security, or encouraging national goals for driver's license standards.

Mandates in areas such as communications, equipment, infrastructure, etc., are seemingly a foregone conclusion. A federal mandate for local drinking water systems to develop vulnerability assessments and action plans has already been enacted, albeit with some federal dollars. Mass transit may very well be next, as national officials consider proposals to require local systems to monitor threats as a condition for receiving federal transit funds. Other key areas of infrastructure will feel the heat of the federal mandates.

- ***Model 3: Partial Preemption***—The other tool of coercive federalism that we've seen recently used is partial preemption where the federal government engages state and local regulatory agencies to serve national protection goals. Frank Thompson has written about this. With this model, state or local enforcement or regulatory resources are marshaled to serve national goals. The INS, for instance, has entered into partnerships with certain local police departments to use their contacts and personnel to track down foreign residents overstaying their visas. The Coast Guard has assumed responsibility for policing ports in 55 major areas, with local police and other authorities working under their leadership. The TSA in a sense has conscripted local police to patrol airports more regularly, often providing federal funds to defray at least some of the overtime costs. Active consideration is being given to imposing national standards for the states' issuance of driver licenses—the *de facto* national ID card.

Which Model Will Homeland Security Use?

I wish the cooperative model would be the prevailing model, but I fear that in homeland security the particular nature of these issues will prompt more reliance on the coercive. And why is that? Well, the cooperative federalism model is appropriate and has the greatest advantage to promoting diversity and experimentation. This works when stakes are lower, when there's limited national consensus and limited knowledge of how to accomplish the goal. We have laboratories of democracy that help us along. For homeland security, we may have limited knowledge but we have high stakes. We also have a much greater consciousness of the interdependence, of the weak link destroying the rest of the chain, whether it's driver licenses or port security—local failure has national consequences.

I'm taken with the model in this wonderful volume that Frank Thompson helped edit for the *Public Administration Review.* George Frederickson and Todd Lapore talked about two types of organizations. They talked about an error-tolerant organization and a high-reliability organization. The error-tolerant organization has a much greater premium on diversity and consensus. With the high-reliability organization (the nuclear power plant, for example) the presumption is to err on the side of safety. The high-reliability organizations could be transported to the idea of intergovernmental networks. The high-reliability network is the kind of network that will be guided by strong standards and low-risk tolerance—this is the reason why we departed from our historical reliance on contractors to screen airline passengers and instead converted to the most significant single increase in civilian federal employment in recent history with the creation of the TSA.

I think this kind of transition is going to take root in intergovernmental management as well, albeit in different forms. For instance, for natural disaster planning and preparedness, FEMA funded states using the error tolerance model. Since most disasters had largely state or regional consequences, FEMA provided discretion and flexibility to states to manage and allocate funds. The accountability for these grants was largely process-oriented. FEMA provided advisory criteria for states to use to evaluate themselves. This model of accountability will not be sufficient for homeland security preparedness grants, and we will see the emergence of more insistent national standards and reviews of state performance.

The Emergence of Protective Federalism

Ultimately, anxious political leaders and restive publics will determine how our federal system responds. The stakes are high, mass publics are engaged and watchful, and responsibility is difficult to assign. The concluding thought is that state and local and federal political leaders are going to grasp for "protective federalism." What are they trying to protect against at the state and local level? They're trying to protect against threats, low-probability threats with high consequences. They're also trying to protect against other governments that might undermine their best efforts, other local governments who might undermine public health protection (for example, other state governments who might be the weakest link in the chain). And they need to protect themselves against the voters and political opponents who can be unmerciful if a crisis occurs on their watch.

The consequences of protective federalism are that state and local governments seek both funding and national standards to immunize themselves and indemnify themselves from political risk. They avoid isolation by seeking partnerships and networks, including regions. They also want to avoid unstable partners like, possibly, the federal government. They want to shift blame before the crisis occurs. "We didn't get that money you promised." And they are tempted to overachieve to immunize themselves from charges that they failed to do enough should a terrorist event occur on their watch.

I would like to think that another strategy of protective federalism is that political officials might see the value of seeking cover in performance standards and measures. That is, relying on professionals to develop an expert consensus on how much protection is sufficient, on what kinds of measures define best practice, and on what kinds of reports can best showcase for the public the level of protections that local or state governments are committed to achieving. Ideally, standards and measures and perhaps even a readiness index of sorts would be a far better way of defining accountability and preparedness than the presence or absence of a terrorist event. So, in my own optimistic view, possibly professionals can save political leaders from themselves.

Notes

1. Paul L. Posner, *The Politics of Unfunded Federal Mandates: Whither Federalism?* (Washington, D.C.: Georgetown University Press, 1998)
2. Paul Peterson, Kenneth Wong, Barry Rabe, *When Federalism Works* (Washington, D.C.: Brookings Institution, 1985).
3. Ibid.

Chapter 3 Review Questions

1. How has the distribution of power between the federal government and state governments changed over time? According to Posner, how does the nation's response to homeland security fit into this pattern?
2. What are some of the different ways through which the federal government exercises power over state and local governments? Explain what is meant by mandates, conditions of aid, and preemptions.
3. What does Kincaid say are some of the forces that have emerged in recent years that may lead to a restoration of state power? What are some of the forces that are working against restoring state power? Why does he believe that devolution is working at a turtle's pace while centralization is racing ahead?
4. What does Posner say are the three models of federalism that are competing with one another in response to homeland security? Which one does he believe will eventually prevail? Why?
5. After reading the essays by Kincaid and Posner, as well as those in the first chapter, do you think that the states can be trusted to govern responsibly and democratically? How capable is your state government in governing? Does it have the capacity to act? Does it seem to be more responsive to public concerns than the federal government? Less responsive? Give examples.

6. How do you think power should be distributed between the federal government and the states? In what policy areas do you think the federal government should play a dominant role? In what areas should the states dominate? What criteria would you use in deciding which level of government should lead?

Key Terms

devolution
dual federalism
progressive federalism
competitive federalism
cooperative federalism
picket fence federalism
Creative Federalism
coercive federalism
New Federalism
centralized federalism
pragmatic federalism
general revenue sharing
unfunded mandates
Republican Revolution
Personal Responsibility and Work Opportunity Reconciliation Act (PRWORA)
homeland security
Help America Vote Act
No Child Left Behind Act
devolution revolution
Unfunded Mandate Reform Act
New Deal
Great Society
federalism
decentralization
flattening hierarchies
individualism
funding formula
mandates
conditions of aid
preemptions
Supremacy Clause
Tenth Amendment
United States v. *Darby*
National League of Cities v. *Usery*
Garcia v. *San Antonio Metropolitan Transit Authority*
destructive interstate competition
laboratories of democracy
race to the bottom
intergovernmentalization
networks
partial preemptions
protective federalism

Suggestions for Further Reading

Conlan, Timothy. *From New Federalism to Devolution: Twenty-Five Years of Intergovernmental Reform.* Washington, D.C.: Brookings Institution, 1998. Superb historical overview of the changing character of federalism from Nixon's New Federalism through the late 1990s.

Derthick, Martha. *Keeping the Compound Republic: Essays on American Federalism.* Washington, D.C.: Brookings Institution, 2001. Collections of essays on the character of federalism in the United States and how it has changed over time.

Donahue, John D. *Disunited States.* New York: Basic Books, 1997. Critical analysis of the distribution of power between the federal and state governments. Argues that whether power should be centralized or devolved to the states depends on the policy issue.

Hanson, Russell L., ed. *Governing Partners: State-Local Relations in the United States.* Boulder, Colo.: Westview Press, 1998. Collection of essays provides a good overview on state and local government relations.

O'Hanlon, Michael E., Peter R. Orszag, Ivo H. Daalder, I. M. Destler, David L. Gunter, James M. Lindsay, Robert E. Litan, and James B. Steinberg. *Protecting the American Homeland.* 2d ed. Washington, D.C.: Brookings Institution, 2003. An early analysis of the nation's effort to fight terrorism since September 11, 2001. The book includes suggestions on how the government can improve security in the future.

O'Toole, Laurence J., Jr., ed. *American Intergovernmental Relations: Foundations, Perspectives, and Issues.* 3d ed. Washington, D.C.: CQ Press, 2000. This collection of writings provides material on a wide range of topics related to intergovernmental relations, including historical, theoretical, political, and fiscal perspectives.

Posner, Paul L. *The Politics of Unfunded Mandates: Whither Federalism?* Washington, D.C.: Georgetown University Press, 1998. Comprehensive study on the use of federal mandates on state and local governments.

Publius: The Journal of Federalism. This quarterly journal, published by the Meyner Center for the Study of State and Local Government, is devoted entirely to federalism and intergovernmental relations. The journal devotes an article each year to provide an update on the state of American federalism.

Rivlin, Alice M. *Reviving the American Dream: The Economy, the States, and the Federal Government.* Washington, D.C.: Brookings Institution, 1992. Presents a stimulating argument on why and how there should be a better "sorting out" of responsibilities between the federal and state governments.

Walker, David B. *The Rebirth of Federalism: Slouching Toward Washington.* 2d ed. Chatham, N.J.: Chatham House Publishers, 2000. This is one of the most comprehensive books on the history and character of the nation's federal system of government.

Related Web Sites

http://www.federalismproject.org/
The American Enterprise Institution for Public Policy Research has an excellent web site devoted to promoting federalism, which includes articles and links presenting different perspectives.

http://www.closeup.org/federal.htm
Provides historical background and links on federalism-related topics.

http://www.dhs.gov
Home page for the U.S. Department of Homeland Security.

4

State Constitutions: The Concept of Distinctiveness

Whether one examines the structure of state constitutions, the range of topics they address, the level of detail they encompass, the changes they have undergone, or the political perspectives underlying them, the conclusion remains the same: state constitutions are different.

G. Alan Tarr

READING 4

Introduction

What should a state constitution contain? This is a question to which most Americans do not give much thought. As voters, we are frequently asked to approve specific amendments to our state constitutions, but we rarely take a step back and give any philosophical thought about what should be included in constitutions generally. Since state constitutions provide the fundamental law for each state, however, it makes sense to give some broader consideration as to what we want them to include.

Political attitudes about what state constitutions should contain have changed over time. When the nation was founded, most state constitutions were short and limited to laying out the basic framework of government. They also included a bill or declaration of rights. The reasons for their brevity and focus on rights are understandable. With little history in writing constitutions, the first authors of state constitutions simply focused on providing for a government structure and addressing concerns that grew out of their political experiences, especially from colonial rule. As times changed, however, and the states confronted new issues and problems, the content and length of constitutions changed with them.

During the nineteenth century, state constitutions were frequently revised or expanded in response to changing political tides. The emergence of Jacksonian Democracy, for instance, spurred states to change their constitutions to expand political participation. After the Civil War, the southern states were forced to rewrite their constitutions as a precondition for reentering the union. When Reconstruction ended, the southern states rewrote their constitutions again, providing for a political and social system that discriminated against African Americans. The Progressive Movement of the early twentieth century brought another wave of change, as reformers sought ways through state constitutions to reduce the power of special interest groups.

In most of these waves of reform, reformers sought to revise or amend the constitution as a way to solve specific problems that they identified in the political system. In many cases, the pressure for change grew out of internal state politics, as different groups within the state jockeyed to advance their political position or interests. In other cases, change came in response to regional or national pressures, such as the passage of new federal laws or in reaction to changes in how the U.S. Constitution was interpreted. As changes were made, little attention was given to the general character of state constitutions themselves.

Some political leaders and legal scholars have been concerned, however, about state constitutions as legal documents. This concern was particularly important during the movement to revitalize the states that began in the 1950s (see Chapter 1). Many of the modern reformers associated with this movement wanted to rewrite state constitutions so that the constitutions would be more rationally composed and structured. The problems with state constitutions were that they were too long and detailed, they were too hard to understand, and they included provisions that were contradictory, irrelevant, or inappropriate. Certainly, the criticisms were understandable. By the mid-1960s, the average length of state constitutions was 27,000 words, which is more than three times the length of the U.S. Constitution. The most egregious example of the length and complexity of state constitutions was Georgia's constitution, which was almost 600,000 words.

Many reformers argued that state constitutions should follow the model offered by the U.S. Constitution, so that they would be limited in length and include only fundamental law. One of the most prominent advocates of this position has been the National Municipal League. The league's interest in reforming state constitutions dates back to the latter part of the Progressive Movement, when it advocated changes in state constitutions to improve the political power of cities. In 1921, the League unveiled a "Model State Constitution" to guide states in what should be included in the state constitution. The league put forward its sixth and most recent model for constitutions in 1968. At the core of the league's proposal was the suggestion that the states should draw from the "simplicity and clarity of the national prototype."[1]

The movement to revitalize the states led to important changes in state constitutions. As discussed in other chapters, these changes opened the door to stronger and more capable state governments. The movement also led to improvement in the structure of state constitutions themselves, as some states sought to reduce the length of their constitutions and remove unnecessary or inappropriate provisions. The most extensive change occurred in Georgia, where the state slashed the size of its constitution to 25,000 words in 1982.

Despite the successes in reforming constitutions over the past forty years, many legal scholars and reformers continue to criticize state constitutions because they go well beyond providing fundamental law and include minute details on how the government should be run. Many also criticize the constitutions for including provisions that are so policy-specific that they seem more appropriate as statutes than as part of a constitution.

Bringing about constitutional reform to shrink state constitutions and remove inappropriate provisions is difficult, however. It is very rare for states today to convoke a constitutional convention that could provide sweeping revisions. Without a constitutional convention, the only way to alter state constitutions is through the amendment process, which is not an assured road to success because it requires building sufficient political support to get the proposed changes on the ballot and approved by voters. Perhaps the most difficult challenge confronting reformers is that many political groups may see the minute details as being in their best interest or in the best interest of the state, whereas the effect of constitutional revision is unknown or perhaps even undesirable. Thus, instead of addressing constitutional reform, states tend to continue expanding their constitutions as they confront new political demands and pressures.

To understand the concerns of reformers as to what should be included in a constitution, one first has to understand the character of state constitutions themselves. In many ways, state constitutions mirror the U.S. Constitution in their general structure and content. Yet in other ways, they are quite different. In the reading that follows, G. Alan Tarr, the Director of the Center for State Constitutional Studies at Rutgers University at Camden, provides a concise introduction to the content of state constitutions and to why they are so different from the federal model. Professor Tarr begins by discussing the most important distinction that separates the U.S. and state constitutions, which is the role of the constitutions in shaping the power of government. Under the U.S. Constitution, the federal government can only exercise those powers that are specifically enumerated in the Constitution. State governments, on the other hand, have what Tarr refers to as *plenary* power, which means a state's authority is not limited solely to specific powers enumerated in the state's constitution. Rather, state governments have the authority to exercise power in all areas except for those in which power is granted solely to the federal government or where the states are expressly prohibited from acting under the U.S. Constitution. The only other restrictions on state government power are those placed in state constitutions. Part of the reason that state constitutions have become so long is that they include provisions that are meant to limit the broad powers of state governments. After discussing this general distinction, Tarr then describes the structure and content of state constitutions.

Questions to Consider

The reading is from the first chapter of Tarr's outstanding book *Understanding State Constitutions.* The rest of his book explores the historical development of state constitutions since the nation was founded. These are some questions to consider as you read Tarr's work:

- How are state constitutions similar to and different from the U.S. Constitution?
- What does Tarr mean when he writes that state governments possess "plenary" power, whereas the federal government does not?
- How much emphasis do state constitutions put on rights and liberties? In what ways are rights more specific and broader under state constitutions than they are under the U.S. Constitution?
- What are some of the factors that Tarr indicates have caused state constitutions to become so lengthy and detailed?

- How long and detailed is your state constitution? How closely does its structure and content parallel the description given by Tarr? Does your constitution include many provisions addressing specific policy issues? Has it been revised or amended frequently?

The Distinctiveness of State Constitutionalism

G. Alan Tarr

In 1982, five years before the nation celebrated the bicentennial of the federal Constitution, Georgia abandoned its constitution of six years duration and adopted a new constitution. The 1982 replacement, the state's tenth constitution, was over four times as long as the federal Constitution. Within a decade it had been amended more times than the federal Constitution has been in over two hundred years.[1] Georgia's experience, though extreme, is hardly unique. Whether one examines the structure of state constitutions, the range of topics they address, the level of detail they encompass, the changes they have undergone, or the political perspectives underlying them, the conclusion remains the same: state constitutions are different. These differences reveal that the United States has not just a system of dual constitutionalism but dual constitutional traditions. This chapter documents differences in constitutional design and constitutional practice that have developed at the state and national levels. Its survey of the structure and substance of state constitutions lays the groundwork for . . . assess[ing] various explanations that have been proposed to account for this state constitutional distinctiveness.

State Constitutional Design

Power and Purpose

Because it furnishes what has become the standard account of American constitutionalism, *McCulloch* v. *Maryland* provides a convenient starting point for identifying what is distinctive about state constitutionalism.[2] In upholding the congressional creation of a national bank and striking down a state tax on it, Chief Justice John Marshall acknowledged that the federal Constitution granted only limited powers to the national government. But this limited delegation did not restrict Congress to only those powers expressly granted to it; for it was probably impossible and certainly undesirable to provide "an accurate detail of all the subdivisions of which [the Constitution's] great powers will admit, and of all the means by which they may be carried into execution." To do so would require that the Constitution "partake of the prolixity of a legal code," which was inappropriate for a charter of government. Rather, it was sufficient that the Constitution's "great outlines be marked, its important objects designated, and the minor ingredients which compose those objects be deduced from the nature of the objects itself."[3] Put differently, because the federal Constitution was created to achieve certain broad ends, its grants of power were to be interpreted as carrying with them the subsidiary powers necessary for the achievement of those ends. If there were any doubts on this score, the grant to Congress of implied powers through the necessary and proper clause effectively removed them. Thus, in *McCulloch* the failure specifically to grant to Congress the power to create a bank did not determine the bank's constitutionality, because the Constitution's language, as well as its overall character, bespoke a willingness to permit Congress broad discretion in determining how the Constitution's aims were to be achieved. As Marshall concluded: "Let the end be legitimate, let it be within the scope of the constitution, and all means which are appropriate, which are plainly adapted to that end, which are not prohibited, but consist with the letter and spirit of the constitution, are constitutional."[4]

What is striking about Marshall's constitutional analysis is how little of it applies to American state constitutions. Whereas Marshall recognized that the federal government could exercise only those legislative powers granted to it by the federal Constitution, state governments have historically been understood to possess plenary legislative powers—that is, those residual legislative powers not ceded to the national government or prohibited to them by the federal Constitution. As the Kansas Supreme Court has observed: "When the constitutionality of a statute is involved, the question presented is, therefore, not whether the act is authorized by the constitution, but whether it is prohibited thereby."[5] State governments are not restricted in the purposes for which they can exercise power—they can legislate comprehensively to protect the public welfare—and because of this, state constitutional interpretation cannot proceed in terms of a state government's "important objects" and "minor ingredients." Furthermore, whereas Marshall viewed grants of power as carrying with them subsidiary powers, what appear as grants of power in state constitutions typically do not operate in that fashion. The state provisions may be included for emphasis, indicating powers that the state government can exercise, without enlarging those powers. Or they may direct state legislatures to exercise powers that they command. Or they may serve to overrule judicial decisions limiting legislative power, to eliminate questions of authority where state power was doubtful, or to indicate exceptions to constitutional prohibitions on the legislature. Most often, however, these apparent "grants of power" function as limitations. For in a constitution of plenary legislative powers, an authorization to pursue one course of action may by negative implication serve to preclude pursuing alternative courses that were available in the absence of the "grant," under the familiar legal canon of *expressio unius est exclusio alterius.*[6]

Length and Detail

Although Chief Justice Marshall cautioned that a constitution should avoid the prolixity of a legal code, state constitution-makers have largely ignored his counsel of constitutional minimalism. Indeed, for those unfamiliar with state constitutions, probably their most striking feature is their length. State constitutions, particularly those adopted during the late nineteenth century, are replete with "constitutional legislation," provisions that in their length and detail are indistinguishable from statutes but that nonetheless have been elevated to constitutional status.[7] During the twentieth century, state constitutional reformers have attacked the proliferation of constitutional legislation as the primary flaw in state constitutions and campaigned to prune their state charters of such provisions. In several states these reformers have prevailed, although in none did they succeed in reducing the state constitution to the dimensions of the federal Constitution. Even a reform constitution such as New Jersey's, adopted in 1947, is three times as long as its federal counterpart. Moreover, in other states constitutional reform has proceeded slowly—Louisiana's constitution of 1921 ballooned to over 250,000 words before it was finally replaced in 1974—or has failed altogether.[8] Finally, those states that have the constitutional initiative have found their constitutions increasing in length, particularly during the late twentieth century, as groups have used the initiative to circumvent the legislature and enact legislation via constitutional amendment. Currently, the unamended text of the typical state constitution remains over three times as long as that of the federal Constitution, and state constitutions on average contain over 120 constitutional amendments.[9]

To some extent this greater length of state constitutions can be attributed to the plenary character of state legislative power. Because legislative power exists in the absence of constitutional limitations and because state courts have characteristically interpreted such limitations narrowly, many state constitution-makers have believed it necessary to detail the limitations they sought to impose on their state legislatures. To some extent, too, this greater length derives from the inclusion of elements not found in the federal Constitution. Donald Lutz has argued that the brevity of the federal Constitution and the length of state constitutions are related.[10] According to Lutz, the federal Constitution is an "incomplete constitution," which depends for its operation on state constitutions that "complete" and consequently form a part of the national constitution. For example, the original federal Constitution did not need to define voting qualifications because state constitutions had already done so. Even today, it can say nothing about education and local government—to choose but two examples—because state constitutions deal with such matters.

Yet neither the plenary character of the state legislative power nor the incompleteness of the federal Constitution fully explains the length of state constitutions. For if these shared features were decisive, then all state constitutions would be roughly similar in length. But in fact they vary widely. The longest current state constitution (Alabama's) is more than twenty-six times as long as the shortest (Vermont's), and nine state constitutions contain over forty thousand words, while eleven contain less than fifteen thousand.[11] Furthermore, state constitutions within individual states have varied enormously over time in both their length and their contents. Many state constitutions during the nation's first half-century resembled the federal Constitution in their length and absence of policy prescriptions, but post–Civil War constitutions grew to enormous lengths. For example, the revised constitutions in Maryland (1867), Arkansas (1874), and Missouri (1875) all exceeded their predecessor constitutions by over ten thousand words.[12] More substantively, whereas nineteenth-century constitutions included lengthy provisions dealing with local government and financial matters, most recent constitutions have eschewed their predecessors' detailed treatment of those topics.

Structure and Substance

Since at least the late nineteenth century, most state constitutions have shared a more or less uniform structure and have dealt with a common set of issues (while differing in the detail of their treatment of those issues and in the range of other issues addressed). In certain structural features these state constitutions resemble their federal counterpart. All fifty state constitutions have eschewed a parliamentary system, established a tripartite division of governmental power, provided for regular elections, and guaranteed a range of fundamental rights, while all but Nebraska's have created a bicameral legislature. However, closer inspection of the structure and substance of state constitutions highlights many features that distinguish them from the federal Constitution.

Rights Guarantees

In contrast to the federal Constitution, the initial article of the state constitution (following the preamble) is typically a declaration (or bill) of rights.[13] This ordering of rights and powers dates from the earliest state constitutions, some of which expressly divided their basic law into a declaration of rights and a constitution, or frame of government (although they typically contained provisions emphasizing that the declaration was part of the constitution and hence obligatory). Many of the early bills of rights included provisions that would not be understood as rights guarantees today. Virginia's famous Declaration of Rights, for example, mandated a separation of powers and admonished citizens to treat each other with "Christian forbearance, love, and charity." Pennsylvania's Declaration of Rights recommended that the legislature "consist of persons most noted for wisdom and virtue" and urged citizens to "pay particular attention to these points in electing officers and legislators." And the Massachusetts Declaration of Rights required local governments to "make suitable provision" for "the support and maintenance of public Protestant teachers of piety, religion, and morality in all cases where such provision shall not be made voluntarily." Due to the widespread interstate borrowing that has characterized state constitution-making, both the precedence given to rights and the inclusion of "nonrights" material have been carried over to constitutions in other states.

Although some states have retained their original constitutional language, over time state bills of rights have come to resemble more closely the federal Bill of Rights. Still, important differences remain. Many state guarantees are more specific than their federal counterparts. For example, in addition to prohibiting governmental establishment of religion, nineteen states specifically bar religious tests for witnesses or jurors, and thirty-five prohibit expenditures for "any sectarian purpose."[14] Several state constitutions not only forbid cruel and unusual punishments but also ban unnecessary rigor in punishments, require that penalties be proportionate to the offense, and/or establish rehabilitation as an aim of punishment; while others expressly authorize capital punishment.[15] In addition, many state bills of rights contain protections that have no federal analogue. Thus, thirty-nine states guarantee access to a legal remedy to those who suffer injuries, and eleven expressly protect a right to privacy.[16] Furthermore, in contrast with federal practice, states have not treated their bills of rights as sacrosanct but have amended them with some frequency. From 1986 to 1993, for example, the states adopted fifty-two amendments to their declarations of rights.[17] Some of these amendments served to expand rights—for example, fourteen states added "little ERAs" to their constitutions between 1971 and 1976.[18] Other served to curtail them—Texas, for instance, has amended its bill of rights to restrict the right to bail and California to permit the use of illegally obtained evidence in criminal proceedings.[19] Finally, although the federal Bill of Rights only protects against governmental invasions of rights, some state guarantees prohibit private violations of rights as well. A few, like the Louisiana Constitution's ban on private discrimination, do so expressly. Other guarantees leave themselves open to extension to private action by not specifying that they are directed against governmental violations. A case in point are those state free-speech guarantees that affirmatively protect freedom of speech without specifying against whom. These provisions have been used to protect speech rights on private property open to the public, such as shopping malls.

Governmental Institutions and the Distribution of Power

The Separation of Powers Both federal and state courts recognize the separation of powers as a constitutional principle, but from the outset several states were not content to leave the principle to implication. Currently, forty state constitutions expressly mandate a separation of powers, rejecting dual office-holding and restricting each branch to the powers appropriate to it. At the same time, many of these constitutions anticipate that the state may not maintain a strict separation of powers, permitting departures from it if authorized elsewhere in the constitution. Wyoming's article 2 is representative:

> The powers of the government of this state are divided into three distinct departments: The legislative, executive, and judicial, and no person or collection of persons charged with the exercise of powers properly belonging to one of these departments shall exercise any power belonging to either of the others, except as in this constitution expressly directed or permitted.

The inclusion of such separation-of-powers provisions in state constitutions serves to illustrate the interesting questions that arise in interpreting state charters. Federal courts enforce a separation of powers even without an explicit constitutional mandate, as do some state courts, treating the requirement as implicit in the constitutional design.[20] What, then, is the effect of constitutionalizing the separation of powers? Some state courts, loath to hold that the constitutional language has no effect, have suggested that the state provisions must impose a more stringent separation than is established by the federal Constitution. Thus, the West Virginia Court of Appeals has insisted that the requirement "must be strictly construed and closely followed," holding that "the plain language of [the separation-of-powers provision] calls not for construction, but only for obedience."[21] Other courts, reluctant to attribute a different meaning to the principle of the separation of powers at the state and federal levels, have read the state provisions as mere truisms and generally rejected constitutional challenges raised under them.[22] However, even these courts have been obliged to recognize that the provisions impose some restrictions on the range of legislative powers that can be exercised by the state's executive and judicial branches.[23] A further question arises: if constitutionalizing the separation of powers has an effect on constitutional interpretation, what is the effect of not constitutionalizing it? Or, put differently, given the inclusion of separation-of-powers provisions in many state constitutions, what implications—if any—should be drawn from the fact that a state's constitution-makers chose not to include such a provision?

These questions reveal some of the complexities involved in interpreting a state constitution in the context of other constitutions that have treated the same issue.

State Governmental Institutions The next three articles found in state constitutions typically establish the legislative, executive, and judicial branches of the state's government. Like Articles 1–3 of the federal

Constitution, these articles create offices and prescribe the qualifications, terms, and mode of selection for their occupants. However, the state articles differ in important respects from their federal counterparts. Article 1 of the federal charter grants a set of enumerated powers to Congress; but state constitutions do not delineate state legislative powers, because (as noted previously) state legislative power is considered to be plenary. This has important implications for state constitutional interpretation. In determining the distribution of powers among the branches of state government, the underlying premise must be that the powers of the executive and judicial branches are defined by the constitution, whereas the legislature's are not, so all powers not clearly granted to those branches are reserved to the legislature. Thus, under state constitutions implied powers reside in the legislature rather than the governor or the courts. In addition, in contrast with federal constitutional interpretation, which historically has focused on the implied powers of Congress, the fundamental interpretive issue under state constitutions is the implied limitations (if any) on state legislative power.[24]

The legislative article in state constitutions focuses primarily on the limitations on the state legislature's powers. Some of these limitations are substantive. State legislatures are enjoined from undertaking various actions, such as lending the credit of the state, or adopting laws on certain topics, such as lotteries. They are also prohibited from enacting certain types of special laws—the list can be very long—such as laws granting divorces or changes of name, and from passing special laws when more general enactments are possible. Other limitations on state legislatures are procedural, regulating the process of legislation in order to ensure a more open and orderly deliberative process. These procedural requirements have no counterpart in the federal Constitution. For example, many state constitutions prescribe the form that bills must take, limit the range of subjects a single bill can encompass, and specify the procedures by which a bill is to be considered and adopted. These requirements might prove onerous if they were consistently enforced. However, state courts usually have allowed state legislatures to police their own observance of these requirements, and thus the requirements have seldom impeded the legislative process.[25]

Like Article 2 of the federal Constitution, the state executive article enumerates the powers of the executive. However, unlike their federal counterpart, most state executive articles establish a nonunified executive. Only New Jersey has no elected executive-branch officers beyond the governor, and many states have several independently elected executive officers who undertake important administrative responsibilities and who need not share the governor's political affiliation. As late as 1920, over three-quarters of the states elected their secretary of state, state auditor, and attorney general; and even today, more than two-thirds of the states have at least four independently elected executive officials.[26] State executive articles therefore must delineate the sphere of authority of each executive officer and the division of responsibility among them, as well as the extent to which the governor or other officials can exercise authority over their fellow executive officers. The executive article may in addition attempt to ensure administrative rationality by limiting the number of executive departments in state government. Finally, state executive articles may create and independently empower executive agencies: Florida's Game and Fresh Water Fish Commission is a prime example. This constitutionalization of executive agencies obviously limits the alternatives available in reorganizing the state's executive branch. It also creates a rather anomalous situation in which rules adopted by the agencies in pursuance of their constitutionally granted authority are superior to statutes enacted by the legislature.

Finally, in contrast with Article 3 of the federal Constitution, several states have chosen to set up their entire judicial system by constitutional prescription rather than by statute. The judicial articles in these states establish all state courts, specify each court's jurisdiction, delineate the boundaries of the districts in which the courts shall operate, and provide for the selection of judges to serve on them. State judicial articles may also institute an administrative office of the courts, create judicial discipline commissions, and provide for officials such as court clerks, prosecuting attorneys, coroners, and sheriffs. For some state constitutions, no detail appears too minor for inclusion. The New York Constitution specifies the quorum for its Court of Appeals, the Nevada Constitution regulates how judges charge juries, and the California

Constitution establishes guidelines for the publication of judicial opinions. Not surprisingly, the detailed prescriptions of state judicial articles have periodically required amendment to accommodate population shifts and changes in the demand for legal services.[27] Often, however, constitutional amendments have merely exacerbated existing problems and have themselves been subject to amendment. Since World War II, many states have reformed their judiciaries by unifying courts and centralizing administrative control in the state supreme court.[28] Others have instituted intermediate courts of appeal, thereby increasing the discretion of the states' supreme courts and lessening their workload.[29] Although these changes have contributed to sleeker, less detailed state judicial articles in some states, these articles remain among the least successful—and most heavily revised—provisions in state constitutions.

Local Government The federal Constitution altogether ignores local government, but it was also largely ignored by early state constitutions. These constitutions accepted the authority of existing local governments and the legitimacy of their prerogatives, in some instances even establishing representation for these governments in state legislatures. However, the state constitutional silence about local power ended during the mid-nineteenth century, when New York adopted the first constitutional provisions expressly regulating cities. Other states soon followed New York's lead. The shift in constitutional design resulted from a reconceptualization of the legal status of local governments. Local governments came to be understood as entities "whose powers are derived from and subject to the sovereign state legislature" rather than as component units of a quasi-federal state government.[30] This understanding of the state as a unitary sovereign and local governments as subordinate units was formalized in legal doctrine as "Dillon's rule," under which municipalities could exercise only those powers that were expressly granted by the state or that were indispensable to accomplish the declared purposes of the municipal corporation.[31] The effects on state constitutional design resulting from this changed understanding were dramatic. If units of local government owed their powers and their very existence to the state, then the state had to establish procedures for creating units of local government and determine the structure and powers of those units in considerable detail. Enshrined in the local government articles of state constitutions, these provisions often came to resemble municipal codes. Moreover, these codes grew and grew, as new eventualities required adjustments in the powers granted to particular localities or the redistribution of power among the various units of local government. Complaints about legislative interference, together with the drain on state legislative energies that detailed supervision of localities required, soon prompted efforts to replace micromanagement by the state government with local self-government. Missouri in 1875 pioneered one solution with the adoption of a "home rule" provision, which granted greater autonomy to local governments, and most state constitutions eventually followed Missouri's lead.[32] Indeed, a few recent constitutions have altogether reversed "Dillon's rule," authorizing local governments to tax, regulate, and otherwise deal with matters of local concern, unless specifically prohibited by statute. These home-rule provisions have had a significant effect on state constitutions, because the broader the grant of local self-rule, the shorter and less detailed the constitutional provisions on local government need to be. In addition, fifteen states have adopted amendments requiring the state government to fund programs that they require local governments to undertake.[33] In 1995 Congress followed the states' lead in curbing unfunded mandates, although it pursued by statute a goal for which the states, with their greater ease of amendment, had sought a constitutional solution.

Public Policy

Relatively few provisions of the federal Constitution directly address public-policy issues, although the Constitution's grants of power can be interpreted as suggesting the purposes for which national power is to be exercised. State constitutions, in contrast, deal directly with matters of public policy, sometimes in considerable detail. State governments share common policy responsibilities, and these are reflected in state constitutions. Thus, many state charters contain separate articles on finance, on taxation, on corporations, and on education. Other policy provisions reflect problems that are peculiar to a region—for example, eight western states adopted constitutional prohibitions on the employment of children in mines during the late nineteenth and early twentieth centuries. Still other policy provisions are distinctive to particular states. A few deal with salient aspects of a state's economy: for example, Idaho's Constitution has articles on water rights and on livestock, and California on water resources development. Others, such as New Mexico's article dealing with bilingual education, reflect the social composition of the state. Some policy provisions are a product of the particular political movements regnant during the era in which they were adopted. For instance, the tax revolt of the late 1970s added to the California Constitution articles dealing with tax limitations and government spending limits, while the environmental movement of the late 1960s prompted Illinois to include an article on the environment in its 1970 constitution. Finally, some state policy provisions are simply constitutionalized statutes. Article 10B of the California Constitution, which is entitled the Marine Resources Protection Act of 1990, is a case in point.

Policy provisions in state constitutions may contain direct prohibitions on legislative action, such as the constitutional bans on the use of public funds in support of any religious institution or for any sectarian purpose. Prohibitions in finance and taxation articles, which may range from limitations on the imposition of ad valorem taxes by local governments to bans on state assumption of local government debt, tend to be particularly detailed and specific. Policy provisions in state constitutions may also take the form of policy directives. They may directly enact policy—the California Constitution's establishment of an eight-hour workday on public works is an example. Or they may establish policy guidelines for legislative enactments. In some instances legislative enactment may still be discretionary, as when the Illinois Constitution listed the types of property that the General Assembly could exempt from property taxes, restricting the range of possible exemptions but leaving the legislature free to decide whether to grant those exemptions. More often, however, constitutional directives for legislative enactments are mandatory, requiring legislative action and presumably permitting judicial enforcement if the legislature fails to act.[34]

Finally, the policy provisions in state constitutions may be statements of principle, committing the state to achieve particular ends.[35] The contrast between the language of these articles and the text of the federal Constitution is crucial. Although the federal Constitution grants Congress various powers, it never requires that these powers be exercised—for example, Congress did not regulate commerce among the several states in any substantial way for almost a century after the ratification of the Constitution, and it failed to enact appropriate legislation to enforce the equal protection clause of the Fourteenth Amendment despite obvious violations by southern states. In contrast, state constitutions impose specific duties on state governments. Thus, New Jersey is required to ensure a "thorough and efficient system of free public schools" for all children in the state; Illinois must "provide and maintain a healthful environment for the benefit of this and future generations"; Alaska must "provide for the promotion and protection of public health"; and Idaho is obliged "to pass all necessary laws to provide for the protection of livestock against the introduction or spread" of various diseases. Although these provisions are not framed as rights protections and are not contained in state declarations of rights, they serve as the functional equivalent of positive rights. Even if these provisions do not specifically direct legislative action, they may be self-executing, providing a cause of action when government fails to meet its affirmative responsibilities.[36] If they are, they prompt litigants to recast what would be rights claims under the federal Constitution in terms of obligations that the state government owes its citizens.[37] If the provisions are not self-executing, they still impose requirements on conscientious legislators and governors who wish to remain faithful to their constitutional obligations.

State Constitutional Practice

Perhaps the most striking contrast with federal constitutional practice is the states' reliance on the formal mechanisms of revision (replacement of one constitution by another) and amendment (the alteration of an existing constitution by the addition or subtraction of material) to promote constitutional change. Since 1791, when the adoption of the Bill of

Rights completed the task of founding the federal government, the federal Constitution has been amended less than once per decade. Moreover, the most dramatic constitutional developments, such as the growth of national power and the expansion of presidential prerogatives, have occurred largely without formal constitutional amendment. In contrast, the American states have regularly revised and amended their constitutions. Only nineteen states still retain their original constitutions, and a majority of states have established three or more.[38] Louisiana's current constitution is the state's eleventh, and Georgia's its tenth. The level of constitutional amendment likewise underscores the states' willingness to initiate formal constitutional change. As of 1996, over 9,500 amendments had been proposed to the states' current constitutions and over 5,900 adopted—an average of almost 120 amendments per state.[39] The Alabama Constitution of 1901 has been amended over 580 times, and the California Constitution of 1879 almost 500 times. Even these figures, impressive as they are, substantially underestimate the states' propensity for constitutional tinkering, because they omit amendments and proposed amendments to the states' earlier constitutions. For example, in 1980, three years before adopting a new constitution, Georgia submitted to its voters 137 proposed amendments—16 general amendments and 121 local amendments; and Louisiana's constitution of 1921 was amended 536 times before its replacement in 1974.[40]

While certain aspects of the federal Constitution—for example, the Bill of Rights and the tripartite governmental structure—have been viewed as too fundamental for amendment, no similar reticence has marked state constitutional change. The states have not only regularly replaced their constitutions but have also submitted sets of amendments to the voters that, taken together, have substantially altered the basic character of the state government. Moreover, the issues addressed by state constitutional amendments are as diverse as the subjects treated in state constitutions. For example, a survey of amendments from 1986 to 1993 found that 13 percent concerned bills of rights and suffrage, 42 percent dealt with the structure of state government, 35 percent involved policy matters, and 10 percent concerned miscellaneous other matters.[41]

Whereas Congress has originated all the amendments to the federal Constitution, the states have devised and utilized a variety of mechanisms to propose constitutional change.[42] Most state constitutional amendments have been proposed by state legislatures. In recent years, the proposed amendments have often originated in constitutional commissions, groups of experts and notables appointed by the legislature or executive to develop proposals either for consideration by the legislature or—in the case of Florida—for direct submission to the people for ratification.[43] In addition, forty-one state constitutions expressly authorize the legislature to convene constitutional conventions—indeed, fourteen require that the legislature periodically poll the populace on whether to call a convention—and state legislatures have assumed the power to call conventions even in the absence of express constitutional authorization. Altogether, over 230 state constitutional conventions have been held to create, revise, or amend state constitutions. Finally, eighteen states have adopted the constitutional initiative, which empowers citizens to propose amendments by petition directly to the voters (sixteen states) or to the legislature before submission to the voters (Massachusetts and Mississippi).

The use of the constitutional initiative illustrates another key difference between federal and state constitutional practice regarding constitutional change. Whereas the federal amendment process provides no mechanism for direct popular participation, the states have structured the process of constitutional change to maximize such participation.[44] Popular participation in the initiation of constitutional change occurs not only through the constitutional initiative but through popular votes on legislative proposals to call constitutional conventions and on the selection of delegates to those conventions. Twelve states require that amendments be proposed by majorities in two successive legislatures, giving citizens an opportunity to express their views on proposed constitutional changes in the intervening election.[45] Furthermore, in every state except Delaware, the people ratify all constitutional changes, however proposed, by referendum.

A final distinctive feature of state constitutional practice regarding constitutional change is the involvement of state courts in overseeing the process of change. The reliance on formal constitutional change in the states has prompted opponents of proposed changes to challenge their legality in the courts. Whereas the United States Supreme Court has dismissed procedural challenges to the federal amendment process as "political questions," state courts have proved quite willing to address a wide range of issues associated with state constitutional change.[46] Several state courts have ruled on whether the state legislature can call a convention despite the absence of express authorization in the state constitution. Others have considered the validity of mechanisms designed to facilitate ratification of amendments in states that required extraordinary majorities for approval or the validity of popular consent to an amendment when publicity about its content and effects had been misleading. The Indiana Supreme Court invalidated the legislature's attempt to convene itself as a constitutional convention, and the Iowa Supreme Court struck down popularly approved constitutional amendments because the proposed amendments were not entered into the legislative journals as required by the state constitution.[47] Some state constitutions restrict amendments to a "single subject," and in those states courts have heard challenges claiming that wide-ranging amendments encompassed more than a single subject. State constitutions also restrict the use of the constitutional initiative to amendment, not revision, and so state courts have had to consider whether the far-reaching changes introduced by some amendments constituted revisions of the state constitution. Some state constitutions impose additional restrictions on the constitutional initiative that have likewise promoted litigation. Taken altogether, these cases reveal that state judges are active participants in the process of formal constitutional change.

Conclusion

This chapter's description of state constitutions and state constitutional change has highlighted what is distinctive in state constitutional design and state constitutional practice. Some of the distinctive features, such as the plenary character of state legislative power, reflect the fundamental premises of the nation's constitutional system. For when legislative power is divided in a federal system, one government must receive grants of power and the other retain residual power. Most of the distinctive features of state constitutionalism, however, arise from political choices by the states. Although state legislatures' possession of plenary legislative power may reflect the character of the nation's constitutional system, the states remain free to choose what sorts of constitutional limits to impose on that power. And the states over time have swung from few limitations in the late eighteenth century, to extensive and detailed restrictions in the late nineteenth century, to somewhat fewer restrictions by the late twentieth century. Although the incompleteness of the federal Constitution in a sense requires that state constitutions deal with local government, it does not determine how state constitutions will do so. Thus, the states have chosen over time to deal with local government in various ways, ranging from implicit recognition of local communities' right to self-government, to detailed regulation of the structure and powers of local governments, to broad grants of home rule. Although the nation's constitutional system assigns to the states the power to structure their state governments, it does not determine whether the states will follow the federal model or will depart from it. Nor does it determine whether states will revise and amend their constitutions frequently or constitutionalize policy matters or establish mechanisms for direct popular rule.

This chapter has for the most part treated state constitutions as a unit, ignoring variations among state charters. Obviously, these differences can be substantial. . . . [C]omparison of state constitutions adopted in different eras reveals significant variations in structure, substance, and underlying political theory. Yet even though the states' political choices have varied over time, the extent and character of the differences among state constitutions are less substantial than those between state and federal charters.

Notes

1. Information on Georgia's constitutional experience is drawn from Melvin B. Hill Jr., *The Georgia State Constitution: A Reference Guide* (Westport, Conn.: Greenwood Press, 1994).
2. *McCulloch* v. *Maryland,* 17 U.S. (4 Wheat.) 316 (1819).
3. 17 U.S. (4 Wheat.) 316, 405 and 407 (1819).

4. 17 U.S. (4 Wheat.) 316, 420.
5. *State ex rel. Schneider* v. *Kennedy,* 587 P.2d 844, 850 (Kan. 1978).
6. Frank P. Grad, "The State Constitution: Its Function and Form for Our Time," *Virginia Law Review* 54 (May 1968): 928, 967–68; and Robert F. Williams, "State Constitutional Law Processes," *William and Mary Law Review* 24 (winter 1983): 178–79 and 202–3.
7. As of 1997, more than half the states—twenty-six in all—were operating under constitutions adopted during the second half of the nineteenth century.
8. Lee Hargrave, *The Louisiana State Constitution: A Reference Guide* (Westport, Conn.: Greenwood Press, 1991), 16.
9. Data on contemporary state constitutions are drawn from Janice C. May, "State Constitutions and Constitutional Revision, 1992–93," in *The Book of the States, 1994–95* (Lexington, Ky.: Council of State Governments, 1994), 19, table 1.1.
10. Donald S. Lutz, "The United States Constitution as an Incomplete Text," *Annals of the Academy of Political and Social Science* 496 (March 1988): 23–32.
11. May, "State Constitutions, 1992–93," 19, table 1.1.
12. Sister M. Barbara McCarthy, *The Widening Scope of American Constitutions* (Washington, D.C.: Catholic University of America, 1928), 25.
13. Preceding the initial article is a preamble, which indicates the general purposes for which the people established the constitution. However, the preamble does not create powers or confer them on the state government. Some states do include short articles before their declaration of rights. . . . But few state constitutions have followed the federal practice of appending the declaration of rights to the end of the constitution.
14. See Ronald K. L. Collins Jr., "Bills and Declarations of Rights Digest," in *The American Bench,* 3d ed. (Sacramento: Reginald Bishop Forster and Associates, 1985–86), 2500–2501; and G. Alan Tarr, "Church and State in the States," *Washington Law Review* 64 (winter 1989): 93–100.
15. Collins, "Bills and Declarations Digest," 2510.
16. On the state constitutional right to a remedy, see David Schuman, "The Right to a Remedy," *Temple Law Review* 65 (winter 1992): 1197–1227; state provisions are listed at 1201 n. 25. On the state constitutional right to privacy, see Ken Gormley and Rhonda G. Hartman, "Privacy and the States," *Temple Law Quarterly* 65 (winter 1992): 1279–1323; state provisions are listed and discussed at 1282–83.
17. May, "State Constitutions, 1992–93," 7, table B.
18. On state guarantees of gender equality, see G. Alan Tarr and Mary Cornelia Porter, "Gender Equality and Judicial Federalism: The Role of State Appellate Courts," *Hastings Constitutional Law Quarterly* 9 (summer 1982): 953, table A.
19. The Texas amendment restricting the right to bail is Texas Constitution, art. 1, sec. 11(a). The California amendment, adopted in 1982, is California Constitution, art. 1, sec. 28, part (d).
20. Representative federal cases include *Youngstown Sheet and Tube Company* v. *Sawyer,* 343 U.S. 579 (1952); *Morrison* v. *Olson,* 487 U.S. 654 (1988); and *Mistretta* v. *United States,* 488 U.S. 361 (1989). State cases in the absence of an express constitutional requirement of a separation of powers include *State* v. *A.L.I.V.E. Voluntary,* 606 P.2d 769 (Alas. 1980), and *State ex rel. Stephan* v. *House of Representatives,* 687 P.2d 622 (Kan. 1984).
21. *State ex rel. Quelch* v. *Daugherty,* 306 S.E.2d 233, 235 (1985).
22. Thus, in *Brown* v. *Heymann,* 297 A.2d 572, 577 (N.J. 1972), the New Jersey Supreme Court denied that the inclusion of an express requirement of a separation of powers made any difference.
23. See G. Alan Tarr and Russell Harrison, "Legitimacy and Capacity in State Supreme Court Policymaking: The New Jersey Supreme Court and Exclusionary Zoning," *Rutgers Law Journal* 15 (spring 1984): 541.
24. Walter F. Dodd, "Implied Powers and Implied Limitations in Constitutional Law," *Yale Law Journal* 29 (December 1919): 137–62.
25. Williams, "State Constitutional Limits," 106–12.
26. McCarthy, *Widening Scope,* 52–55; and "The Executive Branch," *Book of the States, 1996–97* (Lexington, Ky: Council of State Governments, 1996), 35, table 2.10.
27. This paragraph follows the analysis in G. Alan Tarr, *Judicial Process and Judicial Policymaking* (St. Paul: West, 1994), 49–53.
28. See Larry Charles Berkson and Susan B. Carbon, *Court Unification: History, Politics, and Implementation* (Washington, D.C.: Government Printing Office,

1978); and G. Alan Tarr, "Court Unification and Court Performance: A Preliminary Assessment," *Judicature* 64 (March 1981): 358.

29. See Roger D. Groot, "The Effects of an Intermediate Appellate Court on the Supreme Court Work Product: The North Carolina Experience," *Wake Forest Law Review* 7 (October 1971): 548–72; Victor Eugene Flango and Nora F. Blair, "Creating an Intermediate Appellate Court: Does It Reduce the Caseload of a State's Highest Court?" *Judicature* 64 (August 1980): 74–84; and John M. Scheb and John M. Scheb II, "Making Intermediate Appellate Courts Final: Assessing Jurisdictional Changes in Florida's Appellate Courts," *Judicature* 67 (May 1984): 474–85.
30. See Daniel J. Elazar, "State-Local Relations: Reviving Old Theory for New Practice," in Stephanie Cole, ed., *Partnership within the States: Local Self-Government in the Federal System* (Urbana, Ill.: Institute of Government and Public Affairs, 1975); James E. Herget, "The Missing Power of Local Government: A Discrepancy between Text and Practice in Our Early State Constitutions," *Virginia Law Review* 62 (June 1976): 1001–5; Michael E. Libonati, "Home Rule: An Essay on Pluralism," *Washington Law Review* 64 (January 1989): 51–71; and Michael E. Libonati, "Intergovernmental Relations in State Constitutional Law: A Historical Overview," *Annals of the American Academy of Political and Social Science* 496 (March 1988): 107–16.
31. *Clinton* v. *Cedar Rapids and Missouri River Railroad,* 24 Iowa 455, 476 (1868); see also generally John Forest Dillon, *A Treatise on the Law of Municipal Corporations,* 5th ed., 5 vols. (Boston: Little, Brown, 1911). A useful overview of the transformation is Gerald E. Frug, "The City as a Legal Concept," *Harvard Law Review* 93 (April 1980): 1059–1154.
32. Missouri Constitution, art. 9, secs. 20–25 (1875). The circumstances surrounding the adoption of these provisions are discussed in Joseph D. McGoldrick, *Law and Practice of Municipal Home Rule, 1916–1930* (New York: AMS Press, 1967).
33. For an overview of constitutional provisions requiring the funding of mandates, see Joseph F. Zimmerman, "State Mandate Relief: A Quick Look," *Intergovernmental Perspective* 28 (spring 1994): 28–32.
34. A useful discussion of mandatory and directory provisions is found in Williams, *State Constitutional Law: Cases and Materials,* 2d ed. (Charlottesville, Va.: Michie, 1993), 412–21.
35. James Willard Hurst, *The Growth of American Law: The Lawmakers* (Boston: Little, Brown, 1950), 246.
36. For a useful discussion, see Richard A. Goldberg and Robert F. Williams, "Farmworkers' Organizational and Collective Bargaining Rights in New Jersey: Implementing Self-Executing State Constitutional Rights," *Rutgers Law Journal* 18 (summer 1987): 729–63.
37. See Jonathan Feldman, "Separation of Powers and Judicial Review of Positive Rights Claims: The Role of State Courts in an Era of Positive Government," *Rutgers Law Journal* 24 (summer 1993): 1057–1100.
38. Unless otherwise indicated, data in this paragraph on the number of state constitutions and on state constitutional amendment are drawn from "State Constitutions," *Book of States, 1996–97.*
39. The data are derived from Janice C. May, "Constitutional Amendment and Revision Revisited," *Publius* 17 (winter 1987): 162, updated on the basis of "State Constitutions," 3, table 1.1.
40. See George D. Busbee, "An Overview of the New Georgia Constitution," *Mercer Law Review* 35 (fall 1983): 3; and Mark T. Carleton, "Elitism Sustained: The Louisiana Constitution of 1974," *Tulane Law Review* 54 (April 1980): 560.
41. These percentages were computed from data reported by May in "State Constitutions, 1992–93," 7, table B.
42. This paragraph relies on May, "Constitutional Amendment and Revision," 153–179; May, "State Constitutions"; Walter F. Dodd, *The Revision and Amendment of State Constitutions* (Baltimore: Johns Hopkins University Press, 1910; rpt. New York: Da Capo, 1970); and Roger Sherman Hoar, *Constitutional Conventions: Their Nature, Powers, and Limitations* (Boston: Little, Brown, 1919).
43. Florida Constitution, art. II, sec. 2. For discussion of the commission mode of amendment, see Robert F. Williams, "Are State Constitutional Conventions Things of the Past? The Increasing Role of the Constitutional Commission in State Constitutional Change," *Hofstra Journal of Public Policy* 1 (1996): 1–26.
44. For a useful discussion of the popular role in state constitutional change, see Harry L. Witte, "Rights, Revolution, and the Paradox of Constitutionalism: The

Processes of Constitutional Change in Pennsylvania," *Widener Journal of Public Law* 3 (1993): 383–476.

45. See "State Constitutions," 5, table 1.2. Three other states—Connecticut, Hawaii, and New Jersey—permit submission of amendments either by an extraordinary legislative majority or by a majority vote in a second session following an intervening election.

46. The leading federal case is *Coleman* v. *Miller,* 307 U.S. 433 (1939). For an overview of state activity, see Michael G. Colatuono, "The Revision of American State Constitutions: Legislative Power, Popular Sovereignty, and Constitutional Change," *California Law Review* 75 (July 1987): 1473–1512. On the relative unimportance of the "political questions" doctrine in state constitutional law, see Tarr and Porter, *State Supreme Courts in State and Nation* (New Haven: Yale University Press, 1988), 44–45.

47. *Ellingham* v. *Dye,* 178 Ind. 336 (1912); and *Koehler* v. *Hill,* 60 Iowa 543 (1883), and *State* v. *Brookhart,* 113 Iowa 250 (1901).

CASE STUDY 4

Introduction

In 1901, the state of Alabama adopted a new constitution, one that disenfranchised African American and poor white voters, severely restricted the power of local governments, and protected industrial and agricultural interests. Today, more than 100 years later, the state is still governed by that same constitution, although it has been amended more than 700 times. At more than 300,000 words long, it is by far the longest state constitution in the nation. To many people, it is also a document that is in dire need of revision.

In June 2000, a group of Alabama residents created an organization dedicated to reforming the state's constitution. The members of Alabama Citizens for Constitutional Reform (ACCR) Foundation offer a litany of complaints against the constitution. Some of the complaints mirror the concerns of the reformers in other states who have sought to revitalize their state government in the recent past. As in these other states, Alabama's constitution is seen as restricting the ability of government to act effectively and efficiently. The citizens group also criticizes the constitution for protecting the power of business and agriculture at the expense of ordinary citizens. In addition, there is concern that the constitution still retains a large number of inappropriate, outdated, and irrelevant provisions that should be removed, including ones that reflect the state's segregated history.

In the case study that follows, Mike Goens, the managing editor of the *Florence TimesDaily,* describes the controversy over Alabama's constitution and the positions of the different sides involved in the debate. Goens's work clearly underscores Tarr's point that state constitutions are distinctive. The difference between the Alabama constitution and the U.S. Constitution is not just in length, but in their treatment of government and politics. Unlike the U.S. Constitution, which grants some specific powers to the federal government and is vague on the limits of those powers, Alabama's constitution has placed severe restrictions on what state and local governments can do. As a result of these restrictions, the only way that the state can address a variety of policy concerns is through the passage of particularized amendments, causing the constitution to swell in length. Perhaps more important than simply illustrating the distinctiveness of state constitutions, Goens's work is valuable because it encourages one to think about the question of what state constitutions should contain.

Questions to Consider

As you read the case study, these are some questions to consider:

- Why does Alabama have such a long and detailed constitution? How is it different from the U.S. Constitution? In what ways is it similar and different from other state constitutions?
- Why do some groups want to rewrite the constitution? What do they say are some of the problems with the current constitution? Why do some groups oppose reform?
- Why do some people see Amendment 328 as an example for successful reform? What did Amendment 328 do? Why was it successful?
- Should state constitutions be modeled more closely after the U.S. Constitution so that they are shorter and simpler? Or are there benefits to including more details? What do you think state constitutions should contain?

Alabama Constitution at Heart of Heated Controversy

Mike Goens

Objectionable language and provisions are sprinkled throughout Alabama's century-old constitution.

> Article XIV, Section 256: "Separate schools shall be provided for white and colored children, and no child of either race shall be permitted to attend a school of the other race."
>
> Article IV, Section 102: "The Legislature shall never pass any law to authorize or legalize any marriage between any white person and a Negro, or descendant of a Negro."
>
> Article VIII, Section 180: "The following male citizens of this state" qualify to register as electors.
>
> Article VIII, Section 181: "The owner in good faith in his own right, or the husband of a woman who is the owner in good faith of 40 acres of land" qualify to register as electors.

Proponents of constitutional reform in Alabama say those and similar sections paint an embarrassing picture of Alabama's past and stand in the way of its future. To some, the passages are examples of why Alabama needs a new constitution.

Others, however, say it is insane to think progress in economic development and education are cursed in Alabama because of segments of the constitution that were written 100 years ago and, for the most part, have been rescinded.

They say writing a new constitution will open the state to gambling interests and higher taxes while jeopardizing the presence of God in the document.

And it is here that the battle lines are drawn in a growing debate over constitutional reform that will likely spill over into next year's statewide elections.

This case study is from a series of articles written by Mike Goens that appeared in the *Florence TimesDaily* on November 18 and 19, 2001. The articles were entitled, "Alabama Constitution at Heart of Heated Controversy" (November 18), "Constitutional Reform: Who's in this Fight and Why?" (November 18), and "Some See Amendment 328 as Proof That Constitutional Reform Can Happen Here" (November 19). Reprinted by permission of *The Florence TimesDaily.*

At the Top

Gov. Don Siegelman has endorsed revision of the constitution primarily as a way to secure consistent funding for the state's education system, which is facing yet another round of cuts in state appropriations.

"If people understand it's our constitution that's forcing us to cut education spending, then I think people will be more receptive to changing the constitution," he said. "If parents become concerned enough about the effect it's having on their children, and if the business community feels strongly enough about a well-educated work force, we can force some changes in the way we fund education."

Other politicians who are considering campaigns for governor, including Lt. Gov. Steve Windom and U.S. Rep. Bob Riley, both Republicans, have also endorsed constitutional reform.

"Education will be the number-one campaign issue next year, as always, but constitutional reform is quickly becoming a major issue," said Wayne Flynt, professor of history at Auburn University and a reform proponent. "Education and constitutional reform are interlinked."

Scholars like Flynt and Bill Stewart, professor emeritus of political science at the University of Alabama, use terms like "dinosaur" and "an embarrassment" when describing Alabama's constitution.

Governing Magazine lists Alabama as the poorest state government in the country, said Thomas Corts, president of Samford University and chairman of Alabama Citizens for Constitutional Reform.

"We've got a lot wrong with the state," he said. "When you look at why state government is not better, you have to look at what established the government, and that's our constitution."

The current constitution was written in 1901, primarily by self-serving business owners, Stewart said. "It was written in the post–Civil War era by industrial leaders at the time, particularly in Birmingham and the Black Belt, who found common interests such as low taxes, cheap labor and less government," Stewart said.

"It was written in such a manner that the state couldn't even engage in improvements such as building new roads, at least until an amendment was approved in 1908."

The constitution restricted voting rights to white men who owned at least 40 acres, or whose wives did.

"To say things have changed in Alabama since that time would be a major understatement," Stewart said. "We can't compete for low-wage jobs anymore because of foreign competition. Since we can't get those jobs, we need to emphasize jobs that require a high level of education."

"Our constitution works against the best interests of our education system. The quality of education in this state is scaring off industry that would offer higher paying jobs."

Flynt said the current constitution was designed to do two things: "Strip local government of the ability to govern themselves and to strip blacks and poor whites of an opportunity to vote."

Jerome Gray, state field director for the Alabama Democratic Conference, said language contained in the constitution should be considered offensive to all Alabamians, regardless of race.

"We had on the ballot during the last election an amendment to end the ban on interracial marriages," Gray said. "The U.S. Supreme Court had already ruled the ban against interracial marriages unconstitutional, but to get it out of our constitution you have to pass an amendment."

Aiding the Powerful

Other proponents of reform say the constitution was designed to maintain low taxes on property, another advantage for major landowners and corporations.

"The populist was a threat to those in control, those who wanted to maintain the power in this state," Flynt said, taking note of the state's former practice of charging voters a poll tax.

David Bronner, chief executive officer of the Retirement Systems of Alabama, puts it more bluntly.

"The 1901 constitution was written to screw over black people and 90 percent of the white people," Bronner told a group at the University of Alabama in Huntsville recently.

Racist and sexist terms appear frequently in the constitution, although most of those sections are no longer in effect.

"The old language is still there today even though we say it no longer pertains," Corts said. "It's not enforced, but it's still there. If you were a minority and a top official of a company that is looking to locate in Alabama, how would you react?"

Flynt said a company was considering locating in Montgomery a few years ago, and a member of the company's site team happened to be black.

"There was talk about the constitution's racist language during those discussions," Flynt said. "The company went to another state."

"Every time Alabama is talked about on a national or international scene, they're quoting from the 1901 constitution," Flynt said. "There's no doubt it's being used against us in industrial development. States in competition with us will talk of how backwards we are and use our constitution as example one."

Gary Palmer, a spokesman for the Alabama Policy Institute, is in favor of "cleaning up" Alabama's constitution and taking out certain language, but he said the debate should avoid scare tactics.

He disagrees that industrial development is being hampered by language included in the constitution 100 years ago.

"A company is not going somewhere else because of language contained in a constitution," he said. "They're going where they can get trained workers. Boeing, Mercedes, Honda and many others have come to Alabama and didn't have problems with our constitution."

"Our constitution is not holding us back. It's our leadership."

Amendment-frenzy

Alabama's constitution is believed to be the world's longest constitutional document with about 315,000 words and 706 amendments and counting. The number of amendments is growing by 15–20 per year. The document is four times longer than Texas', the next largest state constitution.

By comparison, the average state constitution contains about 120 amendments. There are 27 amendments and 7,842 words in the U.S. Constitution.

Stewart and others who favor constitutional reform said amendments will continue to be necessary even with a rewritten constitution.

"It won't be perfect, but it's absolutely impossible to believe it won't be better," Stewart said.

The controversy involved in constitutional reform lies primarily in two areas—tax reform and home rule.

Opponents say rewriting the constitution can be dangerous because it could lead to increased taxes by giving local governments more power. Proponents counter by saying politicians on any level will be cautious in adding taxes. They say the state and local tax burden in Alabama is the nation's lowest, resulting in problems in education, public health, roads and bridges, prisons and other major services.

For instance, Alabama ranks 44th in the country in total spending on education and 43rd in per-pupil spending. Siegelman said tying education money directly to sales tax revenue has created budget shortfalls that are difficult to predict.

The constitution places restrictions on the Legislature. Nearly 90 percent of revenue collected in Alabama is earmarked before it's collected. In comparison, most states earmark about one-fourth of their revenue, according to a recent study by the Public Affairs Research Council of Alabama.

On the issue of home rule, nearly 70 percent of the 706 amendments to Alabama's constitution involve single cities or counties.

The amendment process requires local governments to seek permission from the Legislature and then state voters to address local issues, such as development of industrial boards, changes in retirement benefits for sheriffs, tax increases to support volunteer fire departments or school systems, even mosquito control. "You can't even ban prostitution in your town or county without a constitutional amendment," Flynt said.

Opponents say the amendment process is healthy and prevents local governments from abusing their power.

"Man is inherently evil, and the constitution restrains evil," said Kayla Moore, wife of Alabama Supreme Court Chief Justice Roy Moore.

Conservative Christian groups like Alabama Citizen Watch, the state's Christian Coalition group, warn that rewriting the constitution will bring higher taxes and legalized gambling. They say without the need for statewide approval cities and counties will have too much power.

"Thank God for these amendments," said Sandra Lane Smith, executive director of the Association of Judeo-Christian Values. "We have probably one of the most solid constitutions in the country," she said. "It gives us protection and puts chains on the Legislature and the governor to keep down taxes."

Up to the Voters

Corts said Alabamians should not fall for "scare tactics" by opponents of constitutional reform.

"I would like to think American democracy is just vital enough for people to get the true facts and realize this must be done," he said. "This is an opportunity to show that grassroots democracy still works, and we can be a lesson for the rest of the world."

Most of the people involved in the escalating debate agree that constitutional revision will happen in Alabama, whether it is cleaning up language and discarding provisions no longer in effect or a total rewrite. Corts said his group, as well as other organizations and individuals who want to see the constitution rewritten, will insist on Alabamians having a say in the process and the final approval on any revision.

"Alabamians won't stand for the kind of things that opponents are mentioning as smokescreens," Stewart said. "Things like taking out references to God won't happen. Alabama people will not stand for those things. The truth is there is nothing to fear."

The constitution can be revised or rewritten by the Legislature or during a statewide convention involving elected delegates from throughout the state.

Palmer agreed that the state is headed toward some form of revision. He suggested the process proceed slowly to make sure Alabama values are protected.

He said local governments should have authority to put in new water lines and decide how much their sheriff will earn. But he does not want to see local governments have the ability to tax residents.

"I don't think the question is if it will happen," Flynt said. "It's a matter of when. I think it can happen in 2003 or 2004 with a constitutional convention."

The other option would be to allow the Legislature to rewrite the constitution. Proponents of reform say that process won't work because of the influence of special-interest groups over many legislators.

Palmer and others say special-interest groups could have a bigger influence in a convention. Instead, he favors the Legislature making the revisions—a new Legislature, that is.

"The lack of trust Alabamians have in their Legislature is well-documented," he said. "We'd be much better off sending new people to Montgomery because too many legislators are not behaving as they should."

"We need new people in the Legislature, people who are honest and intelligent. At that point, maybe we would be able to say with confidence that our rights would be protected in such an undertaking."

Constitutional Reform: Who's in this Fight and Why?

"There's no turning back once the constitution is open to reform," said Smith, executive director of the Association for Judeo Christian Values. "God help us if it ever happens."

Smith's group has been the most outspoken against constitution reform. She said the reform effort is being led by people with a liberal agenda who want legalized gambling, increased taxes and the elimination of references to God in the constitution.

"They will slip things in that will tear down our state and tear down our moral values," Smith said.

Academics and others who favor constitution reform are just as passionate.

Proponents stop short of saying they want to rip out everything in the constitution and start over, but most agree a major overhaul is needed.

Somewhere in the middle are lobbyists and other special-interest groups that want to see the state take a cautious approach to constitution reform. They would like to see some of the old and embarrassing verbiage taken out of the document, but they also want to protect their own interests.

Bill Stewart, retired professor of political science at the University of Alabama, said Smith's group is the most openly hostile to constitution reform, "but the association won't be as big of a factor as some groups" like the Alabama Farmers Federation.

"Several interests might be quiet right now, but if the ball gets rolling, you'll find other groups that won't be supportive," said Stewart, a constitution scholar and a proponent of reform. "There are amendments by the score that benefit specific areas of our economy. They don't want to risk losing those benefits with a rewritten constitution. They will be very eager to make sure that any new constitution won't put them in a worse position."

Stewart and others in the academic field who support reform say they have heard opponents accuse them of self-serving agendas. They say nothing is further from the truth.

"There's no way I can personally benefit, nor can this university benefit," said Thomas Corts, 60, president of Samford University and director for the Alabama Citizens for Constitution Reform group. "I'm not after any job, and Samford doesn't get any money from the state. My tent is pretty well pitched. My only motive is to see this state be the best it can be."

Smith, although conceding there are "things in there that shouldn't be there," said the current constitution serves as a protector of individual rights and keeps government from raising taxes without permission of the people.

"The constitution is our moral foundation," she said. "When you take God out, you're taking our cover out."

Smith takes exception to a revision of the state constitution's bill of rights written by state Rep. Jack Venable, D-Tallassee. The revision, which has not been passed, states that "men and women are created equal." Smith said men and women already are considered the same and the word *man* in the constitution is considered mankind.

"That's just part of the feminist movement that wants to bring in things that are really bad," Smith said.

Taxation and Proration

Other opposing groups seem to focus on what constitution reform would do to the tax structure in the state, given that there is little question that a revision likely would address the way tax revenue is collected and distributed.

Gov. Don Siegelman and others say budget shortfalls for education are directly tied to an outdated constitution. They contend that "constitutional loopholes" that protect corporate landowners are shortchanging schools and other state services.

"It is time that we remove the unfair tax burden placed on the working families of Alabama by this constitution," said Stewart Burkhalter, president of the Alabama AFL-CIO, which claims 130,000 members in the state. "It's time that we make the large corporate landowners of this state stop hiding behind the family farm and pay their fair share of property taxes."

"This is the only way we can avoid future proration in education funding. It's the only way for the working people of Alabama to have a fair chance at getting and keeping good jobs."

Paul Hubbert, executive director of the Alabama Education Association, is a proponent of constitution reform. Opponents say Hubbert, perhaps the most powerful lobbyist in Alabama, will try to manipulate any reform process to make sure education gets more than its share.

However, Hubbert steers clear of any debate about how his membership and the education system could benefit from constitution reform.

"They wrote the constitution as an almost sure-fire way to disenfranchise at least half of our citizens at that time," he said.

Smith said Hubbert and others are trying to "manipulate people through a liberal agenda."

"The black community in Alabama is being used, and I have several close friends who are black who understand that," she said. "Prejudice no longer exists in our constitution."

Hubbert says the constitution limits the state's ability to have a fair tax structure and lays the foundation for unfair taxation.

"Alabama treats its working class more shabbily than any other state," he said. "Some workers are paying up to 12 percent of their checks to the state, while some corporations pay less than a penny on the dollar because of tax breaks. That whole document is predicated on the needs of the so-called ruling class of landowners and big-city industrialists."

To Alfa, Eagle Forum and similar groups that want the state to take a cautious approach to constitution reform, tax reform is paramount.

"We have been closely studying this issue for several years and we've determined that what's driving this debate is radical tax reform," said Mike Kilgore, executive director of Alfa. "If the people are going after tax reform, then they shouldn't hide behind the curtain of rewriting the constitution."

Kilgore said Alfa favors the limitations on taxing that is provided in the constitution. He said the group has concerns about home rule and doesn't want regulatory control over agricultural issues handled individually by all 67 counties.

The Alabama Eagle Forum, Alabama Policy Institute and many other groups share that view on taxes. They say local governments should not have the authority to approve additional taxes.

"Alabama's regressive tax code needs to be repaired, but one of the biggest issues that needs to be addressed is spending," said Gary Palmer, a spokesman for Alabama Policy Institute. "Our government simply spends too much money. When they don't have enough money left, they want to raise taxes. We need the protection our constitution provides us."

Eunie Smith, state president of the Alabama Eagle Forum, said she's concerned that some proponents want to remove the requirement that the people must vote on any proposed tax increase.

"That is very wrong," she said. "We don't need to give government any more authority than they already have when it comes to tax increases. They should not be allowed to add taxes without consent of voters."

Smith said Eagle Forum does not oppose "cleaning up the constitution," but wants the process to proceed slowly. She said her group would like to see unconstitutional provisions removed. The group also wants amendments dealing with specific counties logged separately from the basic text of the constitution.

Alfa does not oppose revision of the constitution, but Kilgore said it should be done article by article instead of calling a constitutional convention.

Corts and numerous proponents say special-interest groups have too much control over the Legislature. Corts said those groups should not be allowed to taint the process.

"Anyone who thinks a convention won't be controlled by special interests is very naive," Palmer said. "Paul Hubbert and several other lobbyists will be heavily involved for their own interests."

"We should all be involved to protect our own interests."

Most legislators want any revision of the constitution to be handled in a convention. State Rep. Todd Greeson, R-Ider, has introduced legislation that would prevent any person seeking to become a delegate at the constitutional convention from accepting contributions from a political action committee. He said the bill is necessary to keep politics out of the process.

Stewart said the toughest task is getting average Alabamians involved.

"Most people don't understand it," Stewart said. "They can't see the relevance the constitution has in their lives and what impact a new constitution would have. We were all taught in school to honor and uphold the constitution. It's just hard to honor a document with so many problems."

Some See Amendment 328 as Proof That Constitutional Reform Can Happen Here

Today, it's known as Amendment 328.

The amendment, which provided Alabama with a new Judicial Article, is hailed by scholars as proof that constitutional reform works. The amendment has also continued to provide the nation with a model for how state court systems should operate.

"Imagine that, Alabama being a model and held up as an example of the way to do something right," said

Wayne Flynt, professor of history at Auburn University. "The Judicial Article is a good example of Alabama at its best."

Modernization of the state's court system was the brainchild of retired U.S. Sen. Howell Heflin of Tuscumbia, who served as the state's chief justice during the early 1970s.

The revision of Article IV of the state constitution did not come without months of political maneuvering, consensus building and compromise.

Shortly after Amendment 328 was finally passed in 1973 by 62 percent of Alabama voters, Heflin and the state's judicial system were tossed into the national spotlight.

Heflin was asked by officials in South Carolina to help write a judicial article there. He also spoke to groups throughout the country about modernization of the state court system.

Checks and Balances

Scholars say the Judicial Article truly defined the separation of powers in the state, stripping the state Legislature of the control it once held over the court system.

Among other things, the document also:

- Unified the court system into a two-tier approach involving the circuit and district courts.
- Mandated that all judges, with the exception of probate judges, had to be certified to practice law in the state.
- Established a code of conduct for judges and set up a judicial inquiry commission, which could file complaints against judges, and a judiciary court to hear and rule on the complaints.
- Required the Legislature to provide money to run the court system.

The document has withstood the test of time and remains viable today, according to constitutional law professors and those involved in the state court system. Even proponents of constitution reform in Alabama say there's little reason to involve the Judicial Article in the process.

"There's no reason to change for the sake of changing," said Thomas Corts, president of Samford University and chairman of Alabama Citizens for Constitutional Reform. "The Judicial Article might need some tweaking, but it's still in pretty good shape. We'd be in a terrible fix had that not been changed."

Article by Article

Gary Palmer of the Alabama Policy Institute, whose group proposes a slow approach to constitutional reform, said the best way to approach revision is article by article.

"What was done with the Judicial Article is a good example of why we should do it article by article," Palmer said. "We have seen that it can be done and quite well."

The process of adopting the new Judicial Article was filled with political land mines that Heflin and those who worked with him had to sidestep.

Gov. George Wallace, perhaps the most powerful politician in Alabama's history, was among those who objected to efforts to rewrite Article IV.

Heflin said Wallace did not work publicly to defeat the effort, "but he got his lieutenants to do their best to stop it."

Political observers at the time said Wallace's opposition was based on, more than anything else, his fear that Heflin would gain political clout during the process. Wallace's men began labeling Heflin as a power grabber.

There were other opposing forces, including some older and more experienced attorneys who had made a reputation and a lot of money by exploiting holes and technical points in the old Judicial Article to win lawsuits, Heflin said. Judges who were seated despite not having license to practice law also opposed it as did about 45 circuit clerks who had made $75,000 or more annually because they were being paid based on the fines they collected.

The Alabama League of Municipalities also opposed the revision initially because the proposed article eliminated municipal courts and placed them under the district court system. The requirement that city judges be lawyers also caused concern.

Tuscumbia Mayor William Gardiner was the league president at the time and helped work out a compromise that gave cities and towns an option of keeping their own courts or having those duties assumed by district courts. The provision requiring judges to be attorneys remained.

Heflin also formed citizens' conferences and committees to build grassroots support for the change.

He also formed a group that became known as the "Muscle Shoals Mafia" to build support and get the reform effort through the legislative process.

Legislators were already being lobbied by Wallace and other groups that opposed the movement, so the undertaking was considered monumental.

While Gardiner worked the League of Municipalities membership, O'Bannon and former Lauderdale County Circuit Judge Ed Tease began lobbying the Legislature.

The first step was to persuade the Legislature to allow a statewide referendum on the Judicial Article. O'Bannon introduced the bill in the Senate calling for the referendum and Rep. Bob Hill of Florence introduced the same bill in the House.

The move nearly stalled in a Senate committee, with Sen. Casey Downing of Mobile holding the key vote. Heflin said he knew the senator was a Roman Catholic so he called Archbishop Oscar Lipscomb to help persuade Downing to vote in favor of the referendum.

There were also efforts in the House to kill the bill. The legislation was placed near the bottom of the House's legislative calendar, meaning that four-fifths of the House membership would have to vote for immediate consideration before it could be brought up for debate on the final day of the session.

After failing earlier, Hill managed to get the House to suspend rules and bring up the bill for a vote. He and fellow Rep. Ronnie Flippo managed to gain enough support to get the needed four-fifths vote.

"We were fighting the establishment that wanted to keep status quo and special interests that had an interest in not wanting to see a modern judicial system," Hill said.

"A tremendous amount of work had been put into this by Howell Heflin and many others. We finally got it through on the last hour of the last day."

Opponents in the Senate attached nine amendments to the legislation, causing the bill to go back to the House for approval.

Heflin said he and others had anticipated the move. They had already typed in several possible changes so they could quickly prepare the new legislation in time for another House vote before the session ended at midnight.

The legislation was approved less than 15 minutes before the session ended.

Heflin then launched a statewide public relations blitz to convince Alabamians that the Judicial Article needed replacing. He made numerous speeches and television appearances throughout the state in an attempt to gain support.

The result was an overwhelming vote of approval by state residents on Dec. 18, 1973. Scholars say that's the day Alabama's judicial system was transformed from the nation's worst to one that continues to be a model.

"There was a lot of people from a diverse population that came together," Heflin said. "We had to compromise on some things, and there will have to be a lot of compromises worked out with potential opponents if constitutional reform is going to happen now."

Heflin said reform is needed in Alabama.

"Don't question the fact that you're going to have special-interest groups that will either want something put in or will oppose some things," Heflin said. "For instance, potentially there will be opposition from religious groups that think freedom of religion will be somehow compromised. Farm groups will want land that's fairly close to cities protected from suburban growth."

"But it can all be worked out and compromises can be formed. In the end, it's worth it."

Editor's Epilogue

In January 2003, Alabama Governor Bob Riley appointed a thirty-four member commission to make recommendations for reforming the state's constitution. In March, the commission reported back with recommendations for changes in five areas, including the removal of racist language from the constitution and the granting of limited home rule to local governments. But as of June 2004, none of the reform proposals had been adopted.

In September 2003, Governor Riley was able to place a tax and accountability referendum on the state ballot, which was favored by reformers. Among other consequences, Amendment One, as the referendum was called, would have raised $1.2 billion a year in more taxes. The referendum was overwhelmingly defeated by state voters. The defeat of the tax reform and the death a few months later of Bailey Thomson, the newly elected chair of the Alabama Citizens for Constitutional Reform, has slowed down the efforts for reform, although the citizens' group is still active.

Chapter 4 Review Questions

1. According to Professor Tarr, how are state constitutions distinctive?
2. How are state constitutions different from the federal Constitution in how they grant and limit power? What does it mean that state governments have plenary power?
3. What do state constitutions contain? What is the basic structure of most state constitutions? What are some of the major provisions that they include?
4. What are some of the criticisms that reformers have against state constitutions in general? What are some of the criticisms lodged against Alabama's constitution?
5. How are state constitutions amended? How does this differ from the U.S. model?
6. The U.S. Constitution has reached a point for many people in which it seems too sacred to amend, yet voters have no qualms about altering state constitutions. Why should we have different attitudes about amending the U.S. and state constitutions? If we are willing to amend state constitutions frequently, why shouldn't we also be willing to amend the U.S. Constitution? Or conversely, if constitutions are too fundamental to change, why should we be continuing to revise state constitutions?

Key Terms

constitutional distinctiveness
declaration of rights
Jacksonian Democracy
Progressive Movement
National Municipal League
Model State Constitution
plenary power
home rule
McCulloch v. *Maryland*
grant of power
necessary and proper clause
separation of powers
nonunified executive
Dillon's Rule
single subject restriction

Suggestions for Further Reading

Adams, Willi Paul. *The First American Constitutions.* Lanham, Md.: Rowman & Littlefield, 2001. Historical study of the first state constitutions.

Elazar, Daniel J. "The Principles and Traditions Underlying American State Constitutions." *Publius* 12 (Winter 1982): 11–26. This was the first of several essays that appeared in the Winter 1982 edition of *Publius* that focused on state constitutions. Elazar argues that there have been three principle philosophical traditions that have shaped the character of state constitutions over time.

Gardner, James A. "The Failed Discourse of State Constitutionalism." 90 *Michigan Law Review* 761, 761–837 (1992). Highly critical analysis on the character of state constitutions.

Graves, W. Brooke, ed. *Major Problems in State Constitutional Revision.* Chicago: Public Administrative Service, 1960. This is a collection of writings on the poor health of state constitutions in the 1950s. The essay by David Fellman on "What Should a State Constitution Contain?" (pp. 137–158) is particularly valuable for thinking about state constitutions.

Hammons, Christopher W. "Constitutional Reform: Is It Necessary?" 64 *Albany Law Review,* 1327–1353 (2001). Empirical analysis of state constitutional change. Argues against the need to reduce the length and remove policy from state constitutions.

———. "Was James Madison Wrong? Rethinking the American Preference for Short, Framework-Oriented Constitutions." *American Political Science Review* 93 (December 1999): 837–1849. Empirical study of the relationship between the length of state constitutions and the frequency in which they are revised. Study tests Madison's argument that shorter, more framework-oriented constitutions are more likely to last longer.

Lutz, Donald S. *The Origins of American Constitutionalism.* Baton Rouge: University of Louisiana Press, 1984. Detailed study of the influence of colonial compacts on state and federal constitutions.

———. "The Purposes of American State Constitutions." *Publius* 12 (Winter 1982): 27–44. Explores the purposes for state constitutions.

———. "Toward a Theory of Constitutional Amendment." *American Political Science Review* 88 (June 1994): 355–1370. Why are some state constitutions amended more frequently than others? This empirical study indicates that states with longer constitutions and easier amending rules tend to have higher amendment rates.

Maddex, Robert L., ed. *State Constitutions of the United States.* Washington, D.C.: Congressional Quarterly, 1998. Complete collection of state constitutions.

Stewart, William H. *The Alabama State Constitution: A Reference Guide.* Westport, Conn.: Greenwood, 1994. Comprehensive legal guide to Alabama's constitution.

Sturm, Albert L. "The Development of State Constitutions." *Publius* 12 (Winter 1982): 57–98. Fine history of changes in state constitutions since 1776.

Tarr, G. Alan. *Constitutional Politics in the States: Contemporary Controversies and Historical Patterns.* Westport, Conn.: Greenwood Press, 1996. Collection of eight essays on the history of state constitutions and the politics involved in several recent state constitutional battles.

Thomson, Bailey, ed. *A Century of Controversy: Constitutional Reform in Alabama.* Tuscaloosa: University of Alabama Press, 2002. This book consists of a collection of essays on the history of Alabama's constitution and the concerns of the modern day reformers.

Related Web Sites

http://www.camlaw.rutgers.edu/statecon/
The web site for the Center for State Constitutional Studies at Rutgers–Camden provides a valuable selection of on-line readings on state constitutions, as well as other valuable resources.

http://www.constitutionalreform.org/
Official web site for the Alabama Citizens for Constitutional Reform includes newspaper articles and other resources on Alabama's reform efforts.

5

Political Participation: The Concept of Civic Engagement

For the first two-thirds of the twentieth century a powerful tide bore Americans into ever deeper engagement in the life of their communities, but a few decades ago—silently, without warning—that tide reversed and we were overtaken by a treacherous rip current. Without at first noticing, we have been pulled apart from one another and from our communities over the last third of the century.

Robert D. Putnam

READING 5

Introduction

Many political observers have grown increasingly concerned in recent years about the health of American democracy, pointing to a number of different signs that suggest something is wrong. Ever since the Vietnam War and the Watergate scandal, the public has become more distrustful of politics and politicians. Voting turnout has declined. Voters have become more willing to elect political outsiders and those who campaign on antigovernment platforms. Many states have adopted term limits to remove professional politicians from office. Citizen groups have sought to reduce the size of government by pushing for limits on taxes. Some groups have tried to circumvent government institutions entirely by turning more frequently to the initiative process in order to change state laws.

One particular concern to many scholars has been the apparent decline of participation by Americans in civic activities. The decline has not just been in overtly political organizations, but in a broad spectrum of groups that brought people together in the past—from labor unions to Elks clubs to the PTA. Many scholars fear that this decline in civic engagement is harmful to democracy, creating greater distrust of politics and making it more difficult for government to function. Interest in civic engagement is not just limited to experts on American politics but also includes those who study the politics of other nations, as well as scholars in a wide range of disciplines, including sociology, communications, community health, education, religious studies, and history.

Robert Putnam, a professor of public policy at Harvard University, has probably done the most to spur interest in civic engagement. Putnam first began to put forward his ideas on the importance of civic participation in *Making Democracy Work,* a book he published in 1993 on democracy in Italy. He argued that regional governments worked more effectively in parts of Italy in which there were more civic and community groups.[1] He argued that these groups, including ones that were not at all political, promoted democracy by teaching citizens values that are essential to effective and stable government. Shortly after *Making Democracy Work* was published, Putnam turned his attention to American politics. The initial result of his efforts was an article he published in 1995 in the *Journal of Democracy,* entitled "Bowling Alone: America's Declining Social Capital." Here, Putnam argued that the problem confronting American politics today is that people are no longer joining civic organizations as they once did, and as a result they are becoming disconnected from each other. A few decades ago, Americans took an active part in political, social, economic, and religious groups. But today, they do not. The title of Putnam's article captures the essence of his point. Instead of joining bowling leagues, today people bowl alone.

The central argument in Putnam's work is that social networks are valuable to democracy because they build trust among citizens and encourage them to work together for mutual benefit. By participating in civic groups, individuals are forced to interact face to face, an experience that instills values that help make democracy work—values such as tolerance, empathy, and a willingness to share information. Putnam uses the term *social capital* to describe the benefits of social networks for democracy.

Putnam's work has spurred a vibrant discussion among scholars on the importance of civic engagement in America. Many researchers have followed Putnam's lead and focused on the problems caused by declining social capital. Others have pursued different lines of research or have come to different conclusions. Some researchers argue that there has not been a decline in civic engagement, as Putnam argues, just a shift in how and where people are participating. Others agree the decline is real, but contend that the consequences are different from what Putnam argues.

Another leading voice in the civic engagement literature is Theda Skocpol, one of Putnam's colleagues at Harvard University. Skocpol has questioned Putnam's argument that the development of trust is essential to democratic government. She points out that democracy arose out of distrust of government, as citizens grew disillusioned with those in power. Instead of being concerned about the relationship between civic engagement and trust, Skocpol focuses on the role of groups in promoting the political concerns of ordinary citizens. She argues that civic engagement has not necessarily declined, so much as it has changed. Whereas individuals once participated actively in large, multipurpose federated organizations, today they participate by writing checks to advocacy groups based in Washington, D.C., by joining narrowly focused local groups, and by volunteering on an intermittent basis. Even though she sees the change in civic engagement differently from Putnam, Skocpol is still concerned about the health of democracy in America. The changed character of involvement, she fears, has strengthened the political position of an upper-middle-class elite, while making it more difficult for ordinary citizens to be heard.[2]

The research on civic engagement represents only a part of a larger body of literature that is concerned with understanding who participates in politics and the effect that participation has on democracy. Historically, much of the scholarly literature has focused on *conventional* forms of participation, such as voting, working on political campaigns, or writing to elected officials, although there has also been research on more *unconventional* forms of participation. Unconventional participation generally refers to forms of political action that are not considered appropriate by the dominant culture in society, such as violent protests or illegal activities. The research on social capital is different because it is concerned not only with these forms of overt political participation, but also with the willingness of individuals to participate in a wide swath of social life.

For many academic and community leaders, the decline in civic engagement has moved beyond a scholarly question to a problem that needs to be addressed in practical terms. As a result, a growing number of organizations, from large national associations to small community groups, have begun promoting programs to rebuild social capital in America. Scholars who study political participation have found that the ways people are socialized into politics play a significant role in their willingness to participate and their political attitudes. Because much of our political socialization occurs during childhood, through the influences of our families, peers, and schools, many of these organizations have focused their efforts on school children and university students. As a result, many schools and universities today encourage service learning, internships, volunteerism, and other activities that are designed to rebuild civic engagement.

The following reading introduces readers to the debates over civic engagement. The reading is meant to encourage readers to think about why people do not participate in group activities in the same way they did in the past and what this change in participation means for democracy at the state and local levels. The reading is taken from a book Putnam published in 2001 to elaborate his ideas more fully and to respond to criticisms of his earlier works.

In this excerpt, Putnam explains what he means by social capital and its importance both to individuals and to society. Central to Putnam's argument is his contention that social capital benefits the wider community by building trust and encouraging individuals to help others without expecting something in direct return. Social capital produces expectations that we will eventually benefit from our actions, but that the reward will not necessarily come immediately or from those we directly help. Rather, social capital encourages what Putnam refers to as a norm of generalized reciprocity. The ultimate benefit of building trust and generalized reciprocity is that it makes society work more efficiently.

The selection ends with Putnam cautioning the reader that the best way to test the accuracy of his argument is to count the number of people involved in groups and other activities over time, to see if there has indeed been a decline in social capital. In the chapters that follow in his book, Putnam presents an immense array of data to support his contention. He then goes on to examine the causes for this decline.

Questions to Consider

In reading Putnam's work, these are some questions to think about:

- What does Putnam say has happened to civic and social life in American communities over the past few decades? What was social life like earlier in the twentieth century? What is it like today?

- In what ways is social capital both a private good and a public good?
- What does Putnam mean by the term *general reciprocity*? How does it differ from *specific reciprocity*? Why does he consider general reciprocity to be valuable?
- What evidence does Putnam provide to support his claim that civic involvement has declined? What evidence does he provide that Americans share a sense of civic malaise?
- Thinking about groups with which you have been involved, do you agree with Putnam's argument that civic engagement instills values that are helpful to democracy? Why or why not?

Thinking About Social Change in America

Robert D. Putnam

No one is left from the Glenn Valley, Pennsylvania, Bridge Club who can tell us precisely when or why the group broke up, even though its forty-odd members were still playing regularly as recently as 1990, just as they had done for more than half a century. The shock in the Little Rock, Arkansas, Sertoma club, however, is still painful: in the mid-1980s, nearly fifty people had attended the weekly luncheon to plan activities to help the hearing- and speech-impaired, but a decade later only seven regulars continued to show up.

The Roanoke, Virginia, chapter of the National Association for the Advancement of Colored People (NAACP) had been an active force for civil rights since 1918, but during the 1990s membership withered from about 2,500 to a few hundred. By November 1998 even a heated contest for president drew only fifty-seven voting members. Black city councillor Carroll Swain observed ruefully, "Some people today are a wee bit complacent until something jumps up and bites them." VFW Post 2378 in Berwyn, Illinois, a blue-collar suburb of Chicago, was long a bustling "home away from home" for local veterans and a kind of working-class country club for the neighborhood, hosting wedding receptions and class reunions. By 1999, however, membership had so dwindled that it was a struggle just to pay taxes on the yellow brick post hall. Although numerous veterans of Vietnam and the post-Vietnam military lived in the area, Tom Kissell, national membership director for the VFW, observed, "Kids today just aren't joiners."[1]

The Charity League of Dallas had met every Friday morning for fifty-seven years to sew, knit, and visit, but on April 30, 1999, they held their last meeting; the average age of the group had risen to eighty, the last new member had joined two years earlier, and president Pat Dilbeck said ruefully, "I feel like this is a sinking ship." Precisely three days later and 1,200 miles to the northeast, the Vassar alumnae of Washington, D.C., closed down their fifty-first—and last—annual book sale. Even though they aimed to sell more than one hundred thousand books to benefit college scholarships in the 1999 event, co-chair Alix Myerson explained, the volunteers who ran the program "are in their sixties, seventies, and eighties. They're dying, and they're not replaceable." Meanwhile, as Tewksbury Memorial High School (TMHS), just north of Boston, opened in the fall of 1999, forty brand-new royal blue uniforms newly purchased for the marching band remained in storage, since only four students signed up to play. Roger Whittlesey, TMHS band director, recalled that twenty years earlier the band numbered more than eighty, but participation had waned ever since.[2] Somehow in the last several decades of the twentieth century all these community groups and tens of thousands like them across America began to fade.

It wasn't so much that old members dropped out—at least not any more rapidly than age and the accidents of life had always meant. But community organizations were no longer continuously revitalized, as they had been in the past, by freshets of new members. Organizational leaders were flummoxed. For years they assumed that their problem must have local roots or at least that it was peculiar to their organization, so they commissioned dozens of studies to recommend reforms.[3] The slowdown was puzzling because for as long as anyone could remember, membership rolls and activity lists had lengthened steadily.

In the 1960s, in fact, community groups across America had seemed to stand on the threshold of a new era of expanded involvement. Except for the civic drought induced by the Great Depression, their activity had shot up year after year, cultivated by assiduous civic gardeners and watered by increasing affluence and education. Each annual report registered rising membership. Churches and synagogues were packed, as more Americans worshiped together than only a few decades earlier, perhaps more than ever in American history.

Moreover, Americans seemed to have time on their hands. A 1958 study under the auspices of the newly inaugurated Center for the Study of Leisure at the University of Chicago fretted that "the most dangerous threat hanging over American society is the threat of leisure," a startling claim in the decade in which the Soviets got the bomb.[4] *Life* magazine echoed the warning about the new challenge of free time: "Americans now face a glut of leisure," ran a headline in February 1964. "The task ahead: how to take life easy."

> As a matter of fact, mankind now possesses for the first time the tools and knowledge to create whatever kind of world he wants. . . . Despite our Protestant ethic, there are many signs that the message is beginning to get through to some people. . . . Not only are Americans flocking into bowling leagues and garden clubs, they are satisfying their gregarious urges in countless neighborhood committees to improve the local roads and garbage collections and to hound their public servants into doing what the name implies.[5]

The civic-minded World War II generation was, as its own John F. Kennedy proclaimed at his inauguration, picking up the torch of leadership, not only in the nation's highest office, but in cities and towns across the land. Summarizing dozens of studies, political scientist Robert E. Lane wrote in 1959 that "the ratio of political activists to the general population, and even the ratio of male activists to the male population, has generally increased over the past fifty years." As the 1960s ended, sociologists Daniel Bell and Virginia Held reported that "there is more participation than ever before in America . . . and more opportunity for the active interested person to express his personal and political concerns."[6] Even the simplest political act, voting, was becoming ever more common. From 1920, when women got the vote, through 1960, turnout in presidential elections had risen at the rate of 1.6 percent every four years, so on a simple straight-line projection it seemed reasonable, as a leading political scientist later observed, to expect turnout to be nearly 70 percent and rising on the nation's two hundredth birthday in 1976.[7]

By 1965 disrespect for public life, so endemic in our history, seemed to be waning. Gallup pollsters discovered that the number of Americans who would like to see their children "go into politics as a life's work" had nearly doubled over little more than a decade. Although this gauge of esteem for politics stood at only 36 percent, it had never before been recorded so high, nor has it since. More strikingly, Americans felt increased confidence in their neighbors. The proportion that agreed that "most people can be trusted," for example, rose from an already high 66 percent during and after World War II to a peak of 77 percent in 1964.[8]

The fifties and sixties were hardly a "golden age," especially for those Americans who were marginalized because of their race or gender or social class or sexual orientation. Segregation, by race legally and by gender socially, was the norm, and intolerance, though declining, was still disturbingly high. Environmental degradation had only just been exposed by Rachel Carson, and Betty Friedan had not yet deconstructed the feminine mystique. Grinding rural poverty had still to be discovered by the national media. Infant mortality, a standard measure of public health, stood at twenty-six per one thousand births—forty-four per one thousand for black infants—in 1960, nearly four times worse than those indexes would be at the end of the century. America in *Life* was white, straight, Christian, comfortable, and (in the public square, at least) male.[9] Social reformers had their work cut out for them. However, engagement in community affairs and the sense of shared identity and reciprocity had never been greater in modern America, so the prospects for broad-based civic mobilization to address our national failings seemed bright.

The signs of burgeoning civic vitality were also favorable among the younger generation, as the first of the baby boomers approached college. Dozens of studies confirmed that education was by far the best predictor of engagement in civic life, and universities were in the midst of the most far-reaching expansion in American history. Education seemed the key to both greater tolerance and greater social involvement. Simultaneously shamed and inspired by the quickening struggle for civil rights launched by young African Americans in the South, white colleges in the North began to awaken from the silence of the fifties. Describing the induction of this new generation into the civil rights struggles of the 1960s, sociologist Doug McAdam emphasizes their self-assurance:

> We were a "can do" people, who accomplished whatever we set out to do. We had licked the Depression, turned the tide in World War II, and rebuilt Europe after the war. . . . Freedom Summer was an audacious undertaking consistent with the exaggerated sense of importance and potency shared by the privileged members of America's postwar generation.[10]

The baby boom meant that America's population was unusually young, whereas civic involvement generally doesn't bloom until middle age. In the short run, therefore, our youthful demography actually tended to dampen the ebullience of civil society. But that very bulge at the bottom of the nation's demographic pyramid boded well for the future of community organizations, for they could look forward to swelling membership rolls in the 1980s, when the boomers would reach the peak "joining" years of the life cycle. And in the meantime, the bull session buzz about "participatory democracy" and "all power to the people" seemed to augur ever more widespread engagement in community affairs. One of America's most acute social observers prophesied in 1968, "Participatory democracy has all along been the political style (if not the slogan) of the American middle and upper class. It will become a more widespread style as more persons enter into those classes."[11] Never in our history had the future of civic life looked brighter.

What happened next to civic and social life in American communities is the subject of this book. In recent years social scientists have framed concerns about the changing character of American society in terms of the concept of "social capital." By analogy with notions of physical capital and human capital—tools and training that enhance individual productivity—the core idea of social capital theory is that social networks have value. Just as a screwdriver (physical capital) or a college education (human capital) can increase productivity (both individual and collective), so too social contacts affect the productivity of individuals and groups.

Whereas physical capital refers to physical objects and human capital refers to properties of individuals, social capital refers to connections among individuals—social networks and the norms of reciprocity and trustworthiness that arise from them. In that sense social capital is closely related to what some have called "civic virtue." The difference is that "social capital" calls attention to the fact that civic virtue is most powerful when embedded in a dense network of reciprocal social relations. A society of many virtuous but isolated individuals is not necessarily rich in social capital.

The term *social capital* itself turns out to have been independently invented at least six times over the twentieth century, each time to call attention to the ways in which our lives are made more productive by social ties. The first known use of the concept was not by some cloistered theoretician, but by a practical reformer of the Progressive Era—L. J. Hanifan, state supervisor of rural schools in West Virginia. Writing in 1916 to urge the importance of community involvement for successful schools, Hanifan invoked the idea of "social capital" to explain why. For Hanifan, social capital referred to

> those tangible substances [that] count for most in the daily lives of people: namely good will, fellowship, sympathy, and social intercourse among the individuals and

> families who make up a social unit. . . . The individual is helpless socially, if left to himself. . . . If he comes into contact with his neighbor, and they with other neighbors, there will be an accumulation of social capital, which may immediately satisfy his social needs and which may bear a social potentiality sufficient to the substantial improvement of living conditions in the whole community. The community as a whole will benefit by the cooperation of all its parts, while the individual will find in his associations the advantages of the help, the sympathy, and the fellowship of his neighbors.[12]

Hanifan's account of social capital anticipated virtually all the crucial elements in later interpretations, but his conceptual invention apparently attracted no notice from other social commentators and disappeared without a trace. But like sunken treasure recurrently revealed by shifting sands and tides, the same idea was independently rediscovered in the 1950s by Canadian sociologists to characterize the club memberships of arriviste suburbanites, in the 1960s by urbanist Jane Jacobs to laud neighborliness in the modern metropolis, in the 1970s by economist Glenn Loury to analyze the social legacy of slavery, and in the 1980s by French social theorist Pierre Bourdieu and by German economist Ekkehart Schlicht to underline the social and economic resources embodied in social networks. Sociologist James S. Coleman put the term firmly and finally on the intellectual agenda in the late 1980s, using it (as Hanifan had originally done) to highlight the social context of education.[13]

As this array of independent coinages indicates, social capital has both an individual and a collective aspect—a private face and a public face. First, individuals form connections that benefit our own interests. One pervasive strategem of ambitious job seekers is "networking," for most of us get our jobs because of whom we know, not what we know—that is, our social capital, not our human capital. Economic sociologist Ronald Burt has shown that executives with bounteous Rolodex files enjoy faster career advancement. Nor is the private return to social capital limited to economic rewards. As Claude S. Fischer, a sociologist of friendship, has noted, "Social networks are important in all our lives, often for finding jobs, more often for finding a helping hand, companionship, or a shoulder to cry on."[14]

If individual clout and companionship were all there were to social capital, we'd expect foresighted, self-interested individuals to invest the right amount of time and energy in creating or acquiring it. However, social capital also can have "externalities" that affect the wider community, so that not all the costs and benefits of social connections accrue to the person making the contact. As we shall see later in this book, a well-connected individual in a poorly connected society is not as productive as a well-connected individual in a well-connected society. And even a poorly connected individual may derive some of the spillover benefits from living in a well-connected community. If the crime rate in my neighborhood is lowered by neighbors keeping an eye on one another's homes, I benefit even if I personally spend most of my time on the road and never even nod to another resident on the street.

Social capital can thus be simultaneously a "private good" and a "public good." Some of the benefit from an investment in social capital goes to bystanders, while some of the benefit redounds to the immediate interest of the person making the investment. For example, service clubs, like Rotary or Lions, mobilize local energies to raise scholarships or fight disease at the same time that they provide members with friendships and business connections that pay off personally.

Social connections are also important for the rules of conduct that they sustain. Networks involve (almost by definition) mutual obligations; they are not interesting as mere "contacts." Networks of community engagement foster sturdy norms of reciprocity: I'll do this for you now, in the expectation that you (or perhaps someone else) will return the favor. "Social capital is akin to what Tom Wolfe called 'the favor bank' in his novel *The Bonfire of the Vanities,*" notes economist Robert Frank.[15] It was, however, neither a novelist nor an economist, but Yogi Berra who offered the most succinct definition of reciprocity: "If you don't go to somebody's funeral, they won't come to yours."

Sometimes, as in these cases, reciprocity is *specific:* I'll do this for you if you do that for me. Even more valuable, however, is a norm of *generalized* reciprocity: I'll do this for you without expecting anything specific back from you, in the confident expectation that someone else will do something for me down the road. The Golden Rule is one formulation of generalized reciprocity. Equally instructive is the T-shirt slogan used by the Gold Beach, Oregon, Volunteer Fire Department to publicize their annual fund-raising effort: "Come to our breakfast, we'll come to your fire." "We act on a norm of specific reciprocity," the firefighters seem to be saying, but onlookers smile because they recognize the underlying norm of generalized reciprocity—the firefighters will come even if *you* don't. When Blanche DuBois depended on the kindness of strangers, she too was relying on generalized reciprocity.

A society characterized by generalized reciprocity is more efficient than a distrustful society, for the same reason that money is more efficient than barter. If we don't have to balance every exchange instantly, we can get a lot more accomplished. Trustworthiness lubricates social life. Frequent interaction among a diverse set of people tends to produce a norm of generalized reciprocity. Civic engagement and social capital entail mutual obligation and responsibility for action. As L. J. Hanifan and his successors recognized, social networks and norms of reciprocity can facilitate cooperation for mutual benefit. When economic and political dealing is embedded in dense networks of social interaction, incentives for opportunism and malfeasance are reduced. This is why the diamond trade, with its extreme possibilities for fraud, is concentrated within close-knit ethnic enclaves. Dense social ties facilitate gossip and other valuable ways of cultivating reputation—an essential foundation for trust in a complex society.

Physical capital is not a single "thing," and different forms of physical capital are not interchangeable. An eggbeater and an aircraft carrier both appear as physical capital in our national accounts, but the eggbeater is not much use for national defense, and the carrier would not be much help with your morning omelet. Similarly, social capital—that is, social networks and the associated norms of reciprocity—comes in many different shapes and sizes with many different uses. Your extended family represents a form of social capital, as do your Sunday school class, the regulars who play poker on your commuter train, your college roommates, the civic organizations to which you belong, the Internet chat group in which you participate, and the network of professional acquaintances recorded in your address book.

Sometimes "social capital," like its conceptual cousin "community," sounds warm and cuddly. Urban sociologist Xavier de Souza Briggs, however, properly warns us to beware of a treacly sweet, "kumbaya" interpretation of social capital.[16] Networks and the associated norms of reciprocity are generally good for those inside the network, but the external effects of social capital are by no means always positive. It was social capital, for example, that enabled Timothy McVeigh to bomb the Alfred P. Murrah Federal Building in Oklahoma City. McVeigh's network of friends, bound together by a norm of reciprocity, enabled him to do what he could not have done alone. Similarly, urban gangs, NIMBY ("not in my backyard") movements, and power elites often exploit social capital to achieve ends that are antisocial from a wider perspective. Indeed, it is rhetorically useful for such groups to obscure the difference between the pro-social and antisocial consequences of community organizations. When Floridians objected to plans by the Ku Klux Klan to "adopt a highway," Jeff Coleman, grand wizard of the Royal Knights of the KKK, protested, "Really, we're just like the Lions or the Elks. We want to be involved in the community."[17]

Social capital, in short, can be directed toward malevolent, antisocial purposes, just like any other form of capital. (McVeigh also relied on physical capital, like the explosive-laden truck, and human capital, like bomb-making expertise, to achieve his purposes.) Therefore it is important to ask how the positive consequences of social capital—mutual support, cooperation, trust, institutional effectiveness—can be maximized and the negative manifestations—sectarianism, ethnocentrism, corruption—minimized. Toward this end, scholars have begun to distinguish many different forms of social capital.

Some forms involve repeated, intensive, multistranded networks—like a group of steelworkers who meet for drinks every Friday after work and see each other at mass on Sunday—and some are episodic, single stranded, and anonymous, like the faintly familiar face you see several times a month in the supermarket checkout line. Some types of social capital, like a Parent-Teacher Association, are formally organized, with incorporation papers, regular meetings, a written constitution, and connection to a national federation, whereas others, like a pickup basketball game, are more informal. Some forms of social capital, like a volunteer ambulance squad, have explicit public-regarding purposes; some, like a bridge club, exist for the private enjoyment of the members; and some, like the Rotary club mentioned earlier, serve both public and private ends.

Of all the dimensions along which forms of social capital vary, perhaps the most important is the distinction between *bridging* (or inclusive) and *bonding* (or exclusive).[18] Some forms of social capital are, by choice or necessity, inward looking and tend to reinforce exclusive identities and homogeneous groups. Examples of bonding social capital include ethnic fraternal organizations, church-based women's reading groups, and fashionable country clubs. Other networks are outward looking and encompass people across diverse social cleavages. Examples of bridging social capital include the civil rights movement, many youth service groups, and ecumenical religious organizations.

Bonding social capital is good for undergirding specific reciprocity and mobilizing solidarity. Dense networks in ethnic enclaves, for example, provide crucial social and psychological support for less fortunate members of the community, while furnishing start-up financing, markets, and reliable labor for local entrepreneurs. Bridging networks, by contrast, are better for linkage to external assets and for information diffusion. Economic sociologist Mark Granovetter has pointed out that when seeking jobs—or political allies—the "weak" ties that link me to distant acquaintances who move in different circles from mine are actually more valuable than the "strong" ties that link me to relatives and intimate friends whose sociological niche is very like my own. Bonding social capital is, as Xavier de Souza Briggs puts it, good for "getting by," but bridging social capital is crucial for "getting ahead."[19]

Moreover, bridging social capital can generate broader identities and reciprocity, whereas bonding social capital bolsters our narrower selves. In 1829 at the founding of a community lyceum in the bustling whaling port of New Bedford, Massachusetts, Thomas Greene eloquently expressed this crucial insight:

> We come from all the divisions, ranks and classes of society . . . to teach and to be taught in our turn. While we mingle together in these pursuits, we shall learn to know each other more intimately; we shall remove many of the prejudices which ignorance or partial acquaintance with each other had fostered. . . . In the parties and sects into which we are divided, we sometimes learn to love our brother at the expense of him whom we do not in so many respects regard as a brother. . . . We may return to our homes and firesides [from the lyceum] with kindlier feelings toward one another, because we have learned to know one another better.[20]

Bonding social capital constitutes a kind of sociological superglue, whereas bridging social capital provides a sociological WD-40. Bonding social capital, by creating strong in-group loyalty, may also create strong out-group antagonism, as Thomas Greene and his neighbors in New Bedford knew, and for that reason we might expect negative external effects to be more common with this form of social capital. Nevertheless, under many circumstances both bridging and bonding social capital can have powerfully positive social effects.

Many groups simultaneously bond along some social dimensions and bridge across others. The black church, for example, brings together people of the same race and religion across class lines. The Knights of Columbus was created to bridge cleavages among different ethnic communities while bonding along religious and gender lines. Internet chat groups may bridge across geography, gender, age, and religion, while being tightly homogeneous in education and ideology. In short, bonding and bridging are not "either-or" categories into which social networks can be neatly divided, but "more or less" dimensions along which we can compare different forms of social capital.

It would obviously be valuable to have distinct measures of the evolution of these various forms of social capital over time. However, like researchers on global warming, we must make do with the imperfect evidence that we can find, not merely lament its deficiencies. Exhaustive descriptions of social networks in America—even at a single point in time—do not exist. I have found no reliable, comprehensive, nationwide measures of social capital that neatly distinguish "bridgingness" and "bondingness." In our empirical account of recent social trends in this book, therefore, this distinction will be less prominent than I would prefer.

On the other hand, we must keep this conceptual differentiation at the back of our minds as we proceed, recognizing that bridging and bonding social capital are not interchangeable.

"Social capital" is to some extent merely new language for a very old debate in American intellectual circles. Community has warred incessantly with individualism for preeminence in our political hagiology. Liberation from ossified community bonds is a recurrent and honored theme in our culture, from the Pilgrims' storied escape from religious convention in the seventeenth century to the lyric nineteenth-century paeans to individualism by Emerson ("Self-Reliance"), Thoreau ("Civil Disobedience"), and Whitman ("Song of Myself") to Sherwood Anderson's twentieth-century celebration of the struggle against conformism by ordinary citizens in *Winesburg, Ohio* to the latest Clint Eastwood film. Even Alexis de Tocqueville, patron saint of American communitarians, acknowledged the uniquely democratic claim of individualism, "a calm and considered feeling which disposes each citizen to isolate himself from the mass of his fellows and withdraw into the circle of family and friends; with this little society formed to his taste, he gladly leaves the greater society to look after itself."[21]

Our national myths often exaggerate the role of individual heroes and understate the importance of collective effort. Historian David Hackett Fischer's gripping account of opening night in the American Revolution, for example, reminds us that Paul Revere's alarum was successful only because of networks of civic engagement in the Middlesex villages. Towns without well-organized local militia, no matter how patriotic their inhabitants, were AWOL from Lexington and Concord.[22] Nevertheless, the myth of rugged individualism continues to strike a powerful inner chord in the American psyche.

Debates about the waxing and waning of "community" have been endemic for at least two centuries. "Declensionist narratives"—postmodernist jargon for tales of decline and fall—have a long pedigree in our letters. We seem perennially tempted to contrast our tawdry todays with past golden ages. We apparently share this nostalgic predilection with the rest of humanity. As sociologist Barry Wellman observes,

> It is likely that pundits have worried about the impact of social change on communities ever since human beings ventured beyond their caves. . . . In the [past] two centuries many leading social commentators have been gainfully employed suggesting various ways in which large-scale social changes associated with the Industrial Revolution may have affected the structure and operation of communities. . . . This ambivalence about the consequences of large-scale changes continued well into the twentieth century. Analysts have kept asking if things have, in fact, fallen apart.[23]

At the conclusion of the twentieth century, ordinary Americans shared this sense of civic malaise. We were reasonably content about our economic prospects, hardly a surprise after an expansion of unprecedented length, but we were not equally convinced that we were on the right track morally or culturally. Of baby boomers interviewed in 1987, 53 percent thought their parents' generation was better in terms of "being a concerned citizen, involved in helping others in the community," as compared with only 21 percent who thought their own generation was better. Fully 77 percent said the nation was worse off because of "less involvement in community activities." In 1992 three-quarters of the U.S. workforce said that "the breakdown of community" and "selfishness" were "serious" or "extremely serious" problems in America. In 1996 only 8 percent of all Americans said that "the honesty and integrity of the average American" were improving, as compared with 50 percent of us who thought we were becoming less trustworthy. Those of us who said that people had become less civil over the preceding ten years outnumbered those who thought people had become more civil, 80 percent to 12 percent. In several surveys in 1999 two-thirds of Americans said that America's civic life had weakened in recent years, that social and moral values were higher when they were growing up, and that our society was focused more on the individual than the community. More than 80 percent said there should be more emphasis on community, even if that put more demands on individuals.[24] Americans' concern about weakening community bonds may be misplaced or exaggerated, but a decent respect for the opinion of our fellow citizens suggests that we should explore the issue more thoroughly.

It is emphatically not my view that community bonds in America have weakened steadily throughout our history—or even throughout the last hundred years. On the contrary, American history carefully examined is a story of ups and downs in civic engagement, *not just downs*—a story of collapse *and* of renewal. As I have already hinted in the opening pages of this book, within living memory the bonds of community in America were becoming stronger, not weaker, and as I shall argue in the concluding pages, it is within our power to reverse the decline of the last several decades.

Nevertheless, my argument is, at least in appearance, in the declensionist tradition, so it is important to avoid simple nostalgia. Precisely because the theme of this book might lend itself to gauzy self-deception, our methods must be transparent. Is life in communities as we enter the twenty-first century really so different after all from the reality of American communities in the 1950s and 1960s? One way of curbing nostalgia is to count things. Are club meetings really less crowded today than yesterday, or does it just seem so? Do we really know our neighbors less well than our parents did, or is our childhood recollection of neighborhood barbecues suffused with a golden glow of wishful reminiscence? Are friendly poker games less common now, or is it merely that we ourselves have outgrown poker? League bowling may be passé, but how about softball and soccer? Are strangers less trustworthy now? Are boomers and X'ers really less engaged in community life? After all, it was the preceding generation that was once scorned as "silent." Perhaps the younger generation today is no less engaged than their predecessors, but engaged in new ways. In the chapters that follow we explore these questions with the best available evidence. . . .

Before October 29, 1997, John Lambert and Andy Boschma knew each other only through their local bowling league at the Ypsi-Arbor Lanes in Ypsilanti, Michigan. Lambert, a sixty-four-year-old retired employee of the University of Michigan hospital, had been on a kidney transplant waiting list for three years when Boschma, a thirty-three-year-old accountant, learned casually of Lambert's need and unexpectedly approached him to offer to donate one of his own kidneys.

"Andy saw something in me that others didn't," said Lambert. "When we were in the hospital Andy said to me, 'John, I really like you and have a lot of respect for you. I wouldn't hesitate to do this all over again.' I got choked up." Boschma returned the feeling: "I obviously feel a kinship [with Lambert]. I cared about him before, but now I'm really rooting for him." This moving story speaks for itself, but the photograph that accompanied this report in the *Ann Arbor News* reveals that in addition to their differences in profession and generation, Boschma is white and Lambert is African American. That they bowled together made all the difference.[25] In small ways like this—and in larger ways, too—we Americans need to reconnect with one another. That is the simple argument of this book.

Notes

1. David Scott and Geoffrey Godbey, "Recreation Specialization in the Social World of Contract Bridge," *Journal of Leisure Research* 26 (1994): 275–295; Suzi Parker, "Elks, Lions May Go Way of the Dodo," *Christian Science Monitor,* August 24, 1998; John D. Cramer, "Relevance of Local NAACP Is Up for Debate," *Roanoke Times,* January 24, 1999; Dirk Johnson, "As Old Soldiers Die, V. F. W. Halls Fade Away," *New York Times,* September 6, 1999. I am grateful to Professor David Scott for information about the Glenn Valley Bridge Club; "Glenn Valley" is a pseudonym for a college town in central Pennsylvania.
2. Christine Wicker, "A Common Thread of Decency," *Dallas Morning News,* May 1, 1999; David Streitfeld, "The Last Chapter: After 50 Years, Vassar Ends Its Famed Book Sale," *Washington Post,* April 28, 1999, Cl; Caroline Louise Cole, "So Many New Uniforms, but So Few Musicians," *Boston Sunday Globe Northwest Weekly,* September 5, 1999, 1.
3. Jeffrey A. Charles, *Service Clubs in American Society: Rotary, Kiwanis, and Lions* (Urbana: University of Illinois Press, 1993), 157.
4. Eric Larrabee and Rolf Meyersohn, *Mass Leisure* (Glencoe, Ill.: Free Press, 1958), 359, as quoted in Foster Rhea Dulles, *A History of Recreation: America Learns to Play,* 2nd ed. (New York: Appleton-Century-Crofts, 1965), 390.
5. *Life,* February 21, 1964, 91, 93.

6. Robert E. Lane, *Political Life: Why People Get Involved in Politics* (Glencoe, Ill.: Free Press, 1959), 94; Daniel Bell and Virginia Held, "The Community Revolution," *The Public Interest,* 16 (1969): 142.
7. Richard A. Brody, "The Puzzle of Political Participation in America," in *The New American Political System,* ed. Anthony King (Washington, D.C.: American Enterprise Institute for Public Policy Research, 1978).
8. George H. Gallup, *The Gallup Poll: Public Opinion 1935–1971* (New York: Random House, 1972); Karlyn Bowman, "Do You Want to Be President?," *Public Perspective* 8 (February/March 1997): 40; Robert E. Lane, "The Politics of Consensus in an Age of Affluence," *American Political Science Review* 59 (December 1965): 879; and Richard G. Niemi, John Mueller, and Tom W. Smith, *Trends in Public Opinion* (New York: Greenwood Press, 1989), 303.
9. See Thomas R. Rochon, *Culture Moves: Ideas, Activism, and Changing Values* (Princeton, N.J.: Princeton University Press, 1998), xiii–xiv.
10. Doug McAdam, *Freedom Summer* (New York: Oxford University Press, 1988), 14–15.
11. James Q. Wilson, "Why Are We Having a Wave of Violence?" *The New York Times Magazine,* May 19, 1968, 120.
12. Lyda Judson Hanifan, "The Rural School Community Center," *Annals of the American Academy of Political and Social Science* 67 (1916): 130–138, quotation at 130.
13. John R. Seeley, Alexander R. Sim, and Elizabeth W. Loosley, *Crestwood Heights: A Study of the Culture of Suburban Life* (New York: Basic Books, 1956); Jane Jacobs, *The Death and Life of Great American Cities* (New York: Random House, 1961); Glenn Loury, "A Dynamic Theory of Racial Income Differences," in *Women, Minorities, and Employment Discrimination,* ed. P. A. Wallace and A. LeMund (Lexington, Mass.: Lexington Books, 1977), 153–188; Pierre Bourdieu, "Forms of Capital," in *Handbook of Theory and Research for the Sociology of Education,* ed. John G. Richardson (New York: Greenwood Press, 1983), 241–258; Ekkehart Schlicht, "Cognitive Dissonance in Economics," in *Normengeleitetes Verhalten in den Sozialwissenschaften* (Berlin: Duncker and Humblot, 1984), 61–81; James S. Coleman, "Social Capital in the Creation of Human Capital," *American Journal of Sociology* 94 (1988): S95–S120; and James S. Coleman, *Foundations of Social Theory* (Cambridge, Mass.: Harvard University Press, 1990). See also George C. Homans, *Social Behavior: Its Elementary Forms* (New York: Harcourt, Brace & World, 1961), 378–98.
14. Ronald S. Burt, *Structural Holes: The Social Structure of Competition* (Cambridge, Mass.: Harvard University Press, 1992); Ronald S. Burt, "The Contingent Value of Social Capital," *Administrative Science Quarterly* 42 (1997): 339–365; and Ronald S. Burt, "The Gender of Social Capital," *Rationality & Society* 10 (1998): 5–46; Claude S. Fischer, "Network Analysis and Urban Studies," in *Networks and Places: Social Relations in the Urban Setting,* ed. Claude S. Fischer (New York: Free Press, 1977), 19; James D. Montgomery, "Social Networks and Labor-Market Outcomes: Toward an Economic Analysis," *American Economic Review* 81 (1991): 1408–1418, esp. table 1.
15. Robert Frank in private conversation.
16. Xavier de Souza Briggs, "Social Capital and the Cities: Advice to Change Agents," *National Civic Review* 86 (summer 1997): 111–117.
17. *U.S. News & World Report* (August 4, 1997): 18.
18. Ross Gittell and Avis Vidal, *Community Organizing: Building Social Capital as a Development Strategy* (Thousand Oaks, Calif.: Sage, 1998), 8.
19. Mark S. Granovetter, "The Strength of Weak Ties," *American Journal of Sociology* 78 (1973): 1360–1380; Xavier de Souza Briggs, "Doing Democracy Up Close: Culture, Power, and Communication in Community Building," *Journal of Planning Education and Research* 18 (1998): 1–13.
20. As quoted in Richard D. Brown, "The Emergence of Voluntary Associations in Massachusetts," *Journal of Voluntary Action Research* 2 (April 1973): 64–73, at 69.
21. Alexis de Tocqueville, *Democracy in America,* ed. J. P. Mayer, trans. George Lawrence (Garden City, N.Y.: Doubleday, 1969), 506. See also Wilson Carey McWilliams, *The Idea of Fraternity in America* (Berkeley: University of California Press, 1973), and Thomas Bender, *Community and Social Change in America* (Baltimore, Md.: Johns Hopkins University Press, 1978).

22. David Hackett Fischer, *Paul Revere's Ride* (New York: Oxford University Press, 1994).
23. Barry Wellman, "The Community Question Re-Evaluated," in *Power, Community, and the City,* Michael Peter Smith, ed. (New Brunswick, N.J.: Transaction 1988), 81–107, quotation at 82–83.
24. *The Public Perspective* 8 (December/January 1997): 64; Robert Wuthnow, "Changing Character of Social Capital in the United States," in *The Dynamics of Social Capital in Comparative Perspective,* Robert D. Putnam, ed. (2000, forthcoming); *The Public Perspective* 10 (April/May 1999); 15, *Wall Street Journal,* June 24, 1999, A12; Mark J. Penn, "The Community Consensus," *Blueprint: Ideas for a New Century* (spring 1999).
25. Emma Jackson, "Buddy Had Kidney to Spare," *Ann Arbor News* (January 5, 1998).

CASE STUDY 5

Introduction

Putnam's work has not only produced a lively intellectual debate among scholars, it has also generated discussion among many outside of academia about the health and direction of American politics. For many, the main question that Putnam's work has raised is what can be done to rebuild social capital and improve democracy in America. In the final chapter of *Bowling Alone,* Putnam addresses this question by calling for "leaders and activists in every sphere of American life" to seek innovative ways to respond. Looking across the states, one can find a large number of organizations, from neighborhood schools to national associations, that have become aware of the problem identified by Putnam and have begun to introduce projects to encourage greater civic participation.

In the case study that follows, Mark Warren describes the efforts of the Industrial Areas Foundation (IAF) to build social capital in San Antonio, Texas, as a strategy to reshape the city's politics. The IAF is an organization that was founded in Chicago, Illinois, in the 1930s, by Saul Alinsky, a nationally known community organizer. Warren's essay traces the history of the IAF and explains how its Texas chapter, under the leadership of Ernesto Cortes, rewrote some of Alinsky's strategies to develop a strong, community-based organization. The key to Cortes's success was in changing the organization's strategy so that it focused on building ongoing cooperative relations among individuals and groups, rather than trying to mobilize citizens on particular political issues. In other words, Cortes focused on building social capital. The IAF was then able to use this social capital to influence San Antonio's politics.

The case study illustrates how organizations can teach democratic skills to individuals who have previously remained outside of politics. To build the IAF in San Antonio, Cortes worked closely with the Catholic churches that serve the Mexican American community. But his focus was not just on church officials; rather, he sought to build networks with the lay people who were active in church affairs, training them to become community leaders and getting them to work together to promote shared values. The case study demonstrates the important role that social capital can play in politics, and it provides some food for thought on how local groups may be able to rebuild their communities to revitalize democracy.

Questions to Consider

As you read the excerpt from Warren's book, these are some questions to consider:

- What does Warren mean when he writes that Alinsky's book *Rules for Radicals* is no longer relevant? How did Cortes rewrite that book?
- How did the IAF build social capital in San Antonio? What strategies did its leader use to get more people involved?
- Given the nation's tradition of separating church and state, do you think it is appropriate to rebuild social capital by relying on local churches? Why or why not?
- In general, what role do you think the government, schools, and other organizations should play to encourage greater civic participation? What do you think could be done to increase participation in your community?

A Theology of Organizing: From Alinsky to the Modern IAF

Mark R. Warren

On a winter's day in 1975 George Ozuna's grandmother asked him to accompany her shopping in downtown San Antonio.[1] The high school senior got his shoes and began the long walk from the Hispanic south side of town to Joske's Department Store, the largest retail establishment in the city. When the pair arrived, George immediately realized something was going on. Hundreds of Hispanic grandmothers, housewives, and churchgoers had gathered outside the store. They entered en masse and began trying on clothes. And they didn't stop. They continued to try on clothes all day, grinding store operations to a halt. The protesters were all members of Catholic parishes active in Communities Organized for Public Service (COPS), a new organization fighting to improve conditions in San Antonio's impoverished and long-neglected south and west side neighborhoods. While they disrupted business, COPS leaders and its organizer, Ernesto Cortes, Jr., met with the store's owner. They demanded that he use his influence on San Antonio's city council to pass COPS' $100 million budget proposal for infrastructural improvements and increased services to Mexican American neighborhoods.

The next day COPS supporters disrupted banking operations on a busy Friday afternoon at the central branch of Frost National Bank by continuously exchanging pennies for dollars and vice versa. Upstairs COPS leaders and organizer Cortes met with Tom Frost, Jr., one of the most influential men in San Antonio. The Joske Department Store manager had refused COPS' demand for assistance, and now Frost, although polite, declined to call the mayor as well. Cortes, as the organizer, was supposed to let COPS leaders do the negotiating; but he watched them fold as Frost stalled.

As Cortes later recounted in a speech to farm workers, "My leaders freeze, and they don't do anything.... I believe in the iron rule of organizing: never do anything for anybody that they can do for themselves. But they ain't doing for themselves! They're collapsing; they're folding. Our people are downstairs waiting with no instruction, no word and they don't know what to do. I decide I've got to do something, so I move my chair over to Mr. Frost, and he's got a blood vessel that's exposed, and I focus on it and I look at it. I just keep moving, he moves away, and I move closer with the chair.

Then finally he says something, and I say, 'Mr. Frost, that's a bunch of balderdash. You're the most arrogant man I've ever met.' And he gets up. We have a priest there and Mr. Frost says, 'Father, you better teach your people some manners and some values.' And finally the priest says, 'Well, Mr. Frost, I don't know about that, but you know, you're apathetic and I think that's much worse.' "[2]

Despite little initial success, COPS continued its protests and the tide began to turn. Prime time television crews started covering the actions, scaring away paying customers. Pressure mounted on business leaders. The head of the Chamber of Commerce came to negotiate with Cortes. But the organizer made him wait until COPS leaders could be rounded up to participate. Through the organizing strategy discussed later in this chapter, COPS eventually won the city's commitment for $100 million worth of desperately needed improvements to its neighborhoods. For the first time, Mexican Americans had flexed their political muscle in San Antonio, and they gained new drainage projects, sidewalks, parks, and libraries for their efforts.

Many Hispanics were surprised to see the Catholic Church become involved in such militant tactics. But according to George Ozuna, his grandmother and her parish friends knew exactly what they were doing. "I'm doing this because we're winning. Your grandfather and I came from Mexico to try to build something. But we were losers. There were things that always worked to keep us down. In Mexico, it was the government taking away our animals and chickens. Here it was poverty again. Grandfather working at Finesilver with no union. All my life I've worked very hard to win, to find something where you're really winning. We've always lost. Now I'm winning. *We're* winning. And we have a say-so in what's going on. And we're going to have more of a say-so."[3]

Militant, direct action tactics geared towards winning put COPS squarely in the tradition started by Saul Alinsky in founding the Industrial Areas Foundation (IAF) in the 1930s. Alinsky codified many of these principles in his books *Rules for Radicals* and *Reveille for Radicals.* After his encounter with Cortes, the banker Tom Frost bought a case of these books and distributed them among the power elite of San Antonio so that they could better prepare to deal with COPS. COPS and the IAF are still known for these militant tactics. The casual observer who sees only these tactics, however, will miss the fundamental changes to Alinsky's way of organizing that Cortes began to make with his work in San Antonio. Twenty years after the tie-up at his bank, Frost, now an influential figure in Texas state politics as well, gave this author his last remaining copy of *Rules for Radicals,* claiming it was no longer relevant. According to Frost, "I told Ernie [Cortes] he's now working out of another book. And I asked him just what is that book? Ernie said he's still writing it."[4]

This chapter is the story of that new book. It starts by examining the organizing efforts of Saul Alinsky in the working class neighborhoods of Chicago in the thirties. Considered the "father of community organizing" Alinsky was the first to attempt to mobilize industrial workers and their families into direct action where they lived, as opposed to where they worked. Although Alinsky's organizing projects scored impressive victories, most were short-lived or failed to maintain the progressive vision and participatory character upon which they were founded. Trained under the IAF in the early seventies, Cortes began organizing COPS using Alinsky's methods. Almost immediately, though, he began to revise Alinsky's approach. This chapter explores those changes, showing how Cortes and his colleagues in the IAF developed a new model of organizing to overcome the limitations of Alinsky's methods. The modern IAF would come to base its local organizations in the institutions and values of faith communities. Its organizers would become a permanent feature of local affiliates using relational organizing to reach beyond pastors to foster the participation of lay leaders. And the IAF would come to link these leaders across racial lines, attempting to build broad-based organizations that would help ensure a commitment to the common good, rather than narrow group interests. While Alinsky took a rather utilitarian view of churches as repositories of money and people to be mobilized, the modern IAF developed a close collaboration with people of faith, fusing religious traditions and power politics into a theology of organizing.

Saul Alinsky and the Origins of the IAF

Saul Alinsky founded his first community organization, the Back of the Yards Neighborhood Council (BYNC), on Chicago's southwest side in 1939.[5] Alinsky formed the organization both to support the union organizing drive of the Congress of Industrial Organizations (CIO) in the nearby stockyards as well as to address the broader needs of the impoverished community. Upton Sinclair had made the Back of the Yards neighborhood famous in *The Jungle,* his expose of filth and degradation in the largely immigrant community surrounding the meat packing industry. Catholic Bishop Bernard J. Sheil played a pivotal role in the creation of the BYNC by helping to convince local pastors to support the CIO unions and the new neighborhood organization. Although the community consisted of a diverse group of white ethnics, 90 percent of them were Catholics. Union leaders, small merchants and local churches worked together in the BYNC, using militant tactics—like sit-downs and boycotts—drawn from the CIO repertoire. Originally seen as a threat by Chicago's Democratic machine, the BYNC early on won many concessions from city hall to improve local services.[6]

After his initial success in Chicago, Alinsky wanted to extend his work to other parts of the country. Through the BYNC project, Alinsky developed a close relationship with Bishop Sheil and the philanthropist Marshall Field III. With their support Alinsky founded the Industrial Areas Foundation (IAF) in 1940 to raise money to assist his efforts to organize in other communities. The Industrial Areas Foundation owes its somewhat anachronistic name to BYNC's roots in the CIO tradition. It was meant to be a foundation that organized in the areas (neighborhoods) surrounding industry.[7]

Alinsky launched several organizing projects in the late forties and fifties. He began hiring and training organizers, setting up projects in Lackawanna, New York, Butte, Montana, and the Chelsea section of Manhattan. Alinsky also worked with Fred Ross to organize Mexican Americans in California through the Community Service Organization, where Cesar Chavez (later the president of the United Farm Workers Union) first trained as an organizer. Catholic pastors invited Alinsky to set up the Organization for the Southwest Council (OSC) to stem racial tensions and violence in southwest Chicago in 1959, and to start another project on the northwest side. Except for the Chelsea project which folded quickly, these organizations all scored significant successes.[8]

Alinsky received widespread public recognition in this period through his work with The Woodlawn Organization (TWO) on the black south side of Chicago. In 1960 a coalition of local ministers asked Alinsky to set up a community organization in Woodlawn, near the University of Chicago. Woodlawn had recently undergone dramatic racial turnover. Within the ten years between 1950 and 1960, Woodlawn's residents changed from being 86 percent white to 86 percent black. TWO represented an important new departure for Alinsky in two ways: Protestant churches supported an Alinsky project for the first time; and Alinsky attempted to organize in a large black community. TWO made use of picketing and boycotts to stop exploitative practices of local landlords and merchants. It also organized to stop plans by the city and the University of Chicago for urban renewal in Woodlawn. Drawing inspiration from the freedom rides in the South, TWO undertook a massive voter registration drive to force the city to give the group representation on a school board and on an antipoverty agency. Through its activities, TWO won improvements in sanitation, public health procedures, and police practices. TWO's victories became well-publicized. The publicity launched Alinsky onto the lecture circuit and generated many requests from local activists for Alinsky to come to their cities and start IAF projects.[9]

After hearing about Alinsky's work in Woodlawn, an interracial group of clergy invited Alinsky to organize in the black community in Rochester, New York. The African American community in Rochester had been largely excluded from employment opportunities at the massive Eastman Kodak plant there, and its neighborhoods were neglected by the city. With Alinsky's help, black clergy formed FIGHT (Freedom, Integration, God, Honor, Today). Alinsky appointed Edward T. Chambers, a white ex-seminarian who got his start with the IAF in Lackawanna, as the head of a staff of black organizers. Reverend Franklyn D. R. Florence, a dynamic black minister fresh from civil rights organizing in the South, became attracted to the potential of the Alinsky model for black power and became FIGHT's president. FIGHT eventually won a pledge from Kodak for a job recruitment and training program for African Americans. When the company reneged on this promise, Alinsky developed a new tactic. He launched a well-publicized campaign that succeeded in gaining control of stock proxies to pressure Eastman Kodak to fulfill its pledge.[10]

In order to expand his efforts, Alinsky set up a national institute to more systematically train organizers and neighborhood leaders. He appointed Ed Chambers who had cut his teeth with FIGHT's work in Rochester, to direct the institute, called by the Industrial Areas Foundation name itself. Moreover, through the Kodak experience Alinsky saw the need to develop allies among the middle classes, and even to organize them directly. In the early seventies he launched his last major initiative, the Citizen Action Program, as a broad metropolitan and multiclass organization to address rising concerns about pollution in Chicago.[11]

Saul Alinsky died in 1972, leaving an organizing legacy that inspired a wide range of populist efforts, from farm worker and welfare organizing to consumer advocacy.[12] Alinsky's legacy derived from the model of organizing he first elaborated in his 1946 book, *Reveille for Radicals.* Alinsky saw community organizations as political institutions with three basic characteristics: indigenous leadership and citizen participation; financial independence; and a commitment to defend local interests while avoiding divisive issues. Alinsky saw conflict as inherent in society, and his community organizations used confrontation as a means to gain recognition and forge compromises with power holders. Alinsky further elaborated his views on organizing in *Rules for Radicals,* published in 1971. In the midst of the highly ideological politics of the antiwar and Black Power movements, Alinsky argued that community organizations must base themselves on the self-interest of individuals and communities in a pragmatic and nonideological manner. These organizations should remain independent from parties and should not endorse candidates. Instead, they should focus on citizen participation through their own independent structures.

Alinsky gained a radical reputation through his efforts to empower the poor and because of his disruptive tactics. But he was not a revolutionary. Alinsky considered the political system, despite its corruption and bias toward the rich, to be open to change if people could organize to demand inclusion. Unfortunately, the only form of inclusion open to many poor communities was through the patronage machine of local bosses, like Mayor Richard Daley in Alinsky's Chicago. Alinsky sought to connect people to politics in a different way, by establishing independent political power. Through IAF organizations citizens could confront the machine and other public and private authorities and negotiate on behalf of their neighborhoods. The establishment of militant, independent organizations in poor communities represented a radical departure in American politics. But Alinsky's acceptance of power politics meant that he did not call for the transformation of the political system itself. He simply wanted to open the system up to a new interest group, that is, political organizations of the poor.

Alinsky insisted that political organizations should be based upon the existing social institutions of a community, like churches, block clubs, and small businesses. These institutions offered the necessary resources to build independent political power. They provided finances for the organization, respected institutional leaders who already had roots in the community, and an organized base of followers who could be mobilized by such leaders to participate in the militant tactics for which Alinsky was so well known. Alinsky's organizations in this period were really coalitions of organizations. Unions, block clubs, and small businesses joined churches to make up the Back of the Yards Neighborhood Council in Chicago, while the black organizations TWO and FIGHT consisted almost entirely of churches. Member institutions sent official representatives to organization meetings and conventions, where they debated formal resolutions and elected officers.[13]

Alinsky was not particularly interested in the culture and belief systems embedded in the churches he recruited. When Reverend John Egan, a Chicago priest who became a long-term supporter of the IAF, advocated more discussion of religious values within IAF organizations, Alinsky responded, "You take care of the religion, Jack, we'll do the organizing."[14] Nor did he often try to reach beyond the established institutional authorities to cultivate and sustain political leadership among the membership of these institutions. The job of Alinsky's organizers was to forge coalitions of institutions, get the projects up and running, and then leave, passing on the responsibility for organizational development to the institutional leaders.

Despite Alinsky's impressive achievements, and the significant legacy he left to American populist organizing, the local organizations he built largely failed to sustain themselves as participatory political institutions. After a string of early successes, Alinsky's first project, the Back of the Yards Neighborhood Council, was gradually taken over by a small group of leaders. The council degenerated in the fifties and sixties into a conservative organization, cooperating closely with Chicago's Mayor Daley. Although Alinsky had taken steps to promote interracial understanding in segregated Chicago, by the fifties the council had come to oppose black demands for racial integration of its neighborhood. In 1968, the council endorsed George Wallace for President, prompting Alinsky to comment, "this is why I've seriously thought of moving back into the area and organizing a new movement to overthrow the one I built twenty-five years ago."[15]

While Alinsky's projects in black communities did not become reactionary, they did lose their grass-roots participatory character. In the sixties, The Woodlawn Organization (TWO) on Chicago's south side became more involved in administering services to the community than in continuing to organize broad participation. TWO set up an innovative job-training program developed with gang leaders as well as an experimental school program. Opposition from the city eventually ended both programs. In the late sixties, TWO launched community development efforts. In a progression common to many activist organizations, as TWO moved toward economic development, it lost its more participatory side as well as its ability to be an independent community advocate.[16] Meanwhile, FIGHT in Rochester also shifted its efforts to economic development programs, taking on administrative responsibilities for these efforts. FIGHT suffered a factional struggle that debilitated the organization, which formally dissolved in the early seventies.[17]

By the early seventies, the IAF could count many individual successes, at least in the short run. But neither the local organizations it formed, nor the IAF itself, had found a way to establish long-lasting institutions that could sustain broad participation and an independent base of power for poor communities. When Alinsky died in 1972, he left a compelling organizing model that served to inspire a new generation of activists. But he also left a weak institution. At the time of Alinsky's death, the IAF had only two professional organizers and a secretary on staff.[18]

Upon Alinsky's death, Ed Chambers took over as director of the IAF, and began to make some significant changes to Alinsky's organizing approach. Chambers had worked for Alinsky in Lackawanna, Chicago, and Rochester, and had been the director of the IAF training institute when it formed in 1969. While Alinsky was the agitator and charismatic orator, Chambers was the classic organization man. To stabilize the IAF's precarious financial situation, Chambers moved to extend contracts with community organizations after the initial two to three year start-up period. Alinsky, in *Reveille for Radicals,* had argued that the IAF should break its ties with these organizations after four or five years at the most. Chambers wanted to develop long-term relationships with local organizations, both to keep the flow of money into the IAF, and also because he thought community organizations needed the kind of extended training that the IAF could provide. Chambers also systematized the training of organizers themselves and promoted the professionalization of the occupation by upgrading pay. While Alinsky liked to run a one-man show, Chambers set up a cabinet of senior organizers to provide collective supervision to the IAF's efforts. In 1979 Chambers moved the IAF's headquarters to New York, after Cardinal Cody broke the ties between the IAF and the Archdiocese of Chicago that stretched back to the thirties.[19]

When Chambers established long-term contracts to supply organizers to local affiliates, he put the IAF on a new road that held out the possibility of mutual interaction and collaboration between professional organizers on the one hand and community leaders from local organizations on the other. Alinsky had an instrumental interest in the kinds of resources churches and other social institutions could provide to organizing efforts. The ex-seminarian Chambers, with his theological training, began to see religious leaders as more than the instruments for mobilizing resources. He thought their ideas and traditions might provide important values to sustain participatory politics. Although Chambers had the germ of these ideas in his head, the new model of organizing would be initiated in practice through the organizing work of Ernesto Cortes. Shortly after Alinsky's death, Cortes began to organize Communities Organized for Public Service (COPS) in San Antonio. Through that effort, and in coordination with Chambers and IAF efforts in other parts of the country, Cortes began to write the new book on organizing to which the banker Tom Frost alluded.

Communities Organized for Public Service (COPS)

Ernesto Cortes, Jr., arrived back to his hometown of San Antonio in 1973, fresh from his training in Alinsky's Industrial Areas Foundation. His goal was to build an organization to give voice to poor and working Mexican Americans in San Antonio's forgotten west and south sides. Within a few short years he and a group of committed Catholic clergy and lay leaders had built a powerful organization, which broke the Anglo elite's monopoly on political power in San Antonio. In the process, the modern IAF came to base its organizing work almost exclusively in religious congregations and to reach deeply into religious networks to build organizations based upon religious values as much as material interests. By doing so, the IAF began to build organizations meant to last and to maintain participation over time.

While Hispanics made up a majority of San Antonio's nearly one million residents by the early seventies, they were almost entirely excluded from political representation at city hall. The Good Government League (GGL), a small association of wealthy Anglos from the north side, had dominated city politics since the fifties and normally placed only one handpicked Hispanic representative on the city council it controlled. While concentrating on Anglo development on the north side, the city neglected Hispanic neighborhoods on the west and south sides of town. Roads there were often unpaved, sidewalks nonexistent, schools poor, and floods a common and deadly occurrence. Mexican Americans were concentrated in lower paying, mainly service occupations. The city displayed an old-fashioned colonial atmosphere, as the growing Hispanic community, reaching a majority of the city's population by 1970, remained a "sleeping giant."[20]

Cortes, however, thought the sleeping giant might be ready to wake up. Cortes had been involved in several efforts to mobilize San Antonio Hispanics in the sixties. In 1966 he worked to elect the Mexican American Johnny Alaniz to the Bexar County Commissioners Court. If Alaniz had won, a coalition between Hispanics and progressive whites would have become a majority of the court. But the city's elite used overtly racist advertising, picturing a black hand descending over San Antonio, to defeat the coalition.[21] The failures of political mobilization in the sixties led Cortes to seek training with Alinsky to find a more effective way to empower Hispanics. When he returned, the Good Government League was starting to show some cracks in its monolithic hold over the city. Builders and developers wanted to push the fairly passive city government to take aggressive action to support growth. Fed up with the old guard in the League, they backed independent candidates for mayor and city council in the 1973 election. Their candidates for mayor and several council seats won the election, signifying the possibility of new opportunities for Hispanic empowerment.

At first, Cortes followed Alinsky's methods and attempted to recruit to COPS a variety of neighborhood social organizations, including churches, PTAs, and social clubs. About twenty-five Catholic parishes, however, soon emerged as the bedrock of COPS, while the other institutions proved too unstable or unsuited for the ensuing political conflict. The Catholic Church hierarchy provided both funds and encouragement of pastoral support for COPS. Initial funding of $40,000 came from a variety of religious denominations, including Unitarians and Methodists. But the Archdiocese contributed $4,000 itself, with the Catholic Society of Jesus (the Jesuits) giving another $3,000. Meanwhile, the U.S. Catholic Bishops' funding agency for social action, the Campaign for Human Development, provided $15,000, beginning a long and consistent tradition of support for COPS and IAF affiliates in Texas and around the country.[22] As COPS became established, the largest part of its budget came from dues paid by member parishes, the funding principle followed by all IAF affiliates. Meanwhile, San Antonio's Archbishop Furey publicly endorsed the COPS effort and gave his blessing to priests who became active in the organization. Auxiliary Bishop Patricio Flores served on the sponsoring committee for the effort.

Support by the Archdiocese of San Antonio for COPS represented the culmination of several trends both in the larger Catholic Church and in the diocese of San Antonio. Vatican II heralded a greater openness in the church, encouraged lay participation, and pushed the church to address concerns for social justice and the plight of the poor. In many ways the diocese of San Antonio was ahead of these trends. Archbishop Lucey had involved the diocese in social reform during his tenure from 1941 to 1968. Known as the "pink bishop," he lent support to labor strikes and school desegregation, and agitated for federal antipoverty money for San Antonio. Archbishop Furey, and Furey's personal secretary Grahmann (who later became Bishop of Dallas), continued Lucey's activist tradition through their support of COPS.[23]

In addition to the support of San Antonio's bishops, a movement of Hispanic clergy contributed to the development of COPS. Historically, the American Catholic Church served the religious needs of Mexican Americans in the Southwest through missions. Many San Antonio churches began as open-air meeting places. Church buildings and the consolidation of parishes came quite late, for many not until the fifties and sixties.[24] The diocese did not staff many of these parishes in the west and south sides, leaving those duties to religious orders. Several of these order priests would become early COPS leaders. In addition, the diocese ordained very few Mexican American priests, only seven in the 250 years up to the sixties.[25] During the sixties, however, Hispanic priests and seminarians began to organize themselves, forming a group called PADRES.[26] Members of PADRES in San Antonio wanted to initiate a diocesan presence in the west side, and they wanted the church to address the poverty and discrimination faced by Hispanics. Their titular leader was Patricio Flores, appointed Auxiliary Bishop of San Antonio in 1970 and Archbishop in 1977, the first Mexican American bishop in the United States. Supported by Bishops Flores and Furey, young Hispanic priests like David Garcia and Albert Benavides took up posts on the west side and became important leaders of COPS. They joined the Jesuit priest Edmundo Rodriguez, the pastor of Our Lady of Guadalupe Church on the near west side, who was Cortes' first ally when he arrived back in San Antonio.

Tapping the funds, legitimacy, and institutional leaders from the Catholic Church conformed to traditional Alinsky methods. But in organizing COPS, Cortes began to make a profound innovation. He went beyond the priests and the usually male presidents of parish councils and began to reach more deeply into the networks of lay leaders that spread out from the church. Parishes on the south and west sides served as the center for a variety of social activities. Cortes met with over one thousand residents active in some way in the community. He started with priests, got the names of potential supporters from them, and moved through the community. He recruited leaders, now mostly women, from the ranks of parish councils, fund-raising committees, and churchgoers who were active in PTAs and social clubs. Many were members of the Guadalupanas, a Catholic association of Hispanic women. Andres Sarabia, the first COPS president, and its last male president, was head of his parish council at Holy Family. Beatrice Gallego, the second COPS president, was a PTA leader and active in the Council of Catholic Women in St. James parish. These new COPS leaders were also different from the Hispanic activists with whom Cortes had worked in the sixties. They were not individual activists committed to the cause. Instead, they were connected to parishes and rooted in the dense networks of extended families and friends that constituted San Antonio's Hispanic neighborhoods. Rather than activists committed to the cause, COPS leaders cared primarily about the needs of their families and the religion that bound them together.

Reflecting on the early years of COPS, Cortes explains that "we tried to bust the stereotypes . . . to see leaders not necessarily as someone who could speak or persuade a crowd. We wanted to see leaders as people who have networks, relationships with other people." These leaders were often women, and many of them were excited about the opportunities the new organization offered. According to Cortes, "Many of the women leaders were real powerhouses in their private families. They had a lot to say about who does what. But that's not enough. The public side of them didn't get developed because they are invisible outside of the home. They may have gravitated to leadership in our organization because of the need to develop this aspect of their personality. We offered them the opportunity."[27]

Once Cortes found someone whom he thought had potential to be a COPS leader, he could be dogged in pursuit. He first met Beatrice Cortez at a parents meeting about the closing of a neighborhood school.[28] Mrs. Cortez was an office worker at the time, married to an electrician, and active in her church, St. Patrick's. She became angry when she heard that the San Antonio Independent School District planned to close her children's elementary school, as well as two others in the community. The school department planned to take the money saved by the school closing to help fund a new administration building. Mrs. Cortez came to a meeting to discuss the matter along with seventy other parents. Inexperienced in politics, and fearful of speaking out, Mrs. Cortez tried to avoid the organizer Cortes at the parents meeting. "There was a man, Ernie, sitting next to me at the meeting. He encouraged me to push for us to take some action. So I was asked to speak with school officials. But I was afraid because I had never spoken in public before. Ernie met me outside the meeting and pinned me down to agree to speak." The parents were not able to stop the school closing. But they did stop the construction of the new administration building and got the school department to use some of the money saved to reduce class sizes in other neighborhood schools. And Mrs. Cortez was hooked. "I told Ernie to teach me everything. I stopped being a victim. Now you know what's going on because you're making it happen. But the quid pro quo with COPS was that I had to bring my church into the organization." Along with other parishioners who became involved over the school issue, Mrs. Cortez did get St. Patrick's to join COPS. In 1981 Mrs. Cortez became COPS' fourth president.

In COPS the IAF began to develop a strategy different from Alinsky's to recruit lay leaders, a strategy the IAF would come to call relational organizing. Rather than mobilize people around an issue, Cortes engaged people's value commitments to their community. He got community leaders to talk with each other about community needs first, before identifying an issue around which to act. Specific plans for action emerged out of conversations at the bottom, rather than issues identified by activists at the top. Relational organizing worked to bring community leaders together to find a common ground for action and to develop the capacity to act in the interests of the broader community.

By reaching beyond institutional leaders, the IAF unleashed the deeper capacities of the communities within these churches. Once women like Beatrice Cortez began to learn to assert themselves in public leadership, IAF organizations could become more dynamic and expansive. Compared to Alinsky's projects, which often stagnated eventually under the same small pool of institutional leaders, COPS had a method to create broader participation. By continuing to recruit from these networks, the IAF generated a continual stream of new leaders to bring fresh energy and new ideas into local organizations.

To unleash the leadership capabilities of these women, however, the IAF needed to innovate again. The organization could not be led by a coalition of official representatives from member social institutions, as Alinsky's organizations had been run. Room had to be made for the leadership of the lay parishioners Cortes was recruiting, many of whom were women traditionally excluded from official church positions. As a result, COPS created a hybrid organizational form. Its members were institutions, that is, churches. But the organization was not a coalition, composed of institutional representatives. Its leadership was drawn more broadly from the membership of those institutions, and leaders operated together in a single organization. COPS' structure allowed member parishes and neighborhood leaders to take action for the needs of their own particular neighborhoods at the same time as the organization could also act with a single will, as something more than the sum of its parts.

Despite widespread poverty, San Antonio's Hispanic neighborhoods offered an especially rich social fabric upon which to ground IAF organizing. In part, segregation meant that it was difficult for upwardly mobile Hispanics to move out, so communities remained more intact as well as more diverse socioeconomically.[29] Furthermore, San Antonio's Hispanic community drew its population mainly from rural Texas, not Mexico. In 1980 only 12 percent of San Antonio's Mexican Americans were foreign-born.[30] As new residents arrived in San Antonio, they often joined family or friends from the same hometown, people who could help them get established. With a modest amount of new immigration, San Antonio's Hispanic community maintained relatively stable social ties.

Hispanic cultural traditions like *compadre* and *comadre,* literally cofather and comother, also contributed to the strength of neighborhood networks. Parents appointed close friends as *compadre* and *comadre,* their child's godparents. Yet, as the name suggests, the relationship reflects and reinforces the tie between the natural parents and the godparents. The church serves as the nexus of these personal relations, as the godparents are selected for the child's baptism in the local parish church. By rooting COPS in churches, the IAF was able to tap the cultural and social resources of the wider community.

COPS mobilized its strong church base to challenge the power monopoly of the Anglo elite. In these early battles for recognition, COPS acquired a reputation for pursuing militant and confrontational tactics. COPS engaged in large-scale protests at city council meetings over flooding and drainage issues. It organized disruptive actions at local symbols of economic power, like the protests at Joske's Department Store and the Frost Bank described at the beginning of the chapter. Drawing upon the legitimacy of the bishop's blessing and the authority of supportive priests, COPS leaders mobilized church-based networks to these actions. Because COPS leaders were embedded in social relationships, they could consistently provide large turnouts of hundreds of Mexican Americans to these actions, something never accomplished before in San Antonio. The deep roots of COPS provided the power to back up the organization's demand for its $100 million counter-budget for infrastructural improvements and increased services to the neglected west and south sides of San Antonio. The budget proposal represented an unprecedented demand from a community long excluded from access to power. San Antonio's public officials and business leaders were not accustomed to such an active and aggressive posture by the Hispanic community. But the militant tactics proved successful, and COPS began to win important victories.

While mass mobilization provided one key source of COPS' power, the organization quickly began to see the importance of voter turnout as well. In 1976 it allied with environmentalists to block the construction of a large shopping mall over the Edwards Aquifer, the city's only source of drinking water. By mobilizing their friends and neighbors, COPS leaders provided crucial votes to block the project and quickly became a force to reckon with on important public issues facing the city.[31]

The next year COPS threw its weight behind a revision in the city charter that would serve to help institutionalize its newfound power. Prior to the mid-fifties the Good Government League had been able to control the city council in part because all of the council members were elected citywide. Anglos outvoted Hispanics and African Americans to elect citywide candidates. Faced with a court suit, San Antonio held a referendum on a single member district plan for its city council in 1977. After some initial debate, COPS endorsed the plan and played an important role in turning out voters in the charter election that approved it. With Anglos overwhelmingly voting against the charter change, many observers credit COPS with supplying the margin of victory by mobilizing Hispanic voters.[32] In the first election under the district system in 1977, five Mexican American candidates and one African American won election, so that a majority of the nine member city council was no longer Anglo. With increased voting by Hispanics and sufficient support from Anglos and African Americans, Henry Cisneros won election in 1981 as the first Mexican American mayor of San Antonio since 1842 and the first Hispanic mayor of a large American city. Meanwhile, COPS expanded its role in determining city policy through its influence on the councilors elected from the five districts where it was concentrated.

COPS also enhanced its power through its intervention in the Community Development Block Grant (CDBG) program in San Antonio. The federal government had established this program to help fund city-authorized projects to promote community development. San Antonio had a particularly corrupt CDBG system at the time, in which officials went so far as to propose that federal funds be used for a golf course. COPS represented most of the neighborhoods that qualified for CDBG funds in the city, and it organized its parishes to present proposals for neighborhood improvement. Through extensive research and planning, backed up by mass mobilization to the public hearings mandated by federal regulations, COPS took control of the CDBG process from city planners. By leveraging its electoral base in five city council districts, COPS wielded tremendous influence over the council's final allocations and commanded the lion's share of CDBG benefits for its long-neglected parish neighborhoods. A study published in the early eighties shows that from the program's initiation in 1974 until 1982, $78.2 million, over half of all the CDBG funds allocated to San Antonio, went to projects specifically requested by COPS. The city approved 91 percent of the projects proposed by COPS.[33] A later study found that from 1974 to 1993, 69.9 percent of CDBG funds went to city council districts in which COPS organizes, with the great bulk of those funds going to projects supported by COPS.[34]. . .

COPS now had an organizing approach that proved powerful in gathering many kinds of resources for its neighborhoods. COPS combined careful research and planning by its leaders with large-scale mobilizations to public actions, and demonstrated its ability to turn out voters too when necessary to win its campaigns. With these methods, COPS secured funds from the county for health clinics, state funds for a community college on the south side, and federal money from the Department of Housing and Urban Development (HUD) for affordable housing programs. Many of these programs were quite extensive. By the mid-nineties COPS' programs had rehabilitated two thousand houses, built one thousand new homes, and assisted two thousand families in purchasing their first homes. By the organization's twentieth-anniversary convention in 1994, COPS had channeled to its neighborhoods close to $1 billion from a wide variety of sources. . . .

The IAF's explicit emphasis on organization building helped COPS move from issue to issue. IAF organizers trained COPS leaders not to think primarily about the cause or the issue, but to consider whether that action would build the power of the organization. In this way, when an issue campaign was over, the organization could build upon the capacity generated in that campaign to begin to initiate another. Although streets and drainage concerns dominated the COPS' agenda in the early days, it was never limited to those issues. Meanwhile, COPS drew upon the shared history and culture of Mexican Americans, but from the beginning, COPS insisted that its purpose was not to advocate for Hispanic causes or to work to elect Hispanics to office. In fact, COPS leaders object that their organization is wrongly perceived as Hispanic, even to this day. COPS co-Chair Virginia Ramirez complains that "other Hispanic organizations approach us to support Hispanic people for positions—like the president of the community college—and we say we support the most qualified. We don't care what color they are. We'll hold *all* accountable [emphasis hers]."[35]. . .

Although many of the Anglo elite in San Antonio despised COPS in its early days, by the end of the seventies the organization had earned a degree of grudging respect from them. In 1976, the San Antonio *Light* newspaper put COPS on its list of the ten most powerful groups in the city. In 1983, the San Antonio city council proclaimed a "COPS week" to honor the organization at its tenth-anniversary convention that year. The council publicly recognized the democratic contributions of the organization in its proclamation.[36]. . .

Conclusion: A Synergy of Faith and Politics

By the early eighties Cortes and the IAF had written a good part of that "new book" to which the San Antonio banker Tom Frost referred at the beginning of this chapter. This book revised Alinsky's model of organizing in a number of significant ways, allowing the IAF to build and sustain local organizations with broad participation in a growing number of cities across Texas. The new model served as the framework for the modern IAF's organizing efforts across the country and pushed community organizers in other networks to take faith, values, and relational organizing seriously as well.

Alinsky essentially followed a traditional interest-group model of politics. His genius was to take organizing into poor communities and to play no-holds-barred power politics. His method involved identifying an issue and mobilizing a community's resources to fight hard to win. Successful as he was in winning issues, Alinsky was never able to build organizations that sustained broad participation over time. Instead, a few ministers, civic association presidents, and other institutional representatives eventually came to dominate the organizations, moving them towards program administration, if not in more conservative directions.

In San Antonio, Cortes began to reach beyond institutional leaders into the social fabric of the churches on the west and south sides of the city. He chose not to start with an issue around which to mobilize. Instead, he asked lay leaders to talk among themselves to identify their concerns and find a basis for cooperative action. By doing so, he unleashed the capacity of indigenous leaders, particularly women who were immersed in and often responsible for community life. These women cared about their families, their communities, and their faith as much as about any particular issue. Where Alinsky emphasized self-interest, and saw his base religious institutions solely as repositories of hard resources like money and people, the IAF began to take faith traditions, and the relational strengths of women lay leaders, seriously.

IAF organizers began to talk about two kinds of power, unilateral and relational, a distinction it took from Bernard Loomer.[37] Unilateral power represents "power over" others, the kind of power Alinsky generated in his projects. But the new IAF sought to create relational power as well, that is, the "power to" act collectively together. The Texas IAF organizations were not the simple interest groups Alinsky formed to mobilize resources to win an issue. Instead, they built social capital, that is, cooperative relationships, to create a more expansive form of democratic participation. The IAF has not ignored interests or power politics. Instead, it has added the "soft arts" of relational organizing in order to combine values with interests, community building with political action.

Notes

1. The following account comes from the author's interview with George Ozuna, May 30, 1994, San Antonio, Texas. Mary Beth Rogers provides a more extensive narrative in *Cold Anger: A Story of Faith and Power Politics* (Denton, Texas: University of North Texas Press, 1990), pp. 113–16.
2. Cortes' remarks to the Farm Crisis Workers Conference were published in Ernesto Cortes, Jr., "Organizing the Community," *Texas Observer,* July 11, 1986, p. 13.
3. Quoted in Harry C. Boyte, *Community Is Possible: Repairing America's Roots* (New York: Harper and Row, 1984), pp. 139–40.
4. Author's interview with Tom Frost, Jr., July 22, 1993, San Antonio, Texas. Frost is referring to Saul D. Alinsky, *Reveille for Radicals* (New York: Vintage, 1969) and *Rules for Radicals* (New York: Random House, 1971).
5. Sanford D. Horwitt has written an excellent biography of Saul Alinsky, which covers the evolution of his thought and organizing work, entitled *Let Them Call Me Rebel* (New York: Alfred A. Knopf, 1989). The account of Alinsky in this chapter also draws from David P. Finks, *The Radical Vision of Saul Alinsky* (New York: Paulist Press, 1984); Robert Slayton, *Back of the Yards* (Chicago: University of Chicago Press, 1986); Robert J. Bailey, *Radicals in Urban Politics: The Alinsky Approach* (Chicago: University of Chicago Press, 1974); Donald C. Reitzes and Dietrich C. Reitzes, *The Alinsky Legacy: Alive and Kicking* (Greenwich, CT: JAI Press, 1987); Neil Betten and Michael J. Austin, "The Conflict Approach to Community Organizing: Saul Alinsky and the CIO," in Neil Betten and Michael J. Austin, eds., *The Roots of Community Organizing, 1917–1939* (Philadelphia: Temple University Press, 1990), pp. 152–61; and Robert Fisher, *Let the People Decide: Neighborhood Organizing in America* (Boston: Twayne Publishers, 1984).
6. For further discussion of the BYNC, see Reitzes and Reitzes, *The Alinsky Legacy,* pp. 66–73; Bailey, *Radicals in Urban Politics;* Slayton, *Back of the Yards,* pp. 188–229.
7. For a detailed discussion of the link between Alinsky and the CIO, see Betten and Austin, "The Conflict Approach to Community Organizing."
8. For a further discussion of these projects, see Reitzes and Reitzes, *The Alinsky Legacy,* and Finks, *The Radical Vision of Saul Alinsky.*
9. Charles E. Silberman's book about The Woodlawn Organization, *Crisis in Black and White* (New York: Random House, 1964), brought Alinsky broad public recognition. For a further discussion of The Woodlawn Organization, see Reitzes and Reitzes, *The Alinsky Legacy;* Finks, *The Radical Vision of Saul Alinsky;* and Horwitt, *Let Them Call Me Rebel.*

10. For a further discussion of FIGHT, see Finks, *The Radical Vision of Saul Alinsky;* Reitzes and Reitzes, *The Alinsky Legacy;* and Horwitt, *Let Them Call Me Rebel.*
11. Reitzes and Reitzes discuss this project in more detail in *The Alinsky Legacy.*
12. Reitzes and Reitzes discuss the variety of organizing efforts that drew upon Alinsky's methods in *The Alinsky Legacy.*
13. See Bailey's discussion of Alinsky's project in the Austin area of Chicago in *Radicals in Urban Politics.*
14. As reported from his interview with John Egan by Harry C. Boyte, *Commonwealth: A Return to Citizen Politics* (New York: Free Press, 1989), p. 61.
15. Quoted in "Playboy Interview: Saul Alinsky," *Playboy Magazine,* March 1972.
16. On the fate of TWO, see Reitzes and Reitzes, *The Alinsky Legacy,* p. 83.
17. On the history of FIGHT, see Finks, *The Radical Vision of Saul Alinsky,* pp. 176–228.
18. On the situation of the IAF at the time of Alinsky's death, see Reitzes and Reitzes, *The Alinsky Legacy,* p. 93.
19. For a further discussion of Chamber's role in the IAF, see Reitzes and Reitzes, *The Alinsky Legacy,* pp. 92–100.
20. Rogers refers to San Antonio's Hispanic community as a "sleeping giant" in *Cold Anger.* The essays in David R. Johnson, John A. Booth, and Richard J. Harris, eds., *The Politics of San Antonio* (Lincoln: University of Nebraska Press, 1983), provide a good overview of the history and structure of politics in that city in the seventies.
21. Rogers discusses the election in detail in *Cold Anger,* chapter 10.
22. Budget information for COPS reported by Rogers, *Cold Anger,* p. 107.
23. For a further discussion of Catholic social action traditions in San Antonio, see Joseph D. Sekul, "The C.O.P.S. Story: A Case Study of Successful Collective Action" (Ph.D. dissertation, University of Texas at Austin, 1984), pp. 157–61.
24. Author's interview with Reverend Al Jost, July 8, 1993, San Antonio, Texas.
25. Peter Skerry, *Mexican Americans: The Ambivalent Minority* (New York: Free Press, 1993).
26. The account of PADRES and the activities of Hispanic priests in San Antonio draws from the author's interview with Reverend David Garcia, July 15, 1993, San Antonio, Texas.
27. Quotations from Ernesto Cortes, Jr., come from Rogers, *Cold Anger,* pp. 108, 123.
28. The following account is based on the author's interview with Beatrice Cortez, July 12, 1993, San Antonio, Texas.
29. The consequences of segregation for San Antonio Hispanics is explored more fully by Rudolfo Rosales, "The Rise of Chicano Middle Class Politics in San Antonio 1951–1985" (Ph.D. dissertation, University of Michigan at Ann Arbor, 1991).
30. For a fuller discussion of the demographic composition of San Antonio's Hispanic population, see the study conducted by the Urban Institute, *Growth Without Prosperity: San Antonio's Experience in the New Economy* (San Antonio: Partnership for Hope, 1993).
31. For a detailed discussion of the aquifer controversy, see Sidney Plotkin, "Democratic Change in the Urban Political Economy: San Antonio's Edwards Aquifer Controversy," in David R. Johnson, John A. Booth, and Richard J. Harris, eds., *The Politics of San Antonio* (Lincoln: University of Nebraska Press, 1983), pp. 157–74.
32. Author's interview with Charles Cottrell, May 30, 1994, San Antonio, Texas. See also Roddy Stinson, "COPS Tastes Victory; ABC Takes Medicine," *San Antonio Express,* January 17, 1977. Heywood T. Sanders provides details on the racial split in voting for the charter change in "Communities Organized for Public Service and Neighborhood Revitalization in San Antonio," in Robert H. Wilson, ed., *Public Policy and Community: Activism and Governance in Texas* (Austin: University of Texas Press, 1997), pp. 36–68.
33. Joseph D. Sekul, "Communities Organized for Public Service: Citizen Power and Public Policy in San Antonio," in David R. Johnson, John A. Booth, and Richard J. Harris, eds., *The Politics of San Antonio* (Lincoln: University of Nebraska Press, 1983), pp. 175–90.
34. Sanders, "Communities Organized for Public Service."
35. Author's interview with Virginia Ramirez, May 22, 1993, San Antonio, Texas.
36. "COPS Tenth Anniversary Program," November 10, 1983.
37. Bernard Loomer, "Two Conceptions of Power," *Criterion* (Winter 1976): 12–29. Ernesto Cortes, Jr., elaborates the IAF's understanding of power in "Reweaving the Fabric: The Iron Rule and the IAF Strategy for Power and Politics," in Henry G. Cisneros, ed., *Interwoven Destinies: Cities and the Nation* (New York: W. W. Norton, 1993), pp. 294–319.

Chapter 5 Review Questions

1. What does Putnam suggest is wrong in American politics today? What does he say has occurred? In your own words, how would you define social capital? Why does Putnam say it is important to democracy?
2. How well does the case study illustrate Putnam's arguments? Does it suggest that social capital is important to strengthening democracy in the way described by Putnam, or is it important in some other manner? Explain your answer.
3. Why does Warren refer to Cortes's work as a "theology of organizing"? What is Cortes's theology? How successful has he been?
4. As you were growing up, how were you socialized into politics? Were you encouraged to participate in politics? Did your family discuss political issues at the dinner table? Were your friends interested in politics? How did these experiences affect your attitudes toward participating in politics? Have the schools you attended required you to perform community service? How valuable have these programs been in making you feel connected with your community and willing to participate in politics?
5. From your experiences, why do you think that some of the traditional groups identified by Putnam are facing declining membership? Why aren't people joining these groups?
6. Do you think the political problems we see today in states and local communities are a result of declining social capital, or is something else to blame? What do you think are the biggest problems confronting democracy in America?

Key Terms

civic engagement
social capital
bowling alone
social networks
conventional participation
unconventional participation
political socialization
generalized reciprocity
private good
public good
specific reciprocity
bridging social capital
bonding social capital
declensionist narratives
community organizing
unilateral power
relational power

Suggestions for Further Reading

Baron, Stephen, John Field, and Tom Schuller, eds. *Social Capital: Critical Perspectives.* New York: Oxford University Press, 2001. This collection of fourteen essays provides a good overview of the literature and theories of social capital.

Coleman, James S. "Social Capital in the Creation of Human Capital," *American Journal of Sociology* 94 (Supplement 1988): S95–S120. This article by sociologist James Coleman is considered the seminal work on social capital. Coleman provides an introduction to the concept of social capital and examines its economic benefits for individuals by studying high school dropouts. Coleman develops his ideas about social capital more fully in *Foundations of Social Theory* (Cambridge, Mass.: Harvard University Press, 1990).

Dionne, E. J., Jr., ed. *Community Works: The Revival of Civil Society in America.* Washington, D.C.: Brookings Institution, 1998. This collection of eighteen essays critically examines the extent to which there has been a decline in civil society in America and its importance to the nation.

Grix, Jonathan. "Social Capital as a Concept in the Social Sciences: The Current State of the Debate," *Democratization* 8 (Autumn 2001): 189–210. This essay gives a fine overview of current theoretical debates in the social capital literature.

Ladd, Everett C. *The Ladd Report.* New York: Free Press, 1999. One of the most comprehensive rebuttals of Putnam's thesis that there has been a decline in social capital. Ladd is the former director of the Roper Center for Public Opinion Research.

Putnam, Robert D. "Bowling Alone: America's Declining Social Capital," *Journal of Democracy* 6 (1995): 65–78. This was Putnam's initial study arguing that there has been a decline of social capital in America and the one that brought the phrase "bowling alone" into the lexicon of social engagement. Putnam also explores this thesis in "Tuning In, Turning Out: The Strange Disappearance of Social Capital in America," *PS: Political Science and Politics* 4 (December 1995): 664–683.

———, and Lewis Feldstein. *Better Together: Restoring the American Community.* New York: Simon & Schuster, 2003. A collection of essays describing how groups in several communities have rebuilt social capital to address social and economic problems.

Sirianni, Carmen, and Lewis Friedland. *Civic Innovation in America: Community Empowerment, Public Policy, and the Movement for Civic Renewal.* Berkeley: University of California Press, 2001. Analyzes recent efforts to rebuild the civic health of American cities and towns, with individual chapters devoted to community organizing, environmentalism, community health, and public journalism.

Skocpol, Theda. *Diminished Democracy: From Membership to Management in American Civic Life.* Norman: University of Oklahoma Press, 2003. Presents Skocpol's argument that there has been a change in the types of associations in America over time, with the rise of more Washington-based groups. The book then explores the consequences of this trend for democracy.

———, and Morris P. Fiorina, eds. *Civic Engagement in American Democracy.* Washington, D.C.: Brookings Institution, 1999. This is one of the best collections of essays on civic engagement, providing an introduction to the different theoretical schools and exploring a variety of empirical trends.

Smidt, Corwin, ed. *Religion as Social Capital: Producing the Common Good.* Waco, Tex.: Baylor University Press, 2003. Valuable collection of essays for those who want to learn more about the importance of religion in promoting social capital.

Related Web Sites

http://www.bowlingalone.com/
This web site is devoted specifically to Putnam's book. It includes the original data used in the book and a link to Putnam's efforts to rebuild civic engagement through the Saguaro Seminar at Harvard University.

http://www.cpn.org
National organization devoted to promoting improved civic renewal in America. Web site includes research on efforts to rebuild civic engagement and information on related organizations.

http://www.industrialareasfoundation.org/
Official web site for the Industrial Areas Foundation, which includes contact information and suggested readings.

6

Political Parties and Elections: The Concept of Candidate-Centered Campaigns

Who sent us the political leaders we have? There is a simple answer to that question. They sent themselves.

Alan Ehrenhalt

READING 6

Introduction

Political parties once played the central role in state and local elections. The party organizations chose the nominees for office. They provided their hand-picked candidates with the resources, staff, and expertise needed to win in the general election. They ran the campaigns and provided workers to help get out the vote on election day.

In many states and big cities, the party organizations were so powerful and well organized that they were labeled party machines. The machines were hierarchical organizations, with a boss at the top and a disciplined organization below. The members of the machine worked together to ensure that the party's candidates were elected to office. Some of the most famous machine bosses include James Curley of Boston, Frank Hague of Jersey City, Tom Pendegast of Kansas City, and William Tweed of New York's Tammany Hall. The Cook County Democratic Party Organization in Chicago may have been the last of the great party machines. Led by Richard J. Daley from 1955 to 1976, the machine controlled most Chicago city council races and the election to other offices in the Chicago area.

Over time, however, reforms in state election laws and changes in political attitudes weakened the political parties. Some of the most damaging reforms came during the Progressive Movement in the early 1900s, when there was an effort in many states to uproot government corruption. The Progressive reformers took particular aim at party organizations, which they saw as some of the leading causes of corruption.

The most important electoral reform championed by Progressives was the introduction of the primary election. The use of primaries was significant because it took away the parties' control over the nomination process, which was the foundation of their political power. Without the power to control nominations, the parties could not control those who were elected. From the candidates' perspective, the introduction of primaries meant they did not need to seek the support of party leaders to be nominated, but could instead simply appeal to voters in the primary elections. The Progressives also championed nonpartisan judicial and local elections, further reducing the parties' control over candidates and government.

Party organizations were further weakened in the 1950s and 1960s by the emergence of political action committees (PACs), the appearance of professional campaign consulting firms, and the development of new technologies, including television and direct mail. The growth of PACs provided candidates with a new source of campaign funding. The appearance of campaign consulting firms gave candidates the opportunity to purchase the expertise they needed to run for office, rather than relying on party leaders. The development of television and direct mail provided candidates with new resources with which to reach voters beyond face-to-face contact, which had been a traditional hallmark of party-led campaigns.

These trends resulted in a change in the role and importance of parties in elections. Whereas elections were once considered party-centered, today they are referred to as being candidate-centered. By the term *candidate-centered,* political scientists mean that individual candidates, not parties, play the critical role in elections. The candidates are no longer selected by the party organizations; rather, they decide for themselves to run. Candidates put together their own personal campaign organizations and manage their own campaigns. Instead of relying on the party organization for funds, candidates depend on political action committees and private donors for contributions. They hire independent political consultants to provide expertise. In addition, candidates often downplay partisanship in elections and simply appeal to voters on issues and personal traits. As campaigns became more candidate-centered, the role of political parties in elections was transformed. Parties had become service organizations that provide professional support to candidates running for office.

Over the last three decades, state political parties have enjoyed a bit of a resurgence. The parties have become more professional, acquiring the resources, expertise, and personnel to play a more significant role in elections than they had in the 1970s. Part of the reason for the resurgence of the parties is that state party organizations have made a more concerted effort to improve their fundraising capacity and to develop more professional operations. The states have also seen the emergence of what are called legislative campaign committees, which are party organizations that are run through state legislative party caucuses. These committees now play an important role in financing state legislative elections. Finally, the state parties have benefited from an increased flow of money from the national parties. The national party organizations began to channel money to state parties in the 1960s. The amount of money being transferred increased dramatically after the passage of the 1979 amendments to the Federal Election Campaign Act. Those amendments allowed state and local party organizations to spend an unlimited amount of money on "party-building" purposes. The national party organizations soon began encouraging donors to contribute to state and local parties as a way to circumvent the federal limits placed on party contributions to federal candidates. The flow of this "soft money" from the national parties to state party organizations reached a combined total of almost $500 million during the 2000 election.

With the increased revenue from the national parties and from their own fund-raising efforts, state party organizations were able to establish permanent offices, hire full-time directors and more professional staff, and offer greater services to candidates. These services include developing advertising campaigns, conducting public opinion polls, running get out the vote drives, and even providing candidates with advice on which campaign consultants to hire. The growing strength of the party organizations has, in turn, encouraged more competitive elections in many states as the two major parties square off against each other to gain control of government.

Despite this resurgence, it is important to remember that the role of the party organization remains considerably different today than in the past. Whereas parties once controlled elections and demanded obedience from members, parties today primarily serve as service organizations to candidates, providing money and resources to nominees. It is possible that the state parties may even see some decline in these activities over the next few years because of the passage of the McCain-Feingold Act of 2002, which banned the use of soft money. Without the national party funds, the state party organizations will have to find alternative money sources if they are to continue to play this resurgent role. It is also important to keep in mind that even though the parties play a less significant role in elections than they did in the past, they often play a central role in state government itself. As has been true at the national level, partisan conflict has become a defining characteristic in the politics of many states in recent years. This conflict can often be seen as legislators battle over major pieces of legislation and in the relationship between the legislatures and governors.

In the following essay, Alan Ehrenhalt, the executive editor of *Governing Magazine,* offers a thought-provoking analysis on the importance of candidates in local, state, and national elections. Ehrenhalt's essay is an excerpt from his highly regarded 1991 book, *The United States of Ambition.* The question Ehrenhalt poses in the essay is "who sent us the political leaders we have?" The answer, he writes, is simple: they have sent themselves. Although he does not use the term *candidate-centered campaign* in the essay, Ehrenhalt provides a superb overview of the entrepreneurial character of modern campaigns and the limited role played by parties. However, Ehrenhalt does more than just describe the character of modern campaigns. His work is also a critical analysis of how the change in elections and the rise of professional politicians have altered campaign politics, helped the Democratic Party, and changed the character of government.

Ehrenhalt begins by describing how journalists and scholars frequently analyze election results to determine what the voters were saying. Ehrenhalt points out, however, that voters are not given a "diverse array of clearly defined alternatives" when they cast their ballots. Rather, they can only choose from among the names of those who have decided to run. As a result, he says, if we want to learn more about election results, we need to learn about the choices on the ballot. In other words, we need to study the people who decide to run. Ehrenhalt then explains how most candidates today are professional politicians and are motivated by ambition when deciding to run. They are entrepreneurs who depend on themselves, rather than on parties, to win office. Moreover, he says, they tend to be people who believe in government, or else they would not be attracted to the job. It is from this last argument that Ehrenhalt makes the case that modern electoral politics favor the Democratic Party, because Democrats tend to be more supportive of government.

Ehrenhalt's work is valuable because it shows how the process we use to elect public officials can affect the type of people we elect. The work is also important because Ehrenhalt's argument parallels many of the ideas suggested in the reading by David Hedge in the first chapter. Ehrenhalt argues that as elections have been opened up to anyone who wants to run, government has become less representative of the people and often less able to govern. In other words, the increase in democracy has led to a decline in representation and responsible government.

Questions to Consider

These are some questions to consider as you read this chapter:

- Why is Ehrenhalt critical of viewing election results as a message from the public? What, if anything, do elections tell us?
- What does Ehrenhalt mean when he writes that our political leaders have "sent themselves"? Why is this so?
- Ehrenhalt argues, "Full-timers drive part-timers out of circulation." What does he mean by this, and why does he say this happens?
- In 1994, Republican Party candidates did remarkably well nationwide, gaining control of Congress and many state legislatures. Do these results suggest that Ehrenhalt's argument is entirely wrong? Why do you think the Republican Party has done so well?
- Given what Ehrenhalt has to say about modern elections, do you think it would help to have stronger party organizations? Why or why not?

Thinking About Politicians

Alan Ehrenhalt

Above San Francisco, in the pretty little towns that spread eastward from the Pacific Coast Highway into the Napa Valley, there are an extraordinary number of elegant places to eat. Any village large enough to claim a post office, it sometimes seems, can be counted on to have a restaurant that serves stuffed quail or roulade of salmon or sautéed Burgundy snails. What are all these French restaurants doing there? Why so much gourmet cooking in such a small and crowded corner of the world? Is it because the demand for expensive food in northern California is limitless?

Not really. Restaurants need customers, of course, or they go out of business. But one could spend a lifetime studying customer taste and never understand how such a collection of haute cuisine came to be concentrated in a relatively few square miles. The truth is that northern California is full of restaurants because restaurateurs want to live there. The summers are cool; the winters are mild; the scenery is lovely; the customers are secondary. As long as there is enough business to stave off bankruptcy, Napa and Sonoma counties will always offer more pâté and

Alan Ehrenhalt, "Thinking About Politicians," from *The United States of Ambition* (New York: Times Books, 1991), pp. 5–24. Reprinted by permission of The Sagalyn Literary Agency.

goat cheese than the available diners can possibly consume.

American politics is not a restaurant, but it does have customers—voters—and people whose job it is to serve them—politicians. A great deal is written every year about political events in this country, and nearly all of it attempts to understand them by asking what is on the voters' minds. Every election year reporters and polltakers spend thousands of hours sounding out the American people on the questions of the day. The moment the polls close on election night, the television networks report their findings on why the electorate made the choices it did. In the weeks and months that follow, journalists and scholars take their turns combing the statistics for clues about just what message the American people were trying to send.

It is not the purpose of this book to disparage all this poking around in the electoral psyche. In a democratic society there is no arguing with the principle that the people doing the governing ought to know as much as possible about what the country thinks. But in the end there is only so much the electorate can tell us. Most of the time it is not trying to send any message. A great deal of what has happened in American politics in the past generation is accessible only through a different set of questions, aimed not at the customers of American politics but at the proprietors—the people who involve themselves in politics, run for office, win elections, and govern the country.

Studying the voters is, for all its statistical technology, a relatively simple matter. There are millions of them, and on any issue one chooses to take up, any random sample of a few hundred will do. It is easy to find out what the voters think.

It is comparatively hard to find out what politicians think, or even who they are and where they come from. They are not interchangeable. In any one election year, fewer than a thousand people are active candidates for Congress. One cannot draw a sample of 10 percent of them and claim to have learned anything meaningful at all. There is scarcely any choice but to approach them on an old-fashioned, unscientific, one-by-one basis.

So it is understandable that scholars and journalists tend to focus their attention on the voters, who are accessible, rather than on the candidates, who are frequently elusive. But the attractiveness of voter opinion as a field of study does not automatically make it the critical factor in understanding the results of an election. Sometimes we need to know other things.

For example:

Concord, California, is a conservative town. In the 1980s it voted twice for Ronald Reagan by decisive margins and twice for George Deukmejian, the state's orthodox Republican governor. Yet in the entire Reagan era it did not elect a single Republican to local office. It was governed entirely by liberal Democrats.

One might argue that the voters of Concord possess a finely developed sensitivity to the separation of powers and decided over the years that they wanted one sort of ideology representing them in Washington and Sacramento, and another in their own city hall. But a few conversations with people who have held office in this community turn up a different answer. Serving in city government in Concord used to be easy work. Businessmen did it in their spare time. As the city grew, governing it became a demanding, time-consuming job. The Republican merchants and insurance brokers who used to do it no longer wanted to take the time. In their place came political professionals, and all the professionals, over an entire decade, were Democrats.

The Colorado House of Representatives does the same sort of work that all legislative bodies in the United States do. There is nothing very unusual about its product. But there has been something unusual about its composition. For much of the 1980s it was nearly 40 percent female, and its instrument of leadership, the Republican Caucus, was at one point 45 percent female. No other chamber in any American legislature has come close to matching those numbers.

Some of this no doubt has to do with the fact that Colorado voters, like those in other western states, have always been more or less hospitable to women candidates. There were three women in the legislature as early as 1895. Colorado was one of the first states to ratify the federal Equal Rights Amendment. But there is a more immediate reason why the Colorado House is the way it is. The position of state representative pays $17,500 a year. It is an interesting job, and an important job, but it is no job for a breadwinner. An increasing number of House members are highly educated people who are married to well-paid professionals and do not need their legislative pay to support their families. There is no reason why these cannot be men, and some are. But the vast majority are women.

Then there is the interesting case of the Fifth Congressional District of Indiana. Its Republican loyalties are rock solid. No Democratic candidate for governor or president has carried it in more than fifteen years. In 1984 it gave its Republican congressman nearly 70 percent of the vote. But two years later the incumbent retired, and it chose a Democrat to replace him.

It helps a little, in explaining that unusual event, to know about some of the economic crises that central Indiana suffered through in the 1980s. Hard times in the automobile industry closed factories all over the Fifth District and lifted unemployment to frightening levels. It is natural enough to assume that the voters were angry about their plight and turned their anger against the Republicans—the party that was governing the country.

No doubt some of them did that. But the event becomes much clearer when one learns something about the Democrat who won the election: that at the age of twenty-two he had won a seat in the legislature by defeating the majority leader of the Indiana House; that in the ensuing twelve years he had worked full-time at politics, seven days a week; that he had raised nearly half a million dollars for his congressional campaign at a time when other underdog candidates were starved for funds. The mood of the voters had something to do with the result in Indiana's Fifth District that year, but the candidate had everything to do with it.

It is central to the folklore of our democratic system that elections reflect in some way the considered judgment of the American people. But one need not be a specialist in public opinion to realize just how far the reality differs from the myth. To begin with, most people do not vote. In a general election for president, the national turnout usually edges slightly above 50 percent of those eligible to participate, but in all other elections those who vote are a minority. Only 36 percent of adult citizens voted in the elections for Congress in 1990; in primaries for Congress the percentage is always lower; in elections at the local level it is usually lower still.

Most people who do vote cast their ballots most of the time without knowing very much about the people running or what they stand for. This was made clear by the massive voter studies begun in the 1950s by the Survey Research Center of the University of Michigan, and it has never been convincingly disputed.

The late political scientist V. O. Key, Jr., challenged the pessimism of the Ann Arbor studies in one important way in the 1960s: He argued that "voters are not fools"; choices for president do reflect the considered values and opinions of those who participate. Key felt that voting is retrospective—that citizens might not have a clear idea of which policies they want a president to pursue, but they know whether things in America are going well or badly, and they make up their minds, rationally enough, either to reward the incumbent party or to punish it for its failings. In the years since then, it has been more or less accepted that voters in presidential elections are not just choosing a friendly face or a party label but expressing themselves as best they can about what they think the country should be like.

And so they are. But a presidential election, however critical it may be, is one event held every four years. In the intervening period, in every community in the United States, dozens of elections are held to choose mayors, city councilors, state legislators, members of Congress, and countless other officials who provide the government that is crucial to people's lives, every day, every year.

I know of nobody who has tried seriously to say of these elections that, in general, they reflect the considered judgment of the voters about the choices that confront them or the people on the ballot. As Thomas E. Mann said of congressional elections a decade ago, "The burden of proof is clearly on those who would argue that a significant part of the public is aware of the candidates." The truth is, most votes that we cast in this country—even those cast by the brightest of us—are stabs in the dark. Readers can test this proposition for themselves by recalling the last time they confronted choices for their state legislature. If they made up their minds on the basis of any coherent policy choice, they are rare voters indeed.

Over the past twenty years, an average of 56 percent of the eligible voters have been unable to identify any congressional candidate in their district at the height of the fall campaign. Only 22 percent have been able to name both candidates. The figures for Senate campaigns have not been much higher. That is not to say that Key was wrong and that voters are, in fact, fools. It is simply to say, as Walter Lippmann observed convincingly more than sixty years ago, that life is too short, work is too hard, and leisure too precious for the average citizen to spend more than a small fraction of his time gathering information about the people whose names confront him on the ballot each election year. . . .

Lippmann did not believe the American voter is a fool. "My sympathies are with him," he wrote in 1925,

> for I believe that he has been saddled with an impossible task and that he is asked to practice an unattainable ideal. I find it so myself for, although public business is my main interest and I give most of my time to watching it, I cannot find time to do what is expected of me in the theory of democracy; that is to know what is going on and to have an opinion worth expressing on every question which confronts a self-governing community. And I have not happened to meet anybody, from a President of the United States to a professor of political science, who came anywhere near to embodying the accepted ideal of the sovereign and omnicompetent citizen.

If he does exist anywhere, the omnicompetent citizen is confronted at the polls with an inevitably narrow set of choices. He is limited, for all practical purposes, to those people who have decided to be candidates. In our society that nearly always means two choices in a general election and a few more, not many more, in most primaries. There is no point in pretending that the American voter is selecting among a diverse array of clearly defined alternatives. American politics does not work that way.

It is possible to argue, as many on the left do, that narrowness of choice at the polls reflects a deliberate effort by those who possess power to maintain themselves in power. Holding a monopoly on the skills and resources needed to conduct a modern campaign, an establishment elite uses that monopoly to win all the important nominations and deny any meaningful voice to the downtrodden and anybody who wishes to speak for them.

But one does not have to believe this notion—I do not believe it myself—to realize that the limited set of choices in American elections all but determines the outcome of the voting and the government we get in the end. Our choices at the polls are not restricted by any power-hungry cabal but by thousands of potential candidates who decide on their own either that running for office is worth the trouble or that they are better off staying home and tending to family and career. If the people who want to hold office in the 1990s are a different group from those who wanted to hold office in the 1960s, the voters are going to end up with a different sort of government—whatever they happen to think about the issues of the day. . . .

If voters are not making informed choices, what in the world are they doing? We know a few relevant things about elections below the presidential level in this country, but they do not explain a great deal.

We know that people are far more likely to vote for incumbents than for challengers, whether they are voting to fill seats in Congress, in a state legislature, or on a city council. It is not hard to see why. In an electoral world where information is scarce, incumbents are far more likely to be familiar, and familiarity is rewarded. But this observation, of course, begs the question of how they got to be incumbents in the first place. It is nice to have a theory of how people win second terms, but it would be more interesting to know how they won their first terms.

We know that when voters are uninformed about the candidates on the ballot, they often make their decisions on the basis of the party they prefer. Republicans do not win election to the Illinois legislature from inner-city Chicago; Democrats rarely get elected to that body from the suburbs of Du Page County. But this observation too begs the real question. If the general election in a particular place is only a formality, then the primary is the crucial event. And there is no evidence that the electorate in a primary is any better informed than the electorate in November. If anything, it knows less. How does one person emerge out of a crowded primary field and lift himself into the security of an easy general election and a safe seat in public office? There has not been a great deal written on this subject.

Officeholders do not necessarily behave as if voters were apathetic or uninformed. Congress is full of veteran members who have not faced a hint of serious opposition in years yet cast each vote in apparent fear that someone back in the district is waiting to turn it against them. This is the hypersensitivity of political professionalism. The more a person's career, livelihood, and self-image depend on remaining in office—rather than on some other work he was trained to do in private life—the more likely he is to magnify the smallest threat to that office.

In any legislative body, though, the norm of political squeamishness masks a diverse array of decisions that even the most hypersensitive legislator can make without having to worry much about public opinion back home. Consider, for example, Rep. Glenn English, a Democrat who represents a hard-pressed wheat-growing district in Oklahoma's western plains. English has built himself a secure seat in Congress by noisily trumpeting the cause of higher wheat prices at every opportunity. At the same time he has devoted much of his legislative career to protecting the Freedom of Information Act, a subject of little or no political sensitivity to his constituents. If we want to understand English's position on wheat, we need to know something about his voters. But if we want to understand his position on personal privacy, we need to know something about him—where he came from and why he believes the things he does. The voters have very little to do with it.

There are all sorts of interesting questions in American politics that we cannot answer by asking the voters, no matter how much time we spend on the task. The voters are the customers. We need to find out more about the people for whom politics is a business. We need to know what sorts of people want to be politicians. And to understand that we need to know how the work of politics itself has changed.

One thing we can say with confidence is that seeking and holding office take up more of a politician's time than they did a generation ago. It is much harder now to combine politics and a career in private life. And this is true, to a greater or lesser extent, at all levels of government.

As recently as the 1950s the U.S. Congress could reasonably be described as a part-time institution. Its members arrived in Washington on the train in January and left in the summer, when heat and humidity made the city uncomfortable. When they returned home upon adjournment in July or August, these politicians had enough time left in the year to practice law or sell insurance or do whatever they had done before they were elected.

Since the early 1960s Congress has essentially been in session year-round. It recesses for a month in August during the odd-numbered years and adjourns for campaigning a month or so before each national election, but the rest of the time it is conducting business. A member can return home virtually every weekend if he chooses, and there are half a dozen week-long recesses scattered throughout the average congressional year, but there is no sustained opportunity to pursue any career at all in private life. When someone is elected to Congress, he gives up his "regular job," assuming he did not give it up months earlier to campaign. He returns to it—assuming it still awaits him—only when he leaves office.

Not all state legislators have to cut themselves off from private life in quite the same way. In some of the least populated states, the legislatures still meet every other year for only sixty days. It is possible to combine service in the Wyoming House or Senate with almost any sort of work—law, ranching, business—and describe oneself accurately as a "citizen-legislator." But there are very few Wyomings left. In 1987 thirty-seven legislatures held regular sessions that lasted one hundred days or more, and most of those stayed in business roughly half the year. Nine legislatures met more or less year-round. When it comes to opportunities for a life outside politics, there is little practical difference between being a member of the Michigan House in Lansing and being a member of the U.S. House in Washington. It is time-consuming work.

Millions of words have been written about the advent of year-round legislating, most of them warning that it leads to too many unnecessary laws and to legislators isolated from the people they represent. We can leave that argument aside. My point is a simpler one: Full-time jobs in Congress and in legislatures attract people who want to devote most of their waking hours to politics. There is no reason to suppose that this is the same set of people who would want to do politics in their spare time.

People in local government—city council members, county commissioners, and their equivalents—nearly all have some discretion in how much time they devote to their work. Their meetings tend to take place at night and, except in the largest cities, no more than once a week. Local politicians can hold down private jobs, and most of them do. But a variation on Gresham's law has come to operate in local politics: Full-timers drive part-timers out of circulation. The city councilman who spends his days building political coalitions, meeting with constituents, and cultivating financial support sets a standard of political sophistication that colleagues pretty much have to meet if they are going to stay effective or even stay in office. Once a city council attracts its first full-time member, it is on the way to becoming a de facto full-time institution, even if it does not think of itself as one.

If it is more demanding to hold office in America than it was a generation ago, it is also far more demanding to seek office. Campaigning at any level these days is almost certain to be a time-consuming, technologically complicated, physically strenuous form of work.

To win a seat in Congress now is frequently to do what Bill Schuette did in Michigan in 1984: devote the better part of a year to meeting people and raising money seven days a week. Schuette was, as of 1984, the state of the art in congressional campaigning. "Amateur night is over in this district," he proclaimed one afternoon, more than six months before the election, as he drove from one campaign stop to another in the middle of a day crowded with political appearances. Schuette was on his way to spending nearly $900,000 on a successful campaign that included a meticulous month-by-month game plan, a summer rehearsal, and a headquarters full of computers. Running for Congress for the first time at the age of thirty, Schuette was essentially the proprietor of a small business.

It is perfectly possible to spend $900,000 on a congressional campaign and lose it badly; people do that every year. But as the enterprise becomes more complex and more sophisticated, those who want to stay in business have little choice but to move with it. There is no reason in principle why congressional campaigns have to last a year and cost a fortune. But candidates who do the things Bill Schuette did rarely lose to opponents who campaign casually and run on a shoestring.

It is not just a matter of sophistication; it is a matter of physical effort. When Jim Moody decided to run for an open congressional seat in Milwaukee in 1982, he did it by campaigning door to door virtually every day for more than a year. That was no surprise. Moody had got himself elected to the state legislature twice by doing exactly the same thing. What was surprising was the effect he had on his large field of competitors. Within a few months virtually all of them were out knocking on doors like a crew of Fuller Brush salesmen, hoping to catch the candidate who had a head start. Any one who refused to campaign that way risked gaining a reputation as lacking the commitment or stamina to win.

In the end nobody caught up with Moody; he was elected to Congress. But the important point is that he had established a political entry barrier, and it is one that exists in many parts of the country in contests for Congress, state legislatures, and local office. Candidates win these offices by selling themselves to the voters, in person, one at a time, day after day. People who do not like to do this, people who do not like to knock on strangers' doors or who find it tedious to repeat the same thirty-second personal introduction thousands of times, are at a severe disadvantage. Many of them decide sensibly that, however interesting it might be to serve in office, the job of seeking office is not for them.

Politics in the 1990s is for people who are willing to give it vast amounts of their time. It is also for people who are not particularly concerned about making money. Time and money are related. If state legislatures met for one week every year, it would not be difficult to find a wide assortment of people willing to serve for very little pay, or even for free. But a job that is apt to require six months or more of full-time work every year is measured against a different standard.

Any time members of Congress receive a pay increase, they are assaulted by complaints from constituents who do not understand why a public servant cannot live on an annual wage several times higher than the median in every community in the United States. An annual wage of more than $90,000 (the congressional salary at this writing) seems lavish to them. But if you or I were pondering a campaign for Congress, the crucial question, of course, would not be whether we could make more than our plumber does. It would be whether a member of Congress makes more than we could make staying home and doing something else. And the answer, for most people with the capacity to win election to Congress, is that they can make considerably more money in private life.

It is an often repeated fact that more members of Congress identify themselves as lawyers than as practitioners of any other profession. But the large number of lawyer-legislators obscures the truth about who these people are. They are not, by and large, successful lawyers who left thriving partnerships to run for public office. Rather, they are political activists with law degrees. This does not mean that they are failures; it simply means that they are lawyers by training rather than by profession. Quite a few of them fit the career pattern of Massachusetts Democrat James M. Shannon, who received his law degree in 1975, won election to Congress in 1978, ran for the U.S. Senate in 1984, and later became attorney general of his state.

Shannon never practiced law before becoming a candidate. Therefore he never had to face a reduction in his standard of living by assuming public office. But nearly any successful lawyer, even in a medium-sized American town, quickly attains a standard of material life well beyond the reach of an average member of Congress, let alone a state legislator. He is very unlikely to give up that life for public office.

What is true of law is true, to a greater or lesser extent, of most other professions. They pay much better than politics. People give them up for political careers only at the beginning of the road, or at the end: before they are really launched, or after they have begun to wind down.

Jim Olin of Virginia, a former vice-president of General Electric, is one of the few Fortune 500 corporate executives in Congress. When he was in his thirties, he tried to combine his business career with service as a town supervisor in Rotterdam, New York. Told by GE to choose either business or politics, he chose business, retired in 1982 after thirty-five years with the company, ran for Congress, and won. That is about the only way anybody can combine careers in Congress and corporate business—do one, then the other. But not many people have the energy or the opportunity to accomplish it. . . .

A political career in America in the 1990s, to summarize, is not easy, lucrative, or a particularly good route to status in life. This places increased importance on one other motive for entering politics: sheer enjoyment. You pretty much have to like the work.

You also have to be good at it. Almost as important as the question of what sorts of people want a political career is the question of what sorts of people possess the skills to do it well. Here too there is no reason to assume that the answers are the ones that would have applied earlier in this century, or even earlier in the postwar years.

The skills that work in American politics at this point in history are those of entrepreneurship. At all levels of the political system, from local boards and councils up to and including the presidency, it is unusual for parties to nominate people. People nominate themselves. That is, they offer themselves as candidates, raise money, organize campaigns, create their own publicity, and make decisions in their own behalf. If they are not willing to do that work for themselves, they are not (except in a very few parts of the country) going to find any political party structure to do it for them.

At one time in American politics, parties represented the only real professionalism that existed. A century ago, when defenders of "good government" complained that public life was being usurped by professional politicians, they did not mean candidates. They meant bosses—the people who chose the candidates. Legislators came and went, in Congress as they did at lesser levels. The institutions of professionalism were the party machines: New York's Tammany Hall, the Republican organization of Pennsylvania, the Cook County Democratic Central Committee. The leaders of these machines were the lifelong political practitioners who reaped the rewards of power and graft that the system offered.

Today's professional politicians are less imposing figures, even to those who do not like them. Their influence as individuals is modest, and their opportunities for graft are few. In most cases they do not control anyone's election but their own. Their ties to any political party are limited. They are solo practitioners. It is a different brand of professionalism altogether.

There is no need to dwell on the evidence of party decline; it is all around us. At the national level, it is true, there were some interesting signs of party renewal in the 1980s, centered in the congressional campaign committees. Both the Democratic and the Republican parties in Washington play a far greater role in recruiting and helping candidates than they did two decades ago. But that does not contradict the fundamental point that in the states and cities across America, where elections are fought and won, parties make little difference. Candidates for all sorts of offices are perfectly capable of going on about their business without them. And it is not just parties that have lost their role of anointing political candidates. Other community institutions that used to perform that task have also lost their authority in recent years.

Elections in Sioux Falls, South Dakota, for example, were never conducted on a highly partisan basis. But the successful candidates a generation ago were those who bore the stamp of approval of the town's informal leadership organization. "When we were kids growing up," a Sioux Falls businessman in his forties recalls, "everybody knew who would win the elections. The person who had been in Rotary and had been endorsed by the Chamber of Commerce always won."

What has happened in Sioux Falls in the past two decades has happened in countless other places as well. Candidates do not win because they have party support. They do not win because they have business or labor support. They win because they are motivated to set out on their own and find the votes that will make a majority. Group support helps. But it is almost never enough. The candidate who possesses every attribute needed for victory except the willingness to thrust himself forward is a losing candidate nine times out of ten.

Who sent us the political leaders we have? There is a simple answer to that question. They sent themselves. And they got where they are through a combination of ambition, talent, and the willingness to devote whatever time was necessary to seek and hold office.

In the age of the entrepreneurial candidate, character traits that used to be helpful turn out to be counterproductive. When Alfred E. Smith entered politics in Manhattan in the early years of this century, the one crucial trait he had to exhibit to win nomination was loyalty—uncomplaining devotion to the organization and leaders who placed him in the state assembly. If his loyalty to Tammany Hall had been less than total, he would not have been rewarded with a seat in the legislature, and if his loyalty had declined when he assumed office, he would have been dumped. But the people who have represented Smith's old territory in Congress or in the New York legislature in recent years have not been there because of loyalty. There has been no organization, even in the old machine strongholds, worth a pledge of allegiance. The quality that nourishes political careers today, in Manhattan as elsewhere, is independence.

Most candidates who succeeded on the basis of loyalty did not have to be especially articulate. Political organizations required spokesmen, but they did not require that all their officeholders be capable of playing a visible public role. A genial young man blessed with the support of the party organization did not need to express himself vigorously on the issues of the moment.

That is no longer true. A candidate for virtually any office has to know how to talk. Voters may not make their choices very often on the basis of public policy, but they do not like to vote for candidates who seem uncomfortable expressing themselves. More than in the old days, campaigns for all offices are exercises in communication: in town meetings, in door-to-door canvassing, on television, in direct-mail literature that the candidate has to write himself. Even if it does not matter a great deal what the candidate says, it makes an enormous difference how he looks and sounds saying it. The politics of the 1990s, unlike the politics of earlier generations, is an enterprise in which the inarticulate have no place to hide. When candidates are left to themselves to orchestrate campaigns and do their own communicating with the voters, it is only natural that the glib will survive and the tongue-tied will be drawn toward other lines of work.

In such an atmosphere, the advantage is not only to individuals who know how to talk but to professions that train people in how to talk. There are many reasons why teachers have been the fastest-growing bloc in American legislatures in the 1980s, but one of the most important has to do with verbal ability. Teachers can translate the skills of their private careers into a job in public life. And unlike lawyers, who possess most of the same skills, they can do so without making any financial sacrifice.

Politics is, then, more than in the past, a job for people who prefer it to any other line of work. About these people one more important point should be made: They tend not only to enjoy politics but to believe in government as an institution. The more somebody is required to sacrifice time and money and private life to run for the city council, for the state legislature, or for Congress, the more important it is for that person to believe that government is a respectable enterprise with crucial work to do.

That principle comes through in interviews with people at all levels of the political system. Ron Mullin expressed it one day in 1987, as he trudged down the streets of Concord, California, campaigning door to door all afternoon in 95-degree heat, an incumbent mayor seeking reelection to the city council. "If I believed government wasn't an institution beneficial to society," he said, "I wouldn't give a tinker's dam about politics. I wouldn't waste my time on it." Robert Torricelli expressed similar sentiments a few years earlier, in the midst of his successful Democratic campaign in New Jersey against an incumbent Republican congressman. "People who believe government should be doing less," Torricelli declared, "should not vote for me." Those are the sorts of words one hears from people who succeeded in politics in the 1980s, people whose zest for the game is reinforced by a conviction that they need not apologize for what they are doing.

Occasionally one hears the opposite. Randy Kamrath was elected to the Minnesota Senate as a Republican in 1981 at age twenty-five and almost immediately began pondering his retirement from a profession whose value he questioned. "If a politician likes his job," Kamrath mused one summer morning, as he drove his tractor across his southwest Minnesota farm, "then I don't think I like the job he's doing." Kamrath was in his second legislative term then, seeking a third, yet he worried that the Minnesota legislature was no place for an honest conservative. The next year the voters solved Kamrath's problem for him; they unseated him and put in a liberal Democrat, freeing him to do the farming he regards as honest work.

There are people like Randy Kamrath at all levels of the American political system—people who are highly suspicious of government yet persuade themselves to run for office, or who hate government but find themselves addicted somehow to politics as a game. But it is hard to find enough of them, in most places, to make a majority on a city council, or in a legislature, or in a congressional delegation.

In another sort of political environment, one in which parties made the important decisions, or in which it did not take much time or trouble to serve in office, belief in government might not be a crucial point. People who disliked government might become candidates and win elections in large numbers whether they found the work exciting or not. But in the current environment belief matters a great deal. Indeed, it is critical.

It may seem to some readers that, in paying all this attention to the personal qualities of the candidates, I am missing something crucial: the importance of media in the modern political process, or the dominating influence of money. Or both.

Money and television are important. It has been true for the past twenty years that TV commercials can sway election results, local as well as national. And even in the smaller media markets, commercials are expensive to produce and to put on the air. Television has pushed up the cost of campaigns for an entire range of offices to disturbing levels. It is very difficult now to win an open seat in Congress without raising and spending half a million dollars. Usually it takes more. A contested state Senate campaign, even in a medium-sized state, often costs $100,000. And it is clear to anybody who follows politics where most of this money comes from. It comes from people and interests with a stake in the policy decisions of the institution whose seats are up for grabs.

But who gets it? How did Jim Jontz, running for Congress in 1986 as a Democrat in Indiana's Fifth District, a thirty-three-year-old full-time legislator with no significant resources of his own, manage to raise and spend nearly $500,000 to get himself elected in an impossibly Republican constituency? One can argue, of course, that Jontz was simply an instrument—a tool of the labor unions and liberal pressure groups who found his politics appealing and provided most of the money. But to say that is to misconstrue the role of these groups—and their business-oriented counterparts on the Republican side—in the American political system.

Special interests reward politicians. They buy access to politicians. They seek to influence votes, and frequently they do. But they do not generate careers. They do not pluck people off college campuses or out of entry-level private jobs and lure them into politics. The candidates who raise the large amounts that campaigns now require are people who launched political careers on the basis of their own values, ambitions, and interests. They throw themselves into politics full-time, and they learn where the money is, just as they learn to campaign door to door, address a town meeting, or put together a piece of direct mail. These are the skills that make them successful.

In a similar sense it is not quite true that television wins elections. The ability to look and sound good on television wins elections. It is true that, in a number of well-publicized campaigns every year, people without any such natural ability are made presentable through the efforts of consultants whom they had the personal resources to hire, but those campaigns are exceptions. The vast majority of candidates who win elections through television are people whose commitment to politics over the course of their adult lives put them in a position to afford it and to understand how to use it.

No matter how much importance we want to place on the roles of money and media in the campaign process, we are driven back to questions about which sorts of people are succeeding in that process. Political office today flows to those who want it enough to spend their time and energy mastering its pursuit. It flows in the direction of ambition—and talent.

To recognize this fact is to begin to solve perhaps the oddest riddle of American politics in recent years: the ability of the Democratic party to thrive at so many levels of the political system in the face of a national conservative tide that has elected Republican presidents five times in the last six elections, overwhelmingly in the last three. How could it be, in the era of Ronald Reagan and George Bush, that Democrats prolonged their control of the U.S. House into its fourth uninterrupted decade; reestablished a comfortable majority in the U.S. Senate after a short Republican interlude; controlled as many as thirty state legislatures, compared with fewer than ten for the Republicans; and consistently elected more than 60 percent of the 7,412 people who serve in ninety-nine state legislative chambers nationwide?

Most of the efforts to answer this riddle have fallen back on psychological examination of the electorate. We vote for Democrats below the presidential level, it is said, to place a check on the Republicans to whom we entrust control of the White House. Or, somewhat more plausibly, we split our vote because we have different expectations about different offices. Republicans win the presidency by offering an ideology that the majority of the country feels comfortable with. Democrats win further down by delivering the personal services and generating the governmental programs that voters, on a day-to-day basis, refuse to give up.

There may be some truth to these answers, but in the end they are answers to the wrong fundamental question. Once we drop beneath the level of presidential politics, there is no reason to believe that voters are trying to tell us much of anything. They are responding in an essentially passive way to the choices placed in front of them. The best candidates and the best campaigns win. It is not really a matter of demand. It is a matter of supply. Over the past two decades, in most constituencies in America, Democrats have generated the best supply of talent, energy, and sheer political ambition. Under those circumstances it has not been crucial for them to match the opinions of the electorate on most of the important national issues of the day.

It should be clear, of course, that we are talking about large numbers of elections. We are talking about a distinction which, over time, enables Democrats to win an extra 10 percent of the seats in a state legislature, or an extra two or three seats in a congressional delegation. It adds up. It does not predict the outcome of an individual campaign. Republicans win their share of elections on the basis of talent all over the country, every election year. They just do not win an equal share.

None of this guarantees the Democratic party majority control of any legislative body anywhere in the system. But it does mean that any party, faction, or interest that wants to compete on equal terms must meet the demands of present-day political life. And doing that requires generating large numbers of people to whom politics is more important, or more rewarding, than money, leisure, or privacy. It is not absolutely necessary that these people believe in government as the ultimate social problem solver. It is helpful if they believe rather strongly in something—something sufficiently compelling to generate the sacrifice involved.

CASE STUDY 6

Introduction

Before Arnold Schwarzenegger's successful bid for California governor in 2003, the most prominent gubernatorial race in recent years may have been the 1998 election of Jesse Ventura, a former professional wrestler, in Minnesota. Schwarzenegger's victory was too recent to find a good study that would fit into this book, but perhaps there is something that can be learned about his success, and about Ehrenhalt's argument, by looking at Ventura's campaign. On the surface, at least, there are some striking similarities between the races in California and Minnesota. In both cases, the victorious candidate was an entertainment star, with good media skills, who ran as a political outsider.

In the case study that follows, political analyst David Beiler provides a thoughtful chronicle of Ventura's campaign, from before Ventura's decision to run through the general election. Even though Ventura was not a professional politician before entering the race, his story nicely illustrates many of the arguments laid out in Ehrenhalt's work.

Urged to run by a former Reform Party candidate, Ventura started his campaign slowly, but then threw himself actively into the race, participating in numerous campaign forums, raising campaign contributions, and meeting frequently with the press. Ultimately, Ventura was able to defeat three of Minnesota's best-known politicians, including the sons of two vice presidents.

Throughout the race, several Reform Party members helped manage Ventura's campaign, but to suggest that Ventura's campaign was party-centered would be inaccurate. Ventura was not nominated by the Reform Party, nor elected by the public, because he was a loyal and long-term member of the Reform Party. Rather, he won, as one political analyst says, because of his "name recognition and media skills." It is certainly surprising for a third-party candidate to win a governor's race, but the way he won is not. In the following essay, Beiler describes a candidate-centered campaign, one in which the winning candidate got into office, to quote Ehrenhalt, "through a combination of ambition, talent, and the willingness to devote whatever time was necessary to" win.

Questions to Consider

As you read the essay, these are some questions to consider:

- How well does the case study support Ehrenhalt's argument? What parts of the study are the most supportive of his argument? What parts do not seem to fit?
- Is it possible that, despite all the author's attention to Ventura's communication skills, the real factor determining the outcome of the race was poor strategy by the two major-party candidates? Why did Ventura win?
- Daniel Elazar identifies Minnesota as a moralistic state. How important do you think the state's political culture was in Ventura's success? How successful do you think a candidate like Jesse Ventura would be in your state's political culture?

- After reading the case study, do you think that Ventura had an appropriate background to serve as governor? Are widespread name recognition, good communication skills, and a job history that was highlighted by both wrestling and shock radio sufficient skills to be elected to the highest office in the state? Should there be some sort of gatekeeper to political office, such as a party organization, that would make sure that whoever is elected is not only popular, but actually has the ability to govern?

The Body Politic Registers a Protest

David Beiler

Dean Barkley sensed there was something out of order. Then a fairly well-known candidate for the U.S. Senate, he was marching in a July 4 parade when he noticed that his aide-de-camp was attracting the crowd's attention.

"Next time, *you* be the candidate," he told Jesse Ventura. A former pro wrestler who now earned his Harleys as a radio shock jock and action flick bit player, Ventura chuckled at Barkley's outrageous thought.

He would be the first of many—including most of Minnesota's political establishment—to laugh at Ventura the candidate. But they're not laughing anymore. Ventura is their new governor.

That Ventura would be so easily dismissed by some of the best political minds in the country is the *real* man-bites-dog story here, though it was largely overlooked by the national media horde that trampled the tundra of the Gopher State in November. True, Ventura's Reform Party held no state or federal offices; true, he was being outspent 15-to-1 by his Democratic and Republican rivals right up until five weeks before the election. But the dynamics of American voter behavior have been changing for years, in ways yet unfathomed by many big-league strategists.

"It could happen anywhere," warns pollster Fred Steeper, who worked the race for Ventura's GOP nominee. State Democratic Executive Director Kathy Czar agrees: "If you're up against a third-party candidate with name recognition and media skills, you'd better take them seriously, even if they're short of money."

The warp-speed rise of Ventura offers more than just a wake-up call; it can provide a crash course in the cartography of a new electoral order.

Heavy to Hero

A notorious bad guy in the repertory theater known as the World Wrestling Federation, Ventura continued to nurture his notoriety after retiring from the canvas in 1986. Stints in such movies as Predator and as a ringside commentator for TBS eventually gave way to a steady gig as a radio talk show host in his hometown of Minneapolis. Ventura's public tough guy image notwithstanding, environmental issues propelled him to his first political involvement.

Concerned that stormwater runoff was being dumped into wetlands near his neighborhood, Ventura complained to the City Council of Brooklyn Park, home to 60,000 suburbanites. Dissatisfied with the official response, the riled 250-pound grappler successfully ran for town mayor in 1990, quintupling voter turnout in the process.

The job was, in essence, to chair a part-time legislative body. At its meetings, Ventura chewed tobacco. He occasionally skipped them altogether as he made movies and personal appearances around the country. But his forceful leadership made its mark, and he left office after one term with his popularity intact.

Meanwhile, Barkley had been paving the way for an outsider's takeover of state government.

David Beiler, "The Body Politic Registers a Protest," *Campaigns & Elections* (February 1999): 34–43. Reprinted by permission of *Campaigns & Elections* Magazine.

Inspired by Ross Perot's example, Barkley launched an independent run for Congress in 1992. The lawyer/marketer spent only $64,000, but received endorsements from the two major Twin Cities newspapers and ultimately won an impressive 16 percent of the four-way general election vote.

Setting his sights higher in 1994, Barkley ran for the U.S. Senate and won official status for the Independence Party with his 5-percent showing. After the IP affiliated with the Reform Party in 1996, Barkley launched a second Senate run and improved to 7 percent.

Campaigning for the Senate often landed Barkley a guest slot on Ventura's radio show, where the host was fond of comparing the major parties to Los Angeles street gangs, dubbing them the ReBLOODicans and DemoCRYPTS. Ventura chaired Barkley's '96 campaign, but resisted Reformers' suggestions he run for governor.

The fledgling party had been gaining ground on other fronts, however: Reformer Steve Minn won a nonpartisan seat on the Minneapolis City Council in '93; two years later, radio talk jock Barbara Carlson—the earthy ex-wife of ex-Gov. Arne Carlson (R)—ran a strong race for mayor of Minneapolis as the Reform endorsee.

By the fall of '97, Ventura had grudgingly agreed to be a gubernatorial candidate, and Barkley—now operating a car wash business—had drafted a campaign plan with designated manager Doug Friedline, proprietor of a pull-tab gambling operation housed in a Minneapolis bar.

Barkley's scenario anticipated that the Democrats and Republicans would nominate pro-life candidates, leaving Ventura the only pro-choice alternative in a pro-choice state. That didn't happen, but everything else in his plan did play out as expected: Get Ventura into the debates and excel there; raise half a million dollars for a last-minute media blitz; hit the '92 Perot mark of 24 percent in mid-October polling; energize the youth vote.

But months would pass before the campaign got off the ground. A New Year's fundraiser went poorly, and the candidate seemed to be dragging his feet. On January 17 of election year, the staff delivered Ventura an ultimatum: Kick in $10,000 of seed money or make an official announcement. Otherwise, they would toss in the towel.

Ventura soon announced, but the treasury remained bare for months.

Back in the Real World

Despite its potential for crowd appeal, the Ventura campaign drew scant attention in the early days of 1998. Gov. Carlson was stepping down, and the Republicans had a wide-open, three-way race to succeed him. But a trio of historic marquee names had kept tongues wagging about the Democratic primary for more than a year.

It was the battle between "My Three Sons"—chips off three of the most venerated blocks of political timber ever produced by Minnesota's Democratic Farmer-Labor Party. One was Mike Freeman son of former governor and Kennedy cabinet member Orville Freeman; the two others (ex-state Sen. Ted Mondale and Attorney General Hubert H. "Skip" Humphrey III) were sons of former U.S. senators who later became vice presidents and presidential nominees. The pedigreed trio were joined by pro-life state Sen. Doug Johnson and state auditor Mark Dayton, heir to a department store chain.

Backed by the party's more liberal elements, such as the AFL-CIO and U.S. Sen. Paul Wellstone, Freeman edged Humphrey for the party endorsement in June, but trailed him in polls for the September primary. A suburban candidate with a suburban running mate, Mondale sounded moderate New Democrat themes that fell flat with traditional Democratic constituencies. Dayton, who lost an '82 Senate race, had feminist backing and imaginative, plentiful advertising. Johnson ran a clever campaign, contrasting himself against the "silver-spoon" candidates, though he seemed out-of-tune with the party's social liberalism.

Humphrey, who had made a disappointing run for his father's old Senate seat, won a $6-billion tobacco settlement for the state in May that many pundits felt would propel him into the governorship. But his flip on the abortion issue (to the choice position) bothered some voters.

The Republican intramural initially had four players. Moderate state Sen. Roy Terwillegar started early and visited all 87 counties and logged 45,000 miles on the campaign trail. But when a March poll had him at 4 percent, he folded his tent.

That left the GOP field to three pro-life conservatives, the most extreme being Allen Quist, who had won the party's gubernatorial endorsement in '94 but went on to lose the primary.

Lt. Gov. Joanne Benson was also running to succeed Carlson—the man who put her there—plainly without his blessings, but backed instead by U.S. Sen. Rod Grams.

The presumed Carlson candidate was St. Paul Mayor Norm Coleman, who had switched from the DFL in '96. A pragmatic conservative, Coleman won support from such luminaries as Cong. Jim Ramstad, House Minority Leader Steve Sviggum and national GOP guru Vin Weber.

Coleman was backed by an organization skippered by ex-party Chair Chris Georgacas. He proved to be an appealing candidate and led the caucuses virtually everywhere in the state. The June convention endorsed him on the fourth ballot.

Bodily Charm

The reputation Barkley had established as the state's leading nonpartisan moderate paid off big dividends in January.

Former congressman Tim Penny, a fiscally conservative Democrat, had recently organized the Minnesota Compact, a good government group devoted to making campaigns more substantive. Highly regarded by both parties, Penny succeeded in making the compact a key part of the upcoming gubernatorial debates. At Penny's request, Barkley became co-director, boosting Ventura's chances for inclusion in upcoming debates.

Minnesota's primaries are not held until September, and the long nomination season also played into Ventura's hand. He was invited to many debates and forums, throughout the spring and summer, sponsored by local civic groups across the state. Barkley's strategy called for his candidate to accept as many such opportunities as possible. The forums were so numerous and the election so far away, little attention was being paid to these events by the press or the public. But they afforded a raw, novice candidate the opportunity to prep for prime time.

"Jesse's style never changed," explains Barkley, "but those early forums let him get comfortable with the format and learn about the issues . . . before the pressure was really on."

Meanwhile, Ventura began building a base among his wrestling fans. They were not hard to find.

As their candidate marched in a seven-block parade down the streets of Minneapolis on St. Patrick's Day, Reformers found eager takers for 10,000 pieces of literature. At a major wrestling event in April, pandemonium broke loose as Ventura made a grand entrance, unannounced, yet well-advanced. A few days later, he energized thousands of protestors on the Capitol steps with a blast against the legislature for its vote to return only half of a $4-billion budget surplus to the taxpayers.

A celebrity in Minnesota's popular culture, Ventura started the campaign with widespread name recognition (64 percent), surpassed by only three other candidates: Democrats Humphrey and Mondale and GOP frontrunner Coleman. Comprised largely of young, disaffected, middle-class males, Ventura's initial audience hardly fit a high-turnout profile or a dowager's idea of decorum, but he did not hesitate to round it up and put it in a political harness.

A typical Ventura event found the candidate regaling college students within easy driving distance of his suburban Minneapolis home, quoting philosophers such as Jim Morrison and Jerry Garcia. His schedule was spotty before he was compelled to leave his radio program in July (having finally filed as a candidate), and even sparse thereafter. Though he began to venture beyond the Twin Cities media market in August, he was soon sticking to the homefront again. The results were telling on election day: He lost only one county within a hundred miles of his base, but lagged elsewhere.

"That was by design," explains Ventura's free-spirited media man, Bill Hillsman of North Woods Advertising. "We had to make efficient use of the candidate's time, and the Twin Cities media cover 80 percent of the state."

The candidate impishly claims his close-to-home schedule was dictated by his determination to not miss a practice of the high school football team for which he serves as a volunteer coach. But in truth, this populist revolution was a front porch campaign, driven by Twin Cities journalists looking for colorful copy. The media mountain came to the Minnesota Mohammed, and it was rarely disappointed.

"The press doesn't go out and make their own story," says Barkley. "You've got to give it to them. They'll take it if you can make it meaningful and interesting. And it helps to be colorful and controversial."

Before a student rally at St. Cloud State, Ventura, a community college drop-out, rejected the idea of further state subsidies for tuition. "If you're smart enough to get here," he bellowed, "you're smart enough to figure out how to pay for it." On the flip side, Ventura was fond of decrying the proliferation of laws designed to "save stupid people from themselves," suggesting to do so was interfering with the evolutionary process.

When a debate moderator tried to preface a question by asserting, "To be governor of Minnesota, you have to be an expert in agriculture," Ventura quickly admonished, "No you don't." His capacity for political sacrilege seemed boundless.

But the refreshing Reformer was not all swagger and shock; he often took substantive positions that resonated with those who felt Minnesota's paternalistic government needed a tug on the reins: Return the surplus, forget subsidies for sports moguls, let people carry a gun so they can protect themselves. And while you're at it, cut the student/teacher ratio.

Faced with a horrendous 4-to-1 gender gap, Ventura named elementary school teacher Mae Schunk his running mate for lieutenant governor. He explained that, if elected, he would leave education policy to the 64-year-old schoolmarm.

"Ventura won all the debates," opines Wy Spano, "because he always gave a straight answer, even if it was 'I don't know the answer.' "

Editor of the newsletter *Politics in Minnesota,* Spano was amazed at how directly Ventura's approach ran contrary to standard professional advice: "Unlike the practiced politicians he was up against, he never stayed on message, deflecting the tough questions. That really set him apart. Voters figured the politicians were just telling them what they wanted to hear, and only Jesse was telling them the truth. . . . They'll vote for someone they disagree with, if he's the only one they can believe."

No More Play Time

Ventura's quest hit a watershed on July 21, when he was finally compelled to formally file his candidacy and was immediately relieved of his radio show. Play time was over.

After six months in the field, the campaign had raised a pitiful $12,000. If they were to qualify for the $326,000 in public matching funds, another $35,000 would have to be raised by the end of August, in contributions of $50 or less.

A Ventura T-shirt—bearing the snarling slogan "Retaliate in '98"—had been introduced at Fourth of July parades and was beginning to sell briskly at $20. Hundreds flew out of the Reform Party booth at the state fair in August, and $62,000 had been collected by the end of the month.

Even though the threshold for the state subsidy had been met, the $326,000 taxpayer subsidy could not be collected until a month *after* the election, and then only if Ventura topped 5 percent on election day. That level of performance seemed assured, as Jesse was posting between 11 percent and 13 percent in the polls. But bankers are not conditioned to take polls as collateral.

A program soliciting small personal loans from supporters was heralded on Ventura's Internet Web site, and produced about $1,500 a day. The candidate spoke at the Reform Party convention in Atlanta, but failed to raise much money from the national party cohorts.

On September 15, the Democratic primary had predictably been swept by Humphrey, piling up 37 percent against 19 percent for Freeman. Enthusiasm was palpably low: Turnout failed to crack 20 percent, the lowest in the 50 years that records had been kept.

The 18 percent third place posted by Johnson proved the biggest surprise. Much of the credit for this obscure pro-lifer's impressive showing went to his quirky TV spots, which engagingly appealed to Minnesota's populist tradition. They had been crafted by Hillsman, the same media iconoclast whose ads had helped win Wellstone a Senate seat in 1990, despite being [out] spent nearly 5-to-1.

Five days after the DFL primary, Barkley received a letter from Hillsman offering his services to the Ventura campaign.

"Bill was a perfect fit," the Reform strategist admits, "but he had always been close to Democrats. I hadn't thought he'd do it."

"I liked Dean and respected his positions for years," explains Hillsman, "and I had watched Jesse at all those candidate forums over the summer. . . . I was impressed."

Coming aboard with less than six weeks left to the campaign, Hillsman immediately returned the Ventura effort to a fixation on Twin Cities free media. His first act was to stop the candidate from taking a three-hour road trip to Mankato for an interview on a public access cable station.

While the scramble continued to get a loan to cover expenses pending payment of the public subsidy, Hillsman began crafting radio ads designed to attract immediate media attention. Drawing on Ventura's tough guy image and background as a Navy SEAL in Vietnam, he composed an attitude-laden jingle to the strains of "Shaft:" "When the other guys were cashing their government checks/He was in the Navy, gettin' dirty and wet/Well, they try to tell you he can't win/But we'll vote our conscience and we'll vote him in."

Right on.

Debunking the Debates

What the major party candidates had in terms of monetary advantage, they made up for in lack of inspiration. In an early debate, Coleman had gaffed that "we're going to have to redefine the family farm," suggesting that small operations simply weren't viable anymore. He had spent months on the cowpaths ever since, desperately catering to farmers and trying to shed his image as a city kid from Brooklyn. He went even further than Humphrey in advocating farm subsidies and in forgiving property taxes on cropland.

"It was an absurd spectacle of someone trying to be something he wasn't," assays Spano. But it finally began to pay dividends in early October. Two state senators recognized as leaders on farm issues—one a Democrat, one an independent—unexpectedly backed the Republican.

Coleman, looking more like a liberal panderer, failed to tie down the swing-vote suburbs, a constituency he felt was safe in against big-spender Humphrey. But there was another wolf at this door, one whose pro-choice position might eventually resonate with suburban Republican women.

The idea that Ventura could siphon off Coleman votes *had* occurred to Humphrey's strategists. Buying the conventional wisdom that the wrestler's macho, libertarian appeal synched better with Republicans than Democrats, Humphrey refused to debate Coleman *unless* Ventura was also included.

Fresh from his primary triumph, and shortly after the death of his mother, Humphrey opened up a huge 20-point lead in mid-September polling, and appeared ready to coast to victory with a prevent defense. Trapped in third place and being outspent massively, Ventura looked less like a threat than a way to pull some votes off of Coleman.

Attention was now focused on the three debates sponsored by the League of Women Voters, all due to be carried on statewide television.

At the first such event, in Brainerd on Oct. 1, Coleman again pitched for rural votes, while Humphrey tried to shoot down charges he would raise taxes as governor. While concentrating on Humphrey, Ventura attacked both major party entries for their partisan posturing and lack of leadership, but drew only condescending smiles from his rivals.

The following day's headline in the *St. Paul Pioneer Press* declared: "Leaders battle, Ventura charms." The entry in Barkley's log reads: "Jesse hits a home run." Media interest in the Reformer began to perk up; money or no money, he was plainly on the move. And at Humphrey's expense.

"The biggest mistake of the campaign was Humphrey's insistence that Ventura be in the debates," declares Coleman pollster Fred Steeper. "Like Perot in '92, Ventura connected instantly with that middle-class swing vote that had been parked with Humphrey, largely from recognition. . . . He became the champion of the little guy against the established powers. . . . Humphrey performed poorly in the debates and couldn't hold them."

Spano agrees, reporting the AFL-CIO phone bank nearly shut down two weeks out, after it was found to be reaching as many voters for Ventura as Humphrey.

By Oct. 10, with his lead cut by a third and Ventura rising into the mid-teens, Humphrey began skipping the lesser, late debates. He was markedly more aggressive in the second televised event on Oct. 11, charging Coleman with running up an astronomical debt in St. Paul. Humphrey's media campaign became so pointed, Coleman filed suit in all 87 counties, charging that Democratic ads had violated the state Fair Campaign Practices Act by lying about his record. Humphrey was such a spendthrift, Coleman charged, "he doesn't know what a budget is."

Rising above the bickering, Ventura continued to endear himself to the public and press with expressions of candor most major party candidates would have considered fatal. Running counter to his macho image—but straight after Humphrey's crumbling support—he endorsed gay rights, declaring "love is bigger than government."

"Ventura could have been stopped by bringing the public's attention to the import of his libertarian, outrageous positions," insists Steeper. "It wouldn't have been difficult. He had left such statements in the public record all year long."

Naked and the Dead

But the big boys weren't biting. The idea that a destitute third-party wrestler could actually win was beyond their concept of plausibility. Pundits and major party pols presumed Ventura's vote would follow the classic third-party pattern of falling away in the closing days of the campaign. Both Coleman and Humphrey tried to position themselves as the beneficiary.

"Neither wanted to be the one to stick Jesse with the "emperor's clothes' routine," offers DFL executive director Kathy Czar. "They didn't want to alienate his voters by bursting his bubble."

The Late Fade Theory of third-party candidates relies on the assumption that such candidates will not have the resources to effectively compete in the final media battle. It also assumes that the "wasted vote" syndrome will kick in, that disaffecteds will grudgingly turn to the major parties—or not turn out at all—once they realize their candidate can't win.

Neither of these assumptions applied to Ventura.

On Oct. 20, a *Star-Tribune* poll reported that Humphrey's lead had vanished and the Reform Party standard bearer was up to 21 percent. That helped the Ventura campaign close in on a $266,000 loan from the Franklin National Bank the next day.

The draft had been arranged by Minneapolis Alderman Steve Minn, chair of the Reform state convention, and it had required the taking out of an insurance policy that guaranteed payment.

The cash infusion came at the precise moment it was needed to launch Hillsman's long-planned TV flights. The first spot used the simple graphic of an American flag, the voiceover decrying the debilitating effects of partisan division as the camera panned over the alternating red and white stripes; it then shifted into a paean to Ventura's unifying influence as the screen zoomed to a star on a true blue field.

The soft allegories were a letdown for the newsies, who expected more fireworks from the Ventura/Hillsman combo. "I could tell the press was disappointed," a sensitized Hillsman recalls, having been inculcated by the Wellstone race in the value of crafting spots for free media attention. "I knew, however, we had something coming down the production line that they would really push."

The press pleaser was a takeoff on Ventura's days as a WWF star, when he had his own toy "action figure" on the market, popular enough to buy him a Porsche with a single month's royalties. Two boys were depicted playing with a new version of the figure—Ventura in a business suit—as he battled "Evil Special Interest Man."

"I don't want your stupid money," one kid had Ventura hoot, as the corrupting lobbyist took a well-deserved sock.

True to its billing, "Action Figure" grabbed gobs of free newscast airtime as campaign money began pouring into Ventura's coffers at the rate of $10,000 per day. And the hoopla over it helped douse the only major media crisis suffered by the campaign on Oct. 21.

Asked if he supported legalizing prostitution and drugs, Ventura answered no, but said that legalizing prostitution might bear a second look, as "Nevada doesn't seem to have a problem with it."

"It was the worst timing," shudders Barkley, who at that very moment was getting ready to ink the bank loan. "I was afraid it would blow the deal."

But in the end, the damage was minimal. Humphrey and Coleman both took their first swings at the issue, but they were too absorbed in the task of destroying each other to bother following up. The news media was simply too enamored of the breaking story of Ventura's new-found viability to risk nipping it in the bud. For the first time, reporters began speculating about a third-party win.

"How would you deal with a legislature that includes no members of your party?" reporters asked, to which the brawny candidate responded by rolling up a sleeve and flexing a bieep. The copy and visuals were just too good to ignore.

The identities of Coleman and Humphrey were becoming merged into one gray, dispiriting backdrop against the vibrant color of Ventura's civic carnival. Coleman's platitudinous ad campaign had been pushing the slogan "Norm Coleman: The Only One." Now Humphrey blended in with spots trumpeting "Only Humphrey."

The dissing duo polluted the airwaves with attacks and counter-attacks at their Oct. 24 debate, Humphrey charging "Norman" with seeking "straight tax dollars for his cronies," while Coleman derided the Democrat's pledge to push for Medicare benefits in Washington as a promise Humphrey had made and broken a decade before. The beleaguered moderator was reduced to endlessly shouting "Stop!"

As the flak thickened, big guns from the major parties rolled into the state to fire a few partisan rounds, led by First Lady Hillary Clinton, USDA Secretary Dan Glickman, and erstwhile former GOP ticket-mates Bob Dole and Jack Kemp. To Clinton's calling him a "sideshow," Ventura drily responded: "If I were her, I'd be more concerned about leaving Bill in the White House."

Now leading among all men and voters under-45, Jesse was looking less and less like a freak to be gawked at. But to push to a winning plurality, he had to sober up his image, tighten his gender gap and maintain a sense of bandwagon momentum that would run over any remaining "wasted-vote" qualms.

Hillsman quickly and effectively met these challenges, one by one. He produced a new version of "Action Figure" that introduced a new "war-wagon" accessory: the RV that Ventura would use to barnstorm the state in a non-stop performance over the campaign's last 72 hours.

To drive home the point that his candidate had a record of public service and had discussed issues more thoroughly than had his opponents, Hillsman produced "The Thinker" spot, playing against Ventura's nickname, "The Body." To assure viewers he hadn't suddenly begun to take himself too seriously, the statuesque statesman winks at the camera in the closing shot.

Filmed a week before the election (with a body-builder double minimizing Ventura's studio time), "Thinker" hit the air on Saturday night, and proved to be the crowning blow. News accounts juxtaposed "Thinker" clips with reports of Ventura rampaging across the countryside, exhorting student masses to storm the polls.

Hi-Tech Nervous System

In addition to the ads and news coverage, the campaign's Web site was a particularly effective mobilization and information tool. Early in the race, Ventura realized that the Internet was "tailor-made" for his kind of low budget, unconventional campaign. "It's reaching a huge amount of people at a very low price," he was quoted as observing.

Phil Madsen, director of the campaign's Web site and an initial organizer of Minnesota's Reform Party, was quoted as saying that the "Internet for us served as the nervous system of the campaign. The Web site was the difference; it was the mobilization."

According to American University researcher Rebecca Strauss, much of Ventura's use of the Internet was as a behind-the-scenes coordinating tool. The campaign's big closing event, a 72-hour final drive through the state, was organized and coordinated entirely by e-mail through its Web site. Madsen sent out an e-mail to his 3,000 member list, called "JesseNet," inviting volunteers to a meeting; more than 250 people showed up to help organize the tour.

Another big factor in Ventura's [favor] was Minnesota's unusual election law. It gives voters the right to register at the polls *on election day.* That made Ventura's impact particularly hard to gauge, especially for pollsters who never showed the full force of the Reform surge.

In the end, voter turnout hit 61 percent of the voting age population (the highest in the country)—and

16 percent of the total election day electorate had registered at the polls, a figure unseen since the law's inception in 1974. Analysts estimate more than three of every four new voters opted for Ventura.

The result would stun political analysts across the country. Only a few local wags predicted a Reform Party win and of the national predictions only this magazine's Internet handicapping service, *The Political Oddsmaker,* came close, calling Ventura an even bet to win. The final vote percentages were Ventura 37, Coleman 34 and Humphrey, the initial frontrunner, 28.

Not surprisingly, the late night comics had a field day with the Minnesota results (make that a field *week*), and Minnesotans soon grew testy about their ridiculed voting behavior. Several days after the Ventura earthquake, David Letterman introduced a special segment titled "What the Hell Happened in Minnesota?" a question he intended to pose to a caller chosen at random from the state's phone books. After identifying himself and his "little podunk show on CBS," Letterman pitched his query. He quickly received a click and a dialtone.

"We've circled the wagons," explains Wy Spano. "Everybody defensively insists Jesse will do just fine."

But there is no shortage of political operatives ready to answer Letterman's question.

"Jesse's participation in the debates was probably the most important factor," says Kathy Czar. "He came across as real and established his credibility. After all, he makes his living in radio and has got the sound bite routine down pat."

Steve Minn points to Minnesota's unusually reform-minded election laws: same-day registration, public financing and a provision by which the first $50 donated to any candidate for state office is rebated by the state. "I don't think it could happen anywhere else," he admits, though he concedes that the threshold for third candidate credibility may have been lowered.

A widely perceived arrogance of the state's power structure was key to Ventura's appeal, an attitude that was sustained "in the elevator," as Minn puts it: reassuring word of mouth among friends and co-workers that bolstered their own inclinations. The vaunted opinionmakers were bypassed and disregarded with revolutionary relish.

"I was fooled because conditions here are so good," explains Spano. "Unemployment is the lowest in the country, home ownership is the highest, test scores are at the top. We have the best-run state in the Union. You naturally assume people who have all that will vote for the status quo."

Although times are good in Minnesota and around the nation for now, more and more voters are coming to the conclusion that a two-dimensional electoral system does not represent their will very well, or even respect their opinions. They see two hypocritical political parties ignoring the public interest while they tear at one another and operate as slaves to a corrupt campaign finance system.

If a Jesse Ventura can win the highest elective office in one of America's most prosperous states in the most prosperous of our national times, political professionals should start asking, then what power structure is, indeed, truly secure?

Chapter 6 Review Questions

1. How do party-centered campaigns differ from candidate-centered ones? What reforms and trends were important in causing the rise of candidate-centered campaigns?
2. What are some of the defining characteristics of modern election campaigns as described by Alan Ehrenhalt? Who runs for office? What factors are important in determining who wins? How important are money and television in campaigns?
3. In what ways does the Jesse Ventura race illustrate some of the key characteristics of modern campaigns? Do any of these characteristics trouble you? Why or why not?
4. Why did Ventura win? What, if anything, can that election teach us about what makes a successful campaign?

5. In explaining the Democrats' advantage in winning campaigns, Ehrenhalt writes, "It is not really a matter of demand. It is a matter of supply." What does he mean by that? Why does Ehrenhalt say the electoral system favors the Democratic Party?
6. Many voters do not like political parties, arguing that they play too large a role in elections and politics. After reading the essays by Ehrenhalt and Beiler, do you think that voters should be more critical of parties? Less critical? Explain your reasoning.

Key Terms

political party
party machine
Progressive Movement
direct primary
nonpartisan election
campaign consulting firm
political action committee
candidate-centered campaign
party-centered campaign
retrospective voting
omnicompetent citizen
uninformed voter
professional politician
citizen legislator
party decline
entrepreneurial candidate
special interests
third party
Late Fade Theory

Suggestions for Further Reading

Appleton, Andrew W., and Daniel S. Ward, eds. *State Party Profiles: A 50-State Guide to Development, Organization, and Resources.* Washington, D.C.: Congressional Quarterly, 1997. Collection of essays detailing the history and structure of the party organizations in each of the fifty states.

Banfield, Edward C., and James Q. Wilson. *City Politics.* Cambridge, Mass.: Harvard University Press, 1963. Provides one of the best explanations of how party machines operate.

Beatty, Jack. *The Rascal King: The Life and Times of James Michael Curley, 1874–1958.* Reading, Mass.: DeCapo Press, 2000. Biography of James Curley, the boss of Boston politics for fifty years.

Beck, Paul Allen, and Marjorie Randon Hershey. *Party Politics in America.* 10th ed. New York: Longman, 2002. Leading textbook on American political parties, with attention given to national, state, and local parties.

Bibby, John F. "State Party Organization: Strengthened and Adapting to Candidate-Centered Politics and Nationalization." In *The Parties Respond: Changes in the American Party System.* 4th ed. Edited by L. Sandy Maisel. Boulder, Colo.: Westview Press, 2002. Provides a good overview on the role of state party organizations in elections today.

Carsey, Thomas M. *Campaign Dynamics: The Race for Governor.* Ann Arbor: University of Michigan Press, 2000. In-depth analysis of gubernatorial campaigns and their effect on how people vote.

Clucas, Richard A. *The Speaker's Electoral Connection: Willie Brown and the California Assembly.* Berkeley, Calif.: Institute of Government Studies, 1995. Examines the involvement of California Assembly Speaker Willie Brown in state legislative elections, and how his campaign activities affected legislative politics.

Cotter, Cornelius P., James L. Gibson, John F. Bibby, and Robert J. Huckshorn. *Party Organizations in American Politics.* New York: Praeger, 1984. Broad overview of the role and importance of political parties in state and local politics.

Frank, Stephen I., and Steven C. Wagner. *We Shocked the World!: A Case Study of Jesse Ventura's Election as Governor of Minnesota.* Fort Worth, Tex.: Harcourt College Publishers, 1999. In-depth study of Ventura's successful gubernatorial campaign.

Grimshaw, William J. *Bitter Fruit: Black Politics and the Chicago Machine, 1931–1991.* Reissue Edition. Chicago: University of Chicago Press, 1995. Historical analysis of one of the nation's most well-known party machines and its relationship with the African American community.

Jewell, Malcolm E., and Sarah M. Morehouse. *Political Parties and Elections in American States.* 4th ed. Washington, D.C.: CQ Press, 2001. This is the most comprehensive book on state parties and elections in print.

Lentz, Jacob. *Electing Jesse Ventura: A Third-Party Success Story.* Boulder, Colo.: Lienne Rienner Publishers, 2002. In-depth analysis of Ventura's gubernatorial victory.

Moncrief, Gary F., Peverill Squire, and Malcolm F. Jewell. *Who Runs for the Legislature?* Upper Saddle River, N.J.: Prentice Hall, 2001. Analysis of state legislative candidates and campaigns in eight states.

Reichley, James A. *The Life of the Parties: A History of American Political Parties.* Lanham, Md.: Rowman and Littlefield, 2000. Reichley provides a detailed history of American political parties from the nation's founding through the beginning of the current century. Considerable attention is devoted to the decline of parties and their recent resurgence.

Salmore, Stephen A., and Barbara G. Salmore. "The Transformation of State Electoral Politics." In *The State of the States.* 3d ed. Edited by Carl Van Horn. Washington, D.C.: CQ Press, 1996. Provides a good overview on the character of state and local campaigns today, including how they have become more candidate-centered.

Shea, Daniel M. *Transforming Democracy.* Albany: State University of New York, 1995. Analyzes the growing role of state legislative campaign committees in elections and their impact on party politics.

Related Web Sites

http://www.nass.org/index.html
In most states, the secretary of state oversees the administration of elections. The National Association of Secretary of States provides information on election-related issues and links to the home page of secretary of states in every state.

http://www.politics1.com/
This web site provides information on campaigns and elections in the states and links to major and minor political parties.

http://www.dnc.org
http://www.gop.com/ContactUs/
The web sites for the national Democratic and Republican Parties include up-to-date links to their state party affiliates.

http://www.vote-smart.org
Project Vote Smart provides information on candidates and elected officials, including campaign finance data, issue positions, and voting records.

http://news.minnesota.publicradio.org/collections/special/1998/11/ventura/index.shtml
Minnesota Public Radio offers a web site assessing Ventura's legacy as governor and providing archived news stories.

7

Interest Representation: The Concept of Group Power

The number one element determining the political clout of a group is how much they are needed by politicians and government.

Clive S. Thomas and Ronald J. Hrebenar

READING 7

Introduction

Many Americans today believe that interest groups have become too influential in all levels of government, drowning out the voice of ordinary citizens and controlling the direction of public policy. Interest groups are regularly seen as a corrupting influence in the nation's democracy, using pressure tactics and campaign contributions to bend political leaders to their will. The media frequently reinforce this negative image, since stories of power and corruption make good copy. Of course, Americans have long been distrustful of interest groups. For example, during the early 1900s, with the emergence of the Progressive Movement, political reformers railed against interest groups and sought to curtail their power in the states by revising election laws, altering governmental structures, and introducing direct democracy. Even the nation's founders expressed concerns about groups. Perhaps the most eloquent statement written about the potential harm of interest groups appears in the writings of James Madison in the *Federalist Papers.* In *Federalist* No. 10, Madison discussed the potential threat that groups of citizens could bring to the rights of others. Madison then argued that the structure of the new nation's government must be designed in such a way as to control the "mischiefs of factions."[1]

How accurate is this image of interest groups? Do they play a corrupting role in democracy? How much influence do groups actually have in state politics? Not all political scientists believe that interest groups harm democracy. During the 1950s, in fact, many political scientists began to subscribe to the ideas of *pluralism,* viewing interest groups as a fundamental part of democracy. Pluralism sees democracy as a political system in which individuals join together into groups that compete against each other to influence government action. Public policy decisions are seen as compromises between these competing groups. Ever since the ideas of pluralism were first laid out in the 1950s, they have received a great deal of criticism and are not as widely accepted today as a good description of the nation's political system. However, most scholars would still argue that interest groups play an important role in democracy by aggregating the views of individual citizens and shaping policy decisions. The questions that concern many scholars today are why some interests are better represented than others, why some groups are more powerful, and just how much influence interest groups actually have on politics.

The question as to why some interests are better represented than others is taken up more frequently by scholars studying interest groups from a national perspective. Scholars of state politics have been more interested in understanding why some groups are more powerful than others and why the influence of interest groups tends to be greater in some states. The work of Belle Zeller in the early 1950s was the first to make a systematic effort to examine the power of interest groups across the states compared with other political actors.[2] Relying on a survey of political experts in each state, Zeller categorized the states into three groups, according to whether interest groups had strong, moderate, or weak influence on state legislatures. A majority of states were considered to have strong groups and were listed in the first category, while only a handful of states reported weak groups. Ever since Zeller's work appeared in 1954, other scholars have developed similar classification systems to analyze the relative power of interest groups.

Clive Thomas and Ronald Hrebenar provide the most recent efforts that follow in this line of research. Since the late 1980s, these two political science professors have regularly surveyed political experts across the states, asking them to rate the relative power of interest groups in their states and to identify the groups that are the most powerful. Interest group scholars often cite Thomas and Hrebenar's research because it provides the most comprehensive comparison of interest group power across the states. The essay that follows presents the findings from Thomas and Hrebenar's survey that was taken in the late 1990s. Since the publication of this essay, which appeared in *Comparative State Politics,* Thomas and Hrebenar have conducted another round of their survey. The *Comparative State Politics* essay is valuable to read, however, because it provides both directions on how to think about group power and a concise explanation of their findings over time. The results of the most recent survey, which was conducted in 2002, parallel those in the 1999 one.[3]

In their essay, Thomas and Hrebenar explain how the notion of group power can have three different meanings. First, group power can refer to the ability of individual groups to obtain the political goals that they seek. Second, group power can refer to the individual groups in any given state that are commonly viewed as having considerable power. Finally, group power can refer to the influence that interest groups generally have in shaping politics when compared with other actors within a state's political system, including political parties, legislators, and governors. In the remainder of the essay, the two authors present the results from their survey, identifying the types of groups that are considered particularly powerful across the states and describing the relative power of groups in general in each state.

Looking at the types of groups that are most powerful, the authors' findings are similar to those earlier studies, including the ones that they have conducted. The two groups that are most frequently mentioned as being "very effective" are teachers' organizations and business groups. These are followed by a diverse array of others, from associations to government organizations to individual institutions. The authors write that the one factor that ties all of the groups together at the top of the list is that they provide some benefit on which politicians or the government depends. Interest group power, in other words, grows out of political needs; groups that can help fulfill those needs are in a better position than others to exercise influence. Looking at the relative power of groups compared with other actors, Thomas and Hrebenar again find considerable similarities to the findings of earlier studies. In general, interest groups are considered quite strong in most states, although they do not entirely dominate state politics.

The work by Professors Thomas and Hrebenar does not tell us everything of importance about the power of interest groups. For example, they make only passing reference to the explosion of interest groups that has taken place at both the state and national level and which may have allowed newer groups, including many citizen ones, to have greater influence over state politics than was true in the past. For some political scientists, this explosion has been a good development, allowing many interests that went unheard in the past to now have a voice in state politics. To other scholars, the appearance of more groups is not necessarily better. Some scholars have grown worried that while the proliferation of groups may make the system more democratic, it has led to *hyperpluralism,* which has made it more difficult for the government to act. With more groups lobbying government, it has become harder for elected officials to find common ground in shaping public policy and to think about what is in the state's overall best interest. Even so, the essay provides an excellent overview of the power of particular types of interest groups in state politics and the relative power of groups across the states.

Questions to Consider

Professor Thomas teaches at the University of Alaska Southeast. Professor Hrebenar is at the University of Utah. These are some questions to consider as you read their work:

- What do Thomas and Hrebenar mean when they write that "it is misleading to talk of *interest group power* in a generic sense"? How do they say one should talk about group power?
- How important are campaign contributions in shaping the clout of interest groups? Why are contributions important? What else can be important in shaping a group's clout?
- What factors are important in shaping group system power in the states? In other words, why do some states seem to have strong interest groups while others do not?
- In general, how strong are interest groups in your state compared with other political actors? Why is their influence so strong or so limited? What specific groups seem to be the most powerful? Why are these groups so effective?

Interest Group Power in the Fifty States: Trends Since the Late 1970s

Clive S. Thomas and Ronald J. Hrebenar

Interest groups have long been recognized as a major force—in some cases *the* major force—in state politics and policymaking. Down to the mid-1960s, the lack of pluralism in most states meant that interest groups had an even greater impact in the states, particularly in killing proposals, than they did in Washington, D.C. Until this time, most states were dominated—in some cases "run"—by a single or a handful of interests. Montana was run by Anaconda Copper. Delaware was dominated by Du Pont. Wyoming was sort of a colony of the Union Pacific Railroad. Michigan's politics reflected the enormous influence of the auto makers and the auto workers. The "big three"—electric power, timber, and textile and shoe manufacturing—were prominent in Maine. And Texas was dominated by the "big four"—oil, chemicals, the Texas Manufacturers Association, and railroads, to name but six states.

Yet, like developments in Washington, D.C., the last thirty years have seen a major expansion in the number and types of groups active in state capitals. The so-called "traditional interests"—business, labor, agriculture, education, and local government—that, more or less, had state capitals to themselves for two generations or more have been joined by a host of so-called new interests. These range from environmentalists to women's groups to gay rights and victims' rights groups to hunting and fishing interests to anti-poverty and senior citizens' lobbies. And the number and diversity of interests has been augmented by increased lobbying by traditional interests. For instance, many individual cities, towns, and special districts (especially school districts) now hire their own lobbyists while remaining part of a state league of cities; and a host of businesses, from IBM to local grocery chains, have their own lobbyists while retaining membership in a state manufacturers or other trade associations.

This major increase in lobbying activity raises questions about interest group influence across the fifty states. Have there been major changes in the interests that wield power in state capitals? Has the influence of the traditional interests been undermined by the new interests? Do these new interests now have major political clout? And how has this increasingly crowded state political playing field affected the influence of interest groups in general? Do lobbies and lobbyists exert less influence today than they did, say, in the late 1970s?

Our fifty-state research project on interest groups—the Hrebenar-Thomas Study—conducted over the last two decades and involving over a hundred political scientists, enables us to offer answers to these questions. Our findings also throw light on two other hitherto little understood aspects of interest group power. One is that we have been able to identify the essential elements of individual interest group and lobby power—is it just money, numbers, and contacts that determine influence, or are there other elements to group political influence? The second is that it is misleading to talk of *interest group power* in a generic sense. Our research reveals that *interest group* or *lobby power* can mean one of three things depending on the perspective from which it is viewed.[1]

Three Perspectives on Interest Group Power

The term *group power,* as used in interest group studies, can mean one of three things. First, it may refer to the ability of a single group or coalition to achieve its

Clive S. Thomas and Ronald J. Hrebenar, "Interest Group Power in the Fifty States: Trends Since the Late 1970s," *Comparative State Politics* 20 (August 1999): 3–16. Reprinted from *Comparative State Politics,* 20 (4): August 1999.

policy goals. Second, it may refer to the most effective interest groups and interests overall in the state over a period of time. Third, it may refer to the strength of interest groups as a whole within a state in relation to other organizations or institutions, particularly political parties. We refer to the first as *single group power,* to the second as *overall individual interest power,* and to the third as *group system power.* Political scientists have long realized that power is not the simple phenomenon that the press and the public often believe. In fact, power is one of the most elusive aspects of interest groups to study, particularly the measurement of overall individual interest power and group system power.

Perspective 1: Single Group Power

Single group power is the ability of a group or coalition to achieve its goals as it defines them. Consequently, the only important assessment of the degree of success is a group's internal evaluation. Some groups can be successful in achieving their goals but keep a low profile in a state and not be singled out as powerful by public officials and political observers. This could be the case for several reasons. It may be that the group is active only when it has an issue to work on, or, it could be an ad hoc group or coalition coming together on one issue and then disbanding when success is achieved. Or it could be that the group's issue is far from public view and of minor public concern. Many groups involved in the regulatory process are successful because they have "captured" their area of concern (gotten control of policymaking) because bureaucrats depend on their expertise. The last thing most of these groups would want is the public attention of being singled out as an effective group.

Though single group power is easy to define, developing a method to assess the relative power of groups is virtually impossible because, as we've said, these groups measure success according to their unique standards. Group leaders and their lobbyists are very reluctant to talk to anyone—particularly academic researchers—about their successes and their failures. Furthermore, even if we could develop a method to research and compare single group power, its value would be little more than academic. This is because there are so many groups and coalitions involved in state politics, most of whom are very minor players. The major contribution to interest group studies and to understanding state politics that a study of single group power offers is insights into the elements that constitute an effective group or lobby. We relate these briefly later in this article.

Perspective 2: Overall Individual Interest Power

This aspect of group power most interests the press and the public, who are less concerned about the minutiae of government and more intrigued with high profile questions, such as "who is running the state" or who has the "juice"—the real political clout? Whereas the only important assessment of single group power is internal to a group, overall interest power is based on external assessments of public officials—elected and appointed—and informed observers, such as journalists and political scientists.

There are several problems involved in such assessments, however. First, political scientists agree that the acquisition and exercise of power involves many factors. Second, it is hard to compare groups whose activity varies over time and from issue to issue. Given these problems, researchers have used three methods, singly or in combination, to assess overall interest power: sending questionnaires to public officials and sometimes conducting interviews with them; drawing on the expertise of political scientists; and consulting academic and popular literature on the states. Our assessment uses the Hrebenar-Thomas study, which combined quantitative and qualitative techniques employing the first two methods. This study has assessed overall interest power in all fifty states on three occasions, in 1989, 1994, and 1998, with a fourth partial assessment in 1985 involving twenty-five states. These four assessments enable us to compare trends over twenty years. Table 1 lists the top thirty groups that have been, overall, the most effective since 1980 and compares these with the groups considered effective in our 1998 survey.

TABLE 1 The thirty most influential interests in the fifty states since 1980 compared with 1998 rankings

Interest/Lobby and Overall/ Average Ranking since 1980	Ranking in 1998	Number of States in 1998 where seen as Very Effective or Somewhat Effective, respectively	
1 School Teachers' Organizations (predominantly NEA)	2	41	8
2 General Business Organizations (State Chambers of Commerce, etc.)	1	40	12*
3 Utility Companies & Associations (electric, gas, water, telephone/ telecommunications, cable TV)	3	26	26
4 Lawyers (predominantly trial lawyers & state bar associations)	4	26	14
5 Bankers' Associations (includes savings & loan associations)	13	16	16
6 General Local Government Organizations (municipal leagues, county organizations, elected officials)	7	20	18
7 Traditional Labor Associations (predominantly the AFL-CIO)	12	14	21
8 Insurance: General and Medical (companies & associations)	6	21	16
9 Manufacturers (companies & associations)	8	22	12
10 Physicians/State Medical Associations	10	18	13
11 General Farm Organizations (mainly state Farm Bureaus)	9	17	18
12 State & Local Government Employees (other than teachers)	11	15	19
13 Individual Banks & Financial Institutions	18	10	13
14 Hospital Associations/Health Care Organizations (excluding physicians)	5	17	26
15 Realtors' Associations	15	11	12
16 Environmentalists	19	7	19
17 Universities and Colleges (institutions and personnel)	20	6	19
18 K–12 Education Interests (other than teachers)	16	11	12
19 Contractors/Builders/Developers	14	11	13
20 Individual Cities and Towns	220	9	8

(cont. on next page)

Interest/Lobby and Overall/ Average Ranking since 1980	Ranking in 1998	Number of States in 1998 where seen as Very Effective or Somewhat Effective, respectively	
21 Retailers (companies & trade associations)	260	7	6
22 Individual Traditional Labor Unions (Teamsters, UAW, etc.)	270	6	8
23 Gaming Interests (race tracks/casinos/lotteries)	17	11	11
24 Truckers and Private Transport Interests (excluding railroads)	21	6	17
25 Liquor, Wine, and Beer Interests	290	4	10
26 Agricultural Commodity Organizations (stockgrowers, grain growers, etc.)	240	8	7
27 Mining Companies & Associations	31	6	5
28 State Agencies	230	9	7
29 Oil and Gas (companies & associations)	33	4	6
30 Senior Citizens	34	1	11

*In this case, the totals add up to more than 50 because elements of this interest/lobby were mentioned within both the "very effective" and the "somewhat effective" categories in the state. Therefore, they are counted once for each category. For similar reasons, in a few cases, the total in the last two columns may slightly overstate the total number of states in which the group is mentioned. For example, utilities are ranked in both categories in North Dakota and thus count for two mentions under utilities.

SOURCE: Compiled by the authors from the 1998 update and previous surveys of the Hrebenar-Thomas study. This table is based on Table 4.1 in Virginia Gray, Russell L. Hanson and Herbert Jacob, eds., *Politics in the American States: A Comparative Analysis*, Seventh Edition (Washington, D.C.: Congressional Quarterly Press, 1999), p. 134–35.

First, we must be clear on exactly what the assessments presented in the table do and do not reveal. They reveal the interests that are viewed by policymakers and political observers as the most effective in the states over a five-year period prior to the assessment. Obviously, for this reason the assessments tend to reflect on the most active groups or those with a high profile. Thus, it could be that some observers confuse visibility with power. The assessment should not be viewed as indicating that the groups near the top of the list always win or even win most of the time; in fact, they may win less often than some low-profile groups not listed. The place of an individual interest in the ranking, however, does indicate its level of importance as a player in state politics over the period assessed and the extent of its ability to bring political clout to bear on the issues that affect it.

Comparing the listings over the years, what comes through most of all is the relative stability both of the types of groups that make the list and their ranking. When changes in ranking do occur, or when new groups appear on the list, the changes appear to be influenced by the prominence of issues at the time, partisan control, and the ideological persuasion of state government.

Gaming, health, and insurance interests, for example, steadily increased in perceived influence as lotteries and casinos, health care, and tort reform became issues in the states. Environmental and other liberal causes, as well as senior citizens groups, wax and wane in strength according to who is in power. This is also true of business and development interests, which have seen a boost in their rankings since the GOP successes in state elections in 1994. The biggest loser over the last twenty years is traditional labor, both individual union and, more recently, the AFL-CIO; though white collar unions—particularly state and local employee groups—have risen to prominence and held on even as partisan control has changed.

Today, as over the past twenty years, two interests far outstrip any others in terms of their perceived influence and continue to vie for the top ranking. These are general business organizations (mainly state chambers of commerce) and schoolteachers, (mainly state affiliates of the National Education Association—NEA). Despite the major expansion in group activity, however, Table 1 indicates that relatively few interests are considered to be effective in a large number of states.

Only the top dozen or so ranked interests are mentioned as effective ("very effective" and "somewhat effective") in more than half of the fifty states.

This combined data from our four surveys also confirms once again what we have known since the first study of the power of state interest groups conducted by Belle Zeller fifty years ago: business and the professions remain the most effective interests in the states (as they do in Washington, D.C.). What is very clear from Table 1 is how few new interests are ranked in the top thirty as being consistently successful since 1980 despite the fact that many of them have been continually and increasingly active in state capitals.

The Elements of Single Group and Overall Individual Interest Power

Our findings on the root of the power of individual groups and lobbies may, at first sight, appear to be obvious. But we now have hard evidence for it across the states plus some new perspectives. Generically, the three most important elements are the possession of resources (money, members, and so forth), the ability to mobilize these resources for political purposes, and the political acumen of the leadership. To be sure, we all know that money and numbers count, but without other factors, like good organizational skills to direct a lobbying campaign and good political timing, money and numbers are of little use.

In terms of specific factors, our surveys reveal that the number one element determining the political clout of a group is how much they are needed by politicians and government. This dependence could stem from campaign contributions (as with many business interests contributing heavily to legislative and gubernatorial candidates), running a state service like education (as with schoolteachers), or simply a state's (thus the government's) dependence on an industry like Boeing in Washington state and coal in West Virginia. What most of the top twenty interests in Table 1 have in common is that, to varying degrees, they have been able to create a dependent, symbiotic relationship with one or more of the branches or agencies of state government that most affects their interests.

This dependent, symbiotic relationship between government and a group, coalition, or interest is based on a combination of factors including financial resources, size, and geographic distribution of membership. And this may well be buttressed by an ideological affinity between policymakers and certain interests, as with business and conservatives, liberals and labor. However, based on our findings, such affinity is less important than the dependent, symbiotic relationship. This is evidenced by the fact that many of the new interests, supported and courted by Democrats and liberals, have not seen sustained influence in state politics in the way manifested by many business and some professional groups.

This crucial factor of dependence as a basis of long-term power offers us one other important insight. While some groups, such as those for victims' rights and the arts, may score short-term victories, the stark reality that government does not need them in the way it needs a major industry or professional group means that these groups will never exert long-term influence and be ranked among the most powerful groups in a state.

Perspective 3: Group System Power in a State

Our third perspective on interest group power is that of group system power. Whereas the power of single groups and the overall impact of individual interests is observed in their political mobilization and their ability to achieve their goals, group system power is much more of an abstraction. It is also even more difficult to assess than overall interest power because of the multiplicity of variables involved. The method most frequently used to assess it has been to garner the observations of political practitioners and political scientists regarding the importance of the players involved in the policymaking process in each state. This was the method used over the last fifteen years by the Hrebenar-Thomas study; however, the recent installment fine-tuned the way of categorizing and understanding changes in group system power.

What, then, can we say about what factors determine group system power? In our study we observed that there is likely a connection between the political culture of a state and the extent of group system power. States that have moralistic political cultures, such as Maine and Vermont, generally have less powerful group systems than states that have more individualistic cultures, such as Nevada and New Mexico. Socioeconomic development also has its effects, usually by increasing the number of groups and reducing the likelihood that the state will be dominated by one or a few interests. One factor, however, appears to affect group system power more than any other. This is the relationship between the group system and the strength of political parties. It is probably true that in measuring group system power we may not be measuring the strength of all groups, but only the most powerful ones in a state. But assessing group system power is still important because of what it reveals about the relationship and relative power of political institutions in a state.

Earlier assessments of group system power used only three categories: strong, moderate, and weak. These are rather general and do not convey the gradual movement between categories. The five categories developed by the 1998 Hrebenar-Thomas study improve on this categorization. Table 2 presents these categories and lists the fifty states according to the strength of their group systems in the late 1990s and indicates changes since the mid-1980s. States listed as dominant are those in which groups as a whole are the overwhelming and consistent influence on policymaking. Groups in states listed as complementary tend to work in conjunction with (or are constrained by) other aspects of the political system. More often than not this is the party system, but it could also be a strong executive branch, competition between groups, the political culture, or a combination of all these. A subordinate group system is one that is consistently subordinated to other aspects of the policymaking process. The absence of any state in the Subordinate column indicates that groups were not consistently subordinate in any state either in 1994 or in 1989. The Dominant/Complementary and the Complementary/Subordinate columns include those states whose group systems alternate between the two situations or are in the process of moving from one to the other.

Comparisons between the 1989, 1994, and 1998 surveys reveal three major things about group system power in the states. First, the changes that do take place are gradual. Two-thirds of the states (34) have remained in the same category during this period. And the 16 that have moved changed positions only one category per survey year: eight states have moved up in strength and eight moved down, with only one state, Connecticut, moving up two categories over the past fifteen years. Group system power changes more gradually than does individual group power since changes on a large scale take longer than changes on a small one. Second, most activity involved the Dominant/Complementary category, which showed the only increase in the number of states (from 18 in 1989 to 25 in 1998). The Dominant category dropped from 9 to 5 states, the Complementary category from 18 to 16 and the Complementary/Subordinate category from 5 to 4. Overall, the general movement has been to stronger, but not dominant, interest group systems. Part of the reason for this since the 1994 survey may reflect short-term changes due to the closeness between many pro-business and pro-development groups and the Republicans in charge of many states. Third, over all three surveys the South remained the region with the most powerful interest group systems, followed by the West and the Midwest; the Northeast remains the region with the least powerful interest group systems. These regional rankings are all unchanged from 1989.

General Explanations and Individual Cases

One final point needs to be made about interest group power in the states in general. Although there are some common influences across the states, the impact of

TABLE 2 Classification of the fifty states according to the overall impact of interest groups in the late 1990s with indication of movement in category over the last fifteen years*

States Where the Overall Impact of Interest Groups is:				
Dominant (5)	**Dominant/ Complementary (25)**	**Complementary (16)**	**Complementary/ Subordinate (4)**	**Subordinate (0)**
Alabama	*−Alaska*	Colorado	Minnesota	
Florida	Arizona	*+Delaware*	Rhode Island	
+Nevada	Arkansas	Indiana	*−South Dakota*	
So. Carolina	California	*−Hawaii*	Vermont	
West Virginia	*++Connecticut*	Maine		
	Georgia	Massachusetts		
	Idaho	Michigan		
	+Illinois	Missouri		
	+Iowa	New Hampshire		
	+Kansas	New Jersey		
	Kentucky	New York		
	−Louisiana	North Carolina		
	+Maryland	North Dakota		
	−Mississippi	Pennsylvania		
	Montana	*−Utah*		
	Nebraska	Wisconsin		
	−New Mexico			
	Ohio			
	Oklahoma			
	Oregon			
	−Tennessee			
	Texas			
	Virginia			
	+Washington			
	Wyoming			

*States that have changed categories since the Hrebenar-Thomas study was first conducted are indicated in italics with a plus or minus sign. A plus sign means that their group system has become stronger, moving to the left on the table. A minus sign indicates that it has become weaker. Connecticut has moved up two categories and thus has two plus signs.

SOURCE: Compiled by the authors from the 1998 update and previous surveys of the Hrebenar-Thomas study. This table is based on Table 4.2 in Virginia Gray, Russell L. Hanson and Herbert Jacob, eds., *Politics in the American States: A Comparative Analysis,* Seventh Edition (Washington, D.C.: Congressional Quarterly Press, 1999), p. 137.

groups in a particular state is a product of the unique ways in which these influences interact and change in that state. In some states, the power of certain single groups and the perception of the power of overall individual interests may hold firm or even increase at a time when the same groups and interests are declining in other states. The number of states that have seen increases in group system power in the past fifteen years is equal to the number in which group system power has declined. Thus, while some common denominators do exist across the states, changes in single group power, overall individual interest power, and group system power often depend on the individual circumstances in a state.

Continuity and Change in Interest Group Power

These findings on interest group power bring to mind the adage "the more things change, the more they stay the same." While this is partly true, a better way to look at it is that interest group and lobby power has reached a new stage of development as part of the constantly evolving state of politics in state capitals.

Change has occurred in that states are no longer dominated by one or a handful of interests, although some states still have a prominent interest—the Mormon Church in Utah, agri-business in Arkansas, gaming in Nevada, for instance. The last thirty years have seen a mushrooming of both new and traditional interests. This increasingly crowded political playing field has made it more difficult to predict who will win and who will lose and has forced the development of all sorts of new techniques on the part of traditional and new interests alike, such as grassroots lobbying and media campaigns, to try to meet new challenges. Most of these new techniques have democratized group activity. And, as a result of all these changes, it may be that in many instances lobbyists are less powerful than they were when a man like Artie Samish "ran" California in the World War II era.

On the other hand, some realities about interest group power, particularly about individual groups and lobbies, remain unchanged and likely will hold fast for generations. Foremost among these is that the possession of resources and a dependent, symbiotic relationship between a group and government is at the root of a group's power. Most new interests do not yet have this symbiotic relationship. So, despite the mushrooming of interests in state capitals, the groups considered powerful in 1998 are not that much different from 1978 when Sarah McCally Morehouse did the first assessment of group power in all fifty states.

What determines the success of an interest group has a host of implications for groups and for state politics. Three are especially important. First, if the "outsider interests"—mainly the new interests—want to become "insiders," they need extensive resources—money, members, and so on—and they need to build up a dependent, symbiotic relationship with government. Second, because some groups will never be able to do this, political inequality and uneven representation will likely always exist in state politics, as it does at the federal level in any country, democratic or otherwise. In this regard, the populist "money talks" sentiment shared by large segments of the population is quite justified. Third, lobby laws cannot even-up the political playing field because they cannot deprive powerful groups of many of the basic elements that constitute political clout. Lobby laws can only provide public disclosure of [who's] lobbying whom and marginally affect group influence by constraining certain activities, such as wining and dining, considered by the public to be potentially corrupting.

Note

1. The material presented in the rest of this article is taken, in part, from the section on group power in Clive S. Thomas and Ronald J. Hrebenar, Chapter 4, "Interest Groups in the States." In Gray, Virginia, Russell L. Hanson, and Herbert Jacob, eds. 1999. *Politics in the American States: A Comparative Analysis,* Seventh Edition. Washington D.C.: Congressional Quarterly Press.

CASE STUDY 7

Introduction

In the foregoing essay, Thomas and Hrebenar provide empirical support for what many Americans already believe: business organizations and professional groups tend to play a particularly influential role in state politics. The following case study is intended, however, to encourage readers to think about the extent to which these types of groups actually influence politics. The study is not of a powerful business group or association, but of an organization that seems entirely unlikely to influence legislative politics, even though it was able to persuade the New York legislature to rewrite state labor laws. What makes the group so fascinating and its success so unexpected is that the group's membership is composed primarily of immigrant Latino workers, many of whom are not legal residents and do not speak English.

The organization is the Workplace Project, a workers center based in the Long Island town of Hempstead, New York. The Workplace Project is one of several nonprofit organizations that have formed in recent years in communities across the nation to help improve the working conditions and pay of immigrants. The organization has a small professional staff and a membership of more than 400 immigrant workers. The organization has used a variety of methods to improve the work situation for immigrants—from providing legal assistance on labor issues, to helping members create their own businesses, to providing educational training. The case study tells the story of its campaign to get the state to enact the Unpaid Wages Prohibition Act of 1997 and offers some thoughts on why the campaign was successful.

The case study is valuable because it demonstrates that organizations other than business groups and professional associations can affect legislative action. But the essay also underscores the important role that these types of organizations actually play in state politics. The primary targets of the Workplace Project's lobbying efforts were the Republican members of the state senate, especially those representing Long Island. When the supporters of the bill approached these legislators, the first concern they heard was the question of how business groups felt about the proposal. It was only after the Workplace Project was able to win over the business community and to limit opposition from the state department of labor that it was able to get the act through the legislature and signed into law.

The case study was written by Jennifer Gordon, the founder and former director of the Workplace Project. Gordon, who is now on the faculty at Fordham Law School, has received considerable recognition for her advocacy efforts and her legal work. Among other achievements, she was named the Outstanding Public Interest Advocate of the Year by the National Association for Public Interest Law in 1998 and received a MacArthur Fellowship Award in 1999.

Questions to Consider

As you read Gordon's work, these are some questions to consider:

- What are some of the problems confronting immigrant workers in Long Island? Why were these problems going unresolved? How did the Unpaid Wages Prohibition Act seek to overcome these problems?
- What four different explanations does Gordon provide for why the lobbying efforts were successful? Why do you think the legislators voted to support the act?
- In what ways does the case study provide support for Thomas and Hrebenar's research findings? Or conversely, how well do Thomas and Hrebenar's arguments about the nature of group power apply to the case study?

The Campaign for the Unpaid Wages Prohibition Act

Jennifer Gordon

Large numbers of Latino immigrants came to the United States in the 1980s, propelled by bloody civil wars in Central America and economic crisis throughout Latin America. Although in many ways this migration echoed others of decades past, in at least one sense it was different: instead of settling first in cities, many immigrants headed straight for the suburbs. Long Island, New York was a major destination, in particular for tens of thousands of families fleeing El Salvador. The path traced by earlier immigrants between El Salvador and Long Island played an important role in guiding resettlement patterns. But work was the real drawing card. In an economy where manufacturing jobs, the traditional first step on the ladder for newcomers, were increasingly scarce, suburban neighborhoods offered the alternative of work in the service sector. At last count, Long Island's Latino population was estimated at over 200,000.[1]

At first glance, suburban work seems an appealing alternative to the garment factories of New York City. But sweatshops followed immigrants to the suburbs. . . . [C]ommon problems on Long Island include restaurants where busboys and dishwashers often labor more than seventy hours a week for wages of less than $3 an hour; small landscaping companies where workers mow up to fifty lawns a day and serious injuries are common; and private homes where isolated and vulnerable domestic workers receive as little as $1.90 an hour for workweeks ranging up to eighty-five hours. Business is transacted in cash, employers close and open under new names, and workers are plentiful and cheap. The economy bears all the hallmarks of sweatshop labor except for its suburban setting. . . .

At first glance, the solution to the problem of subminimum wages seems obvious. Minimum wage laws exist—why not simply enforce them? In practice, the situation is much more complex. First, drastic underfunding of federal and state government agencies means that there are not enough inspectors even to begin to cover the number of legitimate, registered business. This situation is unlikely to change, because workers who receive subminimum wages are not perceived as an important political constituency, and thus there is little political will to press the issue. Second, many of the worst exploiters are part of the underground economy. Paying cash, unlicensed and unregistered, these businesses require more time and effort to locate than the established variety. Third, the search for such violators is further hampered by the reluctance of many undocumented immigrants to report subminimum wages to government authorities, a reluctance which is exacerbated by the federal Department of Labor's policy of cooperation with the Immigration and Naturalization Service (INS).[2] Fourth, penalties for non- or under-payment of wages are so low, particularly at the state level where many immigrants bring cases, that they represent no deterrent at all.[3]

Although the Workplace Project and other workers centers use a variety of strategies to ensure the payment of minimum wages, they constantly are hampered by the problem of scale. One small organization can create only so many pickets, press conferences, and court cases. The campaign for the Unpaid Wages Prohibition Act is an example of a strategy that attempts to confront the problem of non- or under-payment of wages more broadly, by focusing on increasing the deterrent factor by increasing fines.

This tactic is premised on the idea that there is such a thing as a penalty high enough to deter employers from paying illegal wages without government or nonprofit intervention. In theory, unscrupulous employers do an informal calculation discounting the profit to be made by paying a subminimum wage by both the likelihood of being caught and the amount of the fine and

Jennifer Gordon, "The Campaign for the Unpaid Wages Prohibition Act: Latino Immigrants Change New York Wage Law," *Carnegie Endowment Working Papers,* Number 4 (Washington, D.C.: Carnegie Endowment for International Peace, 1999) www.carnegieendowment.org. Reprinted by permission of the publisher.

degree of criminal penalty if discovered. Low or nonexistent penalties mean that even if an employer is caught, he will only have to pay back the money that he should have paid in the first place, or a little more, months or years after the fact. This amounts to a long-term low-interest loan from the government, essentially an incentive to pay below-market rates.

If the fine and criminal penalty are high enough, on the other hand, reason suggests that the employer will begin to raise the wages he is paying before he is caught, even if he is unlikely to be detected, because the risk to his profit and reputation is much greater. At the very least, once caught, an employer would be much more likely to pay than fight, because fighting and losing could result in a financial and personal disaster.

Wage Law Enforcement in New York State

In the early to mid 1990s, New York State provided a textbook case of a situation where employers were encouraged to pay subminimum wages by both low penalties and a scattershot approach to enforcement.

Under the administration of George Pataki, elected in 1994 as the first Republican governor of New York state in twenty years, the Labor Standards Division of the New York State Department of Labor (DOL) was moving from a pro-worker stance to a vision of itself as an agency that had business and workers as equally important "customers." . . .

In our experience, the new vision was reflected in an execution of the DOL's wage enforcement responsibilities that bordered on negligence. The DOL on Long Island had one inspector for approximately every 7,000 private workplaces, thwarting any real attempt at curbing the problem of nonpayment of wages. Under then current New York state labor law, an employer who repeatedly or willfully failed to pay minimum wages was subject only to a 25 percent civil penalty. The crime of repeat nonpayment of wages was only a misdemeanor.

Staffing shortages and weak laws were compounded by the DOL's lack of political will to fight unpaid wages. A 1994 study by the New York state comptroller Carl McCall showed that the Labor Standards Division had failed to effectively implement even the minimal existing penalties effectively. McCall concluded that the division imposed penalties in only 2 percent of settled cases over a three-year period, thus sacrificing as much as $6.7 million in revenues, and that "the division does not have adequate procedures to identify and deal with repeat violators of the Labor Law."[4] In our attempts to work with the DOL, we had seen delays of up to eighteen months in initiating investigation of cases it had accepted; frequent refusal to accept claims brought to local offices by undocumented or off-the-books workers; Spanish translation available only once every other week for three hours; case investigations going back only two years although the law permitted six; and—in New York City—the practice of investigators settling for a payment of 50 percent of what the employer admitted to owing, with no penalty levied.

We had ample evidence of the effect of these problems on workers who had not been paid. Beginning in 1993, the Workplace Project kept records of three things: case outcomes, DOL treatment of immigrants seeking assistance at the Long Island office, and DOL handling of cases it accepted. By the end of 1995, the results of this statistic-gathering effort were clear. Our computer database contained records of the over 900 Latino workers who had sought help from our legal clinic over the previous three years. It showed that only two of the 72 cases that we had filed with the DOL over three years, or just 3 percent, resulted in even partial payment to workers. By contrast, over the same period, our office, with only one person working half-time on these cases at any point, accepted 234 wage cases for representation and resolved 71 percent of them, winning over $215,000 for 166 workers during that time. . . .

By late 1995, frustration with this situation was building within the Workplace Project's staff, board, and membership. Members were angry that their wage claims were not being taken seriously by the government; staff were tired of filing cases into what felt like a black hole. The organization decided to undertake an organizing campaign to improve both wage enforcement laws and the DOL's treatment of immigrant workers. Our members focused on two issues: (1) dramatically increasing penalties against repeat or willful violators of wage laws, on the theory that this would deter employers even without the intervention of the DOL and (2) addressing the major problems in DOL mismanagement of cases. Much more for the learning experience than because we felt it was possible to win, we decided to try to do this by changing New York state labor law.

We launched the campaign with testimony of Workplace Project staff and members at a public hearing called in February 1996 by the chair of the New York Assembly Committee on Labor, Catherine Nolan. Although a bill reflecting some of our concerns was introduced in the Assembly Committee on Labor, little happened during the 1996 legislative session.

Dissatisfied by the lack of progress, our membership was forced to decide whether they would drop the issue or commit to a real legislative campaign. In the summer of 1996, they voted to begin a serious effort to pass a bill in 1997. Together with members of the Latino Workers Center and the Chinese Staff and Workers Association, they developed a series of proposals based on their analysis of what needed to be changed at the Department of Labor. . . .

The proposed Act included the following provisions:

- The civil penalty for repeat or willful nonpayment of wages would increase from 25 percent to 200 percent of the amount owed.
- The criminal penalty for nonpayment would change from a misdemeanor to a felony.
- DOL investigations would be *required* to go back the full six years permitted by law, instead of the two that the DOL currently reviewed.
- Settlements of less than 100 percent of the wages owed would not be permitted without the worker's consent.
- When an employer failed to keep adequate records of wage payment, the burden of proof would shift from the worker (to prove nonpayment) to the employer (to prove that he had paid).
- Workers would be informed of the process that their claim would follow when they filed and at regular intervals as the claim was investigated.
- Labor unions could file wage claims on behalf of workers.[5]
- Spanish and Chinese translation would be guaranteed.[6]
- An ombudsman's office on behalf of low wage workers would be created to oversee the division's work.

None of us thought that such a bill would be an easy win. . . . [N]othing becomes law in New York state without strong Republican support, as both the Senate and the governorship are controlled by conservative Republicans. If we were going to make a serious effort to pass our bill, we would have to seek out not only the votes but the sponsorship of legislators who had been in the lead of recent anti-labor, anti-immigrant efforts. And their first concern—as we quickly learned when we began to contact them—was to know what position business groups would take on our proposal.

With this in mind, a group of fifteen of our members worked with me over a period of weeks to refine our message, basing it on the relationships we saw between the legislation we had drafted and what we perceived to be the interests of Republican legislators and industry organizations. . . .

Over the first half of 1997, we built a list of endorsers for the bill that included unions, labor councils, community organizations, religious groups, and, most notably, two of Long Island's most powerful business associations. . . .

With letters from these allies, but otherwise unaccompanied, our immigrant members (sometimes joined by the Latino Workers Center) carried out over fifteen visits with senators or, more often, their staff. Some were in Albany and others took place in local offices. We coordinated these visits with media exposés of the abuses suffered by immigrant workers on Long Island and of the Department of Labor's ineffectual response. . . .

Initially very reluctant, ten Republican senators had signed on by the end of June as co-sponsors in the Senate—five from the Long Island delegation and five from other districts. The bill emerged from the committee process after its ombudsman and translation provisions were cut, revisions which our members agreed to once it became clear that they were necessary for the bill to be released to the Senate floor for a vote.

On June 30, the Unpaid Wages Prohibition Act went to the Senate floor. On July 1, both the Senate and the Assembly unanimously passed the bill. On September 17, after a ten-week battle, Governor Pataki signed the bill over the strong objections of the Farm Bureau, his ally and the powerful representative of agricultural interests in a state where agriculture is still the largest industry.

Political Analysis: How Did the Campaign Win?

. . . To try to pass legislation in New York state is to enter a world of seeming impossibility. The Assembly, with districts drawn by population and therefore heavy with New York City liberals, is staunchly Democratic. The Republicans of the vast upstate farm counties and Long Island control the Senate. . . . The governor is from an upstate farm family himself.[7] In each house of the legislature, one person, who has absolute say about what reaches the floor, rules: in the Assembly, the Speaker; in the Senate, the Majority Leader. The power of the controlling political party in each house, and the level of animosity between the houses that has grown up over time, can seem impenetrable. . . .[8]

Bills benefiting workers face a particularly tough road. Agriculture is still the top industry in New York state, and the Farm Bureau, a private industry organization representing farmers, exerts powerful influence over the Senate. Unions are not a strong force in the legislature.[9] In this context, ostensibly simple legislation can become tangled in debate and rancor for years. For example, a bill guaranteeing clean drinking water to farmworkers in the fields had to be reintroduced five times over as many years before finally passing in 1996.

Long Island's delegation to the Senate plays a critical role in this political system—moderate to conservative, very powerful, tightly adherent to party discipline, it is made up of nine staunch Republicans. In fact, Long Island has never sent a Democratic senator to Albany.[10] With the support of the majority of the Long Island delegation, almost any legislation can pass in the Senate; without it, it can easily wither and die.

Looking at this system with an eye toward winning passage of the Unpaid Wages Prohibition Act, one thing was clear: the Assembly would be easy. The active support of the Chairwoman of the Committee on Labor, Assemblywoman Catherine Nolan, and the thirty-three Democratic co-sponsors that she gathered for the legislation, virtually guaranteed passage in that house. But without strong Republican backing in the Senate, the bill would go nowhere.

This meant that the bill had to be introduced in the Senate by a Republican, preferably by the Chair of the Senate Labor Committee, Senator Nicholas Spano, and it had to have co-sponsorship that demonstrated serious Republican support. For a Long Island organization, the Long Island delegation was a natural target. We set ourselves the goal of winning the sponsorship of Senator Spano plus any five Long Island senators, to make a majority of the delegation. . . .

Conventionally, power in the legislative system is seen to come from two sources: either votes or money. And conventionally, immigrant workers are thought to wield neither. How, then, did this campaign move a Republican Senate and governor to support strong legislation written by and for immigrant workers. . . .

A few simple political factors suggest themselves. First, the bill required no additional expenditures—that is, it had no impact on the budget. In fact, through increased penalty revenue and reduced welfare rolls, it promised to bring additional money into the state's coffers. Although this does not explain the support the bill received, it does highlight a barrier we avoided. Had we, for example, written in a provision funding additional wage inspectors, it is clear that the bill would have required a great deal more organizing on our part to win passage. Second, the bill came along at a time when the Senate, long accustomed to blocking social justice legislation in order to stymie the will of a Democratic governor, was recognizing the need to send some bills to Governor Pataki, a Republican, that would make him look sympathetic to working people. The Unpaid Wages Prohibition Act represented a relatively painless way to do that.[11]

But in some ways, this last explanation begs the question. Why was our bill painless to a Republican Senate and administration not known for its support of immigrant or worker issues?

There is no clear answer to this question, but there are several interesting theories.[12] One possibility is that Republicans did in fact perceive immigrant workers as controlling money and votes, if not now then in the future, and saw this legislation as a relatively painless way to secure Latino support in upcoming elections. . . . Another is that the campaign attracted a mix of unexpected allies who represented powerful interests; their power made up for the political weakness of the immigrant community and shifted the focus away from the tough "immigrant question." A third is that the message that we crafted and spread through the media made it very difficult for legislators and the DOL to oppose the bill without looking like they supported employers who did not pay their workers. A fourth is that immigrant participants in this campaign and their stories of hard work thwarted by unpaid wages convinced supporters through moral strength—a power outside of the money/votes dichotomy. I suspect that each of these four factors played a role in the eventual passage of the legislation.

Theory 1: A Growing Part of the Republican Constituency

The first theory, that Republican senators supported this legislation because they saw Latino immigrants as a group soon to have economic and voting power, is rational given the demographics of Long Island and the state. It becomes more complicated, however, given the demographics of our membership and the other beneficiaries of the legislation.

Nationally, the Republican Party is engaged in a battle to win the hearts of Latino voters. Latinos have recently been portrayed in media and policy discussions as potential Republican Party members by virtue of their social conservatism who are nonetheless increasingly turning to the Democrats out of anger at Republican support of anti-immigrant legislation. The Republican National Party responded to the resounding rejection they received from Latino voters after passing restrictive immigration legislation in 1996 by hiring a Hispanic outreach coordinator, creating a committee to court Hispanic voters, putting out a booklet on "common-sense tips on how to reach out to Hispanic voters," and, most importantly, beginning to backpedal on their anti-immigrant rhetoric.[13]

On Long Island, the percentage of Latino residents has surged over the past decade and a half, increasing by 80 percent between 1980 and 1990, even according to census data that most advocates believe represents a drastic undercount. In New York state generally, the Latino population grew by 50 percent over the same period. While many of these residents are not yet voters, immigrants are becoming citizens at rates unheard of in previous years.[14] Although Latinos still do not control large amounts of money in the state, their importance as consumers and increasingly as a voting bloc is undeniable, even outside the traditional stronghold of New York City. And the local Republican Party has responded in kind. . . .

Theory 2: Unexpected and Diverse Allies Brought Power to the Campaign

Given that we were running a legislative campaign with almost no voters, we realized that we needed a wide range of allies to show support for the Act. Although the endorsement of labor, religious, and community groups was crucial for the success of the campaign, in the end our most important allies would be the ones no one expected we could get: business groups.

The first question that Long Island senators asked us in our early lobbying forays was: "what is the industry associations' point of view on this?" It quickly became clear that we would have a difficult time finding the sponsors that we wanted unless we could show business backing for the proposal.

The process for gaining the support of the Long Island Association (LIA), Long Island's most respected business group, was simple. We sent them a letter setting forth the unfair competition arguments and others that our members had developed. I met with Mitchell Pally, the LIA's vice president for legislative and economic affairs, and we discussed the proposal briefly. He then presented it to their committees and board, won approval, and wrote a letter of support.

In a recent interview, Pally told me that the main factor behind the LIA's support was the "equity issue."[15] Eighty to eighty-five percent of the Association's membership is made up of small businesspeople, largely in the retail and service industries. (Significantly, few of their members are in the landscaping and restaurant industries, which do a considerable amount of underground hiring of immigrant workers.) According to Pally, "a lot of small businesses on Long Island are impacted when other employers do not pay legal wages, so this is a matter of fairness that affects our members." Pally also feels that the timing for the legislation was right: "The economy is good, so people feel better about making sure everyone gets a piece of the pie. It would have been more difficult for us to support this in hard times," given the perception that the legislation put money into the pockets of immigrants. . . .

The New York State Restaurant Association was slightly harder to convince. This is not surprising, given that restaurants are among the biggest violators of wage and hour laws. We were eventually able to win the endorsement of their Long Island chapter by approaching them as the representative of the "good" employers in the restaurant industry, with the argument that it was precisely the good restaurant owners who were in greatest need of such legislation because they were being directly undercut by the subminimum wage employers in their industry. This put the association in a position where saying no would have been tantamount to admitting that their members were the "bad" employers who routinely violated the law. After a letter and several phone conversations, the Long Island chapter wrote a letter of support, and subsequently made several positive statements to the press. . . .

To emphasize the role that business support played in this campaign is not to downplay the importance of our community, religious, and labor endorsers. Without the broad-based support that they represented, the bill would not have had the numbers of presumed voters, the potential for economic benefit or harm to senators, or the moral weight that these organizations were able to generate. . . .

Theory 3: The Message of the Bill Was Hard to Oppose

. . . Strong media support was crucial to our effort to make the bill unopposable. Through media coverage, we built a climate of outrage about the treatment to which immigrant workers were subjected, made our issue into a hot topic, put pressure on legislators, and gained supporters for our cause.

Our media message related to the campaign was threefold and specifically targeted at the Long Island delegation of the New York State Senate. First, given the invisibility of immigrants on the Island, we had to show that sweatshops were a common local phenomenon, though not in the traditional form. Unless the public knew about the scores of busboys and dishwashers earning less than $2.50 an hour for eighty-hour weeks, the gardeners and landscape workers who often went without pay for weeks on end, and the domestic workers who labored from 6:00 A.M. to 11:00 P.M. for wages of less than two dollars an hour, they would have no reason to support this legislation. This was a real challenge: in 1996, although many on Long Island were aware of some immigrants in their midst, few were cognizant of the sweatshop-like working conditions that prevailed in many service industries.

Second, we wanted to make clear that part of the fault for these circumstances lay in weak state laws and inadequate New York State Department of Labor enforcement practices. Third, we wanted the press to communicate our "universal appeal" points: that the bill was supported by business organizations and that it would bring revenue to the state in a number of ways.

We were largely successful both in shaping the message about the problem and the legislation that appeared in the press and in timing press coverage to crucial points in the campaign. *Newsday*'s first Sunday cover piece in January 1996 coincided with our launching of the campaign; their second in April 1997 put the issue on the map as a Long Island problem and gained us our first sponsors. The *New York Times* featured the legislation the day before it was passed in the Senate and Assembly, and ran a lead editorial on Labor Day weekend that preceded the governor's signature by a week. The Schenectady *Daily Gazette,* an influential paper in Albany, published an editorial a week before the bill passed urging the legislature, "this one's too important to get lost in the shuffle."[16] . . .

The message that we crafted and were successful in communicating played an important role in preventing the campaign from becoming a fight about illegal immigrants and jobs. In part, we gained legislative support from our members' decision to cast this bill as being positive for the state budget because it brought in additional funds through penalties and because it cut welfare rolls by insuring that workers were paid for their labor and thus did not need to rely on public benefits. More important still was the shaping of the language of the bill itself. We had written the bill so that the severe punishment it imposed, a 200 percent civil fine and a felony with a maximum $20,000 criminal penalty, only applied to repeat or willful violators of wage payment laws. In addition, the bill applied to all employers and all workers, mentioning immigrants nowhere in its text. In essence, this meant that any organization or individual who wanted to oppose the bill had to come out publicly in favor of companies that repeatedly failed to pay their workers. . . .

The uncomfortable position in which this put the opposition was evident in the nature of their statements in much of the press coverage of the legislation. For example, a *New York Times* news article that ran the day before the bill passed had a lead sentence that stated ". . .many are facing a growing and particularly painful form of exploitation: unscrupulous employers who fail to pay some or all of their relatively low wages," and its sole pull quote was "Unscrupulous employers fail to give immigrant workers their full wages." The best that the Farm Bureau, our staunchest opponents, could do was to state, "No matter what the penalties are, you'll have unscrupulous individuals out there who may want to take advantage of workers." Their particular reasons for opposing the bill were both weak and vague: "If this becomes law, it will have a very punitive impact and send a negative tone through the employer community about what the state of New York thinks about employers."[17] . . .

Despite their objections, the Farm Bureau never circulated a memo in opposition to the bill, standard practice in Albany for groups that come out against legislation. Significantly, with the exception of the *New York Post* editorial, the above quotes were the only two negative comments about the bill that we are aware of in the over twenty newspaper articles and television or radio stories covering the campaign and the legislation. Other than the *Post,* not one opponent publicly brought up the immigration question.

Lack of public opposition thus characterized the bill's passage through the legislature. No senators led crusades against the bill, and no memos in opposition were filed during the course of the legislative session, although after the bill passed there was apparently vigorous behind-the-scenes lobbying by the Farm Bureau and other business interests to keep Governor Pataki from signing the bill into law.[18] In the end, upstate Republican senators voted for the bill—and Governor Pataki signed it—over the Farm Bureau's continued protests.

The fact that the bill and its message were crafted so that only a "really bad person" could oppose it also put the New York DOL in a difficult position. Early conversations with us made clear that the agency was not in favor of new legislation. But to oppose the bill publicly would have made it appear to be against a measure designed to improve collection of unpaid wages, an important part of its responsibility. Instead, the DOL first fought behind the scenes, and then acquiesced in the legislation's passage.

Despite its poor collection record, the DOL's Division of Labor Standards was rarely in the news and had not received any major negative publicity in at least a decade. Thus, the criticism that we leveled at the division at the public hearing and in the press apparently came as a rude surprise. Our complaints were hard to refute because of the database we began in 1993 and the statements we had collected starting in 1994. These made it possible for us to produce both statistics and affidavits related to individual cases to illustrate the problems with the DOL that we were alleging and to complement the stories of the workers who came forward.

Unable to deny our litany of problems with their work, the DOL's initial strategy was to claim that the difficulties we had encountered were merely small quirks due to staffing problems in the Hempstead office or outdated department policies, and then to bring up the "illegal alien" issue as a veiled threat that things could get worse instead of better if we pursued reform efforts. . . .

As the legislative session neared its conclusion and the Act was stuck in committee, it became clear to us that the reason it had not left the Labor Committee was that the senators were waiting for the Department of Labor's assent. This was confirmed when Bill Busler, the DOL's legislative counsel, called me in mid-June to tell me what they were and were not willing to accept in the bill. If we agreed, they would support it. If we continued with the bill as it was, they would not support it, and—we had been told by Senator Spano's office—the bill would never reach the floor.

Busler asked us to remove three things: the translation guarantee, the office of the ombudsman, and the division of the 200 percent penalty between the worker, the state, and the DOL. . . . All of these statements were made in private correspondence or conversations. In public, the Department of Labor and the Pataki administration said nothing. To have taken a stand against legislation that reinforced their supposed mission would have put them in a too compromised position.

At the end of the day, it seems that the DOL, legislators, and interest groups perceived the public cost of standing up against the bill as much higher than the cost of living with it, whatever their initial negative reactions might have been, given that opposition would have made them appear to be defending repeat willful violators of the most basic provisions of the labor law.

Theory 4: The Role of Empathy and the Power of Moral Suasion

Finally, it is worth considering that some part of what moved the senators had nothing to do with money or votes but instead with empathy for the workers before them, a sense of identification with the immigrant stories that they presented, and thus a moral discomfort with the suffering they described.

During the lobbying visits, immigrant workers spoke directly to the senators or their staff about the abuse that they and their families faced. These were not sob stories or tales from a token "client" brought along to speak on an advocacy visit. Instead, immigrants ran the entire meeting, mixing their personal experiences with statistics from the Workplace Project database, appealing to the senators' own interests, answering their questions and responding to their concerns. The fact that the bill's provisions were developed by immigrant workers to remedy the problems that they faced, rather than being designed by advocates on behalf of the workers, gave the workers a passion for the bill that would have been impossible to achieve otherwise. For these reasons, our meetings had an immediacy and a strength that is all too often lacking in traditional lobbying visits on behalf of poor people. . . .

The opportunity to speak directly with an organized and prepared group of immigrants may have moved senators from possible sympathy—a common but ineffectual reaction to sad stories—to empathy, the ability to see the victims of the abuse as in some way the same as themselves. Almost all of the Long Island and other sponsoring senators were second or third generation immigrants.[19] They had justified their support of Proposition 187-like legislation with descriptions of illegal aliens who had come to this country to take from the system,[20] an image safely distant from stories about their own family's immigration experience, which inevitably featured hard work and sacrifice. But it was hard for the senators to separate *these* immigrants, sitting before them with dignity and talking about their struggle to be paid for their labor, from their own family's experiences of building a life in the United States. . . .

The Role of Immigrant Workers in the Campaign

. . . We had initiated the campaign for the Unpaid Wages Prohibition Act in the belief that it would be an opportunity for our members to learn about power, politics, and the legislative process, whatever the outcome. Because the Workplace Project is a member-led institution with organizing as its primary goal, we wanted to run the campaign in a way that maximized our members' leadership and participation. . . .

The decision to put immigrant workers in the lead was a practical as well as a philosophical one. We had very limited resources to dedicate to this campaign. In addition, our ability to spend money was limited by the restrictions on lobbying by nonprofit organizations. The campaign had to be carried out in a way that leveraged what we had, without spending too much or interfering with the other work of the organization. Relying heavily on members and volunteers was one way that we did this. . . .

The first thing that our membership decided to do to support the campaign was to collect signatures on letters directed toward the Majority Leader of the Senate, Joseph Bruno; the chair of the Senate Labor Committee, Nick Spano; and the Speaker of the Assembly, Sheldon Silver, representing both individual and institutional support. Using packets of materials that we prepared, about thirty of our members worked on this throughout the summer of 1997. Our first instinct had been that this was a good and easy way for people to promote the campaign. Reality provided a quick check.

As we should have anticipated, members encountered reluctance and even hostility when they asked fellow immigrants to put their name and address on a letter to be sent to a government official. In the words of Workplace Project member Jose Ramirez:

> When I asked people I knew to sign, some wouldn't even hear of it. Some, out of fear, said "will it hurt me?" And I would explain, and even then they wouldn't sign. . . .

Another member was thrown out of her cousin's home. "You must be crazy!," the cousin said. "The government is doing everything it can to throw us out and you want me to give them my name and address? Why not a map to our front door!". . .

Despite the obstacles they encountered, our members collected over 400 letters from other immigrants during this time. Each one of those contacts, difficult though it was, served a dual purpose in addition to adding another letter to the pile: it gave our members practice in outreach and organizing skills, and it spread the word in the community about the work of our organization. . . .

Members found different barriers as they tried to get institutional support. Although many of them belonged to local institutions—churches, labor unions, civic associations from a particular country, and the like—few held positions of power or were connected to those within them. For example, a request from a member to her shop steward that the union support our campaign repeatedly got lost before it made its way up through the business agent to anyone with decision-making authority in the local or international union, if it was initially taken seriously at all. Likewise, a Catholic member's presentation to the nun in charge of parish outreach for the Latino community had to be passed to the priest who presided over Spanish-language mass, who then had to discuss the request with the priest in charge of the parish, who then had to take it up the Catholic hierarchy on Long Island. The topic was always dropped somewhere along the chain. Only a few members, those who were active in Latino Protestant churches, small but intense congregations run by charismatic pastors, were able to approach a religious leader directly to ask for support; only one gave a letter in response. In the end, perhaps not surprisingly, it turned out that the Workplace Project as an institution was much more successful in recruiting institutional support than our individual members. . . .

The other principle challenge for our members during this campaign was how to communicate with the legislators that they needed as sponsors. Almost none of our members can speak English fluently; almost none can vote. Their initial assumption about this situation was summed up by Rony Martinez: "When we started, I thought it would be very hard to change anything in the system. . . . It's worse because we're immigrants, even worse because some of us don't have any papers at all. If you're not a citizen, how can you make demands? If I can't vote, I'm no one. I'm invisible. How can I protest?" . . .

Nevertheless, it made no sense for our members to get so far into the campaign and then to hand over one of the most interesting parts to English-speaking, voting outsiders. We decided to go ahead with having our members carry out the legislative visits on the theory that at the very least we would learn from the experience of fielding the first all-immigrant lobbying teams in these senators' careers.[21]

With the help of Terry Maroney, our law student volunteer, we developed roleplay trainings for our members on how to carry out an effective lobbying visit. . . . Much of the material was conventional, the same ground that any lobbying group would cover. In other areas we went down less well-trodden paths: what would we say if the senator asked who in the room could vote? How should we deal with a senator who balked at putting on the translation equipment headphones? What should we do if the senator insisted on speaking with the only white or English-speaking person in the room, namely the translator, and ignored the workers?

The question of how to handle immigration status was one that we rehearsed frequently. With almost entirely nonvoters, including undocumented workers, as lobbyists, we were prepared for trouble. At the same time, we all strongly believed that, as people living in and contributing to the senator's district, our members were the senator's constituents. If the issue arose, our members had decided to respond honestly by saying that only some of them could vote, but that they believed that as residents of the community being affected by a widespread problem within it, they had a right to inform the senator of their views and they believed he would be interested in hearing their ideas about solutions. In the end, we never brought the issue of immigration status up, and much to our surprise neither did the senators.

The language problem had a relatively simple solution: simultaneous translation through radio transmitters. Upon entering, we would hand the senator or his staff-person a translating receiver that looks something like a radio-only Walkman, and ask him to put on the headset. As the team leader began to speak in Spanish, the senator would hear the words in English. All of our members could communicate directly with the senator and his staff, and vice versa, as the entire conversation was being simultaneously translated by one of our staff-people. . . .

These visits had significant impact, both on the senators and their staff. . . . From the senators' perspective, it was the first time that most if not all of them had participated in a meeting with immigrants that was run by the immigrants themselves, who spoke to the senator's political interests and made a request that the senators could relate to their own family histories. . . . The unusual structure of the visit made it stand out in a legislator's mind; the image it presented of immigrant workers as hard-working, engaged members of a community made it stay there. . . .

In emphasizing the role that our members played in the campaign, I do not want to ignore the importance of the role that the Workplace Project and its staff and volunteers played. The Workplace Project as an institution had contacts with allies that the individual immigrants would never have been able to reach. The Project had staff and volunteers whose knowledge of the United States political system and ability to access people within that system were instrumental in providing members with the information that they needed to make strategic decisions. English-speaking staff and volunteers were also able to serve as contacts for legislators and DOL administrators outside of group meetings. . . .

Effect of the Campaign and the Law

. . . [W]e can look at two things at this early stage to assess how effective the law may be in the long run: its use to date by both advocates and the Department of Labor. . . .

Soon after the law passed, the Workplace Project noted a rise in the numbers of groups of workers coming to its legal clinic. Presumably, these workers were drawn by both publicity about the changes and a new sense of possibility that recalcitrant employers would be forced to pay. The Project has also found that, when faced with a letter informing them that they may have to pay a fine equivalent to an additional 200 percent of what they owe, employers settle much more quickly than they did when threatened with a 25 percent penalty. In 1998, the first full year after the law went into effect, the Project legal clinic saw 44 percent more workers than the previous year and recovered a record amount of wages for unpaid workers, a surge due in large part to the new law.[22] Other advocacy groups and individuals have made similarly effective use of the law. . . .

The story with regard to the Department of Labor . . . is a different one. It is true that the pressure from our campaign brought about significant changes in the practices of the DOL locally and throughout New York state. On Long Island, the agency hired a full-time Spanish-speaking investigator for the Hempstead office, developed Spanish language versions of their forms, began to process cases in under three months, and built a relationship with our staff that allowed us to coordinate work with them—all without new regulations. Statewide, the DOL has developed a series of new forms and procedures in compliance with the law, including multilingual updates on case progress, the right for workers to be present at the DOL conference held with the employer, and the guarantee that a case will not be settled for less than the full amount owed unless the worker consents. The DOL also implemented a central docketing system for unpaid wages claims in response to our pressure for swifter processing of cases.[23] . . .

But there is little evidence that . . . the administrative changes are improving the Department's wage collection record. Once it was out of the spotlight, the DOL made little use of the new tools afforded it by the law. Out of 304 orders issued in the first six months after the Unpaid Wages Prohibition Act went into effect, the DOL issued 24 "orders to comply" (their final stage in a civil case) with the full 200 percent penalty; uncounted others were given fines of 50 percent or 100 percent—higher than the previous law permitted although not the full amount allowed under the Act.[24] In contrast, out of 758 orders issued in the sixteen months that followed that initial burst, DOL issued only 6 additional orders to comply with a 200 percent penalty.[25] Similarly, in the initial six-month period, the DOL investigated 174 cases for periods going back up to six years, where previously they would have looked no further back than two years;[26] in the following sixteen-month period, they investigated only an estimated 75 additional cases.[27]

Given this pattern, it is disturbing but not surprising to note that early gains in wage collections during the first few months after the law went into effect have fallen back over ensuing months to levels even lower than in the years before the law.[28]. . .

These results suggest several critiques of the Workplace project's strategy. First and foremost, it is now clear that two of the reasons that the bill was able to pass—no additional money for enforcement and no direct attack on DOL practices—have also undermined its effectiveness. Without any new inspectors or any funded mechanism to ensure that the DOL would do its work differently, the agency has been able to claim that it is working to capacity and within the letter of the law, and yet put no meaningful additional effort toward enforcement. Second, because the Workplace Project did not continue to focus its organizing and advocacy work for the implementation of the law as it had for its passage, the Department of Labor was let off the hook. Without ongoing activism and bad publicity, the DOL had little incentive to do things differently after the bill became law.

It is important to remember, however, that the campaign for the Unpaid Wages Prohibition Act was intended to increase the deterrence factor so that the law would be more self-enforcing *in the absence of an effective DOL*. Deterrence is a very difficult thing to measure. No one can count how many employers changed their practices as a result of the law if their previous violations were not detected by the DOL; a dip in DOL wage recovery could as easily be proof of effective deterrence as of DOL inactivity. Despite this lack of hard proof, it seems likely that even without a positive effect on the Department's enforcement practices, the law and others like it can potentially have a real impact on employers who decide on their own to pay legal wages in order to avoid a high penalty. This is particularly true where advocates and organizers work to make effective use of the law and keep it in the public's eye.

Notes

1. Beth Whitehouse, "The New Long Islanders," *Newsday,* July 12, 1994, p. A7.
2. Until November 1998, when the federal Labor Department went to any workplace to investigate wage violations, they also were required to review the business's I-9 forms, on which employers note the documents that each of their employees presented to prove authorization to work at the time of hiring. The federal Labor Department then had to file a report with the INS, noting both whether the I-9 forms were properly filled out and whether the Labor Department inspector noted anything else that would lead him or her to suspect that the employer had violated "the provisions against knowingly hiring or continuing to employ unauthorized workers". . . .
3. For a comprehensive survey of state minimum wage and wage enforcement laws, *see* "A Survey of State Wage Enforcement Laws: Models for Successful Reform," National Employment Law Project, 1997.
4. H. Carl McCall, "Department of Labor: Recovery of Unpaid Wages on Behalf of Claimants," Report 94-S-56, State of New York, Office of the State Comptroller, Division of Management Unit (Executive Summary).
5. This and the previous provisions were part of the bill that passed.
6. This and the following provision were cut from the bill before it passed.
7. Andy Logan in "Family Business," a review of Pataki's autobiography, *Pataki* in *New York Times,* July 12, 1998, p. 24.
8. This chronic dysfunction has resulted in New York state's receiving the lowest credit rating of any state except for Louisiana. Clyde Haberman, "Albany Sets Bad Example for California," *New York Times,* July 25, 1997, p. B1. See also "Scorn for Albany Unites Forces Urging a New Constitution," *New York Times,* October 26, 1997, p. 31; "Call a Constitutional Convention," *New York Times,* editorial, October 28, 1997, p. A22.
9. Although New York City is more heavily unionized than the country as a whole, the same is not true for the rest of the state. In addition, unions had grown used to doing business in Albany during the long reign of Democrats in the governor's seat. They have had a difficult time developing an effective strategy to promote their legislative agenda under a Republican governor.

Jennifer Gordon interview with Geri Reilly, Associate Counsel for Labor, New York State Assembly, October 2, 1998 (hereinafter "Reilly interview").

10. For a discussion of the history of the formation of the Long Island Republican machine, see Michael Dorman, "A Legacy of Kings: LI's Suburbs Produced Two Republican Bosses Whose Political Imprint Remains," *Newsday,* May 31, 1998, p. A14.
11. Reilly interview.
12. I am deeply grateful to Janice Fine, whose thoughts about the campaign helped me to form the theories that I discuss here. She discusses this campaign further in her forthcoming dissertation for a Ph.D. in political science from MIT, "Community Unionism: Beyond the Politics of Particularism."
13. *See,* e.g., Lisette Alvarez, "G.O.P. Tries to Win Hispanic Support Reagan Once Had," *New York Times,* November 21, 1997, p. A30; Todd Purdum, "California G.O.P. Faces a Crisis as Hispanic Voters Turn Away," *New York Times,* December 9, 1997, p. A1; Adam Nagourney, "Badillo Is Said to Be Switching to the Republicans," *New York Times,* June 25, 1998, p. B1.
14. In 1990, 234,000 people around the country applied to become U.S. citizens. In 1994 the number had more than doubled to 543,000. By 1997 the number of applicants had almost tripled again, to 1,564,000 (INS Statistical Yearbooks, 1990 and 1994; INS Monthly Statistical Report, September FY 1997, Year End Report).
15. This and all other quotes from Mitchell Pally are from a telephone interview with the author, June 8, 1998.
16. "Pay Them for Their Labors," *The Daily Gazette,* editorial, June 25, 1997.
17. Steven Greenhouse, "Bill Seeks to Make Sure Immigrants Get Paid," *New York Times,* June 30, 1997.
18. Reilly interview.
19. Interviews with Senator Marcellino on July 2, 1998, and Senator Skelos on July 23, 1998; conversations with press offices of Senators Maltese, Marchi, Trunzo, and Volker on July 31, 1998; Joseph Berger, "When County Politics Is a Family Business; Westchester Feels the Spanos' Presence," *New York Times,* April 26, 1996, p. B1. I was unable to obtain information about Senators Hannon and Vellela; Senator Levy is deceased.
20. For example, Unpaid Wages Prohibition Act sponsor Senator Marchi was quoted in *Newsday* a few years earlier as saying "It is street knowledge around the world that we're under a mandate to provide relief. . . We've become a magnet, saying, 'Come to New York, and we'll take care of you." Nicholas Goldberg, "Move in State to Cut Aid to Poor," *Newsday,* March 11, 1993. . . .
21. Both senators that I interviewed confirmed that they had never before or since had a lobbying session held in a language other than English. The reaction we received during our visits leads me to conclude that this was true for most if not all of the senators we saw.
22. Workplace Project legal program coordinator. Rhina Ramos, telephone conversation with the author, October 18, 1999.
23. Author's notes from her meeting with Rhina Ramos and Michael Hoffman, then-Workplace Project executive director, and Richard Polsinello, Joaquin Bermudez and Manuel Fruchter, DOL, July 2, 1998 (hereinafter "July 2 DOL meeting").
24. The total number of cases investigated during that period was 5,649; only 174 of those cases had claims for periods going back longer than two years, and all were investigated for the full length of time worked. Statistics regarding the first six months of implementation were provided by Richard Polsinello during July 2 DOL meeting, through subsequent faxes, and in a follow-up interview by telephone on October 7, 1998.
25. Richard Polsinello, telephone interview with the author, October 12, 1999 (hereinafter "Polsinello interview, October 12, 1999").
26. The total number of cases investigated during that period was 5,649; only 174 of those cases had claims for periods going back longer than two years, and all were investigated for the full length of time worked. Statistics from same sources as in n. 24.
27. Polsinello interview, October 12, 1999.
28. All statistics about wage collections were taken from charts provided to the author by Richard Polsinello. Unpaid wage information is from New York State Department of Labor, Wage and Hour Division, 1998, Report LS 50105; fringe benefit information is from New York State Department of Labor, Wage and Hour Division, 1998, Report LS-50110.

Chapter 7 Review Questions

1. What are the three different meanings of group power? What are the characteristics of each?
2. What are the most powerful types of groups across the states? What makes these groups so successful?
3. How would you categorize the power of interest groups generally across the states? What factors seem to make interest groups more powerful in some states than in others? What kinds of changes are occurring in group system power?
4. What strategies and tactics did the Workplace Project use to influence the passage of the Unpaid Wages Prohibition Act? Why was the group successful? What does the case study tell us about the distribution of power among different types of interest groups?
5. As you think about some current political issues that are being fought in your state, what interest groups seem to be important in shaping the outcome? Why are these groups important? Do you think that interest groups play too large a role in shaping the outcome of this and other battles in your state? In general, do you think that interest groups play a harmful or beneficial role in your state's politics? How are they harmful? What are some of their benefits?
6. The case study in Chapter 5 on the Industrial Areas Foundation suggests that individuals can have greater influence on government through greater civic engagement. The reading by Thomas and Hrebenar, however, suggests that groups can only enjoy long-term success if they develop a symbiotic relationship with politicians and government. Is there a conflict between these two arguments? Do Thomas and Hrebenar's findings suggest that it is difficult for citizen groups to obtain power, or is there reason to believe that these groups can reach a position where they can regularly exercise power? How so?

Key Terms

interest group
Federalist No. 10
pluralism
group power
citizens group
hyperpluralism
single group power
overall individual interest power
group system power
symbiotic relationship
dominant influence
complementary influence
subordinate influence

Suggestions for Further Reading

Baumgartner, Frank R., and Beth L. Leech. *Basic Interests: The Importance of Groups in Politics and in Political Science.* Princeton: Princeton University Press, 1998. Provides a comprehensive overview of the scholarly literature on interest groups in America.

Berry, Jeffrey M. *The Interest Group Society.* 3d ed. New York: Longman, 1997. This book provides a fine overview of interest group politics at the national level, with considerable attention devoted to many of the important theoretical concerns within the literature.

Gray, Virginia, and David Lowery. "Interest Representation in the States," in Ronald E. Weber and Paul Brace, eds., *American State and Local Politics: Directions for the 21st Century.* New York: Chatham

House, 1999. Excellent overview of the research on state interest group systems by two of the foremost experts on the topic. Includes discussions of important theoretical concerns and recent empirical trends.

———. *The Population Ecology of Interest Representation: Lobbying Communities in the American States.* Ann Arbor: University of Michigan Press, 1996. Groundbreaking study analyzing the density and diversity of interest groups across the states.

———. "State Interest Group Research and the Mixed Legacy of Belle Zeller," *State Politics and Policy Quarterly* 2 (Winter 2002): 388–410. This essay provides a valuable overview of the research on state interest groups. The authors devote special attention to the influential work of Belle Zeller.

Hrebenar, Ronald J., and Clive S. Thomas, eds. *Interest Group Politics in the American West.* Salt Lake City: University of Utah Press, 1987. This was the first of several collections of essays edited by Hrebenar and Thomas on the role and influence of interest groups in the states. Three later volumes focused on interest groups in the South, the Midwest, and the Northeast.

Nownes, Anthony J., and Patricia Freeman. "Interest Group Activity in the States." *Journal of Politics* 60 (February 1998): 86–112. By studying their activities in three states, this paper provides insights on what groups do and the techniques that they use.

Olson, Mancur. *The Logic of Collective Action.* Cambridge, Mass.: Harvard University Press, 1965. This highly influential book introduced the use of economic ideas for understanding the development and impact of groups.

Portes, Alejandro, and Ruben G. Rumbaut. *Legacies: The Story of the Immigrant Second Generation.* Berkeley: University of California Press, 2001. Highly praised book by two sociologists on the experiences of modern immigrants and their children in the United States.

Rosenthal, Alan. *The Third House: Lobbyists and Lobbying in the States.* Washington, D.C.: CQ Press, 1993. This book provides the most comprehensive analysis of lobbying in state legislatures.

Thomas, Clive S., and Ronald J. Hrebenar. "Interest Groups in the States." In Virginia Gray and Russell L. Hanson, eds., *Politics in the American States.* 8th ed. Washington, D.C.: CQ Press, 2004. This essay provides a fine overview on the state of interest group politics in the states. The essay includes the results from Thomas and Hrebenar's 2002 survey on interest group power.

Truman, David B. *The Governmental Process.* New York: Alfred A. Knopf, 1951. A seminal book that is often credited with laying the foundation for the concept of pluralism and spearheading scholarly interest in interest groups.

Waldinger, Roger, ed. *Strangers at the Gates: New Immigrants in Urban America.* Berkeley: University of California Press, 2001. Collection of nine essays provides valuable insight into the economic problems confronted by immigrants to the nation's urban centers.

Related Web Sites

http://www.publicintegrity.org/default.aspx
The Center for Public Integrity monitors lobbying and campaign finance at the state level. The web site includes information on state lobbying laws and links to the state agencies that oversee lobbyists.

http://www.followthemoney.org/
The web site for the Institute on Money in State Politics provides data and research findings on campaign contributions and their impact on public policy debate.

http://www.uspirg.org/
The web site for U.S. Public Interest Research Group includes links to individual state and student chapters.

http://www.empirepage.com/
This web service provides links to New York government and politics. The links are free, but access to the service's newspaper articles requires a paid subscription.

8

State Legislatures: The Concept of Professionalism

While there is debate as to the policy impact of professionalized legislatures, few can deny that the institution itself is very different than it was only two or three decades ago.

Joel A. Thompson and Gary F. Moncrief

READING 8

Introduction

State legislatures have changed significantly since the 1960s. Until that time, most state legislatures met only briefly, every year or every other year, to consider legislation and to handle their other duties. The legislatures hired few secretaries and little professional staff to help legislators handle their work. Facilities were often inadequate, with little space set aside for committee meetings and few private offices for members. The legislators themselves were paid less than a living wage, and thus needed a job outside of the legislature in order to survive financially. Ethics rules were nonexistent or poorly enforced.

A movement began to emerge after World War II to improve or modernize state legislatures to make them better able to function. The movement started slowly, with a handful of states taking steps to provide better staff support and to improve the legislatures' ability to conduct research. Even though the history of the movement can be traced to the period after World War II, state legislative scholars frequently link the movement's rise to the U.S. Supreme Court's decisions in *Baker* v. *Carr* (1962) and *Reynolds* v. *Sims* (1964). These two court decisions forced states to redraw their legislative district boundaries so that all districts for a given chamber had approximately equal population. The court's actions, and the subsequent redrawing of district lines, are considered to have brought in a large influx of new members who supported modernization.

The movement received a boost in 1971 with the publication of *State Legislatures: An Evaluation of Their Effectiveness* by the Citizens Conference on State Legislatures.

The book, which included critical evaluations of the legislatures in all 50 states, helped motivate state after state to pursue modernization. Among other actions, reforms were enacted allowing the legislatures to meet more frequently and for longer periods, providing greater staff support for members, upgrading legislative facilities, reorganizing legislative structures and procedures, raising legislators' pay, providing members with health and retirement benefits, and establishing ethics rules.

State legislative scholars have long been interested in understanding the effect of the Legislative Reform Movement on legislative politics, making it the central focus of a large body of research. Past studies have examined how the changes brought by this movement have affected such things as the success of female candidates, the competitiveness of elections, the prevalence of particular legislative norms, the role of legislative leaders, and the influence of governors in legislative politics.

Instead of looking at the effect of the reform movement on politics, however, some legislative scholars have been interested in understanding the causes that brought about the changes themselves. To understand this research, it is important to recognize that state legislatures have actually changed in at least two very important ways since the 1960s. On one hand, the legislatures have developed more professional work environments. Today, for example, most legislatures have better facilities than in the past, including private offices for members and more rooms for committee meetings. Most legislators now have their own private staffs, and legislatures employ more policy experts to help analyze state issues and policy proposals. The legislatures meet for longer periods of time, allowing legislators to give more thought to proposed legislation. The legislators are also paid a more livable wage and face a heavier workload. On the other hand, beyond these changes in the work environment, the legislatures have also changed in the sense that the members who serve in them are more likely to make a career out of legislative service. To distinguish between these two different trends, legislative scholars sometimes refer to the changes in the work environment as the spread of *professionalism* and the changes in members who serve as the rise of *careerism.*

In general, many legislative scholars suggest that the rise in careerism is a result of the more professional work environment. Meeting in longer sessions, with heavier workloads and better pay, the part-time legislators were forced out of office. Replacing them were individuals who were willing to make legislative politics a career. Not all scholars, however, agree with this scenario. In fact, some argue that the relationship may be reversed, with the rise of careerism actually preceding the growth of the professional environment. These scholars argue that once legislators began to make legislative politics a career, the legislators restructured the organization to meet their own needs.

Joel A. Thompson and Gary F. Moncrief provide an alternative, and more complex, explanation for why state legislatures have changed so much over the past three decades. Thompson and Moncrief are leading experts on state legislative politics and frequent coauthors. Thompson is a professor at Appalachian State University and Moncrief at Boise State University. Drawing from organizational theory, the two tie changes in state legislatures to broader changes in society, including population growth, increased urbanization, and greater social complexity. As the broader society changes, they argue, it places external stresses on the legislatures. Many of the reforms adopted by state legislatures are designed to accommodate these stresses and allow the legislatures to function in the changing world. The reforms, which they refer to as *adaptive changes,* create new internal tensions in the legislature. In response to the internal tensions, legislatures adopt other reforms, or what the two call *consolidative* changes. Whereas adaptive changes are meant to help the legislature cope with changes in the external environment, consolidative changes are made to address legislators' changing needs.

The research on the modernization movement is of interest to scholars because it provides insight into how and why legislatures change, and the effect of those changes on legislative behavior. Yet the modernization effort should be of interest to nonscholars as well, because it reveals the difficulties that often occur in trying to create a governmental structure that fulfills all of our expectations about good government. The Legislative Reform Movement represented a serious effort to improve the ability of state legislatures to function. Using Hedge's terminology again, the movement sought to make the legislatures more *responsible.* In many ways, the movement was a great success, strengthening the legislatures' capacity to govern, making them more independent, and opening up elected office to a more diverse group of representatives. Yet although the movement was clearly a success in many ways, it also produced new problems. Among the most troubling is that it helped make the public grow increasingly disillusioned with state legislatures and legislators. Today, many Americans see state legislators as being overly concerned with reelection, obsessed with raising campaign contributions, beholden to special interests, and unconcerned about the voters who elected them. Not all scholars view the reforms so harshly, yet state legislators are clearly more concerned about reelection than in the past and more attentive to raising campaign funds. The reforms may have also made legislators less willing to work together to address state problems, as they focus instead on furthering their individual career goals. The reform movement also harmed the legislatures' legitimacy in the public's eye and encouraged the feeling among many Americans that they are poorly represented. In other words, the movement has produced a tradeoff in which the legislatures have become better at fulfilling some of the goals we expect from them, but worse at others. They are more capable, more independent, and more diverse. Yet the reforms have also encouraged the election of more career-minded politicians who may not always be as willing to work together, and the public has become less trusting of government. The question for future reformers is what can be done to make the legislatures better able to fulfill all of these different goals, or whether a tradeoff is inevitable.

Questions to Consider

The following selection by Thompson and Moncrief provides an overview of the changes that have swept state legislatures over the past few decades and lays out the authors' theory on institutional change. More importantly, the essay also explains how the changes have improved state legislatures, yet also have created new problems. As you read this selection, keep the following questions in mind:

- What do Thompson and Moncrief mean by *adaptive* and *consolidative* changes? What are the different forces that encourage these changes?

- What do Thompson and Moncrief mean when they write that there is a "new breed of state legislator"? What is this new breed like, and how has its appearance altered legislative politics?
- After reading this selection, do you believe that the changes in state legislatures have been for the better or for the worse? How so?
- How is Thompson and Moncrief's argument similar to and different from Ehrenhalt's argument in Chapter 6?
- How has your state legislature changed over the past few decades? Has the work environment become more professional? Do legislators make a career of legislative service?

The Evolution of the State Legislature: Institutional Change and Legislative Careers

Joel A. Thompson and Gary F. Moncrief

For anyone interested in the variety of historical patterns of organization presented by the (U.S.) House and Senate in the nineteenth century, the current range of state legislative practices have a quite familiar look. One does not need to go, like Darwin, to the Galapagos Islands to rediscover long missing species of legislative operation. (Price 1975, 20)

American state legislatures have changed remarkably in recent years. It can be argued that state legislatures have experienced greater internal change in the past twenty-five years than any other of our governmental institutions and that they have changed more rapidly than during any other period in their history. (Pound 1988, 1)

State legislatures are becoming like the U.S. House of Representatives. (Rosenthal 1989, 78)

Modern (state) representatives aggressively pursue political self-interest, which usually translates into advancing the interests of their district and their political career. (Van Horn 1989, 211)

These observations of state legislative life in the United States, made less than fifteen years apart, attest to the profound changes that have occurred in state legislatures in the past three decades. Price's statement was based on his observation of state legislatures in the mid-to-late 1960s. He found that many of the characteristics that affected their functioning and operations were similar to arrangements found in Congress at the turn of the century. Pound notes the rapid and significant changes that have occurred in state legislatures, and Rosenthal observes that many of these changes mirror those made in Congress. Finally, Van Horn posits a relationship between changes in the institution and changes in the career orientation of its members. These observations are central to the discussion in this chapter.

This change in the legislative institution has not gone unnoticed. Indeed, a whole literature on state legislative change, often couched in terms of legislative reform and professionalism, has developed. While there is debate as to the policy impact of professionalized legislatures (Moncrief and Thompson 1988), few can deny that the institution itself is very different than it was only two or three decades ago.

While the initial scholarly impetus was to assess either the impact of legislative change on public policy or

Joel A. Thompson and Gary F. Moncrief, "The Evolution of the State Legislature: Institutional Change and Legislative Careers," from *Changing Patterns in State Legislative Careers*, ed. Moncrief and Thompson (Ann Arbor: University of Michigan Press, 1992), pp. 195–206. Reprinted by permission of The University of Michigan Press.

the impact of change on the internal order of the body, subsequent research efforts have begun to examine changes in those individuals who make up the institution—the state legislators. Just like the institution itself, the job orientation or career of the state legislator has changed dramatically. We believe that these two changes are not independent phenomena. Yet little scholarly work has attempted to connect, in some theoretical way, the relationship between *institutional* change and *individual* change. It is the purpose of this essay to explore this relationship. . . .

Organizations exist in relation to their environments. As Davidson and Oleszek note, "In order to survive, an organization must adjust both to its external environment and its internal needs. . . ." (1976, 39). As the environment changes it creates pressures on the organization to change—to adapt. In relation to legislative organizations, terms such as *institutionalization, professionalization,* and *modernization* have often been used to describe their evolution. These terms fit within the theoretical framework developed by Davidson and Oleszek, who refer to these changes as *adaptation* and *consolidation.* Adaptive and consolidative changes are adjustments that organizations make in relation to external and internal stresses respectively. . . .

It is our contention that over the past three decades state legislatures have been subjected to significant external stresses and that adaptive changes made to address these external stresses have created additional internal stresses, which subsequently have led to consolidative changes. These consolidative changes have important implications for state legislative careers.

External Stress and Adaptive Changes

Few studies have examined the impact of environmental changes on state-level political institutions in general (Thompson and Lanier 1987) or the state legislature in particular (Moncrief 1985; Brace and Ward 1989). Although these studies used different indicators and time periods, all found linkages between measures of social or economic change and legislative development. Other sources of external stress include political and legal changes.

The *Baker v. Carr* decision served as the legal shock to a system that had already begun to feel the pressures of changing societal forces. Pound notes that "some significant reform trends were evident before [*Baker v. Carr*]" (1988, 1), primarily the development of staff and research capabilities. But the pace of legislative modernization increased dramatically in the mid-1960s. The first sixty years of the twentieth century was a period of rapid growth, increased urbanization and industrialization, and technological change. Societal forces affected state legislatures. For example, Rosenthal and Forth explain the significant increase in the number of bill introductions and enactments in state legislatures as partly a function of the changing political and social environment: "much of what legislators introduce comes in response to conditions in the environment. The more people, the more problems, the more complexity, the greater the amount of legislation proposed" (1978, 287). As a result, governing became a more complex task than at the turn of the century.

Yet state legislatures were ill equipped to meet the demands of a changing society. They had not adapted rapidly enough to changing external stresses and were, in the words of Davidson and Oleszek, operating "on credit," as pressures were "allowed to build up and resolution of the conflict delayed" (1976, 42). This observation was verified by others. Writing in 1966, Heard notes:

> Even if all legislators were models of efficiency and rectitude . . . most state legislatures would remain poorly organized and technically ill-equipped to do what is expected of them. They do not meet often enough nor long enough; they lack space, clerical staffing, professional assistance; they are poorly paid and overworked; they are prey to special interests, sometimes their own; their procedures and committee systems are outmoded; they devote inordinate time to local interests that distract them from general public policy; they sometimes cannot even get copies of bills on which they must vote. They work, in short, under a host of conditions that dampen their incentive and limit their ability to function effectively. (1966, 1–2)

Heard cites the *Baker* decision as a "radical development" that solved the malapportionment problem, considered to be the most serious problem with state legislatures. With reapportionment came "a change in outlook toward the whole future of state legislature" (1966, 2).

The twenty-five-year period following Heard's observations has witnessed a partial fulfillment of the changes that he anticipated and that others advocated. Many of these are similar to changes in Congress during its process of institutionalization (Moncrief 1985; Brace and Ward 1989). . . .

Institutionalization is not necessarily the same as professionalization. But as Squire notes, "The two are, however, likely to occur together, because the dynamic element leading to the development of an institutionalized legislature is closely related to the result of professionalization" (1989, 9).

Squire goes on to make an argument that is very similar to ours concerning consolidative and adaptive changes: "A professionalized body is likely to be one where members look on their service as being their career. . . . Legislators who adopt this long-term perspective are likely to try and mold the organization to meet their needs: that is, to institutionalize it" (1989, 9). . . . Squire shows that the career needs in the California Assembly are not the same as in Congress, and therefore, some of the norms and structures are different (1989). These findings suggest that there is more than a single path that leads to professionalization of the state legislature.

There is, however, an apparent consensus on what factors constitute the major elements of professionalization at the state legislative level. These factors include increases in session length, members' compensation and benefits, and staffing. These factors contribute to the internal complexity and institutional autonomy of the legislature.

Session Length

As society has become more complex and technical, perhaps no other aspect of legislative performance becomes more paramount than adequate time to gather information, deliberate, legislate, and oversee. In 1940, only four state legislatures (N.Y., N.J., R.I., and S.C.) met in annual sessions. This number grew to nineteen by the early 1960s, thirty-five by 1975, and today, forty-three legislatures meet annually. Twenty-nine states now have the authority to convene themselves in special session. Overall, the average length of legislative sessions has increased and in California averages approximately 250 days. Even states that have maintained biennial or limited sessions have found it increasingly necessary to utilize interim and special committee activities, sometimes to nearly a year-round schedule (Pound 1988).

Compensation

Although salaries remain low in many states, especially for the amount of time spent on legislative matters, they are much improved. It is difficult to compute salary figures for some legislatures because they are tied to the number of session days and daily expense reimbursements. But for thirty-nine of the forty states that have established annual salaries (New Hampshire excluded), the average compensation now approaches $20,000 per year (plus expenses in most cases). Some states still pay extremely low salaries—New Hampshire, $100, West Virginia, $6,500, Texas, $7,200, and Arkansas, $7,500. Others, however, have salaries that are comparable to those in the private sector for requisite education and skills—$57,500 in New York, $52,500 in California, and in excess of $40,000 in Michigan, Ohio, and Pennsylvania. At least ten states now have annual salaries of $30,000 or more. Better legislative salaries should result in a more careerist orientation and, according to Brace and Ward, are "the most important catalyst for stimulating institutional adjustments" (1989, 1a).

Staffing

. . . State legislators have enhanced their capabilities vis-à-vis other political actors by increasing staff resources and research capabilities. The National Conference of State Legislatures estimates that the permanent staff of state legislatures is now between eighteen thousand and twenty thousand persons, compared to about five thousand in the mid-1960s. The number of full-time professional staff now exceeds fifty in all but twelve state legislatures. Thirty-six states hire more than one hundred additional staff members during legislative sessions. Of the fourteen that do not, only four have less than one hundred full-time professionals. In addition, thirty-five states now have full-time staff support for standing committees.

Weberg (1988) reports that for all fifty states legislative staffs grew by 24 percent between 1979 and 1988. The largest increases in the past decade have occurred in personal staff. Finally, Pound notes that *every* state legislature has enhanced its research and fiscal capabilities, although some still lag (1988, 16–18). In short, the level of staff and technical support in most state legislatures today is in sharp contrast to that of twenty-five years ago.

The result of these adaptations is greater legislative autonomy and independence. Limitations of time and staff support, coupled with high turnover, and hence little expertise, resulted in the inability of any legislature, except perhaps California's, to carry out its oversight function "with any degree of adequacy" (see Citizens Conference on State Legislatures 1971, 126–27). When oversight was accomplished, it tended to be "episodic, partial, and selective" (Keefe 1966, 46).

But many state legislatures have made adaptive changes to meet the challenges of a strengthened executive branch. One scholar observes that "during the 1970s, state legislatures discovered oversight" (Gormley 1989, 132). Also, they became much more involved in other administrative aspects of governing. For example, in 1967, only two states engaged in administrative rules review. By 1988, at least forty-two states were active to some degree in this process (Pound 1988, 3). Sunset legislation also became a mechanism utilized by approximately two-thirds of the states, and approximately one-third continue to use the legislative veto, although it has been invalidated in at least eight states (Gormley 1989, 132). The result of these and other adaptations may provide "more occasions for legislative oversight and more incentives for individual legislators to engage in oversight" (Gormley 1989, 133).

The results of adaptive changes made by state legislatures have been profound. These changes are perhaps best summarized by Rosenthal:

> Thus, the decade from about 1965 to 1975 can appropriately be termed the period of "the rise of the legislative institution." Traditional assemblies became modern ones, and reformed legislatures emerged. They had developed the capacity to do their jobs, to perform the functions that they could be expected to perform. (1989, 70).

Internal Stress and Consolidative Changes: Implications for Legislative Careers

According to our theoretical framework, byproducts of adaptive changes made by state legislatures include internal tensions, which are "an inevitable concomitant of all organizational innovation" (Davidson and Oleszek 1976, 40). Consolidative changes . . . are designed to accommodate as much as possible the *individual* needs of members. . . . [C]onsolidative changes in the state legislature after the rapid period of modernization are more closely linked to the needs, goals, and motivations of individual legislators. If we assume that the goal of some is a legislative career (see Rosenthal 1989), then consolidative changes should enhance this goal.

In addition to the socioeconomic changes chronicled in the literature on institutional change, other political, legal, and structural changes have had profound consequences for the state legislature. The most notable result is the new breed of state legislator—"professionals who want to stay in public office for the long haul" (Rosenthal 1989, 76; also see Loomis 1990, 13). Women constitute a larger proportion of this new breed; Patricia Freeman and William Lyons note . . . that the number of females serving in the states has quadrupled since 1969. Women hold more than 25 percent of legislative seats in at least five states—New Hampshire, Maine, Colorado, Vermont, and Washington—and make up a sizable contingent in many others (Van Horn 1989, 211). Overall, however, women are still underrepresented. . . .

Reapportionment and the preclearance provisions of the Voting Rights Act have had a significant impact on the number of African-Americans and Hispanics elected to state legislatures. Charles S. Bullock notes . . . that the number of blacks has increased from 172 in 1969 to 400 in 1987. As of 1987, thirty-six states had at least 1 black senator and forty-one states had at least 1 black house member. Sixteen states had at least 10 blacks in the lower house. The number of Hispanic representatives has increased also. By 1988, 120 Hispanics held seats in state legislatures. Hispanics are most predominant in states where they constitute a significant proportion of the population (Van Horn 1989, 211). . . .

Another difference between the new breed and the old breed relates to occupations. The old breed (lawyers and businesspeople) are being replaced by "career politicians who come from the ranks of unseasoned lawyers, teachers, preachers, spouses of professionals, single people who can live on a legislative salary, public organizers, legislative aides, and others of like ilk" (Rosenthal 1989, 75). Another part of the new breed is made up of "the younger, newer members—men and women alike—who come out of college, graduate school, or law school and go directly into politics" (Rosenthal 1989, 75). They are more mobile and less parochial. A final contingent of this group has a unique occupation—legislator. Today, more than 10 percent of all state legislators consider their occupation to be legislator, up from 1 percent only a decade earlier (Bazar 1987). In the more professional bodies the proportions are much higher: approximately two-thirds in Michigan and Pennsylvania; half or more in Illinois, Massachusetts, and New York; and only slightly fewer in at least seven other states. Wisconsin is illustrative of the trend (Loomis 1990, 13–15). In 1963 no member listed legislator as his or her primary occupation. By 1969, only about 5 percent were full-time. This proportion grew to about 55 percent by 1983 and today approaches 70 percent (Rosenthal 1989, 71–72).

As a result, the legislature is much less homogeneous than it used to be. Perhaps more importantly though, it is made up of individuals who have few outside interests and distractions. In short, the legislature is their vocation. Thus, to reduce occupational uncertainty, electoral concerns become paramount (Loomis 1990, 20). After all, for the old breed, electoral defeat was a disappointment; for the new breed it may be the end of a career.

Electoral considerations have significantly affected the legislature and the careers of its members. One of the most obvious is money, "the mother's milk of politics." The cost of running for a legislative seat has risen dramatically in the last decade (Alexander 1991, 7). Sorauf (1988, 266) reports that candidates for the Assembly in California spent $56,300,000.00 in 1986, or $3.20 per vote. This figure approaches the average expenditure per vote for Congress that year—$4.59. In Ohio a competitive seat now costs about $300,000.00, in Michigan about $250,000.00, and in Wisconsin about $100,000.00 (Rosenthal 1989, 79). Even in smaller, more rural states where media are not used extensively, competitive campaigns can cost $25,000.00 and more.

As a result of the increase in campaign costs, candidates are forced to seek larger and larger war chests. Quick to fill this void, political action committees (PACs) have proliferated. Jones (1986) reports that the number of PACs has increased significantly: up 500 percent in Arizona, approximately 400 percent in Louisiana and New York, and about 100 percent in Wisconsin. In North Carolina, the number of PACs has increased tenfold since 1974 (Thompson and Cassie 1990).

Of course, there has been a corresponding, almost geometric, increase in the amount of money flowing into electoral coffers. Between 1976 and 1982, the amount of money contributed by PACs increased by 240 percent in Florida, over 400 percent in Montana, and over 1,500 percent in Arizona (Wagner 1986). This money constitutes a substantial proportion of the funds generated and spent by candidates, ranging on the average from about 25 to 75 percent. Studies indicate that PAC contributions go disproportionately to incumbents (Giles and Pritchard 1985; Jones and Borris 1985), giving career legislators another electoral advantage. Although political party organizations may attempt to offset this advantage to some extent, the proportion of incumbents who are reelected to state legislative seats now approaches that of members of Congress.

Money has also become a consideration of legislative leaders. Increasingly, leaders are expected to raise and distribute campaign funds for party members. This practice can help insulate individual legislators from PACs and their influence and strengthens the role of the legislative leadership.

Electoral considerations are also a force behind the increase in the proliferation of personal staffs. Approximately twenty states now provide personal staffs for members. In addition, at least ten states have made some type of provisions for district offices, where staffs can maintain close ties with local citizens and provide assistance to constituents. Unlike professional staff, the major function of personal staff is "delivering service to constituents and reelection to members, two very compatible tasks" (Rosenthal 1989, 83).

Increases in money and staff support are related to another aspect of careerism—a decrease in turnover. The steady decline in turnover in state legislatures is well documented (Rosenthal 1974; Shin and Jackson 1979; Niemi and Winsky 1987). Turnover rates are a product of (1) the relative attractiveness of the position and (2) the relative competitiveness of the district. Salary increases and the availability of personal staff have made the state legislature a more attractive place to work. Large campaign war chests have enhanced the reelection chances of incumbents who run and discourage those who want to challenge.

Stabilization of membership is followed by other consolidative changes like the development of a seniority system, curtailment of the Speaker's power, and the decentralization of power within the chambers. There are surely differences here between the types of changes that occurred in Congress and those that may occur in some state legislatures, because the career opportunity structures are somewhat different (see Squire 1988, 1989). Nonetheless, the patterns of institutionalization and professionalization are very similar.

The rising costs of campaigns, the proliferation of personal staff, the appearance of district offices, and the increase in the number of full-time legislators are indicative of the "congressionalization" of the state legislature (Van Horn 1989). Whether we call it "reform," "professionalization," "modernization," or "congressionalization," the institution has changed dramatically. And so have those who occupy it.

The most recent external shock to the system—the movement to limit legislative terms—may have profound effects. . . . [S]ome of the short-term effects may be positive ones—positive in terms of making the legislature more representative: women and southern Republicans would likely benefit from the sudden increase in open seats, increasing the possibility that their numbers in the legislature would more accurately reflect their proportion in the general population.

But some of the effects of term limits may adversely affect the evolution of the institution. Certainly leadership positions will change hands more frequently. In some states this may open up the chambers to some of the new breed who may disperse power among the members and open the legislative doors to new ideas and innovative state programs. On the other hand, the departure of those members with long service will result in a substantial loss of legislative and policy expertise, making the remaining members more dependent on lobbyists, the bureaucrats, and the governor. In the long-term, term limits may cause other unintended results: fewer effectively contested elections and an increase in the influence of legislative staff (see Copeland and Rausch 1991 or Moncrief et al. 1992). . . .

Conclusions

State legislatures today are very different institutions than before. Changes in the socioeconomic, political, and legal environment generated substantial stresses that required organizational change. Twenty-five years of reform resulted in a stronger, more capable, and more independent branch of government. . . . As a result, many state legislatures are becoming more like their national counterpart, the U.S. House of Representatives.

Adaptive changes and system "shocks" (reform, reapportionment, and the Voting Rights Act) have facilitated the election of a new breed of state legislators. The new breed is different from the old in many ways. Its impact has been to make the institution less homogeneous, more representative of its constituents, and more inclined to shape the institution to meet its career needs.

But while some consolidative changes have enhanced the career opportunity structures of state legislatures, others have detracted from the legislative process by contributing to its fragmentation. Members are more concerned with reducing electoral uncertainties than with advancing programmatic or party agendas. As a result, campaign costs have soared, and the pursuit of money has become a time-consuming task. Individual staff members spend more time satisfying constituents' needs and less time researching legislative proposals (see Rosenthal 1989). Citizens are becoming disenchanted with career politicians who give the appearance of placing their electoral welfare over that of the state. These actions and perceptions have contributed to the nascent term limit movement.

These changes carry individual costs as well. The transition from part-time to full-time legislatures has brought with it "a serious source of tension" between public and private affairs (Francis 1985, 641). For some, the added costs of more time away from family plus more energy directed toward legislative matters outweigh their individual rewards, personal achievements, or desires for a legislative career (Francis and Baker 1986).

An important question for subsequent research is the extent to which state legislatures and legislative careers will continue to evolve in ways similar to Congress. Will they become so fragmented that they lose their capacity to function effectively as governing bodies? Will members become so individualistic and parochial that the public interest becomes lost in a myriad of private interests? "If the case of the U.S. Congress is an indication, then state legislatures . . . face the prospect of an unraveling organizational coherence and approaching paralysis" (Rosenthal 1989, 97). If this prediction comes true, state legislatures will have come full circle, from virtual paralysis due to institutional handicaps and external stress to near paralysis because of individual motivations and internal stress. One is then left with a Darwinian question: Are state legislatures evolving into a stronger species or an endangered one?

References

Alexander, Herbert. 1991. *Reform and Reality.* New York: The Twentieth Century Fund Press.

Bazar, Beth. 1987. *State Legislators' Occupations: A Decade of Change.* Denver: National Conference of State Legislatures.

Brace, Paul, and Daniel Ward. 1989. "The Transformation of the American Statehouse: A Study of Legislative Institutionalization." Paper delivered at the 1989 annual meeting of the Midwest Political Science Association, Chicago, Ill., April.

Citizen's Conference on State Legislatures. 1971. *Report on the Evaluation of the 50 State Legislatures.* Denver, Colo.: Citizen's Conference on State Legislatures.

Copeland, Gary, and John Rausch, Jr. 1991. "The End of Professionalism? The Dynamics of Term Limitations." Paper presented at the annual meeting of the Southwestern Political Science Association, San Antonio, Tex., March 27–30.

Davidson, Roger H., and W. Oleszek. 1976. "Adaptation and Consolidation: Structural Innovation in the U.S. House of Representatives." *Legislative Studies Quarterly* 1:37–66.

Francis, Wayne. 1985. "Costs and Benefits of Legislative Service in the American States." *American Journal of Political Science* 29:626–42.

Francis, Wayne, and John Baker. 1986. "Why Do U.S. State Legislators Vacate Their Seats?" *Legislative Studies Quarterly* 11:119–26.

Giles, Michael W., and Anita Pritchard. 1985. "Campaign Expenditures and Legislative Elections in Florida." *Legislative Studies Quarterly* 10:71–88.

Gormley, William T. 1989. "Custody Battles in State Administration." In *The State of the States,* ed. Carl E. Van Horn. Washington, D.C.: CQ Press.

Heard, Alexander, ed. 1966. *State Legislatures in American Politics.* Englewood Cliffs, N.J.: Prentice Hall.

Jones, Ruth. 1986. "State and Federal Legislative Campaigns: Same Song, Different Verse." *Election Politics* 3:8–12.

Jones, Ruth, and Thomas J. Borris. 1985. "Strategic Contributing in Legislative Campaigns: The Case of Minnesota." *Legislative Studies Quarterly* 10:89–105.

Keefe, William J. 1966. "The Functions and Powers of the State Legislatures." In *State Legislatures in American Politics,* ed. Alexander Heard. Englewood Cliffs, N.J.: Prentice Hall.

Loomis, Burdett. 1990. "Political Careers and American State Legislatures." Paper presented at the Eagleton Institute of Politics Symposium on "The Legislature in the Twenty-first Century," Williamsburg, Va.

Moncrief, Gary. 1985. "The Correlates of Adaptation in State Legislatures: A Comparative and Diachronic Application of Organization Theory." Paper presented at the annual meeting of the Western Political Science Association, Las Vegas, Nev.

Moncrief, Gary, and Joel A. Thompson. 1988. "The Policy Consequences of State Legislative Reform." Paper presented at the annual meeting of the Midwest Political Science Association, Chicago, Ill.

Moncrief, Gary, Joel A. Thompson, Michael Haddon, and Robert Hoyer. 1992. "For Whom the Bell Tolls: Term Limits and State Legislatures," *Legislative Studies Quarterly* 17:37–47.

Niemi, Richard, and Laura Winsky. 1987. "Membership Turnover in U.S. State Legislatures: Trends and Effects of Districting." *Legislative Studies Quarterly* 12: 115–23.

Pound, William. 1988. "Twenty-five Years of State Legislative Reform." Paper presented at the annual meeting of the Midwest Political Science Association, Chicago, Ill.

Price, H. Douglas. 1975. "Congress and the Evolution of Legislative Professionalism." In *Congress in Change: Evolution and Reform,* ed. Norman J. Ornstein. New York: Praeger.

Rosenthal, Alan. 1974. "Turnover in State Legislatures." *American Journal of Political Science* 18:609–16.

———. 1989. "The Legislative Institution: Transformed and at Risk." In *The State of the States,* ed. Carl E. Van Horn. Washington, D.C.: Congressional Quarterly Press.

Rosenthal, Alan, and Rod Forth. 1978. "The Assembly Line: Low Production in the American States." *Legislative Studies Quarterly* 3:270.

Shin, Kwang, and John Jackson. 1979. "Membership Turnover in U.S. State Legislatures: 1931–1976." *Legislative Studies Quarterly* 4:95–114.

Sorauf, Frank J. 1988. *Money in American Elections.* Glenview, Ill.: Scott, Foresman/Little, Brown College Division.

Squire, Peverill. 1988. "Career Opportunities and Membership Stability in Legislatures." *Legislative Studies Quarterly* 13:65–81.

———. 1989. "Reform and Institutionalization of the California Assembly." Paper presented at the annual meeting of the Midwest Political Science Association, Chicago, Ill., April.

Thompson, Joel A., and William Cassie. 1990. "Milking the Cow: Campaign Contributions to State Legislative Candidates in North Carolina." Paper presented at the annual meeting of the North Carolina Political Science Association, Salisbury, N.C.

Thompson, Joel A., and Mark Lanier. 1987. "Measuring Economic Development: Economic Diversity as an Alternative to Standard Indicators." *Policy Studies Review.* 7:77–90.

Thornburg v. Gingles. 1986. 105 S. Ct. 2137.

Van Horn, Carl E. 1989. "The Entrepreneurial States." In *The State of the States,* ed. Carl E. Van Horn. Washington, D.C.: CQ Press.

Wagner, Holly. 1986. "Costly Campaigns Attract Special Interest Dollars." *State Government News* 29 (October): 19–20.

Weberg, Brian. 1988. "Changes in Legislative Staff." *State Government* 61:190–97.

Editor's Addendum

State legislatures have continued to change since Thompson and Moncrief's essay was published in 1992. In many ways, the changes represent a continuation of the trends over the past few decades, with legislatures growing more professional and diverse. One of the most important events has been the continued growth in the number of full-time professional staff. According to data from the National Conference of State Legislatures (NCSL), there were more than 28,000 permanent staff members employed by state legislatures nationwide in 2003.[1] Nearly 7,000 more staff members were hired when the legislatures were in session. The pay given to state legislatures has also continued to grow. As of 2003, the average pay for legislators in the thirty-nine states cited in Thompson and Moncrief's work was over $30,000, not counting additional benefits and per diems. Many states, including New Hampshire ($100/year) and Texas ($7,200/year) continue to pay low salaries, but others have improved considerably. West Virginia legislators, for example, are now paid $15,000 a year, compared with the $6,500 cited in Thompson and Moncrief's work. California legislators are the highest paid in the nation, receiving $99,000 a year.

State legislatures are also continuing to attract a more diverse membership. As of 2004, 1,661 of the 7,382 state legislators nationwide were women, or more than 22 percent.

The number of African American legislators had reached above 8 percent and the number of Latinos just below 3 percent.

Yet not all of the changes have been a continuation of the trends of the preceding decades. Perhaps the most important trend has been the efforts in many states to make the legislatures less professional through the introduction of term limits. When Thompson and Moncrief's essay was written, only three states (California, Colorado, and Oklahoma) had adopted term limits. Over the next decade, another eighteen states adopted them. The imposition of term limits has had an important effect on politics by increasing turnover, reducing tenure, changing members' career goals, and altering power relations in state government. Since the late 1990s, however, the movement to limit terms has lost much of its momentum, and in six states the term limit laws have either been repealed by the state legislature or thrown out by the state courts.

CASE STUDY 8

Introduction

Professors Thompson and Moncrief's work offers an explanation of why state legislatures have experienced so much change over the past few decades. Yet to many individuals, the real concern about these changes is not why they have occurred, but how they have affected legislative politics. There is a sense among many citizens that these changes have harmed state legislatures. Many of the critics' concerns are laid out in the latter part of Thompson and Moncrief's essay. Legislators seem to place reelection above all other concerns. Campaign costs are soaring and election war chests expanding. Larger staffs are not being used for research, but to help members get reelected. The legislatures are becoming more fragmented.

The case studies that follow consider whether the changes associated with the modernization movement and the rise of career legislators have actually harmed state legislatures by making legislators too concerned about getting reelected. Two short essays are presented. The first one was written by Charles Mahtesian and appeared in *Governing* magazine in 1997. Comparing the Tennessee legislature with the more professional Minnesota one, Mahtesian suggests that professionalism encourages partisan conflict, greater incivility, and a dysfunctional legislature. Mahtesian's critique of professionalism stimulated a great deal of discussion among state legislative scholars when it appeared, leading several scholars to write responses to his work in a newsletter for professors who study legislative politics. Peverill Squire, a University of Iowa professor, contributed one of the responses. In his short essay, Squire discusses how the problems identified by Mahtesian are not limited to professional legislatures, and suggests that their cause may lie elsewhere. The debate between the two sides is valuable to consider because it covers some of the leading criticisms lodged against professionalism, and it provides insights into how to evaluate claims about professionalism's effects.

Questions to Consider

As you read these two pieces, you might think about the following questions:

- What are the symptoms of the Sick Legislature Syndrome that Mahtesian sees in professional legislatures?
- From what you have seen or read elsewhere, do you concur with Mahtesian's assessment of professionalism? What have you seen that makes you support or oppose Mahtesian's argument?
- What evidence does Mahtesian use to make his case? What evidence does Squire provide to counter Mahtesian's claims?
- What else besides professionalism may have caused the conflict in Minnesota's legislature?
- How well does the legislature in your state seem to function? Does it have the type of work environment that it needs to handle its responsibilities? Does it have the type of conflict seen in Minnesota? What seems to be the cause of the conflict in your legislature? Or conversely, why does it seem to avoid conflict?

The Sick Legislature Syndrome

Charles Mahtesian

One quick look at the Minnesota legislature tells you that it is a state-of-the-art political institution, all fitted out for the interactive democracy of the next century.

There is gavel-to-gavel televised coverage of every session, something very few states provide. Voters can use the Internet to peruse bill texts and bill status, committee schedules, press releases and biographies of the members. Every Friday, *Session Weekly*, an informative and readable journal published by the nonpartisan House Public Information Office, reports on the highlights of each week's activity. All of this is provided to the public free of charge.

The same brief glance at Tennessee's legislature suggests that the Volunteer State is, one might say, a little amateurish. There is no televised coverage, and there is no Internet site. Tennessee is one of only two states that don't have one. In Nashville, they brag about how they rank 48th out of 50 in per-capita legislative branch expenditures. In fact, Tennessee spends less than half of what Minnesota spends—despite being home to a half-million more residents.

Over the past couple of decades, while Minnesota was winning national praise for innovations such as public campaign financing and gender pay equity, Tennessee's legislature went almost completely unnoticed until recently, when frivolous arguments over a Ten Commandments resolution and the teaching of creationism attracted nationwide ridicule.

It probably won't surprise you to learn that last year, one of these two bodies conducted an efficient, productive and thoroughly civilized legislative session, something it has done every single year during the 1990s. Or that the other has sunk into a humiliating morass of bitter partisanship and personal scandal.

What will surprise you is which of these legislatures is which.

In the past four years, voters in Minnesota have been bombarded with tawdry tales of errant members

Charles Mahtesian, "The Sick Legislature Syndrome," *Governing* (February 1997): 16–20. Reprinted with permission.

nabbed for shoplifting, fraud, drunk driving, spousal assault and spreading false rumors about constituents. A scandal surrounding the misuse of state phone card privileges led to the resignation of the House majority leader and the eventual ouster of the speaker in 1993. All in all, lawmakers there have exhibited a stunning knack for discrediting their institution, accumulating a body of offenses that equals, if it does not surpass, some of the more egregious transgressions of their colleagues in other states.

By last fall, all sense of collegiality had vanished from the Minnesota House. Since nearly all of the turmoil had occurred on the Democratic side of the aisle, Republicans took the opportunity to portray the ethical chaos as the arrogant excesses of an entrenched majority. Governor Arne Carlson's spokeswoman herself openly mused about the "thieves and drunks" of the state legislature.

Meanwhile, the Democratic caucus itself was in full-scale revolt against its speaker, the combatively partisan Irv Anderson. Two of Anderson's fellow Democrats took their criticism to the editorial pages of the *St. Paul Pioneer Press,* blaming Anderson for gridlock and calling for his removal. Within a week of last November's elections, he was unceremoniously dumped from the speakership.

As for the voters, they apparently found the Republican tactics almost as unappealing as the scandals themselves. Democrats actually survived the election with one more House seat than they had before it. But the voters made their feelings clear. They not only stayed home from the polls in record numbers, but overwhelmingly approved a ballot measure permitting recall of virtually anyone holding elected office. The entire episode suggests one compelling lesson: If the Minnesota legislature is the state of the art, there must be something wrong with the art.

In Tennessee, meanwhile, the year concluded as inconspicuously as it began. There were few surprises at the ballot box, and legislators' personal foibles remained largely out of the public eye. The 1996 legislative product was steady, if unspectacular; nearly all interested parties received a little of what they wanted with a minimum of rancor. Republican Governor Don Sundquist's welfare reform package passed, but with more than 40 amendments. Business and labor both claimed small victories on workers' compensation. State employees received a raise that was not quite what they asked for, but about what they could reasonably expect. "We all don't get what we want with every piece of legislation that passes," says House Speaker Jimmy Naifeh. "We need to remember that half a loaf is better than none."

In short, it was a typical year in the Tennessee legislature, displaying the balance that has enabled it to compile a consistently impressive record of substantive work throughout the 1990s. While most states were engaged in futile hand-wringing over exploding Medicaid expenditures, Tennessee created TennCare, the nation's most ambitious Medicaid overhaul. Long before higher education accountability issues were on the national radar, Tennessee established a performance-based funding mechanism that linked dollars to outcomes—the first of its kind in the nation. Over the course of the decade, the Volunteer State has enacted a wide-ranging K–12 education package and comprehensive campaign finance, ethics and lobbying legislation.

And it has done all that while holding to a level of comity and bipartisanship that is foreign to most chambers these days. "In Tennessee," says Senate Speaker John Wilder, who by statute also holds the position of lieutenant governor, "we don't have to shut down the government before we sit down and talk."

Even under Sundquist, a more partisan figure than any of his recent predecessors, the Republican governor and the Democratic legislature have exhibited a pronounced ability to coexist. Of all the freshman Republican governors who came into office in 1994 facing sizable Democratic opposition, Sundquist arguably has registered the most success in enacting his agenda.

That is no coincidence. Because while Tennessee's legislative system is far from perfect, it speaks to the value of simple qualities such as civility that have been largely lost in the legislatures that have rushed headlong toward professionalism. The Minnesotas and the Californias of American politics aren't laughing at Tennessee anymore. What they want to know is how they can get some of that old-fashioned decency back.

California, the flagship of legislative professionalism, remains the most dramatic exhibit. Stable leadership is nonexistent there. Within the last year and a half alone, five different speakers have held the House gavel. The sense of angry partisanship reaches beyond chamber doors and into the electoral arena, where opposition members are targeted for recall for the slightest provocation. Within the capitol, the halls are choked with representatives of special interests—1,100 registered lobbyists at last count—all narrowly focused and a constant reminder of the high stakes of modern legislating.

Not all of the 10 state bodies classified as "professional" by the National Conference of State Legislatures bear all of these symptoms. But enough of them do to make the pattern unmistakable. Professionalism creates an institution filled with able, full-time legislators, talented staff and generous resources. And yet many of these institutions become hopelessly polarized, from the back benches to the rostrum. It isn't difficult to find professionalized legislatures elsewhere in the country that have shown symptoms of the Minnesota problem in one way or another.

In Pennsylvania, for example, the Senate shut down for much of 1993 because the result of a single special election threatened the razor-thin Democratic numerical advantage. Few were surprised by this tactic: The previous year, Republicans had pulled a similar stunt for fear one of their own would switch party allegiance. It is the cutthroat competition for control in a close partisan situation that explains why, during the past decade in Pennsylvania, ethically tainted members from both sides of the aisle have routinely escaped discipline.

In New York, sharp-elbowed partisanship between legislative leaders virtually guarantees an annual budget standoff. Since a threesome comprised of the governor, the Democratic Assembly speaker and the Republican Senate leader dominates in Albany, there is no effective mechanism for resolving the partisan differences. Last year, New York set a new record by delivering a budget that was 103 days past due.

Illinois is not much different in its partisan ferocity. In 1996, for example, when Republican Governor Jim Edgar offered a wide-ranging school finance package amidst an all-out GOP effort to retain its recently acquired House majority, his proposal was immediately rejected and scorned by his own party. The potential political consequences, it seems, were too great. And Democrats were too close to winning back the House for Republicans to want to take the risk. (As it turned out, the Democrats won the House back anyway.)

Meanwhile, there are signs that the "sick legislature" syndrome is spreading to states that have been relatively free of it thus far. In Florida, where Republicans took control in 1996 for the first time since Reconstruction, Democrats insisted on challenging the credentials of six victorious GOP legislators. Republicans, in turn, registered two challenges of their own. During the legislature's organizational session, a group of lawmakers angrily objected not only to the content of the opening prayer but to the composition of the veterans' delegation that led the Pledge of Allegiance.

The irony was hard to miss. Only recently Florida had been recognized as the 10th and latest state to join the ranks of fully professionalized legislative bodies.

Not everyone in the Minnesota legislature accepts the notion that the onslaught of professionalism is at the root of the recent years' embarrassments. But an increasing number of members, past and present, are beginning to acknowledge that professionalism, partisanship and incivility are linked to each other in some unholy way. "The legislature was less partisan when it was more of a part-time body," says John Brandl, a former leader in the Minnesota House and Senate who now teaches at the Hubert H. Humphrey Institute in Minneapolis. "People are becoming so dependent on their position in the legislature and so self-protective that they can't see the institution for what it is."

There is no simple explanation for how Minnesota got that way, but there is a history, and it stretches back at least as far as 1979—the year the Minnesota House was split evenly between the two parties. Democrats, seizing on campaign practice violations against newly elected Republican Representative Robert Pavlak, moved to expel him, then took advantage of his absence to seize control of the chamber, 67 votes to 66.

To a Republican caucus comprised mainly of first-term members, it was a jarring introduction. And they have never forgotten it. "That was my eye-opening to Minnesota legislative politics," says Steve Sviggum, the current GOP House leader. "That was the absolute worst power politics I've ever seen."

Over the course of the 1980s, with party control up for grabs, those same tensions hardened into a conviction on both sides that they were entitled to pursue their goals by any means necessary. "As each party assumed power," political scientist Royce Hanson wrote in 1989, "it used its organizational and procedural power to humiliate the minority, producing a thirst for revenge among the members who could hardly wait for their turn in power to get even."

The growing partisan hostilities of the Minnesota House are reflected in simple physical changes. At one time members chose their seats on the House floor by seniority, regardless of party. Now the parties face each other across a dividing aisle. And the members' offices, once scattered haphazardly through the legislative building across from the Capitol, are now on two different floors, one for the Democrats, one for the Republicans.

About the only remaining link to an earlier era in the Minnesota House is the continued presence of Irv Anderson, the Democrat who engineered the Pavlak expulsion ploy in 1978 and served as speaker during the party's recent time of troubles in 1995 and 1996. Anderson missed most of the changes of the 1980s after losing his bid for reelection in 1982, but he returned to the chamber in 1990, and by 1993 he was the presiding officer. A gruff, acerbic and brilliant tactician from International Falls, the coldest city in America, Anderson acceded to the speakership in 1993 promising a kinder, gentler, "new Irv." But by last April, the updated Anderson did not seem at all different from the vindictive and iron-fisted leader both parties remembered. He ran the institution with the same single-minded goal he had emphasized in his earlier tour of duty: maintenance of partisan control at any cost. Republican parliamentary concerns were routinely ignored and dismissed. Their committee placement requests went unheeded.

In the end, whatever Anderson's motives were, his campaign strategy worked—Democrats held the House. But he paid for it by losing the speakership.

There is one difference between Tennessee and Minnesota that you won't pick up just by listening to the rhetoric or watching the proceedings on the floor. It is in the composition of the membership.

In Minnesota, NCSL classifies at least 30 members as "full-time legislators," and that is certainly fewer than the actual number, because many who do little else besides legislating still list some other occupation for the record. There is, in addition, a sizable contingent of government employees, teachers and labor officials. In Tennessee, only one legislator lists his occupation as full-time. The largest number are farmers or lawyers, or are drawn from the ranks of business. A 1993 NCSL study ranked Tennessee second in the nation (after Alaska) in the percentage of business owners serving as legislators.

None of this is to say that any one profession is better suited to lawmaking than another. But it is hard to avoid noticing some degree of correspondence between professionalism and partisan acrimony. If professional legislatures attract more talented and better-informed members—and few dispute that they do—it is equally certain that these same members have difficulty avoiding partisan collisions with each other.

Members who have devoted lives and careers to legislative service have a tendency to bristle at any perceived threats to it. In moments of conflict, they are all too aware that a reversal of fortune is only a controversial vote and one election cycle away. "There's more members who see their position as their full-time or primary occupation," says Minnesota's Robert Vanasek, who served as House speaker from 1987 to 1991, "and one of the consequences is that thinking about reelection is much more on their minds."

Within the framework of the professional legislature, there is a certain inevitability to those partisan confrontations, because a body filled with capable legislators and skilled staff is unlikely to content itself with passing innocuous resolutions. Minnesota's 1995–96 regular session alone saw the introduction of 6,185 bills that touched nearly every industry, interest and enterprise in the state, ranging from wind-power energy to wine-tastings at bed-and-breakfasts.

Not only do interest groups grow more active and more sophisticated but some of the largest and most influential of these groups gradually evolve into appendages of the state parties—or perhaps vice versa. "It's not that we can't do things," says Senator John Marty, the 1994 Democratic gubernatorial nominee. "It's that there are pressures stopping them."

In the Minnesota legislature, a liberal, labor-dominated Democratic conference collides with a Republican conference of anti-tax zealots, anchored in affluent suburbs and rural areas where anti-tax and low-spending pressures are the greatest. Between one caucus grounded in the notion of an activist government and another committed to de-funding and dismantling it, consensus has been almost impossible to find. The two parties are no longer merely at odds, they are now diametrically opposed to one another. "The worlds they are representing," observes University of Minnesota political scientist Frank Sorauf, "are increasingly divergent and homogeneous."

Witness the wildly disparate assessments of the 1996 legislative session offered by each party's leaders. "We did what we promised to do last January," Speaker Anderson declared in April. "Pass legislation that makes streets safer, government more accountable, jobs more rewarding and education more effective." If that was indeed the outcome, then Republicans missed it altogether. "The people of Minnesota were the losers," concluded Steve Sviggum. "This was a frustrating session for those of us who expect accountability and responsibility in government."

Tennessee passed a partisan milestone in 1995, but it did so in a remarkably civilized way. Late in the year, two party switches handed Republicans a tenuous one-vote Senate majority. The first thing the GOP did was to allow John Wilder, the Democratic Senate speaker, to remain in the job he had held since 1971. Then, with control of the chamber up for grabs in the coming general election, they actively discouraged GOP opposition to Wilder in his home district.

As implausible as those decisions might have seemed in most other states, in Tennessee they barely raised eyebrows. Wilder was simply reaping the returns on his own style of stewardship. It was he, after all, who had initiated the practice of naming Republicans as committee chairs while they remained in the minority in the mid-1980s.

Even the most partisan senator would agree that Wilder harbors an abiding preoccupation with maintaining the chamber's civility and a collegial approach toward policy making. Last year, when the legislature

Legislatures: Three Flavors

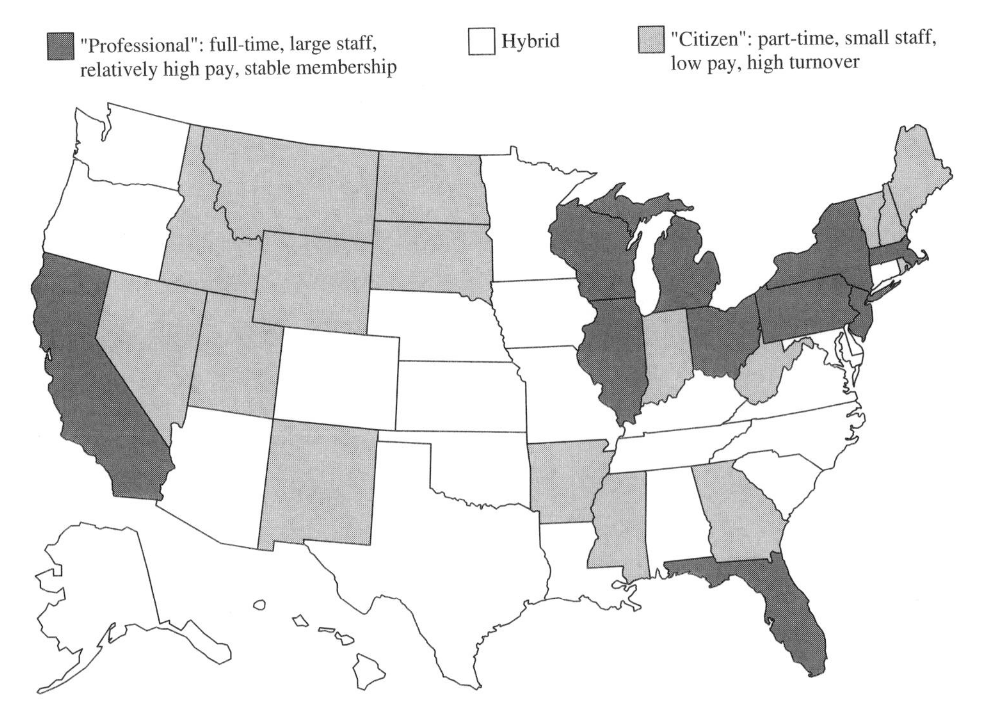

Source: National Conference of State Legislatures

passed a resolution naming a new state golf course after Wilder, the joke went around that one of the rules of the new course would be to require bipartisan foursomes.

The House, too, has benefited from an unusual degree of leadership stability. Since 1973, when Ned McWherter began a 14-year run as speaker before serving two terms as governor, only three individuals have presided over it. McWherter, the dominant legislative presence in Tennessee over the past generation, believed in an independent legislature that was entitled to full partnership in the state governmental process. And he continued to believe it after he had left the speakership for the governor's office. "McWherter recognized," says Bill Purcell, the former House majority leader, "that the enhancement of the legislature was good for the executive."

Indeed, it has been. After agreeing to cede authority to McWherter for the creation of the controversial TennCare program in 1993, lawmakers have been careful to avoid picking it to death in their oversight capacity. They have worked in relative harmony with both McWherter and his Republican successor, Sundquist, on a whole range of other major issues in recent years, including prison system reform, school finance and welfare and the delivery of children's services.

In Tennessee, unlike in Minnesota, members still arrange themselves on the floor the old-fashioned way, by region instead of by party. "In my 10 years in the House," Purcell says, "there were only two issues that broke down along party lines. Literally, only two out of thousands."

The chamber's longtime lobbyists agree. "There's not a whole lot of ideological difference between the majority of legislators," says Dick Williams, a veteran of 24 years as chief lobbyist for Tennessee Common Cause. "Most of them still don't view themselves strictly as Republicans or Democrats."

The House is not as imbued with quite the same bipartisan spirit that Wilder nurtures in the Senate. Some complain that Speaker Jimmy Naifeh wields a heavy gavel. But even Republicans concede that Naifeh shows no interest in humiliating or embarrassing the opposition. If there are grievances, there is an opportunity to air them for an hour and a half every Wednesday, when the leaders from both parties in the House and Senate meet with the governor to flesh out issues. "It gives us an opportunity to talk if someone has their feathers ruffled," says House Republican Leader Steve McDaniel. "If you ever stop communicating, it would be like if a husband and wife stopped talking—things would get pretty bad. After all, we are a family."

You don't often hear that kind of talk in Minnesota these days. It would be a tropical winter day in International Falls before Irv Anderson and Steve Sviggum ever described themselves as members of the same family.

Not that there aren't a few signs of a turnaround at the Minnesota state capitol. After the turbulent 1996 session and the brutal fall campaign, there at least seems to be a recognition that the notions of consensus and bipartisanship are worth recovering, if it is not too late. To signify his intentions, newly elected Speaker Phil Carruthers announced this year that his first move would be to decentralize authority. He says he envisions a body that is "more participative, less bitter, less top-down, with an emphasis on less partisanship." His goal, he says, is to involve both parties in the process.

At the same time, there are those who insist that stronger medicine is needed. A number of elected officials, including GOP Governor Arne Carlson, are backing the idea of scrapping the current system entirely and replacing it with a unicameral legislature, like the one that exists in Nebraska.

In Tennessee, legislators would find that idea hard to comprehend. Their professed interest is in protecting a system that they believe works. Still, there are some warnings about the dangers of creeping partisanship: The past few years have witnessed an increased number of intense campaigns and the growing use of tax issues as a partisan wedge. Naifeh has been challenged by aggressive opposition at home over the last two elections. Indeed, some legislators of both parties are predicting the next session will be the most partisan in years.

If that is the case, though, neither Speaker Naifeh nor Republican leader Steve McDaniel is losing much sleep over it. At a recent meeting between the two, they even joked about the predictions of conflict. "I never said that," Naifeh told the Republican.

"Neither did I," McDaniel replied.

Is Professionalization a Pathogen?

Peverill Squire

Every so often a talented journalist examines the nitty gritty of legislatures in such a way as to highlight important relationships that might otherwise escape the typically more distanced political science community. Such a service was performed by Charles Mahtesian, whose February 1997 *Governing* article, "The Sick Legislature Syndrome and How to Avoid It," posits the idea that as state legislatures professionalize they become less civil places to work and, ultimately, less successful governing bodies. This is an important hypothesis that deserves serious attention.

According to Mahtesian, the sick legislature syndrome results from the needs of politically ambitious careerist legislators whose personal electoral needs drive them to ignore institutional norms of civility as they pursue their individual goals. Far fewer violations of good behavior are to be found in less professionalized legislatures because their members are legislators of a different breed: less ambitious, less concerned with their own political futures, and, therefore, more willing to work together for common goals. This relationship seems plausible, but it runs contrary to Polsby's (1968) observation about institutionalization, which holds that norms of civility increase as members adopt long-term perspectives about their service. The notion is that as members serve together longer they have greater incentive to figure out ways to do that civilly.

The cases Mahtesian studies in depth certainly appear to support his hypothesis. Minnesota, among the more professionalized bodies, has suffered from bitter partisanship and near gridlock for much of this decade. In contrast, the much less professionalized Tennessee legislature has enjoyed a more tranquil atmosphere and, arguably, more productive sessions, despite spending less time in session and having fewer staff resources to support its members' efforts.

It is California, however, that Mahtesian cites as the "flagship of legislative professionalism" and as the "most dramatic exhibit" of sick legislature syndrome. There is little doubt that Mahtesian's characterization of the current California Assembly as a sick legislature is correct. After all, recent sessions have witnessed numerous uncivil outbursts, with members calling each other names and making rude gestures toward each other. One recent story in the *Los Angeles Times* (Gladstone 1997) began by noting, "California's 80-member Assembly has been called disorderly, dysfunctional and as unruly as an elementary school playground during a food fight." But, at the same time the Assembly is justifiably held in low regard, the state Senate, while no bastion of exemplary manners, has managed to maintain a reasonable level of civility and productivity. Yet, of course, the state Senate is operating in the same political culture and electoral system as the more troubled Assembly. Thus one possible problem with Mahtesian's analysis of sick legislature syndrome is that if professionalization is the cause, then the problems it causes should be found in both houses in a state and to the same degree. It is not clear if that is the case in California.

There are, of course, other ways of assessing the possible causes of troubled legislative bodies. One way is to look at the development of the legislature as an institution. In the case of the California Assembly, we know when the professionalization movement took off—the adoption of Proposition 1A in 1966 (Squire 1992). If the Mahtesian thesis is correct, we should see a legislature which is better behaved, and as a consequence more productive, before professionalization than after. Indeed, as the legislature continues to professionalize sick legislature syndrome ought to become more pronounced.

Looking at the behavior in the California Assembly over time, the picture is actually quite murky. The legislature acquired a poor reputation early in its history. The initial session was called the "session of a thousand

Peverill Squire, "Is Professionalization a Pathogen?" from *Extension of Remarks,* January 1998, pp. 10–11. Reprinted by permission of the author.

drinks" because of the long bars set up outside the meeting chambers by lobbyists, U.S. Senate candidates, and patronage seekers (Goodwin 1916, 261). Things improved little over the next half century. By 1911 the body's reputation was so low that the legislature's chaplain began that year's session by beseeching members to "give us a square deal, for Christ's sake" (Mowry 1963, 139). The Progressive era reforms were intended in part to improve the legislature's reputation and performance. What followed the reforms, however, was a period where the legislature was dominated by the legendary lobbyist, Artie Samish, referred to as the Secret Boss of California (Samish and Thomas 1971). Samish influenced legislative behavior by providing members campaign funds and money to help meet their Sacramento living expenses (Samish and Thomas 1971, 122; Buchanan 1963, 59–60). Even after Samish was removed from the political scene by a conviction for income tax evasion, corruption festered in the legislature. Indeed, at the time Jesse Unruh entered the Assembly in 1955, two former Speakers were under indictment for bribery (Buchanan 1963, 55–6).

There is little on the record to suggest that the Assembly Unruh took over was a particularly healthy institution. Moreover, even as he endeavored to improve the legislature's lot, there were episodes of sick legislature syndrome. Take, for example, the fight over the state budget in 1963. Assembly Republicans demanded to see an agreement that Speaker Unruh had reached with the state Senate on an education budget. The Speaker denied the GOP a look, and the minority party exercised its prerogative not to vote. (California requires an extraordinary majority to pass the budget, thus giving the minority party considerable leverage.) According to one recounting of the events that followed (Richardson 1996, 114),

> at 1:40 A.M. on July 30, after an evening of heavy drinking, Unruh ordered the Republicans locked into the Assembly chambers until they voted. . . . That night Republican State Chairman Caspar Weinberger swiftly issued a press release denouncing the lockup as the tactics of "Stalin, Hitler and other dictators." . . . Unruh retreated to a bar at the El Mirador Hotel and got even more drunk. . . . Finally, after twenty-two hours and fifty minutes, Unruh caved in and showed the Republicans the school budget.

The great lockup would seem to be an acute episode of sick legislature syndrome, and it preceded the big professionalization push. And from the picture painted by a member at the time, while the great lockup was the most visible evidence of problems, it was not the only example that could be offered (Mills 1987).

After the reforms of the 1960s, the legislature in general, and the Assembly in particular, enjoyed an excellent reputation. California, for example, placed at the head of the class in The Citizens Conference on State Legislatures (1971) rankings of legislatures. Close observers claimed there were fewer alcoholics and that members were more serious about their duties than in the pre-reform legislature (Fisher, Price and Bell 1973, 69; Salzman 1976, 79–81). A much larger percentage of members live year-round in Sacramento with their families—70% according to one survey (Dodd and Kelly 1989, 25). Decorum and appearance mattered, as evidenced by the uproar over one member's attempt to go without a tie on the floor (Endicott 1975) and concerns with another member's intemperate comments on the floor (Hoover 1989). All of this happened after professionalization took hold.

Professionalization, then, does not appear to lead directly to sick legislature syndrome. The case of California suggests that the disease may well manifest itself before professionalization. The available evidence suggests that like herpes, sick legislature syndrome flares from time to time and then it seemingly disappears.

Other possible causes may be suggested by looking across the fifty state legislatures. By most definitions, a handful of state legislatures are professionalized, the rest lag those bodies by a little or a lot. Those that are the farthest along the road toward professionalization—those identified by Mahtesian as the most likely to suffer problems—are not a random sample of all states. The most professionalized legislatures are found in the largest and most socially and economically diverse states (Mooney 1995). Thus, if these are the legislatures that are most likely to have problems it may be that they are the organizations that are most under stress from the multitude of demands being made of them.

Additional variables that might contribute to sick legislature syndrome are term limits and heightened partisanship. If term limits are a cause, it would appear to substantiate Polsby's (1968) claims; as members are forced to adopt short-term time frames they lose the incentive to establish norms that encourage civility. But it may be the case that term limits in professionalized legislatures create the best possible scenario for sick legislature syndrome, with ambitious career-minded legislators competing with one another during legislative service of short duration. Heightened partisanship, with the memberships of the two parties anchoring the opposite ends of the political spectrum, may also lead to sick legislature syndrome for obvious reasons. It is not clear, however, if professionalization leads to heightened partisanship or not.

There is little doubt that sick legislature syndrome as described by Mahtesian is a real malady with real consequences for legislators and the people they represent. What is not clear is the cause of the disease. Professionalization is not a likely source because many of these problems can be found before it took hold. But it may be that for other reasons sick legislature syndrome is more apt to be found in more professionalized legislatures.

References

Buchanan, William. 1963. *Legislative Partisanship.* Berkeley: University of California Press.

Citizens Conference on State Legislatures. 1971. *State Legislatures: An Evaluation of Their Effectiveness.* New York: Praeger.

Dodd, Lawrence C., and Sean Q. Kelly. 1989. "Legislators' Home Style in Traditional and Modern Systems: The Case of Presentational Style." Presented at the annual meeting of the Midwest Political Science Association, Chicago.

Endicott, William. 1975. "Meade Takes Case of Attire to the Voters." *Los Angeles Times,* 28 February.

Fisher, Joel M.; Charles M. Price and Charles G. Bell. 1973. "The Legislative Process in California." Presented at the annual meeting of the American Political Science Association, Washington, DC.

Gladstone, Mark. 1997. "State's Lower House Sinks a Bit Lower." *Los Angeles Times,* 6 June.

Goodwin, Cardinal. 1916. *The Establishment of State Government in California.* New York: MacMillan.

Hoover, Ken. 1989. "Can Pugnacious Ross Johnson Unify Fractious Caucus?" *California Journal* 20:15–17.

Mills, James R. 1987. *A Disorderly House.* Berkeley: Heyday Books.

Mooney, Christopher Z. 1995. "Citizens, Structures, and Sister States: Influences on State Legislative Professionalism." *Legislative Studies Quarterly* 20:47–67.

Mowry, George E. 1963. *The California Progressives.* Chicago: Quadrangle Books.

Richardson, James. 1996. *Willie Brown.* Berkeley: University of California Press.

Polsby, Nelson W. 1968 "The Institutionalization of the U.S. House of Representatives." *American Political Science Review* 62:144–68.

Salzman, Ed. 1976. "The Deceptive Image of the State Legislature." *California Journal* 7:79–81.

Samish, Arthur H., and Bob Thomas. 1971. *The Secret Boss of California.* New York: Crown.

Squire, Peverill. 1992. "The Theory of Legislative Institutionalization and the California Assembly." *Journal of Politics* 54:1026–54.

Chapter 8 Review Questions

1. In what ways have state legislatures gone through profound change over the past forty years? Provide a brief history of the Legislative Reform Movement and its impact on state legislatures.
2. What is the difference between legislative professionalism and careerism? What are the three major elements associated with professionalism? What is careerism?
3. What do the terms *adaptive* and *consolidative* change mean? What forces cause these types of changes to occur?
4. What do the case studies say about the impact of professionalism on state legislative politics?

5. Based on what you have read, what do you think are the main problems and benefits of both professionalism and careerism? List some of the pros and cons of both.
6. What reforms do you think should be enacted to improve state legislatures? Why do you support these reforms? What effect do you think these reforms will have on legislative politics? In light of Hedge's reading in the first chapter, is it likely that your reforms would improve some aspects of governing while harming others? What are the tradeoffs involved?

Key Terms

professionalism
careerism
modernization
Legislative Reform Movement
adaptive change
consolidative change
Baker v. *Carr*
Reynolds v. *Sims*
institutionalization
Citizens Conference on State Legislatures
sick legislature syndrome
partisanship
term limits

Suggestions for Further Reading

Benjamin, Gerald, and Michael J. Malbin, eds. *Limiting Legislative Terms.* Washington, D.C.: CQ Press, 1992. One of the first books to appear on legislative term limits. Provides insights on the history of term limits and their potential effect.

Carey, John M., Richard G. Niemi, and Lynda W. Powell. *Term Limits in the State Legislatures.* Ann Arbor: University of Michigan Press, 2000. Provides the findings from a nationwide study on the impact of legislative term limits. The study draws from an impressive survey of 3,000 legislators across the fifty states.

Citizens Conference on State Legislatures. *State Legislatures: An Evaluation of their Effectiveness.* New York: Praeger, 1971; *Sometime Governments: A Critical Study of the 50 American Legislatures.* New York: Bantam Books, 1971. The Citizens Conference on State Legislatures was one of the leading advocates for modernizing state legislatures. These two books provide insight into the character of state legislative politics prior to the reform movement.

Clucas, Richard A. "Improving the Harvest of State Legislative Research." *State Politics and Policy Quarterly* 3 (2003): 387–419. Provides a comprehensive overview on the state of state legislative research, including efforts to study legislative change.

Farmer, Rick, John David Rausch, Jr., and John C. Green, eds., *The Test of Time: Coping with Legislative Term Limits.* Lanham, Mass.: Lexington Books, 2003. This compilation includes research findings from some of the leading state legislative scholars on the impact of term limits.

Maestas, Cherie. "Professional Legislatures and Ambitious Politicians: Policy Responsiveness of State Institutions." *Legislative Studies Quarterly* 25 (2001): 663–690. Examines the linkage between professionalism, political ambition, and legislative responsiveness.

Moncrief, Gary F., and Joel A. Thompson, eds. *Changing Patterns in State Legislative Careers.* Ann Arbor: University of Michigan Press, 1992. This is the most comprehensive book on the rise of professionalism and career legislators. The book consists of a collection of studies by some of the nation's leading experts on state legislative politics.

Polsby, Nelson W. "The Institutionalization of the U.S. House of Representatives." *American Political*

Science Review 62 (1968): 144–168. This is the seminal work on legislative institutionalization.

Rosenthal, Alan. *The Decline of Representative Democracy: Process, Participation and Power in State Legislatures.* Washington, D.C.: CQ Press, 1999. Provides an excellent introduction to state legislative politics generally and how they have been transformed over the past few decades.

———. "The Legislative Institution—In Transition and at Risk." In *The State of the States.* 2d ed. Edited by Carl E. Van Horn. Washington, D.C.: CQ Press, 1993. Provides a particularly critical commentary on how state legislatures have changed because of professionalism.

———. "State Legislative Development: Observations from Three Perspectives." *Legislative Studies Quarterly* 21 (1996): 169–198. Provides the most succinct overview of the theoretical literature on state legislative change, including professionalism and institutionalization.

Squire, Peverill. "Career Opportunities and Membership Stability in Legislatures." *Legislative Studies Quarterly* 13 (1988): 65–81. Squire's essay provides an explanation for how a legislature's structure can influence whether members make a career of legislative service.

———. "The Theory of Legislative Institutionalization and the California Assembly." *Journal of Politics* 54 (1992): 1026–1054. Examines the meaning of institutionalization at the state level, and why it may differ from how it has affected Congress.

Stonecash, Jeffrey. "The Pursuit and Retention of Legislative Offices in New York, 1870–1990: Reconstructing Sources of Change," *Polity* 26 (1993): 301–315. This study lays out the debate over whether professionalism produces careerism, or careerism produces professionalism. Stonecash's findings suggest that careerism came first.

Related Web Sites

http://www.ncsl.org
The National Conference of State Legislatures provides data and other information on state legislatures, including reports on professionalism, term limits, and campaign finance rules. The web site also provides links to the state legislatures.

http://www.cawp.rutgers.edu/
The web site for the Center for American Women and Politics provides data and research findings on women in all levels of American government, including state legislatures.

9

Governors: The Concept of Gubernatorial Success

Gubernatorial achievements are dependent on more than intellectual and managerial prowess. A successful governor also possesses the skill and will to engage in the elemental activities of public life: "persuading, bargaining, battling, compromising, co-opting, committing, catering, arm twisting," and public rhetoric.

Robert E. Crew, Jr.

READING 9

Introduction

What makes some governors more successful than other governors in shaping the direction of state politics? This question is of central concern to scholars of state politics. Many early scholars who studied gubernatorial politics focused on the importance of formal powers, such as the type of veto a governor can exercise, in shaping a governor's success. Over time, however, researchers have examined other factors, including personal attributes and the broader political environment. As a result of these efforts, the discipline now has a much better understanding of the influence that governors have on politics.

The seminal work on the study of gubernatorial power is that of Joseph Schlesinger.[1] In 1965, he published an essay on governors' roles in leading their state bureaucracies, in which he provided an index to the formal powers of governors across the states. The index relied on four separate measures to rank the power of governors. These measures were the amount of freedom that a governor has in appointing the heads of state agencies, the degree of responsibility a governor has over the budget process, the strength of a governor's veto, and the potential length of time that a governor can serve in office. Schlesinger argued that governors who can directly appoint other administrators are going to have greater influence than those who must submit their nominees to the legislature for confirmation. Governors also have greater influence if they have full responsibility for putting together the state budget than if they must share that responsibility with others. A governor's power can also be affected by the type of veto that he or she can exercise and the number of votes that are required for the legislature to override the veto. Governors who have access to the item veto will have greater influence than those who only have the general veto or do not have the veto at all. Finally, Schlesinger argued that governors who serve two-year terms and face legal restrictions on the number of terms in which they are allowed to hold office will be weaker than those who serve four-year terms and do not face such limits. Schlesinger then combined these four measures to create a general index of the governor's formal powers across the states. At the top of the list was New York, while North Dakota, Texas, South Carolina, and Mississippi were tied at the bottom.

Since Schlesinger's work appeared, it has repeatedly served as a model for other indices. In the late 1980s, the National Governors Association (NGA) offered an updated version of Schlesinger's work, although it added two new categories, one measuring the strength of the governor's party in the legislature and the other the power of the legislature to alter the governor's budget. In more recent years, Thad Beyle, a professor at the University of North Carolina and perhaps the nation's leading expert on governors, has published several revised versions of Schlesinger's findings, although like the NGA he has expanded the index to include two other measures. One of these measures is the number of other elected executives in the state. The second one is the extent to which the governor's party controls the legislature.[2]

In the 1970s, several scholars began to question whether Schlesinger's index provided a reasonable measure for assessing gubernatorial power. One of the major complaints was that although Schlesinger's index focused on formal powers, many governors seemed to be helped by more informal resources. In 1974, E. Lee Bernick conducted a survey of legislators in eleven states to determine what they thought were the governors' most important tools for influencing the legislature.[3] The survey respondents ranked three of the formal powers identified by Schlesinger (budget authority, administrative control, and veto) as among the top tools, but they also identified several informal powers as being important as well, particularly a governor's popularity, his or her ability to use the mass media, and the prestige of the office.

As a result of this dialogue, textbooks on state politics and research on governors routinely discuss the importance of both formal and informal powers in shaping a governor's success. In 1990, Alan Rosenthal, a professor at the Eagleton Institute of Politics at Rutgers University, offered one of the best descriptive overviews of governors' powers.[4] Drawing from past research and his own experience working with legislators in many states, Rosenthal identified nine powers that help governors succeed. These include the governors' power to initiate legislation, veto bills, and provide patronage and other benefits to legislators to encourage their support. Governors benefit from serving as the leader of their political party and from the attention they garner from the media. Many have served in a variety of offices before becoming governor, which helps them as they work with legislators. They are also helped by their popularity among voters, at least when their popularity is high. In addition, whereas state legislatures are filled with a collection of voices, governors speak with one voice, which makes it easier for governors to provide leadership.

More recently, Margaret Ferguson has offered one of the most comprehensive studies of gubernatorial success.[5] Relying on a sophisticated quantitative analysis of nearly 90,000 pieces of legislation across the 50 states, Ferguson explored the factors that were most important in explaining the success for a governor's legislative agenda. She found that the formal powers identified by Schlesinger were not particularly important in shaping legislative action. Among the factors that did matter were the size of the governor's agenda and a number of institutional factors, including the presence of divided government and the professional character of the state legislature. Governors are more successful when they have smaller agenda, when their party controls both houses of the legislature, and when they face a more professional legislature. The findings from Ferguson's study do not mean that formal powers are unimportant. Rather, they suggest that scholars may need to give more attention to determining which formal powers matter and where these powers affect decisions.

The successes of Minnesota Governor Jesse Ventura and his successor, Tim Pawlenty, provides a good illustration of the importance of both formal and informal powers. Ventura's record was far less noteworthy than his campaign, which was the focus of the case study in Chapter 6. Ventura is credited with reducing state taxes and directing more dollars to light-rail transit, yet he was frequently criticized for ignoring policy details and bullying opponents. The result was a record of few legislative accomplishments. On the other hand, Pawlenty was credited with numerous successes in his first year of office alone, including placing new restrictions on abortions, loosening the state's gun control laws, and balancing a $4.5 billion deficit without increasing taxes. Pawlenty's success reflected both formal and informal factors. Despite the media's continual interest in Ventura, Pawlenty was considered better able to use the media to build policy support. As a former legislator, he had a good understanding of legislative politics and had developed considerable skill in getting legislators to work with him. Not all of his success can be credited to these informal factors, however. Unlike Ventura, who served as an independent, Pawlenty benefited from his party's strong position in the legislature. During Pawlenty's first session, the Republican Party held a commanding majority in the Minnesota House and was close to gaining power in the Senate.

The essay that follows provides a valuable overview of the different factors that have been identified as playing an important role in shaping gubernatorial success. The essay was written by Robert Crew, a professor in the School of Public Administration and Policy at Florida State University. What makes the essay particularly helpful is that it offers a conceptual model for thinking about gubernatorial success. Crew argues that there are five different factors that shape a governor's performance: the governor's personality, his or her political skill, the types of political resources at the governor's command, the nature of the political context, and the strategies that governors use to obtain their goals.

Crew presents his model to provide a framework to use in examining a governor's success and to encourage scholars to think about the interactions between these factors. Even though Crew does not test his argument, the research by Beyle, Ferguson, and other gubernatorial scholars provides strong support for Crew's argument. Crew's essay was taken from the second chapter of a book edited by Beyle on how governors were dealing with the difficult economic problems of the early 1990s. The rest of the book includes case studies of ten of the nation's most prominent governors.

Questions to Consider

As you read Crew's work, these are some questions to consider:

- What problems does Crew see in past research on governors? Why does he say that a framework or model is needed?
- What are the five factors that Crew says affect a governor's success? Can you explain each one?
- How good a job does Crew's model do in capturing the important powers identified by Schlesinger, Beyle, and other scholars discussed in the introduction to this chapter? Has he left out some powers identified by these authors? Are there ones he has added? From what you have read, do you think his model does a good job in capturing what these others have written?
- What factors do you think are important in shaping a governor's power? If you were to create a model to explain gubernatorial behavior as Crew did, what would it look like?

Understanding Gubernatorial Behavior: A Framework for Analysis

Robert E. Crew, Jr.

Much, if not most, of the writing about the behavior of governors and of other political executives exhibits two characteristics: reliance on only a few (often only one) variables to explain that behavior, and use of anecdotal examples rather than systematic, empirical data. Thus the accomplishments of political executives are attributed to political style, to political skill, or to ingenious strategies; rarely are the effects of all of these—and other—variables combined. Further, much of the analysis that forms the basis of speculation about these executives comes from "reporters' comments, newspaper editorials, biographies and autobiographies, as well as political arguments by [legislators] or the administration."[1] Such data are impossible to evaluate adequately without knowledge of comparable situations and statistics. A framework, or model, is needed that incorporates the major variables identified by research as being important to an understanding of executive behavior. It is also important to pay attention to the nature of the data upon which assessments of executive behavior are based. This chapter proposes a model for the analysis of gubernatorial behavior and suggests which data can be used to test hypotheses about the interaction of the variables contained in the model.

Determining Gubernatorial Success

Despite differences in their approaches, those who study the activities of governors are interested most generally in the success the governors achieve—success in reaching goals set either by the governors themselves or by other interested parties, including constituents, the media, or scholars. The standard, or measure, of success is the subject of energetic debate and varies substantially among interested parties. Within the field of presidential studies, at least two camps exist. The first, identified most closely with Richard Neustadt, defines success somewhat narrowly in terms of maximization of administration goals. The second, identified with Fred Greenstein, celebrates a broader view of success, that of "public harmony and governmental legitimacy."[2]

The debate over the appropriate conceptualization of success is normative, not objective, and must be resolved in the minds of the people involved. Nonetheless, the use of systematic, and where possible empirical, data in discussing gubernatorial success will reduce the number of misinformed judgments made about gubernatorial behavior and improve the quality of explanation.

Several kinds of empirical data may be put to use in the study of gubernatorial success. Some of the richest sources of these data are each governor's State of the State address, inaugural address, and budget messages. Each of these identifies goals of varying specificity, which can be tracked through the legislative, judicial, or administrative process. Measures of administration success can be calculated from these data, and indicators of gubernatorial priorities and positions can be developed. Such measures can be used for comparative purposes, particularly within individual states.

Gubernatorial success can also be examined through the use of systematic data on appointments to administrative, advisory, and judicial positions. Appointments provide governors the opportunity to insinuate broad political and governmental philosophies into the politics of their states and to satisfy campaign promises. Appointments offer researchers a basis upon which to assess gubernatorial success on these levels. Has the governor been successful in moving state courts or agencies in new directions? Have new philosophies been introduced into state government? Have specific groups benefited or been disadvantaged? These and other questions can be addressed systematically through the analysis of data on appointments collected over time.

Finally, systematic examination of gubernatorial vetoes can provide insight into what a governor thinks must be prevented. Some scholars view the veto as an admission of failure on the part of the governor; yet an examination of vetoes categorized by policy area can provide information that complements what is developed from analyses of gubernatorial messages. An analysis of vetoes can fill out the picture of gubernatorial priorities and positions. And studying attempts to override vetoes offers another way to assess gubernatorial success and political strength.

A Framework for Studying Gubernatorial Behavior

Most studies of gubernatorial behavior focus on success in achieving policy purposes, variously defined. How the governor develops and uses his or her political resources and how he or she shapes political strategies to achieve policy success within a particular environment are also of concern. These issues can be examined within the framework of a model of leadership that links policy success to the governor's role in bringing it about. The model is displayed in Figure [1]. It includes personal, institutional, and environmental variables.

Gubernatorial performance in office is postulated as depending on five separate factors. First is the governor's personality, "the thumb-print"[3] of perception and

Figure 1: A Model of Factors Affecting Gubernatorial Policy Success

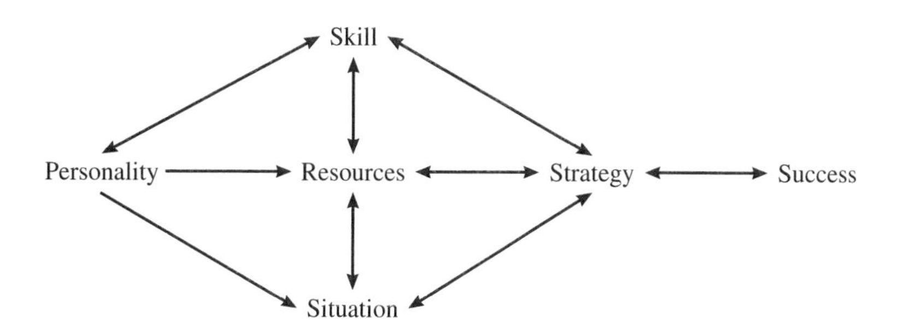

inclination created as one adapts to the situations of his or her life. Several aspects of personality may be important in examining gubernatorial behavior. These include motivation, character, and cognitive and behavioral styles.

The second factor affecting a governor's performance is political skill. Gubernatorial achievements are dependent on more than intellectual and managerial prowess. A successful governor also possesses the skill and will to engage in the elemental activities of public life: "persuading, bargaining, battling, compromising, co-opting, committing, catering, arm twisting,"[4] and public rhetoric.[5] Experience in government helps one develop these skills[6] and assists one in confronting and dealing with the ambiguities, pressures, and uncertainties of the job.

Leadership success is also associated with a third variable: the nature of available political and personal resources. In the political arena a governor is dependent on party support within the legislature, public approval, and professional reputation.[7] At the personal level the resources are "time, attention and political influence."[8]

The fourth variable that affects gubernatorial performance is the nature of the situation he or she faces. To what extent are conditions favorable to the accomplishment of goals inherent in the particular situation facing a governor? To a large extent, leadership success is structured by the opportunities faced. Thus, one question to be asked about all governors is whether they made the most of their opportunities. Skill in specifying objectives, using political resources, and shaping political strategies must be examined against the backdrop of the existing "political time"[9] and the presence of governmental, political, and personal resources.

Finally, gubernatorial performance is affected by a fifth variable: the governor's design or strategy—that is, the specific means chosen to implement his or her expressed goals and intentions. Governors have their own ways of approaching the opportunities and problems of office, and each has a method of pursuing his or her purposes. "His way is bound to capitalize on what he is good at, to minimize what he is not good at, and to reflect on what he has learned from experience about what works and what does not work."[10]

I suggest that the interrelationship among these variables is the most important focus for scholars and that the skill with which the governor creates unity among them is the key to gubernatorial success. Gubernatorial performance cannot be explained solely by reference to any one of these factors. "A dynamic interaction is always at work. In the final analysis, effective . . . leadership that achieves policy goals depends upon how the [governor's] agenda matches the political 'temper' of the times as well as on [gubernatorial] skill in making the most of historical opportunities and political resources."[11]

Politics and Personality

The belief that the personality of an elected official is related to his or her public performance is widely accepted in social science. A rather large body of research has been directed to identifying the important elements of executive personality and to relating these elements to the performance of individual presidents, governors, and other elected officials. Despite the methodological problems associated with this research, it can be useful in analyses of gubernatorial behavior. Indeed, in the absence of some attention to personal differences among governors, analyses of their performance are mechanistic, abstract, and unrealistic. Thus, attention to the topic is necessary. Following are three lines of research that may be useful in bringing attention to the subject.

Cognitive Style. Personality theorists have demonstrated systematic differences among individuals in the way that they assimilate and interpret information affecting their decisions and their view of the world. Some elected officials think in rigid, simplistic categories, conceive of the world in terms of polarized stereotypes, and display a conscious intolerance for ambiguity in their environment. Others display a capacity for "integrative complexity" in their thinking, a capacity that requires finely differentiated and fully integrated representations of an event or environment. These differences have been shown to have implications for a variety of political leaders, ranging from revolutionaries[12] to generals[13] to U.S. senators[14] and may contribute to an understanding of gubernatorial behavior.

The Paragraph Completion Test, the most widely accepted test for determining individual placement on the dimension of personality, has been adapted for use with documentary materials. Thus scholars interested in the relationship between personality and gubernatorial behavior can perform content analyses of gubernatorial speeches, interviews, and other methods of gubernatorial communication.

Gubernatorial Motivation. Common sense suggests that cognition alone cannot account for all executives' behavior; and personality theorists agree. Theorists believe that a motivating force must reside behind each decision and each activity. Leaders differ not only in the way they process information, but also in their fundamental drives; and such differences may have political manifestations and implications. The three drives widely considered to be of political relevance are power, achievement, and affiliation. Research has shown that leaders who score high on each of these motivations behave differently than those who score low.

Thus presidents who score high on the power motive may be more likely to involve the United States in a war,[15] expand U.S. territorial holdings,[16] and enjoy a good relationship with the press,[17] but are at a greater risk of an assassination attempt on their lives.[18] Presidents who score high on the achievement motive may be willing to sacrifice continuity and conviviality to get a job done,[19] and affiliation-driven presidents tend to be more flexible in dealing with issues.[20] However, those motivated by the last drive are also more likely to select advisers who make better friends than expert advisers.[21]

While motivation may be of great importance to gubernatorial leadership, the measurement problems associated with tapping this dimension have been substantial. Fortunately this problem has been mediated by the adaptation of the Thematic Apperception Test—a standard instrument for scoring motivational drives when used with the written materials of leaders.[22] Thus scholars of gubernatorial performance now have an opportunity to examine the extent to which motivation affects performance.

Gubernatorial Character. A third element of personality—character—has been widely touted as an important explanatory variable in the assessment of political leaders, especially American presidents. Character is the way a political leader orients himself toward life and can be arrayed along two dimensions. The first, psychological satisfaction from office, can range from positive to negative. The second, energy invested in the job, is anchored by activity and passivity. As articulated by James David Barber,[23] presidents who exhibit active-positive character traits are better candidates for success than are those with passive-negative traits.

At least one attempt has been made to apply Barber's schema to the study of gubernatorial behavior. In *Florida's Gubernatorial Politics in the Twentieth Century,*[24] David Colburn and Richard Scher place the twenty-one men who held the Florida governor's office from 1900 to 1986 into the categories identified earlier. The authors did not, however, go on to the next logical step and use the placement as an independent variable to explain gubernatorial behavior. Further, their effort illustrates pitfalls that are inherent in the methodology.

First, such analyses are rooted in the examination of childhood and early adult experiences and require substantial biographical data. Most governors, I suspect, have not been the subject of enough early biographical research to provide the data necessary to determine with any security their placement along the two dimensions described by Barber. (This did not, however, deter Colburn and Scher who had biographies or studies of only seven of the twenty-one governors they studied.) Second, the psychological interpretations required in such analysis, "stressing the ways interpersonal experiences shape the person's self-image," are fraught with subjectivity. In the absence of precise rules guiding such interpretations, different scholars are likely to differ on the placement of individual governors. Thus, while the concept of presidential (or gubernatorial) character continues to capture the imagination of some, its usefulness in explaining behavior has yet to be demonstrated.

Nevertheless, attention to the personalities of governors can help explain the larger picture of gubernatorial behavior and should be part of any analysis of gubernatorial performance.

Political Skill

A dominant theme in the literature of executive leadership has been that the potential and limitations of the executive are a function of his or her own behavior and particularly of his or her political skill.[25] Although this theme has been modified,[26] there is still agreement that the success attained by a president or governor will depend to some degree on that person's skill in the political arena. Thus, in analyzing the performance of individual governors, some attention must be directed to an assessment of the political skills they use in their efforts to achieve their goals.

Two problems emerge for researchers interested in relating political skill to gubernatorial success. The first is how to decide on what skills are required. The second is how to determine the extent to which a governor possesses those skills. Since more attention has been devoted to the first of these problems than to the second, some consensus has been achieved regarding the required skills. Although this consensus comes in the absence of supporting research, most scholars refer to one of two sets of skills when identifying those necessary for political success: the effective use of informal sources of power (persuasion, bargaining, and negotiation)[27] and, in an age of mass communication, positive presentation of self.[28] In the absence of an alternative list, these skills seem to have achieved some acceptability and should be examined in any analysis of gubernatorial performance.

Political Resources

There is an old saying in the South, "You can't make chicken salad out of chicken manure." This saying certainly seems relevant to executive leadership. Many scholars argue that success is directly related to the nature of the resources, or capital, available for addressing governmental problems. "Given low levels in [gubernatorial] capital, even the most positive and most active executive could make little impact."[29]

According to Paul Light, political resources come in two "packets": internal and external. The internal packet includes the resources of time, information, expertise, and energy. The external packet reflects the incumbent's political strength and includes party support in the legislature, public approval, electoral margin, and professional reputation.[30] Some of these resources, particularly the external ones, are quantifiable and quite easily brought to bear on an analysis of gubernatorial performance.

For example, some measures of party support in the legislature—the distribution of Democrats and Republicans—are easily collected and others—key votes, nonunanimous support—can be calculated from sources that exist for virtually all states. Electoral margins are also easily gotten, and data on public approval are increasingly available. It is essential to use these data when examining the performance of individual governors. Gubernatorial success starts with party, and party support is related in some degree to the nature of the governor's electoral margin. The size and loyalty of the governor's legislative coalition are major explanatory variables and contribute to a systematic explanation of gubernatorial behavior. Use of data measuring these variables in a time series analysis of several governors will contribute to a theoretical understanding of the institution within a particular state.

The Context

The first scholars who attempted to explain the success of political executives focused on differences in character and skill. These analysts placed the executive at the center of attention and assumed that differences in their will or skill accounted for variations in success. Typical of this genre are Richard Neustadt's *Presidential Power,* Barbara Kellerman's *The Political Presidency,* and the work of a long line of organizational theorists who have used the "trait" approach.

While individual variations in the skills of leadership undoubtedly account for some of the differences in success, there are "bounds to what even the most skilled [governor] can accomplish under some circumstances—indeed under 'normal' circumstances."[31] All governors accept the mantle of leadership at a unique time and face a particular constellation of political and economic circumstances. These circumstances may be so complex and intractable that they defeat even the most capable governor. Thus, analysis of these circumstances is clearly important to an understanding of gubernatorial behavior and may result in a lowered standard of gubernatorial performance and less disappointment with "failures" of leadership.

Two elements of the environment in which governors operate are of particular importance to their performance. These are the general economic conditions of the state and the overall political situation. Variations in these factors can be identified fairly precisely.

State Economic Conditions. Gubernatorial priorities and strategies are constrained or enlarged by economic circumstances. Declining revenues and a stagnant economy often limit new initiatives and reduce service levels. Abundant economic resources may have opposite effects. Further, the nature of changes in these resources—their trend—is also important. An economy buoyed by optimistic predictions has a different effect on gubernatorial strategies than does an economy about which there are gloomy predictions.

Data describing variations in economic circumstances help establish precisely the nature of the situation within which an individual governor labors. Used in a time series, these data reduce the tendency to exaggerate or to downplay the importance of such circumstances.

The Political Environment. The nature of the political environment within which a governor operates can be described at two levels. Both can be measured fairly precisely. Analyses of gubernatorial behavior should be placed in their context.

At one level the political environment can be conceptualized as the distribution of partisanship and political ideology within a state and as a sequence of changes in the nature of the "political time"[32] during which the governor serves. At a more immediate level we can examine the distribution of political power within the legislature and the executive office, the extent of the governor's electoral mandate, her or his personal popularity and professional prestige, and the occurrence of short-term events that affect the nature of political opinion. Most such events are conceptualized as political resources and will, therefore, be treated later in this chapter.

The distribution of partisanship within a state's populace is a broad constraint on gubernatorial activity. While a specific distribution of Democrats and Republicans within the electorate may not be transferred into an analogous distribution within governmental institutions, a governor's actions are likely to be different if 65 percent of the population identifies with the Democrats than if 35 percent does. Public opinion polls that discern the distribution of partisanship within states are now widely available. Although the time series is short in some states, in others (such as Minnesota, Iowa, and California) such polls have been conducted since the 1940s. Analyses of gubernatorial behavior can be placed in the context of the existing distribution of partisanship and in the context of any changes that are occurring.

Gubernatorial behavior can also be placed in the context of a time series distribution of citizens along the liberal-conservative ideological dimension. This abstraction is the most widely used and accepted measure of political attitude. It focuses upon the "degree to which the government should assume interest, responsibility, and control over [various] sectors of endeavor."[33] The distribution of such attitudes has obvious implications for the behavior of governors. Like the measure of partisanship, the distribution of ideological predispositions within a state is usually available, and for some states a fairly long time series is available.

Explanations of gubernatorial behavior will also be enhanced by consideration of the "political time" during which the governor serves and by examination of the extent to which this time is changing. The political history of any state is characterized by periods of dominance by specific coalitions representing geographical regions, ideological predispositions, or political cultures. Stephen Skowronek labeled such periods political times; they exhibit a "distinctive set of institutional arrangements and approaches to public policy questions."[34] These arrangements and approaches affect mightily the nature of gubernatorial strategies and actions. Different political challenges face a governor at different political times, and the quality of gubernatorial performance may be related to the changing shape of the dominant political order. Therefore, some attempt must be made to characterize political times and to assess their implications for gubernatorial success.

Efforts to analyze the effect of political time on gubernatorial activity will take both quantitative and qualitative forms. The nature of the legislative environment at various points in time can be characterized by placement of the legislature along a quantitatively derived centralized-decentralized continuum. The measure is an index constructed by standardizing the sum of two standardized variables: the number of committees and subcommittees in the state legislature, and the percentage of state representatives and senators having served some specific number of years in these bodies.[35] Beyond this, attention can be focused on the personalities in positions of influence within both state government and state political parties, the interrelationships among political elites, and the ideological predispositions and policy preferences of these elites. The results of this latter analysis will be less precise than the quantitative analyses suggested earlier. But its contribution to an understanding of gubernatorial behavior will be as great.

One other element of the political environment is also important to an understanding of gubernatorial behavior and performance: the unexpected event that triggers a political reaction and attracts the public's attention. Research on the presidency reveals that six kinds of events are likely to engender such a reaction: threats to peace, domestic disruptions, political scandals, the conduct of diplomacy, policy initiatives, and incidents that focus on the personal and political health of the incumbent.[36] Systematic efforts to identify and relate such events to gubernatorial performance will enhance explanations of that performance.

Strategy

To achieve their goals "in the face of uncertainty, surprise, ambiguity, inadequate information, and centrifugal forces, public executives need a . . . set of premises deliberately chosen to provide direction to their thinking, choices, and administrative behavior."[37] This set of premises is referred to as a strategy and is a major variable in the equation linking public executives to successful performance in office. Indeed, one observer of presidential performance argues that "if a president does not want to leave his legacy to chance or be merely a caretaker in office, he must take a self-conscious strategic approach to the presidency."[38]

All governors employ some form of strategy to guide their actions. The strategies can be defined by scope, character, and timeliness. One strategy assumes that the size of the governor's agenda is related to success and that "each extra proposal submitted reduces the probability of passage for every proposal."[39] A second strategy is based on the assumption that the governor is more effective at some points in his term than at other points.[40] A third posits a direct causal link between the substantive nature of policy proposals and the response they generate. An empirical measure of the size of the governor's agenda can be calculated by a simple count of the measures proposed in the messages given by the governor. The time at which proposals are introduced by governors can be divided into categories such as honeymoon/first year, midterm election year, post-midterm election year, and gubernatorial election year. The type of policy represented by the governor's initiatives can be categorized by distributive, regulatory, redistributive, and constituent policies using the procedures in the work of Robert Spitzer.[41]

Use of these, or other, conceptualizations of gubernatorial strategy will permit the examination of the contribution of strategy to gubernatorial success.

Conclusion

This chapter advances two unremarkable propositions: that the understanding of gubernatorial behavior will be improved by the integration of several perspectives and that the conclusions drawn from such analyses will be made more meaningful if they are based on systematic and empirical time series data. It suggests a framework for use in combining five variables that are often employed separately into an explanation of gubernatorial performance. The scholarship on this topic should focus on the interaction among these five variables; gubernatorial performance cannot be adequately assessed in the absence of attention to each.

Notes

1. Gary King and Lynn Ragsdale, *The Elusive Executive* (Washington, D.C.: CQ Press, 1988), 4.
2. Bert Rockman, "The Leadership Style of George Bush," in *The Bush Presidency,* ed. Colin Campbell and Bert Rockman (Chatham, N.J.: Chatham House, 1991), 156.
3. David Keirsey and Marilyn Bates, *Please Understand Me* (Del Mar, Calif.: Prometheus Nemesis Books, 1978), 27.

4. Barbara Kellerman, *The Political Presidency* (New York: Oxford University Press, 1984), xi.
5. Jeffrey Tulis, *The Rhetorical Presidency* (Princeton, N.J.: Princeton University Press, 1987).
6. Richard Neustadt, *Presidential Power* (New York: Wiley, 1964).
7. Paul Light, *The President's Agenda* (Baltimore: Johns Hopkins University Press, 1982).
8. Laurence Lynn, *Managing Public Policy* (Boston: Little, Brown, 1987), 39.
9. Stephen Skowronek, "Presidential Leadership in Political Time," in *The Presidency and the Political System,* ed. Michael Nelson (Washington, D.C.: CQ Press, 1984).
10. James Young, Foreword to Erwin Hargrove, *Jimmy Carter as President* (Baton Rouge: Louisiana State University Press, 1988), xiii.
11. Hargrove, *Jimmy Carter,* xxiv.
12. P. Suedfield and A. D. Rank, "Revolutionary Leaders: Long-Term Success as a Function of Change in Conceptual Complexity," *Journal of Personality and Social Psychology* 34 (1976).
13. P. Suedfield, R. Corteen, and C. McCormick, "The Role of Integrative Complexity in Military Leadership," *Journal of Applied Social Psychology* 16 (1986).
14. P. E. Tetlock, "Personality and Isolationism," *Journal of Personality and Social Psychology* 41 (1981).
15. D. G. Winter, *The Power Motive* (New York: Free Press, 1973); and Winter, "Leader Appeal, Leader Performance and the Motive Profile of Leaders and Followers," *Journal of Personality and Social Psychology* 52 (1987).
16. Ibid, *The Power Motive.*
17. H. W. Wendt and P. C. Light, "Measuring Greatness in American Presidents," *European Journal of Social Psychology* 6 (1976).
18. Ibid; Winter, *The Power Motive.*
19. D. G. Winter and A. J. Stewart, "Content Analysis as a Technique for Assessing Political Leaders," in *The Psychological Examination of Political Leaders,* ed. M. G. Hermann (New York: Free Press, 1977).
20. Ibid.
21. Ibid.
22. Richard Donley and David Winter, "Measuring the Motives of Public Officials at a Distance: An Exploratory Study of American Presidents," *Behavioral Science* 15 (1970): 227–236.
23. James David Barber, *The Presidential Character* (Englewood Cliffs, N.J.: Prentice-Hall, 1977).
24. David Colburn and Richard Scher, *Florida's Gubernatorial Politics in the Twentieth Century* (Tallahassee, Fla.: University Presses of Florida, 1980).
25. Neustadt, *Presidential Power;* Kellerman, *Political Presidency.*
26. George Edwards, *Presidential Influence in Congress* (San Francisco: W. H. Freeman, 1980); George Edwards, *At the Margins* (New Haven: Yale University Press, 1989); Lynn, *Managing Public Policy;* Hargrove, *Jimmy Carter.*
27. Neustadt, *Presidential Power;* Kellerman, *Political Presidency.*
28. Samuel Kernell, *Going Public* (Washington, D.C.: CQ Press, 1986); Tulis, *Rhetorical Presidency.*
29. Tulis, *Rhetorical Presidency.*
30. Light, *The President's Agenda,* 34.
31. Tulis, *Rhetorical Presidency,* 146.
32. Skowronek, "Presidential Leadership."
33. Angus Campbell, Phillip Converse, Warren Miller, and Donald Stokes, *The American Voter* (New York: Wiley, 1960), 194.
34. Skowronek, *Presidential Leadership.*
35. Mark Peterson, *Legislating Together* (Cambridge, Mass.: Harvard University Press, 1990), 316.
36. Charles Ostrom and Dennis Simon, "Promise and Performance: A Dynamic Model of Presidential Popularity," *American Political Science Review* 79 (June 1985).
37. Lynn, *Managing Public Policy,* 130–131.
38. James Pfiffner, *The Strategic Presidency* (Chicago: Dorsey, 1988), 156.
39. Richard Forshee and Russell Renka, "The Price of Ambition: Presidents, Agenda Size and Legislative Success," 8 (paper presented at the annual meeting of the American Political Science Association, Washington, D.C., 1991).
40. Neustadt, *Presidential Power.*
41. Robert Spitzer, "Presidential Policy Determinism: How Policies Frame Congressional Response to the President's Legislative Program," *Presidential Studies Quarterly* 13 (Fall 1983).

CASE STUDY 9

Introduction

As the preceding essay makes clear, a variety of factors influence a governor's success. Crew does not talk directly about the work by Schlesinger and others on formal powers, but the essay suggests that these powers can be important because they provide valuable resources to governors that can be used to influence legislative action. Yet Crew's work also reveals why other factors are also important, some that are more personal in nature and others that reflect the situation faced by the governor.

In the introduction and conclusion to his essay, Crew argues that it is impossible to develop a good understanding of gubernatorial behavior by focusing on only one or two variables to explain that behavior and by not comparing "situations and statistics." In essence, Crew is arguing that scholars must go beyond anecdotal case studies if they want to develop more meaningful explanations for gubernatorial success. To build knowledge about gubernatorial leadership, state scholars need to compare gubernatorial performance and look at more than one explanation for success. They must also draw on valid and reliable data, rather than just relying on anecdotes.

Crew makes a good point for anyone who is interested in conducting any type of study of state politics. To understand how state government and politics work generally, you need to compare cases, draw on good data, and evaluate competing explanations for what is observed. Yet case studies also have value in research. On some occasions, scholars use case studies to test specific theories. If a case study provides findings that are not what was anticipated from theory, it can lead to a revised theory, one that provides a better explanation of events. When the findings are consistent with a theory, the case study builds support for that theory. Case studies can also be important for illustrating the findings from more systematic analyses. They can allow for more in-depth analyses of specific events, which can provide a richer and more comprehensive understanding.

In the case study that follows, E. J. Dionne, Jr., an award-winning columnist from the *Washington Post,* provides a thoughtful look at George W. Bush's record as Texas governor. The essay was primarily meant to provide some insights into the leading Republican candidate a year before the presidential election. In looking at Bush's record, Dionne credits a great deal of his success to personal factors, especially Bush's warm personality. Yet Dionne also suggests that there was skill and strategy involved. Bush chose his words carefully and made symbolic gestures that enabled him to build support in the public and from both Democratic and Republican legislators. Combined, these factors helped make the Republican governor a successful leader, even though he faced a Texas legislature that was controlled by Democrats. Dionne's essay does not provide a systematic analysis of data of the kind advocated by Crew, but it does nicely illustrate how many of the factors described by Crew can be important to a governor's success.

Questions to Consider

These are some questions to consider as you read Dionne's essay:

- How would you describe Bush's personality? Why does Dionne say that Bush's personality helped make him a successful governor? What other factors seem to have helped Bush?
- What does Dionne mean when he writes that Bush's talk about "his religious faith solves three problems at once"? What is his faith, and how does it solve these problems?
- Thinking back on Crew's essay, what other factors could explain Bush's success but were not considered by Dionne? What else would you like to know about Bush's administration to judge for yourself why he was successful?

In Search of George W.

E. J. Dionne, Jr.

When they talk about George W. Bush in Texas, it's the man and not his deep thoughts they dwell on. He "brings people together," says a businessman at a community college rally. He's "an inspiration," proclaims a Fort Worth woman. "Down to earth," asserts an official in Grapevine, who declares that this man who has carefully harvested more support from fellow politicians than any non-incumbent presidential candidate in recent history is "not a politician's politician."

Maybe such attributes will help Bush survive the acres of newsprint that will be devoted to serious investigation of his youth and its excesses, his business career, his private habits, his military record, his friendships. Almost certainly, people will tire of the endless analysis of his relationships with his father, his mother, his wife, his children.

They'll tire of this stuff because in presidential campaigns, ideas have consequences and can trump even the strongest personalities. So the core character issue confronting the front-runner for the Republican presidential nomination will not be booze, babes or drugs. It will revolve around the question: What does George W. Bush believe, and why does he believe it?

His allies will tell you that the governor of Texas has given some very clear answers. Bush's campaign Web site lists nearly a hundred positions on issues, and many of them are quite specific—on China policy and trade, taxes and tort reform. And he has, after all, staked out a personal philosophy with a name: compassionate conservatism. It's a term whose use was pioneered by others, but Bush is the first to make it the centerpiece of a presidential campaign. "On this ground," he declares at one campaign stop after another, "I'll take my stand."

But what exactly does Bush mean by compassionate conservatism? Here, the mystery begins.

If you ask him what the Republican Party has done wrong since 1994, he'll offer you a quick answer. "It hasn't put a compassionate face on our conservative philosophy," he replies during an interview in the governor's wood-paneled, uncluttered Austin office. "People think oftentimes that Republicans are mean-spirited folks. Which is not true, but that's what people think."

Those sentiments make Bush appealing to many moderates and even liberals alienated over the years by the Republican Party. In his fullest account of compassionate conservatism (a July 22 speech in Indianapolis), he even went out of his way to separate himself from Republicans who have insisted that the "armies of compassion" in religious institutions could substitute for government.

Bush, of course, loves those armies and talks about them all the time. But, in the Indianapolis speech, he insisted that "there are some things that government should be doing—like Medicaid for poor children"—and that "government cannot be replaced by charities." That certainly seems to put a decent distance between Bush's genial Republicanism and the fire-eating right.

But examine his words carefully. Note what W., as he's known in media circles, actually says in the interview: that the Republicans need to put a compassionate face on their party. That's not the same as transforming it. On the contrary, Bush seems to be saying there's nothing wrong with the Republican Party that a different face won't cure. We know whose face he has in mind.

Yes, people may think the Republicans are "mean-spirited." But Bush quickly adds that this impression can't possibly be true. Which raises the question: Is Bush about public relations or political philosophy, better principles or better cosmetics?

Bush's statements are worth parsing carefully because he has been so successful in getting people of very different views to believe he is one of them.

Many Texas Democrats say that Bush is a centrist who agrees with them on many things. "George has been at odds with some of the leading Republican figures in the state," says one Democratic state legislator who doesn't want his name used for fear of offending Bush and his fellow Democrats simultaneously. "You talk to him in private, and there are a lot of things that, as a Democrat, you agree with him on. He's a moderate."

But talk to conservative Bush fans and you hear the opposite: He's a true conservative who knows how to talk moderate. "More conservative than his father, George W. has a proven record of conservative accomplishment that the media have largely ignored," Ralph Reed, former executive director of the Christian Coalition, wrote in the *National Review* this July. "A Bush victory in November 2000 would be a conservative triumph, not a moderate one."

Reed's view may be biased because he's a Bush consultant whose job involves winning over the right. But Reed was only echoing what other conservatives are saying.

Somebody has to be wrong here. How can Bush be all things to all people? Maybe it's because he doesn't have deep beliefs. Or maybe he's hiding something from somebody. Maybe he really is on the trail of the grand synthesis Republicans have been searching for since Ronald Reagan left office.

One of the secrets of W.'s success in appealing to almost everybody is his mastery of the very oldest political art: He just gets people, all kinds of people, to like him. In person, he's warm, he mugs, he jokes. He clues in fast to the particular thing that makes the somebody in front of him tick.

At a winery in Grapevine, for instance, he doesn't talk too long. He wants time to work the crowd, to put an arm on friends, to look everyone in the eye and remember things about their kids. "He's not looking over your shoulder at the next guy's name tag," says a friend, Republican state Rep. Tom Craddick.

Bush conveys a merry irony about the very political game he takes so seriously. Bush doesn't feel your pain; he counts you in on the joke. In late June, he walked up to *New York Times* reporter Rick Berke as Berke was doing a tarmac commentary in Austin for MSNBC. Bush joshed him for delaying the campaign plane, and practically pulled him off the screen. But in the process, Bush granted Berke an impromptu interview and won some free air time. Good nature has its uses.

And W. profits immensely from being a Republican in Texas. Liberals there are accustomed to conservative tough guys like Reps. Tom DeLay and Dick Armey and Sen. Phil Gramm. Compared with them, Bush is a sweetie. Start with state Rep. Glen Maxey, an openly gay member of the Texas legislature. Maxey disagrees with Bush on most things and is one of his most articulate critics. But here's Maxey on Bush: "As a liberal gay activist in the Texas House of Representatives, I say: He's not as bad as he could be."

Some endorsement. But Maxey goes on. "This place can be very mean. It can be very mean-spirited. There are many of us who are so pleasantly surprised that he's AWOL on issues that could be so detrimental to Texas." Far better to be AWOL than mean.

Or take the way in which W. won over a large share of Texas's Latino community. He made Hispanics and many liberals happy by voicing opposition to California's Proposition 187, which called for cutting off public services to illegal immigrants, including children.

It's true that the local political risk to Bush was small. Even among conservatives and Republicans, the immigration issue plays very differently in Texas than it does in California. But Maxey's maxim applies: Seen by those outside the conservative orbit, Bush is not as bad as he could be.

And few politicians are better at seizing symbolic opportunities. Juan Sepulveda, a young community activist in San Antonio, notes that when the grand marshal of the city's Diez y Seis parade, a local music legend named Flaco Jimenez, could not march because of illness, Bush volunteered to take his place.

The gesture, of course, entailed not a single concession on a single issue. But as Sepulveda explains, Bush's move underscored the political shrewdness of this very political man. "He understands the importance of building relationships, and that came across in a pro-active way," Sepulveda says. In Bush's reelection campaign, footage of W. on the parade route appeared in his Spanish language television ads. And he now boasts of winning almost half the Latino vote.

State Rep. Miguel Wise, a Democrat whose predominantly Latino district in the Rio Grande Valley is racked by poverty, says this about Bush: "He is an Everyday Joe. He's the guy you run into and watch an NBA game with in a sports bar." That Wise says such a thing about a Republican educated at Andover, Yale and Harvard Business—and who doesn't even drink anymore—tells you something about the power of the one piece of discernible ideology Bush has forged: the ideology of personality.

Like Bill Clinton, Bush is the sort of man who leaves an 80 percent approval rating in his wake as he passes through any room. He truly loves the business of connecting, relating, persuading.

But persuading to what end? To understand what W. believes, it helps to know about his religious faith, his business background and his family legacy.

This year, it seems the first requirement of any presidential candidate is to describe his or her personal relationship with Jesus Christ. Bush does this better than most. As he talks, he lets you know that he knows how embarrassing it would be if he laid it on too thick. He suggests that his religious experiences are not something he likes to talk about. And then he will talk about them at length.

"First of all, I generally don't spend a lot of time talking about my religion unless I'm asked," he says, "or unless there's a purpose." The nice reluctance. Then: "I was raised in a Christian household by a mother and father who really gave me the greatest gift of all, which is unconditional love. That in itself is somewhat biblical.

"But I think everybody has to come to terms with their own religion," he continues. "And I always say God works in mysterious ways and I renewed my spirit. It means precisely that I've accepted Christ as my savior, that's what that means."

Bush is a nondenominational sort of guy. He began life in a good Episcopalian family and then adopted the Methodism of his wife. Methodists constitute a much larger religious tribe than Episcopalians, and their church's history is rooted in the experiences of the working class, not the upper class.

Methodists also have a long history of social action, and their church has always had an important progressive wing. Hillary Rodham Clinton, a Methodist from birth, is very representative of the church's social justice tradition. Bush's Methodism reflects a parallel tradition that emphasizes self-improvement through self-discipline. Faith has a functional, 12-step-program quality for him.

"For me, it means understanding and accepting whatever comes with life. I mean, it helps prepare me for my own daily struggles and my own thinking. I believe in prayer. I read the Bible. It helps strengthen me as a person. It helps me understand the priorities in life of family and faith."

Many who know Bush affirm that his conversion was linked to the time his daughters were born in 1981. In talking about his sense of responsibility, he manages to take an oblique but tough shot at Bill Clinton.

There is, he says, "a certain maturation that happens when you assume the responsibility of being a father and a husband . . . I mean, I take solemn oaths very seriously and I can remember when our twins were born. I remember feeling how much my life changed the moment they were born and in anticipation how much it was going to change over time. And there's no question that if you assume your responsibility as a dad as seriously as we should, it changes your life."

And from here, Bush moves easily to answering questions about his compassionate conservatism, which is rooted in all the good work performed by religious institutions on behalf of the poor.

"In terms of government policy," he says, "probably the most profound impact that religion has had on me has led me to help, in our state, forge this relationship between church, synagogue and mosque and people who need help . . . and [we] have welcomed people of faith into the public arena to help people. I mean, the theory is that let's change your heart first, and good results will follow."

The way Bush talks about his religious faith solves three problems at once. Speaking with compassion about the poor takes the hard edges off conservatism. It allows him to relate easily to Christian conservatives, without having to spend too much time on the hard issues—abortion, gay rights, creationism—that turn off moderates. And his conversion allows him to draw a sharp line between his self-described young and irresponsible past, and his presidency-seeking present. He's the prodigal son, the repentant sinner, the transformed man.

Bush resists the view that he is putting his faith to work for his campaign: "People will see through that in a minute." No one, including those among Bush's political opponents, doubts the sincerity of his conversion, the apparent seriousness of his faith, or the fact that his life did seem to change when he turned 40 in 1986. But the content of his faith is harder to pin down. The evidence, especially of his own words, is that it's less an intellectual calling than a matter of feelings and will. Ask him about favorite passages in the Bible, for instance, and his answers are surprisingly vague and general—"Well," he says, "the Beatitudes are great. I mean a lot of the Bible."

"Religion is a very personal matter to me—as it should be to everybody," he says. "I also understand that everybody comes to have religion different ways. All I know is—I know the pathway for me is what I know. And I'm not going to try to tell you the pathway for you." This is a very nonjudgmental, end-of-the-century, good-vibes religion.

Yet compassionate conservatism Bush-style is clearly rooted in personal experience, in the notion that religious faith offers the most effective path to solving problems—private and public problems. He seems to be promising to help every American who wants one to have a religious experience, the Ultimate Political Pledge.

"I ask the question, Does it work?" he says. "And to answer your question, from firsthand knowledge I know that changing your heart can work. It's worked for me. Will it work for everybody? Probably not. But, for example, if in fact we've reduced recidivism by changing hearts first, the state of Texas and, for that matter, America ought to say, 'Thank you, Lord, let's do more.' "

Religious language also enables Bush to take hard, controversial political questions and move them to the soft, friendly ground of personal obligation and faith. He doesn't talk about social justice, minimum wages, unions or monopoly power. He preaches everybody's obligation to be kinder and gentler, to create a thousand points of light.

"Getting tough on crime is easy," says the man who boasts about his aggressive anticrime laws, "compared to loving our neighbors as ourselves. The truth is, we must turn back to God and look to Him for help."

Bush's compassion talk is never about the failure of the economic system, or the rights of those who are poor, or systematic injustices. He always comes back to individuals.

"I know many conservative thinkers and people who adhere to the notion of heralding the individual and individualism and less federal government are people who really do care about the future," he says in the interview. "Because they know what I know: Government can't make people love one another. There have really been a lot of false promises over the last 30 years as well: 'Oh don't worry, you know, we'll make you love each other.' Well, unfortunately it doesn't happen that way. Love comes from a more powerful source."

He's proposing God, not government. It's how he squares his talk about compassion with his insistence on small government. How small? In Texas, at least, it's pretty small. In one legislative battle with the Democrats, for instance, Bush wanted to limit the number of poor children covered by a federally financed health care program. Eventually the governor compromised, but the larger point was made: Compassionism, as perhaps it should be called, is not liberalism.

Compassionate conservatism has very old roots in the Republican Party. But even in its recent incarnation, it has an ambiguous paternity. One iteration was popularized by Newt Gingrich when he championed the writings of Marvin Olasky. This version emphasized the work of religious charities in helping the poor more effectively than any government program could. The upshot was that government should drop dead to bring the religious charities to life.

Olasky, a University of Texas journalism professor and a Bush campaign adviser, argued in a 1996 book, *Renewing American Compassion,* that in an ideal world Congress would simply abolish the federal safety net. "Congress should phase out federal assistance programs and push states to develop ways for individuals and community-based groups to take over poverty-fighting responsibility."

"We must place in the hands of state officials all decisions about welfare and the financing of it, and then press them to put welfare entirely in the hands of church- and community-based organizations." Smash the state in the name of God.

Ask Bush about Olasky, and he says this: "I think that our society can change one heart, one soul, one conscience at a time. That's what I believe. And I believe that Olasky understands that, and I believe that many people of faith understand that, and I'm proud that Olasky wants to try to figure out ways to make society respond to the call."

Bush clearly shares a good deal of Olasky's skepticism about government programs, despite his defense of government in his Indianapolis speech this summer. Here is what Bush said in April 1996: "As government did more and more, individuals were required to do less and less, and they responded with a vengeance. Dependency and laziness are easy when someone else is to blame. We became a nation of victims. Blame it on the parenting, the Prozac, the bossa nova—take your pick."

The man who says he'll go to Washington to change the country doesn't think there's much Washington should do—or at least didn't back in 1996. "We must reduce the role and scope of the federal government, returning it to the limited role our forefathers envisioned when they wrote the 10th Amendment to the Constitution, giving the states all power not specifically granted to the federal government."

If Olasky offers one version of compassionate conservatism, there's a more modest version, formulated by congressional Republicans such as former senator Dan Coats and Sens. Rick Santorum of Pennsylvania and John Ashcroft of Missouri. They argue that if Republicans want to reduce the size of government, they have an obligation to come up with alternative ways of helping the poor. Their ideas have gained so much ground that Vice President Gore has endorsed government cooperation with faith-based organizations.

By turns attacking and defending government, Bush has managed to straddle the entire field of compassionate conservatism. He and his advisers have been ingenious at devising formulas that can be read as friendly by pro- and anti-government voters alike. "My guiding principle," he once said, "is government if necessary, but not necessarily government." Those words might, in principle at least, be spoken as easily by Ted Kennedy as by Jesse Helms.

If you ask Indianapolis Mayor Steve Goldsmith, Bush's top domestic policy adviser, about Bush's leanings, he gives an entirely open answer that simultaneously clarifies and deepens the mystery of W.'s commitments. Bush, he explains, will seek advice anywhere—as long as potential advisers are willing to stick with a short list of core principles.

"I believe in states' rights," Goldsmith says, paraphrasing his marching orders from Bush. "I believe in federalism. I believe individuals ought to have choices and that government has a role in this. Now bring me the best ideas you can." H. J. "Tex" Lazar, who ran unsuccessfully for Texas lieutenant governor on Bush's ticket in 1994, says that in keeping his list of principles short and in delegating most of the details to others, W. "resembles Ronald Reagan more than he resembles his father."

But for all of Bush's warm invocations of "mercy" and "love," there remains a hard—or, if you prefer, tough love—side to his compassion.

Ask Bush why people are poor, and he speaks almost entirely about their shortcomings. "Oftentimes people are poor because of decisions they make," he says. "Oftentimes people are poor because they didn't get a good education . . . [and aren't] making right choices and staying in school and working hard in school."

Are there any social reasons for poverty? "I think if you grow up in an impoverished world that's full of drugs and alcohol, it makes it very hard to break out of the environment which you're in," he says.

Compassionate conservatism is a work in progress, and in this sense, Bush is very different from Bill Clinton, who spent years honing his ideas at the National Governors Association and the Democratic Leadership Council. Clinton arrived on the national scene with bulging packets of proposals. Bush, on the other hand, has shrewd political instincts, some experience—especially in education reform—and a very smart stump speech. Ideas will come later.

In all the analysis and hype surrounding compassionate conservatism, it's possible to lose track of how deeply rooted this idea is in the very old Republican doctrine that voluntary action is better than government action.

Here's Bush's inaugural address this year: "Reducing problems to economics is simply materialism," he declared. "The real answer is found in the hearts of decent, caring people who have heard the call to love their neighbors as they would like to be loved themselves. We must rally the armies of compassion in every community of this state. We must encourage them to love, to nurture, to mentor, to help and thus to offer hope to those who have none."

Now consider these words: "Our national resources are not only material supplies and material wealth but a spiritual and moral wealth in kindliness, in compassion, in a sense of obligation of neighbor to neighbor, and a realization of responsibility by industry, by business and by the community for its social security and its social welfare . . . We can take courage and pride in the effective work of thousands of voluntary organizations for the provision of employment, for the relief of distress, that have sprung up over the entire nation."

The speaker? Herbert Hoover, in 1932, in the midst of the Great Depression. When Bush insists that he truly is a conservative, he has a good case to make and a powerful pedigree to invoke.

Of course Hoover is not exactly a Republican icon, precisely because he failed to use government effectively in a time of national catastrophe. One way to summarize what Bush will need to explain about compassionate conservatism is whether he thinks Hoover was right—or, alternatively, where he and Hoover differ. For in his basic attitudes toward government's role in the economy, Bush is decidedly a traditional Republican.

The fabulously renovated chambers of the Texas legislature feel as opulent as the interests that stalk its halls. Under the rules, representatives of those interests can even get onto the floor to catch the people's representatives as they go in and out. It's a place where oil and gas are sacred words and where the term "taking care of business" means precisely what it says.

Even though the Texas House is under Democratic control, the legislature is a place W. knows how to work. He has lost sometimes—in the case of education reform, at the hands of his own party. But, in general, he's done well—in part because of The Personality. He assiduously courted Democratic allies, notably the late Bob Bullock. Bullock served as lieutenant governor in Bush's first term, guided him through the arcane ways of Austin politics, and became a Democrat for Bush in the 1998 campaign.

But Bush also did well because he was in tune with his party and Texas's Tory Democrats on the imperative of being good to business by keeping taxes low, curbing lawsuits and resisting regulation. It's no wonder, as *National Journal* reported recently, that Texas ranks 50th among states in total per capita spending, 35th in per capita education spending, and still has a state minimum wage of $3.35 an hour.

It's worth remembering that one of W.'s central campaign themes when he defeated popular Democratic Gov. Ann Richards in 1994 was tort reform. It was one of the major legislative achievements of his first term. Limiting the ability of plaintiffs to bring suits, notably against businesses, is a cause most corporate executives hold dear. By winning, Bush made his business backers happy, while striking a blow at trial lawyers, one of the most durable sources of Democratic campaign money.

Bush's biography is the story of a man who ran a single, unsuccessful campaign for Congress in 1978, tried to make it in business and came back to politics later. By Election Day 2000, he will still have had less than six years of experience in elected office. Most of his life has been about business, not politics.

Bush's own business career was, for many years, an uneven journey through oil exploration and dealmaking. In both endeavors, he had more than a little help courtesy of his father's connections. Bush didn't achieve real success until he put himself in the middle of the sale of the Texas Rangers and became the baseball team's managing partner. This is a deal on which he did very well indeed: He paid $600,000 for his share of the Rangers and sold it a decade later for nearly $15 million. It's not a surprise that he loves capitalism and his business friends, or that phrases such as creating "an environment in which people are willing to risk capital" routinely cross his lips.

Bush's love affair with business interests is certain to be an issue in the coming campaign, especially in light of the astounding amounts of cash he's raised.

Does business get what it pays for? Texas environmentalists and labor leaders think so. One of the big environmental issues this year involved Texas industrial plants, many of them in the oil and gas industry, that won exemptions in 1971 from various emission and pollution control standards.

Bush fought for, and eventually won, a voluntary program to clean up the plants. Environmentalists wanted a mandatory program. They denounced Bush and made public a long list of contributions to his presidential campaign from the protected companies and their attorneys.

Bush's fiscal conservatism was on display in the battle over federally subsidized children's health insurance, a program that had to be implemented by the states. Bush wanted to limit the program to only those children who were in families with an income of 150 percent of the poverty level or less. Democrats in the Texas legislature wanted the cutoff to be 200 percent of poverty, to cover roughly 200,000 additional kids.

Bush justifies his stand in the name of fiscal responsibility. "There is a lot of uncertainty," he says. "One of my jobs is to create certainty in the budget and to look beyond the short term, and I will tell you, in times of plenty, the government must not overcommit because we may not have times of plenty in the future."

Yet, Bush did not worry about committing $1.8 billion in state money in these "times of plenty" for tax cuts. To protect those cuts, Bush's legislative allies resisted proposals by his sometime partner on education reform, state Rep. Paul Sadler, a Democrat, who wanted a smaller tax cut to leave room for financing kindergartens throughout Texas. (Sadler eventually got much of what he wanted but not universal kindergarten.)

Nor was Bush at all reluctant to provide a $45 million tax break to the oil and gas industry, which he signed into law this year. State Rep. Dale Tillery drew a direct contrast to the child health care bill. "I know a whole lot of uninsured children," he told the *Dallas Morning News,* "but I don't know a lot of poor oilmen."

If Bush is the Everyday Joe that Rep. Wise says he is, that does not make him an ally of organized labor, which remains positively hostile. "We just don't have that great relationship with him that everybody else says they have," says Rick Levy, legal director of the state AFL-CIO. Bush has never forgiven the unions for opposing certain pet measures early in his first term, Levy says, accusing Bush of routinely breaking deals that labor negotiated with his staff. "He can be very vindictive if you oppose him," Levy says.

Bush's many conservative stands might be music to anti-government, anti-labor ears. But in the biggest fight of his time as governor—a fight Bush lost—he found himself at odds with many staunch conservatives.

In 1997, Bush pushed for a new way of financing the state's schools. It was designed to cut property taxes and dramatically increase the state's share of education funding. To do that, he proposed a series of tax increases, including increases in sales and business taxes.

The result would have been a net cut in taxes. But many conservatives focused on the increases. "This is not a Republican philosophy in this bill," Tom Paulken, then the GOP state chairman, complained at the time. Bush's plan was rewritten by the legislature and Bush embraced a version created by Democrats. The bill Bush endorsed won more Democratic than Republican support in the House.

At the end of a tortured process, the school financing reform failed. Bush had to settle for using part of the state's large surplus for a property tax cut. As luck would have it—and Bush is definitely lucky—the failure of his ambitious plan and its replacement with a simple tax cut turn out to be a boon to him in the current campaign. He doesn't have to explain business or sales tax increases, and he can boast about cutting taxes.

In the interview, that's exactly what he does: "It fell apart, and we ended up cutting taxes by a billion dollars." Different people draw different lessons from the education fight. It's true that though Bush lost, he took a large political risk in an attempt to accomplish something. Texas voters, he says, "appreciate the fact that I took a stand, fought for something I thought was right."

Yet the education battle was also an example of Bush's flexibility, his willingness to work with members of the other party. You can see this flexibility as a mark of realism, or of something less than principle.

Texas state Rep. Bob Junell, a Democrat who supported Bush for reelection and supports him for president, calls him a "bottom line guy" with "lots of flexibility as to how we get there." But Maxey takes a different view: "It's all political. I fundamentally don't know where he stands on anything."

Which leads to one safe conclusion: You can't know what a Bush presidency would be like until you know who'll control Congress. A Republican-led Congress would accentuate Bush's conservative side; a Congress with at least one Democratic chamber would bring out the deal-maker.

Remember that child health care bill, the one Bush worried might "overcommit" state resources if it covered kids at 200 percent of the poverty level? In May, Maxey, the bill's leading House sponsor, predicted that the legislature would ignore Bush, pass the 200 percent proposal—and that Bush would praise it and sign it. That's exactly what Bush did.

You cannot understand W. without sitting down and talking to his top political strategist, Karl Rove.

Sandy-haired and slightly balding, Rove spits out ideas in automatic-weapon bursts. He combines many roles within himself. Like James Carville, he is a shrewd strategist. Like Democratic pollster Stan Greenberg, he has an academic side that includes a strong feeling for history. And like the late Lee Atwater, Rove is good at keeping in touch, lining people up, keeping supporters on board.

Rove is almost single-handedly responsible for the political comeback of William McKinley. He has pushed his theory that the 2000 election has the same epoch-making potential as the election of 1896, when McKinley produced a new and enduring Republican majority. Rove argues that McKinley understood that the issues surrounding the Civil War, which had dominated politics for three decades, were no longer relevant.

McKinley also understood that immigration and industrialization had changed the character of the country. If Republicans did not make a bid for the votes of immigrants and the working class generally, they would lose preeminence. Rove, for whom archival research is a hobby, can cite letters McKinley wrote describing the party's problem, and meetings he held with immigrant leaders to bring them around to his party's promise of the "full dinner pail."

Rove's analysis represents a sharp break with the popular conservative assumption that all that's required for a Republican victory is to re-create Ronald Reagan's appeal and reassemble his coalition. The electorate has changed in the 15 years since Reagan's last election—baby boomers and younger voters are now at its heart, and voters generally are less partisan. And Reagan's best issues are gone: The Cold War is over and hostility to government programs has ebbed.

It's not hard to see how the McKinley parallel plays itself out in 2000. W.'s quest for Latino votes, a large factor in California, Texas, Florida, New Jersey and Illinois, is directly comparable to McKinley's wooing of Czechs, Slovaks, Italians, Bohemians and Irish.

Similarly, Bush's minuets on social issues such as abortion and affirmative action reflect a sense that—whatever Gary Bauer or Pat Buchanan might hope—creating a durable Republican majority requires converting suburban independents and Democrats whose social and moral views are more moderate than conservative.

And it's clear that Bush has taken into account the failure of House Republican revolutionaries' strategy of assailing government. He wants Republicans at least to look less hostile to government. However vague it may be, Bush's formula—"government if necessary, but not necessarily government"—resonates very differently from Ronald Reagan's bold proclamation that "government isn't the solution, government is the problem."

Identity crises in the Republican Party are nothing new, and another Bush once struggled with the problem of the party's image in an era of transition. "Differences between our major parties are blurred," he declared. "Factions mark splits within each party. Slogans and labels are used today much as they were in Lincoln's time to create differences where none exist, or to cover up the real differences which honest reason and discussion would expose."

That's Sen. Prescott Bush, W.'s grandfather, from a 1955 Lincoln Day speech. Bush was a partisan of Dwight Eisenhower's "Modern Republicanism," which involved, as historian Leonard Schlup has written, "absorbing Democratic programs while cutting the costs." It was an approach that "permitted Republicans to incorporate Democratic issues." Sound familiar?

Like the grandson, the grandfather sought a catch phrase. Prescott Bush drew his from Eisenhower. "It is a philosophy of progressive moderation, as the president has called it, or of moderate progressivism, as others name it," he said.

It is a sign of the great change in the Republican Party that in 44 years and two generations, progressive moderation has transmogrified into compassionate conservatism. Yet the grandson's purpose doesn't differ much from the grandfather's. Both have sought a formula for Republican success. Both have sought to strike, as Prescott Bush put it in his Lincoln Day speech, "a responsive chord in the minds and aspirations of the American people."

Which still leaves the question: Is Bush about political philosophy or political positioning? Pragmatism with a purpose or electoral calculation? Does he represent good-natured compromise or is he just looking for action?

Even Rove's McKinley parallel is ambiguous. It's true that McKinley launched a Republican era. Republicans won seven of the nine presidential elections from 1896 to 1928. But McKinley was assassinated in 1901 and Theodore Roosevelt took over. He launched the first great progressive era, which lasted nearly 20 years, through the end of Woodrow Wilson's Democratic administration. If Rove's Great Transition Election theory about 2000 is true, it's not clear what we're transitioning to.

If there is a safe bet, it is that W. is instinctively more conservative than he looks, and very conservative where the interests of business are concerned. Those big campaign contributors, a sophisticated lot, know what they're doing.

But on so many other issues, Bush is cultivating what you might see as a brilliant ambiguity. Take affirmative action.

On June 30, the *New York Times* ran the headline "California, Here Bush Comes, a Moderate on Immigration and Racial Quotas." On the same day, the headline in the *Washington Times* read: "Bush favors ending quotas."

What Bush actually said is this: "I support the spirit of no quotas, no preferences. But I think what's important to say is not what you're against—[but] what you're for. I'm for increasing the pool of applicants and opening the door so that more people are eligible to go to the university systems."

As John J. Miller, a *National Review* writer who called attention to the dueling headlines, wrote, "Until Bush states clearly where he stands on race and sex preferences, headline writers won't be the only people who are confused."

Or take abortion. Bush's record tilts strongly against it. The National Abortion and Reproductive Rights Action League lists 18 provisions in bills Bush signed that it sees as threatening to abortion rights or birth control. Bush says he supports a constitutional amendment to ban abortion. But he also says there is no chance such an amendment could pass.

He has refused, to the consternation of social conservatives, to say he would appoint antiabortion judges. He says he opposes "litmus tests," a term that offends abortion foes because it was invented by their opponents. Yet he has said that his favorite Supreme Court justice is Antonin Scalia, perhaps the most ardent critic of *Roe* v. *Wade* on the court. On this issue, Bush is madly sending signals to everybody.

The most interesting thing of all is that the Bush of many ambiguities, of deal-making and compromising, insists that he really wants to be the Bush of ideas.

Ask him about his family's tradition of public service, and rather than embracing his father, he puts some subtle distance between himself and the former president whom the right wing of his party so mistrusted.

"Obviously it's a proud tradition," he says. Yet, referring to himself and his brother Florida Gov. Jeb Bush, he adds, "I believe we have that sense of service, but I believe that we're both driven as well by ideas and philosophy. That we have come to realize, particularly in our respective roles as governors, how powerful an idea can be. And that it's important to serve but it's also important to achieve results. To set goals, clear and measurable goals, and to lead."

But where? Bush could prove to be the man who brought his party back to a modulated view of government that his grandfather would understand. Or he could parade into office under the banner of compassion and turn out to be one of the most conservative presidents in recent history. The maddening thing for voters may be this: He has absolutely no interest in resolving this mystery until after the votes are counted on Election Day 2000.

Chapter 9 Review Questions

1. How has the literature on gubernatorial power evolved over time? What powers did Schlesinger identify as being important? How have later scholars built on his work?
2. What is Crew's model for explaining gubernatorial success? What does his diagram look like? What different factors does he say are important in shaping a governor's performance?
3. What does Crew mean when he writes that "the understanding of gubernatorial behavior will be improved by the integration of several perspectives and that the conclusions drawn from such analyses will be made more meaningful if they are based on systematic and empirical time series data"? How might this be accomplished?
4. What was George W. Bush like as governor of Texas? What factors does Dionne say were important in shaping his success?
5. How applicable are these ideas about gubernatorial performance in explaining presidential leadership? Looking at Bush's presidency, what factors would you say best explain his success or failures? Are these factors captured in Crew's model?
6. How successful is the governor of your state? What factors do you think have made the governor successful? What has constrained his or her success?

Key Terms

formal powers
item veto
general veto
informal powers
budget authority
administrative control
patronage
legislative agenda
divided government
professional legislature
personality
cognitive style
gubernatorial motivation
character
political skill
political resources
context
political time
strategy
compassionate conservatism
Moderate Republicanism

Suggestions for Further Reading

Bernick, E. Lee, "Gubernatorial Tools: Formal vs. Informal." *Journal of Politics* 47 (1979): 656–664. Valuable early study comparing the impact of formal and informal tools on gubernatorial success.

Beyle, Thad. "Enhancing Executive Leadership in the States." *State and Local Government Review* 27 (Winter 1995): 18–35. This empirical study examines the impact of formal and informal powers on gubernatorial performance, and provides a brief history of how the governor's power has changed over time.

———. "The Governors." In Virginia Gray and Russell L. Hanson, eds., *Politics in the American States: A Comparative Analysis.* 8th ed. Washington, D.C.: CQ Press, 2004, pp. 194–231. Succinct overview on the state of gubernatorial politics. Includes up-to-date tables of the governors' powers.

Cannon, Lou. *Governor Reagan: His Rise to Power.* New York: Public Affairs, 2003. Highly praised history of Ronald Reagan's tenure as California governor.

Dometrius, Nelson. "Measuring Gubernatorial Power." *Journal of Politics* 41 (1979): 589–610. Early effort to assess and revise Schlesinger's index of power. Professor Dometrius has written several influential articles analyzing the governors' formal and informal powers. Another much-cited essay is "Changing Gubernatorial Power: The Measure vs. Reality," *Western Political Quarterly* 40 (1987): 319–333. In this essay, Dometrius argues that Schlesinger's index does a poor job in capturing the formal powers of governors.

Ferguson, Margaret Robertson. "Chief Executive Success in the Legislative Arena." *State Politics and Policy Quarterly* 3 (2003): 158–182. Sophisticated quantitative analysis on the forces that shape gubernatorial success.

Hamilton, Gary C., and Nicole Woolsey Biggart. *Governor Reagan, Governor Brown: A Sociology of Executive Power.* New York: Columbia University Press, 1984. Fascinating study by two sociologists comparing the leadership styles and effectiveness of two California governors.

Marshall, Drenda DeVore, and Molly A. Mayhead, eds. *Navigating Boundaries: The Rhetoric of Women Governors.* Westport, Conn.: Praeger, 2000. An interesting collection of essays on the leadership of the sixteen women to serve as governors.

Minutaglio, Bill. *First Son: George W. Bush and the Bush Family Dynasty.* New York: Three Rivers Press, 2001. Written by a respected reporter for the *Dallas Morning News,* this is considered one of the best books available on Bush's life before he was elected president.

Morehouse, Sarah McCally. *The Governor as Party Leader: Campaigning for Governor.* Ann Arbor: University of Michigan Press, 1998. This book examines the impact of party politics in state elections on the governor's influence over legislative action.

Rosenthal, Alan. *Governors and Legislatures: Contending Powers.* Washington, D.C.: CQ Press, 1990. Excellent overview of the battle between governors and legislatures in shaping the direction of state politics.

Sabato, Larry. *Good-bye to Good-Time Charlie.* 2d ed. Washington, D.C.: CQ Press, 1983. This is the best single book describing the changes that have created the modern governorship.

Schlesinger, Joseph A. "The Politics of the Executive." In Herbert Jacob and Kenneth N. Vines, eds. *Politics in the American States: A Comparative Analysis.* Boston: Little, Brown and Company, 1965, pp. 207–237. This is the seminal work that has shaped comparative state studies on gubernatorial power and success.

Van Assendelft, Laura A. *Governors, Agenda Setting, and Divided Government.* Lanham, Md.: University Press of America, 1997. Valuable study on how divided government affects governors' political strategies and their influence over legislative action.

Related Web Sites

http://www.nga.org
The web site for the National Governors Association includes links and information on the governors and their staff in all fifty states. The site also includes historical, legal, and background information on important public policy issues.

http://texaspolitics.laits.utexas.edu/index.html
This on-line book provides a broad overview of Texas government and politics.

10

State and Local Bureaucracies: The Concept of Privatization

To the extent that the goal is to make government more cost-effective, a proper use of contracts does have much promise. But it must be a use based on an understanding of the limits of contracting and the value of creating good public organizations. More narrowly, the question is one of how we are to make decisions about the relative costs and benefits of contracts and enhancements of direct service provisions.

Elliott D. Sclar

READING 10

Introduction

State and local governments provide a wide array of services that touch our lives every day. Among other activities, these governments run our public schools, community colleges, and universities. They build and maintain roads, issue drivers licenses, regulate automobiles, and manage public transportation. They provide police and fire protection, health care, welfare, consumer protection, and recreational opportunities. They provide for our water supply, trash collection, and utilities. They also oversee hospitals, public housing, parks, ports, libraries, and prisons.

Given the pressure from the public to keep taxes low, and their own concern about doing a good job, state and local officials are routinely forced to consider how to provide these services in a manner that is as efficient and effective as possible. Over time, there have been important changes in attitudes among political leaders and scholars as to the best way to provide services. Historically, responsibilities for handling public services were given to state and local bureaucracies. In other words, the state and local governments provided these services directly, relying on public employees to handle the job. When government officials decided that a government bureaucracy was performing poorly, the primary solution for improving performance was to reorganize the bureaucracy. In particular, political reform proposals often sought to streamline bureaucracies, reducing the number of departments, consolidating programs, and centralizing control. Since the 1920s, this type of structural reorganization has been a mainstay of bureaucratic reform efforts at the state and local level.

During the past few decades, however, many reformers have argued that the problems that bureaucracies face cannot be solved simply by restructuring, as had been done in the past, but requires more wholesale change. One of the alternatives that is frequently put forward to improve government services is to *privatize* them. Privatization involves the transfer of governmental responsibilities and assets to the private sector. Privatization advocates argue that by relying on private companies to handle traditional bureaucratic activities, many of the benefits of the free market system could be brought into the government's operation, including increased efficiency and lower costs. Privatization is touted as a valuable way to improve service delivery by introducing competition among service providers.

How does privatization work? The most common method that state and local governments use to involve the private sector in handling governmental responsibilities is through *contracting out* services. Contracting out involves hiring private companies and nonprofit organizations to handle public services. For example, a city may decide to hire a waste disposal company to handle trash collection rather than creating a government agency to provide the service directly. Similarly, a state may decide to house some state prisoners in privately run prisons rather than relying entirely on prisons directly operated by the state.

Another well-known method used to privatize government is the use of vouchers. In voucher programs, the government distributes vouchers to individuals who need some type of government service. The individuals can then use the vouchers to buy that service from the private sector. Vouchers have generated considerable attention in recent years as a way to improve the nation's education system by allowing students to choose the schools they want to attend, including private ones. The vouchers are used to pay the schools to cover each student's education. Advocates of *school choice* argue that vouchers will improve education by encouraging competition among schools as the schools try to attract more students. Vouchers are also advocated as a better way to provide housing to the poor than through traditional housing projects, allowing the poor to have greater choice in where they live.

Privatization remains popular among many reformers today, especially the use of contracting. In recent years, state governments have been turning over a wide variety of responsibilities to private companies, including transportation programs and road maintenance, building supervision, social services, prison management, and job training programs. Similarly, many cities and other local governments have been hiring private companies to handle such diverse tasks as waste management, food services, janitorial work, bill collection, and street repair. There has been some use of vouchers, although this practice is less common.

Not everyone supports privatization, however. Opponents argue that private business can be just as inefficient in handling many responsibilities as government bureaucracies. Moreover, many critics argue that it is inappropriate to turn some government functions over to private companies, even if such a transfer would reduce costs. These opponents argue that governments should not be held to the same standards as private businesses because governments need to be concerned about factors beyond just how to deliver services at the lowest costs. Unlike private businesses, governments need to be concerned with treating recipients equally and fairly, allowing citizens to be involved in service decisions, and protecting individual rights.

Perhaps the most prominent battles over privatization have revolved around public schools and prisons. Two of the most established school voucher programs are in Milwaukee, Wisconsin, and Cleveland, Ohio. The Wisconsin schools began to introduce vouchers in the 1990–1991 school year. Cleveland began in 1996–1997. Opponents of vouchers argue that these types of programs have the potential to drain money away from public schools, thus harming those who remain behind. They also argue that vouchers may lead to a balkanization of America as different groups leave the diversity of public schools and move their children into more homogeneous private ones. Supporters point to the program in Milwaukee, in particular, as evidence that school choice can improve student performance without the negative impacts predicted by opponents.

The debate over privatizing prisons is split between those who argue that privatization will lower costs and reduce overcrowding of inmates versus those who reject those claims and present a litany of criticisms of privatization. Among other concerns, opponents argue that private prisons often have inadequate facilities and poorly trained staffs. Many point at the track record of the Corrections Corporation of America (CCA), the nation's largest operator of private prisons, as an example of the problems that can occur. In 1996, two sex offenders escaped from a CCA-operated minimum security prison in Houston, Texas. Two years later, four convicted murderers and two other prisoners escaped from a CCA-operated prison in Youngstown, Ohio. The Youngstown prison also saw thirteen stabbings and two murders during that period. Opponents also fear that privatization has produced a private-prison industry that lobbies for tougher sentencing rules in order to create jobs, not to address criminal justice problems.

In the essay that follows, Elliott Sclar offers a brief history of privatization in America and then provides an economics-based analysis of the problems that often confront the contracting of services. As Sclar makes clear early in the essay, there is more to the debate over privatization than simply finding the most efficient and effective way to provide government services. Rather, privatization is seen by many conservatives as an important step toward reducing the size of government. It is part of an ideological debate in the nation as to the proper size and role of government in society.

The major criticism that Sclar has against the contracting of services is that the economic model frequently used to support it often does not capture the economic realities that confront public agencies and private service providers. Whereas privatization advocates see contracting as a way to introduce competition into the delivery of services, Sclar argues that the private providers of government services often lack competitors themselves. He writes that "the automatic case for the *intrinsic* political and economic superiority of privatization" cannot be sustained. Ultimately, Sclar argues that governments must make economic calculations in deciding whether to contract out for services rather than providing them directly themselves. However, he makes it clear that the calculations are not as simple as just comparing an agency's direct production costs with the cost of purchasing a standard service from a private provider. Rather, the decision requires a more complex calculation, one that recognizes that there are a variety of hidden costs involved when contracting for a specialized service over an extended period of time.

Sclar's essay provides valuable food for thought because it encourages approaching privatization from a rational perspective, rather than just viewing it from an ideological perspective as either a panacea or an inherent evil. Sclar is a professor of Urban Planning and Public Affairs at Columbia University and a leading expert on local economic development planning. The excerpt was taken from Sclar's *You Don't Always Get What You Pay For,* which received the Louis Brownlow Book Award from the National Academy of Public Administration.

Questions to Consider

As you read Sclar's essay, these are some questions to consider:

- According to Sclar, how have attitudes toward government's role in society changed over time? What forces caused attitudes to change? How do current political attitudes affect support for privatization?
- What is the standard market model? What factors does it take into consideration when assessing the value of privatization? Why is Sclar critical of this model?
- What economic factors does Sclar say should be taken into consideration when deciding whether to privatize public services or rely on public agencies?

The Urge to Privatize: From the Bureaucratic State to the Contract State

Elliott D. Sclar

The dawning of the twentieth century brought a widespread belief in the power of government to serve as an agent of positive social change. Through the application of rational analysis to social problems, it was believed that plans and programs would be developed that could overcome those problems. This notion of rational public action taken in the name of the people (progressivism) evolved in response to social dislocation, overcrowding, environmental pollution, and wrenching poverty, which were byproducts of the new era of urbanization and industrialization brought on by the prior century. The laissez-faire capitalism that transformed society and created unprecedented levels of wealth also produced severe destabilization. Not only was a belief in public intervention *widely* held, it was *deeply* held, too. It was embedded in ideologies throughout the political spectrum. State power was the only countervailing force capable of checking the antisocial excesses of the emergent class of economic oligarchs or "robber barons" spawned by the new industrialization. Hierarchically organized and professionally trained bureaucrats would exercise this state power. It was believed that such a system of public service was capable of imposing necessary order and stability where markets left only disorder and instability.

For a good part of the twentieth century, the only real debate among reformers concerned how much intervention would be sufficient. In the extreme, it was believed the state itself should run the entire economy in the name of "the people"—socialism. For socialist advocates, this through-going reform was the only way to permanently end the social problems caused by capitalism. For more moderate reformers, the "third way" involved some variant of the social democratic welfare state that came to characterize all the world's industrialized nations for much of the century. It is noteworthy that no less an admirer of the virtues of unbridled capitalism than the brilliant Joseph Schumpeter, standing at almost the midpoint of the century, observed that it was only a matter of time before capitalism succumbed completely to socialism.

> Can capitalism survive? No. I do not think it can. But this opinion of mine, like that of every other economist who has pronounced upon the subject, is in itself completely uninteresting. What counts in any attempt at social prognosis is not the Yes or No that sums up the facts and arguments which lead up to it but those facts and arguments themselves. (Schumpeter 1947, 61)

The essence of his argument was that capitalism was a wonderful system for generating wealth and encouraging creativity. However, it was not capable of equitably distributing the fruits of its effort. Accordingly, even though capitalism had solved society's production problem, socialism, although it would never produce great art or music, would come to dominate the world because it was better prepared to tackle the distribution problem. The widespread belief in either the inevitability of socialism or the continuation of some form of welfare state capitalism persisted halfway into the final quarter of the twentieth century.

But then things quickly changed. By the beginning of the 1980s, political and economic cracks in the foundations of the structures of Eastern European socialism became gaping holes. By decade end, the entire structure imploded. Simply put, although production and distribution are distinctive economic acts, they are not unconnected. In the aftermath of this seismic shift, governments everywhere, even democratic ones, were no longer viewed as the logical solution for the world's social problems. Indeed, they were increasingly viewed as an important source of these problems. As a new century begins, the alternative to government direction and the employment of public bureaucracy to carry out its commands is a fresh belief in the social beneficence and effectiveness of the marketplace.

While in the extreme, the differences in the stylized political conventional wisdom at the beginning and end of the century appear as distinct polar opposites; the distance that actual policy debates can traverse almost invariably falls short of these ends. The activist and expansionist consensus about government that dominated American politics for much of the century, compared with the contemporary debate, merely allowed for more regulation and intervention in what has always been a predominately market-oriented society. Contemporary debate, although marked by far fewer politically viable options for active government but many more for market-sustaining programs, is far more nuanced in reality. Indeed, disgruntled conservatives mutter that in the two decades or so since they ascended to real political power with the election of Ronald Reagan as president, regulation of society has increased not decreased. Evidence exists in every area of social life, from the environment to the right to bear arms. It does not appear to matter whether the conservatives politically control the White House and/or Congress. At the same time, liberals are forced to confront the reality that there is no effective political interest in the types of large-scale interventions, such as urban renewal and public housing, that marked the middle decades of the century. On balance, it is fair to say that while the range of policy choices has shifted more in the direction of nonintervention, it has not been and is not a straightforward move. The notion that government is still the proper bulwark to contain social distress abides. People merely expect government to do more with less. Now the public believes that markets can shoulder far more of the burden than they have been permitted to do in the past.

Consistent with this newfound belief in the efficacy of the market, the question of how government should organize to provide public service is prominent on the policy agenda. In the U.S. political context, this question is characterized as "privatization." The term, as used here, describes initiatives to introduce market relationships into the bureaucratic production of public services. The intention is to force public bureaucracies to be governed by the same competitive forces that make private markets socially beneficial. Conversely, it is important to remember that the welfare state, which evolved under progressive and New Deal political philosophies earlier in the century, assumed that government programs must be staffed by government employees. Consequently, every expansion in state activism was matched by expansion in the public payroll. This was especially the case among the professionals who were needed to deliver the more complex services created by social policies intended to invest in society's human capital, particularly its poorest members. Thus, not only did the public sector require professional police officers, fire fighters, corrections officers, and school teachers, but it also began to need social workers, an expanded public university professorate, doctors, nurses, lawyers, and accountants, among many others. All these professions began to have sizable numbers of members who earned their livelihoods as public servants.

Because the services provided by these workers remain valuable, their continued public employment seriously impedes the larger laissez-faire goal of shrinking both the size and role of the state in society. Advocates for smaller government have been more successful in convincing the citizenry that the *size* of the public sector could be diminished than they have been in convincing them that its *responsibilities* also could be reduced. Privatization, in the form of public contracting with private parties to deliver public services, has much to offer in this regard. If the size of the public workforce could be diminished, then the second half of the chore, namely, gathering popular support for a diminished level of public responsibility, would be easier to achieve in the future.

The case for privatization is built on the assertion that contractual relationships will give the public sector all the advantages of the market without undermining the level of public service. If laissez-faire advocates could demonstrate that private sector employees working under contract and disciplined by market imperatives provide comparable or better service at equal or lower cost, at least a first step could be taken to diminish government activism. In contrast, if the case is not as open and shut as hoped by these proponents, then the role of government in the life of society will not be reversed easily. Consequently, the political debate about privatization is significantly more than a discussion of pragmatic issues in public service management. Although that element does exist and is important—indeed it is the principal focus of this book—it is not the driving force in this debate. Ideology that places market concerns ahead of those of equity and access animates the larger political discourse in which privatization is advocated.

To the extent that shrinkage of government itself is the ultimate goal of a number of the proponents of privatization, I believe they will be disappointed in their quest. By now the notion that government is central to the life of society is deeply rooted and will only expand with the scope of the global marketplace. To the extent that the goal is to make government more cost-effective, a proper use of contracts does have much promise. But it must be a use based on an understanding of the limits of contracting and the value of creating good public organizations. More narrowly, the question is one of how we are to make decisions about the relative costs and benefits of contracts and enhancement of direct service provision. If we fail to address this admittedly less ideological but more practical question, then we run the risk of moving further into an arena of ambiguous contractual arrangements that will be neither discernibly better nor worse than present ones.

To say that not much will change one way or the other does not mean that we won't pay a price. We risk losing a valuable opportunity to meaningfully improve public service. The debate initiated by the change in attitudes toward government presents us with a rare chance to move the issue of improving the efficiency and effectiveness of public service provision from the policy back burner to the front. Indeed, with changes in communications and information technologies we have many more ways to solve public management problems and enhance public services. When I worked for the federal government, we obtained our office supplies from a central government store. One of our employees had to go "shop" and bring back supplies. In an age when large private firms such as Staples and Office Max can ship overnight at low prices, the rationale for using a public agency to store and track a large inventory is difficult to sustain. It is equally difficult to justify using valuable employee time to physically shop for needed items. On the other hand, there are many public functions that are similar to private functions, which are still better done directly. But, how do we know which to contract out and which to retain?

In the following chapters, it is my intention to outline the concerns that must be part of any policy decision to reorganize public service. In too much of the present debate there is an implicit assumption that contracting is identical to organizational reform. Privatization is often presented to public workers with a "shape up or ship out" set of choices. Officials in essence say to their employees, "You figure out how to meet the price of an outside competitor or give up your job." But, as every good manager knows, organizational change is neither a bottom-up nor an easily mandated initiative. By the same token, every good manager also knows that contracting is not an automatic blessing. It takes much hard work and planning to avoid the serious problems and expenses inherent in the misuse of this option. Contrary to near conventional folk wisdom that privatization almost invariably represents improvement, this is simply not true. If we want our public services to really improve, then it is important to combine the judicious use of contracting with a strategy of internal agency reform.

I propose to scrutinize the economic reasons why privatization as a reform strategy in the form of public contracting often bogs down. By understanding the problems, it is possible to construct solutions. . . . My goal is to present readers with a better understanding of the approaches that we might take to balance the use of contracting and internal reform to enhance the operation of public agencies. No one can predict when or how the political pendulum may shift in the future. Regardless of when or how, it is important to the survival of the values of a humane and progressive democracy that public services be as efficient, responsive, and democratically administered as possible.

Since the early 1980s, with the backing of newly empowered conservative political leaders, many ambitious attempts have been made to transform public service from direct to contract provision. Results have fallen far short of promises. However, they have not been the abject failure predicted by opponents. This outcome should not have been surprising. Privatization American style is essentially old-fashioned public contracting writ very large. Privatization inherits and aggravates difficulties already present with this genre of public management. Similarly, it also extends the advantages. Despite approximately twenty years of agitation for more contracting, the proportion of public money spent via contracting is about the same as it has always been—one-half. The underlying problem is the sometimes useful but always limited way that contracting achieves public policy goals. The reasons for this are similar to the reasons why private organizations find outsourcing useful but limited.

The Standard Market Model

To begin to understand the strengths and weaknesses of public service privatization, it is necessary to understand the theory behind the policy. The competitive contract market generally envisioned by privatization advocates is derived from modification of the standard market model, the core element in neoclassical economic theory. A quick review of its essential components is the proper starting point for evaluating the role of privatization as a method of providing public service.

The standard market model envisions a world of markets, each of which is composed of a large number of unrelated buyers and sellers. Each is assumed to be pursuing his or her own gain independent of the others. All are sufficiently small relative to the size of the market to ensure that any individual actions have little or no appreciable impact on the price, quantity, or quality of the product, which are shaped by the aggregation of individual decisions made by the larger market. From the perspective of individual buyers or sellers, these market conditions are viewed as uncontrollable givens on which they base individual decisions to buy, sell, or leave the market. There are no appreciable impediments to the entrance or exit of any buyer or seller from the market in question. Hence, no concentration of market power can accrue because of such barriers. All buyers and sellers are assumed to share equally all relevant knowledge (or ignorance) about the key factors determining product quality and prices in the market. Thus, the aggregate key market characteristics of price, quantity, and quality change only through the concerted action of the equally informed participants. The quality of goods traded in such a market is assumed to be sufficiently uniform and known so that buyers need merely to seek out the lowest priced seller.

On the production side, the pressures of many sellers vying for the dollars of the most buyers leads sellers to discipline their production methods to keep costs as low as possible. Sellers seek to keep their individual production costs low to achieve maximum gain, regardless of the ups and downs of market price. It is assumed that every producer is aware of and has access to all the technical possibilities for producing the goods in question and that each chooses the least costly means to do so.

If all these conditions hold, the market is said to be competitive. A competitive market is similar in many respects to an election: no single vote carries the day, but the collective weight of all votes is decisive. From a social standpoint, the collective interests of buyers and sellers generate countervailing pressures that ensure the sale of products that consumers wish to buy. Prices are determined, not by any coercive power on the part of an individual or small group, but by underlying production costs. Production costs, in turn, reflect the most technically efficient production methods.

It is but a small conceptual step to move from this model of a single competitive market that gives customers what they want at prices that cover legitimate costs to an economy that is an infinite aggregate of such markets. It is a world in which knowledge, technology, product, prices, and costs are all givens. Hence, the profit-maximizing position for each producer and the satisfaction-maximizing position for each consumer become highly predictable. The complexities, uncertainties, and ambiguities of imperfect information, inadequate distribution of existing information, barriers to market entry, and product differentiation are all assumed to be either nonexistent or trivial. In such a world, economic decision-making essentially reduces to a technical matter—a mere mathematical algorithm.

Textbooks of economic theory usually present this standard model, with more or less mathematical sophistication depending on their intended audience, as the starting point for the rest of their analysis. If the conditions for such a competitive market economy hold, then society can attain a state of being in which all individuals are as well off as they can be, given their initial endowment of wealth (i.e., labor skills, capital, raw materials). The standard market model makes no judgments about the quality of initial endowments. The model merely demonstrates that, given each individual's initial wealth, the state of technology, and the state of market prices, the optimal amount of output will be created at the lowest possible cost. At that point, no rearrangement of production or markets can make any individual better off unless another becomes worse off. Labeled a "Pareto optimum," after the early twentieth-century economist Vilfredo Pareto, who first articulated the notion, the idea is quite powerful. Following the teachings of Adam Smith, it implies that not only will a competitive market society enhance material wealth, but that as each individual acts in pursuit of his or her own gain, everyone is in fact helping to create the optimal possible amount of material satisfaction for everyone else in society. The individual optima are, of course, constrained by the initial distribution of wealth. Any change in the distribution of wealth would lead to a recalculation of the optimal result.

Since the standard market model makes no judgments about the fairness of any wealth distribution, it has nothing to say about the fairness of any Pareto optimal outcome. It merely asserts that, given the initial wealth distribution, a society of competitive markets ensures the best possible deal for everyone given their resources. As the Nobel prize winning economist Amartya Sen has succinctly put it, "A society or an economy can be Pareto optimal and still be perfectly disgusting" (Sen 1970, 22). Any policy change that induces a redistribution of wealth is a question of values and not efficiency, according to the model's designers, who have never claimed any special expertise on such matters.

The extent to which one views the standard market model as a more or less complete description of an actual market-oriented economy typically correlates with the strength of one's belief that privatization is more efficient than direct public service provision. The critical issues here pertain to the accuracy of assumptions about the ease of seller access to the contract market and the ready and inexpensive availability of relevant contract information. The first assumption speaks directly to the existence of sustainable competition, and the second pertains to the ability to obtain low cost and effective contract enforcement. To the extent that these conditions hold, contracting in a market-oriented society can typically be expected to be more efficient and effective than the work done by public employees.

However, the extent to which one questions the validity of the presumption that market entry barriers are sufficiently low that many *qualified* sellers will appear and the extent to which one believes that public officials have relevant market information correlate strongly and directly with the strength of individual skepticism about the relative efficiency of public contracting. The higher the barriers to market entry for additional sellers and the greater the lack of inexpensive access to good information on the part of public purchasers, the less likely it is that contracting will provide meaningful improvement. In this case, the notion that privatization is a quick and easy way to overcome bureaucratic inefficiency and move us closer to a state of Pareto optimality is seriously compromised.

Competition and Privatization

The standard market model grossly oversimplifies many important connected issues of economic and political power. This is of special concern when the focus of our analysis is a process of public contracting. There are numerous ways in which arm's-length relationships between government buyers and outside contractors may be breached. Unlike the standard market model, the real economy is not a flat playing field on which a host of atomistic and more or less equally endowed economic agents perpetually compete with one another in pursuit of wealth. The economic playing field is more realistically conceived as mountainous terrain that includes several high peaks from which well-endowed corporate and individual warriors swoop down to seize targets of opportunity. Among these high peaks are some flat areas where market battles akin to the competitive ones described by the standard market model do occur. But the players are not always as equal as the model assumes, and these comparatively level plateaus are seldom where the real economic action takes place.

Because privatization policy emphasizes these small, flat interstices and neglects the dominant peaks, it does not concern itself with the existence and persistence of powerful economic and political concentrations, nor is it able to explain why they would disappear if government increased its use of contracting. By sidestepping the issue of how concentrated economic power arises and sustains itself in the actual operation of contract markets, privatization advocacy often amounts to little more than an endorsement of changing rather than correcting the problems we face with public agency performance.

Atomistic competition almost invariably gives way to concentrated economic power because the competitive market is not a desirable or sustainable long-term condition for sellers. Sellers seek to end this distasteful condition as quickly as possible. Why eke out a marginal profit while battling an unending string of challengers in a style akin to a "good guy" against a host of "bad guys" in a martial-arts movie? To counteract this, sellers continually attempt to attain a strategic high ground from which to drive away their competitors. Although it is possible to conceive of economic situations in which all contractors survive endless rounds of competition, that is not the typical state of the contract market in either the public or the private sector. The more typical situation is one in which success is achieved by driving rivals out of the market or absorbing them through mergers and acquisitions. Sellers try to undermine competition because monopolistic situations are significantly more profitable. In competitive situations, sellers slug it out with each other for slim to nonexistent profit margins. Diminished competition increases profits for the remaining firms. The greater the market power achieved by a seller, the more easily he or she can maintain market prices significantly above production costs. It is also important to remember that in the real world, unlike the standard market model, all competitors do not start from a more or less equal position. Consequently, the probability that any particular market will either sustain competition or trend toward it, as the standard market model assumes, is unlikely.

In general, the tendency for erosion of competition in individual contract markets is exacerbated in the public realm because economics and politics are not separate spheres. Instead, there is a strong tendency for the imbalance between the public and those who stand to gain from anticompetitive behavior to increase because the winners use their advantage to exert political leverage. Although, collectively, taxpayers stand to gain the most through sustained market competition, they have less individual incentive to politically defend competitive public contracting than sellers have to undermine it. Thus, even though competitive contracting seemingly promises more choice and better prices, the potential benefit for individual taxpayers is often insufficient for them to justify the investment of time and money to enforce sustained competition. Contractors, on the other hand, typically stand to reap a great deal individually by ensuring that the public market structures work to their advantage. Therefore, they are willing to invest the necessary resources to shape public markets in anticompetitive ways.

Replacing the assumption that markets are level playing fields with a more realistic and complex political and economic topography yields a clearer view of the possibilities and limitations of privatization. Clarity comes at the price of certainty, however. Although one can find instances in which particular markets bear some resemblance to the standard market model, more often than not they are exceptions to the rules of engagement used by public buyers and private sellers.

The Economic Ideology of Privatization

Depending on where one looks, virtually every public service is now considered a candidate for privatization, including public schools, public hospitals, social services, penal institutions, police and fire departments, and transit systems. All these initiatives are proposed or implemented in the name of managerial efficiency and effectiveness. The most vehement advocates of privatization believe that government should, indeed could, be all but put out of business. In 1991, when Stephen Goldsmith first ran for the office of mayor of Indianapolis, he asserted that he could run the entire city with just four contract managers (Fantauzzo n.d., 2). His bold assertion was the practical elaboration of an idea popularized eleven years earlier by Robert Poole, architect of the libertarian Reason Foundation, which has been perhaps the staunchest proponent of privatization in the United States. In his 1980 book, *Cutting Back City Hall,* Poole envisioned a city run entirely via contractual arrangements between a small government and a host of private providers.

The case for privatization made by Poole and others (Savas 1987; Osborne and Gaebler 1992) always rests on an appeal to a theory of competitive contractual behavior derived from the standard market model. The notion rests on an assumption that contracting takes place in a competitive market environment. Based on that assumption, it is possible to construct a rationale that endows the cause of privatization with a strong political and economic legitimacy in the context of U.S. values. Politically, the existence of competition assumes an environment in which anyone wishing to vie for the right to contract can freely enter the fray and obtain public work. Moreover, the notion implicitly assumes that the barriers to market entry are either nonexistent or so minimal that this freedom of entry is not notional but real. Hence, political legitimacy is achieved because the existence of contract competition essentially sweeps away the need to address the problem of political favoritism, which in practice often dogs public contracting.

Economically competitive contracting sets incentives in place that ensure production of the best possible product for the lowest possible price. The action of many bidders seeking to win the government's business leads each of them to try and deliver the product most desired by the government at the lowest price consistent with costs. To do otherwise could risk loss of the business to a lower priced competitor.

However, privatization and competition are not as inevitably linked as are love and marriage in the 1950s song "Love and Marriage": you *can* have one without the other. Only in a highly constrained set of conditions is it possible to sustain competitive contracting. When competitive contracting cannot be sustained, neither can the automatic case for the *intrinsic* political and economic superiority of privatization compared with direct government service provision. A case may still be made for private contracting, but it is a very different case. It must be sustained on the basis of unique situational factors, not because competition ensures that there are incentives to make it the best possible outcome (Sappington and Stiglitz 1987).

Because of the strong intuitive appeal of the simple competitive market model as adapted to the case for privatization, many of the richest insights of modern economic and organizational theory regarding the relationship between organizational performance and contracting have been notably absent from the privatization debate to date. Most of the resultant claims for the superiority of private contracting borrow little from modern social science literature beyond the crude notion that competition is preferable to monopoly. This truism is then generalized into an abstract theory of organizational behavior in which contracting is either typically competitive or easily made competitive and, therefore, intrinsically efficient. By inference, anything else is just monopoly and inefficiency by another name. To the extent that the case for the ease of competitive contracting can be sustained, it is then possible to pursue privatization as a matter of general public policy. Situations of direct service provision can then be reduced to the status of anomalies. However, if the case cannot be sustained, then each proposed privatization must be examined on its individual merits. The conservative desire to diminish the role of government in society via the easy adoption of a policy of widespread privatization becomes a far more elusive goal.

Experience demonstrates that not only is sustaining competitive contracting for complex services difficult, but other factors also prove to be far more crucial for the ultimate success or failure of the venture. Contracting for services, regardless of whether a public agency or private firm undertakes the task, involves elaborate and generally difficult to anticipate relationships between purchasers and vendors. Much hinges on the institutional and historic context that defines the parameters of relationship between the organizations bound together by contract. Absent a broader analysis of these contextual complexities, the privatization policy debate largely has been little more than dueling anecdotes. Those favoring privatization tell their favorite stories, and those opposed peddle theirs. Like the blind men who each touch a single part of an elephant and self-assuredly contradict each other, they extrapolate their narrow experiential evidence into general descriptions of entirely different creatures.

If we are truly concerned about the long-term efficiency and effectiveness of the public sector, then we need to move the analysis beyond anecdotal assertions. Regardless of number, they do not make a case one way or the other. They become useful only when integrated into a comprehensive conceptual frame of reference that enables analysis of the potentials and limits of contracting for fulfilling the mission of the public sector. To the extent that this frame of reference diminishes the superficial generality of the appeal of privatization as a management strategy, it serves two beneficial social purposes: we can bring more powerful management tools to bear on the challenge of (1) efficient and (2) effective public agency operation.

The Limited Condition of Contractual Competition

Unlike hiring a contractor once every few years to paint the family house over a few days, privatization usually requires establishing a long-term relationship between a government agency and an outside service provider. Because of the complex nature of most public services, privatization contracts are typically written for multiyear periods. Therefore, they foreclose easy competitive access to alternative providers if the product is not up to par. As a result, the characteristics of the contractor–agency relationship principally determine service quality and cost savings, not the competitive marketplace. The longer the term of the contract and the more complex the service provided, the smaller the role played by market competition in the costs and benefits of privatization.

If, for example, a local government must decide whether to replace its own management of a wastewater treatment plant with an outside operator, three factors structure the outcome. The first factor is the nature of the contracting process used to choose the manager. If there are many potential providers operating in an environment of no collusion, hard bargaining for any work, and an agency knowledgeable about all that the work entails, it is possible to envision structuring a management contract highly favorable for the agency. When there is only a handful of professionally interconnected providers with the relevant expertise and the agency is disadvantaged by a lack of relevant internal know-how, the agreement is likely to be more advantageous for the winning provider.

Regardless of the level of competition in the contracting process, once the deal is signed, its success depends critically on the second and third factors: the technological constraints of the work itself and the interpersonal skills of the agency personnel and contractor personnel. Wastewater treatment, for instance, is inherently a monopolistic operation. Because a wastewater treatment plant represents an enormous fixed capital investment, it is most economical to construct a single plant large enough to serve an entire community. A municipality does not build lots of small plants. Since sewer hookups are fixed and rigid, even if there were lots of small plants it would be prohibitively expensive for customers to deliver their wastewater to competitive providers for small price incentives. Once an operator is in place, the learning curve is such that the transaction costs, both financial and in service quality, of frequently changing management effectively reduce outside competition to a theoretical possibility. In practical terms, it would take severe mismanagement to compel the public agency to switch operators once the contract is in place.

Finally, the ultimate success or failure of the arrangement depends in no small measure on the quality of the long-term relationship that develops between the contractor and the public agency. The noncompetitive nature of wastewater treatment means that replacement of the public plant operator with a private one effectively equals the choice of a monopolist with whom the community will coexist for the long haul. No one can foretell the future, and no contract can take every contingency into account. Thus, the dollar amount of a contractor's initial bid may matter less than the contractor's reputation for honest dealing and technical expertise. Although price competition becomes a minor factor in the wastewater treatment decision, this does not necessarily mean that the local government is making a mistake by converting from public to private operation. It does mean that the long-term decision implicit in privatization must be made on a far more complex basis than a belief in the beneficence of competitive markets. . . .

The "Make-Buy" Decision

When is it less expensive to expand the size of an organization to accomplish tasks necessary for a firm's mission? When is it more economical to purchase needed goods or services from outside vendors? Together these questions comprise the essence of what is known as the "make-buy" decision. From an organizational perspective, when are the internal bureaucratic costs that accompany larger size less than the external transaction costs of using the market?

The wrenching tragedy of the explosion and crash of a ValuJet flight in the Florida Everglades in 1996 transformed a mundane organizational make-buy determination into front-page news. In its drive to establish itself as a low-price and low-cost air carrier, ValuJet relied heavily on a strategy of outsourcing as much as possible of its operation in order to avoid high fixed overhead costs. Aircraft maintenance, an expensive part of daily operation and a task vital to the organizational mission of the airline, was outsourced. The Federal Aviation Agency (FAA) determined that the explosion of spent oxygen generators that were improperly stored in the cargo hold by the aircraft maintenance contractor, Sabretech, caused the crash. The FAA has since imposed new rules that explicitly prohibit such shipments in the future. However, even before these explicit rules were effected, the shipment of such generators, long classified as hazardous materials, in the enclosed cargo holds of aircraft was well known to be potentially dangerous. The generators are the property of the airline, not the contractor. Consequently, contractors are eager to return such hazardous materials to the rightful owner as quickly as possible, which is apparently the situation that predicated that fateful day. In the day-to-day rush of activity between ValuJet and Sabretech, the remote risk posed by the shipping decision seemed less important than other tasks. As a result, no one appeared to be in a position to clearly stop the loading of these generators into the cargo hold of the plane. Each party blamed the other for the mix-up as the heirs of the crash victims wended their way through legal proceedings to collect liability damages. In May 1998, the Federal Aviation Administration levied a record fine of $2.25 million against Sabretech. In the fall of 1999, the justice department charged Sabretech and several of its employees with criminal negligence.

It is not my wish to second-guess this tragedy, but the experience does starkly point out the full range of transaction costs that properly should be considered in the use of contracting for such a day-in and day-out type of service. The crash may have been avoided if ValuJet had invested significantly more personnel resources in supervising its maintenance contractor's activity in greater detail. Or ValuJet simply may have avoided the entire problem of such transaction costs by establishing in-house maintenance. But either decision would have been more costly and diametrically opposed to the company's business plan for maintaining low overhead in order to maintain low prices. In the aftermath of the crash, ValuJet decided to switch to in-house maintenance balanced by some outsourcing, which is more typical in the commercial airline industry. Whether this is a more fully costed decision in terms of the full risks that the company bears or merely a public relations ploy is difficult to know from the outside. The larger issue here is the range of tangible and intangible but potentially real costs involved in make-buy decisions. Different firms in the same industry may come to very different decisions depending on their business plans, market position, and resource base. Such decisions do not lend themselves to simple formulaic rule making. Privatization decisions, if driven by management concerns and not ideology, are essentially just a class of make-buy decisions. As such, they too need similar detailed analyses.

When an organization decides to buy rather than make a product, it must go shopping in either a spot market or a contract market. Spot markets are analogous to "buying off the rack," and contract markets are similar to custom tailoring. Spot markets are typically used to acquire products such as office supplies and motor vehicles, which come in sufficiently standardized forms that commercial vendors routinely maintain inventories that are virtually impossible for the firms to make for themselves. However, some long-term services that organizations can readily perform themselves also fit in this spot market category. A business may prepare its payroll internally in its own bookkeeping office or hire an outside payroll service. A periodical publisher may process its own subscriptions and mail its own journals or hire an outside fulfillment company.

When the choice is between spot purchases of standardized products or internal production, the decision rule is essentially a matter of comparative direct production cost analysis. The organization must compare its internal production costs with the cost of purchase. The transaction costs are virtually zero as a result of the standard units in which the product is traded and used. Learning the price often entails little more than two or three phone calls. Typically, goods available in spot markets are sold in competitive environments. Product quality is usually obvious to all buyers and sellers. Competition ensures that retail prices hover just above the level of wholesale prices and that average quality suits the taste of average buyers.

Such simplicity is not the rule when the make-buy decision involves contracting for ongoing specialized services. The choice of sellers is more limited, and both product quality and the relation of contract price with underlying costs are governed more vaguely by market competition. Consequently, decisions to contract out usually involve complex transaction costs related to the specification of product, the negotiation of prices, the close monitoring of quality, and the need to anticipate unforeseen contingencies. In such cases, the managerial decision process involves analyzing not only the comparative production costs typical of spot markets but also the transactions costs associated with contract design and monitoring. In such situations, obtaining all the relevant information can be difficult or require considerable time and money.

Much of the privatization debate in the political sphere ignores such costly transactional complexity. The contracting process is treated as a trivial modification in essentially a spot market. All one need do is announce the availability of the contract through a request for proposals, or RFP, specify the relevant contract contingencies and terms to all the potential bidders, and allow the bidders to set the price competitively. Typically, the lowest bid wins. When the process is that simple and straightforward, contracting for the long term is identical with spot market purchasing. But when contracts are sought for less-standardized outputs with less readily discernible quality and under conditions of greater uncertainty, a more complex managerial calculus is needed. That is typically the case with privatization.

It is also important to remember that privatization via contracting relies heavily on the belief that most contracts can be almost self-enforcing. Yet, the necessity for a written contract arises because each party of a transaction fears that the other party or parties may fail to deliver or perform. Thus, contracts contain descriptions of the future behavioral obligations of all parties to the extent that such behavior can be anticipated and the sanctions to be imposed if any party fails to hold up its end of the bargain. Such future-oriented obligations, created in an atmosphere of uncertainty, place parties in a far different relationship with each other than the cut-and-dried transactions of either the spot market or the idealized contract market cum spot market envisioned by privatization advocates. The extent of this divergence of market types is critical in determining the comparative efficiency of the privatization option.

Bibliography

Fantauzzo, Stephen, N.d. "Competitive Government: A Labor Perspective of the Indianapolis Model." AFSCME Council 62.

Osborne, David, and Ted Gaebler. 1992. *Reinventing Government: How the Entrepreneurial Spirit Is Transforming the Public Sector.* Reading, Mass.: Addison-Wesley Publishing Company.

Poole, Robert W. 1980. *Cutting Back City Hall.* New York: Universe Books.

Sappington, David E. M., and Joseph Stiglitz. 1987. "Privatization, Information and Incentives." *Journal of Policy Analysis and Management* 6, no. 4: 567–82.

Savas, Emanuel S. 1987. *Privatization: The Key to Better Government.* Chatham, N.J.: Chatham House Publishers.

Schumpeter, Joseph A. 1947. *Capitalism, Socialism, and Democracy.* New York: Harper Brothers.

Sen, Amartya K. 1970. *Collective Choice and Social Welfare.* San Francisco, Calif.: Holden-Day.

CASE STUDY 10

Introduction

In the preceding essay, Professor Sclar discusses the importance that political ideology plays in shaping the debate over privatization. Whereas many Americans once believed that government should play an active and positive role in society, the 1980s brought new support for limited government and greater use of the marketplace to deliver public services. Many conservatives see privatization as a path for reducing the "size and role of the state in society." Sclar suggests that ideology not only affects support for privatization, but also the economic analyses used to assess public services. He writes that attitudes on the standard model used to analyze the benefits of privatization tend to "correlate with the strength of one's belief that privatization is more efficient than direct public service provision." Ultimately, Sclar argues that the decision to contract out must be made by using a more complex calculation of the costs than is offered in this standard model.

In the following essay, Professor Jonathan Richmond examines the decision of the Colorado legislature to require Denver to privatize a fixed percentage of its transportation system. What Richmond finds was that the legislature did not base its decision to privatize on economics or an understanding of organizational behavior, but on ideology, with the free enterprise conservatives winning out against pro-labor Democrats. The results of the privatization, however, have been neither all good nor all bad. On the one hand, privatization may have led to some savings from using private contractors and from union concessions. On the other hand, it created some problems in service delivery.

Richmond's essay provides a valuable lesson on the importance of political considerations, including conservative ideology and union activism, in shaping the debate over privatization. The political considerations can be seen not only in the legislative battle to privatize the transit service, but even in the economic analyses of the results, with neither side presenting a clear picture of the costs and benefits of the contracting. Richmond's essay underscores Sclar's points about the importance of ideology in shaping attitudes toward privatization and the need for comprehensive economic analyses. It is worth noting, as Richmond does, that Sclar had a voice in the debate in Colorado, providing an economic report for the transportation union that was critical of the privatization of the transit service.

Questions to Consider

Richmond conducted this study while working as a research fellow in the A. Alfred Taubman Center for State and Local Government at Harvard University. He is currently a Visiting Fellow at the Asian Institute of Technology in Thailand. As you read his essay, these are some questions to consider:

- Who was supporting the privatization of Denver's bus system? Who was opposed? What seemed to be the motivating factors for the different sides? Specifically, what did the legislature decide to do?
- What different groups studied the economic impact of the bus privatization? What did each group find? Why might one be skeptical of some of each group's findings?
- What conclusions can you draw as to the impact of the privatization on bus service in Denver? Did it bring costs down? Did it improve service?

Denver

Jonathan E. D. Richmond

In 1988, Denver became the first city mandated by state statute to begin privatizing its bus system. Wendell Cox, a former Los Angeles County Transportation Commissioner who operates a consulting practice in Illinois, had started the ball rolling in 1986 with a presentation to the Denver Regional Transportation District (RTD) Board on "Competitive Contracting as a Strategic Option." The board showed little interest in contracting but, two years later, Republican state Senator Terry Considine (together with Wendell Cox as his consultant) authored SB 164 to require privatization to commence.

Top of Considine's agenda was reduction of the wage bill. In a *Denver Post* column (Considine 1988), he complained that the average $32,992 salary and $7967 benefits of RTD drivers were 60 percent higher than those of school bus drivers "to whom we entrust our children's lives." He estimated that his proposal, which called for privatizing the entire RTD operation, would save $40 million out of $100 million in annual operating costs.

Pitched in this way, the battle became drawn along classic pro/anti-labor lines. Most Republicans backed Considine on principle. As Senator Ray Powers said, for example, "I'm a privatization type of person, a Republican who believes in free enterprise." Business interests supported Considine, with chamber of commerce lobbyists active. The Colorado Public Interest Research Group sided with Considine as well.

Michael Feeley, Colorado Senate minority leader, admitted that "perhaps we're not as objective as we should be. Pressure to keep wages down is anathema to a traditional Democratic line." Democrats felt in a fragile minority position, "and we rely on the unions for financial support and for arguments." It was natural for Democrats to oppose the bill since its author's

Jonathan E. D. Richmond, "Denver," from *The Private Provision of Public Transportation* (Cambridge, Mass.: Harvard University Taubman Center for State and Local Government, 2001), pp. 26–41. Reprinted by permission of the author.

principal cause was the cutting of wages. Most of the RTD's Board of Directors were members of the Democratic Party and did not support Considine's bill, citing concern at union busting, safety issues, and data suggesting contracting didn't work. Potential private bus operators, aware that they would ultimately need to find favor with the RTD to win contracts, took a low-key position.

Bill Jones, political director of the Amalgamated Transit Union, Local 1001, points out that if Denver-only representatives had voted, the bill would have been killed, but that the state-level action was precisely an attempt to override the left-leaning RTD Board and its Denver constituency. The ATU local hired John Singer as lobbyist and the international also sent in a lobbyist.

The ATU staged a vigorous effort, with a focus on winning over moderate Denver-area Republican votes. Their principal argument was that the proposal would not save money and would lower safety and reliability standards as well. The union also claimed that the bill put federal funding at risk by infringing on mandatory collective bargaining rights, that the RTD would lose its ability to raise tax-free revenue bonds, and that private companies would focus their purchasing out-of-state.

Considine expressed his upset at the vigor of union lobby actions in his *Post* editorial. The ATU, he said, was "using all their influence, a number of misstatements and as much propaganda as they can muster to drive this legislation into the ditch. And they're being helped by taxpayer-paid lobbyists from the Regional Transit District."

Concerned at the union's efforts, Considine offered to compromise and set initial contracting at only five percent of total service. The national union, however, refused to negotiate, declaring they wanted the bill dead. On March 15, Democratic Governor Roy Romer sent a letter to legislators, calling for a "cautious and deliberative approach," providing for privatization up to 20 percent over a two-year period; loss of RTD employees by attrition, not firing; and an analysis of the results of this experiment before further action was taken. The bill the legislature approved and the governor ultimately signed—much to the surprise of its opponents—required "at least" 20 percent of service to be privately contracted, but did provide for the labor protections and reviews Romer had requested.

RTD management now put together three packages of routes to contract (the routes had to be representative of RTD service as a whole, according to the legislation, and were therefore spread throughout the system, requiring extensive supervision, according to a member of RTD staff). Contracts were awarded to three national firms, ATC/Vancom, Laidlaw, and Mayflower (which was later taken over by Laidlaw). The initial solicitation had been for 20.8 percent of service, but 19.1 percent was contracted as some bids had been above RTD's service cost. One further local route was subsequently contracted to get contracting to 20.2 percent of service (Kongs 1996).

One beneficial initial consequence of this first phase of privatization was the ability to close the Alameda bus operating division in March 1990, avoiding the need for substantial renovation expenses, as well as enabling the elimination of a number of support positions and supervisory personnel, according to a member of RTD staff.

The legislation had required an "independent certified public accounting firm" to perform a "neutral and unbiased performance audit" and report the results to the General Assembly by December 1, 1990. KPMG Peat Marwick were retained for the work, but Mundle and Associates and Wendell Cox also participated (although RTD, in an August 11, 2000 e-mail, says Cox was not retained to do so). The ATU says that the involvement of Cox was improper since he had been a primary force behind privatization and an actor in the political process which created it (interview with Bill Jones).

Two studies were produced. The first, covering the first year of private operation, was issued in two versions, a *Final Report,* dated November 14, 1990 (KPMG et al. 1990a), and a *Revised Final Report,* more favorable to the private operations, issued on December 24, 1990 (KPMG et al. 1990b), following a review by Wendell Cox (Jones 1999). Both versions found that over the first year of operation (to June 1990), the private operators lost $217,000 out of total expenses of $10.4 million, assuming startup and leasehold costs amortized over three years (KPMG et al. 1990b, 17). "The privatized RTD services may effectively be a "loss-leader" which provided these contractors a "foot in the door" in the Denver market place," according to KPMG et al., although higher than expected labor, fuel and vehicle costs could also have been responsible (1990b, 16–18).

The two reports differ in reporting impacts on RTD. The *Final Report* estimated that the first year privatization experience had a negative $3.7 million fiscal impact on the RTD on an incremental basis. This changed to negative $1.0 million in the revised report (14, 8 respectively). The *Final Report* estimated that privatization promised to save $21 million on a fully-allocated cost basis over a five-year period. This represented a 19 percent savings of what RTD would otherwise have spent to operate the privatized services in-house. The *Revised Final Report* set the estimated savings at $29 million, however, a 24.5 percent projected reduction over RTD's in-house costs.

The second-year report shows private operators making a profit of $337,000 on total expenses of $14.0 million for the 12 months ending June 1991 (KPMG et al. 1991, 12). A short-term incremental cost analysis for that period showed savings to the RTD of $2.5 million, 12.5 percent of costs (8). Savings increased to $7.5 million, 31.0 percent of costs, when considered on a fully-allocated cost basis (10). More than half the savings in actual operating costs were found to be due to lower wages and fringe benefits paid by the private operators (12a). While this led to higher turnover, the study found no indication that safety or quality of service was affected (41).

Cal Marsella came in as new RTD general manager in August 1995, with a focus on managing the system's privatization efforts, and with the support of Wendell Cox as well as right-leaning board members. Within a week, he was making a presentation on privatization to the state legislature (Duffy 1999, 12). Marsella retained Mundle & Associates and Wendell Cox to report on the performance of the contracting program. The resulting report stated that in incremental cost terms contracting had saved RTD $51.5 million up to 1995, and was estimated to save $88 million for the full decade to 1999 (Mundle et al. 1996, 28).

In February 1997, Elliott Sclar, a professor at Columbia University, submitted *Paying More, Getting Less* (Sclar 1997), a study commissioned by the ATU to respond to the 1996 RTD-sponsored report. Sclar found that the RTD lost $9.2 million as a result of privatization over 1990–1995. Sclar says that 1990 actual expenditures were $112.3 million—an increase, not decrease, over the $99.2 million 1988 expenses. Sclar criticized the use of forecasts based on planned budgets and productivity factors in estimates produced by Mundle et al., arguing that actual costs should have been used as the basis. Looking at these actual costs, Sclar observed that the costs of contracted services increased three times as fast as overall system costs. From 1989 to 1995, RTD staffing actually increased by 7 percent, putting into question, he said, how any claimed savings could have been possible.

In a rebuttal (Denver RTD undated), RTD documented mistakes which it says Sclar made. Sclar misunderstood allocation of fixed and variable costs and failed to account for the fact that, while contract costs did increase over the period in question, so did the levels of service provided. RTD found it unacceptable for Sclar to complain about increased RTD staffing when it had been necessary to increase the workforce to accommodate the new light rail program (RTD staff pointed out that implementation of paratransit service and of bus service to the new Denver International Airport over the period also required additional internal staffing).

If the comparison is based on actual costs, RTD saved $20.5 million over 1991–1995, RTD said, a reduction of 16.7 percent compared to the cost of providing the services in question in-house for the period (note that RTD, interestingly, did not include the first year, 1990, for which KPMG et al. had reported a negative fiscal impact). Perhaps most significantly, this new RTD estimate shows a significantly lower cost savings than the earlier $51.5 million consultant estimate based on modeling work that had required subjectively-chosen assumptions on a wide variety of cost allocations.

Different cost and savings estimates were to play center-stage in the war of the experts that dominated the next major legislative debate, over House Bill 1030 of 1999, which would raise the required percentage of service to be contracted to "at least 35 percent" (this bill followed two failed legislative attempts to increase the proportion of privatization). RTD's initial estimate of cost savings from the increased privatization proposed by the bill, included in a fiscal note of December 21, 1998 attached to the bill, came to $24.3 million by 2004 (Office of the State Auditor 1999, 10).

A Booz-Allen Hamilton report faulted RTD's method of calculating operator wages in estimating potential cost savings from privatization. RTD had assumed that labor costs would be saved based on average wage rates. Booz-Allen pointed out, however, that actual savings would depend on the reduced need to hire new labor at only the lowest incoming rates. (Office of the State Auditor 1999, 7–8). The implication was that the savings shown, both in the Mundle/Cox study and in RTD management's submission to the state on savings from HB 1030 contracting expansion, were exaggerated.

At a January 28, 1999 presentation, RTD showed that adjusting wage calculations as called for by Booz-Allen reduced the hourly cost of internally produced RTD bus service (Group X routes) from $62.39 to $54.38 for the period September 1999–August 2000. This 12.8 percent reduction in the estimate took projected in-house costs to only slightly more than the quoted private contract rate for Group X of $51.84 (Denver RTD 1999b, 22). The same month, RTD issued a reduced (19.8 percent less than the original) estimate of $19.5 million in likely savings from implementing 35 percent privatization in the period to 2004, having incorporated the Booz-Allen recommendations into its model. (Denver RTD 1999a, 18).

The ATU stood firm on its insistence that further privatization would lose money. Declaring that HB 1030 was "a bill based on doctored numbers that deserves to meet with Dr. Kevorkian" (ATU 1999), the union publicly displayed an internal RTD cost report which actually showed RTD costs as lower than for Laidlaw contracts, if still above those for contracts awarded to ATC/Vancom. RTD replied that these numbers didn't have the appropriate inputs of fixed/marginal costs to make a valid comparison and were never intended for such a purpose.

The Office of the State Auditor performed a review to try to unravel the confusion (Office of the State Auditor 1999). It found that the model used by RTD to determine bus service costs had been improved and that the overall structure of the RTD cost model met standards of professional practice. It had only minor issues with the methodology, recommending that a change Booz-Allen had recommended on allocating facility costs be implemented to remove overstatement of costs, and calling for a more extensive annual independent audit.

Regarding the controversial ATU-obtained RTD internal cost numbers, the report stated: ". . . neither RTD nor the Operations Department was able to specifically explain how the bus operating cost/hour figures in the Operating Department's Performance Indicator Program report are to be used. In addition, they could not explain why figures which are different from the cost model are produced at all. In fact, Operations Department management could not think of any specific individual who used this particular information" (Office of the State Auditor 1999, 13). The ATU's conclusions were found to not be supported by use of this data.

Testimony took place before the House Committee on Local Government and the Senate Committee on Transportation. An array of union witnesses argued before the latter that contractors performed poorly; that their buses were dirty and not properly maintained; that inadequate driver training was being given; and that drivers were told not to use the radio to report accidents (since the radio was monitored by RTD). One driver testified that she was one of eight paid by Laidlaw to take defective buses to an empty lot for the day so they would not be seen by RTD inspectors (ATU 1999b). (RTD management acknowledges that there have been certain problems with contracts, but states that contract service has mostly been as satisfactory as that provided by RTD). Laidlaw sent two witnesses to argue for the bill, and two RTD board members testified in favor as well.

Cal Marsella provided testimony, but did not officially announce a view for or against the legislation. "I never established nor furnished an agenda of increased competitive contracting. I provided honest, documented testimony when required," according to Marsella (letter to author, May 15 2000).

Senate Minority Leader Michael Feeley, however, saw Marsella's testimony and the fact that the legislature was aware of Marsella's support for privatization as significant: "Marsella . . . a master politician, has his own agenda, and counts his votes on the board very carefully. . . . There's a Republican majority in the state. Cal recognizes that." RTD board member Karen Benker commented that "privatization was very divisive and he [Marsella] received a number of warnings. There was an issue of whether he should testify [to the state]. Half the board didn't feel he was going to present the board's viewpoint, but he was still doing policy memos favorable to privatization. . . . He plays constant political games."

President of the Senate Ray Powers, who sponsored the bill in the Senate, noted that this time round RTD had not provided opposition, while private providers testified to the potential for success, and "the unions did not fight us at a very high level. And the battle ground was not as intense as it was in 1988," he said.

John Singer had now switched from being lobbyist for the unions to lobbying for the private operators who have become increasingly active in the political process. He does not feel that the numbers put forward by either side ultimately carried the day, saying the debate was essentially about ideology "from day one." Understanding this, his personal lobbying approach emphasized broad philosophy rather than details. Bill Jones, lobbying for the ATU, would agree that the debate was "mostly ideology. They're oriented to what their favorite lobbyists tell them."

Michael Feeley criticizes the ideological perspective of the Republicans: "When the Republicans meet, they reinforce their own thinking and they really don't listen to the population as a whole." Feeley admits, however, that when the bus contractors' lobby came to see him "I listened to what they had to say politely and then discounted it. Perhaps I'm as guilty as the next person at buying the party line."

Dick Sargent (since resigned from the board) was one of few board members to publicly support the bill, citing improvements when a new supermarket arrives to compete with a previous monopolist. Board member Rick Garcia expressed his concern that the "arbitrary percentage" privatization requirement takes flexibility away from the RTD Board. At times the labor market and other factors might lead the board to wish to contract more than the 35 percent specified, at other times less, he said. The bill, requiring the increase to 35 percent service privatization, was passed and signed into law by Governor Bill Ownes, a Republican, on May 28 1999.

The following September 5 another drama unfolded as a new private operator, TCT Services of Tennessee, began a contract arranged the previous January. TCT had won the contract on the basis of an unusually low bid, but was unable to hire the necessary drivers at the wages it was offering—wages which began at only $6.50 per hour during training. The company advertised "No experience necessary" and "20 years old with good MVR," but still could not recruit the drivers it needed at its planned low wages. The result was missed runs, stranded passengers and—in a particularly well-publicized event—a driver brought in from California at short notice who ran a red light and crashed her bus into a light rail train.

RTD drivers were ordered to work overtime to replace some of TCT's absent service, with TCT billed for the cost. The union handed out buttons reading "RTD Employees WORK. Private contracting Doesn't." RTD managers made the drivers remove them, according to an ATU handout (ATU 1999a).

Karen Benker, a union-supported board member, who said she had "people yelling and screaming at me on the telephone because their bus never showed up," moved to fire the company, but was defeated by board vote, with TCT's service load reduced instead. With the service still unworkable after further route cutting, TCT's contract was terminated by mutual agreement, effective November 20, 1999. TCT's drivers were offered the opportunity to work for RTD.

On January 13, 2000, RTD once more issued reduced estimates of savings from an increase to 35 percent privatization through 2004 (Denver RTD 2000). A "High Cost Estimate" of $6.3 million savings and a "Low Cost Estimate" of $9.8 million savings were both substantially below the estimates produced by RTD when arguments had been made for HB 1030. Surprisingly, the "Low Cost Estimate" included in its basis the low-cost contract with TCT terminated because it was not viable. Both estimates assumed that using RTD service would require building a new $8 million maintenance facility at a depreciated cost of $266,667 per annum, and that, if the service was contracted instead, interest of $400,000 would be earned on the unspent $8 million.

Board member Benker, who has accounting experience through her job with the state, does not believe the maintenance facility would be needed in the absence of the further privatization, and calls the information management provided the legislature "biased towards privatization." More efficient maintenance practices and possible adoption of a third shift could increase capacity at existing facilities, Benker said.

Benker also noted that it was not proper public sector accounting practice to take depreciation as RTD had done, and that allocating interest earnings on the notional $8 million saved in addition to taking depreciation was double counting any possible benefit. Removing the impact of the $8 million facility reduces expected savings through 2004 to $3.6 million or 4.7 percent of the RTD-operated budget, assuming the "Low Cost Estimate." Benker does not believe even those benefits would accrue. RTD management denied the claim that proper accounting procedures had not been followed (Smith 2000).

ATC/Vancom, in contract operation since December 1989, has modest facilities compared to RTD. Outdoor bus storage is cheaper, if less protective of buses during the Colorado winter, than RTD's heated indoor facilities. ATC's modest management building symbolizes a low-cost ethic. ATC pays drivers a starting rate of $9.50 per hour compared to $12.06 at RTD. Both ATC and RTD have problems recruiting adequate numbers of drivers in Denver's high-wage economy. ATC says it has an annual turnover rate of 170 percent and must continually train new drivers to replace those who leave. Not only does training impose costs, but constant turnover of freshly-trained drivers mean that there are few well-experienced personnel.

As one RTD manager admitted, "The fundamental problem driving our service troubles is that during an economic downturn, union contract wages remain high, creating a wide margin for private contractors. During an economic boom, union contract wages lag rising market wages, and that narrows the margin." This effect has reduced the advantages which might accrue to contracting, while upward pressure on contractor wage bills or from the unexpectedly high costs of training needed to produce drivers—who only stay for the short-term—may well drive contract costs higher.

A member of RTD management also said that "the biggest service flaws from privatization are caused by the short length contracts [initially for three years, with the option to RTD to extend twice for one year each time]. This greatly adds to the turnover issue, and creates turmoil on the equipment side. TCT was hampered in its training program because the outgoing contractor still had the buses, and then they had to go through an RTD inspection to avoid defects being palmed off onto RTD or TCT. This resulted in equipment shortages, causing cancellations or training delays at RTD and at both of the contractors." The privatization law had an "anti-union," edge, this manager said, "and that is almost certainly the reason for the short contracts, making wage and work rule suppression more important in winning bids than any other factor, such as equipment depreciation, facility costs, service quality, etc."

Managerial efficiency had benefited overall from privatization efforts, according to one RTD staff member. While thoughts of privatizing management functions in addition to operations were dropped due to concerns that elected officials would lose control, a staff buyout program was introduced during the summer of 1990, accompanied by a reorganization of staff functions. This reflected reduced needs in areas such as operations and payroll occasioned by the service privatization, but the program was made available throughout the RTD organization. With generous severance packages made available by the board, due to an expectation that alternative employment would be hard to find, according to the RTD staff member, one-third of white-collar workers left. Many took jobs in the private sector, which was entering an expansionary phase.

The loss of staff created gaps in management functions, but also provided the opportunity for subsequent reorganizations to enable the agency to operate with a smaller management structure in many areas. There were 14 service planners and schedulers before the 1990 buyout, for example, but only 6 afterwards. The number grew back to 10, but has come back down to 6 under General Manager Marsella, and with a much larger transit system to manage than in 1989. Capital projects for bus and rail developments have, however, required additional managerial staff.

According to an RTD staff member, concessions have also been won from the driver's union as a result of pressures induced by privatization, increasing the efficiency of in-house operations: "I have observed numerous examples of flexibility by our union, as they try to keep us from shifting more work to the contractors."

While the recent departure of certain vocal critics from the board may promise greater calm, the RTD board—which is formed by direct popular local election—has had a history of fractured behavior. Interviews for this study revealed a high level of anger amongst board members, aimed both at each other and at RTD management. Jack McCroskey, the subject of a board motion of censure passed 10–4 for "mean-spirited" and "belittling" attacks on RTD employees, made frequent use of four-letter words indicating his state of warfare with the general manager.

Karen Benker, marginalized by both right-of-center board members and management for her left-wing views, was polite, but deeply critical of staff. Benker was particularly concerned at management's allegedly politically-inspired manipulation of numbers. Dick Sargent, the subject of criticism for saying bus passengers smelled bad prior to his resignation from the board, referred to the people running RTD operations as "a bunch of slugs." "Competition is basically good," he said. He criticized the board for failing to take action. "The reason it went to 35 percent was that the legislature said we perceive it's good, and if you don't take the leadership role, we will." Perhaps, however, the level of discord at RTD has in itself promoted an environment in which decisions have been taken out of RTD's control.

Conclusions

The Denver experience, in short, has been one of the play of ideology. Decision-making on the details of how to operate an essentially local or regional service was taken away from the RTD board, which would not have implemented contracting of fixed-route bus service on its own volition, reflecting both the union connections of some of its membership and fractured relationships between board members which precluded arrival at a consensus.

The state level is dominated by broader general political concerns, with less of a penchant for the nitty-gritty, and views and votes were essentially drawn on ideological lines for both pieces of approved legislation. Lobbyists played a key role in fueling political preconceptions. General Manager Marsella insists he was not a political actor, but his praise for privatization and willingness to implement it, helped give the legislature the confidence to go ahead, providing Marsella a mandate he could not secure from his own board.

For a legislative body to mandate that a given percentage of privatization take place without understanding the underlying organizational or financial policy issues, and to give responsibility for the consequences to a board that would not agree to the privatization in the first place, seems like poor policy decision-making. What if the costs of contracted service continue to escalate? The RTD board must still legally increase contracting to the mandated 35 percent, and will also be answerable for the results.

There was a potential conflict of interest in the participation of Wendell Cox in providing the legislated requirement for an unbiased appraisal of the legislation which Cox had himself proposed. Estimates of contractor savings produced by RTD management and their consultants have, furthermore, been used for political purposes, with assumptions on cost allocations leaning towards the support of contracting. Karen Benker, who has studied the financial data more carefully than management would like to admit, is surely correct in questioning some of the accounting practices she has identified.

The numbers produced by the unions are also unreliable. Sclar, the Columbia professor, who says in an e-mail (April 30, 2000) that he "never had direct access to meaningful data," clearly made mistakes which show he did not have the benefit of an adequate understanding of RTD's costing systems. And the internal RTD numbers the union discovered cannot be shown to provide an adequate conception of the alternative sets of costs, either. What does appear clear is that the savings from further contracting at this point seem likely to be at best marginal given rising wage pressures, while further service disruption could be risked if contractors continue to be forced to use a low-wage, high-turnover workforce to keep costs low.

Some benefits from privatization can be identified. While positions have been added to deal with capital programs, RTD managerial positions related to operations have been reduced or kept stable, while overall service has expanded. In addition, the threat of privatization has led to greater flexibility from the ATU, improving the efficiency of use of in-house drivers.

The November 2000 elections gave the Democrats a Colorado Senate majority of one. Republicans remain in control of the House. The possibility of consequent shifts in state policy on transit privatization illustrates the potential for disruption from ideologically-driven state-level intervention in issues of local service delivery.

References

ATU [Amalgamated Transit Union, Local 1001, Denver] (1999a). *Letter* from Bill Jones, political director, and attached information packet sent to state senators.

ATU [Amalgamated Transit Union, Local 1001, Denver] (1999b). *Witnesses AGAINST House Bill* 1030. Summary of witness testimony.

Considine, Terry (1988). "Private buses would be a plus for taxpayers." "Speak Out" column in *Denver Post.* March 4.

Denver Regional Transportation District (1999a). *RTD Bus Cost Model Workshop.* January 21.

Denver Regional Transportation District (1999b). *RTD Legislative Presentation.* January 28.

Denver Regional Transportation District (2000). *Memorandum* and attached data from Sherry Ellebracht to Chris Ward, Legislative Counsel.

Denver Regional Transportation District (undated). *Rebuttal of "Paying More, Getting Less" by Elliot* [sic] *Sclar.*

Duffy, Jim (1999). "Managing by the numbers at Denver RTD." *Mass Transit,* Vol. xxv, no. 5. September/October. 10–28.

Jones, Bill (1999). *A Very Brief History of RTD Privatization.* Contained in ATU (1999).

Kongs, Thomas F. *Privatization Experience of the Denver Regional Transportation District.* Denver Regional Transportation District. October.

KPMG in association with Mundle & Associates (1990a). *Performance Audit of Privatization of RTD Services, Final Report.* November 14.

KPMG in association with Mundle & Associates (1990b). *Performance Audit of Privatization of RTD Services, Revised Final Report.* December 24.

Mundle & Associates and Wendell Cox Consultancy (1996). *Management/Administration Study for the Regional Transportation District. Final Report.* March 29.

Office of the [Colorado] State Auditor (1999). *Regional Transportation District Bus Service Costs.* March.

Sclar, Elliott D. (1997). *Paying More, Getting Less. The Denver Experience with Bus Privatization 1990–1995.* Prepared for the Amalgamated Transit Union AFL-CIO/ CLC. February.

Smith, Joseph T. (2000). *Letter* from manager of finance, Denver Regional Transportation District to Jonathan E. D. Richmond.

Chapter 10 Review Questions

1. What is privatization? What are some of the different forms that it can take? Why do some reformers see privatization as being beneficial? What are some of its potential drawbacks?
2. Why is Sclar critical of many economic analyses of privatization? Why does he argue that a more complex economic calculus needs to be used in deciding whether to privatize a public service? What factors does he say need to be taken into consideration that are often ignored?
3. Why did the Colorado legislature decide to privatize Denver's bus service? Did the legislature seem to be motivated primarily by ideology or by economic considerations? What effect did the privatization have on the cost and quality of bus service?
4. What are Sclar's concerns about privatization? Are they supported by the evidence of the case study? What response might be made by those who support privatization to the case study? Does the case study provide evidence to support privatization? How so?
5. Does your local government provide most public services directly, or does it rely on contracting out to private companies and nonprofit organizations? What types of services does it provide directly? What types does it contract out? Does the contracting out seem to improve service delivery? Are there problems with it?
6. Under what circumstances do you believe that state and local governments should privatize their services? What services should be privatized? What factors need to be considered in considering whether to privatize? Why are these factors important?

Key Terms

privatization
bureaucracy
bureaucratic reorganization
free market system
contracting out
vouchers
school choice
progressivism
laissez-faire capitalism
socialism
welfare state
marketplace
standard market model
Pareto Optimum

Suggestions for Further Reading

Andrisani, Paul J., Simon Hakim, and Eva Leeds, eds. *Making Government Work: Lessons from America's Governors and Mayors.* Lanham, Md.: Rowan and Littlefield Publishers, 2000. Collection of essays on successful administrative reform efforts at the state and local level, including the use of privatization.

Brudney, Jeffrey, F., Ted Herbert, and Deil S. Wright. "Reinventing Government in the American States: Measuring and Explaining Administrative Reform." *Public Administration Review* 59 (1999): 19–30. This study presents the findings of a nationwide survey of 1,200 state agency directors on the extent to which states are reinventing government reforms.

Buchanan, James M., and Richard A. Musgrave. *Public Finance and Public Choice: Two Contrasting Visions of the State.* Cambridge: MIT Press, 2000. A fascinating collection of essays on the proper role of government by two leading economists.

Chi, Keon S., and Cindy Jasper. *Private Practices: A Review of Privatization in State Government.* Lexington, Ky.: Council of State Governments, 1998. Presents findings from a nationwide survey on trends and issues related to privatization in the states.

Chubb, John E., and Terry M. Moe. *Politics, Markets, and America's Schools.* Washington, D.C.: Brookings Institution, 1990. Frequently cited book on the value of introducing market incentives through the use of vouchers to improve public education.

Friedman, Milton. *Capitalism, Freedom, and Democracy.* Chicago: University of Chicago Press, 1962. This classic work by Milton Friedman, a University of Chicago economist, is frequently credited with laying out some of the key theoretical foundations for privatization.

Henig, Jeffrey R. "Privatization in the United States: Theory and Practice." *Political Science Quarterly* 104 (1989/1990): 649–670. This essay presents an excellent discussion on the history and theoretical underpinnings of privatization in America.

National Research Council. *Contracting for Bus and Demand-Responsive Transit Services: A Survey of U.S. Practice and Experience.* Washington, D.C.: National Transportation Board, 2001. Comprehensive study of the contracting of transit services across the United States, includes analysis of the extent of and reasons for contracting.

Osborne, David, and Ted Gaebler. *Reinventing Government: How the Entrepreneurial Spirit Is Transforming the Public Sector.* New York: Penguin Books, 1993. This is the seminal book in the movement to reinvent government.

Poole, Robert. *Cutting Back City Hall.* New York: Universe Books, 1980. An influential book on the benefits of privatizing local government programs and services.

Savas, E. S. *Privatization and Public-Private Partnerships.* New York: Seven Bridges Press, 2000. Written by a leading advocate of privatization, this book offers a valuable discussion on the benefits and shortcomings of different types of privatization arrangements. Also see Savas's *Privatization: The Key to Better Government* (Chatham, N.J.: Chatham House Publishers, 1987).

Self, Peter. *Government by the Market? The Politics of Public Choice.* Boulder, Colo.: Westview Press, 1993. This book provides an excellent overview of the literature on public choice theory and offers a critical assessment of the application of market concepts to government services and programs.

U.S. General Accounting Office. *Privatization: Lessons Learned by State and Local Governments.* Washington, D.C.: General Accounting Office, 1997. This study of privatization efforts in five states and one city provides helpful insights into successful privatization efforts.

Related Web Sites

http://www.statelocalgov.net/
This web service provides links to state and local government web sites, including a host of different agencies in each state. The service allows searches for links by state or by topic.

http://www.privatization.org/
This web site from the Reason Public Policy Institute provides information on privatization efforts across the nation, as well as links to a wide variety of other web sites on the topic.

State Courts: The Concept of the New Judicial Federalism

Over the years, state judges in numerous cases have interpreted their state constitutional rights provisions to provide more protection than the national minimum standard guaranteed by the Federal Constitution.

Robert F. Williams

READING 11

Introduction

In 1975, the Alaska Supreme Court ruled in *Ravin* v. *State* that Alaskan residents have a constitutional right to possess marijuana in their home for personal, noncommercial use. In making this ruling, the court did not rely on the United States Constitution, but rather on the Privacy Clause of Alaska's constitution. The state passed a ballot initiative in 1990 making it a criminal offense to possess marijuana in a private residence, but whether the *Ravin* decision could be overturned by the simple passage of a statutory initiative remains an unanswered legal question.[1]

How is it possible that a state supreme court could rule that a person has a right to possess marijuana when the federal courts have ruled on more than one occasion that such a right does not exist? The answer lies in the fact that the nation has a federal system of government in which power is shared between the federal government and the states. Even though the U.S. Constitution is the supreme law of the nation, all the states have their own constitutions, which all include a bill or declaration of rights.

For many years, state courts ignored the rights that were spelled out in the state constitutions, and based rights decisions on the federal Constitution and U.S. Supreme Court rulings. In the mid-1970s, however, state courts and constitutional scholars discovered that state constitutions could be used as a new means to protect rights and liberties. This discovery led many state high courts to begin rendering decisions based on the rights spelled out in state constitutions. The Supreme

Court has since recognized that the U.S. Constitution represents a floor for individual rights, and that the states can provide greater protection of rights in their constitutions.

The *Ravin* decision represents one of the first modern cases in which a state supreme court used the more expansive rights guaranteed under a state constitution as the basis for its decision. This new willingness of state high courts to use state constitutions for providing greater rights protection is called the new judicial federalism.

In the essay that follows, Robert Williams, a Rutgers University School of Law professor, provides a short history of the new judicial federalism, describing it as going through three different stages and perhaps entering a fourth. Williams's essay jumps right into the history with little introduction. He begins by tracing the emergence of this significant change in state supreme court behavior to several early state and federal court decisions. The first of these cases was *People* v. *Anderson,* a 1972 California Supreme Court ruling that declared the death penalty unconstitutional under the state constitution. After that decision, support for the new judicial federalism began to spread across the nation, as other state courts began to issue rulings based on their readings of state constitutions. Williams also points out the important role that several U.S. Supreme Court justices played in promoting the new judicial federalism, especially Justice William Brennan. Williams's essay may not emphasize strongly enough how widely the new judicial federalism began to spread. One early study found more than 400 state high court rulings had been issued between 1970 and the mid-1980s based on state constitutional grounds, while only a handful had been issued on those grounds before 1970.[2]

Williams concludes his overview of the first stage by pointing out the importance of the 1983 Supreme Court case, *Michigan* v. *Long.* It was in this case that the U.S. Supreme Court laid down some guidelines as to when it would not review state court decisions based on state constitutions. The Court ruled that a state court's decision must clearly be based on "adequate, and independent state grounds" for it to avoid being reviewed by the federal court.

Despite the spreading popularity of the new judicial federalism, not all state courts and constitutional scholars were initially supportive of it. As Williams describes, the second stage represented a backlash against the new judicial federalism in the 1980s. Williams writes about some of the criticisms, but there were others in addition to those he mentions. Many opponents argued that the more liberal state courts were simply using their state constitutions to circumvent the decisions of the U.S. Supreme Court, which had been growing more conservative under the leadership of Chief Justice Warren Burger. To be sure, most of the first courts to adopt the ideas of the new judicial federalism were in more liberal states. These include Alaska, California, Colorado, Michigan, Oregon, New Jersey, and New York. There was also concern that since many state high court judges were elected, they would be more focused on politics than on participating in a serious constitutional discourse.

One of the most articulate critics of the new judicial federalism in this period of backlash was James Gardner, a professor at the Western New England School of Law.

Williams does not discuss Gardner in this essay, although he does in other works. In a frequently cited 1992 article, Gardner argued that state constitutional law was "a vast wasteland of confusing, conflicting, and unintelligible pronouncements."[3] Part of the problem with state constitutions, he wrote, is that they contain a vast amount of statutory detail, much of which simply represents political compromise and not any type of coherent philosophy. Gardner argued that state constitutional discourse was "impoverished" because of these failures of state constitutions.

The third stage of the new judicial federalism brought a change in attitudes within the legal community. There tends to be more acceptance today, Williams writes, that state high courts have the right to grant greater protections under state constitutions than those spelled out in the U.S. Constitution. As a result, the conflict over judicial federalism has quieted down. Even though the new judicial federalism is more broadly accepted, there remain inconsistencies in its application. There are frequent instances in which state high courts do not turn to the state constitutions in deciding rights cases or they do not recognize the distinctions between wording in the federal and state constitutions.

Williams concludes the essay by discussing the desire among many scholars and judges to conduct more discourse on the appropriate relationship between federal and state constitutional law. Williams suggests that this desire for discourse may be the beginning of new stage in the new judicial federalism. Williams's essay, which was part of a series of articles on state constitutional law in the *NYU Annual Survey of American Law,* was meant to encourage that dialogue.

Questions to Consider

In reading Williams's essay, these are some questions to consider:

- What events spurred on the emergence of the new judicial federalism? How is the new judicial federalism a departure from the past?
- Why might Justice William Brennan's law journal article be considered the "Magna Carta of state law"? What did Brennan write? How is it comparable to the Magna Carta?
- Why were some scholars and judges opposed to the new judicial federalism? How did some states react against it?
- What was the "Montana Disaster"? Why would the court decisions in Montana or Pennsylvania be considered disasters? How was Arkansas's response different?
- Should state supreme courts play an active role in overturning the laws passed by the state legislature and signed by the governor? Under what circumstances do you think state courts should be able to overturn the decisions of state legislators, who have been elected by the people?
- Thinking back to the problems of Alabama's constitution described in Chapter 4, should one be wary of using state constitutions as the basis for establishing rights and liberties? Does Florida's effort to give constitutional protection to pregnant pigs make you any more wary?

The Third Stage of the New Judicial Federalism

Robert F. Williams

State constitutions are coming out of the archives into the legal literature and into the classroom. They are coming out of the literature and the classroom into the courtroom. State constitutions will go from the courtroom back into the legal literature and into the classroom, and maybe back to the courtroom, through the lawyers trained in the 1980s.[1]

Shirley S. Abrahamson
Wisconsin Supreme Court Justice

The New Judicial Federalism dates from the early 1970s and, of course, cannot be described as "new" anymore.[2] Over the years, state judges in numerous cases have interpreted their state constitutional rights provisions to provide more protection than the national minimum standard guaranteed by the Federal Constitution. In addition, scholarly publications by state judges have helped develop the doctrines included within the New Judicial Federalism. . . .

The First Stage: The Thrill of Discovery

There were a number of factors contributing to the rise of the New Judicial Federalism. Probably the most important early case was *People v. Anderson*[3] in 1972, where the California Supreme Court declared the death penalty unconstitutional under its state constitutional prohibition against cruel *or* unusual punishment.[4] This decision stimulated a substantial academic response, as well as the initial recognition that state courts could evade decisions of the United States Supreme Court by relying on their own state constitutions.[5] In 1973 the wave of litigation on equality and adequacy in school finance was launched in New Jersey,[6] and it is still going on today.[7] In 1980 the United States Supreme Court decided *PruneYard Shopping Ctr. v. Robins* upholding . . . the California Supreme Court's recognition of free speech rights under the California Constitution in privately owned shopping malls.[8] In this way the United States Supreme Court placed its "seal of approval" on the New Judicial Federalism. Individual justices of the United States Supreme Court also gave their imprimatur to the New Judicial Federalism in individual opinions. For example, Justice John Paul Stevens wrote a number of opinions encouraging independent interpretation of state constitutions.[9]

Justice William J. Brennan, Jr., is also credited with stimulating the reemergence of *state* constitutional law. His 1977 *Harvard Law Review* article, *State Constitutions and the Protection of Individual Rights,*[10] has already taken its place among "the most frequently cited law review articles of modern times."[11]

In that article, Justice Brennan noted the rise of federal constitutional rights protections, and the influence of that development on the work of state courts. He also criticized the trend toward lesser protections reflected in the United States Supreme Court's pronouncements and pointed out that state courts had been "step[ping] into the breach" by interpreting their state constitutions to provide more rights protections than required under the Federal Constitution.[12] In now oft-quoted words, he stated:

> State constitutions, too, are a font of individual liberties, their protections often extending beyond those required by the Supreme Court's interpretation of federal law. The legal revolution which has brought federal law to the fore must not be allowed to inhibit the independent protective force of state law—for without it, the full realization of our liberties cannot be guaranteed.[13]

. . . Justice Stewart G. Pollock of New Jersey referred to Brennan's article as "the Magna Carta of state constitutional law."[14]

Finally, during this first stage in 1983, questions of United States Supreme Court jurisdiction in mixed federal and state constitutional cases were ironed out with the Court's adoption of the "plain statement" require-

Robert F. Williams, *Introduction: The Third Stage of New Judicial Federalism,* 59 *NYU Annual Survey of American Law* 211, 211–219 (2003). This article is excerpted from a work originally published in the *NYU Survey of American Law.* Reprinted with permission.

ment for invoking the adequate and independent state ground doctrine in *Michigan v. Long*.[15]

The Second Stage: Backlash

Beginning in the 1980s, but finding its roots in the reaction to the 1972 California decision in *People v. Anderson*,[16] a backlash against the New Judicial Federalism arose. Academics, government officials, and judges spoke out in various forums opposing state decisions "going beyond" the national minimum standards. Prosecutors were particularly critical of state constitutional criminal procedure decisions providing more protections than those required by the United States Supreme Court.[17] They argued that state court judges' disagreement with the outcome of similar rights claims in the United States Supreme Court did not justify such judges' substitution of their judgment for those federal outcomes at the state level.[18]

In some states, amendments to state constitutions were proposed to the electorate that would overturn state court interpretations that were more protective than federal constitutional rights. The development of the New Judicial Federalism therefore has shown that the exercise of popular sovereignty, or voting by the electorate, can not only be used to add new rights, but also to literally overturn or "overrule" judicial interpretations of state constitutional rights guarantees. . . . Such overruling can be accomplished either through legislatively-proposed amendments, constitutional convention proposals, or, in those states that permit it, popularly-initiated constitutional amendments. There are two different approaches. First, state constitutional decisions can be overruled simply by amending the constitution to say that the judicial interpretation no longer applies. For example, several states have overturned state judicial decisions declaring the death penalty unconstitutional by inserting language in the relevant constitutional clauses to indicate that capital punishment will not be deemed to violate the clause. Illustrating a different approach, . . . Florida's search and seizure clause was amended in 1982 to require the state courts to interpret the provision the same way as the United States Supreme Court interprets the federal clause. This also happened in California to eliminate a line of state constitutional interpretations that went beyond the federal requirements in the area of school busing. This Florida and California "lockstep" or "forced linkage" amendment approach can be seen as undesirable because it constitutes a blanket adoption, *in futuro*, of all interpretations of the United States Supreme Court, thereby abdicating a part of a state's sovereignty and judicial autonomy. In a few states, notably California[19] and Oregon,[20] campaigns were mounted against judges associated with independent interpretation of the state constitution.

Another feature of this middle stage of the New Judicial Federalism was the attempt, in a number of states, to develop criteria to guide and limit state courts in their decision about whether to interpret their state constitutions to provide more rights than were guaranteed at the federal level. I have described the "criteria approach" as follows:

> Under this methodology, the state supreme court . . . sets forth a list of circumstances (criteria or factors) under which it says it will feel justified in interpreting its state constitution more broadly than the Federal Constitution. These criteria, then, are used by advocates to present, and judges to decide, claims made under the state constitution in cases where there is also a federal claim that is unlikely to prevail. . . .[21]

This approach is still attracting adherents today. For example, the Wyoming Supreme Court justices engaged in debate through the 1990s on the proper methodology to apply in cases where litigants argued for greater protection under the state constitution. The debate began in 1993 in *Saldana v. State*, which produced four opinions based on methodology.[22] In 1999 the court appeared to settle on the criteria approach,[23] which it now applies.

The Delaware Supreme Court has also recently expressed reliance on the criteria approach.[24] The California Supreme Court continues to assert the requirement that "there must be cogent reasons for a departure from a construction placed on a similar constitutional provision by the United States Supreme Court."[25] Ohio seems to apply a similar approach, as do Illinois, Hawaii, and Tennessee. Pennsylvania has eased up on the rigidity with which it had been applying the criteria approach. I have argued that the criteria approach gives improper deference to the United States Supreme Court, which is interpreting a different constitution under different, national, circumstances.[26]

The Third Stage: The Long Hard Task

[T]o make an independent argument under the state clause takes homework—in texts, in history, in alternative approaches to analysis.

Justice Hans A. Linde[27]

The most vitriolic reactions to the New Judicial Federalism now seem to have died down. More and more members of the public, lawyers, judges, academics and members of the media have learned that state constitutions may, in fact, be interpreted to provide more rights than the national minimum. This fact is no longer such a surprise to people as the maturation process of the New Judicial Federalism has continued.[28] Still, independent state constitutional interpretation can, as Justice Linde noted, be difficult work. The following comments reflect on some of the issues currently arising in state constitutional rights cases.

Several state courts have recently abandoned their interpretations of the state constitution after the United States Supreme Court revised its interpretation of a similar or identical federal constitutional provision. For example, after the Pennsylvania Supreme Court ruled that both the state and federal constitutional search and seizure provisions were violated,[29] the United States Supreme Court vacated the Pennsylvania Court's judgment on the federal ground[30] and remanded in light of its earlier decision.[31] On remand, the Pennsylvania court reversed its original state constitutional interpretation.[32] Judge Zappala dissented:

> I find the majority writer's present change of position regarding our disposition of this matter pursuant to Article 1, Section 8 perplexing. In our original opinion addressing this matter, we relied upon *both* the Fourth Amendment to the United States Constitution and Article I, Section 8 of the Pennsylvania Constitution in holding that the police officer here did not possess the requisite cause to stop appellant based upon flight alone. . . . While the United States Supreme Court's decision in *Wardlow* impacts upon our analysis as it relates to the Fourth Amendment, the Court's decision is not dispositive of our state constitutional analysis. Moreover, regardless of the majority writer's *current* disagreement with his prior disposition of the case pursuant to Article 1, Section 8, principles of *stare decisis* mandate that such disposition, a majority opinion of this Court, remains the law of this case and of the Commonwealth.[33]

A similar state constitutional turnaround took place in Washington in 1997.[34] Analyzing the same phenomenon in Montana in the 1980s, a commentator referred to this type of changed opinion as the "Montana Disaster."[35]

Despite the development of the New Judicial Federalism nearly two generations ago, lawyers still fail to properly argue the state constitutional grounds where available. In many states the courts refuse to reach the state constitutional argument under such circumstances. In this context, the colorful imagery of the Supreme Court of Appeals of West Virginia is relevant: "[w]e have said many times that a skeletal argument, really nothing more than an assertion, does not preserve a claim . . . . Judges are not like pigs, hunting for truffles buried in briefs."[36]

In *State v. Sullivan,* the Arkansas Supreme Court acknowledged what the United States Supreme Court had already confirmed—a state supreme court may not interpret the *federal* constitution to provide *more* rights than recognized by the United States Supreme Court.[37] In the original adjudication of *Sullivan* in the Arkansas state court system, the Arkansas Supreme Court had required suppression of the fruits of a pretextual arrest, concluding that even if the United States Supreme Court had rejected that result, it could still base its decision on its view of the Federal Constitution.[38]

The United States Supreme Court reversed.[39] On remand, the Arkansas Supreme Court, by contrast to those courts discussed earlier that abandoned their views of their state constitutions after the Supreme Court reversed on the federal ground, affirmed its earlier decision "on adequate and independent state grounds."[40] The court further noted that it could make this determination, even after stating in earlier opinions that it would follow the United States Supreme Court's interpretation of the Fourth Amendment, explaining, "[c]urrent interpretation of the United States Constitution in the federal courts no longer mirrors our interpretation of our own constitution."[41]

The State of Florida has what has been referred to as the most amendable state constitution in the country.[42] A proposed state constitutional amendment to be placed on the ballot by a citizens' initiative, mandating humane treatment for pregnant pigs, was evaluated by the Florida Supreme Court for its validity prior to the referendum.[43] The court approved the proposed amendment, letting it go to the ballot; Justice Barbara Pariente concurred, noting:

> [T]he issue of whether pregnant pigs should be singled out for special protection is simply not a subject appropriate for inclusion in our State constitution; rather it is a subject more properly reserved for legislative enactment. I thus find that former Justice McDonald's observations made when this Court reviewed the net fishing amendment continue to ring true today:
>
>> The merit of the proposed amendment is to be decided by the voters of Florida and this Court's opinion regarding the wisdom of any proposed amendment is irrelevant to its legal validity. I am concerned, however, that the net fishing amendment is more appropriate for inclusion in Florida's statute books than in the state constitution.[44]

Many state constitutions contain a wide variety of equality clauses, yet it is very common for state courts to interpret the disparate provisions as identical to the Equal Protection Clause of the Fourteenth Amendment.[45] Still, other states that initially equated their equality clauses with federal doctrines have begun to move in the direction of independence. States like Indiana, Vermont, Minnesota, Alaska, and Idaho have been moving to decouple their state constitutional equality doctrines from the formerly dominant federal equal protection analysis.

A Fourth Stage? State and Federal Constitutional Dialogue

A number of scholars and judges have called for a true dialogue among state and federal judges and constitutional scholars. Professor Paul Kahn has argued that state constitutional rights cases should not necessarily "rely on unique state sources of law. Those sources include the text of the state constitution, the history of its adoption and application, and the unique, historically identifiable qualities of the state community."[46] Kahn described constitutionalism, including state constitutional law, as "not a single set of truths," but rather as an ongoing national discourse about "ideas of liberty, equality, and due process."[47] Professor Kahn argued that state courts and federal courts should work together, using both state constitutions and the Federal Constitution to pursue the "common enterprise" of providing interpretive answers to great constitutional questions. . . .[48]

Still, it must be remembered that each state constitution has its own text. The textual focus is an important way to distinguish the interpretation of a state constitution from the United States Supreme Court's interpretations of the Federal Constitution. This point was emphasized by Justice Hans Linde of Oregon, one of the most influential scholars and judges in the rise of New Judicial Federalism, when he cautioned that state constitutions are not common law.[49] He has noted that:

> [S]tate courts find themselves pulled between fidelity to the state's own charter and the sense that constitutional law is a shared enterprise. Fidelity to a constitution need not mean narrow literalism. Most state bills of rights leave adequate room for modern applications, as well as for comparing similar guarantees elsewhere. But fidelity to a constitution means at least to identify what clause is said to invalidate the challenged law, to read what one interprets, and to explain it in terms that will apply beyond the case at issue, not to substitute phrases that have no analogue in the state's charter. . . . A demand that each state's court reach whatever desired result courts in other states have reached, in the common law manner of generic judge-made formulas, denies significance to the lawmaking act of choosing and adopting the constitutional provisions on which claims of unconstitutionality rest.[50]

The move to overrule state constitutional rights decisions seems to have slowed down. This is a positive development. A constitutional ruling about people's rights is really something quite special. We invented it here in the United States and it is now the envy of the world. Rights decisions should be seen as different from constitutional rulings about separation of powers, state-local relations or other matters of state constitutional interpretation. Such matters are extremely important but are qualitatively different from rights rulings.

Rulings about rights often protect unpopular people or groups who cannot gain a legislative or electoral majority. If a decision about constitutional rights becomes nothing more than the springboard for a proposed constitutional amendment to overrule it, we can damage our fundamental system of state constitutional rights. That system depends on independent courts for its operation.

Constitutional interpretation, especially in controversial rights cases based on older, generally worded clauses, is not an exact science. This is true despite the assertions of strict constructionists or originalists. Decisions based on similar clauses, which rule against the asserted rights, are not necessarily correct either. Either way, we should leave those decisions in the hands of independent judges.

Those who disagree with a controversial rights decision often argue that there is no constitutional underpinning for the decision and that the court was just implementing its policy preferences. These people often feel a particular decision cries out for a constitutional amendment to overrule it even though they may not feel that way about other controversial rights decisions in such areas as free speech, criminal procedure rights, and religious freedom. Those who feel strongly about the other decisions, however, may propose amendments to overrule them. This reaction can have a snowball effect.

When such people are legislators, rather than ordinary citizens, the slippery slope problem becomes obvious. The legislator who believes passionately about a particular amendment, and believes just as passionately that the decision to be overruled was rendered without legal basis, will need to enlist the support of other legislators, forming a majority or even a supermajority.

If some of these other legislators have amendments about which they are passionate, the stage is set for a logrolling process on constitutional rights. Support for one amendment may depend on, or even stimulate, support for others. This is not a climate that is conducive to independent interpretation of state constitutional rights provisions.

Notes

1. Shirley S. Abrahamson, *Reincarnation of State Courts,* 36 Sw. L.J. 951, 971 (1982).
2. *See* Ronald K. L. Collins, *Foreword: Reliance on State Constitutions—Beyond the "New Federalism,"* 8 U. Puget Sound L. Rev. vi (1985).
3. 493 P.2d 880 (Cal. 1972).
4. *Id.* at 899. *Anderson* was overruled by Article I, § 27 of the California Constitution, ratified only a few months later.
5. Donald E. Wilkes, Jr., *The New Federalism in Criminal Procedure Revisited,* 64 Ky. L.J. 729 (1976); Donald E. Wilkes, Jr., *More on the New Federalism in Criminal Procedure,* 63 Ky. L.J. 873 (1975); Donald E. Wilkes, Jr., *The New Federalism in Criminal Procedure: State Court Evasion of the Burger Court,* 62 Ky. L.J. 421 (1974).
6. *See* Paul L. Tractenberg, *The Evolution and Implementation of Educational Rights Under the New Jersey Constitution of 1947,* 29 Rutgers L.J. 827, 892–930 (1998).
7. *See* Abbott v. Burke, 798 A.2d 602 (N.J. 2002); Tractenberg, *supra* note 6, at 930–36.
8. 447 U.S. 74 (1980).
9. *See* Ronald K. L. Collins, *Justice Stevens Becomes Advocate of States' Role in the High Court,* Nat'l L.J., Aug. 27, 1984, at 20.
10. William J. Brennan, Jr., *State Constitutions and the Protection of Individual Rights,* 90 Harv. L. Rev. 489 (1977).
11. Ann Lousin, *Justice Brennan: A Tribute to a Federal Judge Who Believes in State's Rights,* 20 J. Marshall L. Rev. 1, 2 n.3 (1986) (citing Fred R. Shapiro, *The Most-Cited Law Review Articles,* 73 Cal. L. Rev. 1540, 1550 (1985).
12. *See* Brennan, *supra* note 10 at 502–03.
13. *Id.* at 491.
14. Stewart G. Pollock, *State Constitutions as Separate Sources of Fundamental Rights,* Rutgers L. Rev. 707, 716 (1983).
15. 463 U.S. 1032 (1983). *See generally* Note, *Fulfilling the Goals of* Michigan v. Long: *The State Court Reaction,* 56 Fordham L. Rev. 1041 (1988). Richard W. Westling,

Comment, *Advisory Opinions and the "Constitutionally Required" Adequate and Independent State Grounds Doctrine,* 63 Tulane L. Rev. 379 (1988).

16. 493 P.2d 880 (Cal. 1972). *See also supra* note 3 and accompanying text.
17. *See generally* John B. Wefing, *The New Jersey Supreme Court 1948–1998: Fifty Years of Independence and Activism,* 29 Rutgers L.J. 701, 721 (1998).
18. I took the position that reasoned disagreement was justified in Robert F. Williams, *In the Supreme Court's Shadow: Legitimacy of State Rejection of Supreme Court Reasoning and Result,* 35 S.C. L. Rev. 353, 389–404 (1984). The Arkansas Supreme Court recently recognized this point in *Griffin v. State,* 67 S.W.3d 582 (Ark. 2002). *But see* People v. Haley, 41 P.3d 666, 679–80 (Colo. 2001) (Kourlis, J., dissenting).
19. Among the most well-known judicial elections was the 1986 California Supreme Court election in which three sitting judges, including Chief Justice Rose Bird, were voted out of office. . . .
20. *See, e.g.,* Fred Leeson, *Oregon Court Seat Fight Gets Bitter,* Nat'l L.J., May 14, 1984, at 3; Wallace Turner, *Law-and-Order Groups Oppose an Oregon Justice,* N.Y. Times, Apr. 2, 1984, at A17.
21. *See* Robert F. Williams, *In the Glare of the Supreme Court: Continuing Methodology and Legitimacy Problems in Independent State Constitutional Rights Adjudication,* 72 Notre Dame L. Rev. 1015, 1021–22 (1997).
22. 846 P.2d 604 (Wyo. 1993).
23. Vasquez v. State, 990 P.2d 476, 486 (Wyo. 1999).
24. *See* Jones v. State, 745 A.2d 856, 864–65 (Del. 1999).
25. E. Bay Asian Local Dev. Corp. v. State, 13 P.3d 1122, 1139 (Cal. 2000). *See also* People v. Monge, 941 P.2d 1121, 1133 (Cal. 1997) (internal quotations omitted).
26. Williams, *supra* note 21, at 1046–55. *See also supra* note 18 and accompanying text.
27. Hans A. Linde, *First Things First: Rediscovering the States' Bills of Rights,* 9 U. Balt. L. Rev. 379, 392 (1980).
28. *See generally* Randall T. Shepard, *The Maturing Nature of State Constitution Jurisprudence,* 30 Val U. L. Rev. 421 (1996).
29. *In re* D.M., 743 A.2d 422 (Pa. 1999).
30. Pennsylvania v. D.M., 529 U.S. 1126 (2000).
31. *See* Illinois v. Wardlow, 528 U.S. 119 (2000).
32. *In re* D.M., 781 A.2d 1161 (Pa. 2001).
33. *Id.* at 1165 (Zappala, J., dissenting).
34. *See* State v. Catlett, 945 P.2d 700 (Wash. 1997).
35. Ronald K. L. Collins, *Reliance on State Constitutions—The Montana Disaster,* 63 Tex. L. Rev. 1095 (1985). Collins referred to the "Problem of the Vanishing Constitution." *Id.* at 1111.
36. State v. Ladd, 557 S.E.2d 820, 831 n.1 (W.Va. 2001) (internal quotations omitted).
37. State v. Sullivan, 74 S.W.3d 215, 216–17 (Ark. 2002).
38. State v. Sullivan, 16 S.W.3d 551, 552 (Ark. 2000).
39. Arkansas v. Sullivan, 532 U.S. 769 (2001).
40. *Sullivan,* 74 S.W.3d at 221.
41. *Id.,* at 222 (internal quotations omitted).
42. *See* Talbot D'Alemberte, The Florida State Constitution: A Reference Guide 146 (1991).
43. *See* Advisory Opinion to the Attorney General Re: Limiting Cruel and Inhumane Confinement of Pigs During Pregnancy, 815 So. 2d 597 (Fla. 2002).
44. *Id.* at 600–01 (quoting Advisory Opinion to the Attorney General Re: Limited Marine Net Fishing, 620 So. 2d 997, 999–1000 (Fla. 1993) (McDonald, J., concurring)).
45. *See, e.g.,* In re Commitment of Dennis H., 647 N.W.2d 851, 854–55 n.3 (Wis. 2002); Mass. Fed'n of Teachers v. Bd. of Ed., 767 N.E.2d 549, 562 (Mass. 2002). *See generally* Robert F. Williams, *Equality Guarantees in State Constitutional Law,* 63 Tex. L. Rev. 1195 (1985).
46. Paul W. Kahn, *Interpretation and Authority in State Constitutionalism,* 106 Harv. L. Rev. 1147, 1147 (1993).
47. *Id.* at 1147–48.
48. *Id.* at 1168.
49. Hans A. Linde, *State Constitutions Are Not Common Law: Comments on Gardner's* Failed Discourse, 24 Rutgers L.J. 927 (1993); Linde, *Common Law?, supra* note 4, at 226–29.
50. Hans A. Linde, *Are State Constitutions Common Law?* 34 Ariz., L. Rev. 215, 228–229 (1992). *See also* Linde, *E Pluribus, supra* note 4, at 195; Robert A. Schapiro, *Identity and Interpretation in State Constitutional Law,* 84 Va. L. Rev. 389, 393–94 (1998).

CASE STUDY 11

Introduction

The Vermont Supreme Court ruled on December 20, 1999, that same-sex couples have a constitutional right to the same "statutory benefits and protections afforded to persons of the opposite sex who choose to marry." The Vermont court, like the Alaskan Supreme Court in the *Ravin* decision discussed previously, did not base its ruling on the U.S. Constitution. Rather, it relied on a passage in the Vermont constitution that states that the "government is, or ought to be, instituted for the common benefit" of the people.

The Vermont Supreme Court's decision in *Baker* v. *State* is one of the most recent and controversial examples of the new judicial federalism. Until the 1970s, the Vermont court would probably have relied on the Equal Protection Clause of the U.S. Constitution to base its decision. And more likely than not, it would have dismissed the case. By relying on the Common Benefits Clause of the Vermont constitution, however, the court extended greater benefits to gays and lesbians than is granted under the U.S. Constitution.

In the case study that follows, Matt McDonald gives an overview of the political battle surrounding the *Baker* decision. As McDonald makes clear, the court's action led to strong reactions from within the state and across the nation. Within Vermont, the reaction was similar to what has occurred in other states when a high court has relied on state constitutional grounds to make an unpopular decision; opponents soon began an effort to rewrite the constitution to overturn the court's decision. Those efforts, however, have been unsuccessful. Nationwide, the decision sparked criticism from conservative opponents who viewed it as a threat to marriage and an inappropriate endorsement of homosexuality. It also spawned talk of creating a U.S. constitutional amendment banning marriages between individuals of the same sex.

After McDonald's article was published, a series of events kept the issue of gay marriages in the political spotlight. In April 2000, the Vermont legislature adopted a domestic partnership bill granting civil unions to gay couples, thus allowing these couples to enjoy the same legal rights as heterosexual couples, although without the title of marriage. A more monumental event occurred on November 19, 2003, when the Massachusetts Supreme Judicial Court ruled that the state must grant marriage licenses to homosexual couples. As in the Vermont case, Massachusetts's highest court based its ruling in *Goodridge* v. *Dept. of Public Health* on the state constitution. The following February, the city of San Francisco began to issue marriage licenses to homosexual couples. Multnomah County, Oregon, soon followed suit. In both of these cases, the state courts ordered the local governments to quit issuing licenses, but the city and county had helped to keep the issue in the news. Then on May 17, 2004, Massachusetts became the first state in the nation to allow gay and lesbian couples to marry.

McDonald's essay does not talk about the events that occurred after the Vermont Supreme Court ruling, but it is valuable because it provides an especially good overview of the constitutional and political issues involved in the case. The one piece that is missing from the essay is that it does not discuss the attitude of many opponents of gay marriages who believe that both courts created a right that does not exist within their state constitutions. The argument put forward by these opponents is a common one among those who oppose the new judicial federalism. The problem with the new judicial federalism, these critics argue, is that it has allowed state courts to become too active in governing the states. As you read McDonald's essay, one of the questions you should consider is how active should courts be in shaping state policy. As in other political debates discussed in earlier chapters, this is a question of what one values. In this case, the question is whether one believes it is important for state courts to play an active role in monitoring the other branches of government, even though the courts may overstep their bounds at times. Or whether one wants these questions of state policy to be decided primarily by democratically elected representatives and through direct democracy, even if the process may result in a diminution of rights and liberties.

Questions to Consider

These are some additional questions to consider as you read McDonald's essay:

- Should states be able to extend greater rights to their citizens than are granted by the U.S. Constitution?
- If rights are universal, which was one of the fundamental ideas of the nation's founders, then shouldn't Vermont's decision be expanded to other states?
- Is there a fundamental right for same-sex couples to be treated the same as opposite-sex couples?
- From the reading, do you believe that the Vermont Supreme Court had a reasonable justification to extend the same rights to same-sex couples? What was its justification?
- Several opponents of the Vermont decision later sought to revise the state constitution to overturn the *Baker* decision. If constitutions reflect fundamental rights, should citizens be able to frequently alter them when they become unhappy with how they are being interpreted?
- Under the Full Faith and Credit Clause, each state is required to recognize the legal actions of other states. If the supreme court in Vermont or Massachusetts recognizes gay and lesbian unions under their constitutions, is it fair that another state would have to abide by that ruling even though such unions are not recognized in the U.S. Constitution?

Common Benefits

Matt McDonald

MONTPELIER, Vermont—This small town, one of the most difficult state capitals for American schoolchildren to remember, could become the birthplace of same-sex marriage.

It almost happened this past December 20. In *Baker* vs. *State of Vermont,* all the state's Supreme Court justices appeared to support the claim made by three same-sex couples that they should have the legal right to a marriage license. But most of the justices were reluctant to impose that claim by fiat, preferring to refer the matter to the state legislature.

Instead, the court ruled that the legislature must offer same-sex couples "the same benefits and protections afforded by Vermont law to married opposite-sex couples." Without telling the legislature exactly what to do, the justices in their decision point to the possibility of offering "domestic partnership"—a status a government grants to unmarried couples that guarantees them the material benefits of marriage without calling their association a "marriage." In other words, domestic partnership is marriage without the title.

The Vermont court, acknowledging that their ruling amounts to "decidedly new doctrine," gave the legislature "a reasonable amount of time" to implement the decision. But the justices threatened, in the event the legislature does not comply, to hear a petition from the plaintiffs for an injunction that would grant them a marriage license.

For same-sex marriage supporters, the ruling was a partial victory, but not everything they wanted. Opponents of same-sex marriage felt that they had dodged a bullet, for now. (One justice had wanted to make an immediate declaration that same-sex marriage is a legal right, and castigated her colleagues for "abdicat[ing] this Court's constitutional duty to redress violations of constitutional rights.")

As *Catholic World Report* went to press, the Vermont General Assembly was considering several proposed bills, none of which appears to have gained the support that will be necessary to ensure passage. Most observers believe the legislature will opt for some sort of domestic partnership arrangement.

But even an "everything-but" bill—a measure that would give same-sex couples all the legal rights of marriage without the actual title—would be vulnerable to a legal challenge brought by the advocates of same-sex marriage, who argue that the ability to invoke the very title "marriage" is itself a benefit. The Vermont Supreme Court noted that possibility, but refused to comment further upon it—thus virtually furnishing an invitation for a further challenge if the legislature does not grant same-sex couples the right to marriage outright.

"I guess we're going to have to wait and see," said Mary Bonauto, civil rights project director at Gay and Lesbian Advocates and Defenders in Boston, Massachusetts. "From our perspective, the only thing that's going to satisfy the court's mandate is marriage."

While the outcome is still unclear, Vermont for now seems to afford the likeliest prospects for legal recognition of same-sex marriage, among the several U.S. states that have considered or will likely soon consider that possibility.

"It's kind of like you've got a dam and the water's rising," said David Coolidge, director of the Marriage Project, an organization based at the Columbus School of Law of Catholic University of America in Washington D.C., which favors traditional marriage. "And the question is: Is it going to recede, is it going to stop, or is it going to breach?"

Taking Sides

Same-sex marriage and its companion issue, domestic partnerships, have now become a political fault line in the Green Mountain State.

On either side of the divide have stood vocal activists. For those in favor of same-sex partnerships there is the Vermont Freedom to Marry Task Force, which likens the prohibition on same-sex marriage to the old legal acceptance of slavery. Standing against the change in Vermont law is Take It to the People, which bills itself as "Vermont's Grassroots Coalition for Traditional Marriage." The latter group is trying to force the legislature to begin the process of amending the state constitution, to nullify the effect of the court ruling. The first step in that amendment process would be for the legislature to send the question before the people, in a public referendum.

When the Vermont House Judiciary Committee held its first public hearing on the amendment question, on January 25, about 1,200 people showed up, despite a snowstorm that hit earlier in the day. An estimated 500 people could not even get into the overflowing State House; 115 citizens testified.

For the second public hearing a week later, Bishop Kenneth Angell, the Roman Catholic bishop of Burlington, whose diocese covers the whole state, joined with an Evangelical Protestant minister to organize a rally against same-sex marriage on the State House steps. Somewhere between 1,000 and 1,800 people attended the rally, and about 1,000 more went on to attend the hearing. Some 110 testified. This was believed to be the largest gathering ever at the Vermont State House.

(Adding to the local color of the political battle in Vermont has been the arrival of Randall Terry, the founder of the anti-abortion group Operation Rescue, who has moved his radio show from New York to Burlington to fight same-sex marriage and is vowing to stay "for the duration." Vermonters are notoriously parochial; octogenarian dairy farmer Fred Tuttle in 1998 waged a successful campaign for the Republican U.S. Senate primary, in part by passing his millionaire opponent, who was originally from Massachusetts, a list of Vermont towns and inviting him to pronounce them. Recognizing that native distrust for outsiders, Take It to the People officials have told Terry he isn't welcome, and have asked him to go home.)

A public poll in January found that 52 percent of Vermont's registered voters disagreed with the court's decision in *Baker* vs. *State,* as against 38 percent who agreed. The proposal for a constitutional amendment limiting marriage to one man and one woman won 49–44 percent support (the difference between those two figures was scarcely more than what the pollsters cited as their survey's margin of error). While the findings of the poll appeared to show that same-sex marriage and domestic partnership are unpopular in Vermont, the margin was narrow enough so that the political balance could easily tilt in the other direction. On the other hand, politicians watch not only for raw numbers, but depth of feeling, and the poll found that only 18 percent of respondents said they "strongly disagreed" with the court's ruling. Only 6 percent said they "strongly agreed."

Nor is it certain that the January poll, sponsored by two leading newspapers of the state (the *Rutland Herald* and the *Barre-Montpelier Times Argus*) along with a local television station (WCAX-TV Channel 3, a CBS affiliate), gave an accurate assessment of public opinion. Poll results attain credibility through repetition and diversity of pollsters; when there is a large number of different pollsters, taking different surveys and producing similar results, the public can place greater confidence in the numbers those surveys produce. But polls, which are usually conducted by media outlets, are expensive. So polls are not usually repeated on a routine basis, except for the national audience, or in the large metropolitan media markets of states which attract intense national interest (such as Iowa and New Hampshire, where the presidential races begin). Vermont fits none of those categories. So to date, there have been no follow-up polls to confirm or deny the accuracy of those first survey results.

Compromise Expected

The muddy political waters reflected in the poll explain in part why most observers expect nothing decisive to come out of the Vermont legislature this year. The state Supreme Court's decision was announced December 20. Most observers have predicted that the legislature will pass a compromise domestic partnership bill this year.

Any bill would need a majority in the 150-member House before heading to the judiciary committee of the 30-member Senate, where it could be debated and amended by committee members and then taken up by the full Senate. If the Senate made any changes, then the House and Senate together would have to agree on a new version before sending the legislation to the governor, who would have to sign it before it became law. (The governor has endorsed domestic partnership, but not marriage, for same-sex couples.) The House leadership hopes to schedule a vote by March 7, which is Town Meeting Day in Vermont. A final vote in the legislature would not come until spring at the earliest.

Already there are signs of what the final product may look like. On February 9, the Vermont House Judiciary Committee voted 8–3 against same-sex marriage, but in favor of a domestic-partnership bill that would provide exactly the same legal benefits. Under the terms of this bill, same-sex couples could obtain a domestic partnership license from town and city clerks, and then have their union "solemnized and certified" by a judge, justice of the peace, or cleric. If they wanted to end their partnership, they could go to family court and get the equivalent of a divorce. The new status promises the same benefits as marriage, without the "Mrs."

Alternatives to the domestic partnership legislation do not appear to have adequate political support. In theory the Vermont legislature could simply ignore the court's decision, and do nothing, but then the state Supreme Court would probably make good on its threat to grant marriage licenses to the same-sex couples who brought the lawsuit. The legislature could also vote to abolish civil marriage altogether, but that radical idea has very little support. A bill that would allow same-sex marriage was filed in the House, but it has only six sponsors. All 11 members of the House judiciary committee are sympathetic to same-sex marriage, but they voted down the proposal on the grounds that the bill could not pass—at least not this year. On the other side of the divide, a bill prohibiting same-sex marriage and refusing to recognize such unions when they are contracted in other states has 57 sponsors in the House, but that is still 19 votes short of the 76 needed for passage. And even if that bill passed, such a law would presumably be vulnerable to a constitutional challenge, since the state Supreme Court has already found that the current system violates the state Constitution.

The only outright victory possible for those who do not want the government to sanction same-sex relationships would have to come through a constitutional amendment, but that looks unlikely, too. Vermont's constitution makes amendments difficult to pass. The process requires a two-thirds vote in the state Senate, followed by a majority vote in the state House of Representatives, followed by a confirming majority vote in both houses during the next legislative session (in this case, beginning in 2001) before the proposed amendment could go to the voters for final approval. If a proposed constitutional amendment does not pass the Senate and House this year, it could not even be taken up again until 2003, because the state constitution only allows the legislature to start the process during every other two-year legislative session. (This session happens to be an amendment session; the 2001–2002 session is not.)

But all that is probably moot, in any case, because supporters of the proposed amendment do not appear to have the votes they would need. Already 10 state senators have announced their opposition to an amendment; if just one more senator joins that opposition, the amendment could not even get out of the Senate.

Why Vermont?

Vermont, the second smallest and whitest state in America, is best known for skiing and maple syrup. It has a reputation for being liberal and at least a bit eccentric. Its two U.S. senators (one Democrat, one Republican) are liberals. Its lone U.S. representative, Bernie Sanders, is a Socialist, one of only two independents in the U.S. Congress. Its state auditor, a long shot in the U.S. Senate Democratic primary this year, is believed to be the only openly homosexual official elected to a statewide position anywhere in the country. The state includes sexual orientation in its anti-discrimination statutes. It includes homosexuals among groups protected in its "hate-motivated crimes" law (which increases penalties for crimes if they are found to be "maliciously motivated" on account of the victim's status). Since 1996, Vermont has allowed same-sex couples to adopt children.

In short, this is not exactly the Bible Belt. So Vermont's reputation as enlightened and progressive makes it prime territory for a challenge to civil laws defining marriage as a more-or-less permanent union between one man and one woman.

Actually, Vermont's own civil laws do not do that, as the state's Supreme Court noted in its ruling. So deeply ingrained is the common understanding of the word "marriage" that the state statutes governing it never explicitly define it, and the *Baker* vs. *State* decision actually spends 643 words laboriously drawing out the inference, from words like "bride" and "groom," that marriage in Vermont has been up to now an opposite-sex affair. Such is the nature of the American campaign for legal approval of same-sex unions. Now playing its third major American engagement since 1993 (after Hawaii and Alaska), the same-sex marriage tour has forced people to reconsider fundamental assumptions about perhaps the most fundamental of all social institutions.

In its December ruling, the Vermont Supreme Court acknowledged that the framers of the Vermont Constitution of 1777 did not envision same-sex marriage, but the justices saw their duty as interpreting the "broad principles" of the constitution's Common Benefits Clause. That Clause, largely based on the Declaration of Rights of Virginia written by George Mason (1725–1792), states:

> That government is, or ought to be, instituted for the common benefit, protection, and security of the people, nation, or community, and not for the particular emolument or advantage of any single person, family, or set of persons, who are a part only of that community; and that the community hath an indubitable, unalienable, and indefeasible right, to reform or alter government, in such manner as shall be, by that community, judged most conducive to the public weal.

The "text and history" of the Common Benefits Clause, the court found, "yield no rigid categories or forms of analysis." Still, the justices concluded that they must weigh laws challenged under the Common Benefits Clause according to "a relatively uniform standard, reflective of the inclusionary principle at its core."

The court's majority opinion states:

> The concept of equality at the core of the Common Benefits Clause was not the eradication of racial or class distinctions, but rather the elimination of artificial governmental preferments and advantages. The Vermont Constitution would ensure that the law uniformly afforded every Vermonter its benefit, protection, and security so that social and political preeminence would reflect differences of capacity, disposition, and virtue, rather than governmental favor and privilege.

In the court's judgment, that fundamental premise of the state constitution effectively put the burden on the state government—to prove that any denial of any benefits to anyone "bears a reasonable and just relation to the governmental purpose." So the court set up a three-part test to judge the validity of the state's restrictions: whether significant benefits were being conferred; whether the exclusion of some people from obtaining those benefits would promote the government's goals; and whether "the classification is significantly underinclusive or overinclusive."

In the United States, it is the attorney general's duty to defend laws against legal challenges. In Vermont, the attorney general's main argument was that the state has a right to promote a link between marriage and child-rearing. But the Vermont Supreme Court ruled that it makes no sense to distinguish between same-sex and opposite-sex couples with respect to children when the state explicitly allows same-sex couples to adopt, as it has since 1996.

The attorney general also claimed that recognizing same-sex unions would bring "destabilizing changes" to marriage, without specifying what they might be. Such claims, the court countered, "may be plausible forecasts as to what the future may hold, but cannot reasonably be construed to provide a reasonable and just basis for the statutory exclusion. The State's conjectures are not, in any event, susceptible to empirical proof before they occur."

Uncharted Legal Waters

Indeed, there is no empirical proof of any kind about the consequences of legal recognition for same-sex marriage, because it has never been tried. According to the Lambda Legal Defense and Education Fund, a New York-based organization that supports same-sex marriage, domestic partnership arrangements that approach the legal status of marriage are now the law in Denmark (since 1989), Norway (1993), Greenland (1994), Sweden (1995), Iceland (1996), the Netherlands (1998), and France (1999). Australia and Israel also recognize same-sex unions for some legal purposes.

In 1995, the Scandinavian countries signed a treaty recognizing each other's "registered partnerships" for same-sex couples, according to Lambda. "[R]ecognition throughout Europe and beyond will develop over time," the organization predicts on its web site. Countries now considering domestic partnerships include Belgium, the Czech Republic, Finland, Germany, Luxembourg, Portugal, Spain, and Switzerland.

Holland appears to be closest to approving actual same-sex marriage. A court in South Africa recently ruled that the government had to allow a foreigner into the country because he was the same-sex partner of a citizen. Courts in Colombia, Hungary, and Namibia have also given some recognition of same-sex associations, according to Lambda.

In May 1999, Canada's Supreme Court ruled that Ontario's Family Law Act must be applied equally to same-sex couples. The Ontario government complied last fall, but refused to broaden the definition of "spouse." The new act is on appeal to Canada's federal Supreme Court, according to Equality for Gays and Lesbians Everywhere, a group based in Ottawa. Last summer, according to the same organization, British

Columbia added to the domestic partnership benefits already available to same-sex couples, and the Quebec National Assembly put same-sex relationships on a par with common-law couples.

At the vanguard of them all is the Vermont Supreme Court, which could mandate same-sex marriage in that state even if the legislature refuses to approve it. The justices certainly seem ready for that task. In *Baker* vs. *State* the court said:

> The challenge for future generations will be to define what is most essentially human. The extension of the Common Benefits Clause to acknowledge [same-sex couples] as Vermonters who seek nothing more, nor less, than legal protection and security for their avowed commitment to an intimate and lasting human relationship is simply, when all is said and done, a recognition of our common humanity.

A Plea for Equality

The argument for same-sex marriage is simple: it is said to be a matter of equality.

Marriage casts a long shadow on the law—as can be seen just from the paper it takes to describe its effects. Marriage confers at least 1,049 material benefits at the federal level, according to a study ordered by the U.S. Congress in 1996. In Vermont and every other state, hundreds of benefits are bound up with "I do." Health insurance, death benefits, pensions, inheritance, property titles, health decisions, hospital visitations, and legally privileged communications are among the entries on the long list of social realities affected by the ultimate social association: marriage.

Opponents of same-sex marriage argue that advocates have exaggerated their deprivations. They note that many benefits that spouses receive by default can be gained by other means. A person can designate anyone to be a medical proxy, for instance, and can leave anyone whatever he wants in his will; health insurance is more expensive when purchased individually, but it is still available.

"There's a lot of room to negotiate, but this is not being presented as an invitation to negotiate," said Coolidge, director of the Marriage Law Project.

But even couples who file all the proper paperwork sometimes lose out, according to Mary Bonauto, who once represented same-sex couples in her private legal practice. She recalled companions who were unable to visit their partners in the hospital because administrators refused to honor a medical proxy, and survivors who had to fight off challenges to a partner's will—challenges brought by relatives who charged the partner had exercised undue influence over the deceased. "So even when you have the documents, there's pervasive disrespect," Bonauto said. "Frankly, people feel very unprotected by the law right now."

Both sides agree that there are many benefits which cannot be obtained outside of legal marriage. A same-sex property owner who wants to transfer the title so that it is held by his partner and himself jointly, for instance, must pay a tax for a title transfer; the law automatically grants joint title to a spouse. If you are not married, you cannot qualify for the Social Security death benefits of a spouse. Communications between husband and wife are privileged in court, but those between mere companions are not.

Moreover, the advocates of same-sex marriage argue that compromise is never the way to achieve full equality. The question for Bonauto—who serves as co-counsel for the three same-sex couples in Vermont—"is whether you're a full and equal citizen or not. It's a badge of citizenship."

Opponents of same-sex marriage make a similar point, from a different perspective.

"What they want is for society to say it's OK," said Dwight Duncan, associate professor of law at Southern New England School of Law in North Dartmouth, Mass., who filed a friend-of-the-court brief in the *Baker* case against same-sex marriage.

Subtler Arguments

While equality is the straightforward claim of same-sex marriage supporters, the arguments against recognizing same-sex relationships are subtler.

Coolidge, who is something of a de facto coordinator for opposition to same-sex marriage and domestic partnerships in the United States, argues that official recognition of homosexual partners' relationships will indirectly undermine traditional marriage. He likens the political situation in America today to the situation preceding the widespread acceptance of no-fault divorce—which was widely viewed in the 1960s as a wonderful idea, but has had unforeseen consequences on families and especially on children.

If same-sex marriage is legalized, Coolidge warns, corporations and local government agencies that do not want to deal with same-sex couples may simply stop providing certain benefits to all married people. School districts may drop marriage-preparation classes for the same reason, he believes. "You'll have a lot less support for marriage as a meaningful legal institution," he concludes.

That is all nonsense, Bonauto counters. If same-sex marriage becomes legal, she predicts, the secondary consequences would amount to nothing. "I don't see the sky falling in, and I don't see any undermining of marriage," she said. "There are plenty of marriage licenses to go around. Gay people wouldn't use them all up."

Even if the world would not fall apart, Coolidge argues, same-sex marriage would amount to the-world-turned-upside-down. He worries about the effect of this new social philosophy. The law is a teacher, he reasons, and its symbols send moral messages. "If the law says a man and a man can marry, then the law's teaching a lie, and it's teaching it with the force of law," Coolidge says. "And anyone with a different opinion is at least a dissenter, and probably a bigot, and likely to do something illegal."

Similarly, the Roman Catholic bishop of Burlington, whose diocese covers the whole state of Vermont, reasons that recognizing same-sex partnerships would encourage homosexuality, an inclination the Church teaches is "gravely disordered." ". . . [O]ne can love and respect others without accepting all their actions and without wanting the government to provide special incentives for their lifestyle," Bishop Kenneth Angell wrote in a January letter to Vermont Catholics, who make up about one-quarter of the state's population.

Supporters of same-sex marriage obviously do not accept such moral judgments. They also note that the opinion of religious leaders is divided on the matter; while orthodox Roman Catholics, conservative Evangelical Protestants, and Mormons have stood together against recognizing homosexual partnerships, many liberal Protestants and dissident Catholics in Vermont have come out strongly in favor of same-sex marriage.

Bishop Mary Adelia R. McLeod of the Episcopal Diocese of Vermont, for instance, has called for an "Emancipation Proclamation" for same-sex couples that would allow them to marry both civilly and within the Church. "The union of two human beings in mind, body and heart is one of God's greatest gifts," she wrote in her "Bishop's February Message." "Heterosexual and homosexual people are equally capable of entering into life-long unions of love, mutual support and fidelity."

Indeed, state Rep. Thomas Little, chairman of the House Judiciary Committee, in his written summation of the testimony delivered before his committee by four Christian and two Jewish clerics, called it inconclusive. Little termed the clerics' comments "powerful," but added:

> However, the testimony was not conclusive with respect to the teachings of the Judeo-Christian texts under discussion. . . . The testimony drew different moral lessons, one disfavoring giving legal recognition to homosexual unions and the other favoring such recognition.

In any event, Bonauto argues that religious denominations can work out their own rules without worrying so much about what rights and responsibilities the government confers. "We see a distinction between civil and religious marriage that is recognized in law. It doesn't seem to be universally recognized by some of our opponents," she said.

Elsewhere in the United States

The Vermont case shows only the front burner of a long-simmering stove. The drive to establish a right to marry for same-sex couples has received widespread attention in the United States since 1993, when the Hawaii Supreme Court found that a state law limiting marriage to opposite-sex couples was "presumptively unconstitutional," and sent a case back to a lower court for trial. The dispute heated up quickly in 1996, when a lower court judge in Hawaii found that state law was unconstitutional. The decision could have legalized same-sex marriage in Hawaii immediately, but the judge stayed his order so it could be appealed to the state supreme court.

The ruling jolted lawmakers nationwide, who realized its implications. Hawaii could effectively make same-sex marriage legal everywhere in the country. The reason is imbedded in the principles of the United

States Constitution, which was crafted and ratified in the late 1780s largely because individual states were acting like independent republics instead of members of one nation. To fix this problem, the framers of the federal constitution approved the following language (Article IV, Section 1): "Full Faith and Credit shall be given in each State to the public Acts, Records, and judicial proceedings of every other State." This is the section that prevents states from charging tariffs on goods from other states or ignoring the laws of other states. This section also allows Congress "to prescribe the manner . . . and the effect" of how laws and court rulings from some states are accepted in others.

But in 1996, since there was no law mentioning same-sex marriage anywhere, if Hawaii made such unions legal, then same-sex couples who married there could move to another state and demand recognition of their union as a marriage. So in September of that year, the U.S. Congress overwhelmingly passed the federal Defense of Marriage Act, which defines marriage as "only a legal union between one man and one woman as husband and wife," and allows states to ignore other states' definitions of marriage that differ from their own. Eyeing his reelection just six weeks later, U.S. President Bill Clinton signed the bill into law.

In 1998, the Hawaii legislature crafted a proposed constitutional amendment, allowing legislators to define marriage as between one man and one woman, and sent it to the voters. Hawaii's state supreme court could have ruled on the pending lower-court appeal at any time during the year-and-a-half amendment process—in effect, the court could have legalized same-sex marriage instantly—but the justices chose to hold off and let the legislative process work. The Hawaii amendment passed on November 3, 1998, by a referendum vote of 69 to 31 percent. Instead of marriage, same-sex couples in Hawaii got domestic partnership.

Meanwhile, a similar thing happened in Alaska. In February 1998, a superior court judge there found that state's marriage law presumptively unconstitutional. That November, voters approved a constitutional amendment limiting marriage to one man and one woman, 68 to 32 percent.

Over the last four years, 30 states have passed laws or amendments to their state constitution defining marriage as an alliance between one man and one woman, and refusing to recognize alternative definitions from other states. These laws are known as "mini-DOMAs," after the acronym formed by the federal Defense of Marriage Act.

Not among the 30 is California, the country's largest state, which is scheduled to vote March 7 on a ballot initiative to bar same-sex marriage. The measure, which is called Proposition 22, was winning the approval of the public by 52 to 39 percent, according to a poll conducted in early February.

What Comes Next?

Thus far, same-sex marriage has not received much popular support. Its supporters' successes have come from courts, not legislatures or ballots. Republican political leaders—including all of the current or recent Republican candidates for the U.S. presidency—oppose same-sex marriage. But even Democrats who are considered friendly to homosexuals, when called to address the question of same-sex marriage, have tended to respond with versions of the same message: "I'm-liberal-but-not-that-liberal." Democratic presidential candidates Al Gore and Bill Bradley, while courting homosexual support, have come out against same-sex marriage. (They both support domestic partnership arrangements.) And it was President Bill Clinton, considered the most homosexual-friendly American president to date, who signed the federal Defense of Marriage Act.

Still, the quest for approval of same-sex marriage appears to have momentum in America today. By finding traditional marriage laws unconstitutional, the Vermont Supreme Court has gone further than any court in the country. The court has explicitly recognized the claims of homosexual couples as deserving the opportunity to secure benefits at least equal to those of heterosexual married couples, if not the title "marriage."

"And that's a message, I hope, that will resonate with lawmakers in all 50 states," Bonauto said. "I think what's next is people in the 50 states have to think about the call for equality from Vermont and see what that means in their states. . . . Equality is a concept we keep building upon."

In the meantime, a few court victories could bring about the desired results, even without legislative action. If Vermont does not legalize same-sex marriage, Coolidge predicts that the next test case will arise in Oregon, where a lower court has already suggested that the state's marriage law may be unconstitutional.

Like Vermont, the case in Oregon would have national importance. If one state ever legalizes same-sex marriage, then its supporters will have a means of challenging the federal Defense of Marriage Act on the basis of the full-faith-and-credit clause in the federal constitution (and probably several other grounds). Although the U.S. Supreme Court would probably hear the case, no one can be sure what it would do. If the nation's highest court ruled that the Defense of Marriage Act was unconstitutional, then same-sex marriage in one state could conceivably become same-sex marriage in every state.

Since opponents of same-sex marriage are forever playing defense in a conflict that gives them 50 potential weak spots, Coolidge acknowledged that same-sex marriage supporters may break through somewhere. But if that happens, he contends it is possible that the country will pass an amendment to the federal constitution defining marriage as between one man and one woman, which would settle the issue—maybe.

Because they require initiative and consensus, amendments to the U.S. Constitution are unusual. Only 27 have passed in 211 years—only 17 since the Bill of Rights in 1790—and history books are littered with proposals that went nowhere. In order for an amendment to be incorporated into the Constitution, two-thirds of each house of Congress must ratify an amendment, followed by three-quarters of the states. (The states may also call constitutional conventions on their own, bypassing Congress, but three-quarters of the states must still vote to ratify.)

Coolidge thinks an amendment could pass muster in the U.S. House of Representatives, although it would be tougher to get the measure through the Senate. And he notes that 30 of the necessary 37 states have already passed defense-of-marriage statutes, many of which employ language similar to that which would be used in an amendment.

"There's a lot left to be played out on this one," Coolidge says. He adds: "One of the things to be played out is not only will it happen, but will it happen for good?" The legislative recognition of same-sex marriage might well "happen someplace, sooner or later," Coolidge concedes. But if and when that happens, defenders of traditional marriage will launch their own offensive to change the law. The battle is only beginning.

Chapter 11 Review Questions

1. What is the new judicial federalism? Why is it considered such an important change in judicial politics?
2. Why do state courts have the ability to grant citizens greater rights than those granted under the U.S. Constitution?
3. What are some of the criticisms against the new judicial federalism? Conversely, why might one support it?
4. How have attitudes about the new judicial federalism changed since it first emerged in the early 1970s? What are some of the issues surrounding it today?
5. What happened in the *Baker* v. *State* decision? How is this case illustrative of the new judicial federalism?
6. Reviewing the arguments for and against the new judicial federalism, do you think that a state should be able to grant its citizens greater rights than those specified in the U.S. Constitution? Why or why not?

Key Terms

Ravin v. *State*
Privacy Clause
supreme law
new judicial federalism
People v. *Anderson*
laboratories of democracy
Michigan v. *Long*
constitutional rights
popular sovereignty
lockstep
forced linkage
criteria approach
Montana disaster
State v. *Sullivan*
textual focus
common law
Baker v. *State*
Equal Protection Clause
Common Benefits Clause
domestic partnerships
Full Faith and Credit Clause
Defense of Marriage Act

Suggestions for Further Reading

Brennan, William J., Jr. "State Constitutions and the Protection of Individual Rights." 90 Harvard Law Review 489, 489–504 (1977). This article, along with the Supreme Court Justice's speech to the New Jersey State Bar Association in 1976, is often credited with helping spawn the new judicial federalism.

Carp, Robert A., and Ronald Stidham. *The Judicial Process in America.* 4th ed. Washington, D.C.: Congressional Quarterly Press, 1998. A scholarly and accessible introduction to judicial politics and procedures across the nation.

Farole, Donald J. *Interest Groups and Judicial Federalism.* Westport, Conn.: Praeger, 1998. Examines the involvement of interest groups in pursuing civil rights and liberties litigation in the state courts.

Gardner, James A. "The Failed Discourse of State Constitutionalism." 90 Michigan Law Review 761, 761–837 (1992). One of the most frequently cited critiques of the new judicial federalism.

———, ed. *State Expansion of Federal Constitutional Liberties.* New York: Garland, 1999. This two-volume set includes some of the most important law review articles, court decisions, and other writings on the extension of state constitutional protections beyond those provided in the U.S. Constitution.

Kincaid, John. "The New Judicial Federalism." *The Journal of State Governments* 61 (1988): 163–169. Good introduction to the history and significance of the new judicial federalism.

Maltz, Earl M. "The Dark Side of State Court Activism." 63 Texas Law Review 995, 995–1023 (1985). Critical perspective on the new judicial federalism.

Moats, David. *Civil Wars: A Battle for Gay Marriage.* Orlando, Fla.: Harcourt Books, 2004. Highly praised historical account of Vermont's battle over same-sex marriages, written by a Pulitzer Prize–winning author.

Solimine, Michael E., and James L. Walker. *Respecting State Courts: The Inevitability of Judicial Federalism.* Westport, Conn.: Greenwood Press, 1999. In-depth study on the impact of and debate over judicial federalism.

Stumpf, Harry P., and John H. Culver. *The Politics of State Courts.* New York: Longman, 1992. A good general textbook on the state court system.

Tarr, G. Alan, ed. *Constitutional Politics in the States: Contemporary Controversies and Historical Patterns.* Westport, Conn.: Greenwood Press, 1996. A collection of eight essays addressing the patterns of state constitutional politics. The book includes several case studies examining state constitutional change.

———. *Understanding State Constitutions.* Princeton: Princeton University Press, 1998. Scholarly overview of the content and importance of state constitutions; includes discussion of the new judicial federalism.

Williams, Robert F. "Old Constitutions and New Issues: National Lessons from Vermont's State Constitutional Case on Marriage of Same-Sex Couples." 43 Boston College Law Review 73, 73–124 (2001). Williams argues that the *Baker* v. *State* decision is a particularly illustrative example of the new judicial federalism. He provides a detailed analysis of the case and explains its value for understanding the new judicial federalism.

Wolfson, Evan. *Why Marriage Matters: America, Equality, and Gay People's Right to Marry.* New York: Simon and Schuster, 2004. Recent book on the national fight for gay marriage rights by one of the nation's leading legal experts on and advocates for gay marriages.

Related Web Sites

http://www.ncsconline.org/
The National Center for State Courts provides extensive information on the structure, administration, and work of state courts. The web site also includes links to the courts in each state.

http://www.usc.edu/schools/annenberg/asc/projects/soin/
This web site at the USC Annenberg School of Communication provides a comprehensive listing of newspaper articles and research on issues related to gays and lesbians, including the debate over gay marriages.

12

Local Government: The Concept of the Model City Charter

The challenge at hand is to somehow capture the range of beliefs and opinions as to how best to organize, govern, and manage the American city.

H. George Frederickson, Curtis Wood, and Brett Logan

READING 12

Introduction

City governments in the late 1800s were often corrupt and poorly run. The problem was that city governments were dominated by party machines that were more interested in retaining control of the government and enjoying the spoils of office than with addressing the problems that confronted the cities. The leaders of the machines—the party bosses—rallied supporters from immigrant neighborhoods, bought votes, and stuffed ballot boxes to make sure that their hand-picked candidates were elected to office. The party's elected officials then distributed public funds and city contracts to party members and supporters within the business community. They accepted bribes from businesses and they paid close attention to the needs of local residents who had voted for them to make sure that these individuals continued to support the machine.

In response to the widespread corruption, a group of civic reformers met in Philadelphia in 1894 to discuss how to reduce the power of the political machines and institute good government. The meeting led to the creation of the National Municipal League, an organization dedicated to improving city government. Today, the group is known as the National Civic League. Three years after the Philadelphia meeting, the league put together a committee of civic activists and scholars to consider how city governments ought to be structured. The result of the committee's deliberations was the release in 1900 of the league's first Model City Charter, a series of recommendations on the ideal plan for how city governments should be structured. Since that initial report was released, the league has put together new committees on seven different occasions to reconsider its recommendations and offer revisions to the model charter.

The Model City Charter is important because it encourages city leaders, political reformers, and scholars to think about how city governments should be structured. The way in which city governments are structured is not set in stone. To be sure, city governments have gone through considerable change over the past one hundred years and many cities today continue to wrestle with the best ways to structure their government. As reformers think about changing a city's structure, the Model City Charter provides them with a framework on which to draw.

What is the best city structure? Even though the National Civic League has been able to identify a preferred alternative, there is no one right answer to this question. In many ways, this is a value question. The answer depends on what one believes constitutes good government. Over the years, reformers have pushed for the restructuring of city government to reduce corruption, expand democracy, empower city leaders, promote professionalism, increase efficiency, and improve representation. All of these efforts reflect a desire to ensure that different values are incorporated into a city's political structure.

The choice of what type of government is best is not just a matter of values, but also of the extent to which these values can actually be incorporated into the structure. The problem confronting many municipal reform efforts is that different reform proposals may help improve governing in one way, but harm it in others. For example, a proposal to increase public input into government, and thus improve representation, can also result in a less efficient government. As in other types of political debate, the battle over restructuring city government often presents a conflict in values. Moreover, there are frequently differences of opinion on which form of municipal government is actually best able to promote a particular value.

It is also worth recognizing that underlying the outward campaign for reform can be other goals that are not being discussed in the open. The structure and rules that govern any type of political body can affect who wins and who loses in policy decisions. Thus, the lofty rhetoric of reformers and their opponents may actually be masking a battle over political power or policy outcomes. Certainly, many political reformers seek to change how government operates out of a sincere desire to improve politics, but it is always valuable to think about the potential winners and losers as one evaluates calls for reform.

The National Civic League's recommendations on the best government have shifted over time in response to changes in the nation's politics and to the emergence of new perspectives on governance. One of the major concerns of the first Model City Charter was to reduce the corruption in city governments, but this was not its only concern. Many of the early municipal reformers had very strong class and ethnic biases. Part of the reason that party machines were so successful is that they were able to rely on working-class immigrants for support. Many municipal reformers not only wanted to rid the cities of the corrupt machines, but to remove the influence of these immigrant groups, who they did not think were capable of governing. The first Model City Charter called for the use of a strong-mayor form of government. Under this system, the mayor is given the veto and other powers to ensure that she or he plays a strong role in leading the city. When the league released its first Model City Charter, many reformers saw a strong mayor as being essential for countering the power of the party machines and for overcoming the decentralized structure that characterized many city governments. It was also seen as a more accountable form of government than the weak-mayor system that dominated at the time. The charter called for the mayor and city council members to be elected citywide in nonpartisan races rather than from districts, as they had been in the past. By making this electoral change, the city reformers hoped to take power away from immigrant groups, who tended to live in concentrated areas of the city, and to increase the influence of the middle-to-upper-class white elite and the business community.

In the late 1890s and early 1900s, many political reformers began to develop new ideas about how government should operate. In particular, a scientific management movement became popular that called for using more businesslike practices in government. Municipal reformers called for removing politics from city government and relying on the expertise of professionals. The movement affected the league's recommendations. When the league came out with its second model charter in 1915, it had replaced the strong-mayor form of government with a council-manager system. With this proposal, the league was still emphasizing the need for strong leadership, but it sought to provide this leadership through a professional administrator rather than through a separately elected mayor. The proposal also called for the city council to play a larger role in shaping the general direction of the city. The council would oversee the work of the administrator, but the administrator would handle the day-to-day concerns of the city. In addition, the proposal called for the city council to select one of its own as mayor, but this person would have limited powers and responsibilities, such as presiding over council meetings and serving as the city's ceremonial leader.

Since 1915, the league has continued to advocate the use of council-manager as the preferred form of city government, although it has made other changes in its recommendations. Of particular note, it began to provide recommendations in 1941 on how to structure the mayor-council form of government if a city decides to use that form rather than the council-manager system. Despite the National Civic League's continued preference for the council-manager system of government, not everyone believes it is always the best. In the 1990s, some reformers began to champion the merits of the strong-mayor system of government for urban areas. These reformers argued that large cities needed to have stronger leadership and greater responsiveness than was being provided by an appointed city manager. In a number of cities, charters were revised to strengthen the hand of the mayor. These cities include Oakland, California; Cincinnati, Ohio; Kansas City; Missouri; and St. Petersburg, Florida.

Some reformers have also been critical of the model's long support for using at-large elections to select council members. At-large elections are considered beneficial because they are thought to decrease conflict on the council. Advocates of at-large elections argue that these elections encourage city council members to think about the needs of the city as a whole, rather than just a particular district or area. Although at-large elections may reduce conflict and improve the government's ability to find consensus, they are criticized for denying representation to racial, ethnic, and other minorities. Thus, this type of election system may promote one value—efficiency—while denying another—fair representation. The only way to ensure minority representation is through district elections or proportional representation.

In early 2001, the National Civic League began putting together a committee to revise the Model City Charter for the seventh time. As part of this project, the *National*

Civic Review, the league's journal, published a series of essays on the charter, in order to provide an overview of problems and issues confronting the league as it embarked on its task. One of the best essays was one written by H. George Frederickson, Curtis Wood, and Brett Logan tracing the history of the Model City Charter and explaining some of the concerns that shaped the changes in the league's recommendations over time. The essay is valuable because it makes clear some of the different values that people expect to see reflected in city government and the difficulty in finding an ideal model that fits all cities. The essay also gives a picture of how city governments themselves have actually changed over time. The most interesting transformation pointed out in the essay is how few cities today have either a pure council-manager or mayor-council form of government. Rather, most cities tend to be moving toward some sort of middle ground in which they try to incorporate the professionalism that is associated with the council-manager system with the responsiveness that is found in mayor-council systems. Thus, these cities have sought to find a structure that captures both of these different values.

Questions to Consider

A professor at the University of Kansas, Frederickson is a well-known and respected expert on public administration. He is the former president of the American Society for Public Administration. Wood and Logan are graduate students at the University of Kansas. Here are some questions to consider as you read their work:

- How did the character of the Model City Charter evolve over time? What did the initial Model City Charter hope to accomplish? What were some of the underlying concerns that led to changes in the league's recommendations in later models?
- How has the structure of city governments evolved over time? What form of government was most common in the past? How has that changed?
- What form of government does your city have? Is it a pure form of one of these types, or does it have a mixture of features? Do you think your city's government should be restructured? How so?

How American City Governments Have Changed: The Evolution of the Model City Charter

H. George Frederickson, Curtis Wood, and Brett Logan

Dynamic is hardly a word associated with government. Neither are *changeable, malleable, adaptable,* and *responsive.* Yet properly understood, many American cities, particularly seen over the long run, are all of those. Their structure and form change a bit here and a bit there, and when these changes are summed it is evident that cities are changeable things and that they change much more than is commonly understood.

H. George Frederickson, Curtis Wood, and Brett Logan, "How American City Governments Have Changed: The Evolution of the Model City Charter," *National Civic Review* 90 (Spring 2001): 3–18. Reprinted with permission of John Wiley & Sons, Inc.

The primary structural features of cities are based on generalized state statutes or specific city charters. They broadly fit into three forms: the mayor-council, or strong-mayor form; the council-manager form; and the commission form. Within each form there are rather wide differences in "detail," differences that are often important in terms of who has power, how democratic representation works, and what the quality of city administration is. These details are often in flux.

In simplified terms, these are the legal-statutory platforms of the three types of American city:

1. The mayor-council or strong-mayor form features separation of powers between the elected mayor and city council members; it also has checks and balances between them. The mayor has all executive powers while the council has all legislative powers. This form is similar to that of the state and federal governments; in comparative national terms it is often called the presidential model. About 40 percent of American cities have the mayor-council or strong-mayor legal platform.
2. The council-manager form features an elected council whose members together choose a professional city manager to whom all city departments report. This model resembles the structure of a typical corporation and also has some similarities to the parliamentary form of national government, with its single executive, chosen by the legislature, to whom all departments report. About 60 percent of American cities use this legal-statutory platform.
3. The commission form is now rare in American cities, but it is still the dominant model of county government. In the commission form, the elected commissioners—there are usually three or five—have both executive responsibilities (such as being the commissioner for public works and roads) and legislative authority to act together to make law and policy for the city or county.

With this background, we return to the claim made earlier that American cities are quite changeable. One simple way to understand these changes is to trace the evolution of the Model City Charter.

The First Model City Charter

This examination of the evolution of the Model City Charter takes us back to January 25, 1894. On that day, in Philadelphia, 147 citizens gathered in response to a "Call for the First National Conference for Good City Government" issued by the Municipal League of Philadelphia and the City Club of New York. The impetus for this call was the wide perception of rampant graft, corruption, patronage, and spoils associated with city bosses and political machines. The reformers included Theodore Roosevelt, then a member of the U.S. Civil Service Commission; Charles W. Eliot, president of Harvard University; Marshall Field, a prominent Chicago businessman; and future cabinet members Charles Francis Adams and Charles J. Bonaparte. The purpose of this gathering was to consider how to rid cities of corrupt political machines. But there was another side to the story: "These primarily white, Anglo-Saxon, and Protestant reformers had looked upon civil service reform as one way to wrench power away from ethnic political machines. Under the spoils system, political parties obtained workers and money via political patronage and assessments . . . to obtain funds, however, the parties had to turn to businessmen and the wealthy for money. Political power was then transferred from the party members to the businessmen and other members of the elite who contributed to the party."[1]

Martin J. Schiesl describes the alternative as "the replacement of the ward system of public affairs with a centralized administration that would organize municipal services according to the business view of what was good for the community [thus reducing] the influence of lower-class groups in city government. . . ."[2] The group assembled in Philadelphia voted to create a national municipal league and to help local leagues.

The National Municipal League (now the National Civic League, or NCL), founded in 1894, began producing and disseminating reports and papers. It was Edmund Janes James, a political scientist at the University of Pennsylvania, who first introduced the concept of a model charter: "A *Model* city charter must be . . . adapted to local and temporal conditions. . . . That scheme of government is the ideal one . . . which under any given set of conditions makes the working of good influence easy and of bad influence hard."[3] A committee of civic reformers and distinguished scholars was assembled in 1897 to develop "a municipal program." The committee reported its recommendations in 1899, and they were "published in 1900 as *A Municipal Program*."[4]

The first Model City Charter recommended the mayor-council form of government. Under this plan, the mayor would be directly elected and paid, have veto power, and serve a two-year term. The members of the council would be elected on a general ticket from the city at large and serve six-year staggered terms without pay. The model charter recommended a city council of at least nine and not more than fifty members, the precise number being determined by local conditions.[5] The charter called for an independent civil service commission, whose "commissioners shall prescribe, amend and enforce regulations for appointment to, and promotion in, and for examinations in the administrative service of the city. . . ."[6] Except for the at-large and nonpartisan components of this model, it is very similar to a unicameral version of the state and federal governments.

The recommendation of a mayor-council form of city government was a drastic departure from prevailing practice, and it gained little support. There was reluctance to give the mayor such extensive powers. As a result, the tendency was to place boards between departments and the elected chief executive, in the desire to prevent scandal, but the result was to diffuse responsibility.[7]

In the same year as the adoption of the first Model City Charter, a tidal wave hit Galveston, Texas. It is argued that "the special commission used to deal with that emergency evolved into the commission form of government,"[8] but there is more to the story. A 1918 doctoral dissertation by a University of Iowa student suggests that "the commission plan of city government, though popularly regarded as being created by the city of Galveston to meet a special emergency, is by no means in its essential principles an innovation of this century. . . . The old colonial system of borough government, the New England town government, the government of the national capital since 1878, the system of county government, and the plan of appointing commissioners to manage their municipal affairs in times of emergency adopted by various cities are all in some very important respect similar to the plan initiated sixteen years ago by the Texas city on the gulf."[9]

The author further contends that Galveston, "which was governed by a mayor and twelve aldermen elected by the people, had been characterized as 'one of the worst governed urban communities in the whole country.' "[10] The commission form of government, which emerged in Galveston after the tidal wave, happened not only because of the emergency but also in response to the poorly managed affairs of the city. The commission plan was also not a new entity but one that had been in existence for many years, particularly in American counties.

In any case, for a brief period the commission plan caught on, spreading to "over four hundred . . . cities" by 1915;[11] "typically, this form [of government] has five commissioners elected at large. Collectively, they serve as the legislative body, but each commissioner heads one administrative department or more."[12] The National Municipal League found itself pressured to endorse the plan: "Then as now, however, the League rejected the commission plan because it fragmented the executive and permitted too little attention to policy development. The question was how to combine the 'short ballot' result that characterized the commission plan with the integrated, responsible executive provided in the League's first *Model*."[13]

Revisions of the Model City Charter

1915 Model City Charter

In 1913, the league established a new committee on municipal reform to review the first Model City Charter and discuss other reform efforts. The man often credited with being the originator of the council-manager form of government appeared to strongly influence the drafting process of what would become the second Model City Charter. Richard S. Childs "promoted the ingenious combination of the experience in commission-governed cities and the basic organizational feature of private business—the appointed chief executive officer. The committee's first report in 1914 endorsed what came to be known as the council-manager plan."[14] The words "came to be known as" were used here because, initially, the plan was referred to as the "commission-manager" plan. Beginning in 1908, Staunton, Virginia, had a general manager serving a two-house council and sharing the executive function with the mayor. In

1912, the city of Sumter, South Carolina, had a manager who was responsible to a single elected council. By the end of 1915, eighty-two cities had adopted the council-manager plan. It is interesting to note that "Richard Childs himself, however, acknowledged in the early 1970s that the council-manager plan may date back to 1904, when the Ukiah, California Board of Trustees appointed an 'Executive Officer' to serve at its pleasure."[15]

The council-manager plan in the second Model City Charter recommended a small council, elected by means of nonpartisan, at-large ballots, that would select a professional executive to manage the administrative functions of the city. The council could choose a ceremonial mayor who would serve a term of one or two years, with no veto power. The council's charge was to "elect one of its members as chairman, who shall be entitled mayor."[16]

The duties of the mayor in this first council-manager charter were as follows:

> The mayor shall preside at the meetings of the council and perform such other duties consistent with his office as may be imposed by the council. He shall be recognized as the official head of the city for all ceremonial purposes, by the courts for the purpose of serving civil processes, and by the governor for military purposes. In time of public danger or emergency he may, with the consent of the council, take command of the police and maintain order and enforce the laws. During his absence or disability his duties shall be performed by another member appointed by the council.[17]

Thus it happened that between 1898 and 1915 the preferred form of American city government, at least as promoted by the reformers of the day, changed from the mayor-council to the council-manager plan.

1927 Model City Charter

In 1925, the 1913 Committee on a New Municipal Program was reconstituted and charged with further revising the Model City Charter, in light of ten years' experience with the council-manager plan. Although no important changes were found necessary, this third edition of the Model City Charter does have a number of innovations. It includes, for example, the first mention of the council selecting a vice-chairman or mayor pro tem. This person would serve if a vacancy occurred in the office of the mayor or if the mayor were absent or disabled.[18]

The first mention of council staff is also in the third edition of the model: "The council shall choose a city clerk and such other officers and employees of its own body as it may deem necessary. The city clerk shall keep the records of the council and perform such other duties as may be required by this charter or the council. Officers and employees of the council shall not be chosen for a definite term but shall continue to serve during the pleasure of the council."[19]

Finally, the third Model City Charter began the first of three editions that did not specify the terms of the mayor or council. With regard to the civil service department, adjustments were made regarding more centralized responsibility for administering city personnel systems.

1933 Model City Charter

By 1933, it was felt that the effects of the Great Depression warranted some revisions to the Model City Charter. National Municipal League President Murray Seasongood appointed a committee that produced a model calling for a department of personnel, development of new provisions on slum clearance, new rules for counting ballots in a proportional representation election, and amplification of the sections on city planning and zoning. This edition of the model alludes to the clerk and other employees of the council being "in the classified service of the city, and shall be appointed, supervised and promoted, and may be reduced and removed by the city manager in accordance with the personnel section of this charter."[20]

1941 Model City Charter

The fifth edition of the model is referred to as the "completely revised fifth edition." The decision to further revise it was made in 1937 "in order that it might remain a modern document embodying the best that practical experience can offer."[21] In light of advances in finance, personnel, planning, zoning, housing, elections, public utilities, and special assessments, eminent specialists were called upon to review and revise the 1933 Model City Charter, with the result that it was completely rewritten.

The 1941 model returns to the question of mayor-council government. The model recommends the council-manager plan, a ceremonial mayor and an assistant mayor to be elected by the council, and a city manager also selected by the council. But it also suggested that many of the advantages of professional administration could be obtained in the mayor-council model of city government by changing the charter to provide for a professional administrator[22]: "The strong mayor form of government should be footnoted as 'second best alternative' to the city manager plan. Motion by Fesler seconded by Bauer, carried unanimously. Amendment to resolution suggested by Upson that in appendix actual draft of strong mayor form should be incorporated. Some difference of opinion left to Drafting Committee. Footnote should make clear that there should be no departure from fundamentals and that strong mayor plan is merely suggested in cities where manager cannot be adopted."[23]

The drafting committee decided to include a draft of the mayor-council form in the document but relegated it to an appendix entitled "General note as to election of Mayor, under a 'strong-mayor' form of government." Although the previous four editions of the model described merit principles such as examinations and classification systems, the fifth edition is the first to use the word *merit.*

The 1941 model charter favors the council-manager system, but it does provide guidelines for electing a mayor. Many features of the mayor-council system offered in the first model reappear in the fifth model. For example, the directly elected mayor would have veto power and his or her election would be at large. Department heads would report directly to the elected executive. However, the fifth model mentions that the elected mayor may appoint an "assistant mayor" who would serve as the administrative officer of the city. In this case, depending upon the duties assigned to that position, department heads could report directly to the mayor or to the mayor through the assistant mayor.

There are other differences between the first and fifth models. The first model, for example, specifies a two-year term for the elected mayor, while the fifth model does not specify term length. A number of changes were recommended regarding city councils. The first model called for at-large elections but does not specify the "Hare system" of proportional representation that is found in the fifth model. The recommended size of the council has decreased considerably, from nine to fifty members in 1900 to five to nine in 1941. The first model did not address the issue of council pay, but the fifth edition of the Model City Charter indicates that some pay is acceptable. Finally, bid and purchasing procedures, along with routinized budgeting, accounting, and auditing procedures, were not outlined in the first Model City Charter but are set out in some detail in the 1941 model.

1964 Model City Charter

The objective of the 1964 Model City Charter was to present a legal document in the form of a plan that was democratic but also capable of promoting efficiency and effectiveness.[24] In the introduction to the sixth edition of the Model City Charter, Terrell Blodgett and William Cassella, Jr., describe two streams of thought concerning the purpose of the Model City Charter: "One view insists that a *Model* present the 'ideal' structure of local government. The other view is to endorse a general principle of organization or process and present alternative means for achieving the basic end."[25] For the first time, the model presents, in addition to the preferred provisions, alternatives for composing and electing the council and selecting the mayor.[26] As Luther Gulick, chairman of the revision committee, stated in the introduction to the sixth model: "We recognize, of course, that there are cities, especially those in the largest population class, where the strong mayor plan is preferred. Provisions of the *Model* are appropriate for such a charter or can be readily adapted. This *Model* is not a text to be followed 'as is' but a guide and checklist, useful for all charters commissions and draftsmen. The charter for any city should be tailored to fit."[27]

This move toward flexibility and tailoring can be seen especially in the alternatives offered with regard to council elections in cities using the council-manager form. These alternatives are at-large election, combination at-large election and nomination by district, combination district and at-large election, and proportional representation. In addition, the 1964 Model City Charter moved away from outlining rules, such as for personnel, instead suggesting that these matters are better dealt with in a separate model administrative code. The 1964 model once again addressed the issue of terms for council members. Having seven members of the council was suggested, with the three candidates receiving the highest number of votes serving for four years, and the four candidates receiving the next highest number of votes serving for two years.

As has been the case since the second edition of the model, the sixth edition endorses the council-manager form of government and describes other forms as options. For the first time, the model describes the option within the council-manager form of a directly elected mayor. A description of the mayor-council form of government is found in an appendix, and it is recommended that the mayor serve a four-year term. There is also a description of how easily the word *mayor* could be substituted for the word *manager* in the language outlining provisions for the mayor-council form of government. Further, the assistant-mayor concept first described in the fifth edition is explained in detail, particularly alternative titles for such a position: city administrator, executive officer, or chief administrative officer.

1989 Model City Charter

James H. Svara writes that there were two major concerns in revising the sixth edition of the Model City Charter: "First there was a perceived need to update the language and style of the charters, and it was feared that local groups considering charter revisions would give little credence to the documents because of their age. Second, there was a pervasive sense that the charters should confront issues regarding leadership and representation that had achieved greater salience since the previous editions were prepared."[28]

This second concern is especially evident in larger-population cities with the council-manager form. As previously mentioned, two streams of thought regarding the purpose of the model—ideal structure, or general principles with alternatives—were considered by this group of model drafters. What emerged was a "*Model* with Alternatives" that "will continue to endorse the council-manager plan, but will present alternatives for certain key provisions *without indicating an absolute preference.*"[29]

The model outlines provisions for a mayor to be elected and to serve a four-year term in a council-manager system. Or the council may select a mayor and deputy mayor, who will serve at the pleasure of the council. In either case, the role of the mayor was expanded well beyond ceremonial duties to include presiding at meetings of the council; representing the city in intergovernmental relationships; appointing, with the advice and consent of the council, members of citizen advisory boards and commissions; presenting an annual state of the city address; and other duties specified by the council.[30] As in the sixth edition of the model, the mayor-council form with a chief administrative officer is included, but it is in the appendix.

Although merit principles were endorsed in all previous models, the description of a full merit *system* appeared only in the seventh edition, which called for the city council to "provide by ordinance for the establishment, regulation and maintenance of a merit system necessary to effective administration of the employees of city departments, including but not limited to classification and pay plans, examinations, force reduction, removals, working conditions, provisional and exempt appointments, in-service training, grievances and relationships with employee organizations."[31]

The seventh Model City Charter describes the role of the mayor in council-manager government: "The mayor fills three facilitative roles that offer enormous leadership opportunities. First, the mayor can coordinate the activities of other officials by providing liaison between the manager and their council, fostering a sense of cohesion among council members and educating the public about the needs and prospects of the city. Second, the mayor provides policy guidance through setting goals for the council and advocating the adoption of policies that address the city's problems. Third, the mayor is an ambassador who promotes the city and represents it in dealing with other governments as well as the public."[32]

From these new roles flow new responsibilities, such as appointing boards and commissions and giving the state-of-the-city message. The seventh charter then begins to rein in the expanding roles and responsibilities of the mayor by saying that "the mayor is preeminently a legislator, a member and leader of the council; the mayor is not an executive and not a full-time official."[33] The charter, however, goes on to say that this nonexecutive will need staff support, which can be provided by the city manager. Working together to offer this support, according to the seventh charter, "can often be arranged as part of a system whereby the mayor and the manager function as a team."[34] The 1989 charter then backs away from this newly forged "team" by saying that "the mayor and council collectively, as a body, oversee the operations of the city by the manager."[35]

Tying the Seven Model City Charters Together

It has been eleven years since publication of the last Model City Charter. The NCL is in the early stages of appointing committees and generally gearing up for the eighth Model City Charter in time for publication within the usual fifteen-year cycle between charters. The International City/County Management Association (ICMA), in a somewhat different fashion, is also considering generalized models of preferred forms of city government. ICMA does this in the form of "recognition."

On January 7–8, 2000, a twenty-one-member task force, convened by the ICMA executive board and chaired by Northeast Vice President Phil Schenck (town manager of Avon, Connecticut), met to examine ICMA's current council-manager recognition criteria and the process by which recognition should be determined in the future. The task force discussed how to simplify the process of determining who is a voting member of ICMA and how to develop a separate process for determining whether a jurisdiction operates under the council-manager government.

The task force recommended that ICMA define council-manager government in consultation with other relevant organizations, particularly the NCL, which develops and produces the Model City Charter. ICMA does not want to be viewed as the "sole, self-serving supporter of council-manager government."[36] But ICMA would like to work closely with the NCL to update and revise the 1989 Model City Charter. If there are "serious reservations either during the process or with the end product," then the task force recommends ICMA decide on another course of action to define council-manager government.[37] The task force recommendations were adopted by the ICMA executive board at its July 2000 meeting and are to be submitted to the membership for approval in early 2001.

As both the NCL and ICMA consider models and criteria for recognition, it is useful to review how things have changed. Fuller understanding of how things have changed is important to informed and reasonable development of future models. . . .

The Model City Charter has evolved from recommending a directly elected mayor with executive powers to recommending a mayor chosen by the council with more limited powers. Then, in 1941 (and ever since), the Model City Charter endorsed the ceremonial mayor in the council-manager form but found a directly elected mayor to be acceptable in both forms. Mayoral veto power was initially supported and then dropped for council-manager cities. Mayoral terms of office have generally moved from two years to four.

For eighty-five years, the Model City Charter has endorsed council-manager government, with a professional city manager chosen by the council on the basis of qualifications. Since 1941, the charters have also recommended an appointed professional executive in mayoral cities, selected on the basis of qualifications and chosen directly by the mayor. The model charter recommends that city department heads report to the manager in council-manager cities and that the mayor retain executive control in mayor-council cities. Finally, all of the primary features of generally accepted good public management practices—a merit-based civil service; strict bid, contract, and purchase controls; an administratively developed budget, and so on—are found throughout the Model City Charters.

With this picture in place, we turn to the present and to the challenges faced by those who will develop the eighth Model City Charter.

Easily the biggest challenge has to do with the structural changes that mayor-council (Type I) cities and council-manager (Type II) cities have made. Over time, many mayor-council cities have changed structure to become more professional, efficient, honest, and accountable. Many council-manager cities have changed structure to foster political responsiveness in the form of directly elected political leadership and direct representation of districts and neighborhoods.

Using data from the 1996 ICMA survey, Frederickson and Johnson studied the institutional structures of 2,484 cities. They found that 3.7 percent of the cities were pure mayor-council (political) cities, 17.5 percent were pure council-manager (administrative) cities, and the balance of 78.8 percent of the cities were adaptations of the two forms, that is, adapted or Type III cities.[38] To further differentiate among the large number of cities in the Type III category, Frederickson and Johnson created three types of adapted city: adapted political, adapted administrative, and mixed. The adapted political and adapted administrative cities are incrementally different from the pure political and pure administrative cities. However, the mixed city is a blending of, and a major departure from, either the mayor-council or the council-manager form.

Mayor-council cities are characterized by separation of powers between the mayor and council, considerable mayoral executive and administrative authority, and maximum political responsiveness for the council through district representation. Council-manager cities are characterized by a mayor who has neither political authority separate from the council nor administrative control and by a council elected by the entire community. Fully adapted cities are neither only political nor only administrative but a mix of both. The mixed city is characterized either by separation of powers between the mayor and council and little mayoral administrative control or by a mayor with ceremonial political authority and considerable administrative control.

The adaptations of mayor-council and council-manager cities have been incremental, step-by-step modifications to the city's charter or statute base. Put another way, most council-manager cities have adopted several structural changes of the mayor-council form, although few have completely changed to the mayor-council form. The strong-mayor cities also have adopted structural modifications of the council-manager form, but few have entirely changed to the council-manager model.

The results of the 1996 ICMA survey were also examined and summarized in an article written by Tari Renner and Victor S. DeSantis.[39] Table 1 shows some of the results of the survey with regard to structural changes found in council-manager and mayor-council forms of government.

TABLE 1 Results of the 1996 ICMA Survey

	Percentage
Mayor-council cities with a chief administrative officer	50.8
Attempts to modify structure or form:	
Mayor-council	13.4
Council-manager	14.9
Council-manager cities with directly elected mayor	61.1 (1992)
Type of election system (all forms):	
At-large	60.9
District only	16.8
Mixed	22.3
Mayor not on council:	
In council-manager form	15.8
In mayor-council form	65.5
Mayor has voting power (council-manager form):	
On all issues	74.8
To break a tie only	22.9
Never	1.3
Other	1.1
Mayor's power to veto in council-manager form	11.1

Ebdon and Brucato's study of 193 cities with a population over one hundred thousand (1990 census number) between 1980 and 1994 found evidence of convergence between the council-manager and mayor-council forms of government.[40] Mayor-council cities still use district elections more than council-manager cities, but the gap is narrowing. They found that more than one half of the larger council-manager cities use district elections. They also found that in 87 percent of the larger council-manager governments the mayor was chosen by direct election. Only 10 percent of the larger council-manager systems still had at-large elections for council members and a mayor who was selected from the council. The researchers conclude that "both forms, then, are increasingly combining these two values in their structural design."[41]

Recently, even more profound adaptations are evident. Some large council-manager cities (such as Cincinnati, Ohio, and Kansas City, Missouri) have enhanced the power of the mayor. Beginning in 2001, the mayor in Cincinnati will be directly elected at large, have veto authority, be able to nominate a city manager, initiate termination of the manager, appoint boards and committees, set the council agenda, present the budget, and hire assistants. In Kansas City, the mayor now has veto authority, can nominate a city manager, can appoint members to boards and commissions, and presents the budget to the council. Yet at the same time, these cities have retained the council-manager form of government. Oakland, California, has recently changed its charter from council-manager to mayor-council. The mayor can now terminate the services of the city manager without the consent of the council. These larger cities appear to have changed their charters in such a way as to be mixed and are no longer clearly either council-manager or mayor-council forms.

It is important not to be preoccupied by the structural changes of a few large cities. The great majority of cities are still based on either the mayor-council platform (following the logic of separation of powers) or the council-manager platform (following the logic of unitary or parliamentary government). It is, however, also evident that the structures built on these platforms have changed—in some cases significantly—over the last fifty years.

To write the eighth Model City Charter, the NCL will be challenged to take these changes into account. Because the differences and distinctions between the two dominant statutory platforms—council-manager and strong mayor—are now blurred, a whole new approach may be necessary.

Bill Hansell, executive director of the ICMA, notes that council-manager cities increasingly have "direct election of the mayor, district or part at-large and part district elections of council members, higher compensation for elected officials, partisan elections, veto power for the mayor, mayoral appointments of council committee and chairs, and mayoral appointments of citizens to serve on authorities, boards, and commissions."[42] He proposes four variations in city government structure:

1. A mayor-council-manager form, where the mayor is selected by his or her fellow council members
2. A mayor (at-large)-council-manager form, where the mayor is elected by the voters to the position of leader of the council with a council vote
3. A mayor (empowered)-council-manager form, where the mayor is separately elected by the people, with special veto power, authority to nominate a city manager, and the power to review the city manager's proposed budget before it is submitted to the council
4. A mayor (under separation of powers)-council-manager form, where the mayor does not serve on the council and does not vote; in this alternative, the mayor serves as the chief executive officer and appoints a city manager subject to approval by the council.[43]

On the basis of their research, Frederickson and Johnson write that "the formal legal description of a given city as either council-manager or mayor-council is less accurate than the particular structural variations that the citizens of a given community have chosen to adopt in order to make their government reflect citizens' preferences and values."[44] Earlier research by Adrian[45] is complemented by Frederickson and Johnson's recent work, which suggests that "distinctions between cities on the basis of their legal platforms are less and less meaningful and have little explanatory power."[46] The eighth Model City Charter will have to respond to these new realities.

For a century, the seven Model City Charters have served as guides and templates to anyone interested in how to organize and manage cities. Looking back, we conclude that the Model City Charters are splendid documents illuminating the changing values and beliefs of the leading city specialists of each era. In the sweep of history, these charters reflect the dynamics of structural adaptation. The evidence is clear: American cities are anything but static.

The challenge at hand is to somehow capture the range of beliefs and opinions as to how best to organize, govern, and manage the American city. The task before the NCL is nothing less than to develop a guide and a template for the American city in the twenty-first century.

Notes

1. Moore, P. *Public Personnel Management: A Contingency Approach.* Lexington, Mass.: Lexington Books, 1985, pp. 34–35.
2. Schiesl, M. H. *The Politics of Efficiency.* Berkeley: University of California Press, 1977, p. 176.
3. Quoted in National Civic League. *Model City Charter, 7th ed.* New York: National Civic League, 1989, p. xv.
4. National Civic League (1989), p. xvi.
5. National Municipal League. *Model City Charter.* New York: National Municipal League, 1900.
6. National Municipal League (1900), p. 23.
7. National Civic League (1989).
8. National Civic League (1989), p. xvi.
9. Chang, T.-S. *History and Analysis of the Commission and City-Manager Plans of Municipal Government in the United States.* Ph.D. dissertation, University of Iowa, 1918.
10. Chang (1918), p. 55.
11. Chang (1918), p. 157.
12. National Civic League. *Forms of Local Government: Meaningful Reform for a New Century.* Denver: National Civic League Press, 1993, p. 12.
13. National Civic League (1989), p. xvi.
14. National Civic League (1989), p. xvi–xvii.
15. National Civic League (1993), p. 16.
16. National Municipal League. *Model City Charter, 2nd ed.* New York: National Municipal League, 1915, p. 13.
17. National Municipal League (1915), p. 14.
18. National Municipal League. *Model City Charter, 3rd ed.* New York: National Municipal League, 1927.
19. National Municipal League (1927), pp. 12–13.
20. National Municipal League. *Model City Charter, 4th ed.* New York: National Municipal League, 1933, p. 24.
21. National Municipal League. *Model City Charter, 5th ed.* New York: National Municipal League, 1941, p. vii.
22. National Municipal League (1941).
23. Model City Charter Committee. "Memorandum as to Decisions Reached at Meeting of Model City Charter Committee." (Memorandum.) Chicago, June 4–6, 1937.
24. National Municipal League. *Model City Charter, 6th ed.* New York: National Municipal League, 1964.
25. National Municipal League (1964), p. xi.
26. National Municipal League (1964).
27. National Municipal League (1964), p. xiv.
28. Svara, J. H. "The Model City and County Charters: Innovation and Tradition in the Reform Movement." *Public Administration Review,* Nov.–Dec. 1990, 50, 688–692.
29. National Municipal League (1989), p. xii.
30. National Municipal League (1989).
31. National Municipal League (1989), p. 33.
32. National Municipal League (1989), p. 20.
33. National Municipal League (1989), p. 21.
34. National Municipal League (1989), p. 21.
35. National Municipal League (1989), p. 21.
36. ICMA Task Force Recommendations, March 27, 2000. *ICMA Newsletter,* 2000, 81 (7), suppl. 1, p. 3.
37. ICMA Task Force Recommendations (2000).
38. Frederickson, H. G., and Johnson, G. Unpublished results.
39. Renner T., and DeSantis, V. S. "Municipal Form of Government: Issues and Trends." In *Municipal Year Book 1998.* Washington, D.C.: International City Management Association, 1998, pp. 30–41.
40. Ebdon, C., and Brucato, Jr., P. F. "Government Structure in Large U.S. Cities: Are Forms Converging?" *International Journal of Public Administration,* 2000, 23(12), 2209–2235.
41. Ebdon and Brucato (2000), p. 2228.
42. Hansell, B. "Revisiting the Reform of the Reform." Public Management, Jan. 1999, pp. 27–28.
43. Hansell (1999).
44. Frederickson and Johnson (unpublished).
45. Adrian, C. R. "Forms of City Government in American History." In *Municipal Year Book 1988.* Washington, D.C.: International City Management Association, 1998, pp. 3–11.
46. Frederickson and Johnson (unpublished).

CASE STUDY 12

Introduction

Since 1900, the National Civic League has provided a framework for municipal government reform through the Model City Charter. The league's recommendations have not gone unheeded. Today, a substantial majority of cities have a council-manager form of government, which the league has preferred ever since the second model charter was published in 1915. In addition, many cities that retain mayor-council governments have moved toward the league's recommendations by hiring professional administrators to provide expertise to the mayor and council members. Despite the league's success, not all cities have gone through reform or adopted all of the league's recommendations. More important, many cities today often find themselves confronting problems that might be addressed by restructuring their governments.

One such city is St. Louis, Missouri. In the essay that follows, Rob Gurwitt, a staff correspondent for *Governing* magazine, provides a critical view of St. Louis's government. Gurwitt writes that the city technically has had a strong mayor form of government for the past hundred years, although its mayor actually has few of the powers associated with strong mayors elsewhere. Most of Gurwitt's essay does not focus on the mayor, however, but on the St. Louis city council. The problem Gurwitt identifies with the council is that its members provide little meaningful leadership for the city, but instead focus on narrow concerns as they try to protect their own neighborhoods. Gurwitt traces the council's problems to its large size and small wards. Each of the 28 aldermen on the council represents a ward of about 12,500 people. The smallness of the wards, Gurwitt suggests, encourages parochialism and allows aldermen to be elected who may lack skill and vision. The problems confronting St. Louis are not isolated to this one city. In fact, the councils in many large cities today frequently find themselves focusing primarily on mundane or narrow concerns, and as a result their relevance to governing is threatened.

In the preceding essay, Frederickson, Wood, and Logan describe the concerns that motivated the authors of the Model City Charter for the past hundred years. Ever since the second charter, the authors of the charter have been particularly concerned with finding ways to provide cities with both expertise and leadership. With a weak mayor and a large city council concerned about localized matters, St. Louis offers a vivid illustration of an unreformed city. As such, it provides a valuable case to consider when thinking about the preceding essay and the recommendations that have been offered in the model charters. It also illustrates how the struggle for power and the desire to change policy outcomes can affect the battle over reform.

Questions to Consider

These are some questions to consider as you read the essay:

- What does Gurwitt say is the problem confronting the city council in large cities? Why has this problem come to be?

- How would you describe politics in St. Louis? What role does the city council play? How has it come to play this role?
- What are the benefits and drawbacks of St. Louis's governmental structure? Thinking back to the preceding essay, what reforms from the Model City Charter do you think might help St. Louis?
- Why does it appear that St. Louis has not changed its governmental structure?

Are City Councils a Relic of the Past?

Rob Gurwitt

You notice two things right off about the 19th Ward in St. Louis. The first is that pretty much everywhere there's construction, there's also a large sign reading, "Assistance for the project provided by Michael McMillan, Alderman." The second is just how limited Alderman McMillan's domain happens to be. Walk a few minutes in any direction, and you're out of his ward. You don't see the signs anymore. You also don't see as much construction.

Within the friendly confines of the 19th, St. Louis looks like a city busily reviving. There are new high schools being built, scattered apartments and loft projects underway, efforts to rejuvenate the historic arts and entertainment district, and a HOPE VI retrofit of an enormous public housing facility. While all this activity has some powerful people behind it, just one person has had a hand in all of it, and that is McMillan himself. Only 31, he has been on the St. Louis Board of Aldermen for six years, and in that time has made it clear that his ambitions for his ward—and by extension, himself—are high. "I don't have other obligations," he says. "I'm not married, I have no kids, I have no other job. It's one of my competitive edges."

Cross the ward boundary, and you find out what "competitive edge" means in St. Louis politics. North of the 19th, and for some distance to the east, stretch a series of neglected, depopulated neighborhoods that do not in any way suggest urban revival. This is, in part, a consequence of private market decisions: These neighborhoods don't have much clout within the corporate suites where such decisions are made. But equally important, they don't have much clout in local government, either—at least not when it comes to large-scale development projects.

That's because in St. Louis, each of the 28 ward aldermen is the gatekeeper of development in his or her little slice of the city. If they're shrewd and well connected, like Michael McMillan, the ward does fine. If they're inattentive, or maladroit at cutting deals, or on the outs with local developers, or just plain picky, which is the case in more than a few wards, hardly anything gets done. "You don't see a Mike McMillan coming out of some of these devastated wards," says one City Hall insider. "They have a voice, but if it's weak, what do they really get?"

To be sure, even the weak aldermen in St. Louis have their uses. They get potholes filled and streetlights fixed, offer advice on how to handle code violations or deal with housing court, and see that garbage gets picked up in alleyways where contractors dump it illegally. This hands-on attention is hardly a bad thing. In the words of Jim Shrewsbury, who as president of the Board of Aldermen runs at large and is its 29th member, the city's deeply entrenched system of political micro-management "protects neighborhoods and gives people a sense of influence." As members of a democratic institution, that's what city councilmen are supposed to do. But when that's about *all* many of them do, in a city that is struggling to emerge from years of economic debility, even Shrewsbury agrees that something

Rob Gurwitt, "Are City Councils a Relic of the Past?" *Governing* (April 2003): 20–24. This article first appeared in the April 2003 issue of *Governing* Magazine.

is wrong. The system, he says, "creates a sense of parochialism and feudalism. We become the Balkans."

Feuding and Hot Air

The concept of balkanization could be applied these days to councils and boards of aldermen in many of America's biggest cities—perhaps most of them. Look around the country and you can quickly compile a dossier of dysfunction.

Sometimes it is a case of pursuing tangents, as the Baltimore City Council likes to do. In a recent commentary about what it called "the hot-air council," the Baltimore *Sun* suggested that frequent resolutions on foreign affairs, hearings on the differences between telephone exchanges, and debate about counteracting "the negative images of Baltimore, as portrayed in 'real-crime' fiction, TV dramas and movies" suggested that the members didn't have enough real work to do.

Other councils become so embroiled in internal maneuvering that they lose their relevance. In Philadelphia, where a former mayor once referred to the city council as "the worst legislative body in the free world," there was a brief period of council influence in the mid-1990s, when John Street was council president and worked closely with Mayor Ed Rendell. Now, however, Street is mayor and finds himself in regular tangles with various council factions. "It's like an opera where everybody has a different libretto," says Mark Alan Hughes, an urban affairs professor at the University of Pennsylvania and columnist for the *Philadelphia Daily News*. "The melodrama is clear, it's just the meaning that's completely obscure."

There are councils where bickering and infighting are so intense that the entire body acquires an image of irresponsible flakiness. In Detroit recently, one member charged that supporters of the city's mayor had sabotaged the electric massager in her desk chair to give her a jolt when she used it. Not surprisingly, the public's response was disdainful—what most people saw was a group of elected officials engaged in sabotaging its own reputation.

There are places where, if you want to find the future of the city being pondered, the council chamber is the last place you'd look. "What you have," says a close watcher of civic affairs in Pittsburgh, "is a group of people who primarily deal with very mundane, housekeeping things in their districts. That's what they do, it's what they're interested in, and it's the way they see their power." The real power lies in the mayor's office and with the city's still-strong civic and corporate leadership.

Finally, there are councils whose problem has not been an absence of energy but a hyperactive compulsion to argue over everyday management decisions and prevent important decisions from being made. In Hartford, Connecticut, the city charter for years gave most of the political power to the council, but the council had a long history of intervening in the day-to-day administration of city services and tying itself up in petty squabbles corrosive to the morale of residents, as well as city employees. In the 1990s, the council essentially torpedoed the program of Mayor Mike Peters, who appeared to have broad voter support for his economic reform and revival ideas. Small surprise that when they were finally given a straightforward chance last November to change things, the city's voters opted to create a new form of government that strengthened the mayor at the council's expense.

None of this is to say that councils in large cities never tackle important issues or play a key role in crafting policy. Council members in Los Angeles, for instance, have a great deal to say about basic infrastructure issues, in their districts and across the city. And for all its infighting, the Philadelphia City Council did help to re-shape Street's ambitious urban renewal program, the Neighborhood Transformation Initiative, to be more responsive to neighborhood concerns.

But in all too many large cities these days, the power of councils is, at most, the power to stop things. The wellsprings of citywide innovation and progress lie elsewhere. It is telling that until this past year, neither of the two major national organizations speaking for cities addressed the specific concerns of big-city councils. The National League of Cities is dominated by small- and medium-sized jurisdictions; the U.S. Conference of Mayors, which focuses on larger cities, doesn't address council members at all. "We're literally locked out of the one national group that deals with big cities," observes Nick Licata, a Seattle council member.

Licata, who was struck by the dearth of representation from places like his when he first attended a League of Cities meeting, has put together a new "Central Cities Council" at the League, for council members in the 100 or so largest cities to share information and strategies on common issues. "We're not communicating on a regular basis, we're not exchanging information on local programs we can learn from, and on the national level, when we should be lobbying, we don't have our act together," he says. "This should help us link up."

Still, the sense of floundering one often gets watching big-city councils isn't really a surprise. Over the years, as mayors have moved to get a handle on crime, economic development and even school management, and as semi-private institutions—redevelopment authorities, stadium authorities, transit authorities, convention center authorities, tax increment finance districts—have proliferated, the role of councils in the most critical issues of urban governance has atrophied. Individual council members, the Michael McMillans of the country, may still have a share of power and influence, but the bodies on which many of them serve have lost their identity. "I think city councils have been neutered in most cases," says Dennis Judd, an urban affairs specialist at the University of Illinois-Chicago. "They are engaging in the most trivial aspects of urban government, rather than the most important aspects."

Under these circumstances, it is hard not to wonder whether city councils are becoming relics of the political past, poorly adapted to making the decisions of 21st-century urban life. In all too many cases, they seem in danger of becoming the dinosaurs of American local government.

Out of the Loop

There was a moment not long ago when the St. Louis Board of Aldermen managed to command national attention, but it's one local politicians would rather forget. In the midst of a tense and racially charged ward redistricting debate in 2001, Alderman Irene Smith was conducting a filibuster when she asked whether she could go to the bathroom. Told by Board President Shrewsbury that the rules required her to yield the floor to do so, she summoned her supporters, who brought in a trash can and surrounded her with improvised drapes while she appeared to urinate into the can. "I was mortified," says a St. Louis politician who happened to be watching on cable television at the time. "If you've been in the aldermanic chambers, they call to mind a time when the city was a powerful city, a grand place. To think of her staging that in there! The stock of the entire board of aldermen went down." Smith was later indicted on charges of public indecency but was acquitted in January on the reasoning that no one could know for sure whether she was actually urinating or simply pretending to do so.

To those who spend their time in City Hall, the incident was puzzling, because Smith, a lawyer and former judge, is generally seen as one of the more careful and thoughtful members of the board. "She's bright, she knows how to read the law, she asks tough questions in committee hearings," says one aldermanic insider. But to many in the city at large, there was little question about how to interpret her outburst: Not even its own members accord the board much respect any longer.

The fact is, for all the opportunities that ambitious aldermen have to promote development within their own neighborhoods, it's been a while since the board has played a significant role in shaping matters of vital interest to St. Louis as a whole. One of the biggest issues on the plate of Mayor Francis Slay—himself a former board president—is a new stadium for the St. Louis Cardinals baseball team, and while pieces of the complex deal he has put together will require aldermanic approval, the board itself has had very little role in constructing it.

"When I was in City Hall," says a former aide to one of Slay's recent predecessors, "I only went to the board if I absolutely had to. The truth is, I never felt the need to involve people there on the front end in order to get something passed on the back end. In the 1970s or '80s, if a mayor had a stadium project, he'd have had to line up five or six people on the board before he even went public with it." Because that didn't happen in the current situation, the aide argues, this stadium deal is just a stadium deal—it is not part of any broader city commitment to, say, refurbishing public sports facilities or community centers in the neighborhoods.

There are any number of theories about what has led the board of aldermen to its diminished citywide import, and many of them focus on its size. The 28 wards were created in 1914, when St. Louis had 680,000 people. They remained in place when the city reached its peak of 850,000 in 1950. And they're still there, half a century later, when it's down to 340,000. This means that each alderman represents about 12,500 people. Chicago's 50-member city council, which is one of the largest in the country, would have to grow to 200 members if its wards were the same size as those in St. Louis.

If all you expect of an alderman is close attention to garbage pickup and street repairs, of course, small wards are just fine. But they have a cost, as well. For one thing, they form a low barrier to political entry. In some wards, a politician needs as few as 800 votes to get elected. When the city was larger, says former Mayor Freeman Bosley Jr., "you had to be a real leader to get on the board, someone who could put together thousands and thousands of votes. That plays into your ability to . . . put people together and pull them in a direction. So as the years have gone by, the number of go-to people has diminished."

To be sure, it's possible to overstate the case. "Just because we were once a city of 800,000 people doesn't mean we had rocket scientists serving on the board of aldermen," notes Jim Shrewsbury. "I don't think someone makes a decision between running a corporation and being an alderman." But it's equally true that city councils are, in essence, a political proving ground—former U.S. House Minority Leader Richard Gephardt, for instance, got his start on the St. Louis Board of Aldermen. The less skill and vision they demand of their members, the poorer a city's civic life is likely to be.

"If you can make the council a place where young people who are interested in public policy think they ought to be, then it serves as a farm system to create people who understand how local government works and who have sympathy for it," says Mike Jones, a former alderman who now runs the regional Empowerment Zone. "Because the real question is, Where do you get local leadership from? On a city council where you've got to work hard to get elected, it takes good political instincts and hones them into political and policy-making skills."

Ironclad Privilege

Over time, the small size of the constituencies and the rules of the institution itself have combined to make the lure of parochialism more and more irresistible. In the 1950s, following passage of the federal Urban Renewal Act of 1949, aldermen in St. Louis suddenly found themselves with real power in their neighborhoods as the arbiters of development. That law, says Lana Stein, a University of Missouri St. Louis historian, "brought a huge pot of money, and the aldermen had to pass bills authorizing urban renewal projects and highway projects. They were courted by Civic Progress [the group of corporate movers and shakers at the time] and by the mayor. Even though there were working-class people and saloon keepers elected to the board, they became a much bigger deal because of what they were voting on."

But if the urban renewal money brought the board instant influence, it also led inexorably to parochialism. As requests grew for new housing or redevelopment in the wards, they ran into the ironclad principle of aldermanic privilege—the notion that no member of the board would interfere in matters affecting another member's ward.

Fifty years later, developers still need help from the city, and that usually means a vote from the aldermen, supporting a "blighting" provision or providing a tax abatement or creating a tax-increment financing district. If you happen to live in a ward with an active, responsive aldermen who knows how to put together development deals, you're fortunate. But there's scarcely anyone left on the board looking at what makes sense for the city as a whole. Aldermen rarely feel any right or responsibility to look closely at deals being made in others' wards.

When a group of downtown residents recently challenged plans backed by their alderman to demolish a historic, marble-fronted building to make way for a parking garage, the board deferred to the alderman's wishes by essentially ignoring the protest. The demolition plans were backed by the mayor and by his allies, and the developers insisted that the garage was vital to their plans, even though there are under-used garages within a block's walk.

The local residents, part of a small but growing group of loft dwellers who form one of the few tangible signs of hope for St. Louis' downtown, attended the one aldermanic hearing on the matter and found no one to talk to. "It was a farce," says Margie Newman, one of their leaders. "There was no opportunity to make our case. Literally, there was an alderman with the Sunday comics held up in front of his face, and of the six on the committee, three were wandering in and out. Remember, this was at our one opportunity to bring our case."

Indeed, confirms Matt Villa, a young alderman who represents the city's far southeast, there is little incentive on the board to pay attention to what others are doing when you don't have to. "In our neighborhood," he says, "there's a neighborhood association and a housing corporation, and we sit down to plan the next five years and never take into consideration what other wards are doing. I don't even know how a citywide plan would be embraced by 28 aldermen."

And because the board itself doesn't have an independent capacity to look carefully at measures that come before it—it has very few staff members, and those who want help, such as Michael McMillan, raise funds on the side to pay for an assistant—it often approves important decisions with scarcely any scrutiny at all. "We give pay raises and pension raises and things like that," Villa says, "without really knowing the fiscal impact. The alderman who's sponsored it explains, we pass it, and years later it turns out it wasn't a $5 million impact, it was a $50 million impact."

Charter Changes

If there's anyone unhappy with this state of affairs, it's Jim Shrewsbury, who as president would like the board to become more independent and active. "The truth is, most legislation and ideas originate with the administration," he says. "The vast majority of bills are administration-sponsored bills; they have the resources and the interest and the concentration. Sometimes, I wish we were more careful and would scrutinize them more carefully. And I wish there were more innovation, that more legislation originated here." But he is also quick to point out that in the calculus of the 28 politicians who serve alongside him, that may be more of a risk than they want to take. "I know that on Election Day, the one thousand people who hate me will be there," he explains. "I don't know how many of the thousands who like me will be. I'm prepared to lose my office for something that was in *Profiles in Courage*. If it's not, you start to wonder whether it's worth getting involved."

Yet it's possible that change will come to the St. Louis Board of Aldermen anyway. Although St. Louis is technically a "strong mayor" city, the political reality is that the mayor is constitutionally among the weakest in the country for a city this size. Power has to be shared with a half-dozen other elected officials; the state controls the police through a board on which the mayor has only his own seat; budget decisions and city contracts have to be approved by two of the three members of the Board of Estimate and Apportionment, which is made up of the mayor, comptroller and aldermanic president. "St. Louis is probably the nation's best case of an unreformed government," says the University of Illinois' Dennis Judd, referring to the nationwide movement early in the last century to give mayors enhanced authority. "It's as if it never was touched by the reformers."

Like the board's awkward size, all of this is a result of the 1914 city charter, which is still in effect. But last November, voters statewide approved a home-rule provision for St. Louis that will allow it to take up charter change. Although most of the attention is likely to go to placing more power in the hands of the mayor, there is plenty of sentiment among civic leaders for shrinking the size of the board of aldermen.

This is happening in other big cities with similar problems. Contraction is on the docket in Milwaukee, where some aldermen themselves have proposed shrinking the Common Council from 17 to 15 members, and in Baltimore, where voters last November approved trimming the city council from 19 to 15. Baltimore's initiative, backed by a coalition of labor unions and community organizations, was opposed by most of the city's elected leadership, but it passed overwhelmingly.

It's unclear how much impact tinkering with council size will really have, in St. Louis or anywhere else.

But it's clear that some fundamental changes will have to take place for city councils such as these to maintain any real relevance at all in coming years.

By any standard, there is still important work for these bodies to do. Cities need robust political institutions, and by all rights, city councils ought to be among them—they are, after all, the one institution designed to serve as the collective voice of residents and communities, whether their members are elected in districts or at large. But when little is expected of them, because a city's most important decisions are made elsewhere, it's no surprise that over time the ambitions of their members shrink to take in smaller and smaller patches of turf.

There are undeniable benefits to this. Two decades ago, voters in St. Louis overwhelmingly turned down an initiative to cut the number of wards. They felt, says Shrewsbury, "that government had gotten so complicated and big, the only way their voice could be heard was having an alderman who paid close attention." It may be that all most people really want from their city council is the kind of personal stroking that is often hard to come by elsewhere in a big city. But it's also hard to escape the feeling that, as Judd puts it, "when citizens are consulted these days, it's about things that are less and less consequential. What we're seeing is the slow strangulation of local democracy."

Chapter 12 Review Questions

1. What are the three primary structures of American cities? Describe each one. What would you say are some of the benefits and drawbacks of each type of structure?
2. Why does the essay by Frederickson, Woods, and Logan suggest that there might be a better categorization of the legal platforms for city governments? What has been happening in cities to make the older classification of city government structure seem less meaningful today? What alternative do the authors discuss?
3. What is the Model City Charter? Why was it created? How has it evolved over time? What has caused its recommendations to change?
4. What are the problems with the city government in St. Louis? What has caused these problems to develop? How might the Model City Charter provide a guide to overcome these problems?
5. What form of municipal government do you think is best? Why do you prefer this form? What criteria do you think are important in choosing a city government structure?
6. What advice would you give the National Civic League in revising the Model City Charter? What would you include in the charter?

Key Terms

Model City Charter
party machine
party boss
National Civic League
strong mayor
weak mayor
mayor-council form
council-manager form
nonpartisan elections
at-large elections
scientific management movement
commission form
ward system
merit system
Hare system

Suggestions for Further Reading

Banfield, Edward C., and James Q. Wilson. *City Politics.* Cambridge, Mass.: Harvard University Press, 1963. Provides one of the best overviews of the municipal reform movement and machine politics in American cities.

DeSantis, Victor S., and Tari Renner. "City Government Structures: An Attempt at Clarification." *State and Local Government Review* 34 (Spring 2002): 95–104. Offers new typology for classifying municipal governments that captures the growing number of cities with mixed forms. Includes brief, but helpful, literature review.

Frederickson, H. George, Gary Johnson, and Curtis Wood. *The Adapted City: Institutional Dynamics and Structural Change.* New York: M. E. Sharpe, 2003. Detailed study of why modern cities no longer rely on the traditional council-manager and mayor-council forms of government. Also see H. George Frederickson and Gary Johnson. "The Adapted American City: A Study of Institutional Dynamics." *Urban Affairs Review* 36 (July 2001): 872–84; and H. George Frederickson, Brett Logan, and Curtis Wood. "Municipal Reform in Mayor-Council Cities: A Well-Kept Secret." *State and Local Government Review* 35 (Winter 2003): 7–14.

Gates, Christopher T., and Robert Loper. "Renewing the Model City Charter: The Making of the Eighth Edition." *Public Management* 85 (April 2003): 4–9. Provides a history of the Model City Charter and an overview of the changes in the eighth edition, which was published in 2003.

Hansell, Bill. "Is it Time to 'Reform' the Reform?" *Public Management* 80 (December 1998): 15–16. Short essay by the executive director of the International City/County Management Association on whether the council-manager form of government is adequate for confronting current municipal problems. Hansell takes up this theme again in two other articles, "Reforming the Reforms, Part 2," *Public Management* 81 (January 1999): 28; and "The Mayor: The Unnamed Partner in Council-Manager Governance," *Public Management* 84 (April 2002): 26.

Hirschhorn, Bernard. *Democracy Reformed: Richard Spencer Childs and His Fight for Better Government.* Westport, Conn.: Greenwood Publishing, 1997. Biography of the man considered the creator of the council-manager form of government.

International City/County Management Association. *The Municipal Yearbook.* Washington, D.C.: International City/County Management Association, 2001. Comprehensive source of information on local governments in the United States. Includes comparative data and research articles.

Judd, Dennis R., and Todd Swanstrom. *City Politics: Private Power and Public Policy.* New York: Pearson, Longman, 2004. Fine textbook on city politics, with chapters on both machine politics and municipal reform.

National Civic League. *Model City Charter.* 8th ed. Denver, Colo.: National Civic League, 2003. The most recent edition of the league's model charter.

Stein, Lana. *St. Louis Politics: The Triumph of Tradition.* Columbia: Missouri Historical Society Press, 2002. This book provides a fuller understanding of the problems in St. Louis politics created by the city's unreformed government structure.

Svara, James H. "Do We Still Need Model Charters? The Meaning and Relevance of Reform in the Twenty-first Century." *National Civic Review* 90 (Spring 2001): 19–33. Published in the *National Civic Review* series from which the reading was also drawn, this essay considers what should be incorporated in the Model City Charter, given changes in city government structures and elections in recent years. Svara was an advisor to the eighth edition of the Model City Charter revision committee.

———. *Official Leadership in the City: Patterns of Conflict and Cooperation.* New York: Oxford University Press, 1990. Study of how the choice of government form, whether mayor-council or council-manager, affects the character of city politics.

Related Web Sites

http://nclweb.org/
Web site for the National Civic League includes information on ordering the eighth edition of the Model City Charter.

http://www.icma.org
The web site for the International City/County Management Association contains considerable information on cities and counties, including material on forms of local government. Access to some parts of the site is limited to members, but there are reduced rates for students.

http://www.nlc.org
The National League of Cities web site provides research reports on issues of importance to municipal governments and links to state affiliates. Many of these affiliate sites provide valuable information on their state.

13

Urban Government: The Concept of New Regionalism

Metropolitan political fragmentation has encouraged unplanned, costly sprawl on the urban fringe. It has imposed longer journeys to work on commuters, allowing them less time for family life. It has undermined the quality of life in older suburbs, hardened conflicts between suburbs and the central cities, hampered financing for regional public facilities such as mass transit, and encouraged disinvestment from central cities.

Peter Dreier, John Mollenkopf, and Todd Swanstrom

READING 13

Introduction

Despite the nation's strong economic growth during the 1990s, central cities in America have continued to confront a host of problems for many years that are far worse than in the suburbs or smaller communities. These problems are well known: fewer jobs, greater unemployment, more poverty, higher crime rates, worse schools, and wider drug abuse.

What can be done to address these ills and create a healthier urban environment? In recent years, many political reformers and urban scholars have focused increased attention on finding regional solutions to the problems confronting American cities. One of the primary difficulties faced by central cities is that they lack the economic base to address the host of social and economic problems they confront. The prosperous suburbs, on the other hand, have fewer social problems, but a stronger economic base, which is better able to pay for government programs and services. By looking for regional solutions, reformers argue, the central cities could tap the strong economic base of the suburbs to address urban problems.

This increased interest in looking toward regional solutions has been labeled the "new regionalism." Since 1990, there has been a publishing boom of books and journal articles focusing on regional governance and planning as a way to address these social and economic problems, as well as a wide array of other issues confronting the nation's urban areas. This research has attracted attention from scholars in a cross section of disciplines, including political science, urban planning, sociology, and education.

Despite the label, interest in regionalism is not new. Some urban politics scholars suggest that regionalism has been considered as a solution to municipal problems ever since the early 1800s, when several metropolitan regions, including New Orleans and Boston, pushed for the consolidation of city and county governments. During the industrial revolution, interest in regionalism grew stronger, as many of the nation's cities began to annex neighboring areas more aggressively in order to strengthen their economic competitiveness and improve government efficiency. The leaders of the municipal reform movement, which is discussed in the preceding chapter, were advocates of regional government. One of the problems these reformers saw was that there were too many local governments in the metropolitan areas, creating a fragmentation in the delivery of government services. By unifying metropolitan areas under one government the efficiency and effectiveness of public services would improve.

Since the early 1900s, regionalism has repeatedly attracted interest among reformers and scholars as a solution to different urban problems. In the 1920s, many of the nation's leading planners spoke out in support of regionalism to address urban planning issues. Among its advocates at the time was the well-known architect and planner Lewis Mumford, who helped to found the Regional Planning Association of America in 1923. In the 1930s, some scholars saw regionalism as an important part of the efforts to address the nation's economic woes. In the 1960s and 1970s, reformers and scholars frequently touted regionalism as the solution to a wide range of urban problems, from fighting crime, to improving the environment, to strengthening schools. The federal government stimulated interest in regionalism during this period by establishing federal requirements and allocating funds in ways to promote regional planning. As a result of the federal government's actions, there was a growth in the number of regional Councils of Governments (COGs), which spurred local governments to coordinate their activities voluntarily and led to better regional planning in specific policy areas, especially transportation and housing. There was also an increase in single-purpose metropolitan districts, which are types of regional governments that oversee one particular policy area, such as water supply, sewage treatment, air quality, or transportation.

In the 1980s, however, support for regionalism declined as many political leaders began to praise the benefits of competition between local governments. These leaders, who subscribe to what is called Public Choice Theory, saw this competition as a good way to encourage efficiency and responsiveness. Instead of regionalism, they supported the existence of many local governments in urban areas. In addition, federal funding for regional projects was reduced after Ronald Reagan became president in 1981. As a result of these trends, interest in regionalism declined.

From this brief history, it should be clear that regionalism is not a new proposal to address the woes of the nation's cities, but reflects a history dating back for many years. Yet there are some aspects of new regionalism that are considered different from the past. In particular, many of the scholars who write on regionalism today focus more attention on the issue of equity than was true of their predecessors. In much of this literature, there is a strong normative perspective. Many of these scholars are concerned about the vast differences that separate the urban centers of America from the outlying suburbs, especially in the concentration of poverty, the availability of jobs, the quality of schools, and the prevalence of crime. They look to regionalism as a way to address these inequities and to improve conditions in the central cities. Not all scholars who are associated with new regionalism, however, focus on the question of equity. Others are concerned about urban issues that were first raised in the 1960s or even earlier. These include how to stimulate economic growth across metropolitan areas, improve government efficiency and effectiveness, and overcome problems associated with urban sprawl, such as long commutes, the disappearance of open space, and poorly designed communities.

Peter Dreier, John Mollenkopf, and Todd Swanstrom are among the scholars studying urban issues who are concerned about the question of equity. In 2001, the three professors joined together to publish *Place Matters,* a highly praised book on the problems confronting the central cities in America. The authors argue that the central problem confronting urban areas is that they are strongly segregated by income levels. This segregation affects the quality of a person's life and the opportunities that a person has to improve his or her situation. For the poor who live in the nation's central cities, the government does not provide the same quality of public goods and services that are provided by the governments in the well-to-do suburbs. More important, it is difficult for the poor to rise out of poverty and improve their lives because the central cities cannot provide the education, social contacts, and job opportunities needed to do so. For those who live in the suburbs, however, the government and private sector provide the opportunities and support needed to succeed. The only way the problems of the central cities can be overcome, the authors argue, is through regionwide solutions. In the latter part of their book, the authors lay out a long list of recommendations for addressing these problems, including creating regional governments, introducing regional tax sharing, and taking steps to help poor families move to more prosperous neighborhoods where the opportunities are greater.

The reading for this chapter, which was taken from *Place Matters,* provides an introduction to many of the topics that are necessary to understand the potential value of regionalism. Of particular importance, the reading reiterates many of the authors' concerns about the current problems confronting urban regions today, and it provides an overview of many of the arguments put forward by others in support of regionalism.

If regional government provides so much potential for addressing the ills of urban America, then why haven't more regional governments been created? There are several answers to this question. One is that suburban residents frequently oppose regional initiatives. As the reading makes clear, many suburbanites don't see urban issues as their problems, and many fear that regionalism may increase their tax burden and transform the character of the communities in which they live. Opposition from suburban residents is only part of the answer, however. Although it is not discussed as much in the reading, another hurdle is that many local government leaders, both in the suburbs and the central city themselves, are reluctant to support the creation of regional governments out of fear that their own political power will be diluted. There is also a conflict in values involved, as there are in many of the other types of political debates covered in this book. Whereas many reformers are concerned primarily with finding solutions to these difficult social problems, many of their opponents value the ideals of local control and are reluctant to support a government that they see as being too far removed from the people. Thus, although regional government may offer a more effective solution to urban problems, it is often politically difficult to get adopted. Conversely, some of the regional initiatives that are considered more likely to be put into place, such as the use of voluntary Councils of Governments, are often seen by reformers as being too weak to address regional problems.

Place Matters was the winner of the Michael Harrington Award from the New Political Science Section of the American Political Science Association. Professor Dreier is a professor of politics and the director of the Urban and Environmental Policy Program at Occidental College. John Mollenkopf is a professor of political science and sociology at City University of New York. Swanstrom is a professor of public policy at St. Louis University. All three have written extensively on urban issues.

Questions to Consider

As you read the excerpt from *Place Matters,* these are some questions to consider:

- How did Hartford, Connecticut, and Memphis, Tennessee, try to use regional solutions to address their problems? Why did their efforts fail?
- What do the authors of the reading say is the problem that needs to be solved?
- What are the different arguments presented by the authors in support of regionalism? Give a brief explanation of each one.
- How do New York and Los Angeles reflect the local experience in governing? In what ways have these cities used regional approaches for public improvements?
- How do the Twin Cities of Minnesota and Portland, Oregon, represent exceptional cases? What do their regional governments do?

Regionalisms Old and New

Peter Dreier, John Mollenkopf, and Todd Swanstrom

[I]t is difficult for central cities by themselves to solve the problems generated by economic segregation and urban sprawl. It is only natural, therefore, for cities to reach out to suburban municipalities and attempt to forge regional solutions to their problems. Regional approaches face their own obstacles, however. Consider the efforts of Hartford, Connecticut, and Memphis, Tennessee.

Hartford is the capital city of the richest state in the nation, but for a long time, it has had one of the country's highest poverty rates and large areas of concentrated poverty. In 1969, Hartford's major employers formed a new organization, the Greater Hartford Process (GHP), to solve the region's problems.[1] Three years later, this elite group unveiled a plan to rebuild the city's low-income areas, create an entire new town

Peter Dreier, John Mollenkopf, and Todd Swanstrom, "Regionalisms Old and New," from *Place Matters: Metropolitics for the Twenty-first Century* (Lawrence: University Press of Kansas, 2001), pp. 173–200.

in the suburbs, and develop new regional approaches to housing, transportation, health care, education, and social services. The plan would affect 670,000 persons in twenty-nine communities in a 750-square-mile area.

The most dramatic impact was on the town of Coventry, fifteen miles from the city. GHP had quietly begun buying land in the all-white town of 8,500 residents in order to create, from scratch, a new town of 20,000; 15 percent of the housing units were to be set aside for low-income families. Coventry officials refused to cooperate with the plan, which was ultimately shelved. One suburban official noted, "I don't see the problems of the central city as my responsibility." Within a few years, GHP had ceased to exist. Although most Hartford residents had responded positively, "some leaders of Hartford's black community claimed that the new-town idea was an attempt to dilute their power in the city, and others objected to the lack of citizen input into Hartford Process plans."[2]

Two decades later, Hartford's newly hired city manager, Raymond Shipman, proposed another regional plan. It required suburbs to join a regional government, provided some public services, enacted a tax on suburban commuters to Hartford, and would raze three public housing projects and relocate their residents to the suburbs.[3] Shipman was soon gone as Hartford's city manager. Then, in 1996, the city council took a different approach to the problem, placing a moratorium on new social service agencies that serve the poor, such as soup kitchens, homeless shelters, and drug treatment centers. Within its 18.4 square miles, the city (with a population of 140,000) had 150 social service agencies, which, city officials said, attracted poor people to the city.[4] Hartford city council members claimed that these programs were "ruining the climate for urban revitalization, hurting business, shrinking the tax base, and scaring away the middle class." They also argued that the suburbs were not doing their share to address the needs of the poor—certainly an accurate statement.[5] It was almost as if Hartford officials had decided that if the suburbs refused to cooperate, the city would stop accommodating the region's poor, potentially forcing them out to the suburbs.

Memphis is another central city with many poor, minority citizens that has attempted regional solutions. In 1971, suburban residents in Shelby County, Tennessee, voted two to one against merging with Memphis. In 1990, an attempt to merge the largely black Memphis school system with the predominantly white county school system also failed, due to suburban opposition. In 1993, Mayor W. W. Herenton, the city's first African American mayor and former school superintendent, took a politically courageous stand and again proposed merging the city with suburban Shelby County. The reason Herenton's proposal was courageous was that if it had been successful, it would have diluted the black electoral power so recently gained with his election.

Between 1940 and 1980, Memphis captured 54 percent of all population growth in the region by annexing suburbs. After 1980, suburban opposition ended Memphis's expansion, and during the 1980s, Memphis lost 6 percent of its population, while that of the surrounding Shelby County suburbs more than doubled. Many African American political leaders, who had recently gained six of thirteen seats on the city council and five on the nine-member school board, argued that the merger would dilute black voting strength and cost blacks "some of the political control we have fought for so long." Herenton, who had been elected mayor in a highly racially polarized election, countered that "blacks gain little by controlling a city that is broke."[6] Herenton garnered support from Memphis business leaders, who predicted that the merger would lessen their tax burden, but many suburbanites opposed the merger, fearing that suburban Shelby County (median household income $43,784) would face additional tax burdens when merged with Memphis (median household income $22,674). The proposal failed at the polls.

These two examples show the difficulty of implementing regional solutions to the problems of concentrated poverty and suburban sprawl. They are not the only examples—we will also point to more positive ones—but they are instructive. In this chapter, we examine regional initiatives over the past 100 years, looking especially closely at the "new regionalism" that has emerged since the early 1990s. We applaud these efforts but argue that under the present state and federal rules of the game most regional initiatives are limited and difficult to sustain.

The Problem

The competition among metropolitan jurisdictions to attract higher-income residents and exclude the less well-off has been a powerful factor promoting the concentration of poor people in central cities. In the typical metropolitan area, dozens, even hundreds, of suburban towns seek to establish their places within the metropolitan pecking order. A "favored quarter" houses upper-income people and businesses that pay taxes but do not demand many services and do not lessen the quality of life.[7] These places use zoning regulations, high prices, and even racial prejudice to keep out the unwanted, or at least the less privileged. Elsewhere, less exclusive residential suburbs, suburban commercial and industrial areas, and aging inner-ring suburbs seek to carve out their own places in the hierarchy of municipalities. Even those aging, economically stagnating working-class suburbs on the city's edge often try to keep out inner-city residents. For those with limited means, living in the central city may be their only choice.

A similar but less keen competition takes place among central-city neighborhoods. Here, neighborhoods do not have their own formal authority to exclude some residents and attract others, but factors such as housing quality and price, neighborhood amenities (particularly a good neighborhood primary school), and city zoning and land-use regulations can serve the same purpose. Unlike exclusive suburban towns, however, even well-off central-city residents pay into the city's common budget. As a result, higher-income central-city residents who do not want to pay for services for the less fortunate, or who do not use the central-city services for which they are paying (such as schools, public transit, and parks), have a strong incentive to move to a more exclusive suburban jurisdiction.

Federal policies heightened this competition and made the suburbs attractive by building freeways, fostering suburban home ownership, and encouraging central cities to specialize in social services for needy constituents. Many suburbs reinforce this arrangement by regulating land uses to maximize property values and tax revenues, by customizing their services for middle-class professionals, and by declining to build subsidized housing or sometimes even any kind of rental housing. Central-city public officials have also contributed to this state of affairs by relying on the growth of social services to enhance their budgets, provide jobs for constituents, and build political support. They are no more willing to give up responsibility for, and control over, these activities than exclusive suburbs are to embrace them. Defenders of this system draw on widely held beliefs that localism, private property, and homogeneous communities are sacred parts of the American way of metropolitan living. . . .

Although this deeply embedded system may seem rational to suburban residents and public officials, it has produced dysfunctional consequences for the larger society. Metropolitan political fragmentation has encouraged unplanned, costly sprawl on the urban fringe. It has imposed longer journeys to work on commuters, allowing them less time for family life. It has undermined the quality of life in older suburbs, hardened conflicts between suburbs and their central cities, hampered financing for regional public facilities such as mass transit, and encouraged disinvestment from central cities. Countries with strong national land-use regulation and regional governments have avoided many of these problems. Indeed, the United States could have avoided them if we had chosen a more intelligent path for metropolitan growth over the last fifty years.

As these problems became increasingly evident, they drew criticism from scholars, planners, and good-government groups. These critics have focused on how metropolitan political fragmentation undermines administrative efficiency, environmental quality, economic competitiveness, and social equity. As early as the 1930s, administrative experts promoted regional solutions as ways to address the overlap, duplication, lack of coordination, and waste in the provision of public services. Concern today is becoming widespread. Even long-time suburban residents have expressed concern over the environmental costs of sprawl as they see their countryside being gobbled up by new development and find themselves in traffic jams even while doing their Saturday morning shopping. They have made "smart growth" a hot-button issue across the country. Executives of large firms, transportation planners, and economic development officials most often express concern that fragmented metropolitan areas undermine the economic competitiveness of urban regions.

Finally, those who crusade for civil rights and racial desegregation, who care about the plight of the inner-city poor, and who champion greater civic participation have criticized the ways in which metropolitan fragmentation has hurt the social and economic fabric of our communities. They argue in favor of fair housing and housing mobility programs, metropolitan administration of economic opportunity programs, tax-base sharing, and metropolitan school districts. Indeed, metropolitan fragmentation, sprawl, and inequality are major causes of the decline in community and civic participation, as is convincingly documented in Robert Putnam's *Bowling Alone.*[8] . . .

Origins of the New Regionalism

The current debate over regionalism echoes earlier concerns. At the end of the nineteenth century, New York, Chicago, and many other cities moved to annex or consolidate most of the adjacent territory likely to be developed in the next fifty years. The formation of Greater New York from New York City, Brooklyn, the hamlets of Queens County, the Bronx, and Staten Island in 1898 was a grand and highly successful experiment in metropolitan government. Indeed, much of the current vitality of cities such as Chicago and New York stems from these early actions. By the 1920s, however, middle-class urbanites, dismayed by the rapidly increasing density and inequality of their industrial cities, and frustrated by their inability to continue to dominate their politics, increasingly fled to the suburbs. Once they established themselves as suburbanites, they persuaded state legislatures to pass laws hindering cities from further annexation. Metropolitan growth would henceforth take place largely outside the jurisdiction of the cental city.

Responding to such trends, an early group of regionalists foresaw, as early as the 1920s, the need for new forms of metropolitan planning and cooperation. Echoing the "garden city" idea first promulgated by Ebenezer Howard in England, Lewis Mumford and his colleagues in the Regional Planning Association of America, formed in 1923, hoped that coherent regions would gradually emerge to dissolve the problems of the industrial city. "The hope of the city," Mumford wrote in 1925, "lies outside itself."[9] Other radical (though less utopian) thinkers called for regional land-use planning as an antidote to fragmentation. In 1927, the Regional Plan Association's magisterial plan for metropolitan New York called for knitting the region together with a comprehensive system of highways and rail transit that would concentrate economic growth in Manhattan and in a few suburban centers. In 1937, the New Deal's National Resources Committee called for federal efforts to foster regional planning, including the establishment of multistate metropolitan planning agencies. In the face of resistance from those who saw such measures as abrogating private property and local democracy, however, none of these visionary blueprints had much impact on the post–World War II evolution of American cities. As a result, many of the problems they anticipated did indeed come to pass.

Efficiency Arguments for Regionalism

The negative consequences of unplanned metropolitan growth triggered new strains of regionalist thinking and new political constituencies that favored the creation of new regional institutions. Public administrators, city planners, and municipal reformers viewed regional planning as the best way to promote regional economic efficiency and maintain a sound environment. . . . Prominent academics and planners such as Charles Merriam, Victor Jones, and Luther Gulick elaborated on these themes in the postwar period. Robert Wood's 1961 classic *1400 Governments* argued that postwar suburbanization in metropolitan New York was irrational, inefficient, and unaccountable. The federal Advisory Commission on Intergovernmental Relations, created by Congress in 1947 and eliminated in 1996, recommended ways to broaden the urban tax base and improve the regional distribution of services.

A common theme was that fragmented metropolitan governments promoted wasteful duplication, uneven standards of public service, and wasteful competition between local governments. These trenchant critiques were no more effective than the work of earlier metropolitan visionaries had been in restraining the construction of freeways, suburban shopping malls, and tract housing in the 1950s and 1960s. It nevertheless remained a key doctrine of public administration that regions required some level of metropolitan planning in order to function well. The 1960s saw the creation of many regional councils of government (often called COGs) and single-purpose regional agencies for functions such as water and sewer systems, garbage disposal, and transportation. City-county consolidation took place in Miami, Nashville, Jacksonville, and Indianapolis, but voters in many other areas rejected proposals to merge city and suburban governments into regional governments. Bucking this trend, in the November 2000 election, voters in Louisville, Kentucky, and its suburbs approved (by a 54 to 46 percent margin) the consolidation of the city of Louisville with Richmond County. This is the first major city-county merger to win approval in thirty years. Fast-growing cities of the South and Southwest, such as Phoenix and Albuquerque, also annexed surrounding territory long after that practice ended elsewhere in the country. Finally, voters and public officials sought to streamline and modernize the governance of suburban areas in the postwar period by enhancing county government and consolidating school districts. All these efforts, however, fell short of the goals espoused by the first and second generations of regionalists.

Environmental Arguments for Regionalism

Concern for administrative efficiency motivated the early advocates of metropolitan governance. Beginning in the 1960s, a new generation of regionalists emerged, concerned about environmental protection, sustainable development, and "smart growth." Development rapidly swallowed the metropolitan countryside after World War II, and the freeway construction of the 1960s and 1970s increased traffic congestion to new, more disturbing levels. Confronting these realities, suburban residents and those who represented them became less enthusiastic about unbridled metropolitan growth.

In 1974, the Council on Environmental Quality issued a report titled *The Costs of Sprawl,* calling for greater regulation of suburban development. Today, several national environmental organizations, including the Sierra Club, are campaigning against sprawl, Oregon and Maryland have adopted state legislation for "smart growth," and many other states are actively discussing similar measures. Some approaches call for the establishment of regional growth boundaries monitored by the state; others merely provide incentives to channel new investment toward already developed areas while attempting to preserve agricultural land uses or otherwise protect undeveloped areas. Regional groups are active in the San Francisco Bay Area, Washington, D.C., Pittsburgh, and Suffolk County, New York. A movement for "new urbanism" has emerged among architects and city planners who favor denser, more pedestrian- and transit-oriented forms of neighborhood development. Despite naysayers who see an adverse impact on housing affordability and consumer choice, a growing consensus has emerged in many places on behalf of rethinking older growth policies. Residents of Cook County, Illinois (an old urban area), and Santa Clara County, California (the high-tech Silicon Valley), both showed overwhelming support for regional approaches to solving urban problems. Voters across the country have approved ballot measures to limit suburban sprawl and preserve open spaces. Responding to such sentiments, Vice President Al Gore made smart growth a central theme in the Clinton-Gore administration's "livability agenda," which focused on preserving open spaces, redeveloping brownfield areas, mitigating congestion, and improving urban air quality.

Economic Competitiveness Arguments for Regionalism

Contemporary regionalists have also argued that metropolitan areas divided against themselves cannot compete successfully in the new global economy. In particular, business leaders and regional planning organizations have recognized that regionally oriented planning and development policies could make metropolitan economies more competitive. Although business-supported regional planning groups have existed at least since the Regional Plan Association was established in New York in 1923, groups like San Francisco's Bay Area Council and Pittsburgh's Allegheny Council for Community Development became more common after World War II. The radical changes in technology, business organization, and global competition since the 1980s gave this perspective new force. The high-technology companies of Silicon Valley took the lead in supporting regional approaches to the South Bay's housing, transportation, and development issues. One scholar, Annalee Saxenian, found that Silicon Valley entrepreneurs' ability to collaborate in this way made that region more successful, over the long haul, than the similar technology complex along Route 128 around Boston.[10]

. . . [S]ocial scientists who examine the interrelationships between central-city and suburban economies find a high correlation between the two, though in some cases, substantial central-city decline has not prevented the surrounding suburbs from prospering. Nevertheless, there are obvious linkages in the economic conditions and income growth rates of central cities and their suburbs. Central cities continue to perform functions and provide services that are critical to regional growth. The evidence suggests that cooperative regions are more likely to prosper than are more competitive, divided regions.[11]

These realities have given impetus to new efforts to form regional public-private partnerships to promote regional growth. Syndicated columnist Neal Peirce, who has given visibility to all forms of new regionalism, and his colleague Curtis Johnson have been particularly active in inspiring and advising a new generation of such organizations. They have not promoted any particular organizational forms, stressing instead the general need for collaboration, trust, dialogue, and leadership.[12] These collaborations have produced many Web sites and a journal, *The Regionalist*. . . .

Equity Arguments for Regionalism

The spatial concentration of urban poverty is another concern motivating many new regionalists. As Michael Schill observed, "although segregating themselves in the suburbs may serve the interests of large numbers of Americans today, the long term costs of doing nothing to alleviate concentrated ghetto poverty are likely to be tremendous."[13] Distinguished public intellectuals, including Anthony Downs of the Brookings Institution, former Albuquerque mayor David Rusk, Minnesota state legislator Myron Orfield, and Harvard professor Gary Orfield, among others, have concluded that regional approaches are the only way that the problem of inner-city poverty can be solved.[14] Increasingly, they have been joined by officials representing the inner-ring suburbs who are facing the growth of "urban" problems that they cannot solve within the limits of their own jurisdictions. . . .

Increasingly, planners are arguing that there need not be a trade-off between equality and efficiency, or growth. Indeed, regional strategies that lift up the central city can make regions more competitive. The Center on Wisconsin Strategy at the University of Wisconsin has advocated that workforce developers and regional employers cooperate to train central-city residents for high-wage jobs in technologically innovative firms. This "high road" approach to regional economic development would simultaneously enhance wages, upward mobility, and employer competitiveness.

The Practice of Metropolitan Cooperation

Although support for new, regional approaches to metropolitan problems has grown steadily stronger over the last several decades, the actual practice of metropolitan government has made less progress. Most regions have some elements of cooperation, but they vary considerably in terms of their institutional arrangements, the political constituencies they bring into play, and their capacity to address their region's social and economic challenges. A variety of constituencies has supported regional cooperation—business leaders seeking to enhance regional economic competitiveness, program administrators concerned with better coordination, community groups seeking regional equity, and suburban advocates of slowing growth. Their aims and interests obviously diverge on many points. In contrast to this diversity, the local interest in autonomy, particularly among suburban jurisdictions, is quite consistent. This has hindered the growth of metropolitan cooperation but may not prevent it in the long run.

What experiences has the United States had with metropolitan cooperation, why have they been so ineffective, and what forms would a more effective regionalism take? In formal terms, regional cooperation ranges from limited, single-purpose activities (such as a regional sewer or transportation authority or a reverse commuting program) through multipurpose cooperative arrangements to full-fledged regional governments. What follows is a brief review of the history and experience of metropolitan cooperation. . . .

The Local Experience: Avoidance and Conflict

In the typical metropolitan area, a region's constituent towns and cities may realize that they belong to a common region, but they seek to retain their autonomy and continue to act independently or compete with one another for economic resources. Savitch and Vogel and their colleagues found that New York, Los Angeles, and St. Louis epitomize this pattern.[15] It is common in older industrial areas with long histories of central city–suburban tension and long-standing racial, class, and social differences. David Rusk has shown that these "inelastic" central cities also have the worst race and class segregation and weak regional economic performance.[16]

The New York City consolidated metropolitan statistical area includes thirty-one counties in New York, New Jersey, Connecticut, and Pennsylvania and houses more than 21 million residents.[17] It contains some 1,787 county, municipal, town, school district, and special district governments. The nonprofit, business-backed Regional Plan Association has advocated three regional plans since 1923, most recently calling for a new emphasis on concentrated development around regional transit nodes and greater emphasis on workforce development.[18] These plans, however, have had more effect on thinking among academics and policy elites than on actual development patterns.

Efforts to create a true regional planning agency with significant authority have failed. The two public agencies that could undertake, this mission have not done so. The Port Authority of New York and New Jersey, created in 1921, operates the region's seaport, its three airports, the Hudson River bridges and tunnels, a commuter railroad, and the World Trade Center office complex. In recent decades, it has responded to the development agendas of the governor, who appoints its board, rather than acting as an agent for the region's municipalities. Mayor Rudolph Giuliani of New York City has campaigned to dissolve the Port Authority, or at least to return the New York airports to city control, and the agency suffers from the need to balance any benefit to one state with an equivalent benefit to the other. On the New York side of the river, the Metropolitan Transit Authority operates the city's subway and bus systems, bridges and tunnels, and a commuter rail system. It, too, is a creature of compromise between the governor and mayor, the city of New York and the adjacent counties it serves. It has had difficulty achieving agreement on new initiatives, such as providing rail service to the airports, although it has substantially upgraded the rolling stock and performance of its constituent properties.

Although New York City dominates the region and the borough of Manhattan draws more than 41 percent of daily commuters, it does not dominate the region's highly fragmented politics. The surrounding states and municipalities compete vigorously to attract business investment away from the city. Since the 1970s, Westchester County and Stamford, Connecticut, have lured away many large corporate headquarters; New Jersey enticed the New York Giants and Jets football teams to the Meadowlands complex, and Jersey City has attracted many back-office operations. In response to "predatory moves" by other jurisdictions, New York City has granted large tax abatements and other concessions to attract corporations to Manhattan or to retain them.

Concerned about these bidding wars, the governors of New York, New Jersey, and Connecticut and New York City's mayor signed a "nonaggression" pact in 1991. They vowed to avoid negative advertising and the use of tax breaks and other incentives to steal investment from one another and agreed to cooperate on a regional development strategy. Within a year, however, the economic rivalry accelerated, all three states launched new business incentive and tax reduction programs, and the "job wars" continued as before. For example, New Jersey induced First Chicago Trust Company to move 1,000 jobs from lower Manhattan by subsidizing the company's office space. Bruce Berg and Paul Kantor note, "The economic competition for jobs among states and localities in the tristate region goes unregulated, to the disadvantage of almost everyone except the corporations that are the objects of subsidies."[19] . . .

Los Angeles is the quintessential "fragmented metropolis."[20] The five-county region (Los Angeles, Ventura, Riverside, Orange, and San Bernardino Counties) contains 16 million people, a land area almost the size of Ohio, and an economy that would rank twelfth largest in the world if it were a separate country. It includes more than 200 cities (33 with more than 100,000 residents) and hundreds of special district governments. The city of Los Angeles, with 3.7 million residents, holds one-fifth of the region's population, but no one center dominates this decentered region. Much of Los Angeles, including the central city, has a "suburban" character, reflecting the area's reliance on the automobile. Its region's population grew 25 percent during the 1980s, most dramatically among Latino and Asian immigrants, and grew another 13 percent in the 1990s. Although black ghettos and Latino barrios are disproportionately located in the city of Los Angeles, the region's minority population is dispersed throughout the region, and high-poverty census tracts have also spread across the metropolitan area. During the 1980s, the poverty rate increased in each county; it is significantly higher in San Bernardino County than in Los Angeles County.

The region's many municipalities compete for private investment. After the passage of Proposition 13 in 1978, which drastically limited property taxes and forced localities to try to increase the collection of local sales taxes to expand their revenue base, this competition accelerated. Cities such as Glendale, Ventura, Pasadena, Anaheim, and Cerritos utilized redevelopment projects to reinvent themselves as office, sports, tourist, and retail centers. This competition has made efforts at regional cooperation more problematic. . . .

Los Angeles once mounted bold regional public works initiatives designed to expand the area's economy. The regional water system required complex land purchases, canals, and aqueducts that diverted water from the Owens Valley and the Colorado River. The Metropolitan Water District, a regional special district, now oversees this activity. Regional leaders also developed a port to foster regional economic growth. Los Angeles and Long Beach now have separate and competing ports, however, and many smaller airports compete with Los Angeles Airport.

Business, environmental, and planning groups have frequently sought to promote regional governance. Business leaders believed that traffic congestion, polluted air, and water shortages hurt their competitive position and funded studies to encourage stronger regional coordination. In 1988, Mayor Tom Bradley appointed a Los Angeles 2000 Committee, which called for a regional planning agency to manage land use, housing, and transportation and a regional environmental agency that would consolidate the regional antipollution agency with its water control and solid waste agencies. It also proposed to strengthen the region's airport authority. Despite much debate and the filing of the necessary bills in the state legislature, municipal leaders intensified their competition during the economic downturn of the early 1990s, and support for regional approaches fell apart.

Like many areas, the region has a council of governments, the Southern California Association of Governments (SCAG). An unwieldy body, SCAG has representation from seventy elected officials (sixty-three selected by municipal elected officials, and seven by county supervisors). The city of Los Angeles has only two members. Membership is voluntary, and SCAG has no authority over its member governments. It can recommend approval or rejection of projects proposed by cities under the federal ISTEA (now TEA-21), which allocates over $1 billion annually for transportation in the region. It can also withhold funds for local road improvements unless cities and counties develop plans to reduce auto usage. To comply, the various county-level transportation agencies embarked on such projects as a subway in Los Angeles, the imposition of tolls in Orange and Riverside Counties, and a high-speed train project.

This is one of the most polluted metropolitan areas in the nation, and the most powerful regional body is the South Coast Air Quality Management District. It has set tough standards for industry and automobile emissions, required construction of new public transportation facilities, caused county government to implement measures such as car-pool lanes, and influenced local land-use decisions. As a result, air quality has significantly improved: exposure to unhealthful ozone levels fell by half, despite population growth and constant business opposition.[21] . . .

New York . . . and Los Angeles typify the experience of most metropolitan regions, especially the older ones. Regional cooperation is restricted to a few specific functions, parts of the region still compete for investment and advantage, and regional rivalries hamper regional planning for public improvements that would spur economic growth. Indeed, these regions have difficulty coordinating even simple functions, such as meshing the schedules of regional mass transit systems. Myriad local jurisdictions take their own approaches to federally funded activities such as the construction and management of subsidized housing, the distribution of housing vouchers, the creation of job training programs, and the like, all of which might be more effective if carried out on a regional basis.

Experiments in Metropolitan Governance

Advocates of regional approaches consistently point to two places that have most fully developed the promise of regional government: the Twin Cities of Minneapolis and St. Paul, Minnesota, where an appointed metropolitan council carries out a number of functions and a regional tax-sharing scheme redistributes revenues from high-growth to low-growth areas; and Portland, Oregon, where an elected metropolitan government regulates suburban land development within a regional growth boundary.

The Twin Cities have a 2000 population of 669,769 in a metropolitan area of 2.9 million people. In 1967, the state legislature created a seven-county Metropolitan Council responsible for land use, housing, transit, sewage, and other metropolitan issues. The governor appoints its members, who set policies that local governments then carry out. In its first decade, the council solved a crisis in wastewater treatment. In the 1960s, the Federal Housing Administration threatened to stop insuring mortgages in burgeoning suburbs that lacked sewage treatment. In response, the Metropolitan Council created a Metropolitan Water Control Commission to finance and run treatment plants and build trunk sewer lines.

By the late 1970s, the Metropolitan Council had created or absorbed regional agencies for transportation, housing, and redevelopment. It had its own tax base and a substantial capital budget, and it received federal grants, which allowed it to provide regional infrastructure, encourage affluent suburbs such as Golden Valley to develop low- and moderate-income housing, and create regional parks where shopping centers might otherwise have been developed. In 1971, the state adopted the Fiscal Disparities Act, which required all metropolitan jurisdictions to pool 40 percent of the growth in their commercial industrial tax bases and to allocate the proceeds according to population and level of tax capacity, thus dampening competition for new development and reallocating resources from affluent, fast-growing suburbs to older, more urban parts of the region. The council also created a regional development framework to contain suburban sprawl and limit the cost of extending public services to outlying areas.

Despite these considerable successes, the Metropolitan Council has disappointed many of its early supporters. It did not provide leadership on the major development issues of the 1980s, including the building of several sports complexes and the world's largest shopping mall. It lacks an independent political base. When its views clash with those of the governor, influential state legislators, or even some local officials, it has difficulty mobilizing support for its agenda. Moreover, the existence of the Metropolitan Council and regional tax sharing has not prevented the Twin Cities from becoming one of the most sprawled-out metropolitan areas in the United States. Minneapolis has actually fared poorly under tax-base sharing because the formula stresses revenue-raising capacity, which counts the city's booming downtown but ignores the spending needs generated by its relatively large poor population.

The council also did not address neighborhood decay in the central cities or restrain the growth of central city–suburban disparities. During the 1980s, the two cities' population remained stable, but the metro area increased by 15 percent. By 1990, median family income in the Twin Cities was $33,364, compared with $43,252 in the metro area; the poverty rate was 18.5 percent, compared with 8 percent in the metro area. Poverty had become markedly greater and more concentrated since 1970. Racial minorities constituted less than 10 percent of the metro area population, but almost 20 percent of the two cities' residents. Most job growth took place in the affluent southern and western suburbs, but many central-city residents (including almost half of black households) lacked cars or public transit access to these areas. . . .

Portland, Oregon, has the nation's only directly elected regional governing body, the Metro Council. It serves twenty-four cities and three counties. Its seven nonpartisan members are elected for four-year terms from districts that each contain about 200,000 constituents; its executive officer, elected at large, is responsible for daily management. The Metro Council formulates and implements policy on solid waste, tourism, transportation, land use, and growth management. The state legislature authorized it in 1977, and the voters of Clackamas, Multnomah, and Washington Counties approved it the following year. Metro's revenue base comes from a variety of taxes and fees; it has the authority, which it has not yet exercised, to seek voter approval for regional income and sales taxes.

In 1970, Portland was a city of 382,619 in a three-county region of 878,676. By 2000, the city had grown to 529,121 and the region to 1.9 million. The region's economy is dominated by shipping, electronics, and manufacturing. In contrast to many cities, Portland's employment base has grown significantly, even though job growth has been greater in the surrounding suburbs. Many believe that the region's planning efforts have been a major factor in this outcome.[22]

Until the 1970s, Portland seemed headed for decline. It lost its ability to annex suburban localities in 1906. By 1956, the three-county area had 176 governmental units, including many special districts. In 1960, the League of Women Voters published *A Tale of Three Counties,* which criticized uncoordinated services and wasteful spending and called for a new, more efficient, more accountable government structure. During the 1960s and 1970s, the legislature and voters approved regional agencies for transportation, the zoo, and solid waste. In 1983, a large budget deficit in Multnomah County (which includes Portland) and the need for services in the unincorporated suburban areas east of Portland led the County Board of Supervisors to encourage Portland to annex some unincorporated areas, provide services to some suburbs, and create a sewer construction program for the county. These reforms created support for a metropolitan-wide governance structure. Nevertheless, heavily dependent on such troubled industries as paper and pulp, timber exports, shipbuilding, fishing, and metalworking, the Portland economy did not appear especially well positioned for future growth.

Following several blue-ribbon study commissions, the voters of the three counties approved the creation of an elected metropolitan government in May 1978. Its first task was to designate a metropolitan urban growth boundary under Oregon's land-use legislation, the nation's strongest. Under it, Metro can compel local governments and counties to coordinate their land-use and development plans. As baby boomers moved to Portland to enjoy its environment, as basic resource exports recovered from their slump in the 1980s, and as employment surged in new industries (including Intel, Tektronix, and Nike), the demand for new development grew steadily, as did the political base for managing this growth. A political alliance between Portland's business interests and residents of older neighborhoods also sought to strengthen the downtown area against competition from suburban shopping malls while saving abandoned housing from the threat of large-scale land clearance and redevelopment. When Neal Goldschmidt was elected mayor in 1972, he incorporated neighborhood activists into his administration (1972–1979) and continued that policy after becoming governor (1987–1990).

This coalition largely achieved its goals for coordinating land-use planning and transportation policy, emphasizing public transit, revitalizing older neighborhoods, and strengthening the downtown business district. These efforts were bolstered by state land-use planning laws that preserved farmland and forests around Portland and directed urban growth into Portland and its neighboring areas. Although more office and retail development has taken place outside the city of Portland than within it, the downtown still accounts for 60 percent of the region's office space and half its upscale retail space. Several highway projects were abandoned in favor of buses and light-rail connections between the central city, outlying neighborhoods, and nearby suburbs. By the 1990s, the region's bus and rail system carried 43 percent of downtown commuters, compared with 20 percent in Phoenix, 17 percent in Salt Lake City, and 11 percent in Sacramento. Portland shows that metropolitan government can succeed. As Orfield observed, its "regional government has been more willing than the Twin Cities' appointed Metropolitan Council to exercise its powers vis-à-vis competing authorities."[23]

Even so, Metro is not all-powerful. It does not provide water, sewer, police, airport, parks (other than the zoo), transportation, subsidized housing, cable television, or many other services for the region. Local school districts remain distinct, eighty single-purpose special districts still have the ability to tax, and twenty cities and three counties provide a broad range of services. Key activities that might help promote mobility of the poor out of the central city—subsidized housing construction and the administration of Section 8 vouchers—are administered by the Portland city housing authority and do not operate on a metrowide basis. Two metrowide agencies with appointed boards, Tri-Met (which runs the transit system) and the Port of Portland (which runs the port, industrial parks, and the airports), operate independently of Metro. Metro's most important function is to set ground rules for development and growth. For example, it selected the site for the region's $65 million convention center. It has enhanced the region's ability to resist costly and inefficient sprawl, but it is not a full-service government.

Portland suffers less from the spatial concentration of the poor in the central city than do most other places. Portland's 1990 poverty rate of 14.5 percent was below that of most other large central cities, and the area's low-income residents were spread out, not highly segregated, concentrated, and isolated. The income gap between the central city and the suburbs remains one of the smallest in the nation.[24] Since Portland has a small minority population (7.7 percent African American, 3.2 percent Hispanic, and 5.3 percent Asian), the relationship between the city and its suburbs has not been racially charged. The state's "fair share" housing and land-use mandates, along with Metro's planning efforts, have encouraged suburbs to develop more low-income housing than in other metropolitan areas. The region's housing prices increased more than the national average during the 1990s, although not as much as in booming cities such as Denver or Salt Lake City, which lack Portland's strict growth management.[25] . . .

The Politics of Regionalism in the New Millennium

Historically, many forces have worked against a regional perspective in urban governance. Suburbs have been happy to benefit from being located in a large metropolitan area while excluding the less well-off and avoiding the payment of taxes to support services required by the urban poor. Central cities, for their part, have made a virtue of necessity by increasing spending on social services as a way of expanding the employment of central-city constituents. This spending has become an increasingly substantial part of municipal budgets and an important form of "new patronage" in city politics. As federal benefits have increasingly flowed to needy people, as opposed to needy places, it has helped to expand these functions. Legislators elected to represent areas where the minority poor are concentrated develop a stake in this state of affairs.

[T]his dynamic is gradually but steadily shifting. The first wave of inner, working-class suburbs has long since been built out, their populations have aged, and their residents' incomes have stagnated since the early 1970s. These suburbs have developed increasingly "urban" problems that they cannot solve on their own. Black and Hispanic central-city residents have increasingly moved to the suburbs. Although minority suburbs have significantly better conditions than inner-city minority neighborhoods, they still have higher rates of poverty and disadvantage than white suburbs and may face some of the same forces of decline that operate on inner cities. Even as metropolitan economic segregation has increased, metropolitan racial segregation has declined and suburban diversity has increased. As Orfield has pointed out, these inner suburbs are coming to realize that they share significant interests with their central cities. And as Juliet Gainsborough has shown, voters residing in more diverse suburbs are substantially more likely to vote like their urban neighbors.

The November 2000 vote in favor of consolidation between the city of Louisville and surrounding Jefferson County shows that elite consensus can be a powerful force in promoting regionalism. After previous defeats in 1982 and 1983, the proposal was backed by the current mayor and county executive, former

Louisville mayor Jerry Abraham, the business community, and the local newspaper. The main opposition came from the local chapter of the NAACP, the gay community, and city and county legislators (whose offices would be abolished in favor of a twenty-six-seat county assembly); all worried that the new form of government would dilute gains they had made in the city of Louisville. A group of African American professionals and the local black newspaper, however, argued in favor of consolidation. The final vote was 54 percent in favor, 46 percent opposed. Part of the appeal was to position Louisville more favorably in its competition with Lexington, which was about to overtake it in size.[26] The Louisville case will be an interesting experiment in how the various forces favoring regionalism will play out.

It has thus become clear that many powerful players, including corporations, foundations, unions, political leaders, and community organizations, think that regional collaboration offers the surest route to competitive advantage in the new global economy. Regions divided against themselves are least likely to be able to undertake the necessary investments in physical, human, and social capital. Emerging metropolitan governance institutions should carry out functions that make the most sense from economic, environmental, and equity viewpoints. These include regional capital investments, transportation, land-use planning, economic development, job training, education, and tax-base sharing. This form of cooperation can generate more widely distributed benefits if they follow a high-productivity, high-wage "high road" instead of engaging in a "race to the bottom" that competes for low-wage, low-value-added jobs in highly mobile industries.

To be truly effective, metropolitan cooperation must develop a broad, democratic base and the organizational capacity to articulate the common good, not merely to sum up the aims of the individual parts of the metropolis. Cooperation of the region's constituent elements must be secured through consent, not through unwanted mandates imposed on resistant local jurisdictions. To achieve this consent, the new regional form must provide tangible benefits to its constituent jurisdictions, and its actions cannot be subject to the veto of an exclusive "favored quarter."

Notes

1. Kenneth Neubeck and Richard Ratcliff, "Urban Democracy and the Power of Corporate Capital," in *Business Elites and Urban Development,* ed. Scott Cummings (Albany, N.Y.: SUNY Press, 1988).
2. Ibid., p. 322.
3. Shipman's plan is described in Vicki Kemper, "Operation Urban Storm," *Common Cause Magazine* (July–August 1991): 10–16, 39–40.
4. Evelyn Nieves, "Homeless Defy Cities' Drives to Move Them," *New York Times,* December 7, 1999; William Claiborne, "From Champion to Chief Critic of the Homeless," *Washington Post,* December 9, 1997.
5. Michael Matza, "Social Service Groups Caught in the Middle," *Houston Chronicle,* August 22, 1996; "Hartford Restricts Social Services to Stem Flow of Poor People," *New York Times,* August 14, 1996; Colman McCarthy, "Heartless Go After Services for Homeless," *Washington Post,* May 14, 1996.
6. Woody Baird, "Memphis' Black Mayor Fears a Bleak Future: Leader Wants to Merge City with Majority-White Suburbs to Relieve the Strain on Tax Base," *Los Angeles Times,* October 3, 1993.
7. Myron Orfield, *Metropolitics: A Regional Agenda for Community and Stability,* rev. ed. (Washington, D.C., and Cambridge, Mass.: Brookings Institution Press and Lincoln Institute of Land Policy, 1997), p. 5.
8. Robert D. Putnam, *Bowling Alone: The Collapse and Revival of American Community* (New York: Simon and Schuster, 2000), chap. 12.
9. Carl Sussman, ed., *Planning the Fourth Migration: The Neglected Vision of the Regional Planning Association of America* (Cambridge, Mass.: MIT Press, 1976), p. 89.
10. Annalee Saxenian, *Regional Advantage: Culture and Competition in Silicon Valley and Route 128* (Cambridge, Mass.: Harvard University Press, 1994).
11. Joel Garreau, *Edge Cities: Life on the New Frontier* (New York: Doubleday, 1991); David Rusk, *Cities Without Suburbs* (Washington, D.C.: Woodrow Wilson Center Press, 1993); Neal Peirce, Curtis Johnson, and John Hall, *Citistates* (Washington, D.C.: Seven Locks Press, 1993).
12. Neal Peirce and Curtis Johnson, *Boundary Crossers: Community Leadership for a Global Age* (College

Park, Md.: Academy of Leadership, University of Maryland, 1997).
13. Michael H. Schill, "Deconcentrating the Inner City Poor," *Chicago-Kent Law Review* 67, no. 3 (1992): 852.
14. Anthony Downs, *New Visions for Metropolitan America* (Washington, D.C.: Brookings Institution, 1994); Orfield, *Metropolitics;* Gary Orfield and Carole Ashkinaze, *The Closing Door: Conservative Policy and Black Opportunity* (Chicago: University of Chicago Press, 1991).
15. H. V. Savitch and Ronald K. Vogel, eds., *Regional Politics: America in a Post-City Age* (Thousand Oaks, Calif.: Sage Publications, 1996).
16. Rusk, *Cities Without Suburbs.*
17. This section draws on Bruce Berg and Paul Kantor, "New York: The Politics of Conflict and Avoidance," in Savitch and Vogel, *Regional Politics;* U.S. Bureau of the Census at census.gov.
18. Robert D. Yaro and Tony Hiss, *A Region at Risk: The Third Regional Plan for the New York–New Jersey–Connecticut Metropolitan Area* (Washington, D.C.: Island Press, 1996).
19. Berg and Kantor, "New York," p. 42.
20. This term was coined by Robert Fogelson, *The Fragmented Metropolis: Los Angeles 1850–1930* (Cambridge, Mass.: Harvard University Press, 1967).
21. Marla Cone, "State Scales Back Clean-Air Plan in Bow to Oil, Trucking Industries," *Los Angeles Times,* November 10, 1994; Marla Cone, "U.S. Unveils Scaled-Back Clean-Air Plan," *Los Angeles Times,* February 15, 1995; Linda Wade and Gail Ruderman Feuer, "'Good News' that Means Dirtier Air," *Los Angeles Times,* August 5, 1996; James Lents and William Kelly, "Clearing the Air in Los Angeles," *Scientific American* (October 1993).
22. Arthur C. Nelson, "Smart Growth = Central City Vitality and a Higher Quality of Life" (paper presented to the U.S. Department of Housing and Urban Development conference "Bridging the Divide," Washington, D.C., December 8, 1999).
23. Orfield, *Metropolitics,* p. 102.
24. Carl Abbott, "The Portland Region" (and comments by Henry Richmond and William Fischel), *Housing Policy Debate* 8, no. 1 (1997).
25. Ibid., p. 35.
26. Rick McDonough, "Merger Wins with Solid Majority," *Louisville Courier-Journal,* November 8, 2000. See www.louky.org/merger/default.htm for the city Web site on the merger. Juliet F. Gainsborough, *Fenced Off: The Suburbanization of American Politics* (Washington, D.C.: Georgetown University Press, 2001).

CASE STUDY 13

Introduction

In the preceding reading, Dreier, Mollenkopf, and Swanstrom describe the difficulties that the political leaders in Hartford and Memphis had in trying to put together regional solutions to their urban problems. The problems these cities faced are not unusual. Opposition from local political leaders and voters makes it difficult to create regional governments. Yet the authors also point to two metropolitan areas in which regional governments have been established: the Twin Cities (St. Paul/Minneapolis) of Minnesota and Portland, Oregon. If creating a regional government is so difficult, then how were these two areas able to establish their regional governments? And just how effective have these governments been in solving urban problems?

The reading that follows presents a case study of the metropolitan government in Portland, Oregon. The study explains how supporters of regional government were able to create Metro, as Portland's regional government is now called, and the effect that this government has had on the area. The author, Professor Paul Lewis, argues that Metro's creation reflected the political dynamics of the 1970s when Portland dominated the politics of the region. When new political leadership emerged in Portland in the mid-1970s that wanted to create regional governing bodies, there was not sufficient power in the suburbs to challenge them. Thus, the combination of a politically strong central city and an activist civic elite helped bring Metro about. Lewis then argues that Metro has had a significant effect on the region, encouraging more center-oriented development, protecting the historical character of the downtown, and reducing the prominence of freeways.

The creation of Metro is not the only important factor, however, that has shaped Portland's development. The city has also been affected by the state's strong growth management rules. Since the mid-1970s, all incorporated cities in Oregon have been required to identify urban growth boundaries, separating the city from rural lands. The purpose of these growth boundaries is to manage growth so that the state avoids the urban sprawl found elsewhere. The state has also mandated that all cities within the Portland metropolitan area provide for multifamily housing. Combined, these rules and the creation of Metro have reduced the concentration of poverty and kept the central city alive.

The reading was taken from *Shaping Suburbia: How Political Institutions Organize Urban Development,* a study of how political fragmentation in urban areas affects development. The book was chosen as an Outstanding Academic Book by *Choice,* the scholarly research journal published by the American Library Association. Lewis is a program director and research fellow for the Public Policy Institute of California, a nonpartisan research organization based in San Francisco.

Questions to Consider

As you read the essay, these are some questions to consider:

- What was the nature of the transformation that occurred in Portland in the late 1960s and 1970s? What was the new direction that the city began to take? How did this affect the creation of Metro?
- What is the idea of a "livable city"? What are some of the ways in which Portland has taken steps to make this idea a reality?
- Can you explain the state's urban growth rules and the metropolitan housing rule? How have these rules affected development in Portland?

Portland: A Regionalized Politics Shapes Growth

Paul G. Lewis

While Denver has found it difficult to cope with the effects of growth, Portland has been widely hailed as a livable metropolitan area, with innovative approaches to growth management. The usual spin put on such discussions in journalistic and planning articles is that Portland is simply more progressive, or has just been more careful at planning than other regions. In short, if any explanation is ventured at all, it is usually of the "Portland is smarter than the rest of us" variety (see Langdon 1992). . . .

I argue instead that political organization in the Oregon portion of the Portland metropolis lends itself to regional policy activity by the public sector, and forces local political elites to consider the regional impacts of their decisions. In a PMSA where the largest suburban municipality in 1970 had a population of 18,500, the dominant central city articulated the only coherent political voice until fairly recently. And in the last two decades, the emerging regional governing institutions have directly shaped the area's orientation toward growth and the region's response to the state planning laws. Portland's distinctiveness owes less to planning genius or public opinion than to political structure. . . .

Organizing the Region to Help the Center

As we have seen, a substantial political counterweight to the city of Portland did not exist in the suburban parts of the metropolis in 1970. Although the suburban counties were occasionally able to block Portland's strategic designs in this period, the lack of a municipally organized suburban presence contributed to the evolution of new governing institutions in the 1970s—the Columbia Region Association of Governments (CRAG), the Metropolitan Service District (MSD, or Metro), and the Tri-County Metropolitan Transit District (Tri-Met). Policies promulgated by those institutions during this period worked to the city's advantage, augmenting the quality of life in inner residential neighborhoods and contributing to the centrality of Portland's downtown. They also helped inculcate an unusual areawide perspective among the region's land-use and transportation decision makers.

In terms of the historical and geographical setting for growth in metropolitan Portland, advocates of the central city and its CBD [central business district] proceeded uncertainly before the new suburban era. In general, the city administration relied on traditional urban renewal strategies.

But a transformation in the membership of the planning staff and of elected officialdom in the late 1960s heralded a new attention to neighborhood revitalization and "use value" considerations. With federal seed money, neighborhood organizations were created and brought into the planning process, eventually participating in small-area planning that enabled change rather than reacting to it. A Citizens Planning Board, for example, directed Portland's Model Cities program. Quality-of-life issues at the neighborhood level proved a source of winning electoral strategies for the popular Neil Goldschmidt, who succeeded Terry Schrunk as mayor in 1973. Goldschmidt served until 1979, during the period when Portland's reputation was perhaps rising the most; he later became United States Secretary of Transportation and then governor of Oregon. In contrast to Denver's mayors, Goldschmidt was able to bring together his two major priorities—livable neighborhoods and downtown redevelopment.

Portland historian Carl Abbott, reporting a discussion with a Goldschmidt campaign strategist, indicates that the internal institutional arrangements of Portland's commission form of government and weak-party politics were something of a double-edged sword

Excerpts from Paul G. Lewis, "Portland: A Regionalized Politics Shapes Growth," from *Shaping Suburbia: How Political Institutions Organize Urban Development* (Pittsburgh, Penn.: University of Pittsburgh Press, 1996), pp. 162–182.

at that juncture. While power appeared slack under the previous regime, the Goldschmidt team concluded that a dynamic leader with sufficient popular appeal would be relatively unencumbered in pulling together decision-making authority. In short, city government was primed for a strong dose of central direction—if an ambitious leader like Goldschmidt were to recognize the opportunity and take charge. Abbott finds that "Goldschmidt was eager to cut across the decision making spheres, to find points of agreement among policy areas, and to make the necessary deals" (Abbott 1983, 180).

Two such points of agreement concerned neighborhood quality of life and the vitality of downtown Portland. Goldschmidt built his electoral popularity around simultaneous attention to these two issues. To create the institutional means necessary for this effort, the mayor used his organizational prerogatives under the commission system. He reorganized the weak planning department and other relevant bodies into a new Office of Planning and Development, which reported directly to him. He also started an Office of Neighborhood Associations to coordinate the many active neighborhood groups. These groups communicated service and infrastructure needs, and testified on land-use, zoning, and budgeting concerns (Abbott 1983, 201). Goldschmidt's restructuring represented an entrepreneurial way of tying together a slack, weak-party polity.

Programmatically, the mayor had been influenced by the ideas of urbanist Jane Jacobs regarding the features of livable city neighborhoods—stressing density and variety but opposing surgical reconstruction of urban space. Many Portland neighborhoods had organized to fight off freeway construction or slum clearance in the 1960s and early 1970s, a movement bolstered by Goldschmidt's reorganizations. Funds for housing rehabilitation and provisions to enable new or denser residential buildings on in-fill or redevelopment sites were part of an attempt by Goldschmidt's administration to encourage families to choose a home in the city rather than the suburbs (Lycan 1987, 117).

The mayor was able to link neighborhood living to downtown development by stressing the issue of transportation alternatives and accessibility. Using the city's relative influence within the state and region to halt suburban freeway construction and improve public transit, Goldschmidt attempted to boost the comparative attractiveness of living and doing business in the central city. In the mid-1970s, work began on a new downtown transit mall, which is a bus-only area along two major CBD streets with an attractive, pedestrian-oriented design. During the same period, city council approved a numerical limit on parking spaces in the CBD, intended to induce transit ridership, improve air quality and congestion problems, and allow parking lots to be converted to more productive uses.

These changes could have been overwhelmed by improved freeway access to suburban areas. However, the region's relationship to the interstate highway system provides a particularly interesting contrast to Denver's situation. In the 1960s, an inner freeway loop encircling central Portland was completed, well in advance of planned suburban bypass highways. This marked an important point of divergence from other metropolitan areas, where the less controversial outer loops were often finished first, fueling growth at the periphery. As Abbott reports, "The inner freeway increased the convenience of the central business district in competition with outlying towns" (Abbott 1983, 201). By demarcating a core, the highway also accomplished what urban renewal generally had not, as neglected land parcels in the area were brought into the downtown sphere.

Goldschmidt boosted his popularity by defending city neighborhoods against freeway construction. The transformations in the institutional structure of the city government during his administration helped enable inner eastside and northwest neighborhoods to be heard and taken seriously; their protests eventually killed the proposed Mount Hood Freeway and the I-505 connector in the mid-1970s. These highways had been planned in the 1960s as part of a system of spokes connecting the downtown Portland loop to suburban areas.

The Mount Hood Freeway alone would have destroyed about 1 percent of the city's housing stock and disrupted several southeast Portland neighborhoods. Instead, Goldschmidt, working with two sympathetic Multnomah County commissioners, "mobilized a movement to create a greater role for transit in the metropolitan area" (Dueker, Edner, and Rabiega 1987, 138; Abbott 1987, 200–01). Importantly, *given the institutional environment,* they did not need to create a *mass* movement. Priority for federal grant applications would be decided by CRAG, which was the region's metropolitan planning organization before it was merged into MSD. CRAG's voting system, weighted to reflect population, allowed the city of Portland, along with Multnomah County and any one other member, to attain a majority. Since the city has always constituted a large majority of the county population, getting the Multnomah delegate's vote usually was not a problem. Moreover, the city had been developing extensive staff resources to deal with newly enacted state planning initiatives, and thus had personnel in place to examine the freeway issue carefully. CRAG technical studies on regional transportation relied heavily on Portland city staff.

Working through policy decisions by the city, its friendly county, and CRAG, Goldschmidt and his allies were able to slow down the Oregon Department of Transportation (ODOT) in its freeway construction schedule. They also pressured Governor Tom McCall, a conservationist Republican, to consider mass transit options as they publicized the environmental impact of highways. In 1975, CRAG supported a radical proposal: canceling the Mount Hood Freeway entirely and replacing it with a major new transit construction project that would link the eastern suburb of Gresham to downtown Portland.

As this new transportation initiative was formulated, Sheldon Edner and G. B. Arrington write, "The sense of known rules and procedures was intermittent" (1985, 2). Therefore, there was room for political entrepreneurship. Goldschmidt and the Multnomah County commissioners, with the eventual acquiescence of the state transportation commission, worked out a political deal in which a downsized eastern beltway loop (I-205) would be completed and would include a right-of-way for a future transit line. The existing I-84 freeway would be improved, and the Mount Hood Freeway canceled. In its place were substituted three transit corridor proposals. Immediate priority was given to one on the east side of the metro area—where the pressure for some transportation improvement, and a jobs project, was greatest. In addition, politically popular road improvements were doled out throughout the region. Ultimately, this "pot of gold" of 140 transportation improvement projects, worth $200 million, helped create the necessary political consensus behind the proposal (Dueker, Edner, and Rabiega 1987, 139).

After technical studies and considerable debate in the mid-to-late 1970s the regional leadership settled on light rail transit (LRT) as the mode of choice for the eastside corridor. The transit district, Tri-Met, concluded that it would come closer to meeting its operating costs with light rail than the major alternative proposal—a high-capacity, reserved busway—since light rail is a less labor-intensive system. At this point, Tri-Met had a very short history having been formed in 1969, and lacked staff and political strength. But it could function as a critic of a politically uninspiring busway idea. It also looked favorably on a project that would give it a visible new role in serving the region's transportation demands. In 1978, CRAG agreed upon light rail.

LRT was recommended, too, with a focus on land-use impacts. Tri-Met anticipated that light rail, more than a busway, would facilitate dense land-use patterns that could be amenable to heavy transit usage and thus strengthen the agency's position in the region (Arrington and Edner 1985; Nelson and Milgroom 1993, 57). While the biggest impact was expected downtown, projects were feasible at many proposed stations. Planners forecast that 20 percent of all the residential development in the portion of the region east of the Willamette River would occur within a five-minute walk of the line.

Given the lack of previous relationships among ODOT, Tri-Met, and the federal transportation agencies, the process of analyzing alternative routes and technologies was largely "played by ear" (Edner and Arrington 1985, 20). Following favorable action by the Oregon legislature in 1979, the federal government approved the project the next year, after some initial delays (by which time Goldschmidt had become United States Secretary of Transportation). During the period when progress was held up, MSD demonstrated the important role of a regional government by coordinating grant proposals from local governments so as to keep the project and consensus alive. Ultimately, construction began, with the lion's share of the funding derived from the canceled Mount Hood freeway.

Portland's superior geopolitical position, as reflected by CRAG's weighted voting procedure, had allowed the transit proposal to make it to the regional agenda. In the construction phase, the city's dominance within Multnomah County also made it possible to overcome residents' preservationist instincts. MAX, as the LRT line was dubbed ("metro area express"), encountered a great deal of resistance in Gresham and unincorporated Multnomah County. Neighborhood activists had to be convinced that the LRT's positive impacts would outweigh the expectations of noise, traffic, and parking problems (Kelley interview 1993; see also Hogue 1988). In a more fragmented urban region, these opposition groups could have gained sway in municipal governments and thereby doomed the proposal.

Once opened for service in 1986, the line proved popular. The proportion of residents of the Tri-Met district saying they use transit at least twice a month rose from 17 percent to 31 percent. Support for transit allowed passage of recent referenda that temporarily increase taxes in order to add spurs to the MAX line.

The Results: Maintaining the CBD's Relative Advantages

The impact of the freeway cancellation and LRT construction have bolstered Portland's competitive position in the metro area's development market. As noted, regional elites had looked to MAX to assist in land-use goals. MSD initiated a Transit Station Area Planning Program in 1980—the first example in the United States of planning for intensive land use *prior* to the initiation of light rail service. Local jurisdictions rezoned for transit-supportive development around the twenty-five LRT stations. Although it is difficult to assess the overall land-use impact of light rail, construction volume along the line was reportedly $800 million by 1993, and more is continually occurring (G. Wilson 1993). The largest share of that has been in Portland's CBD and the Lloyd district on its inner east side. Some observers credit the dramatic infusion of new construction in downtown Portland in the 1980s to MAX. But it is impossible to separate the rail line's effects—and those of the downtown bus mall—from the region's general economic boom of the mid- to late-1980s.

In the unincorporated portion of Multnomah County and in Gresham, where a fair amount of vacant land was available along the LRT route, significant increases in zoning densities were undertaken. On this portion of the line, placed along an older local arterial (Burnside Street), attempts were made to redesign a low-density suburban commercial district in order to provide a "sense of place." Development has been sparser on this easternmost end of the line, but a handful of office and commercial sites have been built near LRT stations. Planners argued that new stores should be built directly at the street side, instead of behind parking lots, in order to create an orientation toward public transit. . . .

About a dozen multifamily developments have been built along the line, creating pockets of transit-supportive density in neighborhoods that were formerly strictly detached houses (Arrington interview 1993). Thus, east Multnomah County's traditional position as a bedroom "feeder" for inner Portland has not been altered. However, it is developing in patterns more oriented toward transit use.

In sum, accessibility to the center has been improved, but has not been associated with the cars, freeways, and parking lots that have obliterated much of the special historical character of other American downtowns. The situation stands in notable contrast to Denver. Not coincidentally, Portland's CBD has held its competitive position well since these regional approaches to governance and development began twenty years ago. The CBD actually *increased* its share of metropolitan employment in the 1960–1980 period—highly unusual in the age of American suburbanization (Abbott 1983, 227). Downtown employment has jumped from fifty-nine thousand to ninety-four thousand since 1970, with office space nearly tripling (Nelson and Milgroom 1993, 60). As of 1989, the Portland metropolitan area had the lowest amount of *non-CBD* office space per capita of any major metropolitan area (4.6 square feet); its Central Business District, meanwhile, boasted 9.1 square feet per capita, a figure well above the national average.

Meanwhile, the suburbs are less heavily penetrated by interstate freeways than in most metropolitan areas. Until the I-205 bridge was completed in 1980, connecting northeast Portland to Clark County, the only interstate highways running through suburban areas were I-5 and I-84, both of which serve to focus activity around inner Portland. I-5, the major north-south route, connects the area to California and Seattle. More than half of the territory it traverses inside the metro area's urban growth boundary is within the Portland city limits. I-84 connects the Portland region to Salt Lake City and points east. It runs through small portions of Troutdale, Wood Village, Fairview, and Gresham, but once again, about two-thirds of its length within the urban growth boundary is inside Portland. Moreover, the freeway ends at I-5 near the CBD, and those travelers wishing to proceed further west, on U.S. 26, must first negotiate a circuitous route through central Portland.

Because of these highway configurations, the intrasuburban traffic flow is underserviced compared to Denver. Much travel is forced onto secondary roads. This situation makes these areas relatively less attractive to strategic developers and firms seeking to relocate, compared to wide-open suburban portions of other metro areas. In metropolitan Denver, four interstates cover large amounts of suburban territory, and portions of a distant ring highway have been completed. Secondary arterials in the counties around Denver tend to be six-lane boulevards laid out in a grid, in advance of development. These roads are more typically two lanes in the Portland area, where the local public sector in suburbia is less highly developed.

Because of the accessibility differences, office development patterns in Portland have proceeded in a less centrifugal manner than in Denver. Downtown Portland continues to dominate the region's market for multitenant office development. Its share declined from a whopping 84 percent of the region's space in 1970 to a still exceptional 53 percent in 1992. . . .

Thus, a center-oriented decision-making network contributes to center-oriented development. But such changes required substantial political entrepreneurship; this indicates that a nonfragmented political structure is not enough. The rapid shift in transportation policy toward light rail, land-use impacts, and new decision-making structures, were part and parcel of one basic change "made possible by the emergence of a new regional political elite typified by Mayor Goldschmidt and [Multnomah] County Commission Chair Don Clark" (Edner and Arrington 1985, 29). Another key figure was Rick Gustafson, who served successively as a senior planner at Tri-Met, a state legislator, and finally as the executive officer of MSD. Only with regional institutions can such regional political elites emerge. . . .

Limiting Fringe Growth: State Growth Management Using Regional Institutions

While the new regional approach to transportation was taking shape, a more fundamental restructuring of the rules and responsibilities of land regulation was under way. The state of Oregon, seeking to conserve farmland, took the initiative and set the major parameters for local rule changes. Its main requirement for each of Oregon's urban areas is for an urban growth boundary, enclosing a land area sufficient to accommodate the growth expected over the next twenty years. Thus, the approach to fringe development in the Portland area can be discussed more succinctly than the situation in Denver. Oregon's requirement of a UGB [urban growth boundary] eliminates most of the possibilities for large-scale peripheral development of the type that Colorado has seen. Nevertheless, it is important to stress the key intermediate position of Portland's regional government in shaping the UGB process.

Regionwide Institutions Shape Portland's Response

Planning scholars Knaap and Nelson argue that the UGB process helps inspire intergovernmental coordination, and does so more effectively than voluntary local agreements on growth boundaries. With state input, "urban growth boundaries in Oregon are more circumspect than they would have been if local governments had drawn them on their own" (Knaap and Nelson 1992, 66–67). Moreover, the state's rules have generally given most discretion in any given urban area to the general-purpose jurisdiction with the largest geographic focus. Thus, where county and special-district plans differ over how extensive infrastructure provision should be, LCDC [Land Conservation and Development Commission] (and state courts) have presumed the county to be better able to make the determination and thus guide service extensions. Counties review municipal plans and identify conflicts, while drawing up their own comprehensive plans. . . .

More important, however, the state legislation gave the Portland area's most territorially extensive government—MSD (initially CRAG)—the power to coordinate county and local plans. Primarily, this involved drawing a UGB for the entire metro area. Rather than having three counties bicker about the line, the state decided that the metro government was a convenient planning entity that could avoid local jealousies.

But MSD, as "the new kid on the block," was not yet prepared to do serious battle with powerful local jurisdictions on a matter of policy (Kelley interview 1993). In particular, Washington County's earlier progrowth decision to extend sewer service across much of the county affected the UGB process there. Sewer construction had put the county in serious debt, and as one respondent describes the situation, "You can't very well tell a farmer he can't sell when he's gone into so much debt" (Seigneur interview 1993). Therefore, Washington County pushed regional officials for a generous UGB. While the Portland area in the late 1970s had 220 square miles of urbanized land, the original boundary proposed by CRAG would have included 367 square miles.

In 1979, the recently reorganized MSD decided to stick with CRAG's boundary proposal. After considerable hand-wringing at LCDC, court actions, and compromises, a Portland-area UGB of 334 square miles was approved in 1984 (Poulsen 1987, 88). The 1000 Friends of Oregon environmental lobby opposed the planned UGB, contending that it included much more than twenty years' worth of vacant land. Indeed, LCDC had accepted MSD's request to include 15 percent "excess vacant land" in an attempt to control land price shocks, with provision for an inner "interim" growth boundary for the first ten years. Local plans in the Portland area have had to specify conversion of agricultural lands within the UGB so as to prevent leapfrog growth. . . .

LCDC's position was difficult, because the agency was reluctant to interfere, given the stable context. All parties involved had made difficult compromises, and LCDC was under criticism from the state legislature for its general lateness in acknowledging local plans. Thus, when LCDC approved MSD's urban boundary with few major modifications, "everyone agreed the decision was baldly political, but LCDC thought the decision necessary to avoid the political consequences that might ensue if the MSD proposal were rejected. . . . The commission felt it could not afford to alienate nearly half the voters of the state in a single decision" (Leonard 1983, 103). Whatever its faults, the line has by and large held. To date, about thirty expansions have been approved, most of them insignificant. The current boundary delineates about 350 square miles within which metropolitan Portland's growth is to be contained. In 1989, MSD conducted a review of the area's UGB, attracting hundreds of area citizens to its forums. Overall, the regional government has been an important instrument in setting and enforcing limits on the geographic expansion of the Portland area.

Regional Governance: Guiding Suburban Development to Achieve Balance

While canceled freeways and the growth boundary may have kept development from spreading thinly, Portland was belatedly experiencing the new suburban era by the late 1980s. Probably the last obstacle to Portland fully joining the process that was long under way in the rest of the country was the delay in completing I-205, the region's final interstate highway. Once finished in 1984, the area had a major freeway that connected suburbs with suburbs and bypassed central Portland (though the city was in the process of annexing lands up to and beyond the highway). Meanwhile, both the prosperity and pain of urban change were being felt in the suburban jurisdictions, as urban ills such as gang activity and toxic waste disposal problems began to appear there. One example of the rapid changes in suburbia: The 1990 Census found that nearly one in four residents of the city of Beaverton had moved to the metro area in the last five years (Friedman 1993, 111).

In contrast to the isolationism that marks municipal pockets of metro Denver, the Portland area has seen the costs and benefits of growth spread more evenly. In particular, fewer disparities in development, such as jobs/housing mismatches, have appeared. In suburban growth areas, workers find they can secure moderately priced housing relatively close to their workplace, if they so choose. And the older business districts of the suburbs generally have held their own. The regional transportation and land-use decision process has helped shape these results, by making it difficult for local growth interests to "go it alone."

Transportation Planning with Teeth: Institutionalizing a Regional Process

In the midst of the chain of events that led to the area's first light rail line, voters empowered MSD by merging it with CRAG. During the process of freeway cancellation and LRT development, the regional government served as a common table for the area's jurisdictions. While MSD was not directly in charge of building light rail, the forum it provided helped avoid cumbersome interlocal consultations. . . .

As an elected government rather than a voluntary council, MSD was much more systematic than Denver's DRCOG in requiring consistency in transportation planning as a condition for federal grants to localities. As one participant put it, "You played ball with the region or you didn't get transportation funds" (Seltzer interview 1993b). MSD formed a seventeen-member advisory committee of local politicians and representatives from state and federal agencies, the Joint Policy Advisory Committee on Transportation (JPACT). An analogous *technical* committee of local, state, and federal staffers was created as well. These committees were formed to meet federal transportation planning rules, which required that all MPOs provide advisory representation for local governments as units; the MSD council, since it was elected by district, did not meet those requirements. Moreover, the MSD council was reluctant to force through its own views, since it did not want to put its legitimacy on the line at such an early stage (Kelley interview 1993). However, the MSD council did cast the final votes on transportation plans. In essence, this created a double-veto system in which MSD's final decisions on transportation improvement priorities could first be grounded in necessary political deal making among county and local officials on the transportation committees. At the JPACT level, "there was a concerted effort to balance the projects out [geographically]," according to Multnomah County's top planner. "You had to get cooperation, build a consensus." The presence of the technical advisory committee "added a technocracy element," and eventually "refined it into a pretty sophisticated political-technical process" (Pemble interview 1993).

In these regular advisory committee meetings, the participants discussed development trends in all parts of the metropolis and eventually came to the realization that population and employment patterns were driving their transportation needs (Pemble interview). Moreover, the group came to see, transportation facilities were being developed to support the land-use planning being done by twenty-six jurisdictions. Seeking to get beyond this vicious cycle—road improvements create more growth, which creates more demand for road improvements—MSD staff began producing pioneering analyses and models to tie together projections of land use and transportation demand. In short, by the mid-1980s the regional dialogue had reached a level of sophistication that anticipated current academic research.

In the process, Metro developed as much, or more, staff competence than the Oregon Department of Transportation (ODOT) on these issues. This has created "an undercurrent of tension," because ODOT is responsible for serving the entire state with transportation, but Metro is by far the most well-organized geographic entity. ODOT must react to Metro's many initiatives (Seltzer 1993). With its unusually large and sophisticated planning staff, MSD (now Metro) has been responsible throughout for modeling planned highway and transit projects, rather than leaving the task to highway agencies or Tri-Met. In fact, ODOT contracts with Metro to provide transportation planning for the area. . . .

. . . Portland's suburbs have come to see advantages in ceding these responsibilities to the metropolitan government. As Abbott writes, the process "creates a level playing ground and agreed rules for dealing with city-suburban and intersuburban conflicts. To some degree, it mitigates the heavy-handed role that Portland played in transportation planning in the early and middle 1970s." The priorities among transportation projects that Metro sets, Abbott notes, "are treated as contracts" (Abbott 1994, 218). This elimination of uncertainty is a valuable political commodity. . . .

Keeping Land Uses Balanced: The Metropolitan Housing Rule

Another policy in which the regional government took a lead role involved promoting lower-cost housing near areas of suburban job growth. As with the UGB process, the regional government played a mediating role in the state land-use program. The issue arose because every Oregon city with a population over five thousand—except Portland—had the housing component of its comprehensive plan rejected on first submission to LCDC. With the exception of the inclusive central city, municipalities were reluctant to zone for the apartments or high-density housing that would provide more affordable shelter, whether because of tax/service calculations or their residents' resistance to density.

MSD attempted to overcome this logjam in 1979 by enacting an Areawide Housing Opportunity Plan. This program doled out federal assisted-housing funds in relation to each jurisdiction's needs. However, the program soon disintegrated when funding for housing programs was significantly reduced in the Reagan years.

At this point, LCDC was in a showdown with the recalcitrant city of Lake Oswego. The prestigious suburb had made statements supportive of affordability in the text of its comprehensive plan, but kept actual zoned densities low in order to maintain "community character." Troubled by what it saw as contradictions such as this, LCDC issued a new regulation for the Portland metro area called the Metropolitan Housing Rule (MHR), which drew upon the original MSD plan. The MHR required a mix of at least 50 percent multifamily or attached single-family housing within MSD's boundaries. It also established a "ten-eight-six" formula, under which the metro area's largest municipalities, along with unincorporated Multnomah County, were required to zone for an average density of at least ten dwelling units per buildable acre. Nearly all the remaining cities were given an eight-unit-per-acre requirement, except for five tiny jurisdictions, where the quota was set at six per acre.

The rule is relatively inflexible, and critics say it lacks a coherent technical rationale. . . . Despite such objections, the zoning changes were made, forced by the state but overseen by MSD. "In calling for such coordination, LCDC comes as close as it can to mandating a lesser form of regional development planning" (Toulan 1994, 106). The metropolitan government is given responsibility to ensure that housing needs are being met in areas with rapidly growing employment, which had already been the goal under its original Areawide Housing Opportunity Plan. The results are dramatic:

> Pursuant to these state goals and assisted by regional planning agency (Metro) guidelines, each jurisdiction in the Portland area has accepted fair share responsibility for affordable housing. The average vacant single-family lot in the twenty-seven Portland metropolitan jurisdictions has decreased through rezonings from 12,800 to 8,500 square feet, and land zoned for multifamily housing has quadrupled to over 25 percent of net buildable acres. (Bollens 1992, 461). . .

Evaluating the Relationship Between Regionalism and State Growth Management

The state program has created a state-regional-local nexus of land-use regulation, and has increased awareness of urbanization and conservation issues. By approaching these topics in a regional manner, it has forced local elected officials to consider the regional impact of local decisions, especially since LCDC has costly sanctions at its disposal. Finally, the state program energized the metropolitan government at a key time, shortly after its creation, making it a politically relevant unit with a clear focus. In terms of policy effects, the requirement for relatively dense housing in areas with increasing employment has helped prevent wide jobs/housing disparities. In recent years, school overcrowding has made some local electorates restless about the housing mandates, but no slow-growth ordinances have yet materialized. . . .

Since the regional government's role has been less visible than that of the state government, which initiated the administrative rules, it is difficult to evaluate what independent effect Metro has had on the success of the UGB and jobs-housing balance. It is certainly reasonable to hypothesize that having a sovereign entity at a middle level, between state technocrats and local politicians, has made state planning easier politically. Parochial jealousies can be resolved within the region before they are played out at the state level. There, regulators must walk a fine line if they do not wish to be seen as technical overlords. Scott Bollens, who has analyzed several state land-use programs, discusses this pattern of implementation and enforcement as a form of "conjoint federalism." He cites evidence that metropolitan Portland has gone further toward realizing the state goals than other urban areas in Oregon, which lack a metropolitan government. For example, one study found that about 95 percent of Portland-area growth took place within its UGB, while three other areas examined allowed 24 to 57 percent of their growth to escape the urban boundary (Bollens 1992, 461).

Several of my interview respondents supported the idea that Metro was responsible for the Portland area's better performance. A few others claimed there was simply a cultural predisposition in favor of planning in their part of the state. Part of the explanation for divergent outcomes may be that county commissioners are given the coordination responsibility in the rest of the state. They may resist imposing restrictions on outlying development because they are sensitive to farmers' desires to maintain their land values. But in the Portland PMSA, Metro officials lack such a bias, since there are relatively few farmers within the agency's boundaries. Moreover, the sustained experience with regional institutions has made the interrelationship of localities clearer to elected officials than in many other urban areas.

Bibliography

Abbott, Carl. 1983. *Portland: Planning, politics, and growth in a twentieth-century city.* Lincoln: University of Nebraska Press.

———. 1987. *The new urban America: Growth and politics in sunbelt cities.* Rev. ed. Chapel Hill: University of North Carolina Press.

———. 1994. The Oregon planning style. In *Planning the Oregon way,* ed. Carl Abbott, Deborah Howe, and Sy Adler. Corvallis: Oregon State University Press.

Bollens, Scott. 1992. State growth management: Intergovernmental frameworks and policy objectives. *Journal of the American Planning Association* 58: 454–66.

Dueker, Kenneth, Sheldon Edner, and William Rabiega. 1987. Transportation planning in the Portland metropolitan area. In *Portland's changing landscape,* ed. Larry W. Price. Portland: Portland State University.

Edner, Sheldon, and G. B. Arrington. 1985. *Urban decision making for transportation investments: Portland's light rail transit system.* Washington, D.C.: U.S. Department of Transportation.

Friedman, Elaine S. 1993. *The facts of life in Portland, Oregon.* Portland: Portland Possibilities, Inc.

Hogue, Kendra. 1988. Ex-mayor wheels into Tri-Met post. *Business Journal—Portland,* July 18.

Knaap, Gerrit, and Arthur C. Nelson. 1992. *The regulated landscape: Lessons on state land use planning from Oregon.* Cambridge, Mass.: Lincoln Institute of Land Policy.

Langdon, Philip. 1992. How Portland does it. *Atlantic Monthly,* November: 134–41.

Leonard, Jeffrey. 1983. *Managing Oregon's growth: The politics of development planning.* Washington, D.C.: Conservation Foundation.

Lycan, Richard. 1987. Changing residence in a changing city. In *Portland's changing landscape,* ed. Larry W. Price. Portland: Portland State University.

Nelson, Arthur C., and Jeffrey H. Milgroom. 1993. The role of regional development management in central city revitalization. Working Paper 6, National Center for the Revitalization of Central Cities, University of New Orleans.

Pouslen, Thomas M. 1987. Shaping and managing Portland's metropolitan development. In *Portland's changing landscape,* ed. Larry W. Price. Portland: Portland State University.

Toulan, Nohad. 1994. Housing as a state planning goal. In *Planning the Oregon way,* ed. Carl Abbott, Deborah Howe, and Sy Adler. Corvallis: Oregon State University Press.

Wilson, Geordie. 1993. Portland, Oregon, MAX has made public transit almost trendy. *Seattle Times,* January 21.

Interviews

Arrington, G. B. 1993. Director of Transit Development, Tri-Met, in Portland, June 28.

Kelley, Sharron. 1993. Multnomah County Commissioner, and former Metropolitan Service District councillor, in Portland, July 1.

Pemble, R. Scott. 1993. Planning director, Multnomah County, in Portland, July 1.

Seigneur, David. 1993. Director, Clackamas County Development Agency, in Oregon City, July 2.

Seltzer, Ethan. 1993. Former land use coordinator, Metropolitan Service District, and currently director, Institute for Portland Metropolitan Studies, Portland State University, in Portland, July 7.

Chapter 13 Review Questions

1. What lessons can one learn from the excerpt from *Place Matters*? What types of problems might regionalism help solve?
2. What are some of the ways that regionalism is practiced today? Why are the Twin Cities and Portland considered such important models?
3. How successful has Portland been in overcoming the problems discussed in the reading by Dreier, Mollenkopf, and Swanstrom? Are there reasons to think that Portland's success could be caused by other factors beside the creation of the regional government? What might these reasons be?
4. What factors were important in bringing about the creation of Metro in Portland? To what extent do you think Portland's experiences in creating Metro can be duplicated elsewhere? Explain your answer.
5. Do you think that the nation's metropolitan areas should adopt more regional approaches to addressing their problems? What are the tradeoffs in creating regional governments? In other words, what are the benefits of regionalism, and what are some of the drawbacks?
6. Are there any types of regional governments within your community or state? What do these governments do? How effective are they in achieving their goals?

Key Terms

metropolitan political fragmentation
new regionalism
city-county consolidation
annexation
single-purpose metropolitan districts
Council of Governments
Public Choice Theory
favored quarter
localism
land-use regulations
smart growth
garden city
sustainable development
urban sprawl
regional growth boundaries
new urbanism
livability agenda

Suggestions for Further Reading

Calthorpe, Peter. *The Next American Metropolis: Ecology, Community, and the American Dream.* New York: Princeton Architectural Press, 1995. Influential regional urban design treatise drawing on New Urbanist concepts.

———, William Fulton, and Robert Fishman. *The Regional City: Planning for the End of Sprawl.* Washington D.C.: Island Press, 2001. Frequently cited in urban planning literature, this book argues that metropolitan design with inner cities surrounded by rings of isolated suburbs have negative consequences, and suggests a regional model as a solution.

Fishman, Robert. "The American Metropolis at Century's End: Past and Future Influences." *Housing Policy Debate* 11 (2000): 199–213. Drawing from a survey of urban scholars and social scientists, Fishman describes the ten most important influences on the American metropolis since the 1950s and the most likely influences in the future.

Garreau, Joel. *Edge City: Life on the New Frontier.* New York: Anchor Books, 1992. Seminal work that chronicles the evolution of American urban development from downtown to suburb to large-scale suburban city located on the edge of the metropolis. Provides a more positive perspective on suburbs than is found in much of the literature on new regionalism.

Judd, Dennis R., and Paul P. Kantor, eds. *Politics of Urban America: A Reader.* 3d ed. Boston: Pearson Longman, 2001. Highly regarded reader highlighting the most important trends in urban politics today.

Katz, Bruce, and Amy Liu. "Moving Beyond Sprawl—Toward a Broader Metropolitan Agenda." *Brookings Review* 18 (2000): 31–34. Addresses the full range of forces that shape metropolitan growth, and calls for a new broad agenda that includes solutions to concerns such as racial separation and affordable housing.

Katz, Bruce, ed. *Reflections on Regionalism.* Washington D.C.: Brookings Institution Press, 2000. Well-respected collection of essays on regionalism from both academic and nonacademic perspectives.

Mitchell-Weaver, Clyde, David Miller, and Ronald Deal, Jr. "Multilevel Governance and Metropolitan Regionalism in the USA." *Urban Studies* 37 (2000): 851–877. Thoroughly referenced overview of metropolitan regionalism. Includes discussions of suburban autonomy and metropolitan fragmentation.

Orfield, Myron. *Metropolitics: A Regional Agenda for Community and Stability.* Washington, D.C.: Brookings Institution Press, 1997. Fascinating book on the development of the regional government in the Twin Cities of Minnesota. The book also describes the polarization that exists between central city neighborhoods and suburbs. Orfield's arguments are applied on a much broader scale in *American Metropolitics: The New Suburban Reality* (Washington, D.C.: Brookings Institution Press, 2002).

Peirce, Neal R., Curtis Johnson, and John Hall. *Citistates: How Urban America Can Prosper in a Competitive World.* Washington, D.C.: Seven Locks Press, 1994. This book examines the importance of regionalism for the economic health of metropolitan areas. The authors argue that cities must develop a regionwide strategic framework if they are to compete in the world economy.

Rusk, David. *Inside Game, Outside Game: Winning Strategies for Saving Urban America* Washington, D.C.: Brookings Institution Press, 1999. Highly regarded work on how regional solutions are necessary for overcoming the economic problems in the central city. Also see Rusk's *Cities Without Suburbs: A Census 2000 Update,* 3d ed. (Washington, D.C.: Woodrow Wilson Center Press, 2003).

Wallis, Allan D. "Inventing Regionalism—The First Two Waves." *National Civic Review* 83 (1994): 170–171. Summarizes efforts to achieve regional governance through structural solutions and procedural reforms. Recently, a third generation of metropolitan reform has emerged and is considered in Wallis's "The Third Wave—Current Trends in Regional Governance." *National Civic Review* 83 (1994): 290–310.

Wheeler, Stephen M. "The New Regionalism: Key Characteristics of an Emerging Movement." *Journal of the American Planning Association* 68 (2002): 267–279. Excellent overview of the new regionalism movement in the United States.

Related Web Sites

http://usmayors.org/
Web site for the U.S. Conference of Mayors provides a search engine to find mayor and city web sites nationwide. The site also includes policy reports on a variety of important municipal and urban issues.

http://www.urbaninstitute.org/
Research institute that focuses on issues confronting America's cities and urban areas.

http://www1.umn.edu/irp/zaboutirp.html
The Institute on Race and Poverty at the University of Minnesota provides information on urban-related issues, including the problems of regional inequity, and links to other web sites.

http://www.metro-region.org/
The web site for Metro, the regional government in Portland, Oregon, includes information on its history, responsibilities, and structure.

http://www.metrocouncil.org/
The web site for the Metropolitan Council, which is the regional government for the Twin Cities, Minnesota.

14

State Finances: The Concept of Budgeting

Because the pie is always limited, the budget pits agency against agency, client group against client group, cities against suburbs, Democrats against Republicans. It also provides a major test in the struggle between the governor and the legislature to determine who decides how much is spent on what for whose benefit.

Alan Rosenthal

READING 14

Introduction

The economic downturn that began in 2001 sent state budgets into the red and state political leaders looking for ways to make ends meet. The states first began to see signs of problems before the end of the fiscal year in June 2001 as tax revenues started to decline. Within a few months, many states began to face fiscal problems. By January 2002, thirty-six states revealed that they were facing budget gaps, some as large as 10 percent of their budgets. Others had taken steps to avoid a gap. Since all states except Vermont are required by law to balance their budgets, state leaders looked for ways to reduce spending and increase revenue. By June, the states had been forced to fill a combined budget gap of $37 billion for the fiscal year just ending and to prepare more austere budgets for the new year. Despite these steps, state leaders were once again looking for ways to overcome growing budget shortfalls within a few months. To be sure, the problem was far from over. For many states, the economic turmoil throughout the beginning of the decade meant that they had to cope with more than four years of dealing with severe budget problems. In total, it is estimated the states had to find ways through tax increases and cuts in services to fill a combined budget gap of $200 billion from 2001 through 2003. The continuing fiscal crisis was a far cry from the situation in the 1990s when the nation's economic boom left the states flushed with funds. The fiscal situation was so bad, in so many states, that Ray Scheppach, the executive director of the National Governors Association, described the problems in 2003 as being "just off the charts."[1]

What caused the states' fiscal problems at the beginning of the decade? Why did state leaders continually find themselves scrounging to fix new budget gaps rather than providing long-term solutions? Whom should we as voters hold accountable for the mess found in many states? Certainly, the economy deserves the largest share of the blame. One consequence that usually results when the nation's economy declines is that state revenues drop and expenses rise, pushing state budgets into the red. A weakening economy creates problems for budget officials because it moves people out of the workforce, lowers profits and payrolls, and causes a decline in consumption. As a result, there is often a drop in sales, income, and other taxes. At the same time, there is greater demand for public services as people lose their jobs and the benefits that come with them. In general, many of the problems confronting the states earlier this decade followed this traditional pattern. The one event that may have had the most impact on state revenue was the decline in the stock market, which led to a drop in personal income tax payments. State revenue collection was also hurt by decreases in capital gains and sales taxes. Along with the decline in revenue, the cost of social services grew, as more people filed for unemployment and welfare benefits. The states were also hurt by a large jump in Medicaid costs. Combined, these economic factors had a profound impact on state budgets, forcing state leaders to battle continually against potential deficits.

Although the nation's economic downturn played a central role in creating the mess in many states, one can also blame state political leaders, at least for poor or undesirable decisions taken to cope with the fiscal crisis. The decisions made by states in response to economic problems are political decisions. When governors and state legislators decide to cut services rather than raise taxes, or to raise taxes rather than cut services, they are making decisions based on their own values and judgments, and the values of their constituents. In other words, the battle over state budgeting represents another arena in which political values come into conflict. When the economy declines and budgets are pushed into the red, the options available to these political leaders are often limited. Yet leaders must still find ways to balance the budget, whether by reducing school funding, cutting social services, raising taxes, borrowing funds, or some other solution. How quickly and wisely they respond may cushion the problems created by the economic downturn, or it may exacerbate them. The specific decisions leaders make on where to cut and how to raise more revenue will determine who will benefit and who will suffer. Thus, when evaluating the problems confronting the states earlier this decade, voters are certainly justified in blaming state leaders who handled the problems poorly or in giving credit to those who handled them well.

The economic problems that began in 2001 repeatedly brought state budgets into the news, yet the budget is almost always among the most important pieces of legislation that state leaders must address every year or, in some states, every other year. The budget is important because it dictates how much money will be spent on most state services. It touches nearly all the activities in which the government is involved, and it brings together most of the actors who have a stake in the governments' activities. Despite the importance of the budget, the budget process is often difficult for the public to follow, which makes it hard both to know why particular decisions were made and to hold elected officials accountable for their actions. The purpose of this chapter is to provide an introduction to the political forces that shape state budgets. The chapter is meant to help readers think about who should be held accountable for budgeting decisions.

The governor routinely plays a leading role in shaping state budgets. There are many factors that give governors a strong say in the state budget, but the most important is that they play a formal role at both the beginning and end of the budget-making process. In most states, the governor has the responsibility to formulate the budget and present it to the legislature for its approval. With this power, the governor is able to set the agenda and influence the direction of debate in the legislature. In addition, all fifty governors have the general veto, and most have the item veto, which gives them an important tool to encourage legislators to heed their wishes. If legislators are unwilling to work with a governor's budget proposal, the governor can always veto the legislation or parts of it.

Yet governors are not the only actors who play an important role in shaping the budget. For a budget to be passed into law, it must clear many hurdles in the state legislature, where a number of political actors can influence its content. Party leaders, party caucuses, committee chairs, budget committee members, and influential legislators can all affect the content of the state budget. There is also a wide array of other actors, from state agency heads to interest group lobbyists, who actively try to shape budget decisions, putting pressure on the governor and legislators to listen to their concerns. With all of these actors involved, it is unfair to place too much blame or give entire credit to the governor for budget decisions. It is also important to understand that budgeting tends to be an incremental process in which one year's budget is used as the starting point for the next year's budget. Moreover, state laws and federal policies may require the states to fund particular programs and services. As a result, governors and legislators can often make only marginal changes in most areas of the budget from one year to the next.

The reading that follows provides an inside view of the budget-making process. The essay was written by Alan Rosenthal, a political science professor at the Eagleton Institute of Politics at Rutgers University and one of the nation's leading experts on state legislatures. The essay explains the importance of both the governor and the state legislature in crafting the state budget. It also gives some insight into all the different hands that affect state budget decisions. The essay is valuable because it shows that the governor is not the only actor who is responsible for creating the state budget, but that state legislatures also play an especially critical role. The reading was taken from Rosenthal's book *The Decline of Representative Democracy,* a fascinating study on the current health of state legislatures.

Questions to Consider

As you read Rosenthal's work, these are some questions to consider:

- How is the budget crafted? Can you provide an overview of the budget process from initial formation to when it is signed into law?
- How early do legislatures become involved in the budgeting process? What are some of the steps in the process in which they are able to influence the content of the budget?
- After reading Rosenthal's work, how would you describe the distribution of power over the creation of the budget? What evidence would you cite to support your case?

- What does Rosenthal say is the most critical stage in the budget process? What happens in this stage, and who is involved?
- What is pork, and why is it often important in the budgeting process? Does Rosenthal seem to suggest that pork is good or bad? What do you think?

Balance of Power: The Case of the Budget

Alan Rosenthal

As good a way as any to see how state legislatures balance the power of the executive is to examine the performance of the legislature's and the governor's budgetary role. The state budget—through which resources are allocated among functions, programs, and interests—is probably the most significant policy that the governor and the legislature promulgate. Budgets, in the view of an experienced budgeter, "are typically the most important legislative actions in a session."[1] Whereas the governor and the legislature may choose whether or not to place most policy issues on the state agenda, they have no choice in the case of the budget. Constitutionally, a budget must be enacted either annually (as in thirty states) or biennially (as in twenty others). Even those states with biennial budgets make adjustments in the off years, with corrective or supplemental appropriation bills, so budgeting in one form or another goes on continually.

The budget is a contest over who gets how much. The claimants are many—the schools, universities, institutions, transportation, health, law enforcement, the young and the elderly, business and labor, environmentalists, and many others. Because the pie is always limited, the budget pits agency against agency, client group against client group, cities against suburbs, Democrats against Republicans. It also provides a major test in the struggle between the governor and the legislature to determine who decides how much is spent on what for whose benefit.

Executive-legislative rivalry in the budget area can manifest itself in various ways—loudly or quietly, publicly or privately, confrontationally or diplomatically. But just about everywhere, the two branches have to work out their differences and reach an agreement. A spokesman for the senate majority leader referred to the process by which New York's governor and legislature work things out as "the annual dance of the budget flamingoes," with an opening gambit "where the birds bow, then strut around flapping their wings."[2] By the end of the process, the birds will have squawked, pecked at one another, and perhaps got into a fierce fight, but they will also have settled on a budget that holds, at least for a time.

Budget Formulation

In most states the executive formulates the budget, and in thirty states it submits a budget bill or bills. Governors may not be intimately involved in shaping the budget, but their broad priorities and goals will be reflected in the budget they propose, and their budget will serve as the state's operational frame of reference.[3] Still, in a number of states, the legislature prepares its own budget and in other states the legislature drafts the initial budget bill.

The initial process in shaping a budget is that of setting budget targets, which limit the amount that executive agencies can request, and then reviewing

Alan Rosenthal, "Balance of Power: The Case of the Budget," from *The Decline of Representative Democracy: Process, Participation, and Power in State Legislatures* (Washington, D.C.: CQ Press, 1998), pp. 306–318.

agency requests. In May or June, the governor's budget agency—such as the Office of Budget and Management (OBM) in Ohio or the Department of Administration (DOA) in Wisconsin—prepares a set of budget guidelines and budget request forms that are sent to the agencies of the executive branch. These guidelines are basically instructions from the governor and usually indicate the administration's policy directions.

Even at this executive-centered stage, the legislature is often involved. In a number of states a legislative agency is consulted. In Ohio, for example, the Legislative Budget Office (LBO) consults OBM on budget guidelines and works with executive agencies on the requests they will be submitting. In Florida, too, the governor's budget staff, housed in the Office of Planning and Budgeting, jointly develops instructions to the agencies with the staffs of the senate and house appropriations committees. Similar procedures are followed in Kentucky, where the Interim Appropriations and Revenue Committee, using the initial draft of the Office of Planning and Management, issues the budget instructions that are circulated to all the agencies. The legislative committee, and not the executive, has the ultimate say over what goes out.[4]

In the next phase—from July to November—agencies submit their budget requests, often asking for more than the governor is proposing. The executive budget agency normally reviews their requests, and may also conduct budget hearings. The executive budget staff analyzes and evaluates agency requests, and then makes its recommendations to the governor. In thirty-seven states the legislature also receives agency budget requests, usually at the same time as the governor, well before the executive budget is prepared. Legislative staffs begin working the budget over in much the same way as executive staffs. Ohio's LBO holds budget hearings with the agencies, as does the OBM, and conducts its own analysis. Florida's appropriations committees receive agency requests at the same time as the governor, and staff analysis begins right away.

One of the executive staff's activities is that of revenue estimation. State spending decisions depend on the amount of revenues available (and on decisions to raise or lower taxes as well). If revenues are high, a larger pot can be shared; if revenues are low, then expenditures have to be held down or cut, taxes have to be raised, or other sources have to be found. Revenue estimates or projections will differ, depending on economic assumptions. If the economy grows, tax revenues will flow to the treasury; if the economy shrinks, tax revenues will decline, and there will be less to spend. Projections are part art, part science, and part politics. No one can know for certain where the economy will go. Whoever makes revenue estimates, however, has the edge in shaping the budget. Exaggerating revenues will allow for higher spending; minimizing revenues will require more scrimping. Revenue forecasts generally are made when budgets are being prepared and are then updated on a quarterly basis.

Until relatively recently, only the executive had the authority and/or ability to produce revenue estimations, thus giving the governor an advantage. Now, however, legislative fiscal staffs in three-fifths of the states prepare their own estimates, and these estimates provide grist for the legislature's budget review and negotiations with the governor. In a number of states now the executive and legislative staffs come together in formal sessions to reconcile the differences in their estimates. Mississippi and Florida are examples of states that use a consensus process. Mississippi reaches an informal agreement, whereas in Florida the law requires that consensus-estimating conferences develop revenue forecasts, as well as economic and demographic forecasts, caseloads, and the like. The purpose is to remove, insofar as possible, political factors and to get agreement on the numbers. This allows both sides to start with the same assumptions.[5]

On the basis of agency requests and the analysis and recommendations of executive budget staff, the governor makes final budget decisions in November or December. It is his or her budget to deliver to the legislature, which already is at work examining the requests made by agencies. Even in states where the governor dominates the budget-formulation stage, legislatures are not without early influence. Such influence is usually exercised by legislative leaders who are consulted informally, and whose priorities find their way into the budget document and budget bill. A governor's close allies will certainly have their pet projects included.[6] In Maryland, where the general assembly is constitutionally proscribed from increasing the budget, the legislature is skillful in influencing the governor up front, before the budget is delivered. Through a process referred to as "spending affordability," the legislature sets a spending target, to which governors normally adhere. In addition, legislative leaders meet with the governor and express individual and collective priorities that run the gamut from local matters to executive departments and agencies to statewide policies. Governors usually try to accommodate these requests so that legislative leaders feel ownership and will push the budget through.[7]

Though the overall pattern is executive-centered, governors share responsibility for budget formulation in Arizona, Arkansas, Colorado, Florida, Kentucky, Louisiana, Mississippi, New Mexico, North Carolina, Texas, and Utah. Texas has its Legislative Budget Board (LBB), which is composed of legislators and the lieutenant governor, who serves as senate president. Instructions to state departments and agencies are drafted jointly by the LBB and the Office of Budget and Planning. Requests are submitted simultaneously to the legislative board and to the governor's office. But it is the LBB, and not the governor's office, that presents the budget bill. While legislators have two budgets before them for consideration—one in bill form and the other a document—only rarely is the executive proposal seriously considered. Normally, the legislature responds to the LBB bill, so that in Texas budget formulation is truly a legislative function.[8]

As in Texas, in Mississippi the legislature receives two budget proposals—one from the governor and one from the Legislative Budget Committee (LBC). The committee is dominated by legislative leaders, who negotiate the budget with which the legislature deals, while it ignores the governor's proposal.[9] Elsewhere, too, the legislature refuses to settle for a reactive role. Colorado's executive budget is said to have about as much status as a child's letter to Santa Claus. Here, the Joint Budget Committee (composed of six legislators, three from each chamber, who also sit on the appropriation committees) assembles the budget after analyzing agency requests and hearing agency testimony.[10]

The two-budget model is also used elsewhere. In New Mexico the Legislative Finance Committee prepares its own budget, which competes in the legislative process with the governor's.[11] Although formally an executive-budget state, Utah's joint appropriations subcommittees can choose between the governor's budget and the legislative fiscal analyst's.[12] The governor submits a budget and a budget bill in Florida, but it is only a starting point. Within a few days it has been completely reworked by the staffs of the senate and house appropriations committees. "For major issues, we do what we want to do," is the way one staffer described the legislative role in shaping the budget.[13]

Legislative Review

In January the governor of Ohio presents his budget message to the public and releases the executive budget document, called the "blue book." Meanwhile the LBO, jointly with the Legislative Service Commission, prepares the budget bill, which is based on the document. Ohio's budget bill for 1993–1995 ran to 1,300 pages and weighed in at 13 lbs. In addition to its biennial operating budget (which includes all the agencies of state government, with the exception of the Department of Transportation and Highway Safety and the Bureau of Workers' Compensation and Industrial Commission), Ohio also has a biennial capital budget, as do many other states. In fact, the majority of states use more than a single budget bill for operating expenses.[14] Virginia and North Carolina have two or three. New Mexico has separate budget bills for highways, state fairs and parks, game and fish, public employee salaries, and education.[15] Illinois deals with 80 bills, one for each executive agency. Mississippi has about 250 and Arkansas about 350 budget bills. The more bills, the greater the fragmentation and the more difficult it is for legislative leaders to maintain control over the entire process.

The legislative budget review process is anything but centralized. Tasks are shared between the house and senate. In Illinois, for instance, half of the eighty budget bills start out in the house, and the other half begin in the senate.[16] They are shared in each house among a number of committees or subcommittees. In Minnesota, for instance, the budget is divided among the appropriations, revenue, and education committees on the house side and the finance, revenue, and education committees on the senate side. Appropriations and finance each have four subcommittees (or divisions, as they are called in the house), with jurisdiction over higher education, health, human services, and corrections, state departments and agencies, and agriculture and transportation.[17]

In all but six states, as a matter of fact, appropriations committees make use of subcommittees, which are organized along programmatic lines.[18] The key work goes on in subcommittees. They review staff analyses, hold hearings, deliberate, and arrive at recommendations. The full committees generally accept their subcommittees' work and recommendations.

While in some states the two houses divide up the budget, in others the budget begins in one chamber and then goes to the other. Take Ohio. In February the budget bill is heard in the House Finance-Appropriations committee. Then its subcommittees review the bill and recommend changes to the full committee. From March until early April, House Finance-Appropriations acts on subcommittee recommendations and amends the appropriations bill. The house then passes the bill and sends it to the senate. During April, May, and early June the Senate Finance Committee and its subcommittees review the agency budget requests and changes. The senate passes the appropriations bill, with senate changes, and it is sent to conference committee.

The legislative role in the budget process hinges largely on the performance of the appropriations committees. These committees are those most sought after by members seeking assignments, and leaders normally appoint the most competent legislators to chair them and their subcommittees. The membership tends to be more stable and experienced than that of other committees. The chairmen tend to be on the ladder to top leadership. Workhorses of the legislature, appropriations committees command respect from legislators and executive officials alike.

Moreover, they are assisted by the premier staffs of the legislature—for example, the Office of Legislative Analyst in California, the Department of Fiscal Services in Maryland, the Legislative Fiscal Bureau in Wisconsin, and the staffs of the senate and house appropriations committees in Florida. In addition, in many states, partisan staffs also back up majority and minority members on the committees and subcommittees. Staff analyses, suggestions, and recommendations play an important part in deliberations of the members.

Weeks of hearings and testimony by agency and public witnesses also furnish legislators with information that goes into their decisions. In the case of most members, experience comes in handy. If they have been through the process before, they already have an idea of how effectively agencies are in administering programs and where the difficulties lie. Often, members have traveled around the state, visiting sites and informing themselves when the legislature is not in actual session. The house appropriations committee in Maryland, for example, made seventeen site visits during the 1995 interim, five by the full committee and the rest by four subcommittees.

Just as with the policy committees in the legislature, those who chair the full committee and the subcommittees of appropriations bear much of the responsibility and play the largest role. Subcommittee and full committee chairs have to work out differences, just as do house and senate committee and subcommittee chairs. The majority leadership in the chamber is almost always closely involved in negotiations and decisions. During the process, Maryland's senate committee and subcommittee chairmen meet every week for lunch. House chairmen do likewise; in addition, they meet once a week with the speaker and others in a "leadership" group of about fourteen.[19]

Although leaders have the most say overall in the legislature's review, a number of members serve on the appropriations committee and come to grips with part of the budget. With the exception of a few states—like Wisconsin, where the Joint Finance Committee has only sixteen members—appropriations committees are the largest in the chamber and participation is reasonably broad. Illustrative is house appropriations in Maryland. In the old days only a few members were in on decisions. Then, under the chairmanship of Buzz Ryan, more and more members were included. The process opened up, debate increased, and more members felt included. Even nonmembers could get through. If they came forward with an amendment that looked good, the committee would absorb it. As a result, the budget bill was never amended on the floor and the committee never lost a bill.[20]

Elsewhere, too, membership of the fiscal committees tends to be large. One-third of the senators and representatives in Ohio sit on the committees that work over the budget. In North Carolina 75 percent of the senators and 60 percent of the representatives are on the budget committees, while the rest of the legislators are on the revenue committees. In a few states, essentially every legislator serves on the appropriations committees and can have some say about what goes into the budget. Of 150 legislators in Iowa, 125 are on one of nine joint subcommittees of appropriations (while the other 25 are on ways and means). Legislative leadership decides how many dollars are allocated to each subcommittee's jurisdiction. In Utah everyone but the speaker serves on one of ten joint appropriations subcommittees. In addition, a joint executive committee of eighteen members allocates dollar amounts for the subcommittees to assign to departments, agencies, and programs. The executive committee has the final word on subcommittee recommendations, not all of which are accepted in their entirety.[21]

In many states the budget bill, after being reported out of appropriations, also has to run the gauntlet of the party caucuses. It used to be that majority-party leaders had little difficulty steering the bill through their caucus, but nowadays caucus approval can require substantial work. Members do not automatically fall in line, and dissident elements challenge leadership abilities to negotiate a settlement. In Wisconsin, majority-party members for some years have managed to alter the budget bill as reported by the Joint Finance Committee. Members insist on their own provisions in return for their support.[22] This process in which the caucus engages, referred to as "auctioning off," involves giving enough members projects for their districts to achieve the fifty-one votes needed to pass the bill on the floor. The process is similar in Colorado, where the so-called long bill, developed by the Joint Budget Committee and reviewed by the appropriations committees, gets worked over by the majority-party caucus.[23]

After all of the preceding negotiations, the floor procedure in each chamber is usually perfunctory. Although the minority may offer amendments, few changes (that have not been agreed to beforehand) are allowed on the floor. In California, where a two-thirds vote of each house is required to pass the budget, even a few holdouts can threaten the process. These dissidents have to be pacified before the budget is voted on the floor.

The most critical stage is the end game, after the house and senate have each passed a bill and have to resolve not only their differences but also those they may have with the governor. If the executive and the legislature are in the same partisan hands, things are more likely to be worked out as the process proceeds and the final stage is less of a hurdle. Otherwise, the conference committee of senate and house members and the negotiations between the legislative leadership and the governor are apt to be intense.

Either way, participation in the final phase of resolution necessarily narrows. A conference committee consists of relatively few members from each house. They work in collaboration with the majority leadership and have considerable scope for shaping the fiscal budget settlement, no matter what went on before. In Mississippi the six-person conference committee in effect writes the appropriations bills during the last three days of the session.[24] In Oklahoma the leadership is said to exercise substantial power controlling its conferees, who can almost rewrite the budget from scratch.[25] In Florida the two houses have traditionally been adversarial in negotiating the budget, with each adopting bills that put it in the best bargaining position in conference. The house speaker and the senate president led the negotiations in what has been characterized as "an undue centralization of power in the system."[26]

In other states even the concluding stage has opened up. Maryland used to limit its conference to three members. Now more members have a say, more people are in the room, and a longer time is spent even on relatively noncontroversial issues. Most issues can be resolved by splitting differences or trading off cuts: "We'll take your cut on this, you take ours on that."[27] Conferees fight for the senate or house version behind closed doors, as in Ohio, but still quite a few people are present in the room. These are referred to as "unclosed, closed" meetings, where everything leaks out and all interested parties know what is transpiring. But because the conference is not held in public, there exists no official record reporting who supports what. Were positions on the record, the process would be altered, and the participants' ability to compromise would probably diminish.[28]

Meanwhile, of course, the governor's preferences have to be taken into account because in all but seven states he or she can item-veto budgetary provisions the legislature wants. California's negotiations in recent years usually involved what was called "the Big Five"—the speaker and minority leader of the assembly, the president pro tem and minority leader of the senate, and the governor. These participants would sit at the conference table in the governor's outer office, along with a few staff aides, and try to work out the final budget. In the 1994–1995 budget, the job was accomplished in the legislature and it was not necessary for the Big Five to meet.[29] The process in New York is roughly similar, with the governor (at times a Democrat and at times a Republican) trying to resolve differences with the Democratic speaker of the assembly and the Republican majority leader of the senate. Every year in Albany the end of the session is a time of last-minute bill trading where almost every important issue is tied to something else and everything is tied to the budget. Upstate Republicans try to get more money for their schools; Democrats try to get more environmental projects; and the governor withholds his support from a final budget deal until he obtains an agreement on workers' compensation and domestic-violence measures. "The second the budget is done, the session is over," declares one of Gov. George Pataki's advisers.[30]

However much the process narrows in the final stage to a few key participants, the rank-and-file cannot be ignored. Indeed, legislative leaders speak not so much for themselves, but for their caucuses. The conference committee report, and any agreements entered into, has to win a floor vote in each chamber in order for the budget to become law. So, as long as they have their votes, legislators have bargaining power and some say over what goes in and what stays out of the state budget.

The Legislature's Impact

In their study of budgeting in the states, Edward J. Clynch and Thomas P. Lauth categorize states in terms of executive-legislative power. At one end of the continuum are the executive-dominant states, such as California, Illinois, and Ohio. At the other are the legislative-dominant states, including Florida, Mississippi, Texas, and Utah. In the middle are states where the legislature has the ability to challenge the executive—Connecticut, Georgia, Idaho, Kentucky, and Minnesota.[31]

The balance within a state shifts depending on circumstances. When the executive and legislature are controlled by the same party, the governor tends to gain power. Tight revenues also favor the governor at the expense of the legislature. Under such conditions legislators frequently let governors take the lead raising revenues or cutting spending, neither of which is popular with their constituencies.[32] Divided government enhances the legislative role, as does favorable economic conditions with revenues in abundance.

Over time legislative involvement has increased practically everywhere. As one indication, consider control within a state over federal funds. Only since the early 1980s have legislatures been involved in the review and allocation of federal funds, which earlier had been deemed a gubernatorial prerogative. They became involved in order to gain control over state spending, advance their own priorities for use of the federal funds, exercise discretion over the purposes to which state matching funds would be committed, and limit future demands for state funds to pick up the costs of federally supported programs when federal funding ended.[33]

Not much of an annual or biennial budget is subject to change. Some of state spending takes the form of transfer payments to local governments and school districts, which are funded on a formula basis and not within the purview of the budgetary process. Other expenditures may also be mandated. Depending on the state, perhaps only 5 to 10 percent of total expenditures are susceptible, as a practical matter, to either gubernatorial or legislative control. Changes in levels of expenditure for specific agencies and programs tend to be incremental, with the past level of activity serving as a base from which the review proceeds in both the executive and legislative branches.

Therefore, we cannot expect the legislature to have a large impact on the total amount budgeted. In Connecticut, it is traditional that the legislature makes few changes in the budget. In one fiscal year, the amount was $23.64 million. That was only 0.38 percent of total spending. But the amount was 36 percent of all new and expanded programs in excess of $1 million that were ultimately approved.[34] Using the former percentage, the legislative role appears negligible. Using the latter percentage, the legislative role appears significant. In Ohio the legislature can affect about 5 percent of the budget. But that includes quite a few important initiatives, such as hospital-care insurance and daycare, that come through the budget.[35]

Ohio is one of a number of states that have increasingly made policy through the budget. Human services, education, an experimental voucher program all find their way into the budget. Sometimes this procedure suits the governor, sometimes the legislature, and sometimes both. It facilitates passage of legislation under the budget umbrella. Wisconsin has pioneered in this area, with its budget bill running to 1,557 pages in 1993 (having been 281 pages in 1973), filled as it was with nonbudget policy items.[36]

Even in Maryland, where the legislature cannot increase proposed expenditures or insert items of its own, its budgetary role is not to be minimized. It has a major say in determining the capital budget, through statute it determines aid to localities, by legislating it helps shape the budget for the following year, and it manages to inject considerable fiscal prudence into the process. The legislature establishes limits through its "spending affordability" process, and is not hesitant to reduce items that cannot be justified by the executive. Maryland's governors have the upper hand, in that their priorities constitute the principal budgetary agenda, but the general assembly rarely accepts as a given what the governor presents.

The influence of legislators in obtaining appropriations for special projects that are located in their districts and that benefit their constituencies is acknowledged—and criticized by virtually everyone outside the legislature. We discussed pork in chapter 1 in connection with representation by individual members. Here, our analytical perspective is that of the legislature and its impact on the budget.

Maryland's capital budget normally contains $15 to $20 million for projects of special concern to members and delegations. Florida's budget used to allot $150 to $250 million for "turkeys." New York allows for several hundred "member items" that in 1995 amounted to about $150 million, averaging $710,000 for each of the legislature's 211 members to use for local purposes.[37] Appropriations measures, in particular, serve as vehicles for items or amendments that fund pet projects for as many members as possible. A member of the minority party in New Jersey referred to the 1995–1996 budget as more than the traditional "Christmas tree" budget but rather, as "a whole winter wonderland of pork." That prompted the governor's chief of staff to respond most diplomatically: "There are some items in his budget which the legislature considers priorities in the local level. We can't forget that the legislature is closer to the local spending needs than, perhaps, we are."[38]

The press delights in exposing appropriations like that for the White Otter Fish and Game Club in the southern Adirondacks of New York. The club received $150,000 for a new clubhouse, thanks to the efforts of the local state senator, who was a club member. But many other items clearly have merit, even though they are not screened through the executive's bureaucratic process before insertion in the budget. In New York, as elsewhere, most of the pork goes to deserving organizations like art museums, volunteer fire companies, cub scout troops, and senior citizen centers, and to deserving projects like highways and convention centers. A sampling of member items in the 1996–1997 New York budget is illustrative. There is $95,000 for the Southeast Bronx Neighborhood Centers, $30,000 for the Seneca Chamber of Commerce, $25,000 for the Hispanos Unidos de Buffalo, $15,000 for the Town of Cicero Historical Society, and $10,000 for the Lion's Club of Katonah.[39] Critics of this practice question legislative judgment, condemn the politics involved in choosing local recipients, charge that much of the money is not well used, and deplore the fact that there is little oversight or public accountability.

The assault on pork has made headway, at least in some states. In Florida, every member used to have a share of the budget in the form of a "turkey." Due to Florida Tax Watch, continuing press criticism, and apparent public opinion, any line item with geographical identification is now out of bounds, unless the executive agency requests it. Whereas previously Florida legislators jockeyed for whose arts and cultural projects would be included in the budget, a newly enacted law authorizes the executive to rank projects. Legislators, of course, can lobby an agency to have their items selected for funding, but getting a turkey is tougher now than formerly; and, thus, fewer turkeys survive.[40]

One result of the diminution of pork in Florida is that it is much harder for legislative leadership to exercise leverage over members with regard to the budget and policy issues.[41] That is because, as much as anything else, pork affords leaders resources with which to build consensus among an increasingly independent membership. Local projects that benefit a legislator's district are an important currency in the log-rolling of the legislative process. If leaders control such currency, their power to get the additional votes necessary to pass the budget or enact a controversial bill is enhanced. Pork makes it easier for pluralities to become majorities. Not surprisingly, the new, meager portions of pork signal a decline in the power of legislative leadership.

The legislature's budgetary activity keeps the executive on its toes. Conflict is endemic in the process. When control of government is divided, settlements are more difficult to come by. Governors and legislatures have even failed to produce a budget by the constitutional deadline; namely, the beginning of the fiscal year being budgeted. California budgets were late in 1983, 1990, 1991, 1992, 1994, and 1995, in one of these years for sixty-three days and in another for thirty-three.[42] New York has had an even rockier road. For thirteen straight years, from 1985 to 1997, the governor and legislature failed to meet the state's March 31 deadline. In 1994 and 1995 they were 68 days late, and in 1996 they were 104 days late, apparently a national record, which they surpassed the very next year.[43]

In these struggles legislatures generally give as good as they take. They prevail over governors on some items, while losing on others. After the smoke settled in Albany in 1996, for example, the New York legislature had rejected many of Gov. George Pataki's proposed policy changes and restored about $1.4 billion to his original spending plan. The governor concluded: "I understand that whether you're a legislator, a speaker, a majority leader or the governor, you never get things 100 percent your way."[44]

On occasion, the legislature emerges from the budgetary process with a clear-cut victory rather than some wins and some losses. Rhode Island in 1996 is an illustration. The legislature opposed Gov. Lincoln Almond's retirement plan and his cuts in education. In the face of his refusal to negotiate, the legislature passed its own budget, sustaining most social services, implementing a plan to reduce the number of state employees, and adding slightly to spending for education. The legislature's proposal also contained provisions rescinding existing statutory authority of the governor to move budget allocations within agencies and to impound monies. Since Rhode Island does not provide the governor with a line-item veto, Almond vetoed the entire budget that the legislature had passed; the very next day the legislature overrode the veto.[45]

Notes

1. Dall W. Forsythe, *Memos to the Governor: An Introduction to State Budgeting* (Washington, D.C.: Georgetown University Press, 1997): 75.
2. *New York Times,* March 9, 1988.
3. James E. Jernberg, "Minnesota: Searching for Stability," in *Governors, Legislatures, and Budgets,* ed. Edward J. Clynch and Thomas P. Lauth (Westport, Conn.: Greenwood, 1991), 73, 75.
4. Malcolm E. Jewell and Penny M. Miller, *The Kentucky Legislature* (Lexington: University Press of Kentucky, 1988), 141–142.
5. Edward J. Clynch, "Mississippi: Does the Governor Really Count?" in *Governors, Legislatures, and Budgets,* ed. Edward J. Clynch and Thomas P. Lauth (Westport, Conn.: Greenwood, 1991), 127; Gloria A. Grizzle, "Florida: Miles to Go and Promises to Keep," in *Governors, Legislatures, and Budgets,* ed. Edward J. Clynch and Thomas P. Lauth (Westport, Conn: Greenwood, 1991), 95.
6. Irene S. Rubin et al., "Illinois: Executive Reform and Fiscal Conditions," in *Governors, Legislatures, and Budgets,* ed. Edward J. Clynch and Thomas P. Lauth (Westport, Conn.: Greenwood 1991), 22.
7. Interview with the author, June 5, 1995.
8. Glen Hahn Cope, "Texas: Legislative Budgeting in a Post–Oil Boom Economy," in *Governors, Legislatures, and Budgets,* ed. Edward J. Clynch and Thomas P. Lauth (Westport, Conn.: Greenwood, 1991), 117.
9. Clynch, "Mississippi," 126, 131.
10. John A. Straayer, *The Colorado General Assembly* (Niwot: University Press of Colorado, 1990), 107, 219–230.
11. Interview with the author, May 17, 1995.
12. F. Ted Hebert, "Utah: Legislative Budgeting in an Executive State," in *Governors, Legislatures, and Budgets,* ed. Edward J. Clynch and Thomas P. Lauth (Westport, Conn.: Greenwood, 1991), 110–111.

13. Interview with the author, March 30, 1995.
14. James J. Gosling, "Budget Procedures and Executive Review in State Legislatures," in *Encyclopedia of the American Legislative System,* ed. Joel H. Silbey (New York: Scribner's, 1994), 766.
15. Interview with the author, May 17, 1995.
16. Rubin, "Illinois," 22.
17. Jernberg, "Minnesota," 76.
18. Gosling, "Budget Procedures and Executive Review," 769.
19. Interview with the author, June 5, 1995.
20. Ibid., March 6, 1996.
21. Hebert, "Utah," 112–113; also Ronald K. Snell, "Bringing More Legislators into the Budget Process," National Conference of State Legislatures, March 1994. Photocopy.
22. Rich Jones et al., "Review of Legislative Operations in the Wisconsin Legislature," National Conference of State Legislature, May 1994. Photocopy.
23. Straayer, *Colorado General Assembly,* 214.
24. Clynch, "Mississippi," 132.
25. Ronald M. Peters and Elizabeth Himmerich, "Policy Shift and Leadership Coalition: The Revolt Against Speaker Barker in Oklahoma" (paper prepared for delivery at the annual meeting of the American Political Science Association, San Francisco, August 30–September 2, 1990).
26. Grizzle, "Florida," 96–97.
27. Interview with the author, June 5, 1995.
28. Ibid., February 24, 1995.
29. Ibid., March 16, 1995.
30. *New York Times,* July 3, 1996.
31. Clynch and Lauth, "Conclusion," 152–155.
32. Ibid., 151–152.
33. Gosling, "Budget Procedures and Executive Review," 774–775.
34. Carol W. Lewis, "Connecticut: Prosperity, Frugality, and Stability," in *Governors, Legislatures, and Budgets,* ed. Edward J. Clynch and Thomas P. Lauth (Westport, Conn.: Greenwood, 1991), 48.
35. Interview with the author, February 24, 1995.
36. In 1993 some of these items started to be removed from the budget and treated as regular legislation. See Jones et al., "Review of Legislative Operations in the Wisconsin Legislatures."
37. *New York Times,* July 14, 1996.
38. Ibid., June 20, 1995.
39. Ibid., July 14, 1996.
40. Interview with the author, March 25, 1995.
41. Ibid. See also Forsythe, *Memos to the Governor,* 70.
42. Steve Scott, "The 1995–96 Budget," *California Journal,* September 1995, 8.
43. *New York Times,* July 14, 1996.
44. Ibid.
45. Maureen Moakley, "The Rhode Island Legislature: The Center Still Holds" (paper prepared for delivery at the annual meeting of the American Political Science Association, San Francisco, August 29–September 1, 1996).

CASE STUDY 14

Introduction

No state election has generated as much national attention in recent years as the effort to recall California Governor Gray Davis in October 2003. The effort to recall Davis began in early 2003 just a few months after Davis had been sworn in for a second term as governor. By July, the recall supporters had gathered some 1.3 million valid signatures, several hundred thousand more than were necessary to place the recall on the ballot. The election brought national attention in part because of the media's interest in California's colorful character and the fact that so few governors have been recalled. In fact, prior to the recall effort against Davis the only other governor in the nation's history to be recalled was North Dakota Governor Lynn J. Frazier, who was removed from office in 1921 after the state's economy went into a tailspin, causing, among other consequences, severe budget problems.

The media's interest grew as more and more people came forward to declare their candidacy to replace Davis. In California voters are given two questions to answer on the recall ballot. The first is whether the elected official who is targeted for recall should in fact be recalled. The second question is who should replace that official. In total, 135 candidates names appeared on the ballot to replace Davis, including the publisher of a pornographic magazine, a nationally known political commentator, the organizer of the Los Angeles Olympics and a former commissioner of major league baseball, the star of the television series *Diff'rent Strokes,* and the first Mexican American to hold a statewide office in California since the 1870s. The nation's attention was drawn even more to the state when well-known actor Arnold Schwarzenegger threw his hat into the ring. When the election finally arrived on October 7, more than 61 percent of the registered voters turned out to vote, removing Davis from office and electing Schwarzenegger in his place.

The story of Davis's recall is instructive for studying state finances because the main issue that brought Davis down was the state's budget. Not long after the economy began to decline in 2001, many states began to grapple with unexpected budget deficits, yet the problems confronting California's budget were among the worst in the nation. When the supporters of the recall effort had finished gathering signatures in July 2003, the state was facing a $38 billion gap in its budget. Dissatisfied with Davis's handling of the budget and other issues, state voters turned against him in the polls, removing him from office less than a year after he had been sworn in.

In the preceding essay, Alan Rosenthal makes it clear that the governor is not all-powerful in shaping the content of the state budget, but that legislatures also play a critical role. In California, however, the voters decided to hold their governor responsible for the state's budget crisis. Was Davis to blame for the problems in California? What role, if any, did the legislature and other political actors have in producing the crisis that brought Davis down? The essay that follows analyzes the forces that brought California to a crisis point and led to Davis's recall. According to the authors of the essay, Davis was partially responsible for the state's fiscal problems, but the state legislature and state voters were also involved. The essay is valuable because it underscores the important role played by both branches of government in shaping a state's budget.

The essay was written by a group of leading reporters and political scientists who study California politics. David Lesher and Jim Evans are editors of the *California Journal,* a respected political magazine in the state. A. G. Block is the journal's publisher. Bruce Cain is the director of the Institute of Governmental Studies at the University of California, Berkeley. Thad Kousser is an assistant professor at the University of California, San Diego. Daniel Borenstein is the political editor of the *Contra Costa Times.*

Questions to Consider

Here are some questions to consider as you read their work:

- What does it mean that a two-thirds vote is required to pass the state's budget? How has this requirement affected budget making?

- How has the partisan redistricting affected competition in state elections? Why does partisan redistricting make it more difficult to reach compromises in the legislature?
- How have term limits affected California politics? What impact have they had on budget making?
- Whom do the authors of the essay blame for the current crisis in California?
- The case study by Charles Mahtesian on "The Sick Legislature Syndrome" in Chapter 8 paints an unflattering picture of professional legislatures. Does this article on the crisis in California support Mahtesian's claims? What does it suggest about the value of professional legislatures and term limits?

California in Crisis

Jim Evans, A. G. Block, Bruce Cain, Thad Kousser, Daniel Borenstein, and David Lesher

Recall attempts and budget deficits are hardly new in California.

Three of the four previous governors have been targeted, including a 1968 charge at Governor Ronald Reagan that gained more than 550,000 signatures. And nearly a half dozen budgets have been in the red, since a 1991 gap that saw a third of the state's revenue vaporized by recession.

This year, the state faced stormy conditions once again. But instead of averting disaster, California has foundered. Government's inability to resolve its latest financial crisis has already cost millions of dollars in missed opportunities and higher borrowing costs, shaping the state's ability to address critical education and health issues for years to come. Chaos surrounding the fate of the governor has also blocked any vision for California beyond the recall date. The crisis is far from over, and the ultimate impact has yet to be measured.

"We are at a defining moment," said Assemblywoman Jenny Oropeza (D-Long Beach), chair of the Budget Committee. "The choices we are facing are really fundamental to our way of life."

How did this happen? Regardless of how the budget deficit is resolved or how the recall is decided, California has suffered a crisis that demands some explanation about its cause as well as a discussion about how to avoid it in the future.

It's also a calamity rooted entirely in Sacramento. There has not been a flood or earthquake or other natural disaster. There is no corruption scandal. And while the economy is sputtering, it isn't to blame. This catastrophe happened while everyone was playing by the rules. Many of the rules, however, were set by an angry and disconnected electorate, trying to restrain the power of government while ignorant or suspect about the human nature behind political collaboration.

The term limits set by voters in 1990, for example, drastically changed the process of lawmaking by removing the entrenched class of career politicians and restricting their rookie replacements to six years in the Assembly or eight years in the Senate. Today, the Legislature is far more diverse in gender and ethnicity, but the critical relationships that develop over time—through confrontations and compromise—are gone. There are no personal histories between individual conservatives and liberals forged during battles past. Today, crossing the aisle is a traitorous act that party leaders have threatened to punish.

Jim Evans, A. G. Block, Bruce Cain, Thad Kousser, Daniel Borenstein, and David Lesher, "California in Crisis," *California Journal* (August 2003): 18–27. Reprinted with permission of *California Journal* Magazine.

"There was a time when they knew that this kind of thermo-nuclear political war was not going to be successful," said Assemblyman Dario Frommer (D-Los Feliz). "We don't have that. It's really disintegrated. . . . It's become very petty, very political."

Political peace missions have been nearly impossible since 2001 when lawmakers drew new boundaries for their political districts. The last reapportionment concentrated Republican and Democratic voters into safe districts that assure re-election for the incumbent party. Instead of the moderate lawmakers who often win politically divided districts, the Legislature today is dominated by idealogues who are rewarded for left or right politics.

So nobody in Sacramento is surprised by this crisis. The building blocks have been piling up for years, clearly evident in the multi-year gridlock over financial restructuring, long-term construction plans and health care. California has weathered deficits and unpopular politicians before. The fact that this year's hardships spiraled into disaster is considered the logical result of a government that has grown more partisan, less experienced, more manipulated and less visionary than ever before.

Interviews and research conducted for this issue of *California Journal* found wide agreement about the five primary contributors to this year's trouble. The reasons go beyond the financial conditions that led to a $38 billion deficit or the political motives of an activist group that qualified the October 7 recall election. They include the missing relationships after term limits and the hardened politics of the last reapportionment as well as the fact that California is one of only three states that require a super-majority—two-thirds of the Legislature—to approve a state budget. Of course, the ingredients also include the first gubernatorial recall to reach a ballot and the incumbent governor with the lowest popularity score in state history.

Without any one of those five ingredients—term limits, a partisan reapportionment, the two-thirds vote, a weak governor and easy recall laws—there is a strong case that disaster could have been avoided. Instead, the combination produced a noxious political cocktail.

The doomsday question is whether Governor Gray Davis is being recalled for failing to govern a state that is no longer governable. If it's any solace, experts say this moment in California history may also be an expression of the tremendous anxieties in America today, stemming from the trauma of the September 11 attacks to the criminal scandals that rocked Wall Street, the jitters about economic uncertainties, the frightening experience of a war and, in California, the unthinkable energy shortage followed by an unprecedented financial deficit. People don't distinguish their fears by city, state or federal responsibility, political consultants say. And perhaps, they continue, the California conundrum is traced to the frustration of a new, more difficult world.

The question for California, however, is whether this year's experience is the sign of things to come. We've already been warned that the losers of this recall may try again. And as lawmakers neared agreement on a budget compromise with heavy borrowing and no tax hikes, it's clear the state will face another significant deficit next year. There is popular support in the Capital for a discussion about systemic reforms after the current crisis is settled. Many insiders recognize there are tangled priorities in a state that has one of the easiest rules for recalling a governor but one of the hardest thresholds for passing a budget. And there is renewed focus on the recall laws, which would remove a governor who gains 49 percent of the vote and replace him or her with a candidate who might receive less than 20 percent support.

"I would think that somebody would say, 'Let's have both sides meet and come up with some better rules for this,' " said Bob Mulholland, political director for the state Democratic Party. "Clearly, all of the faults for this are coming to bear here."

Following is a closer look at the five reasons California is in crisis.

The Two-Thirds Vote

The most direct factor contributing to the crisis that California finds itself in is the two-thirds vote requirement to pass a budget in the Legislature. In fact, if a budget could be passed with a simple majority, the Legislature would probably pass a budget on time every year.

But for a budget to be enacted, the law requires 54 of 80 Assembly members and 27 of 40 senators to vote for it. While the Democrats hold a significant majority in both houses this session, they still need eight Republicans to cross lines to craft a budget deal.

California is one of three states—including Arkansas and Rhode Island—to have such a law.

Historically, the constitutional two-thirds requirement—which was passed by California voters in 1933—has been a significant obstacle, but one that could be overcome by an experienced Legislature in which lawmakers on both sides could reach across the aisle. After term limits and the latest reapportionment, however, getting two-thirds is near impossible, said former Assembly Speaker Willie Brown (D-San Francisco).

"It's the 100 percent reason why we're in the mess we're in," said Brown, now in his last term as Mayor of San Francisco. "The advent of term limits and the latest reapportionment help get us here, but the two-thirds requirement for budget passage is the trigger that has the state in a crisis."

Brown and other critics argue that term limits and a partisan reapportionment are the bad medicine that made the two-thirds requirement the poison pill. The problem? Term limits took away the experience and camaraderie in the Legislature and reapportionment made lawmakers less accountable and more partisan.

"When I was in Sacramento there were always 20 percent [of legislators] who wouldn't vote for any budget, no matter what, but everybody else recognized the need for a budget, and I could deal with them," Brown said. "Now, the person who crosses the line to vote on a budget is viewed as a traitor, not as a patriot."

A good example of that might be Republican Mike Briggs, the former assemblyman from Fresno. Briggs—along with only three other Republicans in the Assembly—voted with Democrats on controversial budgets in both 2001 and 2002. The first year, Democrats rewarded Briggs for his vote by passing a tax credit that helped farmers in Briggs' district. In the second year, Briggs voted for the budget when some taxes were stripped out. When Briggs ran for Congress in 2002, he lost in the primary, and his vote on the first budget was a key reason. Assembly Speaker Herb Wesson (D-Culver City) subsequently hired Briggs to work on contract for the Assembly Democratic Caucus for $8,250-a-month. When the story got out, however, Briggs' contract was terminated.

"Once Briggs was toast, that play was no longer possible," Brown said.

Many Republicans argue that the two-thirds vote requirement keeps them involved in governing the state. Historically, Democrats have enjoyed large majorities in the Legislature—some even larger than the current 16-seat disparity in the Assembly and 10-seat gap in the Senate. The vote requirement provides an important check on that majority, said former Republican Assemblyman Bill Leonard.

"Without the two-thirds, California would be in a state fiscal crisis worse than it is," Leonard said. He said this year is particularly acrimonious in the Legislature because of the way the Democratic majority treated Republicans in the last two budget years. In both, most Republicans didn't vote for budgets.

"The minority feels like it's never consulted," Leonard said. "The Democrats are like a company that has tried to break its union, but the union succeeds—then the company still has to sit down with them."

Not all Republicans agree with Leonard's view that the two-thirds requirement restrains Democratic spending. Senator Tom McClintock (R-Thousand Oaks) said that rather than restrain spending, the requirement has increased the amount of pork in the budget because Democrats dangle pet programs in front of Republicans to entice a few to vote on a budget.

"If two-thirds was effective in restraining spending, we wouldn't have seen a 40 percent increase in spending in the past four years," McClintock said. "It makes the budget process a bidding process."

In fact, in the years leading up to the current crisis—when the state economy was booming and there were surpluses—Democratic and Republican lawmakers made deals that directly affected the size of the budget deficit today, said Jean Ross, director of the California Budget Project. Ross said that Democrats, who wanted to increase spending to pay for schools and other programs, got Republicans to agree to budgets in the late '90s by offering billions of dollars in tax cuts (like cutting the vehicle license fee and giving tax breaks to businesses). In effect, Ross said, legislators made a Faustian bargain to increase spending dramatically while lowering the revenue the state took in.

"The two-thirds deal was enacting tax cuts in exchange for increasing spending," Ross said.

While lawmakers blame each other—or the governor—for the current mess, Ross said that ultimately the two-thirds requirement allows both parties to escape responsibility for budget quagmires.

"The Democrats say, 'Don't blame us, we can't pass a budget with a simple majority,' and Republicans say, 'Don't blame us, we're in the minority,' " Ross said. "What we need is to allow the majority to govern, and then if the people don't like what they are doing, they can vote them out."

That may happen. Interest groups are collecting signatures to place an initiative on the March 2004 ballot that would lower the threshold for budget passage from a two-thirds majority to 55 percent of lawmakers. According to a recent Field Poll, 45 percent of those polled oppose the idea.

For now, Sacramento lawmakers will have to make due with the existing system. That makes former Speaker Brown, who moved from office in Sacramento to San Francisco in 1996, glad he left when he did.

"I love being the residential expert," Brown said. "I got out before the rain, and I clearly don't have an umbrella."

—*Jim Evans*

Partisan Reapportionment

In recent years, the philosophical gap between legislative Republicans and Democrats has widened and hardened, with the two sides having increased difficulty resolving differences over a myriad of issues, from taxes to tort reform. Partisan brawls tend to bring the Legislature to a standstill whenever a two-thirds majority is needed to approve legislation that must be passed; notably, the state budget.

One significant factor contributing to Capitol gridlock is the bipartisan redistricting adopted in 2001 and based on the 2000 Census. The vast majority of legislative and congressional districts created by that plan are so safe that most lawmakers effectively win their office in partisan primaries rather than in the general election.

The result is a Legislature that is ideologically polarized, said Allen Hoffenblum, a Republican consultant and co-author of "The Target Book," which tracks campaign activity in contested districts. "In primaries," he said, "hardcore liberals and hardcore conservatives dominate the selection process."

That contributes to gridlock because "a lot of what happens in legislatures these days is driven solely by ideology," said Alan Rosenthal, a professor at the Eagleton Institute of Politics at Rutgers University and a national expert on state legislatures. Republicans want to curtail government spending, and Democrats want to provide services, said Rosenthal, and "people in safe districts can indulge their ideological positions."

A consequence of the redistricting is the disappearance of the political middle—the moderate lawmakers who often provide compromise votes on contentious issues. In years past, budgets were passed when majority Democrats peeled off a few moderate Republicans willing to help reach the required two-thirds vote.

But as former Assemblyman Fred Keeley (D-Boulder Creek) noted, the new redistricting has made it very difficult to coax votes out of GOP caucuses. "Democrats get rewarded for providing services," Keeley explained. "Republicans get rewarded for cutting taxes"—a dynamic with no common ground.

The new, safe districts also change the political calculation for what it means to be at risk in an election. In competitive seats, incumbents facing challenges from the other party are wary of being considered too extreme. In safe districts, however, "extreme" can be an asset, and serious challenges are likely to come from even more ideologically dogmatic members of one's own party—a risk that keeps incumbents and candidates honing to the right or left.

As a result, Keeley said, redistricting stripped Democrats of another tool once used to pressure Republicans on the budget—pointing out the consequences of cutting services in their districts. Democrats tried that tactic this June, sending their members into solid GOP districts to warn local officials about cuts supported by their Republican representatives.

"We discovered," Keeley said, "that Republicans suffer greater consequences in their districts for tax increases than for [spending] cuts. For that kind of pressure to work, a district has to be so marginal [between the two parties] that a particular candidate can't be seen as ideological."

And these days, safe districts far outnumber competitive ones.

By defining a competitive district as one where 10 percent or less separates Democratic and Republican voter registration, the most current data from the Secretary of State's Office (February 2003) indicates that six of 53 congressional districts, four of 40 state Senate districts and 14 of 80 Assembly districts are competitive—24 of 173 districts, or 13.9 percent.

But even that small percentage is inflated when results of the 2002 general election are considered. In that election, only one congressional and one Senate winner (of 20) had margins of victory under 10 percent. The Assembly produced five races where the victor won by less than 10 percent. That is seven close shaves in 153 contests, or 4.6 percent. Put another way, 95.4 percent of primary winners cakewalked through the general election.

The way new districts were drawn also enhanced the clout of legislative leaders when enforcing caucus discipline, a factor effectively demonstrated this past June by Senate Republican Leader Jim Brulte (R-Rancho Cucamonga). Brulte threatened to campaign—in the primary—against any GOP incumbent supporting a tax increase, a threat delivered in person to Senate and Assembly Republicans and widely reported in the media. Afterward, no Republican even hinted at support for a tax hike.

Although no Democrat so bluntly intimidated members of his or her caucus, the message still resonates, according to Hoffenblum. "Democrats don't want to face the wrath of [state Senator] Sheila Kuehl," he said, "any more than Republicans want Brulte coming into their districts and saying to their base voters, 'You sold out to Democrats.' "

Especially in nice, safe districts where the only voters who matter at all are from a legislator's own party.

—*A. G. Block*

Term Limits

One thing seems certain: If anyone thought that solving a fiscal crisis would be easier after Proposition 140 took effect than it was before, today they are sorely disappointed. Term-limited legislators are no more likely to pass difficult budgets on time than their predecessors. Their "fresh" perspectives and "real world experiences" apparently succumb to partisan pressures and personal ambitions pretty quickly. California's budget process is predicated on compromise and bipartisanship, but political forces still pull in the opposite direction.

It is impossible to attribute all of the troubles that the state is having in overcoming its massive deficit to term limits, because of the many other factors discussed in this edition. Term limits, though, have left the current crop of legislators ill prepared to deal with a budget crunch compared to the veterans who faced a similar crisis a decade ago. Our studies indicate that the Legislature's collective experience level, knowledge of the budget and willingness to engage in oversight activities are way down. Since the process is more flawed than in the past, it is likely that the product will be as well.

One very dramatic difference between pre- and post-term limit legislators is the level of experience and expertise they bring to the process. In the Assembly particularly, committee chairs and staffs are often new to their positions—and sometimes new to Sacramento. The Senate benefits from the regular flow of assembly members and their staff into the upper house. This is a positive thing in the sense that the Senate's experience balances off the Assembly, but it also causes gaps in the way that the two houses see problems like budget deficits. For better or worse, some of this experience differential will disappear as the last of the pre-term limit members like Senate President pro Tem John Burton (D-San Francisco) finally term out in 2004.

This lack of experience might not matter so much if members had the incentive to learn as much as they could about the budget as fast as possible. Some do. But our interviews with experienced budget staff suggest that many members do not invest much time and effort in building the budget. Budget subcommittees theoretically offer opportunities for legislators to immerse themselves in the nitty-gritty of agency spending and policy evaluation—information that might lead to a bipartisan consensus on informed cuts when they are needed. But senior staff reported to us that new legislators, out to make names for themselves quickly, often do not take their subcommittee work seriously.

This relates to another problem: the decline in oversight activities. Good oversight allows legislators to discover whether money is being spent well, and whether programs are being implemented the way they were intended. However, digging into the details of agency behavior requires expertise and time that new members cannot afford. With only six years in the Assembly, the ambitious new member has an incentive to avoid the unglamorous work of oversight in favor of headline-catching legislation.

The inexperience of new members cannot by itself explain the remarkable partisan polarization that has made today's fiscal crisis especially difficult to solve. In part, this has occurred because term limits prevent legislators from anticipating a future in their house. This means that they have much less incentive to cooperate across party lines because there will be no time for a "go along to get along" attitude to pay off. Without a future voice in the policy that their house makes, they cannot cooperate with tax increases during a time of fiscal crisis (as Governor Pete Wilson and top Republican legislators did in the early 1990s) and then fight another day to cut back these very taxes (as Wilson and his allies did during the mid-1990s). Term limits can take away opportunities and incentives to govern responsibly.

Yet the great hope of term limits was that they would lead to above-the-fray statesmanship precisely because they erased everyone's political future. Proposition 140 would send legislators back to the farms, homes and schoolhouses from which they came, thus freeing them to stand up to tyrannical party leaders and greedy interest groups in order to do what is best for California. Predictably, however, the initiative failed to create a new brand of citizen legislator. Our analysis shows that newly elected assembly members after term limits are not much different from their predecessors, other than being a bit younger and more likely to have served in a local government. They do bring new ideas and tremendous energy, but most report that it takes them a few sessions to learn how to channel their ideas into policy. By then, their term is up. Bitten by the public service bug, more than three-quarters of them decide to run for the state Senate, Congress, or another state or local office. Instead of being freed from electoral pressures by term limits, they are ever more reliant upon the favor of party leaders and campaign contributors as they seek to impress a new set of voters. Ironically, by severing the link between legislators and the constituents who know them as individuals, term limits have heightened the partisan solidarity that makes the budget stand-off so intractable.

—*Bruce E. Cain and Thad Kousser*

Recall

The stage was set for the recall of Governor Davis when less than one of every four registered voters cast a ballot for him the day he was re-elected in 2002. "When I was asked, 'Could it be done?' " said Dave Gilliard, a Republican campaign consultant who helped lead the signature-gathering, "I said, 'This guy doesn't have support. He won because he was the lesser of two evils.' "

Across the nation, only one governor has ever been recalled. North Dakota voters removed Lynn Frazier from office in 1921. Since Californians adopted the progressive reforms of Governor Hiram Johnson in 1911, there have been plenty of opportunities to oust this state's leader. Yet none of the 31 attempts has reached the ballot.

Why now?

Call it the political "Perfect Storm," a confluence of events that has left even some Democrats convinced that Governor Davis' political career will soon end.

Blame events. The energy crisis and the state budget implosion are the leading culprits.

Blame the recall system. Most states have no provisions for a gubernatorial recall. But, of the 18 that do, California has one of the lowest qualification thresholds. It takes the signatures of just 12 percent of the vote for governor in the last election to force a statewide vote.

Blame California. In the Golden State, voters love using the ballot box to second-guess their leaders. The recall is merely a derivative of the initiative process that political consultants here love so dearly. The signature-gathering operations were already in place.

Blame money in politics. The recall drive languished until Representative Darrell Issa (R-Vista) came along with a $1.7 million jump start.

But also, blame Davis. His inability to work with the Legislature leaves him isolated in his time of need. His negative campaigns and his poor communication keep him detached from the voters of the state he leads.

Tim Hodson, executive director of the Center for California Studies at California State University, Sacramento, criticized Davis' "refusal or inability to recognize that his re-election was not a confirmation of his leadership."

One irony of the Davis recall is that the governor made it easy for his opponents. His negative campaign against Republican businessman Bill Simon not only depressed turnout in the November 2002 election to record-low levels, it also reduced the threshold for qualifying the recall.

Of more than 21 million adults eligible to vote, 15 million were registered before the November 2002 election. Only about 7.5 million voted in the governor's race and 3.5 million voted for Davis. Recall proponents needed signatures of just 12 percent of that roughly 7.5 million. The magic number was just 897,158.

Davis is a governor with little popular support and few loyalists in Sacramento. "When you get in trouble and you don't have friends to rally around you and rally to your defense, it's pretty hard to get yourself out of trouble," said Gilliard.

To be sure, Davis has demonstrated that one should never underestimate him. But this could be his toughest battle.

Just two and a half years ago, the Public Policy Institute of California's poll showed 62 percent of likely voters approved of his job performance. Today, it's down to 22.

In his defense, Davis is a victim of the state's increasingly partisan politics. His top political strategist, Garry South, said the governor can't get cooperation from the state Legislature because it has become dysfunctional.

Term limits produced inexperienced lawmakers most concerned about their next elective office. The state's closed primary election system that bars Democratic and Republican voters from crossing party lines creates more partisan nominees. And, perhaps most significant, the highly partisan districts created by the 2001 redistricting allow legislators to move far from the political center.

South called it the "unholy trinity of the California political system" that has made the state "ungovernable." It helps explain why Davis has had a tougher time forging alliances than his predecessors.

That's clear in the state budget. "Gray is a moderate in the middle of this discussion," said former Assemblyman Phil Isenberg (D-Sacramento). "The discussion has been very polarized."

Many have blamed the recall for making the budget negotiations tougher. Clearly, the issues are intertwined. But the relationship is complex. The recall didn't cause the stalemate, Isenberg noted. "The recall didn't get rolling until April or May. The Democrats and Republicans were locked into their [respective] positions of no cuts and no taxes from December on."

But as the recall got rolling, things changed. In May, Davis backed away from cuts he proposed four months earlier, leading critics to say he was pandering to liberal interests to save his job. And in July, after the recall election was scheduled, Democrats began to capitulate to GOP demands that a budget solution contain no new taxes.

Even while some lawmakers insisted the recall and budget were unrelated, voters thought differently. A Field Poll in July showed 19 percent of likely voters said they would be less inclined to recall Davis if the state budget were satisfactorily resolved.

—Daniel Borenstein

A Weak Governor

Even with all of the contributors to the current crisis, the disaster may have been averted if the state was run today by a popular and powerful governor. Davis had that authority when he took office in 1999 following a landslide election victory and poll ratings over 60 percent. He stood up to special interests, and he persuaded reluctant Democrats to pass several controversial reforms.

But signs of unhappiness with Gray Davis were showing before he was even sworn into office. The same labor unions that went all out for his election threatened to picket the governor's inaugural because Davis declined to support their contract demands. A few weeks later, the California Teachers Association refused to endorse the governor's signature education reform plan because it included new accountability rules. Consumer groups also complained they were being shut out of meetings with the health care industry. And in April, Davis had a very public falling out with his Democratic lieutenant governor, Cruz Bustamante, over immigration issues.

"Our candidate, Gray Davis, seems to have forgotten how he got to the governor's mansion," said a petition signed that spring by hundreds of Democratic activists.

The early misgivings about the first Democratic governor in 16 years culminated in July when Davis complained to the *San Francisco Chronicle* that lawmakers in his party were ignoring his politically centrist direction. "It was my vision that commanded a 20-point [election] victory, the largest victory in 40 years," Davis insisted. "Nobody else in the Legislature ran statewide. Their job is to implement my vision. That is their job."

Clearly, Davis had few friends in Sacramento. But his poll ratings remained high for several years, giving him the authority to win legislative victories and to raise a record-shattering $70 million for his re-election campaign.

His support collapsed quickly, however, in 2001 when California suffered an unfathomable energy crisis. Electricity prices soared 900 percent, and some cities experienced blackouts with no end in sight for the diasaster. National Republican operatives seized the opportunity to launch a television advertising campaign blasting Davis for the problem. Their plan worked. Davis' rating in the independent Field Poll dropped from 57 percent in January 2001 to 36 percent in May. It never recovered. Today, just more than 20 percent of the electorate approves of the job Davis is doing, the lowest rating ever recorded for a California governor.

Davis attributes his poor standing to anxieties about war, security and the economy that are affecting politicians nationwide. In interviews recently, he often notes that other politicians are equally out of favor.

"I really believe it's all about economics," Davis said in July. "Californians are in a funky mood. California is a victim of the national economy. In the early part of 2001, I had 58 percent approval ratings, and they said what they liked. . . . the most was the strong economy in California. People's lives were much better off in the first two and a half years of my governorship than they are now, and the governor is just held accountable. He gets more credit than he deserves in the good times, and the reverse is true in bad times."

Davis has signed major legislation on gun control, auto emissions, health care oversight and expansion, family leave, domestic partners, student testing and teacher training, and farm worker protection. But his tenure in office has also been marked as much by crisis as by accomplishment.

The energy mess is still not resolved, but a few months after it calmed down in late 2001, the governor faced a prominent fund-raising scandal. The controversy involved a $95 million state contract with the Oracle software company that was found to be overpriced and unnecessary by the state auditor. Three aides to Davis were fired or resigned after it was disclosed that the governor's technology adviser accepted a $25,000 campaign donation shortly after the contract was signed.

The scandal fueled cynical media coverage of the governor's unprecedented fund-raising for his 2002 re-election, including stories about other state awards to Davis contributors and strong-arm tactics by the governor. The media coverage, along with criticism from political challengers, prevented Davis from running a positive campaign. Instead, the 2002 race between Davis and Republican Bill Simon turned into one of the most negative contests in recent state history. Davis outspent Simon by more than 2-to-1, but he barely won.

After the election, a humbled Davis took an aggressive posture to try and head off an obvious budget crisis on the horizon. He ordered a special session of the Legislature to convene last December, and he proposed more than $10 billion in immediate, mid-year budget cuts to reduce the shortfall.

But in a clear sign of the governor's flagging authority, lawmakers ignored the governor's plan and adjourned the special session after only a few hours. And in January, they quickly rejected most of Davis' proposal for the 2003–2004 fiscal year budget. Instead, they quickly passed an increase in the vehicle license fee that the governor had explicitly opposed. And when Davis threatened a veto in February, the confrontation devolved into an angry meeting of the Democratic caucus.

Today, insiders believe the solutions to the current crisis will be found outside of the governor's office.

"We have a governor who has not distinguished himself through collaboration," said state Senator John Vasconcellos (D-San Jose). "He's managed to alienate everyone. It's about his personality. He has experience, but his experience was getting ready to run for governor."

—David Lesher

Chapter 14 Review Questions

1. How does a downturn in the economy generally affect state budgeting?
2. How does the budget process work? What are the different steps involved?
3. How much influence do governors have on the state budget in comparison with state legislatures? What factors help make the governor powerful? Where and how is the legislature able to influence budget making?
4. According to the authors of the case study, what are the five factors that led to the crisis in California?
5. Are there lessons we can learn from California's experience about budgeting that are not captured in Rosenthal's essay? Looking at the case study, can you add anything to Rosenthal's essay to give a richer explanation about the forces that shape budgets? Or, conversely, are there aspects of Rosenthal's work that are helpful for clarifying the events in California?
6. What issues have been important in battles over your state's budget in recent years? Who have been on the different sides of the battle? How were the battles resolved? How influential were the governor and the state legislature in resolving the conflict?

Key Terms

fiscal year
sales tax
personal income tax
Medicaid
general veto
item veto
party caucuses
incremental
budget formulation
budget bill
governor's budget agency
appropriations committee
conference committee
executive dominant
legislative dominant
Christmas Tree budget
pork
recall
term limits
two-thirds vote
partisan realignment

Suggestions for Further Reading

Abney, Glenn, and Thomas Lauth. "The Item Veto and Fiscal Responsibility." *Journal of Politics* 59 (1997): 882–992. This article provides the results of a survey of budget officials on the effectiveness of the item veto as a tool of fiscal responsibility.

Alt, James E., and Robert Lowry. "Divided Government, Fiscal Institutions, and Budget Deficits: Evidence from the States." *American Political Science Review* 88 (1994): 811–828. Valuable study examines how state governments respond to fiscal shocks that may cause budget deficits to occur. The findings show that the party that controls government, whether Republican or Democrat, affects fiscal policy, as does whether a state has divided government.

Clynch, Edward J., and Thomas P. Lauth, eds. *Governors, Legislatures, and Budgets: Diversity Across the American States.* New York: Greenwood Press, 1991. One of the best studies of the impact of governors and legislatures on state budgets. Includes case studies from thirteen states.

Forsythe, Dall W. *Memos to the Governor: An Introduction to State Budgeting.* Washington, D.C.: Georgetown University Press, 1997. Straightforward introduction to state budgeting. Written in the form of memos to an incoming governor.

Gold, Steven D., ed. *The Fiscal Crisis of the States: Lessons for the Future.* Washington, D.C.: Georgetown University Press, 1995. Collection of essays on how the states responded to the severe fiscal crisis of the early 1990s. Includes comparative research on all fifty states as well as in-depth case studies of California, Connecticut, Florida, Massachusetts, Michigan, and Minnesota.

Gosling, James J. "Budget Procedures and Executive Review in State Legislatures." In John H. Silbey, ed., *Encyclopedia of the American Legislative System.* New York: Charles Scribner's Sons, 1994. This essay provides a comprehensive overview of past research on state budgeting politics.

Krolak, Richard. *California's Budget Dance: Issues and Process.* 2d ed. Sacramento: California Journal Press, 1994. An excellent overview of the budgeting process in California.

Lowry, Robert C., James E. Alt, and Karen E. Ferree. "Fiscal Policy Outcomes and Electoral Accountability in American States." *American Political Science Review* 92 (December 1998): 759–774. This study examines the impact of state fiscal policies on gubernatorial and legislative elections from 1968 to 1992.

National Association of State Budget Officers and National Governors Association. *The Fiscal Survey of the States.* Washington, D.C.: National Association of State Budget Officers, biannual. This twice-a-year report provides the most comprehensive picture available on the current status of all state budgets.

Raimondo, Henry J. *Economics of State and Local Government.* New York: Praeger, 1991. Comprehensive textbook on state and local government economics and finance.

Rosenthal, Alan. *Governors and Legislatures: Contending Powers.* Washington, D.C.: CQ Press, 1990. The sixth chapter of this book provides a more detailed discussion of the politics of state budgeting than the excerpt written by Rosenthal that is reprinted in this chapter.

Smith, Robert W., and Thomas D. Lynch. *Public Budgeting in America.* 5th ed. Upper Saddle River, N.J.: Prentice Hall, 2003. Comprehensive textbook for those who would like to know more about the budgeting processes at the state level. Another good text is James Gosling's *Budgetary Politics in American Government,* 3d ed. (New York: Routledge, 2002).

Related Web Sites

http://www.nasbo.org/
The National Association of State Budget Officers provides links to all state budget offices and research information on state budgets, including the *Fiscal Survey of the States.*

http://www.pbs.org/now/politics/statebudgets.html
PBS web site devoted to the recent fiscal problems in the states includes data on state budget deficits and links to state budget offices.

http://www.governor.ca.gov/state/govsite/gov_homepage.jsp
Home page for California Governor Arnold Schwarzenegger.

15

Education: The Concept of School Reform

School reform is political at its heart.

Clarence N. Stone, Jeffrey R. Henig, Bryan D. Jones, and Carol Pierannunzi

READING 15

Introduction

The National Commission on Excellence in Education released its report *A Nation at Risk* in 1983, lamenting the quality of education in America. The report warned that the education system was being eroded by a "rising tide of mediocrity that threatens our very future as a Nation and a people." Although education reform has long been a major concern in the United States, the release of the commission's report and its dire tone moved education more prominently up the nation's political agenda. Since the mid-1980s, the public schools have been a target of wave after wave of reform proposals. Some reformers have called on state governments and local school boards to take steps to improve teacher quality by raising salaries, introducing merit pay, and requiring more training. Others have proposed changes in pedagogy and the content of instruction, such as through smaller classes, more interdisciplinary courses, greater reliance on experiential learning, the use of magnet schools, or a return to basics. Some have sought to decentralize authority so that teachers and principals have greater control over education through what is called site-based management. Conversely, others have proposed the creation of standards for student achievement with penalties for schools that do not meet those standards, as mandated by the No Child Left Behind Act of 2001. There have also been proposals to apply economic principles to education so that there is greater competition among schools. For example, some reformers have called for hiring private businesses to run public schools, allowing students to choose the schools they want to attend, and creating charter schools that are free from many government regulations.

The need for reform in urban schools has been seen as especially critical. Although suburban and rural school districts certainly face significant challenges, urban school systems confront a broader array of more intractable problems. Because the nation's urban areas tend to have greater poverty, urban school systems often have to deal with a wider range of complex social problems. Many of the children in urban schools do not have the same support structure at home to help them achieve, which makes the tasks for the schools more difficult. The economic problems in the nation's urban areas also mean that urban school districts do not have as strong a tax base as those in the suburbs. As a result, urban schools often find themselves facing more difficult problems with fewer resources. In addition, some urban school districts have become so large and bureaucratic that they are resistant to change.

What can be done to fix the schools in the urban areas where the need to improve education is the greatest? The proposals listed above provide a variety of options that have been championed in recent years. Although these proposals offer different approaches to addressing the problems, they are all similar in that they seek solutions by looking to the schools themselves for change, be it by improving teaching, revising curriculum, or altering how the schools are managed. There is a growing belief among many social scientists today, however, that none of these proposals alone can solve the schools' problems. The reason these solutions won't work is that the problems confronting the urban schools are not just the product of the education system, but are intricately connected to the broader social and economic problems of the nation's urban areas. For these reformers, the answers to the problems will not be found by simply looking for one particular educational approach that will provide a silver bullet. Rather, the solution requires a political response that addresses the problems in a systemic way over time. More important, the solution demands that all the major actors within the urban community work together to help the schools, including teachers, administrators, community leaders, business people, and parents. In other words, the answer to the urban school problems is to build civic capacity.

In the reading that follows, Clarence N. Stone, Jeffrey R. Henig, Bryan D. Jones, and Carol Pierannunzi describe the major political issues that confront urban schools and explain why reform efforts must include the broader community, not just the schools. The reading begins by explaining why urban school reform is a different type of policy problem than urban redevelopment, but why both of them require the attention of governmental and nongovernmental actors. The authors then identify five major components or strands of education politics: raising revenue, the composition of students in the classroom, the interface between the schools and the community, bureaucratic politics, and classroom management. In this section, the authors provide a straightforward overview of the myriad of different political issues that confront schools. The last part of the essay explains how the complexity of the problems can lead to "the failure syndrome" and why mobilizing civic capacity is essential for making a difference.

The essay is valuable for explaining the complexities of urban school politics and the difficulties in finding a solution that will work. The four authors are respected experts on education and community politics. Stone is a professor of government and politics at the University of Maryland and the editor of *Changing Urban Education: The Politics of Urban Development* (Lawrence: University Press of Kansas, 1998). Henig is a professor of political science at George Washington University. He is the author of *The Color of School Reform* (Princeton: Princeton University Press, 1999). Jones is the director of the Center for American Politics and Public Policy at the University of Washington.

Pierannunzi is a professor of political science at Kennesaw State University. The excerpt is from *Building Civic Capacity: The Politics of Reforming Urban Schools,* which was the recipient of the APSA Urban Politics Section Best Book Award.

Questions to Consider

As you read the essay, these are some questions to consider:

- What is social reconstruction? How do the authors say that it is similar to and different from physical reconstruction?
- What are the five strands of education politics? What are some of the key political struggles associated with each one?
- What do the authors mean by "the failure syndrome"? What causes it? What solutions do the authors advocate for overcoming this syndrome?
- What are the different groups that have a stake in the public school system? What does each of these groups want from the schools? The authors talk about the importance of getting these different groups to work together, but do you think that is always possible? Are there often too many conflicts in values and goals to bring them together?

The Challenge of Change in Complex Policy Subsystems

Clarence N. Stone, Jeffrey R. Henig, Bryan D. Jones, and Carol Pierannunzi

The Civic Capacity and Urban Education Project began with an observation and a puzzle. Physical and economic decline, in the middle of the last century, was so common among central cities that it was seen by some individuals to result from an overpowering "logic of metropolitan growth" that could not be effectively ameliorated.[1] Concerted action by business leaders and politicians in some cities stemmed or even reversed the seemingly unstoppable spiral of deterioration. Yet, we observed, some of the same cities—indeed some of the very same coalitions of actors—appear to falter when faced with the challenges of addressing social inequality and investing in human capital. Why should this be so? Why should the coalitions that were so effective in addressing physical decline be so impotent when facing the challenges of human capital development?

Social reconstruction, typified in efforts to improve the performance of urban school districts, differs fundamentally from the politics of physical reconstruction. Although both physical and social reconstruction have private and collective dimensions, social reconstruction is tied to the pursuit of a collective good in a way that physical reconstruction is not. Physical reconstruction has collective benefits; if economic vitality is stimulated, businesses, unions, and government services (via an improved tax base) all reap the rewards. But particular business interests and construction unions directly benefit through the subsidies that they receive. Moreover, politicians, by being able to focus attention on the massive and obvious changes that occur downtown, can raise their profiles and improve election possibilities.

Clarence N. Stone, Jeffrey R. Henig, Bryan D. Jones, and Carol Pierannunzi, "The Challenge of Change in Complex Policy Subsystems," from *Building Civic Capacity: The Politics of Reforming Urban Schools* (Lawrence: University Press of Kansas, 2001), pp. 32–54.

Investment in human capital development has collective benefits, and some interests benefit more than others. A changing urban economy requires a more educated workforce, so businesses can benefit disproportionately. But educational improvement lacks the direct, particularistic benefits of physical redevelopment. Underinvestment in the education of the poor is thus a distinct possibility.

In American cities, redevelopment has enjoyed backing from powerful business interests with a direct and immediate stake in the effort. Moreover, the activity of redevelopment itself opens up abundant opportunities for contractors, developers, and others . . . to benefit materially from the process. By contrast, school reform runs the risk of being perceived as an activity that takes individual material benefits away from these influential stakeholders. Education costs plenty of money, much of it raised via the local property tax. Increases in taxes can drag economic development down, threatening jobs in the already job-scarce economies of the nation's cities. Even if it is true that a strong school system ultimately contributes to economic development and growth, such a payoff is neither immediate nor assured. Although education might objectively fit Peterson's definition of a developmental policy, key political actors often perceive it as more akin to a redistributive policy and gauge their actions accordingly.[2] As a consequence, the traditional focus of business interests has been on economy and efficiency in schools rather than on the development of human capital.

Thus, social reconstruction involves a different kind of politics. Unlike the prime beneficiaries of redevelopment, in social reconstruction people in position to benefit in the most immediate ways are largely poor and unorganized. Whereas material benefits and personal incentives are primary *drivers* of efforts to physically rebuild central cities, such benefits and incentives are more likely to divert or *co-opt* the collective pursuit of social goods. Although investment in human capital can provide particular benefits in the form of jobs and career possibilities, for example, these can readily become ends in themselves rather than steps toward a collective goal. All the results of human capital development are long-term and uncertain. Many of the benefits of physical redevelopment are immediate and visible. All things considered, there is little wonder that physical reconstruction has held a more central place on the urban action agenda.

Yet, despite past frustrations, especially those accompanying the antipoverty efforts of the Great Society, social reconstruction has gained new prominence.[3] Education especially is a matter of great concern at all levels of government and across several sectors of society. Among other considerations, many actors now see that the economic vitality of the city is irrevocably tied to social conditions, and social conditions, in turn, are closely linked to education and related matters of youth development. School reform has thus emerged as a major policy initiative among those concerned with the revitalization of the city.

The aim of educational improvement represents a collective good in another way. As a policy initiative, it requires that various elements of the city be drawn into the effort. Neither businesspeople, educators themselves, nor any other segment of the community is sufficient alone to ensure that substantial progress occurs; success depends on a collective effort. Democratic theorists see the process as one in which diverse players are brought to understand that *political* change is not a matter of what each separately wants, but of what, working together, they are able to accomplish collectively.[4] Yet in a nation in which an adversarial approach to politics is deeply ingrained, participation in a shared effort is no easy matter.

As embodied in educational reform, the social reconstruction of the city is, then, a special kind of policy. If the physical reconstruction of the city represents a collective good that can be advanced by a heavy mixture of selective benefits, social reconstruction has no comparable base in distributive politics. Educational improvement thus poses the question of what are the conditions under which a diverse set of players, governmental and nongovernmental, can be brought together around the aim of a social good.

If the politics of redevelopment does not suggest a satisfactory answer to that question for education, it nevertheless reminds us that, from initiation through implementation, policy making is a meld of governmental and nongovernmental actions, and that is no less true in education than it is in redevelopment. . . .

The One and the Many: Five Strands of Education Politics

In a very real sense, the education arena has "not one politics, but many."[5] The politics of urban education is thus not a single activity, but, as Kenneth Wong argues, a mixture of many activities and interacting processes.[6] Many of these activities are widely studied and easily recognized: the politics of the board of education, the politics of the superintendent's office, the intergovernmental links between the local school system and education programs and mandates at the state and federal levels, the locally minded moves of governors and other state officials, the local links between the school district and city hall, the politics of the PTA and other community groups as they interact with school officials, collective bargaining by the teachers' union and other employee organizations, and the watchguard activities of taxpayer groups, to name a few. There is also a school-level politics involving the principal's office, principal-teacher interaction, parent-school interaction, and, of course, the most basic of all education interactions—teachers and students in the classroom. The student-teacher relationship is a case of the micropolitics of education, but no less political for being "micro."[7] The varying mix of control, cooperation, resistance, and bargaining in which teacher and student play roles inescapably has a political dimension. Even this long list of activities and processes is only part of the picture. Schools are what organization theorists call "open systems," profoundly affected by their external environment. The "exit" process by which families make housing choices or opt for private schools to seek educational opportunities for their children shapes schools, sometimes more profoundly than the combined activities of the many interest groups at work. Broadly understood, the politics of education encompasses as well those actions through which families and communities imbue children with expectations, provide opportunities, and bring to bear a range of social supports. Because these processes do not occur in a vacuum, the politics of education also intertwines with the system of stratification of the larger society. Hence the politics of urban education reaches far beyond those activities directly connected to formal school organizations.

Although education politics takes place on many levels and at various sites, there are connecting strands that tie these levels and sites together. Moreover, the various elements of an education system react to a shared context. As a city's demography, economic base, and political position change, so also do its schools. We need, then, to acknowledge the varied dimensions of a locality's education system while seeing how they might form a connected experience.

There are at least five major strands of education politics. Although they are conceptually distinct, in practice they have enormous effects on one another, and it is these effects that need close attention. These five strands are raising and spending money, . . . who sits in the classroom with whom, . . . the school-community interface, . . . bureaucratic politics, . . . [and] classroom interaction. . . . Exploring these five strands, we can see how urban education has evolved over time. As cities change, education politics changes, and the way these five strands interrelate also changes.

Revenue. Schools need money. We spent, in the United States, an average of just over $6,900 to educate each public elementary or secondary student in the nation in 1998. In the United States, money for schools comes from different levels of government. At one time, the bulk of the revenues came from local governments. In 1929, local revenues constituted about eighty-three cents of each dollar spent, with the states accounting for almost all of the rest. Today, states and local governments each account for about forty-seven cents, with the national government chipping in a little less than seven cents.[8] Each of these levels comprises a decision-making arena with its own array of competing interests, institutional tendencies, and traditional priorities.

Money is power, at least potentially. For many years, the growing state role in funding was not accompanied by dramatic increases in state influence; traditions of local autonomy, generally weak state legislatures, and dubious political gains to be made combined to induce most states to adopt a hands-off approach. Over the past two decades this has been changing fairly dramatically. Governors, legislatures, and state judges increasingly have insisted on a say in how local schools are run. This has been happening at the same time that central cities have become politically weaker within the state arena. That has meant oftentimes that interests and values more prominent in suburban and rural areas have been imposed on local schools. At the extreme, states have taken over local school systems.

Although this intergovernmentalization of school finance is important, it also is the case that much of the decision-making authority continues to be exercised at the local level. Much of the money coming from states and the national government comes with few or weak strings attached. Although the threat of greater intervention looms, on a day-to-day basis the key maneuvering to set educational priorities and practices tends to be at the local level.

Historically, the local politics of spending money on education pitted business interests, as primary sources of revenue, against parents, as the primary service users, and against educators themselves. In an earlier era, business managed to keep down spending in most cities, producing modest salaries for teachers, construction programs that often lagged behind population growth, and, in some cases, large classes and even shortages in textbooks and other classroom supplies. Yet for many years, with enrollment on the rise and a sizable middle class as a core constituency, urban schools were a growth industry and could generate political support, a high degree of internal peace, and increasing budgets.

Collective bargaining has advanced salaries, but sometimes at the expense of deferred building maintenance. Textbook shortages and antiquated equipment also remain as significant problems, in some instances owing as much to bad management as a lack of funds. Urban schools face special needs from the high level of poverty among students, the number of children for whom English is not the native tongue, and the costliness of meeting special education mandates.

Costs have risen concurrently with declining city tax bases, as both business activity and middle- and higher-income wage earners have become increasingly suburban. Cities have thus become substantially dependent on state funds to meet education costs. However, city political clout in state politics has perhaps reached an all-time low. Suburban predominance in state legislatures has become an overriding fact of life, as is the large suburban vote in gubernatorial and other statewide contests. Greater state funding for education is thus no guarantee that special financial needs of cities will get a receptive hearing. Even litigation over funding inequity has had limited results. Well-off suburbs are reluctant to take any less for themselves than what they pay into the state tax coffers. Hence, funding formulas to target students from disadvantaged backgrounds often encounter determined resistance.

The political disjuncture between taxpayers and service users has widened. Not only does business resistance to increased taxation continue, but many individual taxpayers have little identity with urban schoolchildren. Urban student populations are overwhelmingly poor and minority, but individual taxpayers are preponderantly white, middle-class, and suburban, and in increasing cases do not have children in the public schools of either the city or the suburb.

Though education expenditures have continued to rise, the prospects for future increases are somewhat dim. Financial resources have tightened and run a major risk of compressing even further. With city school systems no longer home to large numbers of middle-class students, political support for spending by these systems has become tenuous. Educators can no longer assume that taxpayers see urban schools as operations in which they have a substantial stake.

Classroom composition. Separating students by ability once enjoyed professional backing, but now is questioned. Whatever professional educators might argue, parents have always had their own inclinations about with whom their children go to school. Thus, many schools have long been segregated de facto by race and class, reflecting the dominant housing pattern in the United States. The consequences of residential segregation are reinforced by the fragmented nature of local school districts.

Urban areas were once the major arenas for struggles over racial desegregation, but with continuing suburban growth the issue has quieted in most large cities. Weariness over past battles might account for that in part. So might the fact that some of the mechanisms developed to handle the desegregation challenge, such as magnet schools and public school choice, have become institutionalized and broadly accepted. Probably most important, though, is the fact that demographic realities simply have changed. The most contentious conflicts around issues of desegregation have involved African Americans, and the size of the black student population in urban areas has dramatically stabilized. In 1972, 32.5 percent of central-city elementary and secondary public school students were black; this crept to a high of 36.0 percent in 1985 and has since fallen slowly to 31.8 percent in 1995.[9] Although the black population stabilized in central cities, it has grown substantially in suburban districts. In 1972, 6.3 percent of suburban elementary and secondary public school students were black; by 1995, this had increased to an all-time high of 10.7 percent.[10] As a result, suburban districts are today the more likely battlegrounds for racial balance issues that take on the traditional form of black versus white.

The hot and sharply defined conflicts involving integration of black students into previously white districts have abated, but today's schools confront a more complex and multidimensional form of heterogeneity. Public schools throughout the nation are now much more likely to have student bodies from multiple racial and ethnic backgrounds. Hispanics constituted 10.8 percent of the central-city public school population in 1972 and 24.3 percent in 1995. The comparable figures rose from 4.4 percent to 11.6 percent in suburban schools and from 3.6 percent to 6.5 percent in rural areas.

At the same time, sensitivities to the socioeconomic composition of student bodies have become more prominent. Large cities typically have predominantly lower socioeconomic status (SES) students, including many from very poor families, and the drive to achieve desegregation seems largely spent. In any case, social class integration was never a policy goal and it remains largely off the education agenda. The ability of middle-income parents to practice the exit option, either by moving to another jurisdiction or placing their children in private schools, stands as an imposing barrier to any effort toward bringing social classes together in the classroom.

Tracking practices, especially at the elementary level, have come under severe criticism but remain widespread. Magnet schools and classes for "gifted and talented" students often serve as a means to prevent or slow the exit of middle-class students from urban school systems. However, in most places, it seems that they contribute little to the aim of integrating diverse students into a common school experience. The reality for most urban city school districts is a huge concentration of poor children, with the integration option long since foreclosed.

The school-community interface. Early in the twentieth century, progressive reforms replaced ward politics with citywide, largely nonpartisan politics. In many communities, business and blue-ribbon groups gained the upper hand on school boards, and professional educators enjoyed wide discretion to shape the agenda and initiate action. Voter turnout was typically low, and school boards more often legitimized policy decisions than formulated them. Even though the authority of professional expertise has declined from its peak earlier, the policy role of most school boards continues to be quite modest, and members play mainly a constituent-service role. Professional educators succeeded initially in presenting themselves as having special expertise and as being largely sufficient on their own to handle the process of education. That belief has begun to yield ground to the alternative view that education requires a broad partnership with parents and others, but it is unclear how much actual practice is changing.

A strong case can be made for parent participation, and parents can reinforce the importance of academic effort as well as be of direct assistance by reading to children, volunteering in school, and monitoring homework. The key to such participation, however, is school staff who are welcoming and encouraging of parent involvement. Parent participation in school governance is a more controversial step, and some parents feel that any form of involvement is resisted by principal and teachers. For their part, street-level educators often see parents as uncaring or indifferent or as a source of bothersome special demands.

Any move toward parent-school partnership faces potential opposition. As Bernard Crick has observed more generally, "the more one is involved in relationship with others, the more conflicts of interest, or of character and circumstance will arise."[11] Educators are keenly aware of Crick's point. With specific regard to schools, Seymour Sarason argues that parent and community involvement, for educators, makes life "more complicated, messy, and even unpredictable." He adds that, though educators have difficulty seeing it, this broad involvement can also make life "more interesting, exciting, less isolating, protective of the existence of public schools, and potentially an aid to their improvement."[12] Oft-criticized as they are, many educators find this possibility highly resistible.

Overall, the issue of school-community interface is in flux. Old beliefs about professionalism have been severely challenged, and the widespread introduction of local school councils, the increasing number of school-business partnerships, and a heightened emphasis on parent involvement, especially when linked to community organization, all serve to change the landscape in potentially significant ways. Of course, middle-class parents have long been involved in school affairs through PTAs as well as on more personal and informal bases. But for urban school systems an unanswered question is the extent to which lower-class and more generally minority parents have come to engage teachers and various school officials, either through formal channels or informal ones. Many lower-SES parents find contact with school staff to be discomforting. Typically they themselves did not have a good experience with school, and they may feel at an educational as well as overall class disadvantage.

Bureaucratic politics. The term "principal" is an abbreviation for "principal teacher." In an earlier period, most school employees were teachers, and most administrators were school-based and thus close to the classroom. Over time, particularly in large urban districts, the superintendent's office grew into a large headquarters staff with numerous areas of specialization. At the school level, the principal's role also increased in administrative scope, and the office of assistant principal took hold and expanded. Federal and state mandates and special grant programs have added to both school- and district-level specialization, and an elaborate array of regulations has grown up around these programs, often focusing their administrators more on satisfying requirements set at the state and federal level than on coordination with classroom teachers and meeting their needs. Collective bargaining has also contributed a body of regulations that are part of the work environment in contemporary schools.

Over the years, then, school administration and the accompanying body of regulations have become increasingly remote from the classroom, particularly from pedagogical matters, often leaving teachers with an increased feeling of isolation. Reformer John Goodlad finds school administrators unduly preoccupied "with collective bargaining, desegregation, declining enrollments, vandalism, and the like, to the neglect of the centrally educational issues."[13] Rules have become so complex that central office staff spend considerable time granting waivers, as schemes of regulation prove to be exasperatingly cumbersome. Careers can be built around the mastery of rule-book detail.

Even the role of principal, although a school-level position, has often become a rung in an administrative career ladder. One observer notes:

> In most large school systems . . . the principalship is now seen as a step in a bureaucratic career—say from counselor to assistant principal to program director to division chief to assistant or deputy superintendent. The requirements increasingly become aptitude for success in the bureaucratic career. . . . Being an outstanding teacher or showing the potential for creating a good educational community are not a salient part of the dossier.[14]

In any big urban school system, administrative career opportunities abound. Taking Baltimore as an example, one finds an administrator for every eight teachers,[15] and that figure is not atypical, but quite in line with other large jurisdictions in Maryland and elsewhere. Because school systems also adhere generally to the "differentiation" principle (hierarchy requires that even lower-level administrators receive greater compensation than the teaching staff), administrators are paid more highly than teachers by a wide margin. There is, then, a significant material incentive for teachers to move into administration.[16]

Intergovernmental programs and mandates create multiple channels of reporting and thus work against school- or district-level coordination. One study refers to the "complex maze of programs, rules, and regulations, and conflicting mandates" in which urban schools operate.[17] On the larger scene, the institutional independence of education makes an integrated policy for children and youth unfeasible. Though there have been a few moves toward greater mayoral involvement in (and in a few cases toward control over) education, channeled thinking along narrowly functional lines remains dominant. Few Social reformers would dispute that fragmentation of effort is the dominant pattern, and a quest for coherence is an understandable theme of school reform.

Classroom interaction. By all accounts, classroom teaching is a demanding and unrelenting job. One observer characterized it as "the educational equivalent of whitewater rafting."[18] The teacher's classroom task centers on producing learning and exerting enough control to maintain order. As the lower-SES composition of a classroom increases, order maintenance tends to become a greater concern for the teacher.

At the same time, we should not overlook the fact that, within the same SES level, there is variation in classroom experience. Some teachers are more skillful than others in advancing learning and some pedagogical approaches are more effective in engaging students. The fact that lower-SES classrooms tend to present greater obstacles to learning increases, rather than decreases, the importance of teachers who *do* make a difference.

Because classroom interaction is the core activity in education, it gives education policy a special character. It is not about the kind of material transactions that abound in urban redevelopment or transportation policy. Although teachers as a group are certainly not unmindful of salary matters, salary has little to do with day-to-day teaching, and faculty norms reinforce that disconnection.

In the student-teacher interaction, inner motivations are central. Much depends on what teachers and students find personally fulfilling. The skill of the teacher can expand what is mutually satisfying and lack of skill can contract it. That is only part of the story, however. For students, especially as they move up in grades and age, their expectations, previous experiences, and cumulative accomplishments have an impact that is largely beyond the control of the teacher. So even highly motivated teachers, especially in the upper grades, find that the nature of their relationship with students depends greatly on the context within which interaction takes place.

For any given classroom, an important part of the context is what is taking place and has taken place in other classrooms. The general norm among teachers is one of mutual noninterference, encouraged by the "egg crate" structure of most classrooms, but the formality of classroom autonomy and the practice of mutual noninterference are not the full reality of the situation. For any given class, student expectations are influenced greatly by previous and concurrent classroom experiences. Teachers, then, are constrained by what their fellow teachers have been and are doing. Moreover, even highly dedicated and skillful teachers have found that their individual efforts "were overwhelmed by the indifference, incompetence, and in some cases the corruption of the larger system."[19]

In addition to what transpires in the school system itself, extraclassroom socialization and experiences also have a large impact on what students bring to their interaction with teachers. Several questions are salient: Do students expect that academic achievement will lead to worthwhile opportunities? Is academic achievement valued by students, or is it seen as a betrayal of one's peers or of one's class, race, or ethnic identity? At the high school level especially, several observers point to an autonomous youth culture and the extent to which it has weakened respect for an academic orientation.[20] Various segments of the youth population see an academic orientation as being a "nerd" or as acting "uppity," "white," or "Anglo." As Goodlad reports, "it may be socially difficult in some schools to be smart unless one is regarded also as good-looking and athletic."[21] Yet a recent survey of American teenagers finds that they see "getting an education" as important to their future.[22] However, academic success is valued more for its instrumental uses than its intrinsic worth. As one high school student put it, "I can't wait to graduate and go to college, get a good job, get rich."[23]

Nevertheless, complex motivations are at work among students, and some teaching situations are more challenging than others are. It is not surprising, then, that teachers display increased stress in lower-SES schools, and given an opportunity to move away from such assignments, many do so, or move out of the teaching profession altogether. The attrition rate among new teachers is particularly high.

With the changing demography of the city, urban school systems have thus experienced a greater challenge, in part because the proportion of lower-SES students has increased. Not only has the population changed, but the expectation has grown that all students will complete high school. With the decline of low-skill industrial jobs, dropouts are now seen as an indicator of school failure, and the pressure is on schools to hold on to youths who, in previous eras, would have drifted into the workforce. This contributes to the proportion of students, especially at the high school level, who are reluctant participants in classroom learning.

Education historians link declining standards to these changes and attribute to it the growing propensity for urban high schools to become "holding" operations for adolescents with limited alternatives.[24] Diversity and unevenness in motivation, in turn, encouraged a trend away from a core-academic curriculum and toward "the shopping mall high school" with its assortment of "life experience" and "entertainment" courses.[25] Even so, these changes and the relaxing of standards did not prevent dropout rates from remaining at a high rate.[26]

Recent efforts to upgrade educational standards and increase the academic content of the curriculum consequently serve to put urban schools through added stress about performing, but without altering the basic conditions that surround these schools and their students. Thus, urban educators find themselves under heightened pressure to show academic improvement, and perhaps the most acute stress is experienced by classroom teachers in the poorest neighborhoods. Teacher burnout has come to be recognized as a widespread problem and one that urban school systems experience at a heightened level.

It should be pointed out that, important as race is in American education, the pattern described above is not attributable solely or even mainly to racial differences between educators and students. Although many big-city school systems have undergone transition and now have preponderantly minority teaching and administrative staffs, stress and burnout continue as problems. After all, the racial composition of school staff does little by itself to alter the larger structure of opportunity and its impact on the experience and expectations of students. Educators might, then, understandably ask if it is appropriate to hold them accountable for the academic achievement of students who have limited confidence that academic effort will improve their life chances.

The strands interrelated: The failure syndrome. As we put together the various strands of urban education, we can see how they might be conducive to a syndrome of failure. The segmenting of American education into local districts, politically and financially independent of one another, puts city school systems into competition with the suburban districts around them and provides suburbs with a strong incentive to maintain independence. So big-city systems face major challenges without a strong political or financial base.

Within the urban community, the tradition of an autonomous education profession puts teachers and administrators in the position of coping with the consequences of a welter of social problems beyond their control, but nevertheless manifest in the experiences, expectations, and habits of mind of their pupils. Students disadvantaged by the larger socioeconomic order pose a particularly sharp challenge to educators. Many of these students lack the same depth of social supports enjoyed by most middle-class students.

That the larger population expects little of those from lower-SES backgrounds is itself a major barrier to academic improvement. The situation is further complicated by the widespread belief that the personal ability of each child, not the effort made, is the key to academic performance. If the long-term prospects for educational achievement and personal success really do depend on a cluster of factors that is pretty much determined by the time a child reaches school age, how could students of whom little is expected be motivated to learn? Or, for that matter, how can their teachers be motivated to try hard to bring about an atmosphere of academic achievement?

Although there is some recognition among experts that background factors strongly influence educational attainment, American ideology of upward mobility and effort has continued to stress excellence in schools. In comparison to an earlier era when education for the poor centered on the basics and on citizenship training, today's school systems that serve the poor are expected to do much more. These expectations, contrasting so vividly with the often cognitively and emotionally impoverished backgrounds of the urban poor, can buffet educators, leading them to feel overwhelmed by the challenges they face and powerless to turn matters around. Schooling may then become a kind of holding operation. To the extent that happens, cynicism has fertile ground in which to grow, and educators can develop a defeatist attitude. They may see themselves not as professionals but simply as "survivors."[27] James Comer talks about schools in the grip of "the hand of hopelessness."[28] That frame of mind, in turn, becomes a further barrier to change as it undermines confidence that new practices can make a difference. It can also weaken personal effort and commitment. In an occupation in which intrinsic reward is so important, an atmosphere of futility is sure to devitalize personal engagement and, even for those who survive the difficult initiation period, the urban school experience may encourage "time-serving."

Because learning is affected by the broad school environment, the number of "time-servers" can have a cumulative effect. In a given school, as the proportion of "time-servers" grows, the teaching task of others becomes increasingly difficult—thereby heightening the likelihood that they too will succumb to feelings of defeat and futility.

As "time-servers" seek less stress-inducing positions, they may gain entry to administrative posts and foster cynicism there as well. Of course, the picture is not totally bleak; capable educators with positive motives also move into administration. No one knows the precise mix that makes up the supervisory staff of various urban school systems, but the level of cynicism is high and the potential consequences are considerable. Given a defeatist attitude, administrators would be little inclined to pursue bold initiatives or see experimentation as a way to foster improvements. Instead, "circling the wagons" to protect against criticism and devising ways to deflect blame are more likely patterns of action.[29] The failure syndrome may also produce a reluctance to involve outsiders in school operations or to seek partnership with parents or other community groups. Nor would those in the throes of futility be inclined to embrace research and evaluation. As one author observed: "Most urban school cultures are resistant to change, even when there is widespread recognition that children are poorly served under current conditions—partly because fear is more likely to breed defensiveness and rigidity than to foster risk-taking behaviors."[30]

Under these conditions, job protection is likely to be an overriding concern, with risk-taking avoided and little energy devoted to efforts at improvement. In failing systems, school administration is likely to resemble the management of a declining industry. Investment in new initiatives is less likely than simply trying to hold existing ground, retrenching to fend off the threat of deeper losses. Deferred building maintenance is especially probable. It is less conflict-laden than reallocations of personnel. With a shrinking pool of resources in relation to need, reallocation poses the risk of internal division and therefore increased political vulnerability for top-level administrators.

Although many urban schools perform well, urban school *systems* overall do not. Nor have suburban systems distinguished themselves as they began to age and face a more diverse and less affluent student body. That some individual schools perform well is evidence that it can be done. That urban school *districts* generally are weak performers is, however, an indicator that systemic problems are a powerful factor, and that education is highly susceptible to the impacts of social inequality. . . .

Requirements of change in complex subsystems. Others, of course, have noted the complexity of the education policy subsystem. School politics has been characterized as "hyper-pluralistic," to highlight the extent to which they are subject to competing demands by a shifting array of stakeholders.[31] School organizations are sometimes described as "loosely coupled" systems, highlighting the senses in which the decentralization of discretion makes it difficult for those in the upper level of the formal hierarchy to effectively exercise oversight, authority, and control.[32]

Although such characterizations are complementary to our characterization of the five strands, we draw a somewhat different set of implications. Most others note the disorder and complexity that confound the process of getting things done and issue calls for administrative restructuring. We suggest, instead, that the interweaving of various strands characterizing the education subsystem sets a higher hurdle for school reform, especially within the urban context. To be successful, school reform must be systemic.

The term *systemic reform* is a popular one these days, but its meaning is often fuzzy. Some use it as little more than a shorthand term for emphasizing that reform needs to be "major." For others, the term also carries a connotation of organizational comprehensiveness; that is to say, systemic reform will require changing all parts of the educational subsystem, not simply a little tinkering here and there.

Our use of the term signals the need to consider the overall picture, far beyond the confines of the educational system alone. Lasting and meaningful change requires acting on a complex set of relationships, both within the school system and in the school-community connection. Yet talk about systemic reform in these senses runs against the grain of a long attachment to specialization. Only reluctantly have education reformers come to recognize that specific needs such as improved math and science training are embedded in a larger context of schooling, and schooling itself is embedded in and influenced by the wide context of the whole community. Even reformers who have come to understand this often shy away from the implication we draw: School reform is political at its heart.

For many observers, the temptation is nearly irresistible to mentally detach school performance from its environment and argue that schools be fixed from the inside out. This inside-out perspective of reform is contradicted by the now overwhelming evidence that schools are powerfully constrained and even shaped by the conditions that surround them.[33] In contrast, we take it as a given that what happens in a particular classroom is *not* independent of the school environment, and the formation of the school environment is *not* unconnected to the larger community from which students, parents, and other stakeholders come.

Rather than buffering schools from external pressures, we believe it is necessary to consider how schools can better align themselves with broader community forces. Rather than focusing on reform as an administrative or technical puzzle, we see it as necessarily a political challenge. It is a political challenge not just in the instrumental sense of politics as power, as a way to bring pressure to bear, but also in the broader sense of politics as a process of reorienting the way society operates collectively by changing public institutions and public ideas. . . .

The Politics of Overcoming the Failure Syndrome

Realistic efforts to improve urban education cannot simply rest on the simple issuance of mandates or declaration of new standards. Improvement almost certainly turns on changing relationships, and such change is fundamentally a political process, whether those involved in the change effort recognize it as such or not. The politics of systemic reform, then, amounts to more than the struggle and resistance that surrounds particular plans. Change is likely to be systemic only if it comes about through the mobilization of a broad set of players in a concerted effort to alter what has been labeled "a culture of failure." Most efforts to change urban education fall far short of that standard.

Because there are many barriers to a broad mobilization and particular barriers are sometimes what is most visible, we need to keep the big picture in mind. The conventional approach to school reform has called for identifying a problem and bringing professional expertise to bear on it. That approach has produced disappointment and frustration. But if broader mobilization is what is needed, how does a community deal with what James Morone calls "a fragmented policy environment"?[34] That issue confronted the early warriors against poverty, and it continues to pose a challenge today. Thus social reform strategists find themselves in search of a comprehensive approach, and for that reason use the language of "bringing stakeholders together." This language and the related term we use, "civic capacity," are thus not about rallying support around particular programs or projects, but . . . they are about reshaping the political life surrounding schools.

Unfortunately, mobilizing civic capacity almost always involves a major dislocation of the existing way of doing things. It means forging a viable consensus on some set of solutions to the complex educational problem. That invariably means some at least limited destruction of the existing policy subsystem, because policy subsystems are invested in the current set of implemented solutions to the educational problem. Harnessing civic capacity to the goal of educational reform means *both* bringing in educational and noneducational actors *and* instituting major changes in the way current educational professionals do business. These coexisting constructive and destructive elements make creating and sustaining coalitions difficult indeed.

Such reshaping does not occur in a vacuum. It pits efforts to change against a set of concrete problems and the political relationships in which those problems are embedded. Thus, we need to set the stage by starting with the diverse elements that, in combination, make up the political picture of urban education. That involves considering the behavior of political stakeholders both within and outside the traditional education community. . . . And it involves considering the particular role of competing issue definitions. . . . But it also involves a more extended consideration of the social and economic context of education, particularly as manifested in the distinct setting of central-city public schools.

Though education is in an important sense a policy subsystem, it does not function with complete autonomy. We need to be realistic about what changes in school practice can accomplish and not ask too much. Tyack and Cuban caution that school reform "has often diverted attention from more costly, politically controversial, and difficult social reforms."[35] Instead of using schools to try to reform society on the cheap, we might better consider how broad social reforms could make the job of schools easier.

Schools, we believe, are not closed systems, capable of being fixed without regard to their surrounding environment. Because the strands of education politics are intertwined, each not only affects the others, but the strands are also connected to the social environment in powerful ways. As a study of Chicago put it, "the root cause of each school failure is not inside each individual school, but rather in the external environments they share."[36] Thus, although up close it might seem that a problem, such as a high dropout rate, can be isolated and treated effectively, in a larger context that problem solving requires a broad set of interrelated approaches. Instead of operating in isolation, specialists need to be part of a comprehensive effort. . . .

Yet structural thinking has its own shortcomings. Unrelenting attention to the big structural picture can cause us to overlook social parallels to what environmentalists call instances of "local robustness."[37] Desirable as structural change to racial and class inequalities might be, awaiting that scope of change would leave urban schools in their plight for an indefinite future. The study of the politics of urban education reported here took as its field of inquiry the middle ground between a continuing flow of incremental reforms and a still-to-be-activated movement to transform U.S. society. Talk about systemic reform is about school-community relationships, but it is more modest in scope than transforming society. Similarly, talk about bringing stakeholders together is a large move, but one far more modest than seeking to launch social revolution. The focus is how school and community can be related in a constructive way. For reformers, the challenge is how to mobilize around a large enough sphere of activities to make a difference, but not so large as to constitute an impossible task.

Notes

1. Edward C. Banfield, *The Unheavenly City Revisited* (Boston: Little, Brown, 1970).
2. Paul E. Peterson, in *City Limits* (Chicago: University of Chicago Press, 1981), notes the somewhat ambiguous status of education in terms of his threefold typology (developmental, redistributive, allocative).
3. Thomas J. Anton and Alison R. Flaum, "Theory into Practice: The Rise of New Anti-Poverty Strategies in American Cities," *Urban News* 5 (Winter 1992): 1 ff; Joan Walsh, *Stories of Renewal* (New York: Rockefeller Foundation, 1997); and Clarence N. Stone, "Poverty and the Continuing Campaign for Urban Social Reform," *Urban Affairs Review* 34:6 (July 1999): 843–56.
4. Benjamin Barber, *Strong Democracy* (Berkeley, Calif.: University of California Press, 1984).
5. Charles E. Bidwell, "Toward Improved Knowledge and Policy on Urban Education," *Politics of Education Association Yearbook* (1991): 193–99.
6. Kenneth K. Wong, "The Politics of Urban Education as a Field of Study," *Politics of Education Yearbook* (1991): 3–26.

7. Betty Malen, "The Micropolitics of Education," in *The Study of Educational Politics,* ed. Jay D. Scribner and Donald H. Layton (Washington, D.C.: Falmer Press, 1995).
8. U.S. Department of Education, National Center for Education Statistics, Statistics of State School Systems; Revenues and Expenditures for Public Elementary and Secondary Education; and Common Core of Data surveys.
9. U.S. Department of Education, National Center for Education Statistics, *The Condition of Education 1998,* Supplemental Table 43-3.
10. Ibid.
11. Bernard Crick, *In Defense of Politics,* 2d ed. (New York: Penguin Books, 1964): 25.
12. Seymour Sarason, *School Change* (New York: Teachers College Press, 1995): 84.
13. John Goodlad, *A Place Called School* (New York: McGraw-Hill, 1983): 354.
14. Gerald Grant, *The World We Created at Hamilton High* (Cambridge, Mass.: Harvard University Press, 1988): 226.
15. Maryland State Department of Education, *The Fact Book* (Baltimore, Md.: Maryland State Department of Education, 1994).
16. Goodlad, *A Place Called School,* 296. See also Allan Odden, "Incentives, School Organization and Teacher Compensation," in *Rewards and Reform,* ed. Susan H. Fuhrman and Jennifer A. O'Day (San Francisco, Calif.: Jossey-Bass, 1996): 226–56.
17. Anthony S. Bryk, Penny Bender Sebring, David Kerbrow, Sharon Rollow, and John Q. Easton, *Charting Chicago School Reform: Democratic Localism as a Lever for Change* (Boulder, Colo.: Westview, 1998), 10.
18. Dennis Shirley, *Community Organizing for Urban School Reform* (Austin: University of Texas Press, 1997), 228.
19. Bryk et al., *Charting Chicago School Reform,* 7.
20. Goodlad, *A Place Called School;* Powell, Farrar, and Cohen, *The Shopping Mall High School;* Paul Haubrich, "Student Life in Milwaukee High Schools, 1920–1985," in *Seeds of Crisis;* and Laurence Steinberg, *Beyond the Classroom* (New York: Simon and Schuster, 1996).
21. Goodlad, *A Place Called School,* 78.
22. Jean Johnson and Steve Farkas with Ali Bers, *Getting By* (New York: Public Agenda, 1997).
23. Quoted in ibid., 13.
24. Jeffrey Mirel, *The Rise and Fall of an Urban School System* (Ann Arbor, Mich.: University of Michigan Press, 1993).
25. Arthur G. Powell, Eleanor Farrar, and David K. Cohen, *The Shopping Mall High School: Winners and Losers in the Educational Marketplace* (Boston, Mass.: Houghton Mifflin, 1986).
26. Official figures on dropout rates are notoriously unreliable and are measured in various ways. Using high school completion by age nineteen as a measure, the rate is about 50 percent in most large cities. The rate of achieving high school diplomas is higher because of the number of young people who obtain GEDs outside the regular high school process. For a close examination of the dropout problem in one system, see Fine, *Framing Dropouts.*
27. Bryk et al., *Charting Chicago School Reform,* 4.
28. James P. Comer, *School Power* (New York: Free Press, 1993): viii.
29. See Robert L. Crain, *The Politics of School Desegregation* (Garden City, N.Y.: Anchor Books, 1969).
30. Shirley, *Community Organizing,* 223.
31. Frederick M. Wirt, *Power in the City: Decision Making in San Francisco* (Berkeley, Calif.: University of California Press, 1974).
32. Karl E. Weick, "Educational Organizations as Loosely Coupled Systems," *Administrative Science Quarterly* 21 (March 1976): 1–19.
33. See, for example, Stephen J. Caldas and Carl L. Bankston, "Multilevel Examination of Student, School, and District-Level Effects on Academic Achievement," *Journal of Education Research* 93 (November/December 1999): 91–109.
34. James A. Morone, *The Democratic Wish: Popular Participation and the Limits of American Government,* rev. ed. (New Haven, Conn.: Yale University Press, 1998), 275.
35. David Tyack and Larry Cuban, *Tinkering toward Utopia: A Century of Public School Reform* (Cambridge, Mass.: Harvard University Press, 1995), 3.
36. Bryk et al., *Charting Chicago School Reform,* 10.
37. Marc K. Landry, "Local Government and Environmental Policy," in *Dilemmas of Scale in American Federal Democracy,* ed. Martha Derthick (Cambridge, UK: Woodrow Wilson Center Press and Cambridge University Press, 1999): 227–60.

CASE STUDY 15

Introduction

The authors of the foregoing reading make the case that the solutions to urban school problems require the commitment of the broader community, not just the education establishment. The success of the Pittsburgh Public Schools provides a good example of the value of building civic capacity in education reform. In 1980, the Pittsburgh School Board hired Richard Wallace to serve as the superintendent of the school system, a position he held for the next twelve years. After being hired, Wallace presented a set of plans to the school board for reforming the schools in six priority areas. Wallace's "excellence agenda" proved to be a remarkably successful program, improving student achievement and the school system's image so much that it stopped declines in enrollment and encouraged students in private schools to enter the public education system. Pittsburgh's schools were soon held up as a national model of education reform, and Wallace was awarded the Harold W. McGraw Jr., Prize in Education, a national award given annually by the McGraw-Hill Corporation to individuals who are committed to improving education.

At the root of Wallace's success was his ability to provide leadership and to build civic capacity. Wallace was also helped by the strong civic commitment that has long characterized Pittsburgh's business community. Since the 1930s, business-related organizations have played an important role in working with Pittsburgh's government to address a host of urban problems. When the city's school system began to confront a series of critical issues in the 1960s, including demands for desegregation, many of these business groups joined with other community leaders to find workable solutions. When Wallace was appointed superintendent, he worked closely with these groups, as well as with the school board and the Pittsburgh Federation of Teachers, to bring his educational visions into reality.

The reading that follows explains Pittsburgh's success and provides a fine lesson on the importance of civic capacity in urban school reform. The reading was written by John Portz, Lana Stein, and Robin R. Jones. Portz is an associate professor of political science at Northeastern University. Stein is an associate professor of political science at University of Missouri, St. Louis. Jones is the coordinator of Community Initiatives for the College of Arts and Sciences at the University of South Florida.

Questions to Consider

As you read their work, these are some questions to consider:

- What was the history of civic capacity in Pittsburgh prior to Wallace's appointment as superintendent? How did the business community initially become active in civic affairs? How important a role have these groups had in Pittsburgh's politics?

- What were the six components of Wallace's "excellence agenda"? How did Wallace's plans address each of these components?
- What do the authors of the reading credit for Wallace's success? What other actors besides Wallace were important in shaping Pittsburgh's educational achievements?
- What were the goals of the New Futures Project? Why did this project fail? What does the failure of this project say about the need for building civic capacity?

Pittsburgh's Public Schools: A Fragile Balance of Leadership and Institution Building

John Portz, Lana Stein, and Robin R. Jones

It is well known that the Pittsburgh region has suffered devastating economic decline in the past forty years. Almost as well known are the attempts to address the crisis through "public-private partnerships." The best-known example is Renaissance I, the redevelopment in the late 1940s and early 1950s of the Point area of Pittsburgh. Mayor David L. Lawrence and banker Richard K. Mellon forged a partnership that served as a model for cities across the country and laid the foundation for a pattern of public decision making in Pittsburgh that continues today.

Renaissance I reflected an earlier political history that included the simultaneous but separate development of political and civic-oriented institutions. During the last two decades of the nineteenth century, Pittsburgh politics was controlled by the Republican Magee/Flinn machine. Early in the twentieth century, however, reform-oriented Republicans implemented several structural changes in the city's political system, including a strong mayor-council form with no term limits and a nine-member, at-large city council. The Republican machine regained control, but these reforms and the rise of a new corporate economic elite profoundly changed how the machine functioned. New business interests, headed by the Mellon family, controlled mayoral elections, but their influence did not extend to the ward level. Therefore, to guarantee that elected leadership did not reestablish a grassroots base, Mellon would not support a mayor for more than a single term. In 1929, however, a mayor who had established independent relationships with the ward chairs defied Mellon and ran for a second term.

Having lost direct control of the public sector, Mellon and his fellow business leaders focused on establishing voluntary civic organizations as extragovernmental public policy vehicles. Thus, as early as the late 1930s, a parallel policy-making system was developing in Pittsburgh that included the political machine and private, civic-oriented organizations. The ward-based electoral machine existed separate from the public policy interest of the business elite. "Private civic nonprofit corporations provided [the business elites] with an organizational base beyond the control of the voting public."[1] These business-sponsored civic organizations produced development studies and plans, but little was accomplished. They were unwilling to cede to the public sector the authority to carry them out.[2]

John Portz, Lana Stein, and Robin R. Jones, "Pittsburgh's Public Schools: A Fragile Balance of Leadership and Institution Building," from *City Schools and City Politics: Institutions and Leadership in Pittsburgh, Boston, and St. Louis* (Lawrence: University Press of Kansas, 1999), pp. 56–69 and 152–153.

In 1933, riding the New Deal wave, Pittsburgh Democrats won their first mayoral race in decades and began to establish their dominance in local politics. David Lawrence, as head of the state Democratic party, worked behind the scenes and used New Deal patronage to build a highly centralized machine in Pittsburgh. Fearing a Democratic defeat in the 1945 mayoral election, Lawrence threw his own hat into the ring. To broaden his base of support, Lawrence adopted the Republican downtown redevelopment agenda for Pittsburgh—an agenda articulated by Mellon's newest civic nonprofit, the Allegheny Conference on Community Development (ACCD).[3] Lawrence's victory and the subsequent joining of his public sector control with Mellon's private sector leadership resulted in the Renaissance I partnership that rebuilt the blighted Point, cleaned the air in the county, and ended the near annual flooding of the central business district.[4]

The partnership of Mellon and Lawrence brought together peak institutions that were themselves transformed. Unlike most business associations of the time, or since, the ACCD was established as a highly formalized institution, capable of garnering the authority, financial resources, and technical knowledge necessary to promote meaningful change. Its membership included the heads of many of the nation's industrial giants. The ACCD hired its own professional planning staff and partnered with major private planning and research organizations of the region. Complementary changes were made on the public sector side. Lawrence centralized the development function within the city bureaucracy by creating one of the nation's first urban redevelopment authorities. He named himself as the authority's chair and placed many ACCD supporters in key administrative posts.[5]

In combination, the two sectors were well positioned to make a significant impact on Pittsburgh's central business district. They provided leadership to initiate and implement key urban projects. Using corporate and foundation financial resources, the ACCD "underwrote the necessary expertise for planning and coordination and leveraged larger sums from private investors and public bodies for redevelopment."[6] Ferman describes these institutional changes as setting up a "corporatist decision making structure that insulated development policy from party control."[7] While private and quasi-private development organizations were able to define economic development in technical terms, the machine's need to reward electoral support was fulfilled through nondevelopment-related public services.

This pattern of decision making has dominated public problem solving in Pittsburgh in the post–WWII era. Except for one, each of Pittsburgh's five mayors since Lawrence has partnered with the ACCD in planning and executing central business district redevelopment. Exemplifying this was Renaissance II, a major reinvestment period during the 1980s.[8] Among the many projects during this period was the creation of a new performing arts center. An earlier arts center was conceived by Pittsburgh corporate leader Howard Heinz and funded through the Howard Heinz Endowment in the 1970s. In 1984, based on a consultant's report that it had commissioned, the ACCD launched the Pittsburgh Cultural Trust. This private nonprofit organization used public, private, and foundation funding to develop a second performing arts center, a smaller theater, a major office tower, and a small movie theater.

Foundation funding was important in this and other projects. Because of its industrial past, the Pittsburgh region is foundation-rich. In a 1994 ranking of cities, although fortieth in population and thirty-fourth in income, Pittsburgh was first in grants from independent foundations and seventh in grants from community foundations and the United Way.[9] Not only generous in financial terms, major philanthropies also are supportive by strategically addressing regional needs. Foundation staff work closely with one another and the staff of grant recipients to develop and implement innovative programs.

The Pittsburgh Cultural Trust exemplified several major themes in the city's approach to civic development: creation of autonomous implementing organizations, utilization of appropriate expertise, and reliance upon foundation funding to support projects. This pattern has been repeated even in policy areas usually defined as outside the purview of the business elite, such as employment for chronically unemployed, minority entrepreneurship, health, housing, and neighborhood development. Urban renewal is a good example. During the late 1950s the partnership of Lawrence and the ACCD used federal urban renewal funding to clear an African-American community bordering the central business district. As in most cities, the federally funded bulldozer prompted the creation of community-based opposition groups. Unlike most cities, however, Pittsburgh's public-private partnership attempted to integrate these demands into its agenda. It created a new nonprofit agency, ACTION-Housing, Inc., to construct affordable units as replacement housing for displaced urban renewal victims. Although the success of this initiative did not compare with Renaissance I, the pattern of community decision making remained the same—a new civic organization with policy expertise was created, insulated from the conflict-ridden electoral arena, and public, private, and foundation funding were combined to achieve desired goals. The result was another addition to an institutional landscape in which nonprofit implementing organizations share space with public and private organizations.[10]

The ACCD has played a central role in this tradition of public-private partnerships. The association has been instrumental in creating an environment of communication and collaboration across sectors. As the ACCD leadership said in 1984, the Conference "is more than a collection of business leaders. It has come to occupy a position at the heart of Pittsburgh's civic activity. As initiator, broker, supporter, monitor or facilitator, it touches nearly every major civic or development undertaking in the city."[11] A former ACCD director described the conference as a "state of mind" more than a real authority. Ferman adds a similar point, noting that "ACCD's early, and at the time quite spectacular, success added a strong dose of deference to the city's political culture."[12] Could this pattern of civic cooperation be applied to public education? It is to that question that we now turn.

Crisis and Response in Public Education

Between the late 1960s and the early 1980s, public education in Pittsburgh faced a series of crises, both within the school system itself and in the external community. In the late 1960s, for example, parents were demanding more input in school policy making. In 1969, the Pittsburgh School Board responded by creating a pyramidal system of elected parent councils. Demands also came from teachers within the system. In 1968, in fact, teachers struck for union recognition. The Pittsburgh Federation of Teachers was recognized, and Al Fondy was elected president, a position he still held in 1999. Between 1968 and 1975, the PFT struck two more times over various contractual issues.[13]

But the most significant crisis came in 1968 when the Pennsylvania Human Relations Commission required the Pittsburgh Public Schools to submit a desegregation plan. Over the next decade four superintendents submitted plans.[14] None of the plans was accepted by the school board, and all four superintendents left office, voluntarily or involuntarily. In 1976, in the midst of this turmoil, the school board changed from a court-appointed, at-large board to an elected, district-based board with nine members. Districts were drawn in an attempt to guarantee at least two African-American representatives on the board. Early elections produced three prointegration members (two African-Americans and one white) who, ironically, often voted against the desegregation plans, arguing that the plans did not go far enough.

Neighborhood-based organizations vociferously advocated both sides of the issue—African-American communities demanded desegregation, while white ethnic neighborhoods called for preserving neighborhood schools. A citywide coalition, the Pittsburgh Neighborhood Alliance, struggled to find a compromise. Even the mayor entered the fray, writing letters to board members asking them to vote against the latest desegregation plan and arguing publicly that the Human Relations Commission's order could not be enforced.[15] The commission held steadfast in its demand and in 1980 issued an ultimatum: submit a desegregation plan within ninety days.

A Citizens Advisory Committee was appointed to bring the warring sides together. Robert Pease, executive director of the ACCD, agreed to serve as chair, and the ACCD granted him a leave with pay so that he could devote himself full-time to the development of an acceptable plan. The ACCD's assistant director, David Bergholz, became head of a subcommittee that ultimately developed the magnet school concept as a strategy of school desegregation. The resulting plan utilized magnets, redrawn feeder patterns, and new middle schools to desegregate the system as much as possible. It also included "school improvement plans" to address achievement gaps in African-American schools that would remain segregated. Thus, the community dialogue spawned by the ACCD during the desegregation crisis forged a compromise between those who defined the issue as "quality education" and those who focused on the equal distribution of educational resources. The ACCD continued its involvement through the plan's implementation stage, conducting a series of public information and troubleshooting meetings in Pittsburgh's neighborhoods. A new mayor, Richard Caliguiri, while not openly endorsing the plan, called for its peaceful implementation.

The ACCD's interest in resolving the desegregation issue reflected a growing awareness that the public schools played a critical role in the community. This approach was the case despite the fact that the Pittsburgh Public Schools were becoming predominantly African-American. Unlike in many cities, where the civic leadership abandoned the public schools as the white population declined, Pittsburgh's leadership became engaged in a constructive way. Instead of criticizing the schools as being inferior or ill managed, they called for an open dialogue. As the ACCD's assistant director noted, "The problems of desegregation, the financial and political climate that faced the schools, and a general insularity of school leadership had created a less than favorable public perception of the schools' administration and on the schools' side, a feeling that the community lacked the understanding and willingness to assist it with its problems."[16]

In consultation with the superintendent, teachers' union, businesses, and foundations, the ACCD established a Public Information Advisory Committee to promote the accomplishments of the public schools. Thus, when the desegregation issue reached crisis proportions, the ACCD had already gained legitimacy in the educational arena and had done so in collaboration with major actors within the school system.

Furthermore, the ACCD created the Allegheny Conference Education Fund (ACEF) in 1978 to provide ongoing dialogue among actors and financial resources to the public schools for innovative projects. The ACEF funded a variety of projects designed to bolster the school staff's confidence that the larger community supported their work. Under the umbrella of the ACEF, the Education-in-Residence program brought national education experts to Pittsburgh to work with education, business, foundation, and community leaders, and the Partnerships-in-Education program fostered partnerships between schools and individual businesses. Also, the Mini-Grants for Teachers and the Grants-for-Principals programs funded innovative school-based projects.[17]

These grants and programs built small yet symbolic linkages between civic leaders and front-line educational professionals—teachers and principals. The ACCD wanted to make sure that the existence of these linkages was quickly communicated to the larger public. It funded a national search for a new position within the Pittsburgh Public Schools—director of public relations—who would answer directly to the superintendent. The candidate selected had public relations experience both in corporate and educational settings.

Thus, by 1980 the Pittsburgh Public Schools had survived a tumultuous decade and a half. The school system had taken initial steps in responding to an onslaught of demands emanating both from within itself and from a wide range of external actors. It was making progress in the formulation of a desegregation plan. In the process, civic leadership had been activated and fragile partnerships established. But much more needed to be done, and the new reform-minded school board lacked confidence in the current superintendent. In March the board voted not to renew his contract, and the ACCD assisted in a national search for a successor.

Superintendent Richard Wallace and an "Excellence Agenda," 1980–1992

Dr. Richard C. Wallace Jr., with impressive academic as well as administrative credentials, was hired in 1980 by the Pittsburgh School Board to implement its new desegregation plan, respond to union and parental pressures, and improve the quality of public education. Wallace quickly developed working relationships with the business community represented by the ACCD, the school board, community organizations, and the educational research community. In forging these relationships he demonstrated leadership skills that extended both inside and outside the school system.

Reform Initiatives

Wallace focused his early efforts on strengthening the school system. As he wrote later, "There is no substitute for constant reinforcement of a vision and an excellence agenda; it is critical to successful leadership."[18] Shortly after arriving in Pittsburgh, he engaged the assistance of the Learning Research and Development Corporation (LRDC) at the University of Pittsburgh to conduct a needs assessment survey of stakeholders within the school system and in the broader community. Using these data he presented the school board with six priority areas: achievement in basic skills, personnel performance, management of enrollment decline (i.e., school closings), enrollment retention and attraction, discipline, and the performance of individual schools, especially African-American segregated schools. The board gave him six months to present a specific program in each priority area. His initiatives in each area represented a willingness to reform the system in significant ways as well as to form partnerships with other stakeholders.

Achievement in basic skills. The first step in supporting student achievement was an effective monitoring system. Wallace developed a student testing program to help teachers monitor progress in such a way that timely corrections could be made. Tests would be administered frequently and also would be "curriculum based" rather than "standardized." The system, known as Monitoring Achievement in Pittsburgh (MAP), was developed in 1981 and implemented in 1982. Curriculum-based objectives were tested in various subject areas every six weeks, and results were returned quickly to teachers and parents for corrective action. This immediate feedback and corrective action led to improvements in basic skills performance among all students, including African-American students. In fact, Pittsburgh became one of the first urban schools to publicize the size of the "gap" between African-American and white students' performance on standardized tests.[19] Between 1979 and 1984 this gap was halved.

With the assistance of the ACCD, Wallace obtained a $200,000 grant from the R. K. Mellon Foundation to establish the MAP testing system, which provided computer-based testing information systems at individual schools as well as at the district level. This approach allowed for more efficient maintenance of student records and implementation of data-based decision making. Wallace enlarged the testing office of the central administration and "changed its orientation to include a strong research emphasis."[20] Teachers, students, and parents showed a high degree of satisfaction with the program.[21] One author stated that MAP was "arguably the most comprehensive internal assessment program in any U.S. school district."[22]

Personnel performance. A second major priority was to improve staff training and development. Superintendent Wallace established a personnel system that trained principals both to encourage teachers to become better teachers (known as PRISM I) and to become more effective instructional leaders themselves (PRISM II). The initiatives that received the most attention concerned teacher training. Over the course of the next several years, all teachers—secondary (PRISM III), elementary (PRISM IV), and middle (PRISM V)—were pulled out of their regular classrooms for six to eight weeks of intensive training at district teachers centers. In an interview with one of the authors, Wallace argued that "firing teachers was the easy way out. The more difficult issue was to make marginal teachers good, good teachers better, and better teachers excellent."

At first, teachers viewed this approach with skepticism. In the same interview Wallace recalled the first group of teachers to attend the Schenley Teachers Center. They were department heads in their schools and were skeptical of Wallace's motives. "They sat there with their arms folded, staring in a hostile way. It took five weeks for them to unfold their arms and to begin to realize that [they were] being treated like professionals and [were] learning something." According to Wallace, among the things teachers were taught was how to get beyond the basic skills tested in MAP and into "higher-order thinking."

This undertaking was expensive. Staffing the training centers and replacing teachers as they took sabbaticals to attend the centers were very costly. Wallace again went to the ACCD for help in raising the money. The ACCD assisted in arranging local and national foundation support for planning and initial costs, but it would not provide ongoing fund-raising services. Mellon Bank Foundation, however, gave Wallace funds to hire a development officer for six months, who succeeded in raising $1.5 million for the teachers centers. The school board was so pleased that they retained the development officer beyond the foundation-funded period.

Wallace's treatment of teachers as professionals formed the basis of a partnership with the Pittsburgh Federation of Teachers. This partnership, which lasted throughout his tenure, resulted in what Kerchner and Caufman call "professional unionism." Under this model, teachers viewed themselves as professional educators rather than technicians, and bargaining became more of a "continuous problem-solving process and less of a periodic tournament."[23]

Management of enrollment decline. Responding to a declining student population posed a major challenge for Wallace and other supporters of the school system. The population of the Pittsburgh Public Schools had dropped 50 percent in the decades before Wallace's arrival, and it was projected to drop another several thousand students by 1990. There was no alternative but to close schools. In a city with strong neighborhood ties, Wallace knew that objections to school closings would be strong.

The successful response that followed attests to Wallace's political skills. He closed nearly a dozen schools and sold several school buildings, but he spread the closing across all nine districts of the school board. Every board member lost a school, but each gained something as well. In one district, for example, South High was closed as a traditional high school but reopened as a vocational-technical magnet, something the community had long wanted. Thus, Wallace succeeded in garnering support from board members while enlisting their assistance to soothe relations between schools and neighborhoods.

Enrollment retention and attraction. Wallace used the magnet concept to desegregate schools as well as attract enrollment. In addition to creating quality magnet programs, an extensive marketing campaign brought schools to the attention of parents. Within a few years, many programs had become so successful that parents camped out overnight to reserve slots for their children. Noting the class bias of such overnight waits—the expense of down parkas and recreational vehicles, not to mention the ability to take a day off from work—the reservation process changed to a lottery system.

A second strategy to enhance enrollment was to emphasize gifted programs. At the elementary and middle school levels, gifted students attended scholars centers one day a week. At the high school level, gifted students attended separate Center for Advanced Studies classes. Treated as "special education" in Pennsylvania, state funding was essential for the maintenance of these programs. State officials challenged Wallace's extensive use of state funding for gifted programs, but he successfully met their objections.

By 1985 not only had the decline in enrollment stopped, but students were entering the system from parochial and private schools at the rate of nearly one thousand per year. Ironically, enrollment retention and attraction policies were so successful that by the time Wallace retired, every school that was closed earlier in the decade had been reopened and the system was buying parochial schools.

Discipline. Wallace's initiatives to address discipline concerns were straightforward—develop a student code of conduct and establish a discipline committee at each school. Although simple, these initiatives addressed the priority in such a manner as to promote other goals, in this case, school-based decision making. Although discipline was not a major problem during the early 1980s, by 1989 gang activity was on the rise in and around schools. Wallace anticipated this problem and was among the first to formulate a response. By the early 1990s, he was concerned that educational excellence had taken a back seat to safe schools.

Performance of individual schools. The final initiative specifically targeted those African-American students who attended schools that, despite the desegregation plan, remained predominantly African-American. Wallace again turned to the concept of personnel training. This time, however, it was peer training among African-American administrators. He selected an African-American principal, who had ten years of success in producing high-achieving students in a predominantly African-American school, to mentor principals from six other minority segregated schools. This "lead principal" was also charged with authoring a model school improvement plan that could be used by any school in the system.

Although this initiative focused on educational equity, quality was the thrust of most of Wallace's reforms. The MAP testing system and the personnel training programs benefited all students, including African-American students. This focus on overall quality was successful, as noted earlier, in narrowing the achievement gap between white and African-American students during the early years of Wallace's tenure.

National Recognition

Wallace began his tenure as a reform superintendent and promoted his "excellence agenda" throughout his twelve years.[24] The reforms he initiated focused on the school system's primary mission—teaching and learning. Most of the reforms, such as the achievement monitoring system and teachers centers, were aimed at directly improving the instructional process. Others, such as data-based decision making and central office positions in public relations and development, were aimed at changing the school system as an organization so that it could better achieve its instructional mission. In recognition of these reforms and his success in Pittsburgh, in 1990 Wallace became the first school superintendent to win the Harold W. McGraw Jr., Prize in Education.[25]

Extending Educational Leadership

Wallace's success depended upon the relationships he nurtured with other educators as well as leaders in the public and private sectors. For most of his tenure, he enjoyed a supportive school board and teachers' union. With the school board, Wallace received strong support for most of the 1980s. The president of the board from 1983 until 1989 was Jake Milliones, an African-American who was an assistant professor of psychiatry and psychology at the University of Pittsburgh. Milliones provided the leadership necessary to bring the disparate board members together, shepherding through much of the Wallace reform agenda. One informant said that under Milliones's leadership most school board votes were 9 to 0. At the same time, Milliones was a strong and informed advocate for the African-American community. He kept Wallace and the board focused on the performance gap between white and African-American students. If it were not for Milliones, the Wallace agenda might have focused exclusively on issues of quality and efficiency in education.

Wallace also established a strong working relationship with the teachers' union. Again, stable leadership was critical. Throughout Wallace's superintendency Al Fondy served as president of the Pittsburgh Federation of Teachers. Wallace recognized the critical role played by the teachers' union, noting that "professional unions are in a powerful position to mobilize their members to embrace and support educational reform; they can also pull the plug on reform."[26] Wallace's reforms that emphasized teacher professionalism elevated teachers and the union to a partnership role in the "excellence agenda." Fondy, a strong and progressive union leader, reciprocated, stating that "if there are problems in the school system, and the union is strong, then the union is responsible either for the fact that the problems exist in the first place, or at least responsible for the fact that they are not being addressed."[27]

Cross-sector Collaboration

Wallace's primary strengths were in leadership within the school system. His focus on educational expertise and achievement fit comfortably with the corporate leadership style of Pittsburgh, characterized by one observer as an "old-style 1960s technocrat, in the Robert McNamara mold."[28] He did, however, venture outside the school system in a number of cross-sector initiatives. In 1991, for example, Wallace, who served on the board of Blue Cross of Western Pennsylvania, brought together a group of health care and foundation leaders to form a School Health Partnership Blue Ribbon Committee. The Blue Ribbon Committee helped Wallace develop broad policy and a funding strategy for the creation of school-based health centers. At the same time, a foundation provided financial support to hire consultants, the Health Education Center, to assist in building relationships between major health providers and individual schools. As a result, in 1992, policy guidelines were approved for the establishment of school health partnerships. These partnerships utilized school facilities and school personnel, a unique integration into the school administration.[29]

Another important cross-sector initiative was the New Futures Project supported by the Annie E. Casey Foundation. In 1987 the staff at the Allegheny Conference Education Fund presented Wallace with an opportunity to participate in the foundation-funded New Futures Project. New Futures would provide multimillion-dollar support to communities to "make long-term changes in the operation, principles, and policies by which education, employment, and other youth services are administered, financed, and delivered at both the local and state levels of government as well as in the private sector."[30]

A proposal planning committee was formed representing, among others, the school district, city and county operating agencies, the Pittsburgh Foundation, and the United Way. Although the program represented a multiagency approach, the proposal had to be written quickly, and the school system's director of development and strategic planning took the lead. The proposal targeted two high schools and their feeder elementary and middle schools, representing one-third of the public school population and four of the city's eleven at-risk neighborhoods. Wallace's administration recognized that the in-school performance of children in these neighborhoods was affected by more than what happened in the classroom. Wallace's director of research, testing, and evaluation had cautioned that the school reforms of the "excellence agenda" had limits. As he noted, "To the degree that those reforms don't pay any attention to multicultural influences or any of the other environmental influences on achievement, there will be clear limits to what you can accomplish. Some of the achievement gap is because schools aren't doing the job well with respect to minority students. Much of it is a consequence of social and economic conditions."[31] Addressing these issues required the cross-sector collaborations anticipated in New Futures.

The proposal was funded, and over the next five years more than ten million foundation dollars were spent for a vast array of programs aimed at building school-to-work relationships, reducing teenage pregnancy, improving attendance, reducing drop-out rates, enhancing achievement, forging community-school relationships, strengthening school building management, and encouraging team teaching.

Educational Challenges and Changing Times

Superintendent Wallace was widely acclaimed as one of the best urban superintendents in the country. His focus on teaching and learning helped raise academic achievement in the schools, and he garnered support and praise from many business and community leaders outside the schools for his educational leadership. By the early 1990s, however, times were changing, and pressures mounted for a different leadership style. Old actors in the education arena—parents, community activists, and board members—were demanding more participation in decision making. New approaches to serving at-risk youth necessitated collaboration with other youth-serving agencies. Wallace was less successful in meeting these challenges to his leadership than in implementing his "excellence agenda."

The first challenge involved participation in decision making. The growing pressure to widen participation in educational decision making did not match well with Wallace's leadership style. Wallace sought the advice of a broad range of interests, but under his leadership task forces and committees were tightly controlled. As he has written, "The superintendent needs to remind [advisory committees] of their proper, yet important, role as advisers; it needs to be made clear from the outset that the superintendent is the final decision maker. Advisory groups sometimes have a tendency to view themselves as decision-making groups."[32] Wallace promoted teacher professionalization and principal leadership, but he resisted decentralization of authority. He very cautiously explored site-based management in 1991, requesting proposals from teachers for two "restructured" elementary schools.

Wallace's relationship with the school board was another important challenge. In 1989 Milliones left the board to join the city council and was replaced in the presidency by Barbara Burns, a community activist first elected to the board in 1983. During the early years of Burns's presidency, conflict developed between the board and Wallace. Several board representatives, also with community activist roots, pressed their individual agendas within the board. One informant described the board during this period as "populist," with individual members attempting to "micro-manage all the way down to the staff level." Indicative of the increased level of involvement was the expansion of board committees: between 1986 and 1992, the number of school board committees expanded from two to eight and the number of subcommittees from eight to twelve.[33]

Individual board members, including the president, hurled a variety of criticisms at Wallace and his agenda—overcentralization, spending too much money, too concerned with his national reputation. The most outspoken critic was Valerie McDonald, an African-American female elected to the board in 1989. Charging that there were improprieties in the district's purchasing and bidding systems, she said that she was "trying to do away with the 'good old boy' system."[34] She objected to spending $150,000 of school funds for a three-year membership in the National Alliance for Restructuring Education (a group the Pittsburgh Public Schools helped to create), describing the alliance as "a lot of fluff and a way to build Wallace's reputation."[35] When Wallace proposed replacing three retiring African-American principals with African-Americans from outside the city, bypassing local African-American educators, McDonald called his actions "racist and elitist."[36] Wallace threatened to sue her for slander, but the dispute died down.

Finally, New Futures provided a significant challenge to Wallace's leadership capacity. Although the project produced a number of important programmatic changes in school operations, it was less successful in reaching its primary goal: to permanently alter the way in which policies for disadvantaged youth were made, financed, and implemented. Midgrant evaluations concluded that such change was not occurring. Several major stakeholders—city and county executives, the corporate sector, public sector workforce agencies—were not at the table. In addition, data generated by the programs under the New Futures umbrella were not being utilized to formulate comprehensive policy initiatives, and service-delivery integration had not been accomplished. Perhaps the single most critical factor was the lack of active involvement by the ACCD. Robert Pease, the longtime director who had guided the ACCD's involvement in a variety of social issues, resigned in 1990 while New Futures was still in a formative stage. The New Futures Board dissolved, and some of the programs were folded into a new regional collaborative, the Allegheny Policy Council for Youth and Workforce Development.

There are many reasons for the failure of New Futures in Pittsburgh—too much money spent too fast, the overly prescriptive agenda of a national foundation, the focus on programs rather than directly on systemic change, and the lack of commitment on the part of major community actors, including the ACCD. Particularly significant is the lack of cross-sector collaboration to address the problems of at-risk youth. The Casey Foundation recognized the need for systemic change through collaboration, but in Pittsburgh the leaders of key institutions were not participating in the effort, and others were only halfheartedly involved. Millions of dollars were spent on add-on, pilot programs in a limited number of schools with no plans for how they would be continued, let alone expanded district-wide, after the New Futures money left the city.

The New Futures Project threw Wallace into a leadership position that he did not seek. The unreasonable time constraints imposed by the Casey Foundation required that a proposal be written quickly, without sufficient time for broad collaborative planning. Wallace's staff stepped forward, and, not surprisingly, the proposal focused on the school system. Sixty percent of the Pittsburgh grant was spent on school programs, leading to unreasonable reliance on the schools to solve complex problems. Yet, New

Futures funding accounted for just 1.2 percent of the school system's budget, allowing for only marginal change. Because the collaborative planning body was weak, Wallace approached the New Futures grant as he did other grants from outside funders rather than as an exercise in multi-institutional collaboration. Wallace, while more than willing to lead the school district in dramatic change in its instructional mission, was frustrated by the inability of the New Futures Project to bring other key actors to the table for a more comprehensive strategy to address the problems of at-risk urban youth.[37]

After twelve years as superintendent, Wallace could point to many accomplishments, but he also recognized that new challenges faced the school system. In 1992, he resigned as superintendent and accepted a joint appointment at the University of Pittsburgh's Learning Research and Development Corporation and its School of Education. . . .

Richard Wallace and Leadership in Pittsburgh

In Pittsburgh in the 1980s, leadership played a central role in expanding civic capacity to include public education. During this decade a number of factors combined to facilitate this critical role for leadership. One major factor was the alignment and long tenure of key leaders in the community, all of whom were supportive of collaborative reform efforts. The alignment and longevity of leaders were indeed striking: Superintendent Wallace served from 1980–1992, Teachers' Union president Al Fondy from 1968–present; School Board president Jake Milliones from 1983–1989; and Allegheny Conference on Community Development executive director Robert Pease from 1968–1990. This continuity allowed an unprecedented sharing of ideas and strategies among this group. Their support for public education was strong and consistent throughout the 1980s. Sustained leadership was critical; as Superintendent Wallace noted, it "takes a decade to institutionalize changes that can produce and sustain positive results for students."[38]

These leaders also were connected to key resources in the institutional environment. Among them, they controlled or had access to school department resources, teachers, and various business resources. The Allegheny Conference on Community Development, in particular, played a key role. Beginning with grant programs through the Education Fund and support for a desegregation plan, the conference provided a "stamp of approval" that facilitated various community connections through foundations and other sources to support the schools.

In addition, the conference applied its model of civic support that included deference to the school department as the lead institution responsible for education in the city. The conference incorporated education into its agenda but relied upon the school department to deliver the product. This model of turning to existing or newly created institutions to implement a civic agenda had been used in housing and other policy arenas. It facilitated a critical connection between leadership at a governance level and implementation through the school department at a programmatic level. For public education, this approach would prove particularly conducive, since it matched the independent nature of Superintendent Wallace's leadership.

Wallace was the linchpin of the reform effort. His leadership skills touched all aspects of a superintendent's role: political, educational, and managerial. Politically, he maintained strong working relationships with actors in the educational field as well as . . . outside. . . . He was well respected by business leaders, who supported the search that led to his appointment as superintendent. He also worked well with other educational leaders, including the presidents of the school board and teachers' union. He recognized the political pressures experienced by other leaders and respected the limits to their actions.

Wallace also was an energetic educational leader and effective manager. Throughout his tenure, he brought a vision to the superintendency that focused on teaching and learning. As he concluded, "There is no substitute for constant reinforcement of a vision and an excellence agenda; it is critical to successful leadership."[39] He carried this vision forward through a number of educational improvements within the school system, including personnel development, basic skills performance, enrollment policies, and discipline. Managing these reform initiatives was another challenge that Wallace met. He closely monitored the implementation of school policies and brought other managers into the school department to assist in this process.

Through these leadership roles, Wallace developed a problem definition that united the community. Crafting a definition began at the outset of his tenure when he hired the University of Pittsburgh to develop a comprehensive assessment of the school system. This assessment became the core of the problem definition. It provided an outline of key strategies to address the educational challenges of the school system, and it raised the overall issue of academic excellence to a position of high visibility on the community's agenda. Wallace and the school board became the sponsors for this definition as they initiated a number of programmatic initiatives to improve teaching and learning in the schools. Based upon the needs assessment, there was a decade of "virtual unanimity among the board on educational matters."[40] This "data-oriented leadership" became a central feature of Pittsburgh's success story.[41]

Notes

1. Donald Stevens Jr., "The Role of Nonprofit Corporations in Urban Development: A Case Study of ACTION-Housing, Inc. of Pittsburgh" (Ph.D. diss., Carnegie-Mellon University, 1987), 24.
2. Roy Lubove, *Twentieth-Century Pittsburgh: Government, Business, and Environmental Change,* vol. 1 (Pittsburgh: University of Pittsburgh Press, 1995); John F. Bauman and Margaret Spratt, "Civic Leaders and Environmental Reform: The Pittsburgh Survey and Urban Planning," in *Pittsburgh Surveyed: Social Science and Social Reform in the Early Twentieth Century,* ed. M. Greenwald and M. Anderson (Pittsburgh: University of Pittsburgh Press, 1996).
3. Michael Weber, "Rebuilding a City: The Pittsburgh Model," in *Snowbelt Cities: Metropolitan Politics in the Northeast and Midwest Since World War II,* ed. R. Bernard (Bloomington: Indiana University Press, 1990), 231.
4. Lubove, *Twentieth-Century Pittsburgh,* vol. 1, chap. 6.
5. Weber, "Rebuilding a City," in *Snowbelt Cities,* 231.
6. Edward K. Muller, "Historical Aspects of Regional Structural Change in the Pittsburgh Region," in *Regional Structural Change and Industrial Policy in International Perspective,* ed. J. Hesse (Baden-Baden, Germany: Auflage, 1988), 38.
7. Barbara Ferman, *Challenging the Growth Machine: Neighborhood Politics in Chicago and Pittsburgh* (Lawrence: University Press of Kansas, 1996), 49.
8. Roy Lubove, *Twentieth-Century Pittsburgh: The Post Steel Era,* vol. 2 (Pittsburgh: University of Pittsburgh Press, 1996), 73.
9. "Community Ties, Income Affect Level of Giving in 50 Big Cities," *Chronicle of Philanthropy* (February 22, 1994), 51–68.
10. Alberta M. Sbragia, "Pittsburgh's 'Third Way': The Nonprofit Sector as a Key to Urban Regeneration," in *Leadership and Urban Regeneration,* ed. D. Judd and M. Parkinson (Newbury Park, Calif.: Sage, 1990).
11. *Allegheny Conference on Community Development: 1983 Report* (Pittsburgh: Allegheny Conference on Community Development, 1984), 2.
12. Ferman, *Challenging the Growth Machine,* 54.
13. Charles Taylor Kerchner, "Pittsburgh: Reform in a Well-Managed Public Bureaucracy," in *A Union of Professionals: Labor Relations and Educational Reform,* ed. C. Kerchner and J. Koppich (New York: Teachers College Press), 45.
14. Richard D. Gutkind, "Desegregation of Pittsburgh Public Schools, 1968–1980" (Ph.D. diss., University of Pittsburgh, 1983).
15. Ibid., 63–64.
16. Valerie S. Lies and David Bergholz, "The Public Education Fund," in *American Business and the Public School: Case Studies of Corporate Involvement in Public Education,* ed. M. Levine and R. Trachtman (New York: Teachers College Press, 1988), 78.
17. *Ten-Year Report: Allegheny Conference Education Fund* (Pittsburgh: Allegheny Conference on Community Development, 1988).
18. Richard C. Wallace Jr., *From Vision to Practice: The Art of Educational Leadership* (Thousand Oaks, Calif.: Corwin Press, 1996), 21.
19. Tina Calabro, "Closing the Racial Achievement Gap: Is the School District Doing Enough to Improve the Achievement of African-American Students?" *Public Voices Public Schools: An Independent Look at the Pittsburgh Public Schools* (January/February 1994).
20. William Cooley and William Bickel, *Decision-Oriented Educational Research* (Boston: Kluwer-Nihjoff, 1986), 18.

21. Paul B. LeMahieu, "A Study of the Effects of a Program of Student Achievement Monitoring Through Testing" (Ph.D. diss., University of Pittsburgh, 1983), 11.
22. Kerchner, "Pittsburgh: Reform in a Well-Managed Public Bureaucracy," in *A Union of Professionals,* 47.
23. Charles Taylor Kerchner and Krista Caufman, "Building the Airplane While It's Rolling Down the Runway," in *A Union of Professionals,* 16.
24. Wallace, *From Vision to Practice.*
25. Bill Zlatos, "Wallace wins national education award," *Pittsburgh Press,* December 5, 1990.
26. Wallace, *From Vision to Practice,* 99.
27. Quoted in Kerchner and Caufman, "Building the Airplane," in *A Union of Professionals,* 19.
28. Rexford G. Brown, *Schools of Thought: How the Politics of Literacy Shape Thinking in the Classroom* (San Francisco: Jossey-Bass, 1993), 196.
29. Joy Dryfoos, "School-Based Social and Health Services for At-Risk Students," *Urban Education* (April 1991): 132–33.
30. Annie E. Casey Foundation, "A Strategic Planning Guide for a New Futures Initiative," 1987.
31. Brown, *Schools of Thought.*
32. Wallace, *From Vision to Practice,* 35.
33. Bill Zlatos, "School board's bickering could scare off candidates," *Pittsburgh Press,* April 12, 1992.
34. "McDonald requires probe of board improprieties," *Pittsburgh Press,* May 20, 1990.
35. Bill Zlatos, "Board weighs cost of joining group it helped start," *Pittsburgh Press,* December 18, 1990.
36. "Valerie McDonald tells Wallace: 'Sue Me,' " *Pittsburgh Press,* March 16, 1991.
37. For a comprehensive assessment of the Pittsburgh New Futures experience, see the various evaluations completed by the Center for the Study of Social Policy in Washington, D.C.: "New Futures in Pittsburgh: A Mid-Point Assessment," 1991; "Pittsburgh New Futures Initiative: Year Three Evaluation Report," 1991; "Pittsburgh New Futures: Year Four Evaluation," 1992; and Melchior, *An Evaluation of the Pittsburgh Promise.*
38. Wallace, *From Vision to Practice,* 93.
39. Ibid., 21.
40. Ibid., 131.
41. Ibid., 120.

Chapter 15 Review Questions

1. Where are some of the key battlegrounds in education politics? How is education politics similar to and different from other types of politics? Do you think there is a significant difference between urban education reform and urban redevelopment as Stone and his coauthors argue? How so?
2. Why do Stone and colleagues maintain that mobilizing civic capacity is critical for urban school reform? Why can't the educational establishment alone address the problems?
3. Why was Wallace successful in strengthening Pittsburgh's public school system? How well does the case study support the arguments put forward by Stone and colleagues? Were other factors important in shaping Pittsburgh's success that were not discussed in the first reading? What were they?
4. Do you think that Wallace's efforts would meet with the same success in other urban areas, or is there something exceptional about Pittsburgh that makes his achievements difficult to replicate elsewhere?
5. What do you think are the underlying problems confronting urban schools? How do you think those problems should be addressed? What role do you see civic capacity playing in solving urban education problems? Explain your reasoning.
6. In Chapter 5, you read an excerpt from Robert Putnam's book *Bowling Alone* that focused on the importance of building civic engagement for democracies. How are these two readings on urban school reform similar to Putnam's work? What do they say about the importance of participation in public policy making?

Key Terms

- *Nation at Risk*
- magnet schools
- site-based management
- standards
- No Child Left Behind Act
- charter schools
- failure syndrome
- civic capacity
- human capital
- social reconstruction
- open systems
- exit process
- collective bargaining
- time-serving
- stakeholders
- systemic reform
- public-private partnerships
- desegregation

Suggestions for Further Reading

Berliner, David C., and Bruce J. Biddle. *The Manufactured Crisis: Myths, Fraud, and the Attacks on America's Public Schools.* New York: Perseus Publishing, 1996. This book challenges the evidence that the public schools are failing, and argues instead that the real problems seen in the schools are economic and social.

Burtless, Gary, ed. *Does Money Matter? The Effect of School Resources on Student Achievement and Adult Success.* Washington, D.C.: Brookings, 1996. A valuable compilation of essays pertaining to the effects school expenditures have on education quality.

Comer, James P., Norris M. Haynes, Edward T. Joyner, and Michael Ben-Avie, eds. *Rallying the Whole Village: The Comer Process for Reforming Education.* New York: Teachers College, 1996. Presents a theoretical model for education reform based on connecting schools more closely with their communities.

Cuban, Larry. "Reforming Again, Again, and Again." *Education Researcher* 19 (1990): 3–13. Frequently cited work on the waves of school reform efforts that have repeatedly swept over the nation.

Ferman, Barbara. *Challenging the Growth Machine: Neighborhood Politics in Chicago and Pittsburgh.* Lawrence: University Press of Kansas, 1997. This is a fascinating book for those interested in learning more about Pittsburgh's politics and political culture.

Henig, Jeffrey R., Richard C. Hula, Marion Orr, and Desiree S. Pedescleaux. *The Color of School Reform: Race, Politics, and the Challenge of Urban Education.* Princeton: Princeton University Press, 1999. A study on the role that race plays in school reform efforts. The authors discuss the importance of civic capacity for improving urban schools.

Hill, Paul T., Lawrence C. Pierce, and James W. Guthrie. *Reinventing Public Education: How Contracting Can Transform America's Schools.* Chicago: University of Chicago, 1997. An argument in favor of reforming public education by relying on private companies to run the schools.

Loveless, Tom, ed. *Conflicting Missions? Teachers Unions and Educational Reform.* Washington, D.C.: Brookings Institution, 2000. Valuable collection of essays on the complex relationship between teachers unions and school reform efforts.

National Commission on Excellence in Education. *A Nation at Risk: The Imperative for Educational Reform.* Washington, D.C.: U.S. Government Printing Office, 1983. This was the early 1980s report that severely criticized "the rising tide of mediocrity" in the nation's schools and moved education reform more prominently up the political agenda.

Ravitch, Diane. *Left Back: A Century of Failed School Reforms.* New York: Simon and Schuster, 2000. Detailed historical analysis of school reform efforts in America and their consequences.

Stone, Clarence, ed. *Changing Urban Education.* Lawrence: University Press of Kansas, 1998. Collection of essays on school reform efforts in nine cities, including Baltimore, Brooklyn, Chicago, and Houston, with an emphasis on the political character of reform.

Tyack, David, and Larry Cuban. *Tinkering Toward Utopia: A Century of Public School Reform.* Cambridge, Mass.: Harvard University Press, 1997. This historical analysis of education reform in America argues that despite all the attention that has been devoted over the years to fixing public schools, most of the reforms enacted have been incremental. The authors argue that the key to successful reform is by helping teachers improve instruction.

Wirt, Frederick M., and Michael W. Kirst. *The Political Dynamics of American Education.* Berkeley, Calif.: McCutchan Publishing, 1997. Outstanding textbook on education politics.

Witte, John F. *The Market Approach to Education: An Analysis of America's First Voucher Program.* Princeton: Princeton University Press, 2000. One of the most comprehensive analyses of Milwaukee's well-known school choice program.

Related Web Sites

http://www.ed.gov
The web site for the U.S. Department of Education provides statistical and other information on the nation's students, schools, and school systems, including an overview of the No Child Left Behind Act.

http://www.cpre.org
The Consortium for Policy Research in Education provides the findings from research on elementary and secondary education and numerous links to other education sites.

16

Social Welfare: The Concepts of Laboratories of Democracy and Race to the Bottom

The landmark legislation of 1996 has given rise to a clash of metaphors used to capture the promise and danger of welfare devolution. Optimists suggest that this loosening of the federal tether will turn the states into 50 "laboratories of democracy" that can develop superior responses to poverty and welfare. . . . By contrast, skeptics caution that the states' new-found discretion might be used to intensify a "race to the bottom."

Sanford F. Schram and Joe Soss

READING 16

Introduction

During the midst of the Great Depression, the federal government created Aid to Families with Dependent Children (AFDC) to provide financial assistance to poor widows and their children. Even though the program was originally intended to help this narrow group, by the mid-1990s AFDC had become the nation's largest and most controversial welfare program. In 1994, when the number of recipients reached an historic high, some 14 million Americans were receiving AFDC benefits. The primary recipients were not widows, but single-parent families headed by divorced or never-married women. Two-thirds of the recipients were children.[1]

Beginning in the 1980s, there was growing public dissatisfaction with AFDC. Critics of AFDC argued that the program created a culture of dependency because it did not include any mechanism to encourage or compel recipients to enter the workforce. Moreover, many felt that the program had helped cause a decline in social mores in America and an increase in the number of out-of-wedlock births. In response to these criticisms, Congress enacted the Family Support Act of 1988, a law that was hailed at the time as being the most comprehensive welfare reform in more than fifty years. At the heart of the new law was an effort to help welfare recipients return to work by requiring them to participate in state-run job skills programs. Despite the rhetoric, the impact of the act was limited, and the number of recipients on AFCD grew in the late 1980s and early 1990s.

The demand for welfare reform remained strong in the 1990s. In his presidential campaign in 1992, Democrat Bill Clinton pledged to "end welfare as we know it." Two years later, the Republican Party unveiled its "Contract with America," a set of policies it promised would be addressed if the party gained a majority of seats in Congress. Among the items on the list was a promise to revise the welfare system. In 1996, with Clinton still in the White House and the Republicans in control of both houses of Congress, the Personal Responsibility and Work Opportunity Reconciliation Act was signed into law, restructuring the nation's welfare system and replacing AFDC with the Temporary Assistance for Needy Families (TANF) program.

TANF included a number of important changes from AFDC. For one, unlike AFCD, TANF is not an entitlement for low-income families. Instead, the program provides block grants to the states for welfare assistance. The states are required to create their own welfare programs, but they are given more flexibility in deciding how their programs will be designed and run than was the case under AFDC. Because of this flexibility, the act is considered by many to give the states greater power over welfare policy than was true in the past. Despite this apparent flexibility, the act does include some rules that the states must follow in their welfare programs. In particular, TANF places restrictions on eligibility that are meant to force recipients off of welfare and into the workforce. When new recipients enter the TANF program, they can only receive benefits for up to two years as they look for a job. The law also establishes a lifetime limit of five years that an adult can receive TANF benefits. Finally, the law places restrictions on the states as to the percentage of recipients that are expected to be participating in work-related activities, including regular jobs and training programs.

For state politics scholars, what makes TANF particularly interesting is that it seems to have given states a greater role in the nation's efforts to address poverty than was true under AFDC. In many of the readings on federal-state relations, TANF is frequently held up as the foremost example of the increased power that was given to state governments in the 1990s through what was called the "devolution revolution." TANF is thus interesting to look at not only for what it means for welfare policy, but for what it says about federal-state relations.

The question that TANF raises is what effect will this devolution of responsibility to the states have on the policies that are enacted to help the poor. Social welfare experts and other political observers have offered two potential scenarios, one that is optimistic and another that is not. The optimistic perspective is that the devolution of power will improve welfare policies because it will allow the states to experiment in how they design and run their programs. This experimentation will lead to the creation of more effective and efficient welfare programs than is possible under a uniform federal program. The less optimistic perspective is that the devolution of power will harm welfare recipients. In particular, critics of TANF worry that states will be reluctant to offer welfare benefits that are more generous than other states out of fear of becoming magnets for welfare recipients. The result will be a downward spiral in benefits as the states try to avoid attracting out-of-state recipients.

For those who study federal-state relations, the two different scenarios on how TANF may affect welfare recipients are not unique perspectives, but can be heard in many different policy debates on the appropriate distribution of power between the states and the federal government. The first scenario presents the perspective that the states can serve as "laboratories of democracy." In many policy areas, political reformers argue that more power should be given to the states because this will lead to more innovative and effective programs. As states try different approaches, other states will emulate programs that prove successful. When there is only one federally run program, there is less opportunity for creativity and innovation. On the other hand, one of the criticisms of state-centered federalism is that it can produce an unhealthy competition among the states. In welfare reform, this competition may encourage the states to set their benefits as low as possible to ensure that they do not become welfare magnets. Similarly, in economic development, this competition may lead states to weaken their environmental regulations or workplace safety rules to try to attract or retain businesses. Instead of producing innovation, state-centered federalism may result in a "race to the bottom."

In March 1998, a group of distinguished scholars met at the Woodrow Wilson Center in Washington, D.C., to discuss the effect of the federal government's new welfare program. The result of that meeting was the publication of an edited book that directly examines the question as to whether TANF produced laboratories of democracy or a race to the bottom. The reading that follows provides a good overview of the book's theme and a distinct perspective on TANF itself. The authors of the reading discuss the meaning of these two different metaphors—laboratories of democracy and race to the bottom—and then examine how well the metaphors actually capture the impact of TANF.

The essay provides a stimulating discussion because it does not see either metaphor as accurately capturing the nature of the new welfare reform. Even though many observers of federal-state relations have hailed TANF for devolving greater power to the states, Professors Sanford Schram and Joe Soss argue that the law does not give the states nearly as much discretion as is often suggested, but it places important restrictions on how state welfare programs are tailored. Moreover, they argue that the fear of creating welfare magnets will put pressure on state leaders to enact welfare policies that are similar to those in other states. As a result of these restrictions and pressures, the authors do not believe that TANF has the potential to create laboratories of democracy.

The law does give the states some discretion, but primarily in allowing them to pursue different approaches for enforcing the law's work requirements and in deciding when to remove recipients from the welfare programs. Schram and Soss argue that the law may cause the states to emulate each other, as is suggested in the race to the bottom metaphor, but they believe the effect will be different from how this race is normally portrayed. Usually, when scholars talk about a race to the bottom in welfare policy, they are referring to the likelihood that states will reduce benefits to avoid becoming welfare magnets. Schram and Soss argue that the real race between the states may not be over lowering benefits, but in setting restrictions on eligibility. As one state places stricter limits on recipients, it may cause other states to follow suit in order to avoid attracting an influx of welfare recipients.

Although the authors' focus is welfare reform, the readings are valuable for thinking about how power should be distributed between the states and the federal government in general. The question this chapter should raise is not just how welfare policy should be handled, but under what circumstances are states likely to serve as laboratories of democracy and when are they likely to participate in a race to the bottom.

The authors of the chapter are both respected experts on social welfare policy. Schram is a visiting professor at the Graduate School of Social Work and Social Research at Bryn Mawr College. Joe Soss is an associate professor of government in the School of Public Affairs at American University.

Questions to Consider

These are some questions to consider as you read their work:

- Why do the authors refer to PRWORA as a dubious devolution? Why do they say the new TANF system "does not move the nation forward into an unprecedented era of state experimentation"? What latitude do the states have under TANF? How are the states constrained in what they can do? Where does the law allow flexibility?
- According to Schram and Soss, why are states likely to produce similar welfare programs? What types of pressures do they face?
- What evidence do the authors cite to suggest that TANF will not cause welfare recipients to migrate to other states to seek out better benefits? What forces do they think could cause migration to occur?

Making Something Out of Nothing: Welfare Reform and a New Race to the Bottom

Sanford F. Schram and Joe Soss

After years of calling for a "new federalism," Republicans in the Congress have finally achieved what some have called a "devolution revolution" in the welfare policy arena. The Personal Responsibility and Work Opportunity Reconciliation Act of 1996 (PRWORA) is said to have reduced federal authority over public assistance programs, providing states more freedom to fashion their own solutions to the problems of poverty and welfare dependency.[1] The most controversial provision of the law expressed this devolutionary spirit by abolishing the 61-year-old federal program that structured how states provided cash assistance to poor families (Aid to Families with Dependent Children, or AFDC) and by replacing it with a new system of state-administered block grants (Temporary Assistance for Needy Families, or TANF).

The landmark legislation of 1996 has given rise to a clash of metaphors used to capture the promise and danger of welfare devolution. Optimists suggest that this loosening of the federal tether will turn the states into 50 "laboratories of democracy" that can develop superior responses to poverty and welfare.[2] Blending references to science and self-government, the phrase "laboratories of democracy" evokes images of careful experimentation conducted in accordance with the will of the people. By contrast, skeptics caution that the states' new-found discretion might be used to intensify a "race to the bottom." In this rival metaphor, the states are cast as competitors engaged in an unruly and self-serving contest. Foregoing the goal of fighting poverty, each state cuts its welfare benefits in order to avoid becoming a "welfare magnet" whose generous assistance attracts poor migrants from other states.[3]

In what follows, we raise critical questions for these two metaphors, and suggest that neither "laboratories of democracy" nor "race to the bottom" do justice to the complexities of welfare reform. As a counter to images of free experimentation, we question whether the 1996 legislation actually promotes diversity or creativity in state policymaking. State officials are not nearly as autonomous in reality as they appear to be in political rhetoric. Along with the block grants that gave more authority to the states, the 1996 law also created new federal mandates that limit state action. In addition to these formal constraints, states also face informal pressures to "keep up" with one another. As fears of becoming a welfare magnet combine with concerns about "falling behind," the new system of decentralization may discourage states from seeking new and creative ways to fight poverty.

We also raise critical questions for the rival race-to-the-bottom metaphor. In an increasingly common tale, it is predicted that the new discretion under the 1996 law will enhance benefit variation, which will produce welfare migration, which in turn will push states into a race to the bottom. First, we offer a reminder that states always had substantial discretion to set benefits under the old AFDC system, and that state attempts to repel poor outsiders have a long history in the United States. These are hardly new creations of the 1996 law. Second, we challenge the key assumption of welfare migration in the race-to-the-bottom metaphor. There is very little empirical support for the existence of welfare migration. Furthermore, new evidence indicates that the value of welfare benefits to recipients does not vary nearly as much in reality as it appears to in common portrayals of the incentives for migration.

Although the benefit differences and migratory behaviors described by the welfare-magnet thesis are largely chimerical, state policymakers still tend to act as if they are real. Thus, to understand the dynamics of federalism under the new TANF system, it is necessary to understand how these fears of migration combine with federal and social pressures to drive down the welfare rolls and promote immediate work. We suggest that in this environment, the recent welfare reforms are likely to produce two ironic outcomes. First, while the 1996 law was ushered in with claims of bold state experimentation, it seems more likely that states will feel strong pressures to emulate one another, and that restrictions initiated by one will be adopted by others. Second, while the race to the bottom was supposed to be driven by welfare migration, it seems more likely that the reverse will occur. As states pursue new restrictions and regulations, they may force recipients to move out in order to survive. In a tragic irony, the procedural race to the bottom may actually turn the myth of migration into a self-fulfilling prophesy.

Welfare Reform: Dubious Devolution

The passage of the PRWORA in 1996 was a major event in the history of United States welfare provision. The shift from AFDC to TANF signaled major changes in the structure of welfare financing, administration, and participation. In some significant respects, the states received real increases in autonomy. The TANF block grant gives state officials more latitude in deciding how to spend federal dollars. In the absence of the old matching formulas, states now bear more of the costs for welfare expenditures, and keep more of the revenue saved through welfare cuts. The 1996 law also ended the federal entitlement that guaranteed aid to low-income families, abridging the web of subsidiary rights and entitlements that went along with it.[4] With the exception of federal civil rights against discrimination, the new law "leaves few remaining federal rights for welfare recipients."[5] These legal changes offer greater latitude to state policymakers, who are now free to "innovate" with less fear that they might provoke litigation by violating the rights of recipients.

This last point deserves more attention than it has so far received in discussions of the discretion given to the states by the 1996 law. The AFDC system established in 1935 allowed programs to vary substantially from state to state. State programs employed a diversity of means tests, benefit levels, forms of surveillance, and disciplinary procedures. Particularly during the first three decades of this system, poor families confronted a patchwork quilt of programs characterized by "length-of-residence requirements, pervasive invasion of privacy, and unregulated state discretion over eligibility conditions and the amounts of grants."[6]

In the 1960s, however, the wide latitude afforded to states under AFDC (and the resulting efforts to deter and discipline welfare recipients) became a target for welfare rights activists. Legal advocates won a series of landmark decisions that strengthened national standards for welfare provision. In *King v. Smith* (1968),[7] the U.S. Supreme Court struck down substitute-father rules on the ground that states could not establish their own criteria for making people ineligible unless authorized to do so by federal law. In *Shapiro v. Thompson,*[8] the Court ruled in 1969 that state durational residency requirements for the receipt of aid penalized the constitutional right to interstate travel and thereby denied equal protection of the law. In *Goldberg v. Kelly* in 1970,[9] the justices ruled that welfare benefits could not be denied without mechanisms of due process.

By recalling these key victories of welfare-rights advocates, one can see more clearly that the new TANF system does not move the nation forward into an unprecedented era of state experimentation. States enjoyed considerable discretion under the old AFDC system, and especially prior to the 1960s, they used this discretion in many "creative" ways to deter welfare receipt and promote work. The passage of the 1996 legislation was a watershed event, in part, because it reestablished some of the conditions of an earlier era in which states were free to exercise discretion without being shackled by the federal system of rights won by welfare advocates. The 1996 legislation marked a critical reversal of the trend toward national standards for the local administration of public aid.[10]

Despite these important changes, the 1996 legislation was not entirely the dramatic act of devolution that it is imagined to be in the laboratories-of-democracy metaphor.[11] To begin with, the new system imposes strict quotas on state policymakers. The percentage of adult recipients in each state who must participate in "work-related activities" was initially set at 25 percent of the caseload working 20 hours per week. These numbers rise to 50 percent of the caseload working 30 hours per week by the year 2002. The law also constrains states by defining "work-related activities" quite narrowly, limiting education and training to no more than one year. After this time, states must force recipients to take immediate jobs or work in community service. As amended, the law further limits the number of clients in education and training programs to no more than 20 percent of those counted as part of the work quota.

Although the 1996 law gives states more latitude in some financial decisions, it also imposes significant new prohibitions on state spending. Just as state officials are barred from using federal welfare dollars to support more than a single year of education and training, they also cannot spend these funds on unemployed clients who have received assistance for more than two years. Additional time limits in the law prohibit the states from using federal funds to assist poor people who have received aid for more than five years in a lifetime. Finally, the federal government also severely constrained state policymakers' abilities to use public assistance to aid legal immigrants.

Thus, it is not entirely the case that the 1996 law was an act of devolution. There is, of course, a grain of truth to the laboratories-of-democracy metaphor. For those who wish to pursue the twin policy goals of enforcing work and paring the welfare rolls, federal restrictions have been significantly cut back. Many states took advantage of waivers to pursue these goals under the old AFDC system. However, the new law provides states with even greater leeway to set strict limitations and impose tough sanctions on recipients, including termination. In addition, under the 1996 law, states' TANF appropriations are only required to be 75 percent of what they were for AFDC in 1994 (80 percent if the state fails to meet its work quota). The law also allows each state to divert up to 30 percent of its federal grant to other, related areas of spending. State officials who wish to emphasize immediate work over welfare are not required to spend this portion of the block grant on cash assistance at all.

With fewer federal constraints, states appear to have pursued new policies, and achieved dramatic results. Early reports have shown significant declines in the number of people receiving assistance. In truth, these declines began in most states in 1993, before PRWORA was enacted in 1996. They can be attributed partly to improvement in the economy, and partly to experimentation by the states authorized through waivers received under the old AFDC program. Still, recent reports suggest that states have indeed been using their new-found discretion under TANF in a variety of effective ways, such as imposing sanctions on families that fail to fulfill the new requirements.[12] The welfare rolls declined 31 percent nationwide from June 1993 to September 1997. In some states, the declines have been much higher, exceeding 50 percent in Alabama, Colorado, Louisiana, Mississippi, Oregon, South Carolina, Tennessee, and Wyoming, while surpassing 60 percent in Wisconsin and 70 percent in Idaho.[13]

With this decline in the rolls, most states have realized a short-term revenue surplus that offers them greater flexibility than was perhaps first anticipated. Because TANF block grants are fixed for each state (based on the state's choice of any annual appropriation received between 1992 and 1995), the 49 states that have experienced declines in their rolls over the last three years now have fewer recipients with the same amount of money.[14] In responses, some states have exercised their new prerogative to cut spending. However, most have not cut as deeply as they are allowed. Instead, they have chosen to invest more on each remaining recipient in a concerted effort to move them out of welfare.[15] In these decisions, we see evidence that the discretion afforded to the states by the new law is both real and effective within the narrow field defined by the goal of moving recipients out of welfare.

By contrast, the image of 50 unfettered laboratories bears little resemblance to the situation confronted by state officials who hope to pursue other welfare policy goals. The 1996 law did not enhance state discretion so much as it redistributed it. The extra latitude granted to state officials who want to eliminate welfare dependency came at the expense of those who view welfare programs as a positive tool of government that can be used to support and invest in poor communities. The great irony of the term "democracy" in the laboratory metaphor is that the new law severely limits policymakers' abilities to use federal funds to pursue inclusive civic goals. State officials cannot use federal funds to support the long-term education of the poorest citizens; they are forbidden from using these funds to ease the incorporation of legal immigrants into the social, political, and economic lives of their communities; and they are forced to turn their backs on those citizens who have remained marginalized from the market for more than five years. For these and other goals, state policymakers now confront stronger barriers from the federal government than they did under AFDC.

Federal standards on the use of the block grants have set strict work quotas and time limits for the states, and have established penalties for failure to meet them. States that realize a revenue surplus are free to cut back on benefits or redirect their savings. But whatever they do, they must now follow the overriding federal objective of moving recipients off of welfare and into paid employment as quickly as possible. This is the nature of discretion under the new federal framework. State policymakers must fit into it or face the consequences.

Welfare Reform in a Federal System and the Specter of Migration

Beyond the specificity of the federal mandates, there are additional reasons to question the blanket claim that the 1996 law dramatically enhanced state discretion. To begin with, this claim generally asserts change without acknowledging the prior state of affairs. As we have already noted, under AFDC, states always retained significant discretion in setting benefit levels and eligibility requirements. In fact, as Theda Skocpol has pointed out, AFDC itself did not radically revise the state focus of public assistance programs that predated its establishment in 1935.[16] The repeal of AFDC has left intact a system that has always relied heavily on the states for provision of public assistance.

Recognizing this strand of historical continuity is important for two reasons. First, it belies the idea that a "devolution revolution" has suddenly liberated 50 servants of the federal government. Second, by examining the history of state discretion before and during the AFDC system, it is possible to see that state policymakers are subject a variety of informal pressures that can limit the ways they use their discretion. Pressures that have little do with federal rules have traditionally worked against innovations that deviate sharply from policies in other states. In particular, policymakers have tended to resist reforms that might make their states less attractive to businesses as well as those that might make their states more attractive to poor people. Through both of these mechanisms, states are pressured to compare their own policies with those of their neighbors—a form of "checking over the shoulder" that undermines each state's ability to be creative in exercising its discretion.

State-run public assistance programs have traditionally been vulnerable to the economic pressures exerted by business mobility. Under the penalty of losing jobs to other states (and sometimes political support to other candidates), state officials experience pressure to create better business climates by using welfare programs to enforce low-wage work as well as by cutting program budgets and related taxes. As Frances Fox Piven and Richard Cloward have argued, "[I]n the twentieth century, it is the state governments that are more sensitive to business political pressures, simply because states (and localities) are far more vulnerable to the threat of disinvestment. This has been true for a long time."[17]

Historically, federal involvement has served as a partial buffer against these sorts of pressures, especially in the nationalized social insurance programs, but also through the AFDC matching formulas that kept states from needing a dollar of additional revenue for every additional dollar spent on public assistance. By contrast, the new TANF system does almost nothing to insulate state officials from business pressures against liberal policy innovations. In fact, by ending federal matching formulas and giving states more control over spending, the new law seems likely to heighten their effect. Evidence suggests that state policymakers are keenly aware of business mobility and its relationship to welfare-policy decisions.[18]

The pressures exerted by the threat of business disinvestment are exacerbated by a second (and far more widely discussed) fear that is equally likely to promote conformity and conservatism in state policymaking—the fear that any state that is too liberal in its approach will become a "welfare magnet" attracting the poor from other states.[19] The idea that more generous benefits will lead to the in-migration of poor people has become a mainstay in welfare policy debates over the past two decades, especially in states offering higher benefits.[20] It is precisely because this idea generates such fear among state officials that some observers have invoked the more unsettling metaphor of a "race to the bottom" to describe the ways states are likely to use their discretion over welfare policy.[21]. . .

By highlighting the issue of welfare migration, and by enhancing some forms of discretion for state officials, the devolution of 1996 has raised interstate policy comparisons to a far more prominent place in the policymaking process. Each state is at risk of being "left behind" by the others, yet cannot be too sure what the others are doing. In this environment, just tracking the activities of other states has become a full-time activity.[22] To the extent that states try to repel would-be migrants by mimicking the restrictive policies of their neighbors, they will retreat from the challenge of serving as innovative "laboratories" seeking out new ways to combat poverty. . . .

Just as formal mandates from the federal government restrict the creativity of state officials to a relatively narrow field of policy goals, fears of business disinvestment and welfare migration also discourage policymakers from pursuing initiatives that might distinguish them from other states. From this perspective, states under the new system seem far less likely to serve as "laboratories of democracy" than to "race to the bottom."

Without Cause or Effect

To this point, we have raised a number of critical questions for the laboratories-of-democracy metaphor. We have challenged its image of free experimentation by underscoring the potential for pack-like behavior that is commonly captured in the phrase, "race to the bottom." Now, we turn to this second metaphor, offering reasons for skepticism regarding the welfare-magnet thesis that serves as its premise. In their most common form, discussions of a race to the bottom have tended to bypass the idea that state responses reflect the real threat of business disinvestment, and have rejected the view that policymakers are simply reacting to unsubstantiated and long-standing fears of the migrant poor. Instead, the race-to-the-bottom metaphor has been premised on the claim that welfare magnetism is quite real; it has a real cause in the form [of] wide benefit variation across the states, and it has a real effect in the form of migration toward states that offer more generous benefits.[23]

Interstate benefit variation and welfare migration are both treated as truisms in welfare policy circles, allowing the myth of welfare migration to shape state actions in ways that may very well produce a race to the bottom.[24] In what follows, however, we suggest that neither the cause nor the effect in this influential tale stand up well to empirical scrutiny.

Empirical research on the effect in question, the migration of welfare recipients to states with higher benefits, has provoked much debate. Successive waves of studies have shifted the consensus among analysts. The earliest studies based on aggregate data suggested that welfare migration did not exist to any great degree.[25] A second wave of studies offered evidence that welfare migration might exist after all.[26] Writing in 1992, at the tale end of this wave, Robert Moffitt concluded a review of the welfare-incentive literature by stating that the research on migration was "suggestive but inconclusive."[27]

Over the past five years, however, a third wave of studies has illuminated a number of weaknesses in earlier measurement techniques, and has consistently pointed to the conclusion that welfare migration is largely nonexistent.[28] In a typical summary of this last wave of research, the authors of one recent study conclude that "the annual level of welfare migration for the 1985–90 period, and probably for other periods, is quite small . . . [and] the migration routes of poor single mothers with children are not associated with higher welfare benefits."[29] In summary, the existing literature does not support the claim that even moderate numbers of recipients move out of state in order to obtain higher benefits. Indeed, while recipients do sometimes move from one community to another, more than 90 percent of their moves are within-state.[30]

We suggest a simple reason why welfare-migration effects do not seem to occur very often. Their purported cause, benefit variation, has been badly overrated. Despite the discretion states always had to set AFDC benefits, it is simply not clear that benefits offered under the old system actually varied enough to matter to recipients. Moreover, there is little evidence to suggest that states have responded to the new TANF block grant by dramatically revising their benefit schedules. In 1997, as in past years, most states left their benefit levels unchanged; three states raised benefits while six lowered them.[31] Thus, the structure of incentives assumed to bring about welfare migration has remained substantially the same in recent periods. According to the welfare-magnet thesis, this structure includes enough benefit variation to motivate migration. We see good reasons to balk at this claim. . . .

. . . Due to declines in the real-dollar value of cash benefits, the basic welfare package of cash assistance and Food Stamps now covers less than two-thirds of the average recipient family's expenditures.[32] Research has shown that welfare checks no longer cover the cost of necessities; recipients must look to close kin, off-the-books employment, and elsewhere to cover additional expenses.[33] Thus, the contemporary reality is that people who rely on welfare checks go broke everywhere. The odds that a recipient family can change this outcome by moving to a state with higher benefits are slim, given that such a move is likely to entail higher housing costs and the loss of informal kin support. Indeed, insofar as recipients cannot be sure how much informal support might lie across the state border, welfare benefits are not likely to offer a clear signal to a better standard of living.

This last observation also suggests an important methodological point. As the gap grows between what recipients spend each month and what they get from government, so too does the amount of "slippage" in studies that measure the economic allure of a state by its welfare benefits. To the extent that welfare migration forces recipients to give up the informal networks of support they enjoy in their home communities,[34] higher benefits in a neighboring state may actually represent a lower overall income.

To sum up, then, we find little evidence suggesting that a "race to the bottom" could be driven by *real* welfare-magnet effects. Consulting the relevant empirical studies, we discover that the effect alleged in the magnet thesis, migration toward higher benefit states, is an exceedingly rare phenomenon. . . . Thus, while the race-to-the-bottom metaphor may or may not offer an accurate image of welfare policymaking in the states, the suggestion that this race is a response to the behaviors of welfare recipients should be viewed with suspicion. Motives for such a race can easily be found in the threat of business disinvestment and in *fears* about the migrant poor. Yet, they cannot be traced to real disparities in benefits or to migration behaviors.

The Uncertainty of Rules, the Irony of Welfare Reform

Having identified weaknesses in both the laboratories-of-democracy metaphor and its counterpart, the race-to-the-bottom metaphor, we are now in a position to draw the two together. Earlier, we acknowledged that states are likely to engage in experimentation under the new system, but suggested that the scope of this activity is likely to be constrained by the narrow federal mandates to enforce work and pare the rolls. In this section, we survey some of the state policy changes that have occurred to date, and ask how they are likely to affect the incentives for welfare migration that purportedly fuel the "race to the bottom."

Despite all the talk about procedural experimentation in the states, surprisingly little consideration has been given to how these changes might influence the likelihood of migration. We suggest that administrative changes in state welfare programs are likely to affect the odds of welfare migration in two different ways, depending on their intensity.

In the short term, if procedural changes proliferate but remain moderate, recipients will face greater uncertainty about their eligibility and the treatment they can expect in other states' programs. Poor family heads who have these sorts of doubts strike us as even less likely to migrate in search of meager increases in benefits. In the long term, however, if states become more restrictive and draconian, the new system may create stronger incentives for migration. Small benefit disparities and moderate procedural differences are unlikely to produce migration because they do not present recipients with clear incentives. By contrast, the denial of essential assistance in one's home state through time limits or sanctions will clarify interstate comparisons quite a bit. Thus, we suspect that while welfare migration is unlikely to arise from the "pull" of slightly more generous benefits, it can effectively be created through the "push" of deprivation.

Significant procedural differences across the states reflect a continuation of developments that began long before the passage of the 1996 law. From 1962 to 1996, Section 1115 of the Social Security Act authorized the Secretary of Health and Human Services to waive federal requirements in order to enable a state to initiate an experimental, pilot, or demonstration project that could help better realize the objectives of AFDC.[35] By mid-February 1996, all but ten states (Alaska, Idaho, Kansas, Kentucky, Maine, Nevada, New Hampshire, New Mexico, Rhode Island, and Tennessee) and the District of Columbia had approval to test departures from specified provisions of AFDC.[36] Under the new law, although states must meet their work quotas, they are still able to obtain some additional procedural discretion through the continuation of waivers. Of the 43 states with waivers in place when the new law was signed, 30 continued them in 1997, 19 on a statewide basis.[37]

These waivers have combined with the new forms of state discretion under TANF to produce a complex and rapidly changing landscape of welfare provision. For recipients, this environment has the potential to foster a paralyzing uncertainty, especially regarding decisions to move to a new state with an unfamiliar welfare program. Eligibility requirements have become so complex and now vary so much that recipients cannot be sure that they will receive any benefits in a neighboring state. Likewise, the proliferation of different participation requirements, oversight mechanisms, and rewards and punishments all make it more difficult for a recipient to predict the treatment she might receive in her new state. States also differ significantly in how they calculate assets and income, grant exemptions from burdensome requirements, and determine access to valuable benefits like housing vouchers.

With increasing frequency, recipients who might consider moving out of state now confront the possibility of restrictive barriers across the border. In response to the federal mandates, widespread fears of welfare migration, and state officials' own desires to end welfare dependency, the direction of recent policy innovations has been, not surprisingly, toward restriction. As states take advantage of their new capacity to tighten requirements and make their programs less attractive, they simultaneously fan fears of welfare migration among their neighbors. As a result, many states have exercised their new freedom to set up different eligibility standards for applicants who have lived instate for less than twelve months.

Beyond these now repudiated barriers to migration, recipients may also find that changes in broader rules make their families eligible in one state but not in another. For example, 21 states have instituted "family caps" which deny additional aid for children born while the mother is receiving public assistance. In addition, states vary in how long they will provide assistance to two-parent families who are needy because their principal wage earner is unemployed. After 30 September 1998, states are free to end such aid altogether—a provision of the new law that returns states to the flexibility they had before the Family Support Act of 1988 required them to offer assistance to two-parent families for at least six months in a year. As of February 1996, 12 states already had time limits on this support: Arizona, Arkansas, Colorado, Florida, Georgia, Nevada, North Dakota, South Dakota, Texas, Utah, Virginia, and Wyoming. These states are likely candidates to think about terminating assistance to two-parent families in 1998.

Recipients may also find that they are ineligible in a nearby state because of individual characteristics. For example, the 1996 law requires states to deny aid to parents if they are under 18 unless they live in an "adult-supervised setting;" but also gives states latitude in determining exemptions. Consequently, young parents are likely to be eligible in some states but not in others. Under the new system, states can also deny aid to persons convicted of drug felonies after 22 August 1996. In 1997, 33 states said they would do so. Eight states, including New York, also exercised their option to require drug testing.

Diversity and restrictiveness in state welfare programs have also been enhanced by the proliferation of new conditions for the continued receipt of aid. In addition to the well-known workfare requirements, states used waivers under the old AFDC system to add conditions such as learnfare (which makes aid contingent on children's school attendance) as well as other "fares" that imposed additional constraints. Under the new system, states can specify all of these conditions and more. For example, some states now require recipients to sign "Individual Responsibility Plans" explaining how they will make the transition from welfare to work, and penalize recipients for not fulfilling provisions of the plans.

As time goes on, recipients will also increasingly confront restrictions arising from time limits; and these too will vary across states. Although states cannot spend federal TANF funds on any recipient who has participated for more than two years without engaging in "work-related activities," they are free to set limits that are stricter than the two-year mark. Twenty-seven have done so, with thirteen requiring immediate work as a condition of aid. Similarly, while states cannot use federal TANF funds to assist any family with a recipient who has exceeded the five-year lifetime limit, states are once again allowed to specify stricter time limits. Twenty-one have done so, with twelve specifying a two-year lifetime limit. In fifteen states, recipients would find *both* shorter lifetime limits and stricter work requirements than are mandated by the federal law.

In the area of work requirements, states vary tremendously in what they count, in the support services they provide, and in the extent to which they grant exemptions. While some states have continued to help recipients pursue an education by allowing their activities to fulfill the work requirement, most have put more stress on immediate paid employment with no support for education and training after the first year. States also vary in the extent to which they provide child-care services. Because large numbers of recipients have traditionally combined welfare and work for at least part of their time on public assistance, the availability of quality child care has always been an important consideration for many welfare recipients. It is likely to become an even more essential support service now that recipients are required by new rules to devote greater portions of their time to seeking out and preparing for paid employment.

Finally, states also vary considerably in how they grant exemptions from various requirements. Under the 1996 law, states can exempt up to 20 percent of their caseloads from time limits, and can exercise some choice over how to allocate these exemptions. For example, some states may exempt parents with children below a certain age, while others may implement the Domestic Violence Option to exempt women at risk of battering and abuse. By the end of 1997, work exemptions included domestic violence in 27 states, medical disability in 33 states, mental health problems in 30 states, and AIDS in 26 states. Such procedural differences across states are, of course, critical determinants of the value of welfare for the large numbers of recipients who have these problems.

In summary, while the administration of welfare programs has always differed across states, this procedural variation has been greatly expanded under TANF. In this climate, it strikes us as untenable to focus narrowly on benefit variation when attempting to determine how state welfare programs might influence the residential decisions of poor families. A broad array of other institutional factors are likely to matter to recipients, and many of these are critical determinants of whether a family will actually be able to receive benefits in a given state.

Our point, of course, is not that recipients are aware of all these details regarding state programs. On the contrary, our argument is that the staggering rate and number of these restrictive policy changes force recipients to reason through their residential decisions under conditions of profound uncertainty. Welfare migration simply does not seem very likely if one considers the plight of a poor single parent who currently survives by relying on informal support and a familiar welfare program, who confronts uncertain conditions across the state border, and who has everything to lose by making the wrong decision.

Thus, in the short term, we expect that there will continue to be an absence of incentives strong enough to motivate welfare migration. Cash benefits continue to vary too little to induce migration, and welfare administration now varies so much that it can hardly be expected to present clear incentives to recipients. This balance of incentives could all be changed, however, in the long term. If absolute time limits come to affect larger numbers of recipients, and if states pursue increasingly stringent exclusionary practices, recipients will no longer have to consider subtle differences between state programs. Like the families who fled the American "dustbowl" in the 1930s, they will simply have to conclude that they cannot survive on "nothing," and that "something" is at least possible elsewhere.

Conclusion

What, then, should we make of the two major metaphors used to describe the current era of welfare federalism? Consider, first, the hopeful image of experimentation in the states. With a bold stroke, devolution was supposed to create 50 laboratories of democracy in which state policymakers act independently to devise better programs for meeting the needs of public assistance recipients. This image is misleading for several reasons. First, it ignores the fact that states have maintained substantial control over public assistance throughout the past two centuries. Second, this metaphor constructs a false image of enhanced state discretion by focusing attention on the new opportunities that have been created in relation to a relatively narrow set of policy goals. The laboratories-of-democracy metaphor obscures the fact that the 1996 laws also imposed significant new federal mandates on the states that now serve as powerful barriers to liberal policy innovations.

Third and finally, images of free state experimentation are misleading because they fail to acknowledge the powerful social dynamics identified by the race-to-the-bottom metaphor. By releasing state officials to act on their fears of welfare migrants, the devolution of 1996 may actually have sown the seeds of conformity. State policymakers have made it clear that they want to avoid becoming welfare magnets. As a result, they seem most likely to follow the pack—to use their newfound discretion defensively to avoid becoming more liberal than other states. Emulation, not innovation, seems to be the name of the new welfare game.

We hasten to add, however, that the rival image of a "race to the bottom," at least in its typical rendering, also has significant limitations. To see these problems, it is helpful to clarify that the race-to-the-bottom thesis does more than predict that states will collectively move toward more restrictive policies; it asserts an explanation for this collective movement. States could follow one another closely in implementing restrictive policies for any of a variety of reasons. For example, they might do so because they must follow the federal government's mandates, or because their elected officials share a common ideology. The race-to-the-bottom thesis presents an alternative explanation for such conformity based on the aggregation of each state's rational response to the problem of welfare-magnet effects. It is this explanation, not the identification of a general tendency toward conformity, that we find suspect.

Specifically, we have raised three complaints. First, discussions of the race to the bottom have typically presumed that it is driven by real disparities in welfare benefits that produce real patterns of migration toward higher benefit states. The evidence suggests that this is not the case. The net value of welfare benefits for recipients does not vary much at all across the states, and recent studies show little evidence of migration toward more generous states. Second, by presuming the reality of welfare migration, discussions of the race to the bottom have obscured more critical factors affecting the actions of state policymakers. Here, we refer to the ways in which anti-welfare advocates have manipulated long-standing fears regarding poor people as well as to the very real threat of business disinvestment.

Third, by focusing attention narrowly on benefit levels, the welfare-magnet thesis has obscured other factors that may be more central to recipients' residential decisions and more central to the states' racing behavior. Put simply, benefit levels are not "where the action is." Recipients do not appear to migrate in response to them, and states do not appear to be using their discretion to revise them. Under the new mandates, states have been far more likely to impose restrictions on eligibility, to develop new forms of sanctions, and to set new conditions for program participation. We find it very plausible that these actions by individual states may, in turn, spur other states to respond in kind. In this scenario, the race to the bottom may turn out to be over who can set the most restrictions and impose the largest number of sanctions.

The great irony of welfare reform is that, as states reshuffle themselves in this game of follow-the-leader, they may actually create the very welfare migration they fear. Although recipients under the old system might not have had strong enough incentives to migrate, the case will be different for recipients who are barred from aid in their current state of residence. States that move expeditiously to tighten time limits and work requirements may actually force poor people to flee to other states. Welfare migration has probably been no more than a ghost haunting welfare reform in the past. But if that ghost succeeds in generating a procedural race to the bottom, it may create a class of impoverished migrants that is very real.

Notes

1. Richard P. Nathan, "The Newest New Federalism for Welfare: Where Are We Now and Where Are We Headed?" (Albany, NY: Rockefeller Institute, State University of New York, 30 October 1997).
2. See John D. Donahue, *Disunited States: What's at Stake as Washington Fades and the States Take the Lead* (New York: Basic Books, 1997). p. 13.
3. Ibid., p. 67.
4. See Gwendolyn Mink, *Welfare's End* (Ithaca, NY: Cornell University Press, 1998), p. 50; Sanford F. Schram and Carol S. Weissert, "The State of American Federalism: 1996–1997," *Publius: The Journal of Federalism* 27 (spring 1997): 1–32.
5. Sherry Leiwant and Yolanda Wu, "Civil Rights Protections and Welfare Employment Programs," *Clearinghouse Review* (January–February 1998): 454.
6. Rand E. Rosenblatt, "Legal Entitlement and Welfare Benefits," *Politics of Law: A Progressive Critique,* ed. David Kairys (New York: Pantheon, 1982), p. 266.
7. *King v. Smith,* 392 U.S. 309 (1968).
8. *Shapiro v. Thomson,* 394 U.S. 618 (1969).
9. *Goldberg v. Kelly,* 397 U.S. 254 (1970).
10. See Mink, *Welfare's End,* pp. 50, 133–139.
11. Schram and Weissert, "The State of American Federalism: 1996–1997," 1–32; Mink, *Welfare's End,* pp. 133–139; John Kincaid, "The Devolution Tortoise and the Centralization Hare," *New England Economic Review* (May/June 1998): 13–40.
12. Barbara Vobejda and Judith Havemann, "Sanctions: A Force Behind Falling Welfare Rolls," *Washington Post,* 23 March 1998, p. A1; "CDF, New Studies Look at Status of Former Welfare Recipients," *CDF Reports* (April/May 1998); National Conference of State Legislatures, "Tracking Recipients After They Leave Welfare: Summaries of State Follow-up Studies" (Denver, CO: NCSL, February 1998).
13. See United States Department of Health and Human Services, *Administration for Children and Families,* August 1998; World Wide Web: Internet Citation: http://www.acf.dhhs.gov/news/caseload.htm.
14. Richard Wolf, "States Plug Budget Gaps with Welfare Windfalls," *USA Today,* 24 March 1997, p. A1.

15. See Jack Tweedie, "Welfare Spending: More for Less," (Denver, CO: National Conference of State Legislatures, March 1998; World Wide Web: Internet Citation: http://www.ncsl.org/statefed/welfare/spendin.htm.
16. See the comments of Theda Skocpol in the symposium "Welfare: Where do We go from Here?" *The New Republic* 215 (12 August 1996): 19–22. Also see Theda Skocpol, *Protecting Soldiers and Mothers: The Political Origins of Social Policy in the United States* (Cambridge, MA: The Belknap Press of Harvard University Press, 1992), pp. 525–526.
17. Frances Fox Piven and Richard A. Cloward, *The Breaking of the American Social Compact* (New York: The New Press, 1997), pp. 71–72.
18. Donahue, *Disunited States,* pp. 56–74.
19. Paul E. Peterson and Mark C. Rom, *Welfare Magnets: A New Case for a National Standard* (Washington, D.C.: The Brookings Institution, 1990).
20. See Russell Hanson and David T. Hartman, "Do Welfare Magnets Attract?" Discussion Paper No. 1028-14 (Madison, WI: Institute for Research on Poverty, University of Wisconsin-Madison, 1994).
21. Peterson and Rom, *Welfare Magnets,* pp. 12–23.
22. See National Governors' Association Center for Best Practices, Summary of Selected Elements of State Plans for Temporary Assistance for Needy Families as of 20 November 1997; World Wide Web: Internet Citation, 3 December 1998: http://www.nga.org/CBP/Activities/WelfareReform.asp, hereafter *State Plans for Temporary Assistance.*
23. The most influential work is Peterson and Rom, *Welfare Magnets.*
24. See Sanford F. Schram, Lawrence Nitz, and Gary Krueger, "Without Cause or Effect: Reconsidering Welfare Migration as a Policy Problem," *American Journal of Political Science* 42 (January 1998): 210–230.
25. Richard J. Cebula, "A Survey of the Literature on the Migration-Impact of State and Local Government Policies," *Public Finance/Finages Publiques* 1 (winter 1979): 69–84.
26. Peterson and Rom, *Welfare Magnets,* pp. 50–83; Thomas R. Dye, "The Policy Consequences of Intergovernmental Competition," *Cato Journal* 10 (spring/summer 1990): 59–73.
27. Robert B. Moffitt, "Incentive Effects of the U.S. Welfare System: A Review," *Journal of Economic Literature* 30 (March 1992): 32–36.
28. Hanson and Hartman, "Do Welfare Magnets Attract?"; James R. Walker, "Migration Among Low-Income Households: Helping the Witch Doctors Reach Consensus," Discussion Paper No. 1031-94 (Madison, WI: Institute for Research on Poverty, University of Wisconsin-Madison, 1994); William H. Frey et. al., "Interstate Migration of the U.S. Poverty Population: Immigration 'Pushes' and Welfare Magnet 'Pulls,' " Research Report No. 95-331 (Ann Arbor, MI: Population Studies Center, University of Michigan, 1995); Phillip B. Levine and David J. Zimmerman, "An Empirical Analysis of the Welfare Magnet Debate Using the NLSY," Working Paper No. 5264 (Cambridge, MA: National Bureau of Economic Research, 1995); Carole Roan Gresenz, "An Empirical Investigation of the Role of AFDC Benefits in Location Choice," Working Paper Series 97-05, DRU-1611-RC (Santa Monica, CA: Rand Corporation, 1997); Schram, Nitz, and Krueger, "Without Cause or Effect," 210–230.
29. Schram, Nitz, and Krueger, "Without Cause or Effect," 227.
30. Ibid., 220.
31. American Public Welfare Association, *State-by-State Welfare Reform Policy Decisions* (Washington, D.C.: September 1997), pp. 22–24; hereafter APWA.
32. Kathryn Edin and Laura Lein, *Making Ends Meet: How Single Mothers Survive Welfare and Low-Wage Work* (New York: Russell Sage Foundation, 1997), p. 43.
33. Ibid., pp. 21–45.
34. Carol Stack, *Call to Home* (New York: Basic Books, 1996), pp. xiii–xix.
35. U.S. House of Representatives, Committee on Ways and Means, *Background Material and Data on Programs Within the Jurisdiction of the Committee on Ways and Means, "The 1996 Green Book,"* WMCP: 104-14 (Washington, D.C.: U.S. Government Printing Office, 1996), June 1998, World Wide Web: Internet Citation: http://www.access.gpo.gov/congress/wm001.html; hereafter *The Green Book.*
36. See APWA, *State by State Welfare Reform Policy Decisions,* pp. 22–24 for the state breakdowns discussed in this section.
37. Ibid.

CASE STUDY 16

Introduction

In the preceding essay, Professors Schram and Soss question whether the TANF program leaves much room for states to play the role of laboratories of democracy. The law does not give the states complete freedom in deciding how they want to handle welfare. Rather it places restrictions on some state activities and allows some flexibility elsewhere. Not everyone, however, sees TANF as being as restrictive as Schram and Soss suggest. Some welfare experts and state politics scholars point to the experiences in many states as indicators of the potential for innovation that is allowed under TANF. Of all the states held up as examples, the one that is routinely cited as the most innovative is Wisconsin.

Wisconsin had already begun to make a name for itself in pursuing welfare reform before the passage of PRWORA. In the late 1980s, for example, the state introduced a new welfare policy that was dubbed "Learnfare," which required teenagers to attend school for their families to receive welfare benefits. In 1992, the state introduced "Bridefare," a program that provided financial incentives to teenage parents to encourage them to marry and refrain from having additional children. In 1993, the state legislature took the extreme step of voting to dismantle the state's welfare system by December 31, 1998. In passing the legislation, however, the legislature did not lay out what would replace the welfare system.

After the legislature's vote, Wisconsin Governor Tommy Thompson worked with policy experts from the Hudson Institute, a conservative research organization based in Washington, D.C., to create a new welfare program. The result of this collaboration was the creation of Wisconsin Works, an ambitious program that sought to eliminate cash assistance to the poor and replace it with work requirements. The program, which is known popularly as W-2, was signed into law in March 1996 and is now considered the state's TANF program. W-2 is considered different from programs in other states both in the harshness with which it requires welfare recipients to look for work and in its willingness to provide additional support to the poor that other states are not providing. For example, Wisconsin requires participants to immediately begin looking for work in order to receive benefits, whereas some states allow for a grace period. On the other hand, Wisconsin has been much more generous than other states in providing childcare support to welfare recipients.

The reading that follows provides an overview of the W-2 program in the late 1990s. The reading describes some of the distinct aspects of Wisconsin's program and suggests that the initial impact of the program was beneficial. Since this essay was published in the *New York Times Magazine,* there has been considerable research on Wisconsin's efforts, and not all of it has been as positive as this story. However, the reading is valuable for shining light on TANF and the extent to which it provides states with an opportunity to act as laboratories of democracy. The author of the article is Jason DeParle, a respected staff writer for *New York Times Magazine.*

Questions to Consider

As you read the essay, these are some questions to consider:

- What are some of the key components of the Wisconsin Works program? In what areas does it seem to be the most innovative?
- How successful has Wisconsin Works been in overcoming poverty and moving the poor back into the workforce? What evidence does the author present to show its success? What other factors may explain why Wisconsin has seen a drop in its welfare rolls?
- Why is Wisconsin a leader in welfare reform? What specific events led it to adopt the new welfare program? What characteristics of the state in general make it more likely than other states to pursue innovative policies?

Getting Opal Caples to Work

Jason DeParle

"Ooooh, I was mad!" Opal Caples says, recalling the notice from the welfare office. "They said we had to start working for our welfare check! I said, 'How could they do this to us?' I didn't feel it was right, to take our money—that's for our children." And as a black woman living in Milwaukee's sprawling black ghetto, Caples detected a hidden agenda. No one talked about work rules in the 1930's, when "welfare was made for middle-class white women," she says. "They're really just targeting the black women."

A bright, animated, street-smart woman who punctuates her speech with knowing glances—you know what I'm talking about, her look insists—Caples is telling her story on the No. 12 bus one July afternoon as it shakes and wheezes down Teutonia Avenue, past the check-cashing counters, liquor stores and lounges. She has dropped her three young daughters with her cousin, Jewel (actually with Jewel's 13-year-old nephew, Little Chuck, since Jewel wasn't around), and before long she'll be toting trash and swabbing toilets in the gastrointestinal lab of a downtown hospital. It's second-shift work and she's unhappy that her girls are asleep by the time the No. 12 shakes home. "They don't even see me at night," she complains.

As the hours wear on, Caples never surrenders her contention that with the strict new work rules pushing people from the rolls, something dangerous and unfair is under way—crime, drugs and prostitution will rise, since "women gonna do what they gotta do." Yet it turns out she enjoys her work. "I like this job," she says that evening, mopping the lab with the radio loud. "Every job I had, you always had somebody gawking over you. This job ain't like that." She also likes the money, which is "more than welfare was giving you anyway." At times she even sounds as if she's campaigning for the work rules she distrusts. "You ain't dealing with the system," she says. "You ain't waiting on no man. You're doing for yourself." Then just as she seems half convinced, Caples mocks herself with a laugh. "Now if I could take a break and come back in a month!"

The program behind this tentative, conflicted handshake with work is by far the most daring to emerge since President Clinton signed last year's watershed law, imposing time limits on welfare recipients and devolving vast new authority to the states. Indeed, Wisconsin's effort represents the most complete rethinking of public assistance in the 62 years since women and children first began receiving Federal aid. For more

Jason DeParle, "Getting Opal Caples to Work," *New York Times Magazine,* August 24, 1997.

than a year, the state has imposed the nation's most stringent work requirements. But a week from now, on Sept. 1, cash assistance in Wisconsin will essentially end. The system that will take its place goes to unprecedented lengths to construct a safety net not around a check but around a job.

It is tougher than anything that has come before: virtually no one is exempt. It is also more generous than anything that has come before: the state is offering child care and health care not just to welfare recipients but to all low-income working families, and it is creating thousands of community-service jobs. It puts new power in private hands: the entire Milwaukee system has been put out to bid, to private job-placement agencies. It is a serious, risky, expensive attempt to offer taxpayers what they claim they want and what, until now, politicians have failed to provide: a system that makes work work.

And it leaves Caples, like 40,000 other Wisconsin recipients, crossing uncertain ground. Falling somewhere between easy cases and the hardest ones, she seems to operate with a kind of dual citizenship, fluent in the language of the streets and of the working world above. She is a high-school graduate of obvious intelligence whom employers like to hire. "I have a personality that attracts people to me—I do," she says accurately. But she loses jobs as fast as she finds them, and a few months after joining the hospital, she has supervisors fretting over her absences. That is to say she's the kind of woman—with untapped talents and unpredictable troubles—that the state, the nation, is seeking to transform.

A year ago, as President Clinton fulfilled his "end welfare" pledge, there was ample reason to worry. What had started four years earlier as a thoughtful plan to fix a broken system had dissolved into an election-year hazing of the poor. The long-term prospects of the new, state-controlled system remain unknown. No state has faced the economic downturn that will test its safety-net commitments. Only a handful of recipients have hit time limits. The competition among states to chase recipients away by withdrawing services and support—the feared race to the bottom—may still ensue.

But whether by luck or by design, the early returns offer three sources of modest reassurance—and all are on magnified display in Wisconsin, where a robust economy and a history of progressive state government may offer a best-case glimpse of what devolution can become. Nationwide, the rolls have dropped 26 percent from their historic high three years ago, and nearly a dozen states have seen declines of 40 percent or more. But none rival Wisconsin, where the rolls have plunged more than 60 percent since their peak a decade ago. While some of those leaving the rolls have fallen into a more abject form of poverty, early evidence suggests the vast majority have not. Like Caples, so far they appear more resourceful than some people feared.

The second welcome development is the cash. Under the logic of block grants—fixed payments pegged to the higher caseloads of a few years ago—the falling rolls have produced a windfall even larger than expected. States will receive about $2.6 billion more from the Federal Government this year than they would have under the old entitlement system, a 16 percent increase. While some of the money is being siphoned into tax cuts and roads, most states are spending at least part of it on new services for the poor. Michigan is investing in caseworkers. Illinois is spending on child care. If Wisconsin's ambitious gamble succeeds, no one should forget the price tag. Last year, the state spent about $9,700 for every family on welfare; this year, after converting to the new, work-based program, it will spend about $15,700. That's an increase of 62 percent, and it gives women like Caples new access to child care, health care and last-resort jobs.

A third hopeful sign—on uneven display elsewhere but unmistakable in Wisconsin—concerns what might be thought of as a new civic energy. Legislation alone cannot move four million welfare families into the work force. The effort will require the attention of governors, bureaucrats, employers, advocates and especially the front-line workers who have major new responsibilities. For years, the welfare office has languished in torpor. But now, across the country, it is becoming a focus of creativity, a locus of hot lines, van pools, clothing closets, resume classes—a place of policy chic.

Not all the news has been good. California and New York have just emerged from rancorous and immobilizing legislative battles that affect nearly a third of the nation's caseload. Texas has squandered its energy on a fight to hire private food stamp and Medicaid workers—peripheral players with no role in the central challenge of putting recipients to work. No major municipal bureaucracy has shown it can overcome the vast problems that take hold when caseloads are counted by the hundreds of thousands. If the race to the bottom is one danger, so is running in place. With the economy alone driving much of the caseload reduction, even a do-little system can look good.

But Wisconsin, the policy petri dish that produced unemployment insurance, might again be on to something big. Having stumbled into a vow to abolish welfare three years before the new Federal law, the state has had to confront, more than any other, the question of what should take its place. The effort to answer has brought a civic transformation along strange-bedfellow lines. The old program was chased away by a Democratic legislator, Antonio Riley, who was once on welfare himself. The new system is being generously financed by a Republican Governor, Tommy G. Thompson, who came to office pushing a welfare cut. It is being implemented in Milwaukee with the support of a Democratic Mayor, John Norquist, who is among Thompson's main rivals.

It doesn't take a crystal ball to picture all that could still go wrong. With her attendance problems, Caples has shown she can get a job—not that she can keep one. There are few opportunities for education and training. There may not be enough jobs to go around, and the jobs women find may not offer a route from poverty. Work may well be its own reward, but will it prove a broader elixir? It's possible that putting women to work will do nothing to shore up the prospects of men, and the absence of fathers may be the more corrosive force in the ghetto. To the extent the new system leads women to work, it also leads them away from their kids, who will be left in arrangements of varying quality. The effect on children is anyone's guess.

The economy could go bad.

Support services could erode.

Some people will surely fall through the cracks.

But these are simply the perennial concerns, and they have paralyzed policy for a generation. What's new, in Wisconsin at least, is that an unlikely constellation of characters has begun the work of addressing them.

The Legislator: He Knew Welfare Up Close

When Antonio Riley says that "67 percent of the people in my district are on some sort of public assistance," he is advertising his dismay and his bona fides. He makes the introduction as he drives west from downtown toward the low-rise ghetto whose 50,000 residents he represents in the state assembly. At 33, Riley has a crisp manner and New Democrat instincts. His shirt is starched. His district is not.

Once a settlement of prospering factory workers, the cityscape is marked by empty lots and hand-lettered signs on corner groceries that invite the use of food stamps. Riley's tour mixes in glimpses of an autobiography that once followed the same downward spiral. There's the house where the family lived before divorce and a stay on welfare; there's the house where Riley himself drew general relief. The tour is capped with a favorite line: "It's sort of ironic that someone like myself, someone who grew up at one point on welfare, was the one to blow up the system."

The plot began at a backyard picnic. In September 1993, Riley attended a party given by his former boss, Mayor John Norquist. Like most Democrats, they were exasperated with the state's welfare politics. Tommy Thompson, the Republican Governor, had fashioned a national reputation out of minor but well-publicized programs, and now he was at it again. Trying to beat Clinton in the race to "end welfare," Thompson was pushing a strict two-year limit—but only in two rural counties. "He was taking credit without doing anything," Riley says. The Democrats could go along as Thompson's popularity soared or continue to be cast as the defenders of a discredited system.

As the party progressed, Riley vented his frustration to an important behind-the-scenes player. Officially, David R. Riemer served as the Mayor's chief of staff. But for years his life had been consumed by an offbeat quest to kill off the welfare system and substitute a program of community-service jobs, like the New Deal's Works Progress Administration; he had even helped start a public-jobs experiment in Milwaukee called

New Hope. Hearing out Riley, Riemer threw down a dare: end it. Respond to the Governor's two-county demo by repealing welfare statewide. Riley was stunned and then intrigued—he considered welfare "a jailer of people." With the Mayor's blessing, he and Riemer met the following week and drafted a daring one-page bill. It would repeal Aid to Families with Dependent Children, then the main Federal welfare program, and replace it with minimum-wage work.

A plan to end welfare would seem to have unlimited appeal. In reality, it raised immobilizing questions about what should take its place. It's one thing to say that women like Caples should work. It's another to explain who will hire them, care for their children and insure they have health care.

Oddly enough it was the Democrats in Wisconsin who had contemplated bolder change, most notably Norquist, who had called for the repeal of A.F.D.C. as early as 1990. But by the fall of 1993, the legislature's Democrats were still deadlocked on the underlying issues. That's when Riley floated his stripped-down idea—end welfare by a specific date and work out the jobs program later. In a surprise move, the Democratic Speaker of the Assembly, Walter Kunicki, embraced the idea (he recalls conceiving it on his own), and it passed without a Republican vote.

Now, in a bizarre inversion of welfare politics, it was the Republicans' turn to squirm. The Democrats had become the welfare repealers. And the man out front was a black official who represented more recipients than anyone in the Assembly. The Republicans complained it wasn't a serious plan, and in a sense they were right. Half the Democrats voted for it just to put Thompson in a bind. Gerald Whitburn, the Secretary of Health and Social Services, denounced the move and all but promised the Governor's veto.

Then Whitburn had breakfast the next morning with the Governor himself. Thompson said he had no intention of a veto, and laid into him for suggesting it. By letting him end welfare without having to spell out the details, the Democrats had given him more of an opening than he ever could have won by himself. A few weeks later he signed the bill, pledging to end welfare no later than 1999.

No one had more than the vaguest idea of what would take its place.

The Program Director: He Hasn't Met a Recipient Unsuited for Work

The 91st Street headquarters of Milwaukee's Goodwill Industries is a 215,000-square-foot monument to the organization's motto: "We Believe in the Power of Work." Washing machines the size of freight cars fill one side of the factory, and a packing business turns the other into a shrink-wrapped cornucopia of soap, furniture polish, calendars and car locks. But the striking thing about the industrial tableau is the sight of some of the workers. There are people crossing the factory floor in wheelchairs. There are men and women with Down syndrome sorting parts through inch-thick glasses. It is the visual embodiment of Goodwill's quasireligious belief that labor is a gift everyone can give. And it is a scene that implicitly challenges the assumptions of the old welfare system, which offered cash to the able-bodied like Caples while expecting nothing in return.

The rethinking of the safety net that began four years ago has led to Goodwill's door. In designing the new program, Wisconsin Works, known locally as W-2, the state tried to make Milwaukee's 25,000 cases more manageable by dividing the city into six districts and inviting bids. Having won the contracts for two districts, Goodwill has become Wisconsin's largest welfare office, with 20 percent of the state's caseload. The $119 million contract brings the group new money to pursue its central mission of reducing the barriers to work. "We believe everyone can give something back," says William Martin, the earnest young executive in charge.

W-2 operates on the same assumption, conceiving a four-rung ladder of "work opportunities" meant to accommodate all recipients, no matter what their background or skills. At the top is a regular unsubsidized job. For those it deems "job ready," Goodwill will provide coaching, job leads and child-care subsidies, but not cash. For those a step behind, the W-2 agencies can create subsidized jobs with private employers. On the next rung down, there are "community-service jobs"—workfare slots that demand 30 hours a week for a grant of $555 a month. And those at the bottom of the ladder, often with addictions or mental illness, will find themselves in something called Transitions. The "work" might consist partly of drug treatment or physical therapy, but it should fill 28 hours a week for a grant of $518. (Thompson is pushing to raise the grants by 20 percent.) The point is that no one should be doing nothing.

In putting the system up for bid, the state hoped to attract new energy and ideas—to attract people like William Martin. Though Martin, 30, spent most of his earlier career in state and local government, he sometimes talks like a business student on No-Doz. He likes to talk about "getting to yes" and finding "win-win opportunities" for his clients. Welfare programs used to define their mission as "income maintenance." Martin's is called Workforce Solutions. He hopes to make Goodwill the city's pre-eminent staffing agency, the place where labor-starved employers can turn for a pool of prescreened, qualified workers. And he is offering bonuses to caseworkers with the best placement rates. "We start from a moral premise that it is simply unconscionable to leave somebody on welfare," he says. "If the goal is to get somebody out of poverty, the only way to do it is to get them a job that pays better."

W-2 pays better (for all but the largest families). Under A.F.D.C., a mother with two children received $9,456 a year in cash and food stamps. Under Thompson's plan, even Transitions would pay $10,668. A community-service job would pay $11,168. That's still 16 percent below the poverty line of $13,330 a flaw worthy of note. But the calculation changes significantly with the move to unsubsidized work. After food stamps and tax credits are added in and co-payments for child care and health insurance are taken out, even a minimum-wage job nets $16,524. (The plan to offer health care, on a sliding scale, to all low-wage workers is still being negotiated with Federal Medicaid officials.)

In theory all the supports should be in place next week when W-2 takes hold. But no one can be sure how it will work. One worry is that the contractors' financial incentives will backfire, and that they will deprive poor women of support. The W-2 agencies are being paid much like health-maintenance organizations—they get a fixed payment to serve a pool of families. The faster they whisk them off the rolls and into unsubsidized work, the more money they make. The longer they leave clients on the bottom rungs, drawing grants and expensive services, the less money they make.

To break even, Goodwill estimates it must cut its caseload in half over a 28-month period. That has never happened, and there's not much, besides good intentions and some vague contract language, to keep a W-2 agency from declaring the most hapless clients "job ready" and withdrawing support. When I assume in passing that someone with a third-grade education would start on the third rung, in community service, Martin interrupts. "That won't keep them from getting a job in this market." Who does he have in mind for Transitions? "An individual with two broken arms and two broken legs, or severe mental illness that has not been stabilized."

That's a long way from income maintenance.

"Look at the people who go to our corporate headquarters," Martin says. "They may have command of only one muscle. And they show up. And work. Every day! All these families can succeed." . . .

The Architect of Reform: He Wants to Make Welfare History

Ruddy, round, rumpled and balding, and smoking a cheap cigar, Jason Turner might sooner pass for a beer distributor than a welfare intellectual. But at 44, he has been puzzling over the subject for nearly three decades. He was still in junior high school in Darien, Conn., when an article on "welfare queens" jolted him. "It hadn't occurred to me that there were whole classes of people who didn't work and who basically existed on Government charity," he says. He wondered what would happen if everyone tried that. While other students scribbled football plays, Turner began sketching plans to replace welfare with work. He was still sketching decades later when Thompson asked him to design W-2.

With the program about to begin in Milwaukee, he took off recently to check on the two sites where it has been running since March. The first stop was Pierce County, a picturesque stretch of farms and factories on the Minnesota border—no one's idea of a welfare zone. Still, even Turner can't believe how much the rolls have fallen. A decade ago, the caseload peaked at 387. By March, when W-2 began, it had fallen to 43. It was reasonable, then, to suspect that those who remained would pose a formidable challenge.

Reasonable but wrong. Now as Turner arrives, there are only eight people still getting cash, and three just haven't been placed in W-2 yet. Two others are briefly exempt because they have infants under 12 weeks old. That essentially leaves a caseload of three, all in Transitions: one applying for disability benefits, one recovering from a car wreck and one on bed rest for a troubled pregnancy.

The rest simply made other plans after being classified "job ready." While some may have slid toward tragedy, the Pierce social workers don't think so. They found that 64 percent were employed and that 19 percent had other income from family or friends. There was no information on the remaining 17 percent, but none wound up in the child welfare system, and none have called for help.

Driving out of town, Turner says he's seeing welfare history in the making. In the past, analysts have warned that the bottom third or so of the caseload may well be unreachable, and with that in mind, most work programs have included sizable exemptions. By contrast, in designing W-2, Turner pushed the principle of immediate, universal work—no exemptions, exceptions or delays. The real test won't occur until next month, when W-2 takes hold in Milwaukee, but the vanishing Pierce caseload deepens his conviction. "We're finding that everyone can work," Turner says.

Not much in his early life would have pointed him toward the poor. His father was an advertising executive who marketed Zest and Crest. But by high school, Turner was planning factories where welfare recipients could assemble Christmas ornaments and reap "the dignity" of work. He joined the 1980 Reagan campaign and spent five years as a Federal housing official. Getting nowhere with his welfare ideas, he left to make his millions as a landlord—only to lose his shirt when the 25 apartments he bought in a poor Washington neighborhood were overrun with crack addicts. Still, he returned to government, as a senior welfare official in the Bush Administration, more street-smart than the average bureaucrat. "I got a ringside view for three years," he says.

Out of a job after the 1992 elections, Turner took a welfare job in Wisconsin state government. He arrived just before the Democrats killed off welfare, and the chance to design its replacement was literally an adolescent dream come true.

What's the hold of welfare policy? Turner, who has just left state government to start a consulting firm, the Center for Self-Sufficiency in Milwaukee, answers in near-religious terms. "It's plumbing the soul—figuring out why people do the things they do."

Arriving in Fond du Lac, the other experimental site, he finds more reasons to be buoyed. The caseloads have crashed—from 791 three years ago to 187 now. And the caseworkers seem, if anything, even tougher than Turner himself. Even a visit with Dick Schlimm, one of the town's leading advocates for the poor, produces only quibbles. If he were to design a system of his own, he says, it might pay higher wages, but "it probably wouldn't look too much different than W-2." An untouched Arch Deluxe graces the dashboard for hours, but Turner is off in the clouds. "Down to the very last line worker, they had taken to heart and acted on the conceptual framework of the reforms," he says.

The Shelter Operator: She Sees No Apocalypse Yet

When Barbara Vanderburgh was 13, her father gave his life to Christ—or more precisely, to the block-long building with the sign that proclaims, "Christ Died for Our Sins." Vanderburgh was sufficiently ambivalent about her father's decision to leave the phone company and run the Milwaukee Rescue Mission that she used to duck when riding in the family station wagon, which had "Rescue Mission" written on the side. "I didn't want people to think I was living there," she says.

Now the question is, how many others will be living there, too? Across the city, soothsayers are predicting disaster. Talk of "Nazism," "slavery" and orphanages abounds, and it brings to mind the more learned warnings offered last year by Senator Daniel Patrick Moynihan. "Just how many millions of infants we will put to the sword is not yet clear," he said, denouncing the new Federal law. "We will have children sleeping on the grates."

Events may still prove Moynihan right, but the apocalypse isn't now. Hunger and homelessness are on the rise: a system that supports families only if they work is bound to leave some more destitute. The question is whether to judge the casualties large or small—alarming or reassuring—in light of the vast changes under way. So far the evidence, while early and mixed, falls more on the reassuring side. "To be honest, we were braced for worse," says Vanderburgh, who now runs Joy House, the mission's family shelter.

The run-up to W-2 began in March 1996 when the city switched to a precursor system, known as "pay for performance." About half the city's recipients were placed in the program, including Caples, who greeted the development with such fury. The rules required her and others to spend 20 hours a week in a community-service job and another 12 hours looking for private work. Over the ensuing months, nearly 30 percent of the city's welfare families vanished from the rolls. Since the state refused to track them, no one can be sure where they've gone. But the evidence doesn't point toward catastrophe.

While homelessness is notoriously hard to measure, Joe Volk, the chairman of the Milwaukee Shelter Task Force, estimates that the number of families in shelters rose by about 25 percent last winter. On a given night that translates into about 41 additional families, or about 120 women and children. It's a lot when measured in human terms, but still a tiny minority of the 10,000 families who have left welfare.

The other available data hint at a similar story, of rising but manageable need. Requests for food assistance are up: the Hunger Task Force of Milwaukee saw activity at its food pantries rise by 14 percent last year. But the increase seems to be leveling off. Reports of child abuse and neglect are up. But they've risen for 12 of the last 14 years, and they are still lower than the 1994 peak. Crime, meanwhile, has declined.

One wouldn't expect the full impact to show up at once, and these numbers can be expected to rise. Inside the shelters themselves, two kinds of stories can be heard. For some women, the loss of a check merely punctuates a life of defeat. With the shelters full during a snowstorm last winter, I found myself driving a woman across town so she could sleep on a church floor. She had known that she would lose her check as soon as her work notice arrived; she was just too despondent to comply. "I stay depressed all the time," she said. It was an indescribably sad night, and one that mocks the word "reform."

But some women insist that the loss of a check can mark a turn for the better. Many of the women who have flooded Joy House are addicts, too distracted by their habits to meet the work requirements. "I'm here because I need to be here," one woman explained. "I was really jacked up." Homelessness isn't a drug treatment plan, but neither, Vanderburgh argues, was a no-strings-attached check. "People are afraid and they're looking for help," she says.

The Governor: He Has Become More Than a Budget Cutter

For years, Tommy Thompson's detractors waved him off as a welfare charlatan—a man grabbing big headlines with small programs while ignoring (or attacking) his critics. A centerpiece of his first governor's campaign was a modest benefit cut, with the savings shifted to job training. He moved on to Learnfare, whose chief virtue was its catchy name. Then came Bridefare and Work Not Welfare, the time-limited experiment he insisted on restricting to two rural counties. Meanwhile, he often addressed the issue with a belligerence that seemed nakedly political. When I spoke with him in 1994, just before he won a record third term, he was boasting that his programs made liberals feel like "their hearts had been cut out." Welfare, he said, was a "fantastic campaign issue."

Now the conventional wisdom about Thompson has changed: whatever W-2 may be, it is not tinkering. Antonio Riley's theory is that abolishing welfare has transformed Thompson, who understands his national reputation will be linked to the program taking its place. "He's come very far," he says. Mayor Norquist also tips his cap. "The Governor should be proud," he says, calling W-2 "perhaps the best welfare reform program in the country." Even Thompson embraces the theory of a New Thompson. "I'm a lot smarter now than I was 10 years ago," he recently told *The Milwaukee Journal Sentinel*. "I'm much more even tempered."

Curious about the change, I traveled to Madison late last month to join him for lunch. I caught him on a Thursday, the day he opens the residence grounds to the public, and our meal was interrupted by a crowd of women, staring through the dining-room windows with their noses pressed to the glass. Had they been able to listen in, they would not have heard an exercise in modesty. "Welfare reform in America would not have happened without me," he said.

At least Thompson has something to boast about now. To his credit, his theme throughout lunch concerned the need to invest. "I have debated conservatives who think that welfare reform is going to save money," he said. "And I have told them that changing a system from dependence to independence is going to cost more, because you have to put money into child care and into job training and medical care and transportation. The liberals have complimented me on that."

And after years of being accused of tinkering, Thompson chose an interesting word to describe his concerns about others. "I think other states are going to tinker with it too much," he said. "I'm somewhat fearful that they're going to have difficulty making the giant leap like we are in Wisconsin."

These are the right worries. Running a work program is costly and consuming—it involves endless skirmishes with legislatures, bureaucrats, advocates and unions of public employees, who fear being displaced. "You have to have a lot of stamina," Thompson warns. Reports from the biggest states are not reassuring. In New York and California, the rhetoric of work has far outpaced the needed bureaucratic change, and the heavy lifting is essentially being left to the counties. (So far, the work program in New York City, while impressive in size, is mostly for single adults.)

Awash for now in Federal money, other states are investing, especially in child care. But many are also pocketing a good part of the Federal windfall. Wisconsin has reinvested the whole Federal increase, raising its spending this year from $451 million to $645 million—a 43 percent jump in the overall budget even as caseloads fall. Thompson is spending large sums on child care, health care and caseworkers.

But his most intriguing move, and perhaps his most revealing, is his push to increase the grant levels themselves. This is, after all, the same Governor who cut benefits within months of taking office, and then froze them for the ensuing decade—spearheading an erosion, in real terms, of about 40 percent.

Now, as a signature move under the new, work-based system, Thompson is pushing for a 20 percent increase in grants. (Community-service jobs would rise to $673 from $555, and Transitions, the work program for the most disadvantaged, would rise to $628 from $518.) In advocating the raise, Thompson overrode his closest welfare aides, and he is battling his own party in the legislature. "We had the dollars to do it and I thought that we ought to do anything we can to make this program successful," he said. "It's brought in a lot of opponents and advocates to help make the system work, instead of standing outside the tent and throwing stones at it."

The hope is that the new support is a sign of things to come, here and elsewhere. In political terms, there are two ways to view last year's epochal debate. The fear, of course, is that killing the Federal entitlement simply insures the erosion of the safety net: that politicians can always find more appealing targets than poor people to spend money on. The counter hope, perhaps a wispy one, is that converting welfare recipients to workers, even in community-service jobs, will transform their political standing. Welfare benefits have dwindled for decades, but support for the "working poor" has recently flourished.

Extending the thought, a few analysts (most prominently, Mickey Kaus) have argued that by signing the law, President Clinton has set the stage for a broader resurgence of activist government. (And a jobs program for the underclass is certainly that.) Welfare wasn't just a political yoke on the Democratic Party; its failures were an impediment to the very idea that government can help the poor.

So far, both sides in the debate—the supporters of the new law and the critics—can claim vindication: the safety net is growing in some places and growing holes in others. But oddly enough, Wisconsin's experiment, in the hands of a Republican Governor, has emerged as the leading hope for what government—more government—might accomplish in the postwelfare era.

Not surprisingly, there are still important battles being fought along those very lines. Perhaps the most significant centers on the community jobs. To truly insure that women like Caples have work when they need it, the state may have to make the jobs an open-ended offer—a safety net of last resort. But Thompson, spooked by worries about "make work" jobs, has defined them only as short-term training. With rare exceptions, a W-2 participant can spend no more than six months in a single community-service job, and no more than two years in community service in a lifetime.

It's a view that, among other things, refuses to acknowledge the realities of recession. And so, when pressed, does Thompson. "We think a good share of the welfare people will not necessarily be the first ones laid off," he said.

What happens if W-2 gets caught in the vice of rising need and falling revenues is impossible to predict. But for now, Thompson has embraced an outline—of jobs, child care and health care for the broad working class—that would have been unthinkable even a few years ago. "I never dreamed we'd be at this point," he says.

The Recipient: Will She Learn to Live With Work?

Lumbering to a halt, the No. 12 bus leaves Opal Caples a half block from Sinai Samaritan Hospital, where she spends her evenings with a cleaning cart. Scrubbing and dusting for the next six hours, she offers a spirited monologue on the changes sweeping the city, but some of her bluntest criticisms are saved for herself. "I've always been able to work," Caples says. "I just don't always want to work."

But work runs in the family. "My mother was never on public assistance—she always worked," Caples says proudly. Indeed, her mother spent 22 years at a Zenith factory, often holding a second job while raising five children on her own. But when Caples is asked what she was like in her youth in Chicago, she breaks out in laughter. "Bad!" she says. "I was smart, but I was out of control. I hung around the gangs." Caples eventually conformed with the conventions of responsible behavior. She graduated from high school and got a job at Wendy's. She waited until she was 22 to marry, then waited a year longer to have children, to be sure the marriage would work. It didn't. Her husband quit his factory job for the flash of a drug hustler's life. He moved in with his pregnant girlfriend and left Caples living on welfare. As for their children—Sierra, 7; Kierra, 5, and Tierra, 4—"he don't call them, he don't see them, he don't buy them nothing."

As her life unraveled four years ago, her cousin Jewel invited her to Wisconsin. A week later, she was stepping off the bus, with five suitcases and three young children to her name. Though some academics dispute it, most people in Milwaukee are convinced that their generous benefits attract women from the immense Chicago ghettos 90 miles south. Caples says nothing to dispel the theory. Her monthly benefits shot up 50 percent (from $411 to $617), while her rent correspondingly fell. "It was easier to survive," she says.

And it was easy to find work on the side. Caples can list seven jobs she has held in the past four years, and there may well be ones she has forgotten. The usual problems arose—child-care emergencies, a terminally ill car—but they aren't what Caples emphasizes. "I knew I always had that welfare check!" she says. But the check got harder and harder to keep. There were "all kinds of goofy classes" and endless job-search regimens. Weary of the hassles, and seeing the W-2 deadline on the way, Caples found the hospital job in February. "With this W-2, you have to work—have to, know what I mean?" she says. "I think it's different for me now."

Is it? On the one hand, she seems to like the job. At $7.69 an hour, it pays more than she has ever made. It offers benefits—medical, dental and life insurance. And it also offers the chance to train for other hospital jobs, which could pay up to $10 an hour. Though it involves emptying trash and cleaning toilets, she seems to feel it offers a certain status. She talks with delight about being invited to a company picnic and having doctors know her name. On the other hand, she hates working second shift, and like many inner-city women, she distrusts center-based child care, worrying about the reports of molestation that travel the ghetto grapevine. She remains convinced that W-2 is racially biased, and she even quotes Malcolm X, to warn what women without welfare may do. "Any means necessary to take care of your kids," she says. "If I don't have a job, who's to say I wouldn't prostitute myself? I pray to God it don't happen, but to some people it will."

It wasn't a complete surprise to discover, earlier this month, that Caples was missing from work. She hadn't called in for three days, and under hospital policy that probably meant she was fired. She doesn't have a phone, so I left a message with her boyfriend's mother, and the next day she placed a collect call back. The verve in her voice was gone. She and her boyfriend had had a fight, and he had moved out. She said she was too distraught the night of the breakup to bother calling work. Then figuring she was fired anyway, she simply didn't go back. Plus she now had day-care problems: Jewel had found a job, and Caples, suddenly single, had no place for her girls. "I don't know what I'm going to do," she said.

But her boss had asked me to pass on a message, and Caples sounded surprised that he wanted to see her. She summoned the courage to give him a call, and a few hours later she was in his office, describing her hapless week. When it comes to supervisors, Caples couldn't have drawn better luck. Having served on the board of a homeless shelter, Charles Lee wasn't looking to see another family on the streets. And it couldn't have hurt that he was taking a master's-degree course called Social Influences on Business Management—and that he had written his term paper on W-2. "I know how tough it can be," he said. "I'm going to do everything I can."

Sitting in his office that afternoon, Caples wrote out a three-page plea for mercy that impressed Lee with its eloquence. She explained what had happened. She pledged to do better. She said she had arranged for child care. Lee passed it on to the hospital vice president. The appeal is pending.

It's a disappointing moment, but the architects of W-2 would call it progress. Caples may still save her job, or she may quickly find another. . . . If things really fall apart, she could find herself doubled up with Jewel—or suddenly out on the streets. The one route no longer open to her is to simply return to the rolls. She's striking off, on shaky legs, into an uncharted, postwelfare world.

Chapter 16 Review Questions

1. What is TANF? How does it differ from AFDC?
2. Why do Schram and Soss argue that TANF will not produce laboratories of democracy? Why are they skeptical of the "race to the bottom" metaphor? What effect do they think TANF will have on states' welfare policies?
3. What is the Wisconsin Works program? Based on what you read in the essay by Schram and Soss, do you think Wisconsin has a particularly innovative program? Are there parts of the program that seem quite different from what you might have expected after reading the Schram and Soss essay? Or does the program seem to fit into the general mold described by those two authors?
4. Thinking about the readings and what you have learned elsewhere, how do you think the states should deal with poverty? Should they compel recipients to work? Should there be exceptions to this? Should states allow recipients to remain on welfare if they are going to school or enrolled in job training programs? How should states handle childcare for recipients?
5. What is the welfare program like in your state? Is it considered to be innovative? Or is it fairly similar to those of other states? What forces would you say have shaped the character of the welfare policy in your state? Is there a concern about being a welfare magnet? Are there broader forces that seem to have shaped the policy, such as your state's political culture?
6. The readings in several other chapters in this book raised questions as to how power should be distributed between the state and federal governments. Thinking about earlier chapters and the readings in this one, how do you think power should be distributed between the two levels of government?

Key Terms

welfare
Aid to Families with Dependent Children
Family Support Act of 1988
Personal Responsibility and Work Opportunity Reconciliation Act of 1996
Temporary Assistance for Needy Families
entitlement
block grants
devolution revolution
welfare magnets
laboratories of democracy
race to the bottom
means tests
King v. *Smith*
Shapiro v. *Thompson*
Goldberg v. *Kelly*
family caps
Individual Responsibility Plan
Learnfare
Bridefare
Wisconsin Works (W-2)
poverty line

Suggestions for Further Reading

Albelda, Randy, and Ann Withorn, eds. *Lost Ground: Welfare Reform, Poverty, and Beyond.* Cambridge, Mass.: South End Press, 2002. Collection of critical essays on recent welfare reform efforts in America.

Barnow, Burt S., Thomas Kaplan, and Robert A. Moffitt, eds. *Evaluating Comprehensive State Welfare Reform: The Wisconsin Works Program.* Albany, N.Y.: Rockefeller Institute Press, 2000. Study of the W-2 program in Wisconsin and its effect on different aspects of state social services. Includes discussion of how to evaluate welfare reform.

Blank, Rebecca M., and Ron Haskins, eds. *The New World of Welfare.* Washington, D.C.: Brookings Institution Press, 2002. A wide-ranging collection of essays on the Personal Responsibility and Work Opportunity Reconciliation Act and its impact.

Ehrenreich, Barbara. *Nickel and Dimed: On (Not) Getting By in America.* New York: Metropolitan Books, 2001. Very readable first-person account of the difficulties confronting the working poor in America.

Harrington, Michael. *The Other America: Poverty in the United States.* New York: Simon and Schuster, 1997. Reprint of classic study on poverty in America. This work is often credited with helping to spark public policy efforts in the 1960s to overcome poverty in the nation.

Katz, Michael. *In the Shadow of the Poorhouse: A Social History of Welfare in America.* 10th ed. New York: Basic Books, 1997. Detailed history of nation's welfare policy, from reliance on the poorhouse to the creation of the welfare state to recent opposition to welfare. Also see Katz's *The Undeserving Poor: From the War on Poverty to the War on Welfare* (New York: Pantheon Books, 1990) for an insightful overview of U.S. policy toward the poor from the 1960s through the Reagan administration.

Mead, Lawrence M. *Government Matters: Welfare Reform in Wisconsin.* Princeton: Princeton University Press, 2004. In-depth study of the history and impact of Wisconsin's welfare reform efforts. Also see Mead's general analysis of the state of America's welfare system and his argument for requiring welfare recipients to work in *Beyond Entitlement: The Social Obligations of Citizenship* (New York: Free Press, 2001).

Murray, Charles. *Losing Ground: American Social Policy, 1950–1980.* 2d ed. New York: Basic Books, 1995. Popular conservative critique of the American welfare state.

Peterson, Paul E., and Mark C. Rom. *Welfare Magnets: A New Case for National Standards.* Washington, D.C.: Brookings Institution, 1990. This book explains why states will reduce their welfare benefits in order to avoid becoming welfare magnets.

Piven, Francis Fox, and Richard A. Cloward. *Regulating the Poor: The Function of Public Welfare.* Updated edition. New York: Vintage Books, 1993. Classic social science study on poverty and social welfare in America.

Sawhill, Isabel V., R. Kent Weaver, Ron Haskins, and Andrea Kane, eds. *Welfare Reform and Beyond: The Future of the Safety Net.* Washington, D.C.: Brookings Institution Press, 2002. This valuable collection of essays was put together by the Brookings Institution to provide insight on welfare and poverty issues as Congress approached the reauthorization of TANF.

Soss, Joe, Sanford F. Schram, Thomas P. Vartanian, and Erin O'Brien. "Setting the Terms of Relief: Explaining State Policy Choices in the Devolution Revolution." *American Journal of Political Science* 45 (April 2001): 378–395. Quantitative analysis of why some states enacted more restrictive welfare policies than other states after the passage of TANF.

Weil, Alan, and Kenneth Finegold, eds. *Welfare Reform: The Next Act.* Washington, D.C.: Urban Institute Press, 2002. Collection of twelve essays on different aspects of the 1996 welfare reform law and its effect.

Weissert, Carol S., ed. *Learning from Leaders: Welfare Reform Politics and Policy in Five Midwestern States.* Albany, N.Y.: Rockefeller Institute Press, 2000. Provides case studies on the welfare reform efforts in five states after the passage of Personal Responsibility and Work Opportunity Reconciliation Act.

Related Web Sites

http://www.acf.dhhs.gov/programs/ofa/
Web site for the Office of Family Assistance, which oversees the Temporary Assistance for Needy Families (TANF). The site provides an explanation of the act, information on state programs, and links to related sites.

http://www.jointcenter.org/devolution/index.html
The Joint Center for Political and Economic Studies conducts research and maintains a web site on TANF. The site's list of internet links is especially helpful because it identifies material that can be found at other TANF research web sites.

http://www.dwd.state.wi.us/dws/w2/default.htm
The Wisconsin Department of Workforce Development provides a valuable web site on the Wisconsin Works Program that includes an explanation of the program, research findings, and other information.

ENDNOTES

Chapter 1 The Changing Position of State Government: The Concept of Resurgence

1. James C. Garand and Kyle Baudoin, "Fiscal Policy in the American States," in *Politics in the American States: A Comparative Analysis,* 8th ed., ed. Virginia Gray and Russell L. Hanson, 290–317 (Washington, D.C.: CQ Press, 2004).

Chapter 2 Understanding Differences Across the States: The Concept of Political Culture

1. Joel Lieske, "Regional Subcultures of the United States," *Journal of Politics* 55 (1993): 888–913.
2. Lawrence M. Mead, "The Culture of Welfare Reform," *Public Interest,* no. 154 (2004): 99–110.
3. "A New Era Dawns," *Times-Picayune,* October 20, 2002, 6; Manual Roig-Franzia, "Edwards Case Shines Light on 'Louisiana Way,' " *Times-Picayune,* May 14, 2000, A1; Robert Travis Scott, "It's Blanco," *Times-Picayune,* November 16, 2003, 1.
4. Adam Nossiter, "New Study Suggests Bias, Ex-Duke Voters Key to Blanco's 2003 Win," *Associated Press State and Local Wire,* April 2, 2004.

Chapter 4 State Constitutions: The Concept of Distinctiveness

1. National Municipal League, *Model State Constitution* (New York: National Municipal League, 1968), p. viii.

Chapter 5 Political Participation: The Concept of Civic Engagement

1. Robert D. Putnam, *Making Democracy Work: Civic Traditions in Modern Italy* (Princeton: Princeton University Press, 1993).
2. See the chapters by Theda Skocpol in *Civic Engagement in American Democracy* by Skocpol and Morris P. Fiorina (Washington, D.C.: Brookings Institution Press, 1999).

Chapter 7 Interest Representation: The Concept of Group Power

1. *The Federalist Papers* (New York: Signet Books, 2003), pp. 71–78.
2. Belle Zeller, ed., *The American Legislatures* (New York: Thomas Y. Crowell, 1954), especially pp. 190–191.
3. See Clive S. Thomas and Ronald J. Hrebenar, "Interest Groups in the States," in Virginia Gray and Russell L. Hanson, eds., *Politics in the American States,* 8th ed. (Washington, D.C.: CQ Press, 2004), pp. 100–128.

Chapter 8 State Legislatures: The Concept of Professionalism

1. The data in this addendum is from the National Conference of State Legislature's web site at *www.NCSL.org.* The one exception is the data on women legislators, which is from the Center for American Women and Politics at Rutgers University (see *www.cawp.rutgers.edu*).

Chapter 9 Governors: The Concept of Gubernatorial Success

1. Joseph A. Schlesinger, "The Politics of the Executive," in Herbert Jacob and Kenneth N. Vines, *Politics in the American States: A Comparative Analysis* (Boston, Mass.: Little, Brown and Company, 1965), pp. 207–237.
2. The most recent index can be found in Thad Beyle, "The Governors," in Virginia Gray and Russell L. Hanson, eds., *Politics in the American States: A Comparative Analysis,* 8th ed. (Washington, D.C.: CQ Press, 2004), pp. 194–231.
3. E. Lee Bernick, "Gubernatorial Tools: Formal vs. Informal," *Journal of Politics* 47 (1979): 656–664.
4. Alan Rosenthal, *Governors and Legislators: Contending Powers* (Washington, D.C.: CQ Press, 1990), pp. 5–38.
5. Margaret Robertson Ferguson, "Chief Executive Success in the Legislative Arena," *State Politics and Policy Quarterly* 3 (2003): 158–182.

Chapter 11 State Courts: The Concept of the New Judicial Federalism

1. Andrew S. Winters, "Ravin Revisited: Do Alaskans Still Have a Constitutional Right to Possess Marijuana in the Privacy of their Homes?" 15 Alaska Law Review 315, 315–344 (1998).
2. John Kincaid, "The New Judicial Federalism," *The Journal of State Governments* 61 (1988): 165.
3. James A. Gardner, "The Failed Discourse of State Constitutionalism," 90 Michigan Law Review 761, 837 (1992).

Chapter 14 State Finances: The Concept of Budgeting

1. Louis Jacobson and Shawn Zeller, "Struggling States Send a Bailout Message," *National Journal,* February 22, 2003, 592–594. For details on the state budget problems, see John Buntin, "Budget Shocks," *Governing,* July 1, 2001, 28–32; Penolope Lemov, "Deficit Deluge," *Governing,* May 2002, 20–24; Corina Eckl, "Roller Coaster Budgets," *State Legislatures,* October/November 2002, 14–18; Corina Eckl, "Beleaguered State Budgets," *State Legislatures,* May 2003, 16–20.

Chapter 16 Social Welfare: The Concepts of Laboratories of Democracy and Race to the Bottom

1. U.S. Department of Health and Human Services, Office of Planning, Research and Evaluation, "ACF-3637, Statistical Report on Recipients Under Public Assistance."

INDEX